Swarm Intelligence
Focus on Ant and Particle Swarm Optimization

Edited by
Felix T. S. Chan and Manoj Kumar Tiwari

Swarm Intelligence Focus on Ant and Particle Swarm Optimization
Edited by Felix T. S. Chan and Manoj Kumar Tiwari

Republished by InTech
Janeza Trdine 9, 51000 Rijeka, Croatia

Additional hard copies can be obtained from orders@intechopen.com

Swarm Intelligence: Focus on Ant and Particle Swarm Optimization,
Edited by Felix T. S. Chan and Manoj Kumar Tiwari

p. cm.

ISBN 978-3-902613-09-7

Preface

In the era globalisation the emerging technologies are governing engineering industries to a multifaceted state. The escalating complexity has demanded researchers to find the possible ways of easing the solution of the problems. This has motivated the researchers to grasp ideas from the nature and implant it in the engineering sciences. This way of thinking led to emergence of many biologically inspired algorithms that have proven to be efficient in handling the computationally complex problems with competence such as Genetic Algorithm (GA), Ant Colony Optimization (ACO), Particle Swarm Optimization (PSO), etc.

Motivated by the capability of the biologically inspired algorithms the present book on "Swarm Intelligence: Focus on Ant and Particle Swarm Optimization" aims to present recent developments and applications concerning optimization with swarm intelligence techniques. The papers selected for this book comprise a cross-section of topics that reflect a variety of perspectives and disciplinary backgrounds. In addition to the introduction of new concepts of swarm intelligence, this book also presented some selected representative case studies covering power plant maintenance scheduling; geotechnical engineering; design and machining tolerances; layout problems; manufacturing process plan; job-shop scheduling; structural design; environmental dispatching problems; wireless communication; water distribution systems; multi-plant supply chain; fault diagnosis of airplane engines; and process scheduling. I believe these 27 chapters presented in this book adequately reflect these topics.

Recent Development of Swarm Intelligence Techniques

The 1st chapter, **"Chaotic Rough Particle Swarm Optimization Algorithms"**, relates to the issues of generating random sequences with a long period and good uniformity. This topic is very important for easily simulating complex phenomena, sampling, numerical analysis, decision making and especially in heuristic optimization. In this chapter sequences generated from chaotic systems will substitute random numbers in all phases of PSO where it is necessary to make a random-based choice. By this way it is intended to develop the global convergence and to prevent to stick on a local solution. Furthermore, this chapter proposes a generalization of PSO based on rough values. The proposed chaotic rough particle swarm optimization algorithm (CRPSO) can complement the existing tools developed in rough computing using chaos. Definitions of basic building blocks of CRPSO such as rough decision variable, rough particle, and different chaotic maps will be provided. Applications of CRPSO in real life problems will be performed and comparisons will be made with others PSO algorithms and different optimization techniques.

The 2nd chapter, **"Integration Method of Ant Colony Algorithm and Rough Set Theory for Simultaneous Real Value Attribute Discretization and Attribute Reduction"**, first discusses the relationship between the problems of real value attribute discretization and attribute reduction in rough set theory. These two problems can be further syncretized as a unified problem based on the notion of distinction table. In this study, the authors consider that both the problems of finding a minimal set of cuts and that of finding a minimal set of attributes preserving the discernability of objects are important. Thus, an objective function with a weight parameter, which can balance these two objectives, is introduced. Secondly, the relationship between the unified problem and the set covering problem is analyzed, and a novel ant colony algorithm is proposed and employed to solve the set covering problem, which can automatically solve the problems of real value attribute discretization and attribute reduction. In order to avoid premature and enhance global search ability, a mutation operation will be added to the proposed ant colony algorithm. Moreover, a deterministic local search operation will be also adopted, which can improve the search speed of the algorithm. Thirdly, the validity and effectiveness of the proposed ant colony algorithm will be illustrated through case studies, and a comparison of different discretization algorithms will also be provided.

The 3rd chapter, **"A New Ant Colony Optimization Approach for the Degree-Constrained Minimum Spanning Tree Problem Using Pruefer and Blob Codes Tree Coding"**, proposes a new ACO algorithm for the degree constrained minimum spanning tree (d-MST) problem that can address this challenge in a novel way. Instead of constructing the d-MST directly on the construction graph, ants construct the encoded d-MST. The authors use two well-known tree-encodings: the Prüfer code, and the more recent Blob code. Under the proposed approach, ants will select graph vertices and place them into the Prüfer or Blob code being constructed. The proposed approach produced solutions that are competitive with state-of-the-art metaheuristics for d-MST.

The 4th chapter, **"Robust PSO-Based Constrained Optimization by Perturbing the PSO Memory"**, reviews the standard PSO algorithm, and several proposals to improve both exploration and exploitation: local and global topologies, particle motion equations, swarm neighborhoods, and social interaction. For all these approaches the common shared feature is the change of the PSO main algorithm. The authors describe a rather different approach: the perturbation of the particle memory. In the PSO algorithm, the next particle position is based on its own flying experience (pbest), and the current best individual in either the entire swarm (gbest), or in a swarm neighborhood (lbest). Since the values for gbest or lbest are determined from the pbest values available at any generation, in the end, it is the pbest which is mainly responsible for the particle's next position. Therefore, a way to reduce premature convergence is to improve the pbest of each particle. The proposed approach aims to prevent convergence to local optima by improving the swarm exploration and exploitation through two perturbation operators. These external operators improve the memory of the best visited locations, and do not modify the main PSO paradigm.

The 5th chapter, **"Using Crowding Distance to Improve Multi-Objective PSO with Local Search"**, a local search and diversity maintaining mechanism based on crowding distance is incorporated into the Multi-Objective Particle Swarm Optimization (MOPSO). The local search procedure intends to explore the less-crowded area in the current archive to possibly obtain better non-dominated solutions nearby. The non-dominated solutions situated in the more-crowded area will be removed from the archive once the archive size reaches a pre-specified level in order to maintain a well-balanced set of non-dominated solutions. Besides these, the non-dominated solutions in the less-crowded area are used to guide the population fly over sparse area of the current archive, such that a more uniform and diverse front might be formed by the optimizer. The proposed approach seeks to reach a reasonable compromise between the computational simplicity and efficiency. Several test problems and statistical comparison techniques are employed to check the performance of the approach.

The 6th chapter, **"Simulation Optimization Using Swarm Intelligence as Tool for Cooperation Strategy Design in 3D Predator-Prey Game"**, the objective of this research is an automatic design of autonomous agents, which situated in inherently cooperative, but noisy and uncertain environments are capable of accomplishing complex tasks through interaction. It is adhered to the methodological holism based on the belief that any complex system or society is more than the sum of its individual entities. As an application example, a problem was taken as a basis where a predators' group must catch a prey in a three-dimensional continuous ambient. A synthesis of system strategies was implemented of which internal mechanism involves the integration between simulators by PSO. The system had been tested in several simulation settings and it was capable to synthesize automatically successful hunting strategies, substantiating that the developed tool can provide, as long as it works with well-elaborated patterns, satisfactory solutions for problems of complex nature, of difficult resolution starting from analytical approaches.

The 7th chapter, **"Differential Meta-model and Particle Swarm Optimization"**, the authors firstly give a brief introduction of the biological model of PSO, and then a differential meta-model is introduced to analysis the PSO evolutionary behavior. Under this method, differential evolutionary particle swarm optimization algorithms with two different types of controllers are discussed in third part. Finally, an extension to this model is illustrated to enhance the velocity information utilization ratio.

The 8th chapter, **"Artificial Bee Colony Algorithm and Its Application to Generalized Assignment Problem"**, introduces a relatively new member of swarm intelligence called Artificial Bee Colony (ABC). ABC tries to model natural behavior of real honey bees in food foraging. Honey bees use several mechanisms like waggle dance to optimally locate food sources and to search new ones. This makes them a good candidate for developing new intelligent search algorithms. In this chapter a review of work on ABC algorithms will be given. Afterwards, development of an ABC algorithm for solving generalized assignment problems which are known as NP-hard problems will be presented in detail along with some comparisons.

The 9th chapter, **"Finite Element Mesh Decomposition Using Evolving Ant Colony Optimization"**, presents the application of evolving ant colony optimization to the decomposition (partitioning) of finite element meshes. The purpose of mesh decomposition is to allow large and complex finite element computations to be conducted in parallel (distributed) environment. The evolving ant colony optimization method in conjunction with a greedy algorithm and the collaboration of a neural network predictor provides the decomposition solutions to finite element meshes. This chapter also provides valuable information on ant colony optimization method which uses the evolutionary concepts in addition to swarm hypothesis for the partitioning of graph systems (special case: finite element meshes). Finite element mesh partitioning (also referred to as domain decomposition or sub-domain generation) has been the subject of interest for many researchers in the areas of Civil, Structural, Aeronautical, Electrical, and Mechanical engineering. The proposed chapter also presents the application of predictive neural networks in collaboration with the ant colony optimization method for the decomposition of finite element meshes.

The 10th chapter, **"Swarm Intelligence and Image Segmentation"**, presents a hybrid algorithm which combines SI with K-means. The authors also use the same method to combine SI with SCL. Their aim is to make the segmentation results of both K-means and SCL less dependent on the initial cluster centers and learning rate respectively, hence more stabilized and more accurate, by introducing hybrid techniques using the K-means and competitive learning algorithms, with Swarm Intelligence including ACO and PSO heuristics. This improvement is due to the larger search space provided by these techniques and their methodology of considering both spatial and intensity features of an image. In this chapter, the authors study the hybridization of PSO with each of the K-means and the SCL algorithms. A thorough comparison study on ACO-K-means, PSO-K-means, ACO-SCL, PSO-SCL, K-means, and SCL algorithms will also be provided.

The 11th chapter, **"Particle Swarm Optimization- Stochastic Trajectory Analysis and Parameter Selection"**, proposes to investigate two important topics in Particle Swarm Optimization (PSO) which are trajectory analysis of particles and parameter selection. In the first part of this chapter, the trajectory of particle in a general PSO algorithm is theoretically investigated, considering the randomness thoroughly. By regarding each particle's position on each evolutionary step as a stochastic vector, the general PSO algorithm determined by five-dimensional parameter tuple {ϕ, c1, c2, a, b} is formally analyzed using stochastic process theory. Because the position of particle at each step is stochastic and cannot be determined directly, its expected value, variance and covariance are investigated instead of the position itself, and corresponding explicit expression of each particle's trajectory is determined. The trajectory analysis leads to a sufficient condition to ensure the convergence of particle swarm system, which is verified by simulation experiments. At the same time, the relationship between convergent speed of particle's trajectory and parameter sets is studied. Those results give some hints on how the chosen parameters can influence the performance of PSO algorithm, and thus parameter selection guideline is given. After that, a set of suggested parameter {ϕ=0.715, c1=c2=1.7} is given, which is compared against three sets of parameters which are proposed in literatures.

The 12th chapter, **"Stochastic Metaheuristics as Sampling Techniques using Swarm Intelligence"**, focuses on stochastic methods, which form the majority of metaheuristics. Stochastic optimization metaheuristics can be viewed as methods manipulating a sample of the objective function, with different probabilistic operators. These operators are often met in several metaheuristics, despite the fact that they are presented as different ones, because of the metaphoric aspects of the algorithmic idea. The authors propose to consider three types of metaheuristics, according to the way they generate the sample: (i) directly; (ii) explicitly; or (iii) implicitly. The first type uses the objective function as a probability density function (pdf) to generate the sample, whereas the explicit methods make use of a specific pdf to do so. Methods of the last type construct an implicit probability density function, they are the most known algorithms. The different operators can be classified into three archetypal behaviors: diversification, intensification and learning. Moreover, one of the key aspects of the metaheuristics is the way these operators are designed. The authors argue that most of these algorithms make use of swarm intelligence techniques for their operators. This feature is evident for operators specialized in learning.

The 13th chapter, **"Artificial Ants in the Real World: Solving On-line Problems using Ant Colony Optimization"**, pointed out several new future directions for Ant Colony Optimization (AGO) researches including (i) how to adjust parameters which depends on the optimization problems; (ii) how to reduce the execution time; (iii) the optimization improvement by using incremental local search; and (iv) the aggregation of different and new concepts to AGO.

New Industrial Applications of Swarm Intelligence Techniques

The 14th chapter, **"Application of PSO to design UPFC-based stabilizers"**, the objective of this chapter is to investigate the potential of particle swarm optimization as a tool in designing an unified power flow controller (UPFC) -based stabilizers to improve power system transient stability. To estimate the controllability of each of the UPFC control signals on the electromechanical modes, singular value decomposition is employed. The problem of designing all the UPFC-based stabilizers individually is formulated as an optimization problem. Particle swarm optimizer is utilized to search for the optimum stabilizer parameter settings that optimize a given objective function. Coordinated design of the different stabilizers is also carried out by finding the best parameter settings for more than one stabilizer at a given operating condition in a coordinated manner.

The 15th chapter, **"CSV-PSO and Its Application in Geotechnical Engineering"**, introduces a new algorithm to recognize the parameters for the visco-elastic-brittle-plastic model of rock masses using a parallel improved practice swarm optimization (PSO). Using case studies, the algorithm is used to recognize parameters of surrounding rocks for a long tunnel excavated at depth of 1500-2500 m, which has serious rockburst and water burst problem during construction. The analysis on tunnel stability based the recognized parameters are good guidance to safe excavation of tunnel and to avoid accident occurrence.

The 16th chapter, **"Power Plant Maintenance Scheduling Using Ant Colony Optimization"**, a formulation has been developed that utilizes ant colony optimization (ACO) to obtain the optimal start times of power plant maintenance tasks of fixed durations and tested on a 21 unit benchmark case study. Subsequently, the formulation has been extended to take into account a number of practical issues commonly encountered in real world optimization maintenance scheduling, such as the shortening and deferral of maintenance tasks, and tested on a 5-unit hydropower system. The above power plant maintenance scheduling optimization formulations are further tested on four case studies, including two benchmark case studies previously solved using genetic algorithms (GAs) and tabu search (TS), and modified versions of the two case studies. In particular, a general heuristic formulation is introduced and its effectiveness in solving PPMSO problems is investigated. In addition, the performance of ACO-PPMSO when coupled with two local search strategies is investigated. The usefulness of both a heuristic formulation and the two local search strategies are assessed using two different ACO algorithms, including the Elitist-Ant System (EAS) and

Max-Min Ant System (MMAS). A wide range of ACO parameters are considered.
The 17th chapter, **"Particle Swarm Optimization for simultaneous Optimization of Design and Machining Tolerances"**, proposes a sophisticated constraints handling scheme suitable for the optimization mechanism of PSO to solve complicated engineering problems. The issue in this work concerns about the application of the constraints handling scheme in tolerances optimization. Tolerance assignment in product design and process planning (machining) affects both the quality and the cost of the overall product cycle. It is a crucial issue to determine how much the tolerance should be relaxed during the assignment process. However, this separated approach in tolerance design always suffers from several drawbacks. This chapter concerns about the simultaneous tolerance optimization in the concurrent engineering context. Generally, this problem is characterized by nonlinear objective, multiple independent variables, and tight constraints. To demonstrate the efficiency and effectiveness of the proposed approach, an example involving simultaneously assigning both design and machining tolerances based on optimum total machining cost is employed. The experimental results based on the comparison between PSO and GA show that the new PSO model is a powerful tool and can be extended into many other engineering applications.

The 18th chapter, **"Hybrid method for the layout problem"**, proposes a method for solving a facility layout problems modeled as a Quadratic Assignment Problem (QAP). It is based upon ant colony optimization with a Guided Local Search (GLS) procedure to escape from local minima. The method is first applied to a particular industrial problem, and then, the performance is evaluated on small instances as well as large instances from the public library QAPLIB.

The 19th chapter, "**Selection of best alternative process plan in automated manufacturing environment: An approach based on particle swarm optimization**", attempts to solve the complex Process Plan Selection (PPS) problem using an Intelligent Particle Swarm Optimization algorithm with modified concept of Local Repeller (IPSO-LR). This chapter formulates the PPS problem in a more justifiable way by the incorporation of a new parameter termed as Similarity Attribute ($\ddot{e}$) that keeps the track of similarity among part types to be manufactured. The algorithm emulates the behaviour of particles in a swarm and explores the search area by interacting with neighbours and utilizes the successes of other particles with regard to reaching towards optima. Robustness and efficacy of the proposed strategy is established by solving the problem of real dimensions and comparing the results with the established solution methodologies in process planning field.

The 20th chapter, **"Job-shop scheduling and visibility studies with a hybrid ACO algorithm"**, solves job-shop scheduling problems and compares different types of ACO variants, namely Elitist AS (EAS), Ant Colony System (ACS), Rank-based AS (RAS), and MIN-MAX AS (MMAS). The post-processing algorithm will be included in the comparisons and similar visibility schemes will also be taken into considerations in this new work. The same well known job-shop scheduling problem MT10 (Muth-Thompson) will be used when evaluating the suitability of the different approaches for solving job-shop scheduling problems.

The 21st chapter, **"Particle Swarm Optimization in Structural Design"**, presents the implementation and application of particle swarm optimization for constrained structural design tasks. This chapter starts by presenting a general background of the particle swarm algorithm, including its basic implementation and convergence properties. Subsequently, it discusses different improvements which can be made to the basic algorithm to handle constrained optimization problems. The improvements include violated point redirection, and the use of different constraint handling approaches such as penalty, adaptive penalty, and augmented Lagrangian formulations. The effect of the swarm setting parameters and the usefulness of the constraint handling improvements are shown for classic structural optimization problems. In the scope of such examples, guidelines for the setting parameters to guarantee proper convergence are shown, and the behavior of the constraint handling approaches are discussed. This chapter finalizes with discussion of outstanding issues regarding the practical application of particle swarms for constrained optimization in structures and other fields.

The 22nd chapter, **"Reserve-Constrained Multiarea Environmental/Economic Dispatch Using Enhanced Particle Swarm Optimization"**, extends the concept of Multiarea Economic Dispatch (MAED) into Multiarea Environmental/Economic Dispatch (MAEED) by taking into account the environmental issue. The objective of MAEED is to dispatch the power among different areas by simultaneously minimizing the operational costs and pollutant emissions. In this chapter, the MAEED problem is first formulated and then an enhanced multi-objective particle swarm optimization (MOPSO) algorithm is developed to derive its Pareto-optimal solutions. The tie-line transfer limits are considered as a set of constraints during the optimization process to ensure the system security. Furthermore, the area spinning reserve requirements are incorporated in order to increase the system reliability. The reserve sharing scheme is applied to ensure that each area is capable of satisfying the reserve demand. Simulations based on a four-area test power system are carried out to illustrate the effectiveness of the proposed optimization procedure as well as the impacts caused by the different problem formulations.

The 23rd chapter, **"Hybrid Ant Colony Optimization for the Channel Assignment Problem in Wireless Communication"**, presents a hybrid ant colony optimization (ACO) algorithm embodied with the sequential packing heuristic to take advantages of both approaches. The ACO algorithm provides an elegant framework for maintaining a good balance between exploration and exploitation during the search, while the sequential packing heuristic is customized to the channel assignment problem and is helpful in intensifying the promising area previously found. The performance of the proposed algorithm is evaluated using a set of benchmark problems named Philadelphia that has been broadly used in the relevant literature. As such the proposed algorithm can be directly compared to previous approaches.

The 24th chapter, **"Case Study Based Convergence Behaviour Analysis of ACO Applied to Optimal Design of Water Distribution Systems"**, focuses on the application of ACO to the optimal design of water distribution systems. The emphasis of this chapter is to: (i) illustrate an example of how ACO can be applied to a long standing engineering problem; (ii) assess the performance of a number of ACO algorithms applied to this problem; and (iii) analyze the algorithms performances at a behavioral level to further understand the algorithms themselves and the nature of the optimization problem.
The 25th chapter, **"A CMPSO algorithm based approach to solve the multi-plant supply chain problem"**, presents the idea behind this proposed CMPSO algorithm which is come from the limitations associated with the existing PSO algorithm under the discussed

problem scenario. The proposed CMPSO algorithm has been applied in multi-plant supply chain environment which has proven to be NP hard problem. In order to prove the efficacy and robustness of the proposed CMPSO algorithm, it has been compared with the existing evolutionary algorithms. Furthermore the authors have also shown the statistically validation of CMPSO algorithm. The proposed research aims towards exploring the applicability of PSO technique under diverse situations by inheriting some new concepts. These hybrid PSO techniques (such as CMPSO) could be applied to efficiently solve number of computationally complex problems prevailing in manufacturing environment.

The 26th chapter, **"Ant colonies for performance optimization of multi-components systems subject to random failures"**, focuses on the use of ant colonies to solve optimal design problems including (i) the reliability optimization of series systems with multiple-choice constraints incorporated at each subsystem, to maximize the system reliability subject to the system budget; (ii) the redundancy allocation problem (RAP) of binary series-parallel systems. This is a well known NP-hard problem which involves the selection of elements and redundancy levels to maximize system reliability given various system-level constraints. As telecommunications and internet protocol networks, manufacturing and power systems are becoming more and more complex, while requiring short developments schedules and very high reliability, it is becoming increasingly important to develop efficient solutions to the RAP; and (iii) buffers and machines selections in unreliable series-parallel production lines. The objective is to maximize production rate subject to a total cost constraint. The optimal design problem is formulated as a combinatorial optimization one where the decision variables are buffers and types of machines, as well as the number of redundant machines.

The 27th chapter, **"Distributed Particle Swarm Optimization for Structural Bayesian Network Learning"**, presents a recent study of the PSO implementation on a cluster of computers using parallel computing tools and algorithms. The PSO is used to discover the best Bayesian Network structure for diagnosing faults in airline engines. This chapter focuses on PSO implementation as well as Bayesian Network learning from large datasets. Learning Bayesian Networks from large datasets is an NP hard problem with disabling computational limits. By applying PSO in a distributed fashion, the computational limits can be eased and better networks can be generated.

I find great pleasure to announce that this book has attracted a great attention and response from researchers in the area of Swarm Intelligence. In particular, these chapters constitute state of the art research-based contributes in the field of swarm intelligence with particular focus on the ant and particle Swarm Optimization techniques. I sincerely hope you find the chapters as useful and interesting as I did. I look forward to seeing another technological breakthrough in this area in the near future.

Felix T. S. Chan
Manoj Kumar Tiwari

Contents

New Industrial Applications of Swarm Intelligence Techniques

1

Chaotic Rough Particle Swarm Optimization Algorithms

Bilal Alatas and Erhan Akin
Firat University
Turkey

1. Introduction

The problem of finding appropriate representations for various is a subject of continued research in the field of artificial intelligence and related fields. In some practical situations, mathematical and computational tools for faithfully modeling or representing systems with uncertainties, inaccuracies or variability in computation should be provided; and it is preferable to develop models that use ranges as values. A need to provide tolerance ranges and inability to record accurate values of the variables are examples of such a situation where ranges of values must be used (Lingras, 1996). Representations with ranges improve data integrity for non-integral numerical attributes in data storage and would be preferable due to no lose of information. Rough patterns proposed by Lingras are based on an upper and a lower bound that form a rough value that can be used to effectively represent a range or set of values for variables such as daily weather, stock price ranges, fault signal, hourly traffic volume, and daily financial indicators (Lingras, 1996; Lingras & Davies, 2001). The problems involving, on input/output or somewhere at the intermediate stages, interval or, more generally, bounded and set-membership uncertainties and ambiguities may be overcome by the use of rough patterns. Further developments in rough set theory have shown that the general concept of upper and lower bounds provide a wider framework that may be useful for different types of applications (Lingras & Davies, 2001).
Generating random sequences with a long period and good uniformity is very important for easily simulating complex phenomena, sampling, numerical analysis, decision making and especially in heuristic optimization. Its quality determines the reduction of storage and computation time to achieve a desired accuracy. Chaos is a deterministic, random-like process found in non-linear, dynamical system, which is non-period, non-converging and bounded. Moreover, it has a very sensitive dependence upon its initial condition and parameter (Schuster, 1998). The nature of chaos is apparently random and unpredictable and it also possesses an element of regularity. Mathematically, chaos is randomness of a simple deterministic dynamical system and chaotic system may be considered as sources of randomness.
Chaotic sequences have been proven easy and fast to generate and store, there is no need for storage of long sequences (Heidari-Bateni & McGillem, 1994). Merely a few functions (chaotic maps) and few parameters (initial conditions) are needed even for very long sequences. In addition, an enormous number of different sequences can be generated simply

by changing its initial condition. Moreover these sequences are deterministic and reproducible. The choice of chaotic sequences is justified theoretically by their unpredictability, i.e., by their spread-spectrum characteristic, and ergodic properties.

In this chapter, a generalization of particle swarm optimization (PSO) based on rough values has been proposed. Furthermore, sequences generated from chaotic systems substitute random numbers in all phases of PSO where it is necessary to make a random-based choice. By this way it is intended to develop the global convergence and to prevent to stick on a local solution. The proposed chaotic rough particle swarm optimization algorithm (CRPSO) can complement the existing tools developed in rough computing using chaos. Definitions of basic building blocks of CRPSO such as rough decision variable, rough particle, and different chaotic maps have been provided. Application of CRPSO in data mining has also been performed.

2. Rough Particle Swarm Optimization (RPSO)

Objects, instances, or records can be described by a finite set of attributes. The description of an object is an n-dimensional vector, where n is the number of attributes that characterizes an object. A pattern is a class of objects based on the values of some attributes of objects belonging to the class.

Let x be an attribute in the description of an object and $\underline{x}, \overline{x}$ represent lower and upper bounds (endpoints) of x such that $\underline{x} \le \overline{x}$. A rough pattern value of each attribute variable consists of lower and upper bounds and can be presented as Eq. (1). It can be diagrammatically seen in Figure 5. It is as a closed, compact, and bounded subset of the set of real numbers R.

$$x = \left(\underline{x}, \overline{x}\right) \tag{1}$$

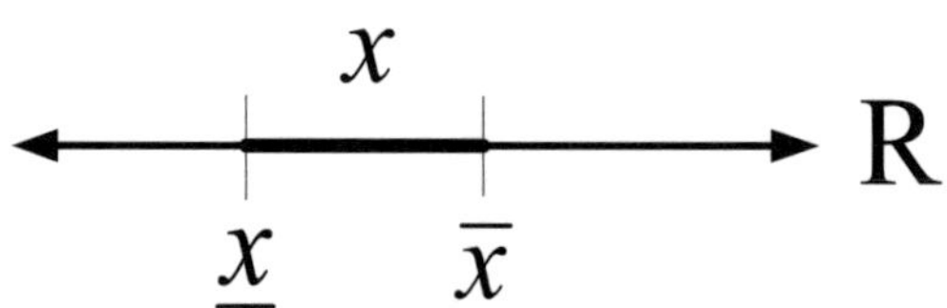

Figure 1. A rough value

If $0 \le \underline{x}$ the rough value is called a *positive rough value*, and we write $x > 0$. Conversely, if $\overline{x} \le 0$ we call the rough value a *negative rough value*, and write $x < 0$. Positive or negative rough values are the two types of *sign coherent rough values*. If $\underline{x} = 0$ or $\overline{x} = 0$ we call the rough value a *zero-bound rough value*. A zero-bound positive rough value is called a *zero-positive rough value*. Similarly, a zero-bound negative rough value is called a *zero-negative rough value*. A rough value that has both positive and negative values is called a *zero-straddling rough value*. These definitions are summed up in Table 1.

Definition	**Condition**
positive rough value (x>0)	Iff $\underline{x}>0$
negative rough value (x<0)	Iff $\overline{x}<0$
zero-positive rough value (x$\geq$0)	Iff $\underline{x}=0$
zero-negative rough value (x$\leq$0)	Iff $\overline{x}=0$
zero-straddling rough value (x<>0)	Iff $\overline{x}>0$ and $\underline{x}<0$

Table 1. Definitions on rough values

The *midpoint (mid), radius (rad),* and *width* of a rough value *x* are defined as:

$$mid(x)=(\overline{x}+\underline{x})/2 \tag{2}$$

$$rad(x)=(\overline{x}-\underline{x})/2 \tag{3}$$

$$width(x)=(\overline{x}-\underline{x})=2rad(x) \tag{4}$$

Since $x = (mid(x)\text{-}rad(x),\ mid(x)\text{+}rad(x))$ rough values can also be represented in terms of midpoint and radius instead of endpoints.

Rough values are useful in representing an interval or set of values for an attribute, where only lower and upper bounds are considered relevant in a computation. It may be very popular for many areas of computational mathematics. For example, by computing with rough values, it is possible (with some error) to evaluate a function over an entire interval rather than a single value. In other words, if we evaluate a function $f(x)$ over some interval of x (e.g. $x\in(\underline{x},\overline{x})$), we know what the possibly overestimated bounds of the function are within that interval. Since working with rough values always produces exact or overestimated bounds, it cannot miss a critical value in a function. Therefore, it is very useful for robust root finding, global maximum/minimum finding, and other optimization problems.

In fact, a conventional pattern can be easily represented as a rough pattern by using both lower and upper bounds to be equal to the value of the variable. Some operations on rough values can be implemented as:

$$x+y=(\underline{x},\overline{x})+(\underline{y},\overline{y})=(\underline{x}+\underline{y},\overline{x}+\overline{y}) \tag{5}$$

$$x-y=(\underline{x},\overline{x})+(-(\underline{y},\overline{y}))=(\underline{x}-\overline{y},\overline{x}-\underline{y}) \tag{6}$$

$$x\times y=\left(\min(\underline{x}\underline{y},\underline{x}\overline{y},\overline{x}\underline{y},\overline{x}\overline{y}),\max(\underline{x}\underline{y},\underline{x}\overline{y},\overline{x}\underline{y},\overline{x}\overline{y})\right) \tag{7}$$

$$\frac{1}{x}=\left(\frac{1}{\overline{x}},\frac{1}{\underline{x}}\right),\quad 0\notin(\underline{x},\overline{x}) \tag{8}$$

$$\frac{x}{y}=\frac{(\underline{x},\overline{x})}{(\underline{y},\overline{y})}=\frac{(\underline{x},\overline{x})}{\left(\frac{1}{\overline{y}},\frac{1}{\underline{y}}\right)},\quad 0\notin(\underline{y},\overline{y}) \tag{9}$$

$$c \times x = c \times (\underline{x}, \overline{x}) = (\underline{x}, \overline{x}) \times c = \begin{cases} (c \times \underline{x}, c \times \overline{x}) & if \quad c \geq 0 \\ (c \times \overline{x}, c \times \underline{x}) & if \quad c < 0 \end{cases} \tag{10}$$

In fact, these operations are borrowed from the conventional interval calculus (Lingras & Davies, 1999).
The algebraic properties of addition and multiplication operations on rough values have been described in Table 2.

Algebraic properties	Description	Condition
Commutativity	$x+y=y+x$	No condition
	$xy=yx$	
Associativity	$(x+y)+z=x+(y+z)$	No condition
	$(xy)z=x(yz)$	
Neutral Element	$0+x=x$	No condition
	$1.x=x$	
Distributivity	$x(y+z)=xy+xz$	If $\underline{x} = \overline{x}$
	$x(y+z)=xy+xz$	If $y \geq 0$ and $z \geq 0$ (non-negative terms)
	$x(y+z)=xy+xz$	If $y \leq 0$ and $z \leq 0$ (non-positive terms)
	$x(y+z)=xy+xz$	If $x \geq 0$, $\underline{y}=0$ and $\overline{z}=0$ (positive factor, zero-straddling terms)
	$x(y+z)=xy+xz$	If $x \leq 0$, $\underline{y}=0$ and $\overline{z}=0$ (negative factor, zero-straddling terms)
	$x(y-z)=xy-xz$	If $y \geq 0$ and $z \leq 0$ (non-negative terms variation)
	$x(y-z)=xy-xz$	If $y \leq 0$ and $z \geq 0$ (non-positive terms variation)

Table 2. Algebraic properties

A rough particle r is string of rough parameters r_i:

$$r = (r_i \mid 1 \leq i \leq n) \tag{11}$$

A rough parameter r_i is a pair of conventional parameters, one for lower bound called lower parameter ($\underline{r_i}$) and the other for upper bound called upper parameter ($\overline{r_i}$):

$$r_i = \left(\underline{r}_i, \overline{r}_i\right) \tag{12}$$

Figure 2 shows examples of rough particles.

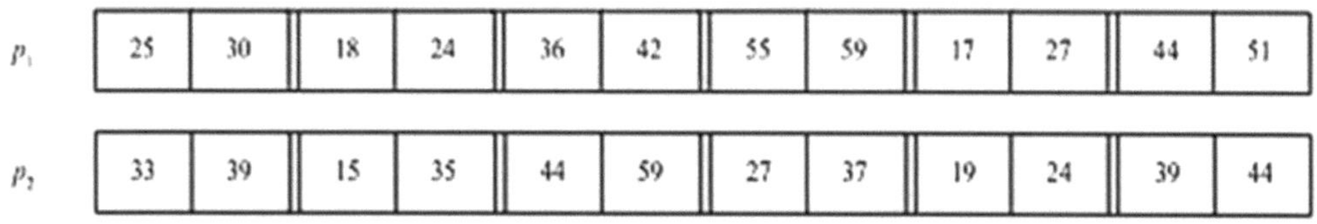

Figure 2. Rough particles

The value of each rough parameter is the range for that variable. The use of range shows that the information represented by a rough particle is not precise. Hence, an information measure called *precision* may be useful when evaluating the fitness levels (Lingras, 1996; Lingras & Davies, 2001).

$$precision(r) = -\sum_{1 \le i \le n} \left(\frac{\overline{r}_i - \underline{r}_i}{Range_{\max}(r_i)} \right) \tag{13}$$

Here, $Range_{\max}(r_i)$ is the length of maximum allowable range for the value of rough parameter r_i.

The conventional parameters and particles used in PSO algorithms are special cases of their rough equivalents as shown in Figure 3. For a conventional particle *p*, *precision(p)* has the maximum possible value of zero.

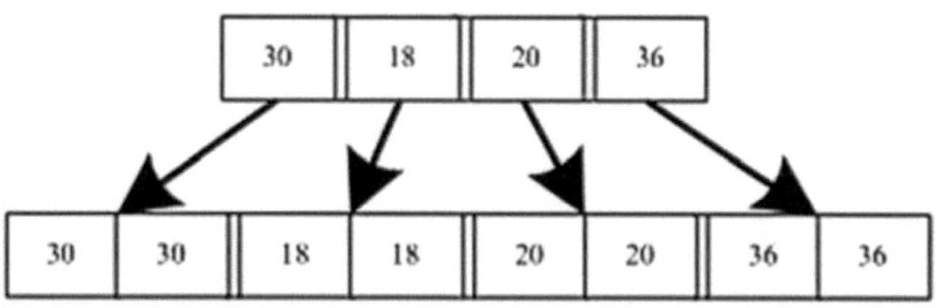

Figure 3. Conventional particle and its rough equivalent

In boundary constraint problems, it is essential to ensure that values of decision variables lie inside their allowed ranges after velocity or position update equations. This technique can also be generalized for RPSO algorithm. Constraint that the lower bounds in rough variables should be less than the upper bounds is already satisfied with RPSO algorithm.

3. Chaotic Particle Swarm Optimization (CPSO)

Generating random sequences with a long period and good uniformity is very important for easily simulating complex phenomena, sampling, numerical analysis, decision making and especially in heuristic optimization. Its quality determines the reduction of storage and computation time to achieve a desired accuracy. Generated such sequences may be "random" enough for one application however may not be random enough for another.

Chaos is a deterministic, random-like process found in non-linear, dynamical system, which is non-period, non-converging and bounded. Moreover, it has a very sensitive dependence upon its initial condition and parameter (Schuster, 1998)]. The nature of chaos is apparently random and unpredictable and it also possesses an element of regularity. Mathematically, chaos is randomness of a simple deterministic dynamical system and chaotic system may be considered as sources of randomness.
A chaotic map is a discrete-time dynamical system

$$x_{k+1} = f(x_k), \quad 0 < x_k < 1, \quad k = 0, \ 1, \ 2, \cdots \tag{14}$$

running in chaotic state. The chaotic sequence $\{x_k : k = 0, 1, 2, \ldots\}$ can be used as spread-spectrum sequence as random number sequence.
Chaotic sequences have been proven easy and fast to generate and store, there is no need for storage of long sequences (Heidari-Bateni & McGillem, 1994). Merely a few functions (chaotic maps) and few parameters (initial conditions) are needed even for very long sequences. In addition, an enormous number of different sequences can be generated simply by changing its initial condition. Moreover these sequences are deterministic and reproducible.
Recently, chaotic sequences have been adopted instead of random sequences and very interesting and somewhat good results have been shown in many applications such as secure transmission (Wong et al., 2005; Suneel, 2006), and nonlinear circuits (Arena et al., 2000), DNA computing (Manganaro & Pineda, 1997), image processing (Gao et al., 2006). The choice of chaotic sequences is justified theoretically by their unpredictability, i.e., by their spread-spectrum characteristic and ergodic properties.
One of the major drawbacks of the PSO is its premature convergence, especially while handling problems with more local optima. In this paper, sequences generated from chaotic systems substitute random numbers for the PSO parameters where it is necessary to make a random-based choice. By this way, it is intended to improve the global convergence and to prevent to stick on a local solution. For example, the value of *inertia weight* is the key factors to affect the convergence of PSO. Furthermore the values of random numbers that affect the stochastic nature are also key factors that affect the convergence of PSO. In fact, however, these parameters can't ensure the optimization's ergodicity entirely in phase space, because they are random in traditional PSO.
New approaches introducing chaotic maps with ergodicity, irregularity and the stochastic property in PSO to improve the global convergence by escaping the local solutions have been provided. The use of chaotic sequences in PSO can be helpful to escape more easily from local minima than can be done through the traditional PSO. When a random number is needed by the classical PSO algorithm it is generated by iterating one step of the chosen chaotic map that has been started from a random initial condition at the first iteration of the PSO. New chaos embedded PSO algorithms may be simply classified and described as Table 3. In this table first column represents the name of PSO. The second column represents which values it effect to. And the last column, divided in to three sub columns, represents the bounds of the values they can take from the selected chaotic maps. For example CPSO3 only effects to second acceleration coefficient (c_2) and the values taken from the selected chaotic map is scaled between 0.5 and 2.5. When rough representation is used these names take a "R" for representing the "Rough" after "C" that represents "Chaotic". Namely when rough representation is used for "CPSO1" it is named as "CRPSO1".

Name	Effect	Scaled Values of Chaotic Maps		
CPSO1	Initial velocities and position	Lower bound - upper bound of each decision variable		
CPSO2	c_1	0.5 - 2.5	-	-
CPSO3	c_2	0.5 - 2.5	-	-
CPSO4	c_1 and c_2	0.5 - 2.5	0.5 - 2.5	-
CPSO5	r_1	0.0 - 1.0	-	-
CPSO6	r_2	0.0 - 1.0	-	-
CPSO7	r_1 and r_2	0.0 - 1.0	0.0 - 1.0	-
CPSO8	w, r_1, and r_2	0.0 - 1.0	0.0 - 1.0	0.0 - 1.0
CPSO9	w	0.0 - 1.0	-	-
CPSO10	w and c_1	0.0 - 1.0	0.5 - 2.5	-
CPSO11	w and c_2	0.0 - 1.0	0.5 - 2.5	-
CPSO12	w, c_1, and c_2	0.0 - 1.0	0.5 - 2.5	0.5 - 2.5

Table 3. Characteristics of CPSO algorithms

Note that CPSO1 can be used together with the other CPSO classes. The chaotic maps that generate chaotic sequences in PSO phases used in the experiments are listed below.

Logistic Map: One of the simplest maps which was brought to the attention of scientists by Sir Robert May in 1976 that appears in nonlinear dynamics of biological population evidencing chaotic behavior is logistic map, whose equation is the following (May, 1976):

$$X_{n+1} = aX_n(1 - X_n) \tag{15}$$

In this equation, X_n is the n-th chaotic number where n denotes the iteration number. Obviously, $X_n \in (0, 1)$ under the conditions that the initial $X_0 \in (0, 1)$ and that $X_0 \notin \{0.0, 0.25, 0.5, 0.75, 1.0\}$. a=4 have been used in the experiments.

Sinusoidal Iterator: The second chaotic sequence generator used in this paper is the so-called sinusoidal iterator (Peitgen et al., 1992) and it is represented by

$$X_{n+1} = ax_n^2 \sin(\pi x_n) \tag{16}$$

When a=2.3 and X_0=0.7 it has the simplified form represented by

$$X_{n+1} = \sin(\pi x_n) \tag{17}$$

It generates chaotic sequence in (0, 1)

Gauss Map: The Gauss map is used for testing purpose in the literature (Peitgen et al., 1992) and is represented by:

$$X_{n+1} = \begin{cases} 0 & , X_n = 0 \\ 1/X_n \bmod(1) & , X_n \in (0,1) \end{cases} \tag{18}$$

$$1/X_n \bmod(1) = \frac{1}{X_n} - \left\lfloor \frac{1}{X_n} \right\rfloor \tag{19}$$

and $\lfloor z \rfloor$ denotes the largest integer less than z and acts as a shift on the continued fraction representation of numbers. This map also generates chaotic sequences in (0, 1).

Zaslavskii Map: The Zaslavskii Map (Zaslavskii, 1978) is an also an interesting dynamic system and is represented by:

$$X_{n+1} = \left(X_n + v + aY_{n+1}\right) \bmod(1) \tag{20}$$

$$Y_{n+1} = \cos\left(2\pi X_n\right) + e^{-r} Y_n \tag{21}$$

Its unpredictability by its spread-spectrum characteristic and its large Lyapunov exponent are theoretically justified. The Zaslavskii map shows a strange attractor with largest Lyapunov exponent for v=400, r=3, a=12. Note that in this case, $Y_{n+1} \in$ [-1.0512, 1.0512].

4. CRPSO in Data Mining

CRPSO has been used for mining numeric association rules (ARs) from databases in which records concerned are categorical or numeric. In a numeric AR, attributes are not limited to being Boolean but can be numeric (e.g. age, salary, and heat) or categorical (e.g. sex, brand). Thus, numeric ARs are more expressive and informative than Boolean ARs (Ke et al., 2006). An example of a numeric AR in an employee database is:

"Age $\in$ [25, 36] $\wedge$ Sex=Male $\Rightarrow$ Salary $\in$ [2000-2400] $\wedge$ Have_Car=Yes"
(Support = 4%, Confidence = 80%).

In this numeric AR, "Age $\in$ [25, 36] $\wedge$ Sex=Male" is antecedent and "Salary $\in$ [2000-2400] $\wedge$ Have_Car=Yes" is consequent part. This numeric AR states that "4% (support) of the employees are males aged between 25 and 36 and earning a salary of between $2.000 and $2.400 and have a car", while "80 % (confidence) of males aged between 25 and 36 are earning a salary of between $2.000 and $2.400 and have a car".
Following subsections are description of CRPSO for mining numeric ARs.

4.1 Particle representation

In this work, the particles which are being produced and modified along the search process represent rules. Each particle consists of decision variables which represent the items and intervals. A positional encoding, where the *i*-th item is encoded in the *i*-th decision variable has been used. Each decision variable has three parts. The first part of each decision variable represents the antecedent or consequent of the rule and can take three values: '0', '1' or '2'. If the first part of the decision variable is '0', it means that this item will be in the antecedent of the rule and if it is '1', this item will be in the consequent of the rule. If it is '2', it means that this item will not be involved in the rule. All decision variables which have '0' on their first parts will form the antecedent of the rule while decision variables which have '1' on their first part will form the consequent of the rule. While the second part represents the lower bound, the third part represents the upper bound of the item interval. The structure of a particle has been illustrated in Figure 4, where *m* is the number of attributes of data being mined (Alatas et al., 2007).

Variable $_1$			***Variable*** $_2$			...			***Variable*** $_m$		
AC_1	LB_1	UB_1	AC_2	LB_2	UB_2				AC_m	LB_m	UB_m

Figure 4. Particle representation

Rounding operator that converts a continuous value to an integer value for the first parts of this representation by truncation is performed when evaluating. Rounded variables are not elsewhere assigned in order to let CRPSO algorithm work with a swarm of continuous variables regardless of the object variable type for maintaining the diversity of the swarm and the robustness of the algorithm.

In the implementation of this particle representation, the second and third part of decision variables will be considered as one value, namely rough value. At first glance, this representation seems to appropriate for only numeric attributes. However it is very straightforward to extend it for discrete, nominal, and numeric attributes. The numeric attributes locates at the beginning of the representation and discrete ones at the end. For discrete attributes only AC_i and V_i where V_i is the value of the attribute are used. Namely, instead of LB_i and UB_i, only Vi is used for values of discrete or nominal attributes.

4.2 Fitness Function

The mined rules have to acquire large support and confidence. CRPSO has been designed to find the intervals in each of the attributes that conform an interesting rule, in such a way that the fitness function itself is the one that decides the amplitude of the intervals. That is why, the fitness value has to appropriately shelter these and it has been shown in Eq. (22).

$$\textbf{\textit{Fitness}} = \alpha_1 \times cover\ (Ant{+}Cons) + \alpha_2 \times \frac{cover(Ant + Cons)}{cover(Ant)} + \alpha_3 \times (NA) - \alpha_4 \times Int - \alpha_5 \times marked \tag{22}$$

This fitness function has four parts. Here, *Ant* and *Cons* are distinct itemsets that are involved in the antecedent and consequent part of the rule respectively. *cover (Ant+Cons)* is ratio of the records that contain *Ant+Cons* to the total number of records in the database. The first part can be considered as support of the rule that is statistical significance of an AR. In fact, the second part can be considered as confidence value. The third part is used for number of attributes in the particle. *NA* is number of attributes in the database that has not '2' in first parts of decision variable of particles. The motivation behind this term is to bias the system to give more quality information to the final user. The last part of the fitness is used to penalize the amplitude of the intervals that conform the itemset and rule. In this way, between two particles that cover the same number of records and have the same number of attributes, the one whose intervals are smaller gives the best information. *Int* has been computed as shown in Eq. (23) where amp_m is the amplitude factor determined for each attribute for balancing the effect of *Int* to the fitness.

$$\frac{UB_m - LB_m}{amp_m} \tag{23}$$

marked is used to indicate that an attribute of a records has previously been covered by a rule. Algorithm is forced to mine different rules in later searches by this way.

α_1, α_2, α_3, α_4, α_5 are user specified parameters and one might increase or decrease the effects of parts of fitness function by means of these parameters. *Int* part of the fitness calculation concerns particles parts representing numeric attributes.

4.3 Mutation

Mutation has also been performed in this study. Mutation operator is introduced which mutates a single decision vector of a particle with probability p_{mut}. Four possible mutations (Mata et al., 2002) have been used for CRPSO algorithms:

- **Shifting the whole interval towards the right**: The values in lower and upper bounds are increased.
- **Shifting the whole interval towards the left**: The values in lower and upper bounds are decreased.
- **Incrementing the interval size**: The value of lower bound is decreased and the value of upper bound is increased.
- **Reducing the interval size**: The value of lower bound is increased and the value of upper bound is decreased.

When a particle is chosen to be mutated each decision value is then mutated by one of this four mutation types or not with probability $1/m$, where m is the number of decision value in the particle. Particle positions are updated only if the mutated particles have better fitness.

4.4 Refinement of bound intervals

At the end of the CRPSO search, a refinement in the attributes bounds that belong to the covered rule is performed. This refinement process consists reducing the interval size until the support value is smaller than the support of the original rule encoded in the related particle.

4.5. Parameter Control

The used parameter values for the experiments have been shown in Table 4. Minimum and maximum values for velocity and position depend on the bounds of the decision values. α_1, α_2, α_3, α_4, and α_5 that have been used in fitness values were selected as 0.8, 0.8, 0.05, 0.1, and 0.2 respectively.

Parameters	Swarm size	No. of generations	Mutation Probability
Values	20	1000	0.5

Table 4. Used parameters for PSO algorithms

5. Experimental Results

Synthetic database is created using the function 2 (Agrawal et al., 1993) to distribute the values in records in such a way that they are grouped in pre determined sets. The function is shown in Figure 5. The goal is to most accurately find the intervals of each of the created regions. Namely, a group is assigned to each record, depending on the values that the attributes *age* and *salary* take. Figure 6 shows a graphic representation of the distribution of 5000 records according to the function where only records belong to Group A are presented.

$$\text{If } ((age < 40) \wedge (50\text{K} \leq salary \leq 100\text{K})) \vee$$
$$((40 \leq age < 60) \wedge (75\text{K} \leq salary \leq 125\text{K})) \vee$$
$$((age \geq 60) \wedge (25\text{K} \leq salary \leq 75\text{K})) \Rightarrow \text{Group } A$$
$$\text{else} \Rightarrow \text{Group } B$$

Figure 5. Function used for the experiment

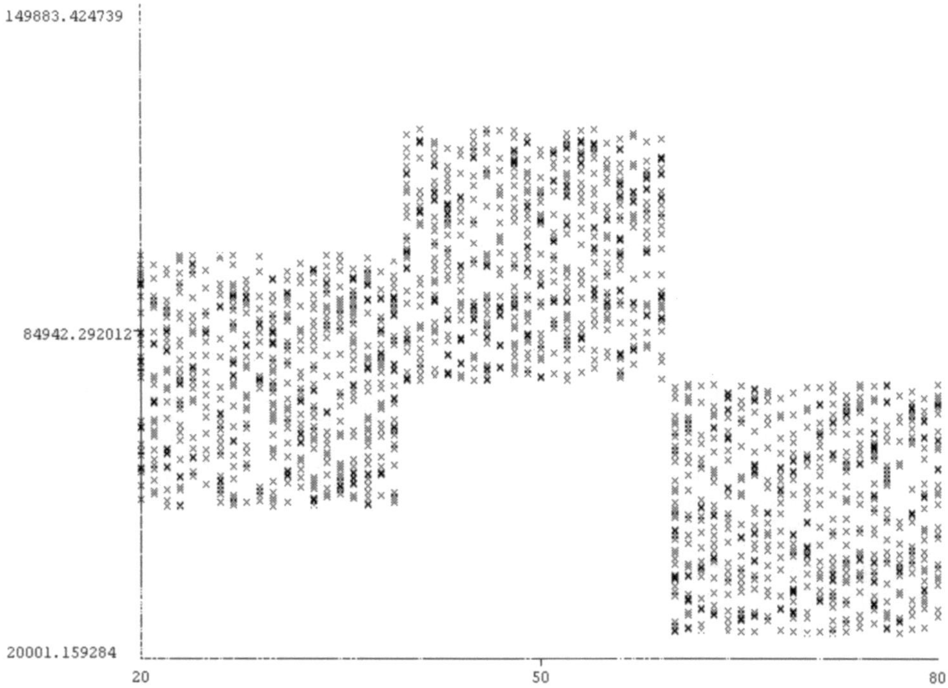

Figure 6. Graphic representation of the function for the experiment

The database has been generated by uniformly distributing the records between the lower and upper values of its domains. For attribute *salary* the extreme values are from 20000 to 150000 and for attribute *age* salary the extreme values are from 20 to 80. The third attribute for the group has also been added. According to the function almost 37.9% of the records belong to Group *A*. the ARs are those that have the attrşbutes salary and age in the antecedent and the attribute Group in the consequent. That is why, representation of the particle respects to this case.

For a fair comparison of the results initial swarm is initialized in a different way. A same record of the database is chosen and the rule is generated departing from it, defining for each value of v_i of the selected attribute a_i, lower limit $v_i - \theta$ and upper limit $v_i + \theta$. θ is a percentage of the value v_i. In this way the swarm is conditioned to cover at least one record. This has not been performed for CRPSO1.

An intuitive measure to verify the efficacy of the CRPSO algorithms, verifying that the mined ARs have larger quality, consists of checking that the intervals of the rules accord to the ones synthetically generated. Mean support and confidence values of mined rules from rough PSO algorithm are 12.21 and 93.33. Acceleration coefficients have been selected as 2 and inertia weight has been gradually decreased from 0.9 to 0.4 for CRPSO1 algorithm.

The obtained results from the proposed CRPSO algorithms are shown in Tables 5. All of the algorithms have mined three rules and mean support and confidence values of these rules have been depicted in this table. If the mean support values are multiplied by 3, values close to 37.9% may be found, which means that the rules have practically covered all the records. Confidence values are also close to 100%, since in the regions there are no records of other groups. Interesting result is that, CRPSO7, CRPSO8, and CRPSO12 have the best performances. CRPSO7 using Zaslavskii map seems the best PSO among others. The mined rules from CRPSO7 using Zaslavskii map is shown in Table 6.

Logistic Map												
	CRPSO1	CRPSO2	CRPSO3	CRPSO4	CRPSO5	CRPSO6	CRPSO7	CRPSO8	CRPSO9	CRPSO 10	CRPSO 11	CRPSO 12
Sup (%)	11.24	10.64	10.96	11.98	10.78	10.80	12.48	12.28	10.82	10.66	11.02	11.54
Conf (%)	98.14	98.12	97.01	97.64	97.42	97.96	99.01	98.98	98.42	98.24	98.56	99.08
Sinusoidal Iterator												
	CRPSO1	CRPSO2	CRPSO3	CRPSO4	CRPSO5	CRPSO6	CRPSO7	CRPSO8	CRPSO9	CRPSO 10	CRPSO 11	CRPSO 12
Sup (%)	11.20	11.24	10.86	11.62	10.86	10.96	12.38	12.28	10.58	10.90	11.06	11.24
Conf (%)	98.48	98.46	98.08	98.06	97.56	97.02	99.08	98.96	98.54	97.98	99.02	98.96
Gauss Map												
	CRPSO1	CRPSO2	CRPSO3	CRPSO4	CRPSO5	CRPSO6	CRPSO7	CRPSO8	CRPSO9	CRPSO 10	CRPSO 11	CRPSO 12
Sup (%)	11.91	11.05	10.86	10.24	10.84	10.97	12.28	12.23	10.81	10.23	9.99	11.98
Conf (%)	97.22	97.62	98.68	98.16	98.26	97.64	99.04	99.06	98.48	97.86	97.56	98.62
Zaslavskii Map												
	CRPSO1	CRPSO2	CRPSO3	CRPSO4	CRPSO5	CRPSO6	CRPSO7	CRPSO8	CRPSO9	CRPSO 10	CRPSO 11	CRPSO 12
Sup (%)	11.05	11.26	10.24	10.22	10.97	10.96	12.62	12.41	10.96	10.82	10.88	11.94
Conf (%)	97.56	97.55	97.22	98.08	98.48	98.69	99.65	99.12	98.62	98.86	97.16	98.84

Table 5. Mean support and confidence values of the rules mined by different CRPSO algorithms

Rule	Sup(%)	Conf(%)
If $age \in [20, 40] \wedge salary \in [50136, 99869] \Rightarrow$ Group A	12.63	98.94
If $age \in [41, 59] \wedge salary \in [76779, 12469] \Rightarrow$ Group A	12.62	100
If $age \in [61, 80] \wedge salary \in [25440, 73998] \Rightarrow$ Group A	12.61	100

Table 6. ARs mined by CRPSO7 using Zaslavskii map

6. Conclusions

In this chapter chaotic rough PSO, CRPSO, algorithms that use rough decision variables and rough particles that are based on notion of rough patterns have been proposed. Different chaotic maps have been embedded to adapt the parameters of PSO algorithm. This has been done by using of chaotic number generators each time a random number is needed by the classical PSO algorithm. Twelve PSO methods have been proposed and four chaotic maps have been analyzed in the data mining application. It has been detected that coupling emergent results in different areas, like those of PSO and complex dynamics, can improve the quality of results in some optimization problems and also that chaos may be a desired process. It has been also shown that, these methods have somewhat increased the solution quality, that is in some cases they improved the global searching capability by escaping the local solutions. The proposed CRPSO algorithms can complement the existing tools developed in rough computing using chaos. These proposed methods seem to provide useful extensions for practical applications. More elaborated experiments by using optimized parameters may be performed with parallel or distributed implementation of these methods.

7. Acknowledgements

This work is supported by Firat University Scientific Research and Projects Unit (Grant. No. 1251) and is supported in part by a grant from Scientific and Technological Research Council of Turkey, National Scholarship Program for PhD Students.

8. References

Agrawal, R., Imielinski, T., Swami, A. (1993). Database Mining: A Performance Perspective, *IEEE Transactions on Knowledge and Data Engineering*, Vol. 5, No. 6, p.914-925

Alatas, B., Akin E., Karci, A. (2007). MODENAR: Multi-objective differential evolution algorithm for mining numeric association rules, *Applied Soft Computing*, Elsevier, http://dx.doi.org/10.1016/j.asoc.2007.05.003

Arena P., Caponetto R., Fortuna L., Rizzo A., La Rosa M. (2000). Self Organization in non Recurrent Complex System, *Int. J. Bifurcation and Chaos*, Vol. 10, No. 5, 1115–1125

Gao H., Zhang Y., Liang S., Li D. (2006). A New Chaotic Algorithm for Image Encryption, *Chaos, Solitons and Fractals*, 29, 393-399

Heidari-Bateni G. & McGillem C. D. (1994). A Chaotic Direct-Sequence Spread Spectrum Communication System, *IEEE Trans. on Communications*, Vol. 42 No. (2/3/4), 1524-1527

Ke, K., Cheng, J. Ng, W. (2006). MIC Framework: An Information-Theoretic Approach to Quantitative Association Rule Mining, *ICDE* '06, 112-114.

Lingras, P. (1996). Rough Neural Networks, *International Conference on Information Processing and Management of Uncertainty*, Granada, Spain, pp. 1445-1450

Lingras, P. & Davies, C. (1999). Rough Genetic Algorithms, 7th International Workshop on New Directions in Rough Sets, Data Mining, and Granular-Soft Computing RSFDGrC 1999, *Lecture Notes In Computer Science*; Vol. 1711, 38-46

Lingras, P. & Davies, C. (2001). Applications of Rough Genetic Algorithms, *Computational Intelligence: An International Journal*, Vol . 3, No. 17, 435-445

Manganaro G. & Pineda de Gyvez J. (1997). DNA Computing Based on Chaos, *IEEE International Conference on Evolutionary Computation*. Piscataway, NJ: IEEE Press, 255–260

Mata, J., Alvarez, J., Riquelme, J. (2002). Discovering Numeric Association Rules via Evolutionary Algorithm, *Lecture Notes in Computer Science*, Volume 2336, Springer Verlag, 40-51.

May R. M. (1976). Simple Mathematical Models with very Complicated Dynamics. *Nature* 261: 459

Peitgen H., Jurgens H., Saupe D. (2004). *Chaos and Fractals*, Springer-Verlag, 0387202293, Berlin, Germany

Schuster H. G. (1995). *Deterministic Chaos: An Introduction*, Physick- Verlag GmnH, John Wiley & Sons Ltd, 3527293159, Federal Republic of Germany

Suneel M. (2006). Chaotic Sequences for Secure CDMA, *Ramanujan Institute for Advanced Study in Mathematics*, 1-4

Wong K., Man K. P., Li S., & Liao X. (2005). More Secure Chaotic Cryptographic Scheme based on Dynamic Look-up Table, *Circuits, Systems & Signal Processing*, Vol. 24, No. 5, 571-584

Zaslavskii G. M. (1978). The Simplest Case of a Strange Attractor, *Physic Letters A*, Vol. 69, 145-147

2

Integration Method of Ant Colony Algorithm and Rough Set Theory for Simultaneous Real Value Attribute Discretization and Attribute Reduction

Yijun He[1], Dezhao Chen[1] and Weixiang Zhao[2]
[1]*Department of Chemical Engineering, Zhejiang University*
[2]*Department of Mechanical and Aeronautical Engineering, University of California, Davis*
[1]*People's Republic of China,* [2]*U.S.A*

1. Introduction

Discretization of real value attributes (features) is an important pre-processing task in data mining, particularly for classification problems, and it has received significant attentions in machine learning community (Chmielewski & Grzymala-Busse, 1994; Dougherty et al., 1995; Nguyen & Skowron, 1995; Nguyen, 1998; Liu et al., 2002). Various studies have shown that discretization methods have the potential to reduce the amount of data while retaining or even improving predictive accuracy. Moreover, as reported in a study (Dougherty et al., 1995), discretization makes learning faster. However, most of the typical discretization methods can be considered as univariate discretization methods, which may fail to capture the correlation of attributes and result in degradation of the performance of a classification model.

As reported (Liu et al., 2002), numerous discretization methods available in the literatures can be categorized in several dimensions: dynamic vs. static, local vs. global, splitting vs. merging, direct vs. incremental, and supervised vs. unsupervised. A hierarchical framework was also given to categorize the existing methods and pave the way for further development. A lot of work has been done, but still many issues remain unsolved, and new methods are needed (Liu et al. 2002).

Since there are lots of discretization methods available, how does one evaluate discretization effects of various methods? In this study, we will focus on simplicity based criteria while preserving consistency, where simplicity is evaluated by the number of cuts. The fewer the number of cuts obtained by a discretization method, the better the effect of that method. Hence, real value attributes discretization can be defined as a problem of searching a global minimal set of cuts on attribute domains while preserving consistency, which has been shown as NP-hard problems (Nguyen, 1998).

Rough set theory (Pawlak, 1982) has been considered as an effective mathematical tool for dealing with uncertain, imprecise and incomplete information and has been successfully applied in such fields as knowledge discovery, decision support, pattern classification, etc. However, rough set theory is just suitable to deal with discrete attributes, and it needs discretization as a pre-processing step for dealing with real value attributes. Moreover, attribute reduction is another key problem in rough set theory, and finding a minimal attribute reduction has also been shown as a NP-hard problem (Komorowski et al., 1998). Two main approaches to find a minimal attribute reduction can be categorized as discernibility functions-based and attribute dependency-based, respectively (Han et al., 2004). These algorithms, however, suffer from intensive computations of either discernibility functions or positive regions. An alternative way to find a minimal attribute reduction is to adopt meta-heuristic algorithms, such as genetic algorithm (Wróblewski, 1995), particle swarm optimization (Wang et al., 2007), and ant colony algorithm (Jensen & Shen, 2003). To our knowledge, there are rare studies about how discretization pre-processing influences attribute reduction and how one integrates these two steps into a unified framework. In this chapter, we will try to give a systematic view into this problem, and will introduce ant colony algorithm to solve it.

Ant colony algorithm (Colorni et al., 1991; Dorigo et al., 1996) is a kind of meta-heuristic algorithms and has been successfully applied to solve many combinatorial optimization problems, such as travelling salesman problem (Gambardella & Dorigo, 1995; Dorigo et al., 1996; Dorigo & Gambardella, 1997; Stützle & Hoos, 1997), sequential ordering problem (Gambardella & Dorigo, 2000), generalized assignment problem (Lourenço & Serra, 2002), scheduling problem (Stützle, 1998; Merkle et al., 2002; Merkle & Middendorf, 2003), network routing problem (Schoonderwoerd et al., 1996; Di Caro & Dorigo, 1998;), set covering problem (Hadji et al., 2000; Rahoual et al., 2002; Lessing et al., 2004), etc. Great achievements of ant colony algorithm have attracted lots of attentions from different disciplinary researchers, and its application fields have been expanded from combinatorial optimization to continuous optimization problems, single-objective problems to multi-objective problems, static problems to dynamic problems, etc.. In this chapter, we just focus on the discrete style of ant colony algorithm, and it is reconstructed to be adapted to simultaneously solve real value attribute discretization and attribute reduction.

This chapter is structured as follows. In section 2, preliminaries of rough set theory will be shortly described firstly, secondly the mathematical definition of real value attribute discretization and attribute reduction will be introduced, and then the relationship between discretization and reduction will be discussed and a unified framework will be proposed by introducing a weight parameter. The relationship between the unified framework and set covering problems will be analyzed in section 3. A detailed implementation of ant colony algorithm for simultaneously solving attribute discretization and reduction will be presented in section 4. The experimental results and discussion will be given in sections 5. Section 6 will make conclusions and provide future research directions.

2. Rough set theory, discretization and reducts

2.1 Preliminaries of rough set theory

In rough set theory, table, also called information system, is often used to organize sample data, where rows and columns of a table denote objects and attributes, respectively. If attributes in a table consist of conditional attributes and decision attribute, the information system will be called a decision table. The mathematical definition of an information system and a decision table can be shown as follows.

Information system and decision table (Komorowski et al., 1998) : an information system is a pair $\mathcal{A} = (U, A)$, where U is a non-empty finite set of objects called a universe and A is a non-empty finite set of attributes such that $a : U \to V_a$ for every $a \in A$. The set V_a is called the value set of a. A decision table is an information system of the form $\mathcal{A}=(U,A\cup\{d\})$, where $d\notin A$ is the decision attribute. The elements of A are called conditional attributes. Let $U=\{x_1,\cdots,x_n\}$, $V_d=\{1,2,\cdots,r(d)\}$, and $A=\{a_1,\cdots,a_m\}$, where n, $r(d)$ and m are the numbers of samples, decision classes, and attributes, respectively. The decision attribute d determines a partition $\{X_1,\cdots,X_{r(d)}\}$ of the universe U, where $X_k=\{x\in U:d(x)=k\}$ for $k=1,\cdots,r(d)$. The set X_k is called the kth decision class of $\mathcal{A}$.

Intuitively, a decision table $\mathcal{A}$ is considered consistent if the following statement is satisfied. If $\forall\, x_1,x_2\in U$ and $d(x_1)\neq d(x_2)$, then $\exists a\in A$, $a(x_1)\neq a(x_2)$.

In other words, for any two objects with different decision class, there at least exists one attribute to discern them. In this study, we assume that the decision table $\mathcal{A}$ is consistent, if not specifically denoted.

Before the discussion of attribute reduction, the notion of relative indiscernibility relation based on decision table $\mathcal{A}$ is briefly introduced as follows.

Relative indiscernibility relation: for any subset of attributes $B\subseteq A$, an equivalence relation called the relative B-indiscerniblity relation, denoted by $IND(B,d)$, is defined by

$IND(B,d)=\{(x_i,x_j)\in U\times U:(d(x_i)=d(x_j))\vee(Inf_B(x_i)=Inf_B(x_j))\}$.

where $Inf_B(x)=\{(a,a(x)):a\in B \text{ for } x\in U\}$ is called B-information function. For any two objects x_i and x_j satisfying relation $IND(B,d)$ are either belonging to the same decision class, or having the same value for every attribute a in subset B. Hence, if any objects x_i and x_j fitting relation $IND(A,d)$ are belonging to the same class, the decision table $\mathcal{A}$ is considered consistent.

2.2 Reduct and Discretization

In this subsection, the notions of reduct and discretization will be firstly introduced, and then the relationship between them will be discussed based on the notion of a distinction table.

An attribute $a\in B$ is relative dispensable in a subset of attributes $B\subseteq A$, if $IND(B-\{a\},d)=IND(B,d)$, otherwise attribute a is relative indispensable. It means that attribute a can not influence the indiscernibility relation if it is dispensable.

A reduct of decision table $\mathcal{A}$ is a minimal set of attributes $B\subseteq A$ such that $IND(B,d)=IND(A,d)$ (Komorowski et al., 1998). In other words, a reduct is a minimal set of attributes from A that preserves the partitioning of the universe and hence the ability to perform classifications as the whole attribute set A does. Meanwhile, the minimal set of attributes $B\subseteq A$ means that every attribute $a\in B$ is indispensable with respect to B.

Now, a formal description of the real value discretization can be presented as follows (Komorowski et al., 1998).

We assume $V_a\in[l_a,r_a)\subset\Re$ to be a real interval for any $a\in A$ and a given decision table $\mathcal{A}=(U,A\cup\{d\})$ to be consistent. Any pair of (a,c) where $a\in A$ and $c\in\Re$ will be called a cut on V_a. For $a\in A$, any set of cuts: $\{(a,c_1^a),\cdots,(a,c_{k_a}^a)\}$ on V_a defines a partition $\mathbf{P}_a$ of V_a into subintervals expressed by $\mathbf{P}_a=\{[c_0^a,c_1^a),[c_1^a,c_2^a),\cdots,[c_{k_a}^a,c_{k_a+1}^a)\}$, where

$l_a = c_0^a < c_1^a < c_2^a < \cdots < c_{k_a}^a < c_{k_a+1}^a = r_a$, and $V_a = [c_0^a, c_1^a) \cup [c_1^a, c_2^a) \cup \cdots \cup [c_{k_a}^a, c_{k_a+1}^a)$. $C_a = \{c_1^a, \cdots, c_{k_a}^a\}$ is used to represent the set of cuts on V_a for convenience, which can uniquely define the partition $\mathbf{P}_a$. Hence any family $\mathbf{P} = \{\mathbf{P}_a : a \in A\}$ is called a partition on decision table $\mathcal{A}$ and can be represented by $\mathbf{P} = \bigcup_{a \in A} C_a$.

Moreover, according to the notion of the set of cuts, a new decision table $\mathcal{A}^{\mathbf{P}} = (U, A^{\mathbf{P}} \cup \{d\})$ can be defined, where $A^{\mathbf{P}} = \{a^{\mathbf{P}} : a^{\mathbf{P}}(x) = i \Leftrightarrow a(x) \in [c_i^a, c_{i+1}^a), x \in U, i = \{0, \cdots, k_a\}\}$.

Using meta-heuristic algorithms for real value attribute discretization, usually one needs to identify an initial set of cuts first and then screen these cuts. In this paper, each cut in an initial set of cuts is also called candidate cut. Assuming an arbitrary attribute $a \in A$ defines a sequence of its different attribute values ($x_1^a < \cdots < x_{n_a}^a$) and the length of this sequence is denoted by n_a ($n_a \le n$), the initial set of cuts on V_a can be represented by $C_a = \{\frac{x_1^a + x_2^a}{2}, \cdots, \frac{x_{n_a-1}^a + x_{n_a}^a}{2}\}$ which includes $n_a - 1$ elements, and the initial set of cuts on decision table $\mathcal{A}$ will be $\mathbf{P} = \bigcup_{a \in A} C_a$. Then, a new decision table $\mathcal{A}^{\mathbf{P}} = (U, A^{\mathbf{P}} \cup \{d\})$ can be established. It should be noticed that the new decision table with the initial set of cuts is consistent if the original decision table $\mathcal{A}$ is consistent.

In order to select cuts from the initial set of cuts, the effect of each cut on classification performance should be analyzed to construct a distinction table DT. Each pair of two objects with different decision classes correspond to a row in distinction table, so the total number of rows in a distinction table is $N = \sum_{p=1}^{r(d)-1} card(X_p) \sum_{q=p+1}^{r(d)} card(X_q)$, where $card(X_p)$ denotes the number of objects in decision class p. Each cut from the initial set of cuts corresponds to a column in distinction table, so the total number of columns is $M = \sum_{a \in A} (n_a - 1)$. Let the ith row and j^{th} column of a distinction table represent one pair of two objects, such as (x_p, x_q) where $d(x_p) \ne d(x_q)$, and one cut of initial set of cuts, respectively. Hence, if the jth column (or cut) can discern these two objects (x_p, x_q), the entry value of the distinction table corresponding to the ith row and j^{th} column, denoted by dt_{ij}, is equal to 1; otherwise, dt_{ij} is equal to 0.

Obviously, a decision table is considered consistent if each row of the distinction table has at least one entry with the value of 1, which also means that there at least exists one discernable cut for any pair of objects from different decision classes.

According to the definition of distinction table, a real value attribute discretization problem can be equivalently represented as searching a minimal set of cuts $J \subseteq \{1, \cdots, M\}$ such that for any row $i \in \{1, \cdots, N\}$ of the decision table, there at least exists one cut $j \in J$ whose value of dt_{ij} is equal to 1. That is to say the minimal set of cuts J from the whole initial set of cuts can preserve the consistence of decision table. Correspondingly, an attribute reduction problem can also be represented as searching the set of cuts $J \subseteq \{1, \cdots, M\}$ corresponding to the minimal number of attributes such that for any row $i \in \{1, \cdots, N\}$ of the decision table, there at least exists one cut $j \in J$ whose value of dt_{ij} is equal to 1.

According to the above definitions, it is concluded that both the real value attribute discretization and reduction can be defined as finding a minimal set of cuts from the initial set of cuts, and the only difference between them is the computation of objective function. Hence, let $f_1(J)$ and $f_2(J)$ denote the number of cuts in J and the number of attributes corresponding to the set of cuts J, respectively. Consequently, a weight parameter w is introduced to balance these two objective functions, and thus both the real value attribute discretization and reduction can be further syncretised into a unified framework, which can be described as equation (1).

$$\begin{aligned} &\min_{J\subseteq\{1,\cdots,M\}} F(J) = [f_1(J)]^w + [f_2(J)]^{1-w} \\ &\text{s.t.} \sum_{j\in J} dt_{ij} \geq 1,\ \forall i \in \{1,\cdots,N\} \end{aligned} \tag{1}$$

where the ith constraint, $\sum_{j\in J} dt_{ij} \geq 1$, represents that there at least exists a cut in J that can discern the pair of two objects in the ith row. This insures the consistence of the obtained reduct decision table with regard to J.

In general, the weight parameter w is dependent on a practical problem and user's preference, so it is usually determined empirically. However, the above problem can also be described as a bi-objective optimization problem, which can be further solved by multi-objective optimization methods to provide a Pareto-optimal solution set. Thus the decision maker can decide to choose one Pareto-optimal solution based on his preference and justification. In this study, we just focus on a single objective optimization problem through introducing the weight parameter w. Moreover, the costs of attributes may be different, so the objective function in equation (1) should be modified while taking account of the costs of attributes. An attribute associated with lower cost will be favored. The proposed algorithm of this study is able to deal with different costs of attributes, but we just focus on the problem with the same costs of all attributes in the case studies of this study.

3. Set covering problem

The set covering problem (SCP) is an NP-hard problem combinatorial optimization problem that arises in a large variety of practical applications, such as resource allocation (Revelle, et al., 1970), airline crew scheduling (Housos & Elmoth, 1997), and so on. In this subsection, we study the relationship between SCP and the unified problem shown as equation (1), which can help us to design a more efficient ant colony algorithm profiting from the existing different heuristic and local search methods for solving SCP.

Given a zero-one matrix $\boldsymbol{S}$ with m rows and n columns, let $cost_j$ be the cost of column j, where $j=1,\cdots,n$. The ith row is said to be covered by column j if the entry s_{ij} is equal to 1. The problem of set covering is to find a subset of columns with a minimal cost to cover all rows, and can be formulated as equation (2), where $\boldsymbol{x}=[x_1,\cdots,x_n]^{\mathrm{T}}$ denotes a solution of SCP and x_j denotes the jth element of the solution $\boldsymbol{x}$ indicating whether column j belongs to the solution based on the value of x_j ("1", belonging while "0", not belonging).

$$\min f(\boldsymbol{x}) = \sum_{j=1}^{n} cost_j \cdot x_j$$
$$\text{s.t.} \sum_{j=1}^{n} s_{ij} x_j \geq 1, \quad i = 1, \cdots, m \tag{2}$$
$$x_j \in \{0,1\}, \quad j = 1, \cdots, n$$

If the distinction table DT is regarded as matrix $\boldsymbol{S}$, the unified problem of simultaneous real value attribute discretization and reduction shown as equation (1) can be handled as SCP, whose main goal is also to find a subset of columns via a minimal objective function to cover all rows. The only minor difference between them is the definition of the objective function. Hence, the existing heuristic methods for solving SCP should be modified to be suited to solve the unified problem shown as equation (1).
Now, we will reformulate the unified problem in equation (1) based on the description form of SCP, as shown in equation (3). In this study, we assume the candidate cuts belonging to the same attribute are arranged together.

$$\min f(\boldsymbol{x}) = [f_1(\boldsymbol{x})]^{w} + [f_2(\boldsymbol{x})]^{1-w}$$
$$f_1(\boldsymbol{x}) = \sum_{j=1}^{n} x_j$$
$$f_2(\boldsymbol{x}) = \sum_{l=1}^{L} cost_l \cdot y_l$$
$$\text{s.t. } y_l = \begin{cases} 1, \text{ if} \sum_{p=1}^{n_l} x_{Index+p} \geq 1, \ Index = \begin{cases} 0, \ l = 1 \\ \sum_{q=1}^{l-1} n_q, l > 1 \end{cases} \\ 0, \text{ otherwise} \end{cases} \tag{3}$$
$$l = 1, \cdots, L$$
$$\sum_{j=1}^{n} s_{ij} x_j \geq 1, \quad i = 1, \cdots, m$$
$$x_j \in \{0,1\}, \quad j = 1, \cdots, n$$

where L is the number of attributes; n_l is the number of candidate cuts on the lth attribute domain; $n = \sum_{l=1}^{L} n_l$ is the total number of candidate cuts on the whole attributes domain, also called the number of columns; y_l is the indicator whether the lth attribute is selected with regard to solution $\boldsymbol{x}$; m is the number of rows. In the case studies, we assume costs of all attributes to be the same.
Up to now, the relationship between SCP and the unified framework is analyzed, and the similarities and differences between them are discussed. In the next section, we will propose a novel ant colony algorithm for solving the problem shown in equation (3).

4. Ant colony algorithm

For simultaneously solving real value attribute discretization and reduction shown as equation (3), solution construction and pheromone update are two key issues for an ant colony algorithm. In the solution construction step, heuristic information should be reasonably designed to improve the optimization efficiency. Moreover, we will also introduce a local search strategy to improve the search speed of algorithm.

4.1 Fundamental notions

In this subsection, we will introduce some notions which will be used for the description of the algorithm.

Search domain, feasible domain and feasible solution: a search domain consists of 2^n solutions, where n denotes the total number of candidate cuts on the whole attributes domain; those solutions in search domain meeting the constraints of equation (3) are denoted as feasible solutions, and all feasible solutions form a feasible domain.

Cover: if s_{ij} is equal to 1, we can say the ith row is covered by the jth column. Let $\kappa_j = \sum_{i=1}^{m} s_{ij}$ denote the number of rows covered by the jth column. In general, the larger the value of κ_j, the more important the jth column.

Node, taboo node set and feasible node set: every element of set $\{1,\cdots,n\}$ is called a node, let $node_j$ denote the jth node, where $j=1,\cdots,n$. Let $tabu_k$ denote the set of nodes that has been visisted by the kth ant and be called taboo node set which is set equal to null initially. Let $allow_k$ denote the set of nodes that remain to be visisted by the kth ant and be called feasible node set which is set equal to an all columns set $\{1,\cdots,n\}$ initially. In nature, the solution construction is a process of iteratively selecting unvisited node from $allow_k$ until a feasible solution is constructed. From another point of view, if $tabu_k$ covers all rows, the solution construction ends and $tabu_k$ is a feasible solution.

Covered rows set and uncovered rows set: Let $CRS = \{i \mid \exists j \in tabu_k, s_{ij} = 1\}$ and $UCRS = \{1,\cdots,m\} \setminus CRS$ denote the set of covered rows and that of uncovered rows by $tabu_k$ respectively. During the process of solution construction, the number of covered rows will increase, and the number of uncovered rows will decrease. The solution construction will continue until the set of uncovered rows $UCRS$ is equal to null set.

Pheromone: let $\tau_j(t)$ denote the quantity of pheromone defined in the jth column at time t. At time 0, all columns' pheromones τ_0 are set equal to 0.5.

Heuristic information: the heuristic information adopted in this study differs from that in other combinatorial optimization problems. Generally, in other combinatorial optimization problems, such as travelling salesman problem, the heuristic information is calculated before the solution construction step, while in this study, it is dynamically calculated during solution construction. Let η_j denote the heuristic information in the jth column, where $j \in allow_k$. In this study, the calculation of heuristic information not only depends on cut infomation (which is usually adopted by the existing heuristic methods in literatures), but also depends on extra attribute information. The concrete implementation for each solution construction step by ant k is shown below.

1. For each cut or column, i.e. $j \in allow_k$, determine which attribute it belongs to, for example, assume the jth column belong to the lth attribute.
2. Obtain the value of CN_l, which denotes the number of selected candidate cuts of the lth attribute during solution contruction.
3. Calculate extra attribute information v_l, defined by equation (4).

$$v_l = \begin{cases} c/cost_l, \text{ if } 0 < CN_l \le CN_{\max} \\ 1/cost_l, \text{ otherwise} \end{cases} \tag{4}$$

where c (c>1) is a prescribed parameter. It means that if none candidate cuts of lth attribute are selected or the number of selected cuts of lth attribute is larger than $CN_{\max}$, the value of v_l is set equal to $1/cost_l$, otherwise, it is set equal to $c/cost_l$. On the one hand, we tend to choose a candidate cut of an attribute whose several candidate cuts have been selected during solution construction, because this may help decrease the number of selected attributes; on the other hand, we would not like to choose too many candidate cuts of an attribute, because this is not conducive to understanding the decision model and could decreases the robustness of the decision model as well. Hence, a prescribed parameter, $CN_{\max}$, which denotes the maximum number of selected candidate cuts for each attribute, is introduced to decrease the probability of the above phenomenon. In this study, the values of c and $CN_{\max}$ are empiricallly set equal to 4 and 5, respectively.

4. Calculate cut information κ_j defined by equation (5), which denotes the number of rows covered by the jth column from the set of uncovered rows $UCRS$.

$$\kappa_j = \sum_{i \in UCRS} s_{ij}, \ j \in allow_k \tag{5}$$

5. Calculate the heuristic information η_j defined by equation (6), using cut information and extra attribute information.

$$\eta_j = \kappa_j \cdot v_l, \ j \in allow_k \tag{6}$$

6. Nomalize the heuristic information via equation (7).

$$\eta_j = \frac{\eta_j}{\sum_{q \in allow_k} \eta_q}, \ j \in allow_k \tag{7}$$

Selection probability: in the solution construction step, let $p_k(j,t)$ denote the selection probability of column j by the kth ant at time t, and be expressed by equation (8).

$$p_k(j,t) = \frac{\tau_j(t) * [\eta_j]^{\beta}}{\sum_{q \in allow_k} \tau_q(t) * [\eta_q]^{\beta}}, \ j \in allow_k \tag{8}$$

where β is a heuristic factor, which determines the relative importance of pheromone versus heuristic information. In this study, it is set equal to 2.

4.2 Solution construction

Unlike the solution construction of travelling salesman problems, where each ant must visit each city node, in this study, each ant will end the solution construction when all rows are covered by the selected column nodes.

The detailed implementation of solution construction by ant k is shown as follows.

Step1 set $tabu_k = \Phi$, $allow_k = \{1,\cdots,n\}$, $CRS = \Phi$, $UCRS = \{1,\cdots,m\}$, and $CN_l = 0$ for all $l \in \{1,\cdots,L\}$;

Step2 calculate the heuristic information η_j based on section 4.1, where $j \in allow_k$;

Step3 generate a uniform random number r in [0, 1]. If the value of r is less than q_0, the next node u is selected by equation (9); otherwise, the next node u is selected based on the probability shown as equation (8). It should be noticed that q_0 can be considered as an exploitation probability factor and is used to control how strongly an ant exploit deterministically the combined past search experience and heuristic information. By adjusting parameter q_0, we can balance the trade-off between exploitation and biased exploration.

$$u = \arg\max_{j \in allow_k} \{\tau_j(t) * [\eta_j]^{\beta}\} \tag{9}$$

Step4 implement local pheromone update operation for column u by using equation (10).

$$\tau_u(t) = (1-\xi)\tau_u(t) + \xi\tau_0 \tag{10}$$

where ξ, $0 < \xi < 1$, is a parameter called local pheromone update strength factor. The effect of local pheromone update is to make the desirability of columns change dynamically: each time when an ant choose a column, this column becomes slightly less desirable for the other ants. Hence, this can prevent ants from converging to a common solution and help increase exploration.

Step5 determine which attribute the selected node u belongs to If this node belongs to the lth attribute, set $CN_l = CN_l + 1$, $tabu_k = tabu_k \cup \{u\}$, $allow_k = allow_k \setminus \{u\}$, $CRS = CRS \cup \{i \mid s_{ij} = 1, i \in UCRS, j = u\}$, and $UCRS = UCRS \setminus \{i \mid s_{ij} = 1, i \in UCRS, j = u\}$;

Step6 if $UCRS$ is not a null set, go back to **Step2**; otherwise, solution construction is finished, and return a feasible solution $tabu_k$.

4.3 Redundant columns remove

After a feasible solution $tabu_k$ is constructed, all redundant columns will be removed from the solution. Column j is considered redundant if $tabu_k \setminus \{j\}$ is also a feasible solution. Let

$\sigma_j = \min_{i \in Cover(j)} (\omega_i - 1)$ represent an associate variable to judge whether column j is redundant, where $j \in tabu_k$, $Cover(j) = \{i \mid s_{ij} = 1\}$ denotes the subset of rows covered by column j, and ω_i is the number of selected columns covering row i. It should be noticed that column j is redundant if and only if $\sigma_j > 0$.

If there is only one redundant column, it is easy to remove this column from the solution. However, if there are several redundant columns, we will remove the redundant column step by step until there is none redundant column. The detailed implementation is shown as follows.

Step1 calculate the value of σ_j, where $j \in tabu_k$, and determine the set of redundant columns, $RCS = \{j \mid \sigma_j > 0\}$. If RCS is equal to null set, stop; otherwise, go to **Setp2**;

Step2 for each column $j \in RCS$, determine which attribute it belongs to. And also let RAS denote the subset of attributes at least one of whose selected candidate cuts is redundant;

Step3 calculate the value of CN_l defined in subsection 4.1, where $l \in RAS$, and sort them by ascending. If the minimal value is equal to 1, go to **Step4**; otherwise, go to **Step5;**

Step4 find the subset of attributes $RAS_{\min}$ with minimal value CN_l from RAS. If there exist several attributes with the same largest cost in $RAS_{\min}$, randomly remove one column which belongs to one of attributes in $RAS_{\min}$; otherwise, remove the column corresponding to the largest attribute cost. Set $tabu_k = tabu_k \setminus \{j\}$, and go back to **Step1**;

Step5 find the subset of attributes $RAS_{\max}$ with maximal value CN_l from RAS. If there exist several attributes with the same largest cost in $RAS_{\max}$, randomly remove one column which belongs to one of attributes in $RAS_{\max}$; otherwise, remove the column with largest corresponding attribute cost. Set $tabu_k = tabu_k \setminus \{j\}$, and go back to **Step1**.

Based on the above discussion about the redundant column removal, it should be noticed that the goal of **Step4** is to decrease the number of attributes in the final solution while taking account of the costs of attributes; moreover, the goal of **Step5** is conducive to creating a final decision model with smaller number of cuts on each attribute domain.

4.4 Local search

To improve the solution quality and global convergence speed, a simple local search procedure is applied after solution construction. The introduced local search consists of two phases, removing columns and adding columns.

In the phase of removing columns, a number of columns determined by a user-defined parameter λ, $0 < \lambda < 1$, are removed from the constructed feasible solution. However it may result in the infeasibility of a new partial solution because some rows will not be covered. The parameter λ is used to control how many columns will be removed from the solution $tabu_k$, and the new partial solution $tabu_k^{new}$ consists of $ceil(|tabu_k| \times (1-\lambda))$ columns, where $|tabu_k|$ denotes the number of columns in set $tabu_k$, $ceil$ denotes a function of round an element to the nearest integer.

In the phase of adding columns, firstly, a size reduction problem is constructed, which is based on the uncovered rows and the columns that could cover these rows, and then this size reduction problem is solved by a greedy algorithm based on the heuristic information discussed in subsection 4.1. The column with the largest heuristic information will be selected step by step until the all rows are covered by the selected columns. The main steps of the column adding procedure are the same as the solution construction described in subsection 4.2, and the only difference between them is the step of column selection. Therefore we just briefly introduce the implementation below. Let $LLmt$ denotes the local search iteration number, which is set equal to 5 in this study.

Step1 set $t=1$;

Step2 randomly remove $ceil(|\,tabu_k\,|\times\lambda)$ columns from solution $tabu_k$, and construct a size reduction problem. Let $tabu_k^{new}$ denotes the new partial infeasible solution;

Step3 solve this size reduction problem by a greedy algorithm based on the dynamically calculated heuristic information. Let $tabu_k^{'}$ denotes the solution of this reduced size problem, and set $tabu_k^{'}=tabu_k^{'}\cup tabu_k^{new}$;

Step4 remove the redundant columns from $tabu_k^{'}$;

Step5 if the objective function value of $tabu_k^{'}$ is less than that of $tabu_k$, set $tabu_k=tabu_k^{'}$;

Step6 set $t=t+1$, and if t is less than $LLmt$, go back to **Step2**; otherwise, stop the local search procedure and return $tabu_k$.

4.5 Pheromone update

When all ants finish the solution construction procedure and the local search procedure, the operation of global pheromone update will be implemented, which includes pheromone release and pheromone evaporate. In nature, pheromone release reflects the positive feedback mechanism in ant colony algorithm; while pheromone evaporate operation follows ant biology background and helps avoid excessive pheromone drowned heuristic information to some extent.

In this study, in addition to the local pheromone update operation discussed in **Step4** of the solution construction in subsection 4.2, two types of global pheromone update operations (iteration-best based and global-best based) are also adopted, defined by equations (11) and (12), respectively.

$$\tau_j(t+1)=(1-\rho)\tau_j(t)+\rho\Delta\tau_j^{ib},$$

$$\Delta\tau_j^{ib}=\begin{cases}\left[f(S^{ib})\right]^{-1}, & \text{if } j\in S^{ib}\\ 0, & \text{otherwise}\end{cases} \tag{11}$$

$$\tau_j(t+1)=(1-\rho)\tau_j(t)+\rho\Delta\tau_j^{gb}$$

$$\Delta\tau_j^{gb}=\begin{cases}\left[f(S^{gb})\right]^{-1}, & \text{if } j\in S^{gb}\\ 0, & \text{otherwise}\end{cases} \tag{12}$$

where ρ, $0<\rho<1$, is the pheromone evaporate factor; S^{ib} denotes the best solution in current iteration; S^{gb} denotes the global best found solution since the start of the algorithm;

$f(S^{ib})$ and $f(S^{gb})$ are the objective function vale of S^{ib} and S^{gb}, respectively; $\Delta\tau_j^{ib}$ and $\Delta\tau_j^{gb}$ are the quantities of pheromone released to column j based on these two pheromone update operations, respectively.

The global-best based pheromone update operation could make the search be concentrated around a current solution and limit the exploration of possible better ones, hence it is prone to trap into local optima; while the iteration-best based pheromone update operation could alleviate the danger of trapping into local optima but it may adversely reduce the convergence speed. Therefore, a mixed strategy, proposed by Stützle & Hoos (2000), is adopted in this study. Moreoever, in this study, another regulating strategy for these two types of pheromone update operations is also introduced, and the probability of the implementation of iteration-best based pheromone update operation is based on a bell-function defined by equation (13). In each iteration, if a generated uniform random number in the interval [0, 1] is less then the value of p_{ib}, the iteration-best based pheromone update operation will be executed; otherwise, the global-best based pheromone update operation will be executed.

$$p_{ib} = \frac{1}{1+\left|\frac{t-c}{a}\right|^{2b}} \qquad (13)$$

where a, b and c are three parameters, specified by user. In this study, a, b and c are set equal to $Lmt/3$ (Lmt denotes the maximal iteration number), 2.5 and 0, respectively. When Lmt is set equal to 100, the curve of number of iteration vs. p_{ib} is shown as Fig.1. In the early stage, the value of probability p_{ib} is relatively large, so the algorithm can benefit from stronger exploration of the search space, which can help escape from local optima and avoid the stagnation phenomenon. In the later stage, the value of probability p_{ib} is relatively small, so the algorithm can benefit from stronger exploitation of all best solution candidates, which can be conducive to improving the convergence speed.

4.6 Framework of ant colony algorithm

In this subsection, we will briefly present the whole framework of ant colony algorithm for simultaneous real value attribute discretization and reduction as follows.

1. Determine the candidate cuts and construct distinction table based on samples.
2. Parameters setting, such as weight parameter w, exploitation probability factor q_0, local pheromone update strength factor ξ, pheromone evaporate factor ρ, local search magnitude factor λ, number of ants $ANum$, and maximum iteration number Lmt.
3. Pheromone initialization.
4. Set $t=1$.
5. For each ant, implement solution construction operation.
6. For each feasible solution, remove all redundant columns.
7. For the set of best solutions in this iteration, implement local search operation.
8. Determine the iteration-best solution, and update the global-best solution.
9. Implement pheromone update operation.

10. Set $t = t + 1$, if t is less than Lmt, go back to step 5; otherwise, terminate and return the best solution.

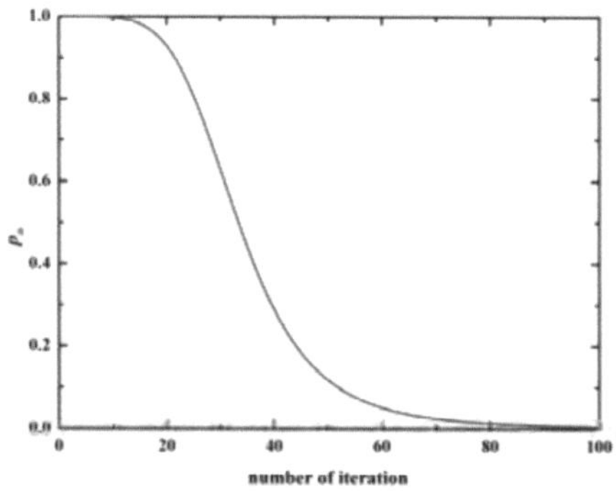

Figure 1. The curve of number of iteration vs. p_{ib} ($Lmt = 100$)

5. Experimental results and discussion

In this section, firstly, four datasets used for this study are briefly described; secondly, the effect of parameters on performance are studied and some suggestions for setting these parameters are presented; finally, the comparisons of our method with other three rough set theory based heuristic methods are provided.

5.1 Description of datasets

In this study, four datasets are used to validate the effectiveness of the proposed method, one dataset is nature spearmint essence (NSE), while the other three datasets are Glass, Wine and Iris obtained from the UCI (University of California, Irvine) machine learning repository available by the link: http://www.ics.uci.edu/~mlearn/MLRepository.html. The main characteristics of these four data sets are summarized in Table 1. The last column shows the number of initial cuts for these four datasets.

Dataset	Cases	Categorical attributes	Continuous Attributes	Classes	Number of Initial cuts
NSE	55	0	56	3	770
Glass	214	0	9	6	930
Wine	178	0	13	3	1263
Iris	150	0	4	3	119

Table 1. Four datasets used for this study

5.2 Parameters setting in ant colony algorithm

In this subsection, we will use the NSE dataset for studying the effect of parameters on performance, and some suggestions for setting these parameters will also be presented. In this study, we focus on the four controllable parameters which affect the performance of ant colony algorithm, exploitation probability factor q_0 shown in subsection 4.2, local pheromone update strength factor ξ shown in equation (10), pheromone evaporate factor ρ shown in equations (11) and (12), and local search magnitude factor λ shown in subsection 4.4. The number of ants $ANum$ is also an important parameter in ant colony algorithm. Dependent on the complexcity of a problem, this parameter must be sufficiently large to explore all potential solutions. In general, the larger the value of $ANum$, the better the final solution quality obtained by ant colony algorithm, and also the longer the execution time. Hence, the selection of number of ants should balance the trade-off between the solution quality and execution time. According to empirical studies, the value of $ANum$ is suggested to set equal to between [5, 20].

In order to study the effect of the parameters on the performance on the NSE dataset, a base value for each parameter is arbitrarily set as: $w = 0.5$, $q_0 = 0.5$, $\xi = 0.1$, $\rho = 0.05$, $\lambda = 0.2$, $ANum = 10$, $Lmt = 100$. When tuning one parameter, the other parameters are kept as their base values. Moreover, to reduce the influence of incidental variation, the tests for each parameter are all executed 10 times independently, and both the average value of objective function and the average iteration number of the first finding of the best solution are used for evaluating the effect of each parameter on performance. However, due to the existence of random factors, the tests can only reflect to some extent the impact of the various parameters on the final results.

5.2.1 Exploitation probability factor

Exploitation probability factor q_0 is used to control how strongly an ant deterministically exploits the combined past search experience and heuristic information. The larger the value of q_0, the larger the exploitation probability. Fig.2 and Fig.3 show the effect of exploitation probability factor q_0 on the average value of the objective function and the average iteration number, respectively. Fig.2 shows that the best algorithm performance when q_0 is equal to 0.4 or 0.7. Fig.3 shows that with the increase of the value of q_0, the average iteration number decreases. The possible reason could be with the large value of q_0, ant colony algorithm focuses on exploiting the space around the best found solution, so the convergence speed may be improved. However, a large value of q_0 may also lead to stagnation and the decrease of the probability of finding global optimum. Hence, the selection of "optimal" exploitation probability factor should balance the trade-off between exploration and exploitation performance. According to this study, the value of q_0 is suggested to set equal to between [0.4, 0.8], but it could vary in other cases.

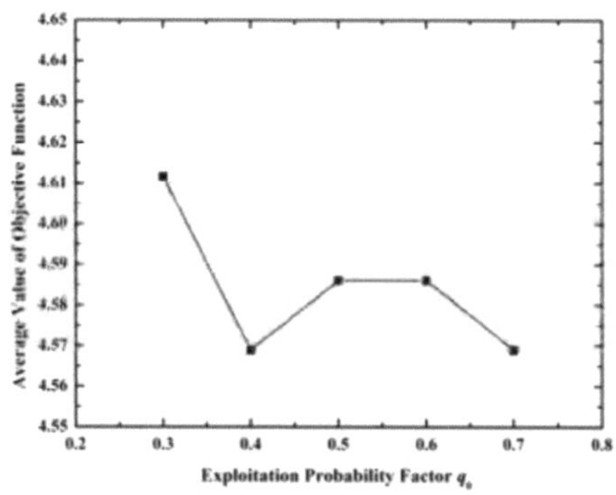

Figure 2. Effect of exploitation probability factor q_0 on average value of objective function for the NSE dataset

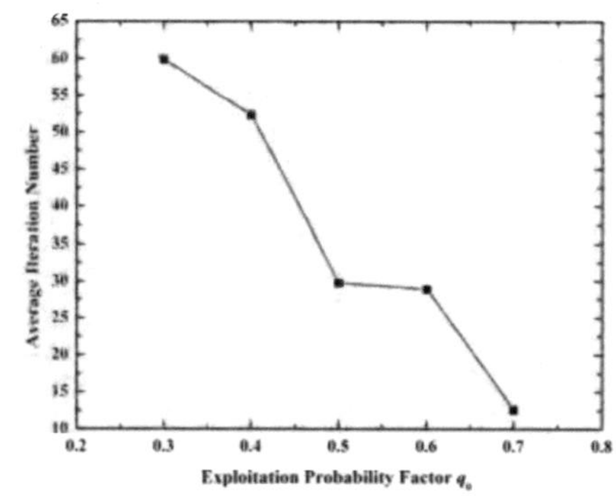

Figure 3. Effect of exploitation probability factor q_0 on average iteration number for the NSE dataset

5.2.2 Pheromone evaporate factor

In ant colony algorithm, cooperation among ants is based on pheromone, and global pheromone update operation can help ants maintain a well coordinated pheromone mediated cooperation. Fig.4 and Fig.5 show the effect of pheromone evaporate factor ρ on the average value of objective function and the average iteration number, respectively.

Fig.4 shows that the average quality of final solution is the best when ρ is equal to 0.05. On the one hand, according to equations (11) and (12), the larger the value of ρ, the more the amount of pheromone released in the best found solutions, which will attract more ants in the next iteration but probably also lead to stagnation. On the other hand, as shown in Fig.5, a large value of ρ can enhance the amount of different pheromone between the relative better solutions and relative worse solutions, so the convergence speed can be improved. However, the final solution could be a local optimum. Extremely, if the value of ρ is set equal to 0, the cooperation among ants will disappear, which would lead to a bad performance. Balancing the trade-off between the solution quality and execution time, the value of ρ is suggested to set between [0.05, 0.2].

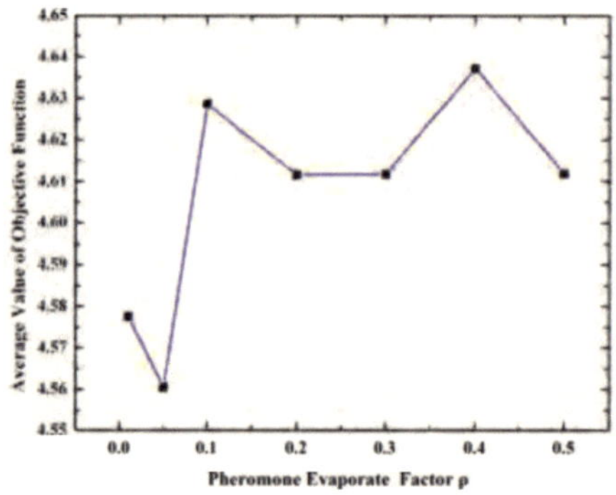

Figure 4. Effect of pheromone evaporate factor ρ on average value of objective function for the NSE dataset

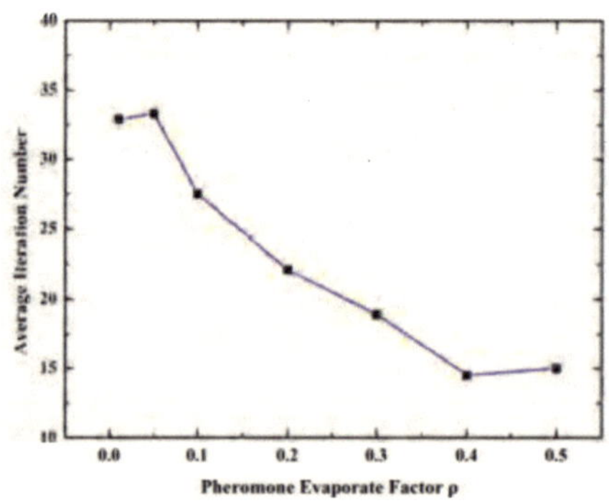

Figure 5. Effect of pheromone evaporate factor ρ on average iteration number for the NSE dataset

5.2.3 Local pheromone update strength factor

Similar to the function of pheromone evaporate factor, local pheromone update strength factor ξ also helps ants maintain a well coordinated pheromone mediated cooperation. Local pheromone update operation helps ants choose those columns that have never been explored previously, which can prevent the ants from converging to a common premature solution. Fig.6 and Fig.7 show the effect of the local pheromone update strength factor ξ on the average value of the objective function and the average iteration number, respectively. Fig.6 shows that the best average quality of final solution is obtained at ξ being 0.01 or 0.1, and Fig.7 shows the least average iteration number when ξ is equal to 0.05. In general, the local pheromone update operation just changes the desirability of columns for following ants, which can be conducive to increasing exploration. The larger the value of ξ, the more likely the probability for the system pheromone to go back to the initial level. Although it can enhance the exploration performance, it also weakens the pheromone level released by previous ants and leads to a lower convergence speed. Hence, we should reasonably select the value of ξ to balance the trade-off between exploration and convergence speed. The value of ξ is suggested to set between [0.05, 0.2] for this study.

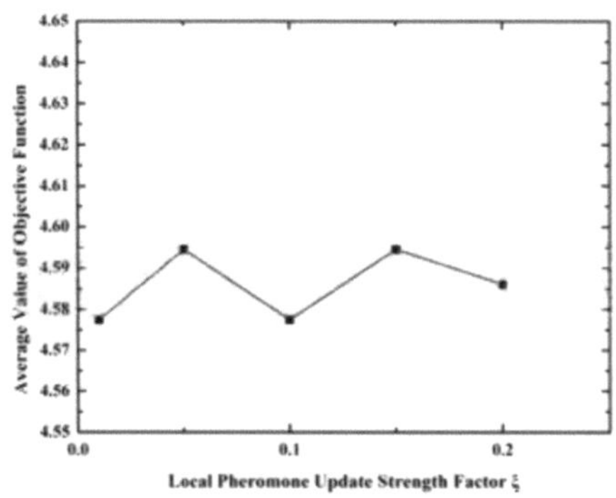

Figure 6. Effect of local pheromone update strength factor ξ on average value of objective function for the NSE dataset

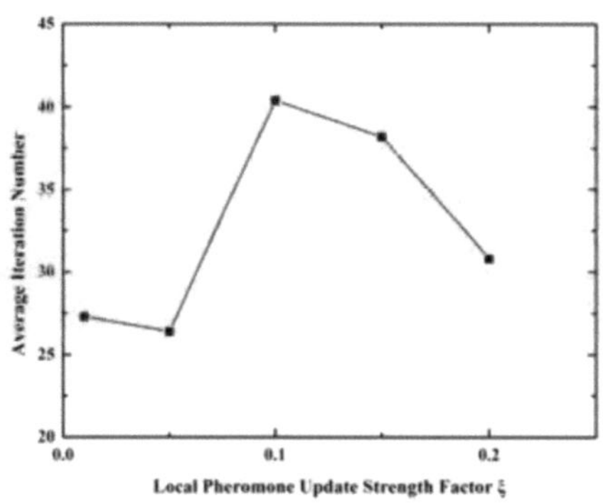

Figure 7. Effect of local pheromone update strength factor ξ on average iteration number for the NSE dataset

5.2.4 Local search magnitude factor

Local search operation usually can improve both the final solution quality and the speed of finding the best solution. Local search magnitude factor λ plays an important role in determining neighbourhood magnitude of a current solution. The larger the value of λ, the larger the neighbourhood magnitude. However, due to a limited iteration number of local search, a large value of λ could decrease the probability of finding a better solution in the neighbourhood area of the current solution. Fig.8 and Fig.9 show the effect of local search magnitude factor λ on the average value of the objective function and the average iteration number, respectively. Fig.8 shows that the best average quality of final solutions is obtained at λ being 0.3. As shown in Fig.9, with the increase of the value of λ, the average iteration number decreases. Balancing the trade-off the final solution quality and execution time, the value of λ is suggested set between [0.2, 0.4].

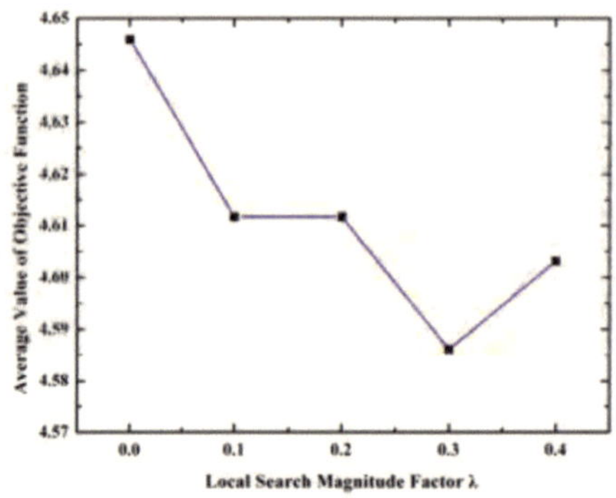

Figure 8. Effect of local search magnitude factor λ on average value of objective function for the NSE dataset

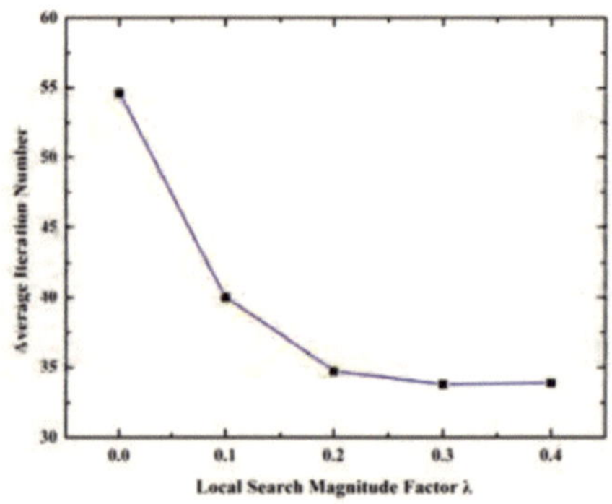

Figure 9. Effect of local search magnitude factor λ on average iteration number for the NSE dataset

5.3 Performance comparison

In this subsection, the other three rough set theory based heuristic methods are used for performance comparison with ant colony algorithm. These three methods include greedy method (Nguyen & Skowron, 1995), modified greedy method, and attribute importance based method (Hou et al., 2000). All of these three methods are deterministic methods, so their obtained results are unique for a given problem. The parameters setting for ant colony algorithm is shown as follows: $q_0 = 0.5$, $\xi = 0.1$, $\rho = 0.05$, $\lambda = 0.2$, $ANum = 10$, and $Lmt = 100$. To reduce the influence of incidental variation, the tests for each dataset are all executed 10 times independently. For performance comparison, on the one hand, we will provide the attribute numbers $AttrNum$ and cut numbers $CutNum$ obtained by these four methods; on the other hand, by introducing the weight parameter, we will give an exponential weighted value EWV, where $EWV = CutNum^{w} + AttrNum^{1-w}$, for a comprehsneive examination of the results obtained by these four methods. Due to the stochastic character of ant colony algorithm, the three performance comparison metrics are the average results of the 10 executations.

Table 2 shows the performance comparison of four methods for the NSE, Glass, Wine and Iris datasets, where the weight parameter w is set equal to 0.5 for computing exponential weighted value. It can be seen from Table 2 that (1) the attribute numbers obtained by ant colony algorithm are remarkably less than those obtained by greedy method and modified greedy method for all the four datasets, (2) although ant colony algorithm yields a little more cuts than the greedy method and modified greedy method for the NSE and Glass datasets, the cut numbers generated by ant colony algorithm are less than or equal to those obtained by these two methods for the Wine and Iris datasets, (3) the cut numbers obtained by ant colony algorithm are remarkably less than those obtained by attribute importance based method for the NSE, Glass and Wine datasets, and (4) although ant colony algorithm requires a little more attributes than the attribute importance based method for the Wine dataset, the attribute numbers obtained by ant colony algorithm are less than or equal to those obtained by that method for the NSE, Glass, and Iris datasets. These superiorities of ant colony algorithm could be supported by the fact that both greedy method and modified greedy method more focus on finding the minimal number of cuts while attribute importance based method more focus on finding the minimal number of attributes. Different from them, ant colony algorithm can simultaneously consider both objectives, minimal numbers of cuts and attributes.

It can also be seen from Table 2 that the exponential weighted value EWV obtained by ant colony algorithm is better than those obtained by the other three methods for the NSE, Glass and Wine datasets; and for the Iris dataset, the exponential weighted value EWV obtained by ant colony algorithm and attribute importance based method both rank top 1. Moreover, in our experiments, the standard deviations of these three metrics in 10 runs are very close to 0 for all the four datasets, which illustrates the stability of the ant colony algorithm.

Metrics		Methods			
		Attribute Importance Based Method	Greedy Method	Modified Greedy Method	Ant Colony Algorithm
NSE	*AttrNum*	3	7	6	3
	CutNum	19	7	7	8
	EWV	6.091	5.095	5.292	4.560
Glass	*AttrNum*	5	8	8	4.4
	CutNum	41	14	14	15.6
	EWV	8.639	6.570	6.570	6.043
Wine	*AttrNum*	2	6	5	3
	CutNum	21	6	6	6
	EWV	5.997	4.899	4.686	4.182
Iris	*AttrNum*	3	4	4	3
	CutNum	6	10	10	6
	EWV	4.182	5.162	5.162	4.182

Table 2. Performance comparison with four methods for four datasets ($w = 0.5$)

Fig.10 shows the exponential weighted values of the four methods for the NSE dataset with different weight parameters. Through changing the relative importance between the cut number and the attribute number by employing the weight parameter w, ant colony algorithm can easily find the optimal cut and attribute numbers, whose corresponding exponential weighted value is better than those obtained by the other three methods. Hence, from a balanced choice of optimal attributes and cuts, ant colony algorithm outperforms the other three methods.

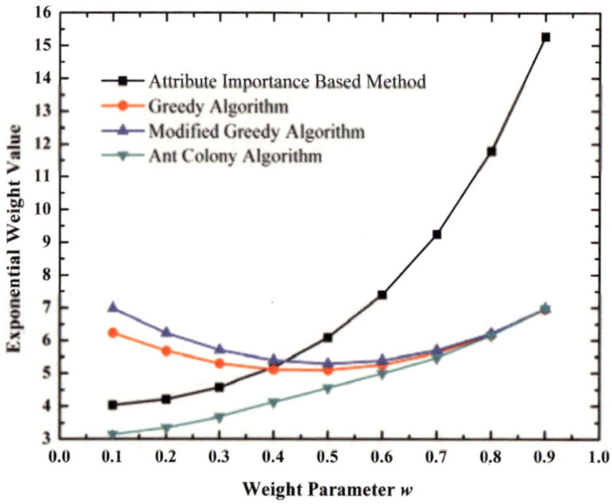

Figure 10. Performance comparison of four methods for the NSE dataset with different weight parameter w

6. Conclusions

In this study, ant colony algorithm is proposed for simultaneous real value attributes discretization and reduction. Based on the concept of distinction table in rough set theory, the relationship between discretization and reduction is discussed, and these two different problems can be integrated into a unified framework. Moreover, the relationship between this unified framework and set covering problem is analyzed. The detailed strategy for ant colony algorithm to solve this problem is proposed and applied to the four datasets. The obtained results demonstrate the effectiveness of the proposed method, showing the better performance than those of the other three rough set theory based heuristic methods.

However, this is a preliminary study, because we only considered the pre-processing step for pattern classification, and how this pre-processing step influences the final classification prediction performance has not been studied. Hence in the future research direction, we will focus on improving the performance of ant colony algorithm including global convergence performance and convergence speed and apply these proposed methods to problems with mass data. Meanwhile, we will combine the present method with any classification methods, such as rough set theory, decision tree, support vector machine, etc., for practical pattern classification problems.

7. Acknowledgements

This project was supported by the National Natural Science Foundation (20276063) of China.

8. References

Chmielewski, M.R. & Grzymala-Busse, J.W. (1994). Global discretization of attributes as preprocessing for machine learning. *Proceedings of the III International Workshop on Rough Set and Soft Computing*, pp. 294-301, San Jose, CA, November 1994

Colorni, A.; Dorigo, M. & Maniezzo V. (1991). Distributed optimization by ant colonies. *Proceeding of the First European Conference on Artificial Life*, pp. 134-142, Paris, France, 1991

Di Caro G. & Dorigo M. (1998). AntNet: distributed stigmergetic control for communications networks. *Journal of Artificial Intelligence Research*, Vol. 9, 317-365.

Dougherty J.; Kohavi R. & Sahami M. (1995). Supervised and unsupervised discretization of continuous features. *Proceedings of the Twelfth International Conference on Machine Learning*, pp. 194-202, Tahoe, CA, July 1995, Morgan Kaufmann

Dorigo, M. & Gambardella, L.M. (1997). Ant colony system: a cooperative learning approach to the travelling salesman problem. *IEEE Transactions on Evolutionary Computation*, Vol.1, No.1, 53-66.

Dorigo, M.; Maniezzo, V. & Colorni A. (1996). Ant system: optimization by a colony of cooperation agents. *IEEE Transaction on Systems, Man, and Cybernetics-Part B*, Vol. 26, No. 1, 29-41.

Gambardella, L.M. & Dorigo, M. (1995). Ant-Q: a reinforcement learning approach to the travelling salesman problem. *Proceedings of the Twelfth International Conference on Machine Learning*, pp. 252-260, Tahoe, CA, July 1995, Morgan Kaufmann

Gambardella, L.M. & Dorigo, M. (2000). Ant colony system hybridized with a new local search for sequential ordering problem. *INFORMS Journal on Computing*, Vol. 12, No. 3, 237-255.

Hadji, R.; Rahoual, M.; Talbi, E. & Bachelet, V. (2000). Ant colonies for the set covering problem. *Proceedings of ANTS' 2000 -- From Ant Colonies to Artificial Ants: Second International Workshop on Ant Algorithms*, pp. 63-66, Brussels, Belgium, September 2000, Springer-Verlag

Han, J.C.; Hu, X.H & LIN T.Y. (2004). Feature Subset Selection Based on Relative Dependency between Attributes. *Proceedings of the Fourth International Conference on Rough Sets and Current Trends in Computing*, pp. 176-185, Uppsala, Sweden, June 2004, Springer-Verlag

Hou, L.J.; Wang G.Y. & Nie. N. (2000). The discretization problems of rough set theory. *Computer Science*, Vol.27, No.12, 89-94.

Housos, E. & Elmoth T. (1997). Automatic optimization of subproblems in scheduling airlines crews. *Interfaces*, Vol. 27, No. 5, 68-77.

Jensen, R. & Shen, Q. (2003). Finding Rough Set Reducts with Ant Colony Optimization. *Proceeding of 2003 UK Workshop on Computational Intelligence*, pp. 15-22, Bristol, UK, September 2003

Komorowski, J.; Pawlak, Z.; Polkowski, L. & Skowron, A. (1998). Rough sets: A Tutorial. In: *Rough-fuzzy hybridization: a new trend in decision making*, Pal S.K. & Skowron A, pp. 3-98, Springer Verlag

Lessing, L.; Dumitrescu, I. & Stützle, T. (2004). A Comparison between ACO Algorithms for the Set Covering Problem. *ANTS' 2004, Fourth Internatinal Workshop on Ant Algorithms and Swarm Intelligence*, pp. 1-12, Brussels, Belgium, September 2004, Springer Verlag

Liu, H.; Hussain, F.; Tan, C.L. & Dash, M. (2002). Discretization: an enabling technique. *Data Mining and Knowledge Discovery*, Vol. 6, No. 4, 393-423.

Lourenço, H.R. & Serra, D. (2002). Adaptive search heuristics for the generalized assignment problem. *Mathware and Soft Computing*, Vol. 9, No. 2-3, 209-234.

Merkle, D.; Middendorf, M. & Schmeck, H. (2002). Ant colony optimization for resource-constrained project scheduling. *IEEE Transaction on Evolutionary Computation*, Vol. 6, No. 4, 333-346.

Merkle, D. & Middendorf, M. (2003). Ant colony optimization with global pheromone evaluation for scheduling a single machine. *Applied Intelligence*, Vol. 18, No. 1, 105-111.

Nguyen, S.H. & Skowron, A. (1995). Quantization of real value attributes: rough set and boolean reasoning approach. Proceedings of the Second Joint Annual Conference on Information Sciences, pp. 34-37, Wrightswille Beach, NC, September 1995

Nguyen, H.S. (1998). Discretization problem for rough sets methods. *Proceedings of the First International Conference on Rough Sets and Current Trends in Computing*, pp. 545-552, Warsaw, Poland, June 1998, Springer-Verlag

Pawlak, Z. (1982). Rough sets. *International Journal of Information and Computer Science*, Vol.11, No.5, 341-356.

Rahoual, M.; Hadji, R. & Bachelet V. (2002). Parallel Ant System for the Set Covering Problem. *Proceedings of the Third International Workshop on Ant Algorithms*, pp. 262-267, Brussels, Belgium, September 2002, Springer-Verlag

Revelle, C.D.; Marks, D. & Liebman, J.C. (1970). An analysis of private and public sector facilities location models. *Management Science*, Vol. 16, 692-707.

Schoonderwoerd, R.; Holland, O.; Bruten, J. & Rothkrantz, L. (1996). Ant-based load balancing in telecommunications networks. *Adaptive Behavior*, Vol. 5, No. 2, 169-207.

Stützle, T. & Hoos, H.H. (1997). The Max-Min ant system and local search for the travelling salesman problem. *Proceeding of the 1997 IEEE International Conference on Evolutionary Computation*, pp. 309-314, Piscataway, NJ, April 1997, IEEE Press

Stützle, T. (1998). An ant approach to the flow shop problem. *Proceeding of the Sixth European Congress on Intelligent Techniques & Soft Computing*, pp. 1560-1564, September 1998, Aachen, Germany, Verlag Mainz, Wissenschaftsverlag

Stützle, T. && Hoos, H.H. (2000). MAX-MIN ant system. *Future Generation Computer Systems*, Vol. 16, No. 8, 889-914.

Wang, X.Y.; Yang, J.; Teng, X.L.; Xia, W.J. & Jensen, R. (2007). Feature selection based on rough sets and particle swarm optimization. *Pattern Recognition Letters*. Vol. 28, No. 4, 459-471.

Wróblewski, J. (1995). Finding minimal reducts using genetic algorithms. *Proceeding of the Second Annual Join Conference on Information Sciences*, pp.186-189, September 1995, Wrightsville Beach, NC

3

A New Ant Colony Optimization Approach for the Degree-Constrained Minimum Spanning Tree Problem Using Prüfer and Blob Codes Tree Coding

Yoon-Teck Bau, Chin-Kuan Ho and Hong-Tat Ewe
Faculty of Information Technology, Multimedia University
Malaysia

1. Introduction

This chapter describes a novel ACO algorithm for the degree-constrained minimum spanning tree (d-MST) problem. Instead of constructing the d-MST directly on the construction graph, ants construct the encoded d-MST. Two well-known tree codings are used: the Prüfer code, and the more recent Blob code (Picciotto, 1999). Both of these tree codings are bijective because they represent each spanning tree of the complete graph on $|V|$ labelled vertices as a code of $|V|$-2 vertex labels. Each spanning tree corresponds to a unique code, and each code corresponds to a unique spanning tree. Under the proposed approach, ants will select graph vertices and place them into the Prüfer code or Blob code being constructed. The use of tree codings such as Prüfer code or Blob code makes it easier for the proposed ACO to solve another variant of the d-MST problem with both lower and upper bound constraints on each vertex (lu-dMST). A general lu-dMST problem formulation is given. This general lu-dMST problem formulation could be used to denote d-MST problem formulation also. Subsequently, Prüfer code and Blob code tree encoding and decoding are presented and then followed by the design of two ACO approaches using these tree codings to solve d-MST and lu-dMST problems. Next, results from these ACO approaches are compared on structured hard (SHRD) graph data set for both d-MST and lu-dMST problems, and important findings are reported.

2. Problem Formulation

In this chapter, a special case of degree-constrained minimum spanning tree where the lower and upper bound of the number of edges is imposed on each vertex is considered. This similar to the problem being solved by Chou et al. (2001), and is named lu-dMST in this chapter. Chou et al. (2001) named this problem as DCMST. The d-MST problem is different since it has only the upper bound constraint. Chou et al. (2001) also proposed the following notation to be used for the lu-dMST problem formulation:
$G = (V, E)$ connected weighted undirected graph.
i, j = index of labelled vertices $i, j = 0, 1, 2, \ldots, |V - 1|$.

$V = \{v_0, v_1, ..., v_{|V|-1}\}$ is a finite set of vertices in the G.
$E = \{e_{ij} \mid i \in V, j \in V, i \neq j\}$ is a finite set of edges in the G.
T = set of all spanning trees corresponding to the G.
$\mathbf{x}$ = a subgraph of G.
C_{ij} = nonnegative real number edge cost that connect vertex i and vertex j.
$L_d(i)$ is lower bound degree constraint on vertex i. Lower bound can vary from vertex to vertex.
$U_d(i)$ is upper bound degree constraint on vertex i. Upper bound can vary from vertex to vertex.

$$\min\left\{ z(\mathbf{x}) = \sum_{\substack{i,j\in V\\ i<j}} C_{ij}X_{ij}. \right\} \tag{1}$$

subject to:

$$\sum_{\substack{j\in V\\ i\neq j}} X_{ij} \geq L_d(i),\ i\in V. \tag{2}$$

$$\sum_{\substack{j\in V\\ i\neq j}} X_{ij} \leq U_d(i),\ i\in V. \tag{3}$$

$$\sum_{\substack{i,j\in N\\ i<j}} X_{ij} \leq |N|-1, N\subset V. \tag{4}$$

$$\sum_{\substack{i,j\in V\\ i<j}} X_{ij} = |V|-1. \tag{5}$$

$$X_{ij} = \begin{Bmatrix} 1, \text{ if edge } e_{ij} \text{ is part of the subgraph } \mathbf{x} \mid i,j\in V, \mathbf{x}\in T; \\ 0, \text{ otherwise.} \end{Bmatrix} \tag{6}$$

The objective function (1) seeks to minimize the total connection cost between vertices. The total cost could be distance, material cost, or customers' requirement cost. The subconstraint ($i < j$) shows that graph is symmetric because vertex i must be less than vertex j where $i, j \in V$. Constraints (2) and (3) specify the lower and upper bounds degree constraints on the number of edges connecting to a vertex. The lower and upper bounds can vary from vertex to vertex. In the d-MST problem, there is only a degree constraint on each vertex. This is given by a constant value d. For the d-MST problem, the lower bound equals 1 and the upper bound equals d on each vertex. Therefore the lu-dMST problem formulation is a generalization of d-MST. At the same time, the lu-dMST problem is also NP-hard because the lu-dMST problem is a general problem formulation that can be used to represent d-MST problem (Garey & Johnson, 1979; Sipser, 2006).
Constraint (4) is an anticycle constraint and constraint (5) indicates that the number of edges in a spanning tree is always equal to the number of vertices minus one. At the same time, the designed networks should not have self-loop, cycles and missing vertices. Equation (6) expresses the binary decision variable X_{ij} equals to one if the edge between vertices i to j is part of the subgraph $\mathbf{x}$, and $\mathbf{x}$ is a spanning tree in T; zero, otherwise. A subgraph $\mathbf{x}$ of G is said to be a spanning tree in T if $\mathbf{x}$:

a. contains all the vertices of G and the vertices can be in non-order form;
b. is connected and graph contains no cycles.

Note that in a complete graph having $|V|$ vertices, the number of edges, $|E|$, is $|V|(|V|-1)/2$, and the number of spanning trees is $|V|^{|V|-2}$.

3. Prüfer code and Blob code tree codings

The Prüfer code of spanning trees is based on Prüfer's constructive proof of Cayley's Formula. Cayley showed that the number of distinct spanning trees in a complete undirected graph on $|V|$ vertices is $|V|^{|V|-2}$ (Cayley, 1889; Gross & Yellen, 2006). Prüfer described a one-to-one mapping between these trees and strings of length $|V|$-2 over an integer of $|V|$ vertex labels (Prüfer, 1918; Gross & Yellen, 2006). Thus, a Prüfer code of length $|V|$-2 whose vertices are the labels {0, 1, ..., $|V|$-1} from a spanning tree of the complete graph on $|V|$ vertices for $|V| \geq 2$ is any sequence of integers between 0 and $|V|$-1, with repetitions allowed. The following Fig. 1 shows Prüfer tree encoding algorithm that constructs a Prüfer code from a given standard labelled tree. It defines a encoding function $f_e : T_{|V|} \rightarrow C_{|V|-2}$ from the set $T_{|V|}$ of trees on $|V|$ labelled vertices to the set $C_{|V|-2}$ of Prüfer code of length $|V|$-2. For example, a Prüfer code (3, 3, 6, 4, 0) corresponds to a spanning tree on seven vertices graph in Fig. 2. The first position value for Prüfer code is 3 because the Prüfer encoding algorithm finds the neighbour of vertex v of degree 1 with the smallest label in the spanning tree T is 3 whereby $v = 1$. Then the vertex labelled $v = 1$ is removed from the spanning tree T. This process is repeated to find the second position value for Prüfer code until only two vertices are remained in the spanning tree T. Two vertices remained in the spanning tree T as in the example mentioned below are vertices labelled 0 and 6. Notice also for example in Fig. 2 that the degree of each vertex in the spanning tree can be easily checked because it is one more than the number of times its label appears in the Prüfer code.

Fig. 3 shows the Prüfer decoding algorithm that maps a given Prüfer code to a standard labelled tree. The Prüfer decoding algorithm defines a function $f_d : C_{|V|-2} \rightarrow T_{|V|}$ from the set of Prüfer code of length $|V|$-2 to the set of labelled trees on the $|V|$ vertices. For example, the Prüfer decoding algorithm identifies the tree's edges in this order: (1, 3), (2, 3), (3, 6), (5, 4), (4, 0), and (0, 6) as in Fig. 2. The Prüfer code's integers appear as the second vertices in the tree's first five edges. The last edge (0, 6) is joined by remaining two integers in list L (line 12 of Fig. 3) to produce the spanning tree with its vertex-labelling. Notice that the tree obtained in Fig. 2 by Prüfer decoding of the sequence (3, 3, 6, 4, 0) is the same as the tree that used by Prüfer-encoded sequence of (3, 3, 6, 4, 0) at the beginning. This inverse relationship between the encoding and decoding functions asserts that the decoding function $f_d : C_{|V|-2} \rightarrow T_{|V|}$ is the inverse of the encoding function $f_e : T_{|V|} \rightarrow C_{|V|-2}$.

```
labelledTreeToPruferCode(T = (V, E), Cij)
code ← ()
Initialise T to be the given tree.
for i = 1 to |V|-2 do
   Let v be the vertex of degree 1 with the smallest label in T.
   Let code[i-1] be the label of the only neighbour of v.
   T ← T - {v}
return code
```

Figure 1. The pseudocode of Prüfer encoding from the labelled tree to its Prüfer code

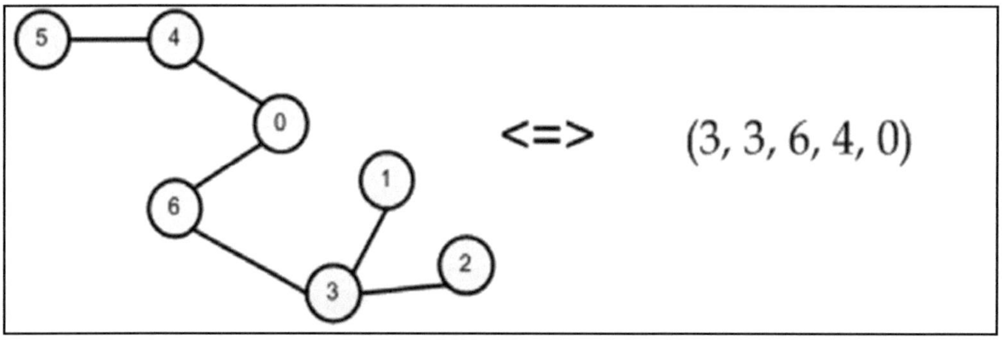

Figure 2. A Prüfer code and the spanning tree on seven vertices that it represents and vice versa via Prüfer encoding and decoding algorithms

```
pruferCodeToLabelledTree(code)
Initialise code as the Prufer input sequence of length |V|-2.
Initialise forest F as |V| isolated vertices, labelled from 0 to |V|-1.
L ← {0, 1, …, |V|-1}
E_T ← { }
for i = 1 to |V|-2 do
   Let k be the smallest integer in list L that is not in the code.
   Let j be the first integer in the code.
   E_T ← E_T ∪ {(k, j)}
   L ← L - {k}
   Remove the first occurrence of j from the code.
Add an edge joining the vertices labelled with the two remaining integers in list L.
return E_T
```

Figure 3. The pseudocode of Prüfer decoding from the Prüfer code to its labelled tree

There are many other mappings from integers of $|V|$-2 vertex labels to spanning trees. Picciotto (1999) has described three tree codings, different from Prüfer code. One of the tree codings is called the Blob code. In Picciotto's presentation, Prüfer codes decoded as Blob codes represent directed spanning trees rooted at vertex 0. In such a tree, there is a directed path from every vertex to vertex 0, and only vertex 0 has no out-edge. Ignoring the edges's direction yields an undirected spanning tree.

Figure 4 shows the Blob encoding algorithm for finding Blob code for a spanning tree. A *blob* is an aggregation of one or more vertices. This algorithm is progressively identifying vertices, starting at $|V|$-1 and ending with a blob-vertex consisting of all the vertices from 1 to $|V|$-1. As the *blob* grows, so does the code; meanwhile, the number of directed edges shrinks. At first, an undirected spanning tree is temporarily regarded as a directed spanning tree rooted at vertex labelled 0 to determine the successor *succ*(v) of every vertex $v \in [1, |V|-1]$ where *succ*(v) is the first vertex on the unique path from vertex v to vertex 0 in a spanning tree. The Blob encoding algorithm uses this directed spanning tree rooted at vertex labelled 0 as a set of directed edges whose vertices are the labels {0, 1, ..., $|V|$-1} as its input. The algorithm uses two functions: *succ*(v) returns the first vertex on the unique path from vertex v to vertex 0 in a spanning tree, and (*path*(v) $\cap$ *blob*) returns TRUE if the directed path (an ordered list of vertices) using those directed edges from vertex v toward vertex 0 intersects the *blob*, FALSE otherwise.

```
1  labelledTreeToBlobCode(T = (V, E), C_ij)
2  blob ← {|V|-1}
3  blobCode ← ( ) //an array of length |V|-2
4  for i = 1 to |V|-2 do
5     if path(|V|-1-i) ∩ blob ≠ Ø then
6        blobCode[|V|-2-i] ← succ(|V|-1-i)
7        E_T ← E_T - {(|V|-1-i → succ(|V|-1-i))}
8        blob ← blob ∪ {|V|-1-i}
9     else
10       blobCode[|V|-2-i] ← succ(blob)
11       E_T ← E_T - {(blob → succ(blob))}
12       E_T ← E_T ∪ {(blob → succ(|V|-1-i))}
13       E_T ← E_T - {(|V|-1-i → succ(|V|-1-i))}
14       blob ← blob ∪ {|V|-1-i}
15 return blobCode
```

Figure 4. The pseudocode of Blob encoding from the labelled tree to its Blob code

An example of a Blob code corresponds to a directed spanning tree on seven vertices graph is given in Fig. 5. The successor *succ*(v) information for this directed spanning tree is shown in Table 1. Once this table has been constructed, the Blob code corresponding to this directed spanning tree on seven vertices graph is equal to (3, 3, 6, 4, 0). Initially on line 2 of Fig. 4, a *blob* containing a single vertex 6 is created, the vertex 6 is the largest label and *blobCode* = ( ). The *blobCode* is an array of length $|V|$-2. The Blob encoding algorithm's first iteration (*path*($|V|$-1-i) ∩ *blob*) = (*path*(5) ∩ *blob*) is FALSE on line 5 of Fig. 4. So the **else** block is followed whereby *blobCode*[4] = 0; delete (*blob* → 0) edge; add an edge from *blob* → *succ*(5) which is 4; delete the edge (5 → 4) and put 5 into the *blob*. The second iteration (*path*(4) ∩ *blob*) is also FALSE. So the **else** block is followed whereby *blobCode*[3] = 4; delete (*blob* → 4) edge; add an edge from *blob* → *succ*(4) which is 0; delete the edge (4 → 0) and put 4 into the *blob*. The third iteration (*path*(3) ∩ *blob*) is TRUE. The **then** block is followed in the algorithm whereby *blobCode*[2] = 6 which is *succ*(3); delete the edge (3 → 6) and put 3 in the blob. This process continues through two more iterations which *blobCode*[1] = 3 and *blobCode*[0] = 3 are obtained, and hence the Blob code of length $|V|$-2 is equal to *blobCode* = (3, 3, 6, 4, 0) is determined. It happened that this Blob code is the same with Prüfer code as in Fig. 2 using the same spanning tree as an example.

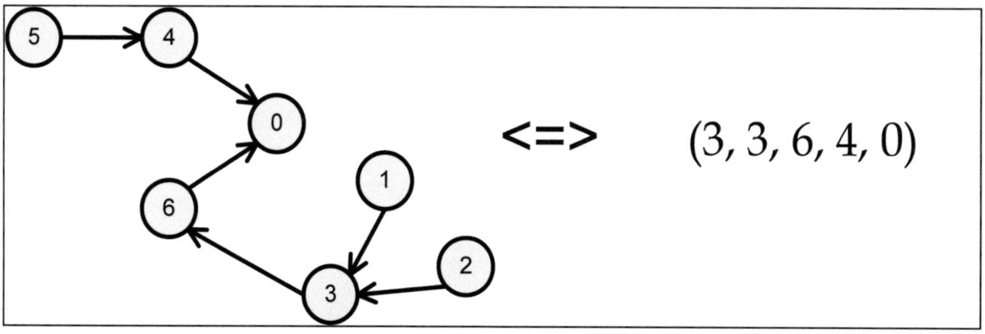

Figure 5. A Blob code and a rooted directed spanning tree on seven vertices that it represents and vice versa via Blob encoding and decoding algorithms

v	$succ(v)$
1	3
2	3
3	6
4	0
5	4
6	0

Table 1. The successor $succ(v)$ information of every vertex $v \in [1, |V|-1]$

Nevertheless Blob code is already proven to be a different coding system from the Prüfer code by Picciotto (1999) in his PhD thesis even tough Blob code contains the same number of times of its vertex label as it appears in the Prüfer code for the same spanning tree representation. The reason for this is the sequences of both Blob code and Prüfer code can have distinct vertex label for each of their sequence position to represent the same spanning tree. An example suffices to prove that Blob code = (2, 4, 4, 6, 2, 4) is different from the Prüfer code = (6, 2, 4, 2, 4, 4) even though these codes are used to represent the same spanning tree.

To identify the directed spanning tree that a Blob code represents, the Blob decoding algorithm begins with a single directed edge from a *blob* to vertex 0. This *blob* contains all the other vertices except vertex labelled 0, and as the algorithm proceeds, it always contains vertices numbered i, i+1, ..., $|V|$-2 as i moves from 1 to $|V|$-2. The algorithm scans the code and adjusts the developing spanning tree depending on whether or not the directed path from each vertex in Blob code toward vertex 0 intersects the *blob*, which shrinks by one vertex on each iteration. The following Fig. 6 summarizes the Blob decoding algorithm, which also uses the same two functions as Blob encoding algorithm: $succ(v)$ and ($path(v) \cap blob$). The edges directions are ignored to obtain the undirected spanning tree that the Blob code represents.

```
blobCodeToLabelledTree(blobCode)
blob ← {1, 2, ..., |V|-1}
E_T ← {(blob → 0)}
for i = 1 to |V|-2 do
   blob ← blob – {i}
   if path(blobCode[i–1]) ∩ blob ≠ Ø then
      E_T ← E_T ∪ {(i → blobCode[i–1])}
   else
      E_T ← E_T ∪ {(i → succ(blob))}
      E_T ← E_T – {(blob → succ(blob))}
      E_T ← E_T ∪ {(blob → blobCode[i–1])}
// now blob is a vertex labelled |V|-1
blob ← {|V|-1} in any edges where the blob appears.
return E_T
```

Figure 6. The pseudocode of Blob decoding from the Blob code to its labelled tree

Figure 5 shows the Blob code (3, 3, 6, 4, 0) and the spanning tree to which it decodes via the Blob decoding algorithm. The algorithm identifies the tree's (directed) edges in this order: (1, 3), (2, 3), (3, 6), (4, 0), (5, 4), and (6, 0). Initially on line 2 of Fig. 6, the *blob* contains vertices 1 through 6 and the tree consists of the single edge (*blob* → 0). The algorithm's first iteration removes vertex 1 from the *blob*. The *blobCode*[0] = 3 and the *blob* contains vertex 3, so that (*path*(3) ∩ *blob*) is TRUE and the edge (1 → 3) is added to the tree. The second iteration removes vertex 2 from the *blob*. The *blobCode*[1] = 3, (*path*(3) ∩ *blob*) is also TRUE, and the edge (2 → 3) is added to the tree. The third iteration removes vertex 3 from the *blob*. The *blobCode*[2] = 6, (*path*(6) ∩ *blob*) is TRUE, and the edge (3 → 6) is added to the tree. The fourth iteration removes vertex 4 from the *blob*. The *blobCode*[3] = 4, (*path*(4) ∩ *blob*) is FALSE. So the **else** block is followed whereby *succ*(*blob*) which is 0; an edge (4 → 0) is added to the tree; delete the edge (*blob* → 0) and add an edge (*blob* → 4). This process continues through one more iteration, each of which increases the number of the tree's edges by one. Then, the *blob* itself is replaced by vertex 6 as on line 13 of Fig. 6. The Blob code's integers appear as the destination vertices of the first five edges. An efficient implementation of the algorithm represents the directed edges in an array that is indexed by the vertex labels. If (i → j) is an edge, then the array entry indexed i holds j. As in Prüfer codes, the degree of each vertex in the spanning tree is one more than the number of times its label appears in the Blob code decoded by the Blob decoding algorithm. This is the same directed spanning tree that was encoded by the Blob encoding algorithm as shown as example above. So, the Blob decoding algorithm has indeed reversed the Blob encoding algorithm.

4. An ACO algorithm using Prüfer code and Blob code tree codings for d-MST problem

In the design of an ACO algorithm, it has been customary to have the ants work directly on the construction graph. For pheromones associated with the graph edges, a common difficulty is the number of pheromone updates is in the order of $O(|V|^2)$, V being the set of vertices of the construction graph. A new ACO algorithm for the d-MST problem is proposed that can address this challenge in a novel way. Instead of constructing the d-MST directly on the construction graph, ants construct the encoded d-MST as solution components. Two well-known tree codings either by using the Prüfer code or the more recent Blob code is used. Under the proposed approach, ants will select graph vertices and place them into the Prüfer code or Blob code being constructed. The advantages of using tree codings as ACO solution components are it reduces the complexity of the number of pheromone update operations to $O(|V|-2)$ attributed to the length of the Prüfer or Blob codes, capable of representing all possible spanning trees from these tree codings, capable of representing only graph spanning trees, and the degree of each vertex in the decoded spanning tree is easily determined whether it's satisfied the degree constraint, d or not. The degree of each vertex in the spanning tree is one more than the number of times its label appears in the Prüfer or Blob codes.

The pseudocode of the proposed ACO approach for d-MST problem is given in Fig. 7. Both of the Prüfer coding and the Blob coding can be applied using this pseudocode. This ACO approach uses local search procedure. The pseudocode of the local search procedure using exchange mutation is given in Fig. 8. Two separate experiments are conducted for the ACO approach in Fig. 7. The first experiment uses the Prüfer encoding and decoding algorithms.

The second experiment uses the Blob encoding and decoding algorithms. Lines from 2 to 4 of Fig. 7 set several parameters for the ACO approach. The parameters are:

- τ_0 is the initial pheromone,
- maximum edge weight cost for SHRD graph is set to 20* | *V* |,
- pheromone trails τ_{vr} be the desirability of assigning vertex *v* to a tree code of array index *r* is initially set to a small value as τ_0 = | *V* |^2*20* | *V* |, where *v* ∈ [0, | *V* |-1] and *r* ∈ [0, | *V* |-3]. Note that, [0, | *V* |-1] is the vertex labels in the spanning tree from 0 to | *V* |-1 and [0, | *V* |-3] is the array indices of the tree code (in array structure) of length | *V* |-2 from 0 to | *V* |-3,
- *mAnts* is the number of ants,
- *antDeg*[*k*][*v*] is the array of ant *k* degree for each vertex *v* in the spanning tree where *k* ∈ [1, *mAnts*] and *v* ∈ [0, | *V* |-1],
- *ant*[*k*].*avlVtx* is the list of ant *k* available vertices to be selected from the spanning tree vertices where *k* ∈ [1, *mAnts*],
- *antTreeCode*[*k*][*r*] is the array of ant *k* tree code of length | *V* |-2 where *k* ∈ [1, *mAnts*] and *r* ∈ [0, | *V* |-3],
- *d-PrimCode*[*r*] is the tree code of d-Prim degree-constrained spanning tree (d-ST) of length | *V* |-2 where *r* ∈ [0, | *V* |-3]. The d-Prim algorithm as described in (Narula & Ho, 1980; Knowles & Corne, 2000) is a greedy algorithm and might not always find the globally optimal solution. It is based upon alterations or additions to Prim's algorithm (Prim, 1957) for finding a MST. The *d-PrimCode* is encoded from its d-Prim d-ST by using tree encoding algorithms,
- *d-ST^{gb}Code*[*r*] is the tree code of global-best degree-constrained spanning tree of length | *V* |-2 where *r* ∈ [0, | *V* |-3]. Initially *d-ST^{gb}Code* ← *d-PrimCode,*
- *ant_d-STCost*[*k*] is the total weight cost of d-ST^k of *antTreeCode*[*k*] where *k* ∈ [1, *mAnts*]. The *antTreeCode*[*k*] cost is computed from its d-ST by using tree decoding algorithm,
- *d-PrimCost* is the total weight cost of d-Prim d-ST. The d-Prim d-ST is determined by using d-Prim algorithm,
- L^{gb} is the total weight cost of d-ST^{gb}. Initially L^{gb} ← *d-PrimCost,*
- a positive integer which governs the influences of pheromone trails α,
- evaporation rate ρ,
- a positive integer Q, and
- *termination_cond* is the termination condition where it can be either a predefined number of iterations has been reached or a satisfactory solution has been found.

The ACO algorithm starts by initialising *d-ST^{gb}Code* of length | *V* |-2 to be equal to the *d-PrimCode* as on line 3 of Fig. 7. d-Prim d-ST is encoded by using tree encoding algorithm to obtain its *d-PrimCode.* Then, the ants start to construct their tree code solutions. Initially, *antDeg*[*k*][*v*] is set to 1 where *k* ∈ [1, *mAnts*] and *v* ∈ [0, | *V* |-1] as on line 8 of Fig. 7. The reason for this is the degree of each vertex in the spanning tree is one more than the number of times label of vertices appears in the Prüfer or Blob codes and initially for each ant their *antTreeCode*[*k*] is emptied. Next, for each ant their *ant*[*k*].*avlVtx* is initially set to {0, 1, …, | *V* |-1} where the spanning tree vertex labels start from 0 to | *V* |-1 (line 9 of Fig. 7). Line 12 of Fig. 7 the ants start to construct their first (index 0) tree code solutions by selecting a vertex *v* from *ant*[*k*].*avlVtx* randomly. A particular vertex *v* will be removed from *ant*[*k*].*avlVtx* so that the vertex *v* won't be available anymore if (*antDeg*[*k*][*v*] = $U_d(v)$). The reason for this is to ensure that degree constraint is not violated. For the remaining tree code position value that is starting from its second position (index 1) to its last position (index $|V|$-3) as lines from 16 to 32 of Fig. 7, every ant will select a vertex v among the available vertices from *ant*[*k*].*avlVtx* probabilistically by applying the roulette wheel selection (Goldberg, 1989; Michaelwicz, 1996; Dorigo & Stützle, 2004) method. According to the probability on line 25 of Fig. 7, only the pheromone trail τ_{vr} indicates the desirability of assigning vertex v to a tree code at array index r is being used. Notice also that this probability formula does not use any visibility measure because the pheromone trail τ_{vr} does not means that an edge cost connecting from vertex v (the ant k tree code array value) to vertex r (the ant k tree code array index) always exists.

After every ant k has completed their *antTreeCode*[*k*] of length $|V|$-2, then the *ant_d-STCost*[*k*] is determined from their *antTreeCode*[*k*] where *antTreeCode*[*k*] is decoded by using the tree decoding algorithm to obtain the ant k d-ST^k. If the *ant_d-STCost*[*k*] is less costly than the current L^{gb} as on line 36 of Fig. 7, then the current *d-ST*^{gb}*Code* will be replaced to be equal to *antTreeCode*[*k*]. Next, the local search procedure by using exchange mutation is applied as on line 39 of Fig. 7. The new mutated tree code will always produce a new feasible d-ST. The detail of exchange mutation is given in Fig. 8. The exchange mutation used here takes the current *d-ST*^{gb}*Code* and the current L^{gb} as its inputs. Then, two different positions from *d-ST*^{gb}*Code* are being selected randomly so that both of the position values can be exchanged. As on line 10 of Fig. 8, the number of times for the exchange mutation procedure that takes the mutated code as its input to be repeated is equal to $|V|/2$ if $|V|$ is an even number, else $(|V|+1)/2$. Notice that, lines from 14 to 30 of Fig. 8, the exchange mutation will be stopped even if the number of repetition has not been completed; if the current new mutated d-ST code is less costly than the current d-ST^{gb} code. Then, the current d-ST^{gb} code will be replaced by the better mutated d-ST code. If the mutated d-ST code is not better than the current d-ST^{gb} code, the current d-ST^{gb} code will be remained without any changes made to its spanning tree code as implied on line 31 of Fig. 8.

```
1  procedure ACO for d-MST
2     Set parameters.
3     d-ST^gbCode ← d-PrimCode //d-Prim d-ST is encoded by using tree encoding algorithm
4     L^gb ← d-PrimCost
5     while termination_cond = false do
6        for k = 1 to mAnts do
7           for v = 0 to |V|-1 do
8              antDeg[k][v] = 1 //each ant k spanning tree vertices initial degree is set to 1
9           ant[k].avlVtx ← {0, 1, …, |V|-1}
10       for k = 1 to mAnts do
11          v ← select from ant[k].avlVtx randomly
12          antTreeCode[k][0] = v
13          antDeg[k][v] = antDeg[k][v] + 1
14           if antDeg[k][v] = U_d(v) then
15              ant[k].avlVtx ← ant[k].avlVtx – {v}
16       r ← 0
17       while (r < |V|-2) do
18          r ← r + 1
19          for k = 1 to mAnts do
```

20 The ant k tree code of array index r of iteration t will select a vertex v
21 among the list of available vertices from *ant*[*k*].*avlVtx*, according to
22 probability:
23–28

$$p_v^k(t_r) = \begin{cases} \dfrac{[\tau_{vr}(t)]^{\alpha}}{\sum\limits_{l \in ant[k].avlVtx} [\tau_{lr}(t)]^{\alpha}}, & \text{if } \forall l \in ant[k].avlVtx; \\ 0, & \text{if } \forall l \notin ant[k].avlVtx. \end{cases}$$

29 *antTreeCode*[*k*][*r*] = *v*
30 *antDeg*[*k*][*v*] = *antDeg*[*k*][*v*] + 1
31 **if** *antDeg*[*k*][*v*] = $U_d(v)$ **then**
32 *ant*[*k*].*avlVtx* ← *ant*[*k*].*avlVtx* – {*v*}
33 **for** *k* = 1 to *mAnts* **do**
34 *ant_d-STCost*[*k*] ← compute the d-ST^k cost from *antTreeCode*[*k*] by using
35 tree decoding algorithm
36 **if** *ant_d-STCost*[*k*] < L^{gb} **then**
37 L^{gb} ← *ant_d-STCost*[*k*]
38 *d-ST*^{gb}*Code* ← *antTreeCode*[*k*]
39 *d-ST*^{gb}*Code* ← Local search by using exchange mutation(*d-ST*^{gb}*Code*, L^{gb}) //Fig. 8
40 The pheromone trails are updated:
41–42

$$\tau_{vr}(t+1) = (1 - \rho)\,\tau_{vr}(t) + \sum_{k=1}^{mAnts} \Delta\tau_{vr}^k,$$

43–44 where
45–47

$$\Delta\tau_{vr}^k = \left\{ \begin{matrix} Q/L^{gb}; \\ 0, \text{ otherwise.} \end{matrix} \right\} \text{as global update only.}$$

48 where L^{gb} is the total weight cost of decoded *d-ST*^{gb}*Code* by using tree decoding
49 algorithms to obtain its d-ST^{gb} cost.
50 **end while**
51 **end procedure**

Figure 7. The pseudocode of the proposed ACO approach for d-MST problem. Both tree codings can be applied using this pseudocode

Back to the last step in an iteration of ACO on line 40 of Fig. 7 is the pheromone update. Only global pheromone update procedure is applied. The global update pheromone procedure decreases the value of the pheromone trails on τ_{vr} by a constant factor ρ and at the same time also deposit pheromone of an amount Q/L^{gb}. The v and r of τ_{vr} is corresponding to be the desirability of assigning vertex v in d-ST^{gb} code of length $|V|$-2 at array index r where $v \in [0, |V|-1]$ and $r \in [0, |V|-3]$. Q is a positive integer and L^{gb} is the total weight cost of decoded d-ST^{gb} tree code of the current iteration by using tree decoding algorithm to obtain its d-ST^{gb} cost.

```
procedure Local search by using exchange mutation(d-ST^gbCode, L^gb)
  mutatedCode ← d-ST^gbCode //tree code of length |V|-2
  indexFirst ← random[0, |V|-3]
  do {
    indexSecond ← random[0, |V|-3]
  } while (indexFirst = indexSecond)
  tempInteger ← mutatedCode[indexSecond]
  mutatedCode[indexSecond] ← mutatedCode[indexFirst]
  mutatedCode[indexFirst] ← tempInteger
  if (|V|%2 = 0) then //if |V| is an even integer
    numberOfTimes ← |V|/2
  else
    numberOfTimes ← (|V|+1)/2
  count ← 0
  do {
    count ← count + 1
    mutatedCodeCost ← compute the mutated tree code length from its
                      mutatedCode by using tree decoding algorithm
    if (mutatedCodeCost < L^gb) then
      L^gb = mutatedCodeCost
      return mutatedCode
    else
      indexFirst ← random[0, |V|-3]
      do {
        indexSecond ← random[0, |V|-3]
      } while (indexFirst = indexSecond)
      tempInteger ← mutatedCode[indexSecond]
      mutatedCode[indexSecond] ← mutatedCode[indexFirst]
      mutatedCode[indexFirst] ← tempInteger
  } while (count < numberOfTimes)
return d-ST^gbCode
```

Figure 8. The pseudocode of the local search procedure by using exchange mutation

5. An ACO algorithm using Prüfer code and Blob code tree codings for lu-dMST problem

Four modifications have been made to the algorithm mentioned in section 4 to solve another variant of the d-MST problem with both lower and upper bound constraints on each vertex. The pseudocode of the proposed ACO approach for lu-dMST problem is given in Fig. 9. The Prüfer coding and Blob coding can be applied using this pseudocode. Again, two separate experiments are conducted. The first experiment is using the Prüfer coding and the second experiment is using the Blob coding. The use of tree codings such as Prüfer and Blob codes have made it easier to solve lu-dMST problem because the degree of the spanning tree is equal to one more of the number of times label of vertices appears in the Prüfer or Blob codes. It is also easy to determine if both the lower and upper bound constraints on each vertex are satisfied.

The first modification is to add new parameter *ant*[*k*].*lwrBndList* for each ant. The *ant*[*k*].*lwrBndList* parameter is the ant *k* lower bound list where $k \in [1, mAnts]$. The intention is that each ant will populate the vertices from *ant*[*k*].*lwrBndList* into *antTreeCode*[*k*] before selecting vertices from *ant*[*k*].*avlVtx*. This *ant*[*k*].*lwrBndList* parameter is needed for the ants to meet their lower bound degree constraint requirement. Each ant initialises their *ant*[*k*].*lwrBndList* as *ant*[*k*].*lwrBndList* ← *ant*[*k*].*lwrBndList* ∪ {*v*} if $L_d(v) > 1$ for each *v* in *V*. Because the $U_d(v)$ can be vary from vertex to vertex and be equal to one, the ant *k* also need to initialises their *ant*[*k*].*avlVtx* as *ant*[*k*].*avlVtx* ← *ant*[*k*].*avlVtx* ∪ {*v*} if $U_d(v) \neq 1$ for each *v* in *V*.

The second modification (line 4 of Fig. 9) is that the *d-PrimCode* is used to initialise the pheromone trails instead of being used as the starting solution for d-ST^{gb} code as in Fig. 7. The reason for this is most of the time, the d-Prim algorithm generates spanning tree that does not satisfy the lower bound degree constraint requirement for lu-dMST problem. The degree constraint for d-Prim is set to the maximum value of $U_d(i)$ where $i \in V$. The d-Prim d-ST is encoded to *d-PrimCode* by using tree encoding algorithm.

The third modification (lines 25 to 45 of Fig. 9) is the ants' tree code solution construction process to obtain their *antTreeCode*[*k*]. According to probability on line 35 of Fig. 9, the ant *k* will select a vertex *v* from *ant*[*k*].*lwrBndList* if *ant*[*k*].*lwrBndList* ≠ { } before the ant *k* can select a vertex *v* from *ant*[*k*].*avlVtx* for their *antTreeCode*[*k*]. The reason for this is to do away with repair function. If the repair option is used extensively it may be computationally expensive to repair infeasible ants' tree code solutions instead of the computation time could be better used for the ants to explore a better solution. A particular vertex *v* will be removed from *ant*[*k*].*lwrBndList* if (*antDeg*[*k*][*v*] = $L_d(v)$) and at the same time the vertex *v* will also be removed from *ant*[*k*].*avlVtx* if (*antDeg*[*k*][*v*] = $U_d(v)$). This is to ensure that both the lower and upper bound degree constraints during the ants' solutions construction process are adhered to. The objective function returns the cost of the lower and upper degree-constrained spanning tree (lu-dST). After every ant has completed their *antTreeCode*[*k*] of length $|V|$-2, then the best *antTreeCode*[*k*] will become the *lu-dST^{gb}Code*. The cost of the best *antTreeCode*[*k*] is determined by using tree decoding algorithms. Then, the same local search procedure by using exchange mutation as for d-MST problem is applied. This local search procedure is already given in Fig. 8.

The final modification is to add an extra pheromone update. The pheromone trails τ_{vr} are updated by using the *v* and *r* of *d-PrimCode* as follows:

$$\tau_{vr}(t+1) = (1 - \rho)\,\tau_{vr}(t) + Q/\textit{d-PrimCost}. \qquad (7)$$

where the d-Prim degree constraint is set randomly between two and the maximum value of $U_d(i)$ where $i \in V$. The d-Prim d-ST is encoded to *d-PrimCode* by using tree encoding algorithm. This *d-PrimCode* can be differed from the *d-PrimCode* as on line 4 of Fig. 9. This additional pheromone update idea is to enable the ants to consider others possible vertex *v* for their tree code solutions.

1	**procedure** ACO for lu-dMST
2	Set parameters.
3	Set L^{gb} to the maximum real number.
4	The pheromone trails τ_{vr} are initialised by using *v* and *r* of *d-PrimCode* as follows:
5	$\tau_{vr}(t+1) = (1 - \rho)\,\tau_{vr}(t) + Q/\textit{d-PrimCost}$

```
where d-Prim degree constraint is set to the maximum value of Ud(i) where i ∈ V. The
d-Prim d-ST is encoded to d-PrimCode by using tree encoding algorithm.
while termination_cond = false do
  for k = 1 to mAnts do
    for v = 0 to |V|-1 do
      antDeg[k][v] = 1 //each ant k spanning tree vertices initial degree is set to 1
      if Ld(v) > 1 then
        ant[k].lwrBndList ← ant[k]. lwrBndList ∪ {v}
      if Ud(v) ≠ 1 then
        ant[k].avlVtx ← ant[k].avlVtx ∪ {v}
  for k = 1 to mAnts do
    v ← select from ant[k].avlVtx randomly
    antTreeCode[k][0] = v
    antDeg[k][v] = antDeg[k][v] + 1
    if antDeg[k][v] = Ld(v) then
      ant[k].lwrBndList ← ant[k]. lwrBndList – {v}
    if antDeg[k][v] = Ud(v) then
      ant[k].avlVtx ← ant[k].avlVtx – {v}
  r ← 0
  while (r < |V|-2) do
    r ← r + 1
    for k = 1 to mAnts do
      The ant k tree code of array index r of iteration t will select a vertex v from the
      spanning tree vertices, according to probability:
```

$$
p_v^k(t_r) = \begin{cases} \left\{ \begin{array}{ll} \dfrac{[\tau_{vr}(t)]^{\alpha}}{\sum_{l \in ant[k].lwrBndList} [\tau_{lr}(t)]^{\alpha}}, & \text{if } \forall l \in ant[k].lwrBndList; \\ 0 & , \text{if } \forall l \notin ant[k].lwrBndList. \end{array} \right\}, & \text{if } ant[k].lwrBndList \neq \{\}; \\ \left\{ \begin{array}{ll} \dfrac{[\tau_{vr}(t)]^{\alpha}}{\sum_{l \in ant[k].avlVtx} [\tau_{lr}(t)]^{\alpha}}, & \text{if } \forall l \in ant[k].avlVtx; \\ 0 & , \text{if } \forall l \notin ant[k].avlVtx. \end{array} \right\}, & \textit{otherwise}. \end{cases}
$$

```
      antTreeCode[k][r] = v
      antDeg[k][v] = antDeg[k][v] + 1
      if antDeg[k][v] = Ld(v) then
        ant[k].lwrBndList ← ant[k]. lwrBndList – {v}
      if antDeg[k][v] = Ud(v) then
        ant[k].avlVtx ← ant[k].avlVtx – {v}
  for k = 1 to mAnts do
    ant_lu-dSTCost[k] ← compute the lu-dST^k cost from its antTreeCode[k] by using
                        tree decoding algorithm
    if ant_lu-dSTCost[k] < L^gb then
      L^gb ← ant_lu-dSTCost[k]
      lu-dST^gbCode ← antTreeCode[k]
```

lu-dST^{gb}Code ← Local search by using exchange mutation(*lu-dST^{gb}Code*, L^{gb}) //Fig. 8
Then, the pheromone trails are updated as global update as follows:

$$\tau_{vr}(t+1) = (1-\rho)\,\tau_{vr}(t) + \sum_{k=1}^{mAnts} \Delta\tau_{vr}^{k},$$

where

$$\Delta\tau_{vr}^{k} = \left.\begin{cases} Q/L^{gb}; \\ 0, \text{ otherwise.} \end{cases}\right\} \text{as global update.}$$

where L^{gb} is the total weight cost of decoded *lu-dST^{gb}Code* by using tree decoding algorithms to obtain its lu-dST^{gb} cost.
The pheromone trails τ_{vr} are updated by using v and r of *d-PrimCode* as follows:
$\tau_{vr}(t+1) = (1-\rho)\tau_{vr}(t) + Q/d\text{-}PrimCost$
where the d-Prim degree constraint is set randomly between two and the maximum of $U_d(i)$ where $i \in V$. The d-Prim d-ST is encoded to *d-PrimCode* by using tree encoding algorithm.
end while
end procedure

Figure 9. The pseudocode of the proposed ACO approach for lu-dMST problem. Both tree codings can be applied using this pseudocode

6. Performance comparisons of Prüfer ACO and Blob ACO on structured hard (SHRD) graph data set for d-MST problem

The Prüfer-coded ACO and Blob-coded ACO are tested on structured hard (SHRD) graphs as used in (Raidl, 2000; Mohan et al., 2001; Bui & Zrncic, 2006) for the d-MST problem. The SHRD graphs are constructed by using non-Euclidean distance as follows. The first vertex is connected to all other vertices by an edge of length l; the second vertex is connected to all vertices bar the first by an edge of length $2l$ and so on. Then SHRD is randomised slightly by adding a uniformly distributed perturbation between 1 and 18 where $l = 20$. The details to generate a SHRD graph is given in Fig. 10. This reduces the likelihood of a large number of optimal solutions existing but doesn't change the underlying complexity of the problem. These are difficult to solve optimally compared to other data sets such as Euclidean data sets of degree 3 or more (Mohan et al., 2001). The MST for SHRD is a star graph where one vertex has degree $|V|$-1 and the all other vertices have degree 1. The SHRD graphs are complete graphs with undirected non-negative weighted edges.

The parameter ρ for Prüfer-coded ACO and Blob-coded ACO is tuned from 0.0 to 0.9. For each ρ, average solution costs over 50 independent runs are recorded. Each run terminates after 274 ($50 * \sqrt{|V|}$) iterations. The setting that produced the lowest average solution cost will be the Prüfer-coded ACO and Blob-coded ACO parameter value used for SHRD data set. Table 2 shows the parameter tuning results for Prüfer-coded ACO and Blob-coded ACO approaches on SHRD data set. The lowest ρ values for Prüfer-coded ACO and Blob-coded ACO from Table 2 are in bold print. Separate parameter values are used for Prüfer-coded ACO and Blob-coded ACO on the SHRD problem instances. The parameter value of $\rho = 0.1$ is chosen for Prüfer-coded ACO while value of $\rho = 0.9$ is chosen for Blob-coded ACO. There is so much difference between Prüfer-coded ACO and Blob-coded ACO parameter value of ρ. One of the probable reasons is the Blob code exhibits higher locality under mutation of one symbol compares to Prüfer code. On average only about two edges for a spanning tree is changed after changing one symbol in a Blob code to be decoded by the Blob decoding algorithm (Julstrom, 2001). Table 3 shows the values of the ACO parameters. All results are obtained using a PC with Pentium 4 processor with 512 megabytes of memory, running at 3.0 GHz under Windows XP Professional.

```
procedure generateSHRDgraph
  Let total number of vertices as |V|
  Let graph edges as edge[|V|][|V|]
  for i = 0 to |V|-1 do
    for j = 0 to i do
      if i = j then
        edge[i][j] = 1000000000.000000
      else
        edge[i][j] = 20*j + random[1, 18]
        edge[j][i] = edge[i][j]
  // Print lower left SHRD triangular graph matrix only
  for i = 1 to |V|-1 do
    for j = 0 to i-1 do
      Print edge[i][j] and " ".
    Print newline.
end procedure
```

Figure 10. The pseudocode to generate a SHRD graph

	Prüfer-coded ACO	**Blob-coded ACO**
$\rho = 0.0$	1554.74	1532.66
0.1	**1551.96**	1533.74
0.2	1554.14	1532.22
0.3	1556.68	1532.04
0.4	1553.48	1533.66
0.5	1554.92	1533.66
0.6	1553.94	1535.20
0.7	1553.90	1533.52
0.8	1552.70	1535.26
0.9	1552.00	**1530.34**

Table 2. Parameter ρ tuning for Prüfer-coded ACO and Blob-coded ACO average results, problem shrd305, $d = 5$, $|V| = 30$, number of iterations = $50 * \sqrt{|V|} = 274$, number of runs = 50

	Prüfer-coded ACO	Blob-coded ACO
ρ	0.1	0.9
mAnts	$\lvert V \rvert$	$\lvert V \rvert$
Q	1.0	1.0
α	1	1
SHRD maxEdgeCost	$20^* \lvert V \rvert$	$20^* \lvert V \rvert$
τ_0	$\lvert V \rvert^2 * 20^* \lvert V \rvert$	$\lvert V \rvert^2 * 20^* \lvert V \rvert$
iterations	$50 * \sqrt{\lvert V \rvert}$	$50 * \sqrt{\lvert V \rvert}$

Table 3. The ACO parameters and their values for artificial ant *k* using Prüfer code and Blob code tree codings on SHRD problem instances

Problem	Prüfer ACO avg.	Prüfer ACO best	Prüfer ACO time	Blob ACO avg.	Blob ACO best	Blob ACO time	Enhanced k-ACO avg.	Enhanced k-ACO best	Enhanced k-ACO time
SHRD153	16.94	18.89	15	17.95	19.84	21	20.26	21.19	120
SHRD154	9.94	12.01	15	12.25	14.37	21	12.29	15.35	120
SHRD155	8.04	9.60	15	7.87	9.60	21	8.95	9.60	120
SHRD203	8.74	10.74	38	10.22	11.39	52	11.72	12.12	180
SHRD204	6.45	7.79	38	7.05	8.47	52	9.22	9.48	180
SHRD205	5.70	7.15	38	6.46	8.03	52	8.17	8.47	180
SHRD253	16.26	18.67	87	17.82	19.13	118	19.81	20.40	360
SHRD254	3.36	4.82	87	4.40	5.55	118	6.41	6.72	360
SHRD255	5.45	7.19	87	7.39	8.29	118	8.91	9.02	360
SHRD303	9.14	10.71	145	9.88	11.52	197	12.30	12.46	660
SHRD304	8.20	10.04	145	9.63	11.06	197	11.61	11.80	660
SHRD305	3.59	5.40	145	4.68	5.96	197	6.37	6.58	660
Total Average:	8.48	10.25	855	9.63	11.10	1164	11.34	11.93	3960

Table 4. Average and best results (quality gains over d-Prim in %), and total times (in seconds) on SHRD problem instances. Label SHRD153 means SHRD graph 15-vertex with degree constraint, *d*=3 and so on

Table 4 summarises the results of Prüfer-coded ACO and Blob-coded ACO on SHRD data set. The Prüfer-coded ACO and Blob-coded ACO were run 50 independent times on each problem instance. Each run is terminated after $50 * \sqrt{\lvert V \rvert}$ iterations. The number of vertices are in the range 15, 20, 25, and 30. The maximum degree was set to 3, 4 and 5. The results for the enhanced kruskal-ACO are adopted from (Bau et al., 2007). At this time, the enhanced kruskal-ACO is used as a performance benchmark. It is one of the best approaches for the d-MST problem on the SHRD graphs (Bau et al., 2007). Besides average gains, the gains of the best run and total times (in seconds) that are required for 50 runs are reported in Table 4.

The total times in seconds for 50 runs is recorded so that the time required between ACO without tree coding and ACO using tree coding can be compared. The enhanced kruskal-ACO is referred to as Enhanced k-ACO but the Prüfer-coded ACO and Blob-coded ACO are referred to as Prüfer ACO and Blob ACO. Between Prüfer ACO and Blob ACO, the highest average gains are underlined.

It can be concluded that Enhanced k-ACO has higher total average results compared to Blob ACO. In turn, Blob ACO has higher total average results compared to Prüfer ACO. Between Prüfer ACO and Blob ACO, Blob ACO almost always identifies trees of higher gains except on a SHRD155 d=5 problem instance. Between Blob ACO and Enhanced k-ACO, Blob ACO achieves results very close to Enhanced k-ACO. On all the problem instances, the maximum average result difference between them is only by 2.42 on a SHRD303 d=3. When all three ACO approaches are compared, the Enhanced k-ACO attains the highest total average compared to the Prufer ACO and Blob ACO. The reason for this is probably due to the fact that Enhanced k-ACO uses visibility measure during the ants' solution construction. However on all problem instances, the Prüfer ACO and Blob ACO performed faster in terms of computation time compared to the Enhanced k-ACO. The Prüfer ACO requires only about 22% and Blob ACO requires only about 29% as much time as does the Enhanced k-ACO.

7. Performance comparisons of Prüfer ACO and Blob ACO on structured hard (SHRD) graph data set for lu-dMST problem

Four networks of varying sizes based on SHRD graphs are generated. The number of vertices are 20, 40, 60, and 80, similar to those used in (Chou et al., 2001). The SHRD 20-vertex problem instance set is labelled as SHRD20, the SHRD 40-vertex problem instance set is labelled as SHRD40 and so on. For each vertex, an integer from a range of one to four is randomly generated for the lower bound degree constraint, $L_d(i)$, and one to eight is randomly generated for the upper bound degree constraint, $U_d(i)$ where $i \in V$. This means that the maximum value for the upper bound degree constraint is eight. The minimum value of $L_d(i)$ and $U_d(i)$ is always equal to 1, and $U_d(i)$ is always greater than or equal to $L_d(i)$. In order to ensure that the network forms at least one feasible solution, the sum for each vertex of lower bound degree constraint is set between $|V|$ and $2(|V|-1)$ as follows:

$$|V| \le \sum_{i=0}^{|V|-1} L_d(i) \le 2(|V|-1). \tag{8}$$

And, the sum for each vertex of upper bound degree constraint is set between $2(|V|-1)$ and $|V|(|V|-1)$ as follows:

$$2(|V|-1) \le \sum_{i=0}^{|V|-1} U_d(i) \le |V|(|V|-1). \tag{9}$$

The reason for this is that a spanning tree always consists of $|V|$-1 edges, an edge consists of exactly two distinct vertices, and the total number of the degrees of an edge is two. Therefore, the sum over the degrees $deg(i)$ of a spanning tree on each vertex i in V as given in (Gross & Yellen, 2006) can be calculated as follows:

$$\sum_{i=0}^{|V|-1} \deg(i) = 2(|V|-1) . \qquad (10)$$

Table 5 summarises the results of these Prüfer-coded ACO and Blob-coded ACO approaches on SHRD graph. The Prüfer-coded ACO and Blob-coded ACO approaches were each run 50 independent times on each problem instance. Each run is terminated after 50 * $\sqrt{|V|}$ iterations. The numbers of vertices are in the range 20, 40, 60, and 80. For each $i \in V$, the $1 \leq L_d(i) \leq 4$, $1 \leq U_d(i) \leq 8$, and $U_d(i) \geq L_d(i)$. Besides average solution cost, the solution cost of the best run and total times (in seconds) required for 50 independent runs are reported in Table 5. The solution cost is used here for performance comparison rather than the quality gain. The Prüfer-coded ACO and Blob-coded ACO approaches are referred to as Prüfer ACO and Blob ACO. The parameter values of Prüfer ACO and Blob ACO for lu-dMST problem are the same as the parameter values of Prüfer ACO and Blob ACO for d-MST problem.

As shown in Table 5, it can be concluded that Blob ACO always has the better results compared to Prüfer ACO. The Blob ACO always identifies trees of lower solution cost for all the problem instances in the SHRD graphs. The overall effectiveness of the Blob ACO compared to Prüfer ACO is probably due to the fact that it uses better tree coding scheme. Prüfer code is a poor representation of spanning trees for EA (Gottlieb et al., 2001; Julstrom, 2001). Small changes in Prüfer code often cause large changes in the spanning trees they represent. However on all problem instances, the Prüfer ACO requires lesser time than the Blob ACO. This does not bring to a conclusion that Blob tree coding always requires more time compared to Prüfer tree coding. In a recent study of the Blob code spanning tree representations, Paulden and Smith (2006) have described linear-time encoding and decoding algorithms for the Blob code, which supersede the usual quadratic-time algorithms.

Problem	Prüfer ACO avg.	Prüfer ACO best	Prüfer ACO Time (secs)	Blob ACO avg.	Blob ACO best	Blob ACO Time (secs)
SHRD20	1429.28	1304	33	1391.56	1286	50
SHRD40	5573.04	4941	330	5034.32	4673	458
SHRD60	12167.48	11003	1345	11448.68	10625	1715
SHRD80	16683.12	14839	3483	15013.24	13844	4610
Total Average:	35852.92	32087	5191	32887.80	30428	6833

Table 5. Average solution cost on SHRD problem instances with both lower and upper bound degree constraints. Label SHRD20 means SHRD graph 20-vertex and so on

8. Conclusion

The design and implementation of Blob-coded ACO and Prüfer-coded ACO for d-MST and lu-dMST problems have been presented. This ACO approaches is different because it constructs the encoded of the solution and can speed up computation time. Performance studies have revealed that Blob-coded ACO is almost always better than Prüfer-coded ACO for both types of problems for the SHRD graphs. However for the d-MST problem, Blob-coded ACO does not perform better than the enhanced kruskal-ACO approach in any single problem instance for SHRD graphs. Finally, the Blob code may be a useful coding of spanning trees for ants' solution construction in ACO algorithms for the d-MST and lu-dMST problems in terms of computation time. There may be other codings of spanning trees even more appropriate for ants' solution construction such as Happy code or Dandellion code as mentioned by Picciotto (1999) in his PhD thesis.

9. References

Bau, Yoon Teck; Ho, Chin Kuan, & Ewe, Hong Tat (2007). Ant Colony Optimization Approaches to the Degree-constrained Minimum Spanning Tree Problem. *Journal of Information Science and Engineering* (in press)

Bui, T. N. & Zrncic, C. M. (2006). An Ant-Based Algorithm for Finding Degree-Constrained Minimum Spanning Tree. *Proceedings of the 8th Annual Conference on Genetic and Evolutionary Computation,* 11-18

Cayley (1889). A theorem on trees. *Quarterly Journal of Mathematics*, 23, 376-378

Dorigo, M. & Stützle T. (2004). *Ant Colony Optimization.* A Bradford Book, The MIT Press, Cambridge, MA, London, England

Garey, M. R. & Johnson, D. S. (1979). *Computers and Intractability: A Guide to the Theory of NP-Completeness.* Freeman, San Francisco, CA

Goldberg, D. E. (1989). *Genetic Algorithms in Search, Optimization, and Machine Learning.* Addison-Wesley, Reading, MA

Gottlieb, J.; Julstrom, B. A., Raidl, G. R. & Rothlauf, F. (2001). Prüfer numbers: A poor representation of spanning trees for evolutionary search. In: *Proceedings of the Genetic and Evolutionary Computation Conference GECCO-2001,* Lee, Spector, Goodman, E. D., Annie, Wu, Langdon, W. B., Hans-Michael, V., Mitsuo, Gen, Sandip, Sen, Dorigo, M., Pezeshk, S., Garzon, M. H. & Burke, E. (Eds.), (343-350), Morgan Kaufmann, San Francisco, California, USA

Gross, J. L. & Yellen, J. (2006). *Graph Theory and its Applications 2nd ed.,* CRC Press, Boca Raton, London, New York, Washington, D.C.

Hsinghua Chou; G. Premkumar & Chao-Hsien Chu (2001). Genetic Algorithms for Communications Networks Design - An Empirical Study of the Factors that Influence Performance. *IEEE Transactions on Evolutionary Computation*, Vol. 5, No. 3, 236-249

Julstrom, B. A. (2001). The Blob Code: A better string coding of spanning trees for evolutionary search. In: *2001 Genetic and Evolutionary Computation Conference Workshop Program*, Annie, S. Wu (Ed.), (256-261), San Francisco, CA

Knowles, J. & Corne, D. (2000). A new evolutionary approach to the degree-constrained minimum spanning tree problem. *IEEE Transactions on Evolutionary Computation,* 4(2), 125-134

Michalewicz Z. (1996). *Genetic Algorithms + Data Structures = Evolution Programs 3rd Rev. and Extended ed.,* Springer Verlag

Mohan, Krishnamoorthy; Andreas, T. Ernst & Yazid, M. Sharaiha (2001). Comparison of Algorithms for the Degree-constrained Minimum Spanning Tree. *Journal of Heuristics,* 7(6), 587-611

Narula, S. C. & Ho, C. A. (1980). Degree-constrained minimum spanning tree. *Computer Operation Research,* 7(4), 239-249

Paulden, T. & Smith, D. K. (2006). Recent advances in the study of the Dandelion code, Happy code, and Blob code spanning tree representations, *In Proceeding IEEE Congress on Evolutionary Computation,* 2111- 2118

Picciotto, S. (1999). *How to encode a tree,* Ph.D. Thesis, University of California, San Diego

Prim, R. (1957). Shortest connection networks and some generalizations. *Bell System Technical Journal,* 36, 1389-1401

Prüfer, H. (1918). Neuer Beweis eines Satzes über Permutationen [New proof of a counting labelled tree sequence over permutations]. *Architecture Mathematics Physics,* 27, 742-744

Raidl, G. R. (2000). An efficient evolutionary algorithm for the degree-constrained minimum spanning tree problem. *IEEE Transactions on Evolutionary Computation,* 1, 104-111

Sipser, M. (2006). *Introduction to the Theory of Computation 2nd ed.,* Course Technology

4

Robust PSO-Based Constrained Optimization by Perturbing the Particle's Memory

Angel Muñoz Zavala, Arturo Hernández Aguirre
and Enrique Villa Diharce
Centro de Investigación en Matemáticas (CIMAT)
México

1. Introduction

A successful evolutionary algorithm is one with the proper balance between exploration (searching for good solutions), and exploitation (refining the solutions by combining information gathered during the exploration phase). Diversity maintenance is important in constrained search space algorithms because the additional pressure set on the population to reach the feasible region reduces the diversity. Since reduced diversity promotes premature convergence, new exploration and exploitation techniques have been incorporated into the PSO main paradigm.

In this chapter the authors review the standard PSO algorithm, and several proposals to improve both exploration and exploitation: local and global topologies, particle motion equations, swarm neighbourhoods, and interaction models. For all these approaches the common shared feature is the modification of the PSO main algorithm.

The present chapter, however, describes a rather different approach: the perturbation of the particle memory. In the PSO algorithm, the next particle's position is based on their flying experience (*pbest)*, and the current best individual in either the entire swarm (*gbest*), or in a swarm neighbourhood (*lbest*). Since the values for *gbest* or *lbest* are determined from the pbest values available at any generation, in the end, it is the *pbest* which is mainly responsible for the particle's next position. Therefore, a way to reduce premature convergence is to improve the pbest of each particle.

Our approach aims to prevent convergence to local optima by improving the swarm exploration and exploitation through two perturbation operators. These external operators improve the memory of the best visited locations, and do not modify the main PSO paradigm.

The rest of this Chapter is organized as follows: In Section 2, we introduce the premature convergence problem. We extend this discussion in the context of constrained optimization, in Section 3. Our approach is introduced in Section 4; giving a brief explanation about every component adopted in the PSO algorithm. In Section 5, a well-known benchmark is used to compare our approach against other PSO based methods and evolutionary algorithms representative of the state-of-the-art. The conclusion is given in Section 6, complemented with future work guidelines in Section 7.

2. Premature Convergence

A natural problem in evolutionary computation is the premature convergence. It means that the evolutionary algorithm could stay trapped in a region containing a local optimum. Premature convergence can be caused by the lost of diversity, which occurs when the population reaches a suboptimal state where evolutionary algorithm can no longer produce offspring which outperforms their parents (Fogel, 1994). A way to attain diversity maintenance is by keeping a balance between exploration and exploitation (Holland, 1975).

2.1 Exploration and Exploitation

The balance between exploration and exploitation is a well known issue in evolutionary computation (Michalwicz & Fogel, 2000). But, why is it hard to find an optimal balance? First, we review the classical concepts: exploration *is the act of searching for the purpose of discovery*; and exploitation *is the act of utilizing something for any purpose* (Agnes, 2004). Then, at the context of evolutionary computation, we could define exploration *as the act of searching through all space regions for discovering promissory solutions*; and exploitation *as the act of utilizing local information for refining the solution.*

Accord with the given definition, Downing explained: *exploitation is encouraged by elitist selection and smaller population sizes or by using lower mutation rates to promote correlation between parent and offspring. Conversely, exploration is encouraged by promoting greater population diversity and selecting parents less discerningly, or by increasing mutation rate.* (Downing, 2006).

We can observe that exploration and exploitation are opposite goals; both compete for limited resources, for instance, the number of fitness function evaluations. So, a trade-off between exploration and exploitation is necessary. The search horizon has to be sufficiently close for maintaining exploitation and at the same time sufficiently distant to discover significant novelty (Jacoby, 2005).

The common approach in evolutionary computation about the control of exploration and exploitation is framed in terms of balancing variation and selection processes. There are several works focused to solve the equilibrium dilemma between variation and selection. Even more, there are proposals from other areas (e.g. management, economics) for solving related problems (March, 1991). In the following sections, we review some approaches and propose a new solution for balancing variation and selection in the PSO algorithm.

2.2 Diversity Control in PSO

In PSO, the diversity comes from two sources. One is the difference between the particle's current position and its best neighbor, and the other is the difference between the particle's current position and its best historical value. Although variation provides exploration, it can only be sustained for a limited number of generations because convergence of the flock to the best is necessary to refine the solution (exploitation).

In an early analysis, Angeline shows that PSO may not converge, neither refine solutions when variation is null, that is, when all the particles rest near by the best spot (Angeline, 1998). A few months after Angeline's work, the first formal analysis of a simple PSO was developed by Ozcan and Mohan (Ozcan & Mohan, 1998), which obtained the PSO trajectories. Based on this work, Clerc and Kennedy analyzed a particle's trajectory and determined the relationship between the acceleration parameters that avoid the divergence of the particle (Clerc & Kennedy, 2002). But, when the problem of converge premature seemed solved; Van Den Bergh proves that the PSO trajectories does not converge to the global optimal (Van Den Bergh, 2002). In his Ph.D. thesis, Van Den Bergh explains the attributes that a hybrid PSO must accomplish to become a global search algorithm. There are several proposes related with developing a global search based on the PSO algorithm. In this context, we can find approaches for dealing with constraints, which is the topic of this chapter.

3 Constraint-Handling in PSO

Real optimization problems are subject to a number of equality and inequality constraints, which can be linear or nonlinear. These constraints determine which areas of the search space are feasible and which are infeasible. In addition to these constraints, boundary constraints are usually imposed to the search space (Michalewicz, 1992). Also, there is the possibility that the feasible space is fragmented and separated by infeasible regions, requiring that both the feasible and infeasible regions be searched.

PSO is an unconstrained search technique. Thus, adopting a constraint handling technique into the main PSO algorithm is an open research area. There is a considerable amount of research regarding mechanisms that allow the evolutionary algorithms to deal with equality and inequality constraints. Some constraint-handling approaches tend to incorporate either information about infeasibility or distance to the feasible region, into the fitness function in order to guide the search. These techniques are based on *penalty functions* (Parsopoulos & Vrahatis, 2002). In their work Parsopoulos and Vrahatis used a multi-stage assignment penalty function without diversity control. Other approaches propose a constraint handling technique based on maintaining a feasible population (El-Gallad et al., 2001), and also some algorithms require a feasible initial population (Hu & Eberhart, 2002; He et al., 2004). In 2003, Coath and Halgamuge presented a comparison of the two constraint-handling methods in PSO: *penalty function* and *feasibility preservation* (Coath & Halgamuge, 2003). Their experiments clearly detect the need of some form of diversity control.

In a more sophisticated approach, Zhang et al. introduced a special technique, called *periodic mode*, to handle inequality constraints. This method consists in keeping the global-best near the boundary thus the flock which is constantly pulled to the border, can sustain exploration (Zhang et al., 2004). A few more sophisticated approaches include applying multi-objective optimization techniques to handle constraints. For instance Toscano and Coello (Toscano & Coello, 2004), use a *feasibility tournament* proposed by Deb (Deb 2000) to handle constraints with PSO. The *feasibility tournament* applies a set of rules similar to the Pareto dominance concept used in multi-objective optimization.

Notably, equality and inequality constraints demand an intelligence exploration of the search space to find the global optimum region. Likewise, an efficient and effective exploitation is required in the boundaries of the feasible region, whenever the inequality constraints are active or equality constraints are present. PSO should find a solution that both optimizes the objective function and satisfies all constraints.

4. Constrained Optimization via Particle Swarm Optimization

A brief analysis of the state-of-the-art in PSO to solve constrained optimization problems was presented. Now, we are going to introduce our approach called Particle Evolutionary Swarm Optimization (PESO) (Muñoz et al., 2005). In this section we explain our approach;

and in the next section we perform a comparison with another PSO-based constraint optimization works.

4.1 Interaction Model

First we should choose an appropriate interaction model for solving constrained optimization problems. In an early analysis, Kennedy provided empirically evidence that the *social-only* model is faster and more efficient than the *full* and *cognitive-only* models (Kennedy, 1997). These models were defined by omitting components of the velocity formula. The *full* model is composed by the cognition component and the social component. Dropping the social component results in the *cognition-only* model, whereas dropping the cognition component defines the *social-only* model. In a fourth model, *selfless* model, the neighbourhood best is chosen only from the neighbours, without considering the current individual. Carlisle and Dozier tested these four models in dynamic changing environments (Carlisle & Dozier, 2000). They empirically prove that the *social-only* model consistently found solutions faster than the *full* model, but the reliability of the *social-only* model is lower than the *full* model.

We test the four models proposed by Kennedy, (Kennedy, 1997). We confirm that the *social-model* is faster than the *full* model, but it is not enough robust due to its premature convergence behaviour. Therefore, we adopt the *full* model which is more reliable for constrained optimization.

4.2 Social Network Structure

In the PSO topology, each particle moves following a leader; this fact is modelled by one of three components of the velocity formula. A leader can be global to all the flock, or local to a flock's neighbourhood. In the latter case there are as many local leaders as neighbourhoods. Having more than one leader in the flock translates into more attractors or good spots in space. Therefore, the use of neighbourhoods is a natural approach to fight premature convergence (Mendes et al., 2004).

Particles in the same neighbourhood communicate with one another by exchanging information for moving towards a better position. The flow of information through the flock, depends on the neighbourhood structure. Figure 1 presents a few neighbourhood structures developed for PSO.

In a highly connected neighbourhood structure, the information about the best particle in the swarm is quickly transmitted through the whole flock. This means faster convergence, which implies a higher risk to converge to a local minimum. Also, Kennedy & Mendes empirically shows that the *star neighbourhood* is faster than the other topologies, but it meets the optimal fewer times than any other one (Kennedy & Mendes, 2002). They suggest trying the *Von Neumann neighbourhood* structure, which performed more consistently in their experiments than the topologies commonly found in current practice. However, in the experiments developed by Kennedy & Mendes, they used a set of unconstrained optimization problems. However, based on their recommendation, we propose a new neighbourhood structure, which we define as *singly-linked ring*.

The *singly-linked ring* rises from analysing the *ring neighbourhood* as a double-linked list; like it is showed in Figure 2-a. Suppose that every particle is assigned a permanent label which is used to construct the neighbourhoods. Then, a particle k has two neighbours, particles $k-1$ and $k+1$. In turn, particles $k-1$ and $k+1$ have particle k as a neighbour. In this way, there is a mutual attraction between consecutive particles, forming overlapped clusters. Also, the slow convergence of the ring structure has been empirically showed (Kennedy, 1999; Kennedy & Mendes, 2002; Carlisle & Dozier, 2000).

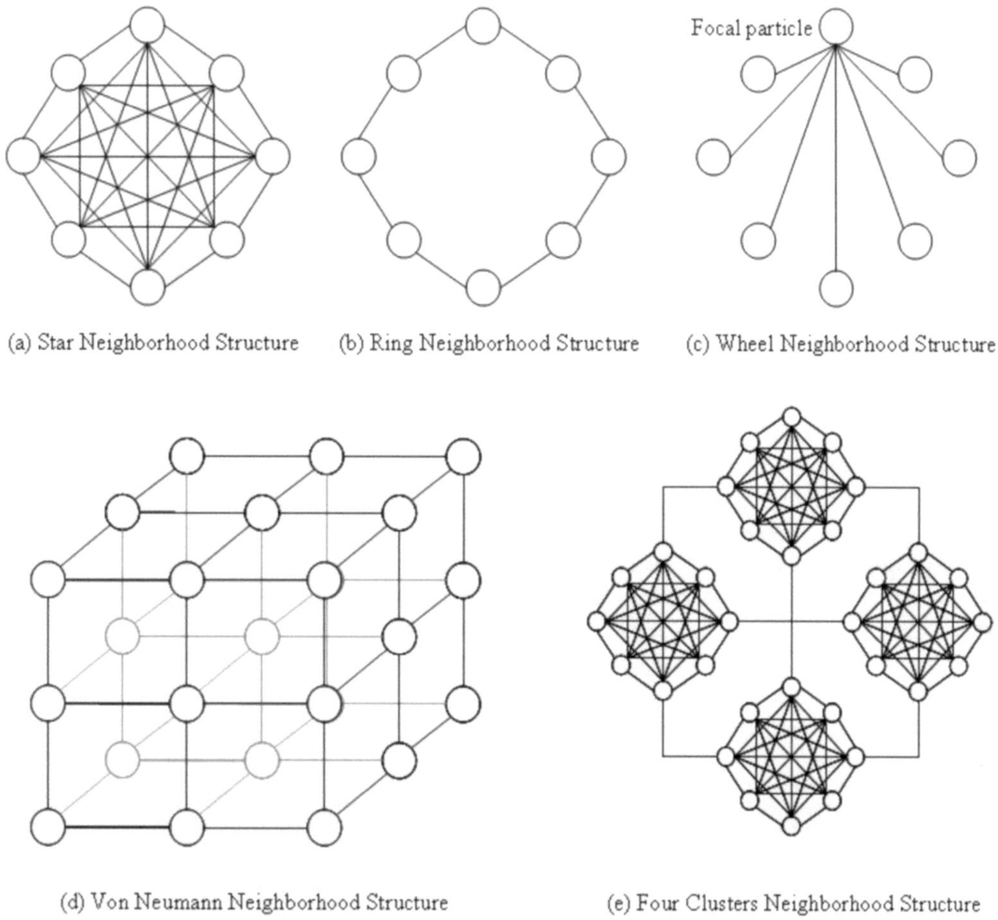

(a) Star Neighborhood Structure (b) Ring Neighborhood Structure (c) Wheel Neighborhood Structure

(d) Von Neumann Neighborhood Structure (e) Four Clusters Neighborhood Structure

Figure 1. Neighbourhood Structures. A representation of the social networks applied in PSO

The successful of the *Von Neumann neighbourhood* is due to the interaction that each particle has with other particles, an average of 5 neighbours. This promotes the exploitation, but unfortunately fails to provide the exploration required by the constrained optimization problems. Thus, we propose the topology presented in Figure 2-b. The *singly-linked ring* keeps two neighbours for each particle, but breaks the mutual attraction between neighbours. Besides, the information through the whole swarm is transmitted faster than in the original *ring* topology. Therefore, the *singly-linked ring* keeps the exploration at the search space, and increases the exploitation of the best solutions (Hernández et al., 2007).

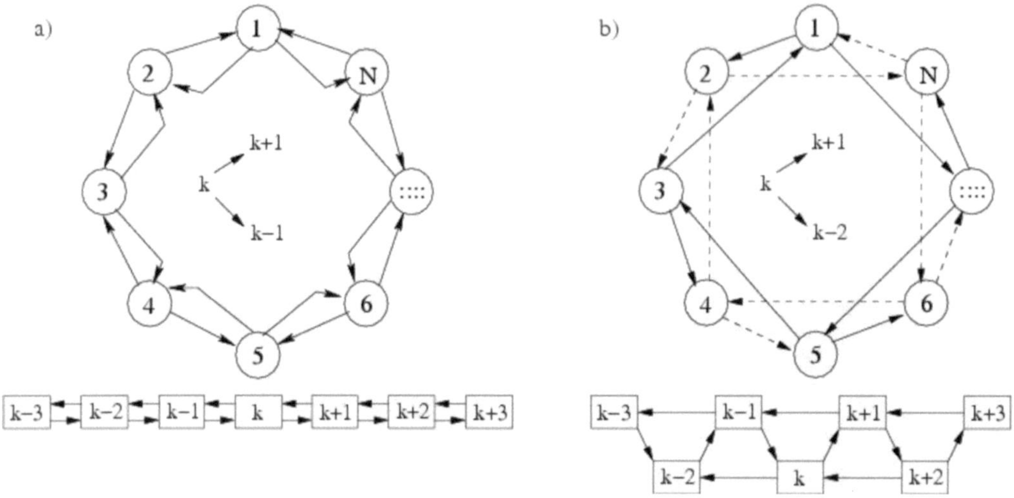

Figure 2. Ring Neighbourhood Structures. a) Original ring topology, b) Singly-Linked ring

4.3 Feasibility Tournament

The first step for developing a PSO-based constraint optimization is to choose a constraint-handling method. There are three methods that have been used by other approaches: *penalty function*, *feasibility preservation* and *feasibility tournament*.

The *penalty function* method involves a number of parameters which must be set right in any problem to obtain good solutions. This fact has motivated sophisticated penalty function approaches and extensive experimentation for setting up appropriate parameters (Michalewicz & Schoenauer, 1996). According with Deb (Deb, 2000), there are two problems associated with the *static penalty function*: the optimal solution depends on penalty parameters and the inclusion of the penalty term distorts the objective function.

Now, we give the details of the *feasibility preservation* method. There are two main problems associated with this method: it needs a feasible initial population and special operators to keep the population into the feasible region. Also, the method could be unreliable handling problems with active constraints, since it does not allow unfeasible solutions and has not information about the boundaries.

The *feasibility tournament* proposes to use a tournament selection operator, where two solutions are compared at time, and the following criteria are always applied:

1. Any feasible solution is preferred to any infeasible solution.
2. Among two feasible solutions, the one having better objective function value is preferred.
3. Among two infeasible solutions, the one having smaller sum of constraint violation is preferred.

The *feasibility tournament* does not require tuning parameters or applying special operators. Just a simple comparison is used to choose the best individual. Even, in any of the above three scenarios, solutions are never compared in terms of both objective function and sum of constraint violation. This method was implemented by Toscano and Coello in a PSO with global topology, obtaining competitive results (Toscano & Coello, 2004). Our approach applies this method in a local topology, allowing feasible and infeasible solutions in the *pbest* particles. It enriches the information about the search space, especially at boundaries. Nevertheless, for handling equality constraints, it is not enough just converting them into inequality constraints:

$$g(x) = \delta - |h(x)| \tag{1}$$

Our approach applies a *dynamic tolerance* for handling equality constraints. First, we rewrite them as inequality constraints of the form $|h(x)| \leq \delta$, where δ is called the tolerance. Then, the tolerance is linearly decremented from 1.0 to a specified target value (1E-06 in our experiments) during the first 90% of function evaluations. For the last 10% the tolerance is kept fixed; thus, the particles have additional time to achieve convergence. This technique proved to be very effective in the test problems that we present in the Section 5.

4.4 Perturbing the PSO Memory

In Section 2, we mention the Van Den Bergh's PhD thesis and his contributions in the PSO context. He gives a set of requirements that an evolutionary algorithm must accomplish to be a global search algorithm. Also, he shows that the PSO algorithm is not in fact a global search algorithm (Van Den Bergh, 2002). Nevertheless, Van Den Bergh gives a theorem which specifies under which conditions an algorithm can be considered a global optimization method. The theorem implies that a general algorithm, without *a priori* knowledge, must be able to generate an infinite number of samples distributed throughout the whole of S in order to guarantee that it will find the global optimum with asymptotic probability 1 (Van Den Bergh, 2002).

This can be achieved by periodically adding randomised particles to the swarm. Nevertheless, resetting the position of the particles is not a trivial task; a bad decision affects directly in the exploitation of the best solutions. We propose, based on the observation that the *pbest* particles drive the swarm, perturbing the *pbest* of each particle.

Our approach has three stages. In the first stage, an iteration of the standard PSO algorithm with the features described in this Section 4 is applied. Then the perturbations are applied to *pbest* in the next two stages. The goal of the second stage is to add a perturbation generated from the linear combination of three different particles for every dimension. This perturbation is preferred over other operators because it preserves the distribution of the population. This operator is used for reproduction by the Differential Evolution algorithm (Price et al., 2005). In our approach this perturbation is called *C-Perturbation*. It is applied to the members of *pbest* to yield a set of temporal particles *tempC*. Then each member of *tempC* is compared with its corresponding father and *pbest* is updated applying the feasibility tournament. Figure 3 shows the pseudo-code of the *C-Perturbation* operator.

In the third stage every vector is perturbed again so a particle could be deviated from its current direction as responding to external, maybe more promissory, stimuli. This perturbation is implemented by adding small random numbers to every design variable. The perturbation, called M-Perturbation, is applied to every member of *pbest* to yield a set of temporal particles *tempM*. Then each member of *tempM* is compared with its corresponding father and *pbest* is updated applying the feasibility tournament. Figure 4 shows the pseudo-code of the *M-Perturbation* operator, where *LL* and *UL* are the lower and upper limits of the search space. The perturbation is added to every dimension of the decision vector with probability **1/d,** where **d** is the dimension of the decision variable vector.

```
For k = 0 To n
  For j = 0 To d
    r = U ( 0 , 1 )
    p1 = k
    p2 = random ( n )
    p3 = random ( n )
    Temp [ k , j ] = P_{i+1} [ p1 , j ] + r * ( P_{i+1} [ p2 , j ] - P_{i+1} [ p3 , j ] )
  End For
End For
```

Figure 3. C-Perturbation Operator. Pseudo-code of the C-Perturbation applies by PESO

These perturbations have the additional advantage of keeping the self-organization potential of the flock since they only work on the *pbest* particles, as we can observe in Figure 5. The current PSO population is not perturbed, but few or may be several *pbest* particles have been moved to a better position. This is an improved form for adding randomised particles to the swarm, compared with those propose by Van Den Bergh (Van Den Bergh, 2002). Our approach not only resets the position of the *pbest* particles, also improves them; probably driving the swarm to a promise region.

```
For k = 0 To n
  For j = 0 To d
    r = U ( 0 , 1 )
    If r ≤ 1/d Then
      Temp [ k , j ] = Random ( LL , UL )
    Else
      Temp [ k , j ] = P_{i+1} [ k , j ]
  End For
End For
```

Figure 4. M-Perturbation Operator. Pseudo-code of the M-Perturbation applies by PESO

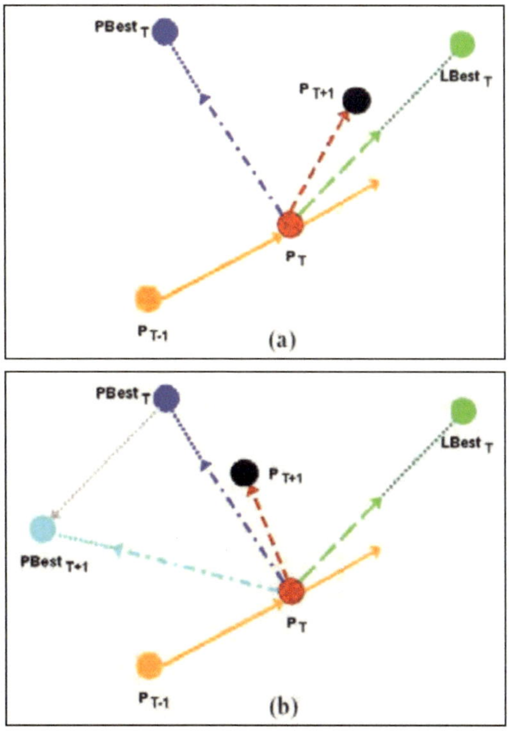

Figure 5. Effects of the perturbation operators. (a) Shows the movement of particle at iteration T+1 without perturbing the PBest in the iteration T. (b) Shows the movement of particle at iteration T+1 with the influence of PBest at iteration T+1, which is the final position after applying the perturbation operators on the PBest in the iteration T

4.5 PSO Parameters

The parameters play an important roll in the successful of any evolutionary algorithm. There are several works that discuss a number of control parameters like swarm size (Van Den Bergh, 2001), neighbourhood size (Suganthan, 1999), or acceleration coefficients (Ratnaweera et al., 2002a; Ratnaweera et al., 2002b).

Our approach generally uses a swarm size of n=100 particles, a neighbourhood size of k=2, and the following set of acceleration coefficients: w=U(0.5, 1.0), c1=1.0, c2=1.0, where U is a uniform distribution. These parameters have not been deeply studied; only the neighbourhood size, which has been explained in this Section. Nevertheless, the acceleration coefficients accomplish the mathematical model gave by Clerc & Kennedy to avoid divergence of the particle trajectories (Clerc & Kennedy, 2002).

4.6 Our Approach PESO

In summary the proposed algorithm, PESO, is a local PSO with a *singly-linked* ring neighbourhood. PESO handles constraints adopting a *feasibility tournament* complemented with a *dynamic tolerance* for handling equality constraints. The main components of PESO are the *C-Perturbation* and *M-Perturbation* operators applied to the *pbest* population.

5. Experiments

PESO is applied to solve the benchmark used in the Special Session on Constrained Real-Parameter Optimization, CEC-06 (Liang et al., 2006). The benchmark is an extended version of 24 functions from the original benchmark of Runnarson and Yao, with 13 functions (Runnarson & Yao, 2000). It is integrated by linear and non-linear functions with linear and non-linear constraints. The benchmark was proposed by Mezura, in his Ph.D. thesis (Mezura, 2004).

TP	Optimal	Best	Median	Mean	Worst	S.D.
g01	-15.000000	-15.000000	-15.000000	-15.000000	-15.000000	0
g02	-0.803619	-0.803619	-0.803617	-0.801320	-0.786566	4.59E-03
g03	-1.000000	-1.000005	-1.000005	-1.000005	-1.000003	3.15E-07
g04	-30665.538	-30665.53867	-30665.53867	-30665.53867	-30665.53867	0
g05	5126.49811	5126.498096	5126.498096	5126.498096	5126.498096	0
g06	-6961.8138	-6961.813876	-6961.813876	-6961.813876	-6961.813876	0
g07	24.306209	24.306209	24.306210	24.306212	24.306219	3.34E-06
g08	-0.095825	-0.095825	-0.095825	-0.095825	-0.095825	0
g09	680.630057	680.630057	680.630057	680.630057	680.630057	0
g10	7049.248	7049.248020	7049.248638	7049.250087	7049.263662	3.61E-03
g11	0.750000	0.749999	0.749999	0.749999	0.749999	0
g12	-1.000000	-1.000000	-1.000000	-1.000000	-1.000000	0
g13	0.053950	0.053950	0.053950	0.053950	0.053965	2.76E-06
g14	-47.764411	-47.761108	-47.747212	-47.741430	-47.670921	2.15E-02
g15	961.715172	961.715171	961.715171	961.715171	961.715171	0
g16	-1.905155	-1.905155	-1.905155	-1.905155	-1.905155	0
g17	8876.98068	8856.502344	8863.875542	8877.812811	8941.344349	30.1195
g18	-0.8660	-0.866025	-0.866025	-0.866001	-0.865568	8.74E-05
g19	32.386	32.349645	32.386872	32.411596	32.571543	6.30E-02
g20	0.096737	*0.204095	*0.209711	*0.212003	*0.233281	6.94E-03
g21	193.778349	205.852693	279.309106	273.298016	303.454837	23.8556
g22	382.902205	*157.5136	*3161.1026	*5376.2265	*18732.7838	5.01E+03
g23	-400.0025	-361.856637	-136.564268	-138.407772	3.775736	84.5217
g24	-5.508013	-5.508013	-5.508013	-5.508013	-5.508013	0

Table 1. PESO results in the Benchmark. *Infeasible Solution

5.1 PESO Results

In Table 1, we present the results of PESO in the benchmark problems, where *S.D.* means standard deviation. For every test problem 30 runs was developed, and in each run 350,000 fitness function evaluations were applied to test our. In only two test problems, g20 and g22, PESO did not find a feasible solution. These problems have 14 and 19, equality constraints respectively. Also, PESO presents a poor performance in test problems g21 and g23, where it did not reach the optimal value, but always found a feasible solution at the 30 runs. In the rest of the benchmark, PESO attains the global optimal. PESO was able to outperform the best know solution in test problems g03, g05, g11, g13, g17 and g19, due the conversion of equality constraints to inequality constraints with a tolerance value of 1E-06. The whole benchmark was resolved using the same parameters, but there are several test problems, which were solved with less than 350000 fitness function evaluations. This fact is showed in Table 2.

TP	Best	Median	Mean	Worst	S.D.	F.R.	S.R.
g01	90800	95000	95396.67	99400	2613.29	30	30
g02	142900	175800	179395.45	232100	28120.18	30	22
g03	315100	315100	315123.33	315600	97.14	30	30
g04	59600	65100	65086.67	70000	2713.28	30	30
g05	315100	315100	315256.67	315900	245.91	30	30
g06	47100	54200	53410.00	57000	2577.80	30	30
g07	185500	227600	233400.00	304500	32253.97	30	30
g08	3600	6850	6470.00	8500	1381.94	30	30
g09	69900	78500	79570.00	102400	7154.65	30	30
g10	167200	221300	224740.00	307200	38407.87	30	30
g11	315100	315100	315100.00	315100	0	30	30
g12	400	6900	6646.67	10400	2606.98	30	30
g13	315100	315150	315546.67	318100	710.87	30	30
g14	326900	326900	326900.00	326900	0	30	1
g15	315100	315100	315100.00	315100	0	30	30
g16	37200	41000	40960.00	45400	2210.88	30	30
g17	315100	316100	316608.70	318800	1061.69	30	23
g18	102200	153600	167088.89	252900	43430.30	30	27
g19	206800	259650	264414.29	331000	36456.84	30	14
g20	NR	NR	NR	NR	NR	0	0
g21	NR	NR	NR	NR	NR	30	0
g22	NR	NR	NR	NR	NR	0	0
g23	NR	NR	NR	NR	NR	30	0
g24	14900	19350	19156.67	22200	1927.24	30	30

Table 2. Convergence of PESO in the Benchmark. NR Optimal not reached

In Table 2, we present the number of fitness function evaluations that PESO requires to attain a value within 1E-4 of the optimal. Also, the number of feasible runs, *F.R.* and the number of successful runs, *S.R.* are showed. We define like *F.R.* that run, which finds at least one feasible solution in less than 350000 fitness evaluations. On the other hand, when the best value found is within 1E-4 of the optimal the run is successful. Only the successful runs were used to calculate the measures presented in Table 2. Test problems with equality constraints require at least 315000 fitness function evaluations, due the dynamic tolerance applied in PESO. The experiments show a poor performance of PESO in test problems g20, g21, g22 and g23. These problems have several equality constraints; in fact the problems g20 and g22 have more than 10 of them. Now, we compare our approach against other PSO based methods and evolutionary algorithms representative of the state-of-the-art.

5.2 Comparison PESO versus Turbulent PSO

First we compare PESO against another PSO approach which applies *feasibility tournament* to handle constrained optimization problems. In Section 3, we mention that Toscano and Coello proposed a constraint handling technique for PSO (Toscano & Coello). Their approach handles constraints through a *feasibility tournament*, and keeps diversity by adding mutations to the velocity vector using a *turbulence* operator. They test the original benchmark with 13 test functions (Runnarson & Yao, 2000). The comparison is shown in Table 3. TC-PSO (Toscano and Coello's PSO) performed 340,000 fitness function evaluations, 10,000 less than PESO, but it is not significative for the comparison. The performance of PESO is better than TC-PSO on test problems g02, g05, g07, g09, g10 and g13.

TP	Optimal	PESO	TC-PSO
g01	-15.000000	-15.000000	-15.000000
g02	-0.803619	-0.803619	-0.803432
g03	-1.000000	-1.000005	-1.004720
g04	-30665.538	-30665.53867	-30665.500000
g05	5126.49811	5126.498096	5126.640000
g06	-6961.8138	-6961.813876	-6961.810000
g07	24.306209	24.306209	24.351100
g08	-0.095825	-0.095825	-0.095825
g09	680.630057	680.630057	680.638000
g10	7049.248	7049.248020	7057.590000
g11	0.750000	0.749999	0.749999
g12	-1.000000	-1.000000	-1.000000
g13	0.053950	0.053950	0.068665

Table 3. Comparison of two PSO with feasibility tournament for handling constraints. Best results of PESO and TC-PSO into 30 runs

5.3 Comparison PESO versus Feasible PSO

Now, we compare PESO against the approach proposes by Hu and Eberhart (Hu & Eberhart, 2002). They apply a global PSO based on *feasibility preservation* for handling constraint problems. They only test the first 12 test functions of the benchmark. The comparison is shown in Table 4. HE-PSO (Hu and Eberhart's PSO) performed 100,000 fitness function evaluations. For developing a real comparison, PESO performed 100,000 fitness function evaluations. Nevertheless, the comparison is not equal since we do not take into account the number of constraint evaluations that HE-PSO performs to preserve feasibility. Also, we must mention that the randomly initialized particles are not always in the feasible space. So initialization may take a longer time. The performance of PESO is better than HE-PSO on test problems g02, g06, g07, g09 and g10. Even, there is not available information about the performance of HE-PSO at test problem g05. We should observe that PESO is robust to the number of fitness function evaluations. It is not a surprise, since in Table 2 we can observe the convergence rate of PESO for every test problem. In the first 12 test problems there are 3 with equality constraints; therefore, their convergence rate is driven by the dynamic tolerance. In the rest, there are 6 test problems with a best convergence rate lower than 100,000 fitness function evaluations. Only test problems g02, g07 and g10 have a best convergence rate upper than 100,000, which cause a little decrease in their best solution found around 30 runs.

TP	Optimal	PESO	HE-PSO
g01	-15.000000	-15.000000	-15.0
g02	-0.803619	-0.803613	-0.7130
g03	-1.000000	-1.000005	-1.0
g04	-30665.538	-30665.53867	-30665.5
g05	5126.49811	5126.498096	-
g06	-6961.8138	-6961.813876	-6961.7
g07	24.306209	24.306248	24.4420
g08	-0.095825	-0.095825	-0.0958250
g09	680.630057	680.630057	680.657
g10	7049.248	7049.250802	7131.01
g11	0.750000	0.749999	0.75
g12	-1.000000	-1.000000	-1.0

Table 4. Comparison of PESO against HE-PSO. Best results of PESO and HE-PSO into 30 runs

5.4 Comparison PESO versus Periodic Mode PSO

In Section 3, we mention the special technique for handling inequality constraints introduced by Zhang et al., called *periodic mode* (Zhang et al., 2004). Their method keeps the global-best near the boundary thus the flock which is constantly pulled to the border, can sustain exploration. They only tested the 9 functions with inequality constraints of the benchmark proposed by Runnarson and Yao (Runnarson & Yao, 2000). The comparison is shown in Table 5.

TP	Optimal	PESO	PM-PSO
g01	-15.000000	-15.000000	-15.000000
g02	-0.803619	-0.803613	-0.64330
g04	-30665.538	-30665.53867	-30665.54
g06	-6961.8138	-6961.813876	-6961.814
g07	24.306209	24.306248	24.306
g08	-0.095825	-0.095825	-0.095825
g09	680.630057	680.630057	680.630
g10	7049.248	7049.250802	7049.5

Table 5. Comparison of PESO against PM-PSO. Best results of PESO and PM-PSO into 30 runs

The PM-PSO algorithm (periodic mode PSO) performed 1,500,000 fitness function evaluations. Although, PESO performed four times less fitness function evaluations than PM-PSO, we did not increase the number of fitness function evaluations, because PESO performance is competitive with the general parameters applied in these experiments. The performance of PESO is better than PM-PSO on test problems g02 and g10.

5.5 Comparison PESO versus Diversity-DE

Now, we compare PESO against other evolutionary algorithms. We believe that could be interesting a comparison against a Differential Evolution algorithm, since PESO applies a *C-Perturbation* similar to the operator used for reproduction in this algorithm. Mezura et al. modified the Differential Evolution algorithm in a way that every parent may have more than one offspring (Mezura et al., 2005). The winner is the best child but then the child is compared to the current parent. Another tournament is performed but this time the winner is found by tossing a coin and comparing by fitness value, or by constraint violation; similar to Stochastic Ranking (Runnarson & Yao, 2000). The comparison of the first 13 test functions is shown in Table 6; the number of fitness evaluations for both algorithms is 225,000. The performance of PESO and Diversity-DE is very similar. A little advantage is shown by PESO on test problems g09 and g13.

TP	Optimal	PESO	Diversity-DE
g01	-15.000000	-15.000000	-15.000000
g02	-0.803619	-0.803618	-0.803619
g03	-1.000000	-1.000005	-1.000
g04	-30665.538	-30665.53867	-30665.539
g05	5126.49811	5126.498096	5126.497
g06	-6961.8138	-6961.813876	-6961.814
g07	24.306209	24.306211	24.306
g08	-0.095825	-0.095825	-0.095825
g09	680.630057	680.630057	680.638
g10	7049.248	7049.248435	7049.248
g11	0.750000	0.749999	0.75
g12	-1.000000	-1.000000	-1.000000
g13	0.053950	0.053950	0.053941

Table 6. Comparison of PESO against Diversity-DE. Best results of PESO and Diversity-DE into 30 runs

5.6 Comparison PESO versus SMES

The extend benchmark was proposed by Mezura in his Ph.D. thesis (Mezura, 2004). Therefore, it is interesting to compare PESO against the approach developed by Mezura, called SMES. SMES works over a simple multimembered evolution strategy: $(\mu+\lambda)$-ES. The modifications introduced into SMES are the reduction of the initial step size of the sigma values to favour finer movements in the search space. A panmictic recombination operator based on a combination of the discrete and intermediate recombination operators. Also, SMES changes the original deterministic replacement of the ES, sorting the solutions by applying a comparison mechanism based on feasibility. This allows remaining in the next generation, the best infeasible solution, from either the parents or the offspring population. In Table 7 we show the comparison of PESO and SMES. In this case both algorithms performed 240,000 fitness function evaluations. It can be seen that PESO is clearly better than SMES in problems g05, g07, g10, g13, g14, g15, g17, g19, g21 and g23. PESO and SMES were unable to find feasible solutions for test problems g20 and g22. But, PESO finds feasible solutions for test problems g17, g21 and g23, where SMES could not find feasible solutions in any single run.

TP	Optimal	PESO	SMES
g01	-15.000000	-15.000000	-15.000000
g02	-0.803619	-0.803618	-0.803601
g03	-1.000000	-1.000005	-1.000000
g04	-30665.538	-30665.53867	-30665.539
g05	5126.49811	5126.498096	5126.599
g06	-6961.8138	-6961.813876	-6961.814
g07	24.306209	24.306211	24.327
g08	-0.095825	-0.095825	-0.095825
g09	680.630057	680.630057	680.632
g10	7049.248	7049.248871	7051.903
g11	0.750000	0.749999	0.750000
g12	-1.000000	-1.000000	-1.000000
g13	0.053950	0.053950	0.053986
g14	-47.764411	-47.760600	-47.535
g15	961.715172	961.715171	*961.698
g16	-1.905155	-1.905155	-1.905
g17	8876.98068	8860.030895	*8890.1826
g18	-0.8660	-0.866025	-0.866
g19	32.386	32.351376	34.223
g20	0.096737	*0.204095	*0.211364
g21	193.778349	236.928359	*347.9809
g22	382.902205	*157.5136	*2340.6166
g23	-400.0025	-369.765012	*-1470.1525
g24	-5.508013	-5.508013	-5.508

Table 7. Comparison of PESO against SMES. Best results of PESO and SMES into 30 runs. *Infeasible Solution

5.7 Comparison PESO versus ISRES

An algorithm representative of the state-of-the-art is the Stochastic Ranking algorithm was proposed by Runarsson and Yao (Runnarson & Yao, 2000). Later, the authors provided a new improved version, called Improved Stochastic Ranking Evolution Strategy, (ISRES) (Runnarson & Yao, 2005). The algorithm is a simple evolution strategy enhanced with a stochastic sorting, which decides, through a probability fixed value, performing a comparison using only the function value or the constraint violation. The ISRES's code is available at Runarsson's page, and we used it, for developing the experiments for test problems g14 through g24. The parameters used were the same as the suggested by the authors (Runnarson & Yao, 2005). The comparison is shown in Table 8. Both algorithms performed the same number of fitness function evaluations, 350000. Note that ISRES finds the best values for test problems g21 and g23. But PESO is better in problems g13 and g17. In test problem g21, PESO found feasible solutions in all 30 runs, whereas ISRES only had 5 successful runs. Both PESO and ISRES were unable to find feasible solutions for test problems g20 and g22.

TP	Optimal	PESO	ISRES
g01	-15.000000	-15.000000	-15.000000
g02	-0.803619	-0.803619	-0.803619
g03	-1.000000	-1.000005	-1.001
g04	-30665.538	-30665.53867	-30665.539
g05	5126.49811	5126.498096	5126.497
g06	-6961.8138	-6961.813876	-6961.814
g07	24.306209	24.306209	24.306
g08	-0.095825	-0.095825	-0.095825
g09	680.630057	680.630057	680.630
g10	7049.248	7049.248020	7049.248
g11	0.750000	0.749999	0.750
g12	-1.000000	-1.000000	-1.000000
g13	0.053950	0.053950	0.053942
g14	-47.764411	-47.761180	-47.761129
g15	961.715172	961.715171	961.715171
g16	-1.905155	-1.905155	-1.905155
g17	8876.98068	8856.502344	8889.9003
g18	-0.8660	-0.866025	-0.866025
g19	32.386	32.349645	32.348689
g20	0.096737	*0.204095	-
g21	193.778349	205.852693	193.785034
g22	382.902205	*157.5136	-
g23	-400.0025	-361.856637	-400.000551
g24	-5.508013	-5.508013	-5.508013

Table 8. Comparison of PESO against ISRES. Best results of PESO and ISRES into 30 runs.
*Infeasible Solution

6. Conclusion

In this chapter, we described a robust PSO for solving constrained optimization problems. We discussed the premature convergence problem, which still is an issue in evolutionary computation. A brief trip was made through several proposals to attain a balance between exploration and exploitation. Also, we briefly review recent works that contribute with interesting ideas for handling-constraints in PSO.

This work presents an algorithm called PESO to handle constrained optimization problems. Based on the empirical and theoretical results of several works, we explain and validate every component applied in PESO. We empirically show the performance of PESO in a well-know benchmark. PESO has shown high performance in constrained optimization problems of linear or nonlinear nature. Three important contributions of PESO are worth to mention: A new neighbourhood structure for PSO, the incorporation of perturbation operators without modifying the essence of the PSO, and a special handling technique for equality constraints.

The first contribution is the singly-linked neighbourhood structure. It increases the exploitation of the algorithm, breaking the double-link that exists between the particles using the original ring neighbourhood structure. PESO implements a singly-linked ring with a neighbourhood of size n = 2, but a general algorithm to build neighbourhoods of size n is given by Hernández et al. (Hernández et al., 2007).
Another relevant idea developed by PESO, is the perturbation of the target to keep flock's diversity and space exploration. Two perturbation operators, *C-perturbation* and *M-perturbation* are applied to the *pbest*. It is equivalent to perturb the particle's memory and not its behaviour; as it is performed by other approaches that tend to destroy the flock's organization capacity.
The last feature of PESO is its special technique to handle equality constraints. It is performed through a *dynamic tolerance* that allows unfeasible particles at the first generations, but it decreases the tolerance value until reach a desired error. The *dynamic tolerance* helps to keep the flock near the feasible region, while exploring promising regions.
The results on the benchmark problems provide evidence that PESO is highly competitive. So far, PESO performed very well at solving the current state-of-the-art problems, but it should be improved to handle problems with a higher number of equality constraints.

7. Future Research

PESO shows a competitive performance solving constrained optimization problems, so global (unconstrained) optimization and multi-objective optimization problems are attractive topics for future research. But, there are other research areas that could be explored in this approach.
As we mention in Section 4, the acceleration parameters have not been studied yet. A set of sub-swarms could improve the robustness of the PSO (Liang & Suganthan, 2006). One of the main research areas in evolutionary computation is the application to real optimization problems. In that field, we used PESO to solve system reliability optimization problems (Muñoz, 2004).

8. References

Agnes, M. (2004). *Webster's New World College Dictionary*, Webster's New World, ISBN 0764571257, May 2004.

Angeline, P. (1998). Evolutionary Optimization versus Particle Swarm Optimization: Philosophy and Performance Differences, *Proceedings of the Seventh Annual Conference on Evolutionary Programming, EP VII*, pp. 601–610, ISBN 3-540-64891-7, March 1998, Springer, San Diego, California, USA.

Carlisle, A. & Dozier, G. (2000). Adapting Particle Swarm Optimization to Dynamic Environments, *Proceedings of the International Conference on Artificial Intelligence, ICAI2000*, pp. 429-434, ISBN 1892512564, Monte Carlo Resort Hotel, June 2000, CSREA Press, Las Vegas, Nevada, USA.

Clerc, M. & Kennedy, J. (2002). The Particle Swarm: Explosion, Stability, and Convergence in a Multi-Dimensional Complex Space, *IEEE Transactions on Evolutionary Computation*, Vol. 6, No. 1, February 2002, pp. 58-73, ISSN 1089-778X.

Coath, G. & Halgamuge, S. (2003). A comparison of Constraint-Handling Methods for the Application of Particle Swarm Optimization to Constrained Nonlinear Optimization Problems, *Proceedings of the 2003 Congress on Evolutionary Computation*, pp. 2419–2425, ISBN 0-7803-7804-0, Rydges Lakeside Hotel, December 2003, IEEE-Press, Canberra, Australia.

Deb, K. (2000). An efficient constraint handling method for genetic algorithms, *Computer Methods in Applied Mechanics and Engineering*, Vol. 186, No. 2-4, June 2000, pp. 311-338, ISSN 0045-7825.

Downing, R. (2006). Neutrality and Gradualism: Encouraging Exploration and Exploitation Simultaneously with Binary Decision Diagrams, *Proceedings of IEEE Congress on Evolutionary Computation 2006, CEC 2006*, pp. 615-622, ISBN 0-7803-9487-9, Sheraton Vancouver Wall Centre Hotel, July 2006, IEEE-Press, Vancouver, BC, Canada.

El-Gallad, A.; El-Hawary, M. & Sallam, A. (2001). Swarming of intelligent Particle for Solving the Nonlinear Constrainted Optimization Problem. *International Journal of Engineering Intelligent Systems for Electrical Engineering and Communications*, Vol. 9, No. 3, 2001, pp. 155–163, ISSN 0969-1170.

Fogel, D. (1994). An Introduction to Simulated Evolutionary Optimization. *IEEE Transaction on Neural Networks*, Vol. 5, No. 1, January 1994, pp. 3–14, ISSN 1045-9227.

He, S.; Prempain, E. & Wu, Q. (2004). An Improved Particle Swarm Optimizer for Mechanical Design Optimization Problems, *Engineering Optimization*, Vol. 36, No. 5, October 2004, pp. 585–605, ISSN 1029-0273.

Hernández, A.; Muñoz, A.; Villa, E. & Botello, S. (2007). COPSO: Constrained Optimization via PSO Algorithm, *Technical Report of the Computer Sciences Department*, I-07-04 (CC), February 2007, Centro de Investigación en Matemáticas, Guanajuato, México.

Holland, J. (1975). *Adaptation in Natural and Artificial Systems*, University of Michigan Press, ISBN 0-262-08213-6, Ann Arbor, MI, USA.

Hu, X. and Eberhart, R. (2002). Solving Constrained Nonlinear Optimization Problems with Particle Swarm Optimization, *Proceedings of the 6th World Multiconference on Systemics, Cybernetics and Informatics 2002 (SCI 2002)*, pp. 203-206, ISBN 980-07-8150-1, Sheraton World, July 2002, The International Institute of Informatics and Systemics, Orlando, Florida, USA.

Jacoby, N. (2005). Exploration and Exploitation Strategies. What kind of analytical models?, *Technical Report Cahiers de la Maison des Sciences Economiques*, May 2005, Université Panthéon-Sorbonne (Paris 1).

Kennedy, J. (1997). The Particle Swarm: Social Adaptation of Knowledge, *Proceedings of the IEEE International Conference on Evolutionary Computation, ICEC'97*, pp. 303-308, ISBN 0-7803-3949-5, University Place Hotel, April 1997, IEEE-Press, Indianapolis, IN, USA.

Kennedy, J. (1999). Small Worlds and Mega-Minds: Effects of Neighborhood Topology on Particle Swarm Performance, *Proceedings of the 1999 Congress on Evolutionary Computation*, pp. 1931–1938, ISBN 0-7803-5536-9, Mayflower Hotel, July 1999, IEEE-Press, Washington, DC, USA.

Kennedy, J. & Mendes, R. (2002). Population Structure and Particle Swarm Performance, *Proceedings of the 2002 Congress on Evolutionary Computation, CEC02*, pp. 1671-1676, ISBN 0-7803-7282-4, Hilton Hawaiian Village Hotel, May 2002, IEEE-Press, Honolulu, HI, USA.

Liang, J.; Runarsson, T.; Mezura-Montes, E.; Clerc, M.; Suganthan, P.; Coello, C. & Deb, K. (2006). Problem Definitions and Evaluation Criteria for the CEC 2006, *Special Session on Constrained Real-Parameter Optimization, Technical Report*, Nanyang Technological University, Singapore, 2006.

Liang, J. & Suganthan, P. (2006). Dynamic Multi-Swarm Particle Swarm Optimizer with a Novel Constraint-Handling Mechanism, *Proceedings of the 2006 IEEE Congress on Evolutionary Computation, CEC 2006*, pp. 9-16, ISBN 0-7803-9487-9, Sheraton Vancouver Wall Centre Hotel, July 2006, IEEE Press, Vancouver, Canada.

March J. (1991). Exploration and Exploitation in Organizational Learning, *Organization Science*, Vol. 2, No. 1, February 1991, pp. 71-87, ISSN 1047-7039.

Mendes, R.; Kennedy, J. & Neves, J. (2004). The Fully Informed Particle Swarm: Simpler, Maybe Better, *IEEE Transactions on Evolutionary Computation*, Vol. 8, No. 3, June 2004, pp. 204–210, ISSN 1089-778X.

Mezura, E. (2004). Alternatives to Handle Constraints in Evolutionary Optimization, Ph.D. thesis, CINVESTAV-IPN, DF, Mexico.

Mezura, E.; Velazquez, J. & Coello, C. (2005). Promising Infeasibility and Multiple Offspring Incorporated to Differential Evolution for Constrained Optimization, *Proceedings of the Genetic and Evolutionary Computation Conference, GECCO 2005*, pp. 225-232, ISBN 1-59593-010-8, L'Enfant Plaza Hotel, June 2005, ACM, Washington DC, USA.

Michalewicz, Z. (1992). *Genetic Algorithms + Data Structures = Evolution Programs*, Springer-Verlag, ISBN 3-540-60676-9, Germany

Michalewicz, Z. & Schoenauer, M. (1996). Evolutionary Algorithms for Constrained Parameter Optimization Problems, *Evolutionary Computation*, Vol. 4, No. 1, 1996, pp. 1-32, ISSN 1063-6560.

Michalewicz, Z. & Fogel, D. (2000). *How to Solve It: Modern Heuristics*, Springer-Verlag, ISBN 3-540-22494-7, Germany.

Muñoz, A. (2004). Diseño Optimo para la Confiabilidad, Master thesis, Department of Computer Sciences, CIMAT, Guanajuato, Gto, Mexico.

Muñoz, A.; Hernández, A. & Villa, E. (2005). Constrained Optimization Via Particle Evolutionary Swarm Optimization Algorithm (PESO), *Proceedings of the Genetic and Evolutionary Computation Conference, GECCO 2005*, pp. 209-216, ISBN 1-59593-010-8, L'Enfant Plaza Hotel, June 2005, ACM, Washington DC, USA.

Munoz-Zavala, A.; Hernandez-Aguirre, A.; Villa-Diharce, E. & Botello-Rionda, S. (2006). PESO+ for Constrained Optimization, *Proceedings of the 2006 IEEE Congress on Evolutionary Computation, CEC 2006*, pp. 231-238, ISBN 0-7803-9487-9, Sheraton Vancouver Wall Centre Hotel, July 2006, IEEE Press, Vancouver, Canada.

Ozcan, E. & Mohan, C. (1998). Analysis of a Simple Particle Swarm Optimization System, Intelligent Engineering Systems Through Artificial Neural Networks: *Proceedings of the 1998 Artificial Neural Networks in Engineering Conference. ANNIE98*, pp. 253-258, ISBN 0-7918-0064-4, Marriott Pavilion Hotel, November 1998, ASME Press, St. Louis, Missouri, USA.

Parsopoulos, K. & Vrahatis, M. (2002). Particle Swarm Optimization Method for Constrained Optimization Problems, In: *Intelligent Technologies from Theory to Applications: New Trends in Intelligent Technologies*, P. Sincak, J. Vascak, V. Kvasnicka, and J. Pospichal, Ed. 76 of Frontiers in Artificial Intelligence and Applications, pp. 214-220, IOS Press, ISBN 1-5860-3256-9, Amsterdam ; Washington DC.

Price, K.; Storn, R. & Lampinen, J. (2005). *Differential Evolution: A practical Approach to Global Optimization*, Springer Verlag, ISBN 3540209506, Berlin, Germany.

Ratnaweera, A.; Halgamuge, S. & Watson, H. (2002a). Particle Swarm Optimization with Time Varying Acceleration Coefficients, *Proceedings of the First International Conference on Soft Computing and Intelligent Systems*, pp. 240-255, At the Auditorium of AIST, October 2002, Tsukuba, Japan.

Ratnaweera, A.; Halgamuge, S. & Watson, H. (2002b). Particle Swarm Optimization with Self-Adaptive Acceleration Coefficients, *Proceedings of the First International Conference on Fuzzy Systems and Knowledge Discovery*, pp. 264-268, ISBN 981-04-7520-9, Orchid Country Club, November 2002, Singapore.

Runarsson, T. & Yao, X. (2000). Stochastic Ranking for Constrained Evolutionary Optimization, *IEEE Transactions on Evolutionary Computation*, Vol. 4, No. 3, September 2000, pp. 284–294, ISSN 1089-778X.

Runarsson, T. & Yao, X. (2005). Search Biases in Constrained Evolutionary Optimization, *IEEE Transactions on Systems, Man and Cybernetics - Part C: Applications and Reviews*, Vol. 35, No. 2, May 2005, pp. 233–243, ISSN 1094-6977.

Suganthan, P. (1999). Particle Swarm Optimiser with Neighborhood Operator, *Proceedings of the 1999 Congress on Evolutionary Computation*, pp. 1958-1962, ISBN 0-7803-5536-9, Mayflower Hotel, July 1999, IEEE-Press, Washington, DC, USA.

Toscano, G. & Coello, C. (2004). A Constraint-Handling Mechanism for Particle Swarm Optimization, *Proceedings of the 2004 Congress on Evolutionary Computation*, pp. 1396–1403, ISBN 0-7803-8515-2, Portland Marriott Downtown, June 2004, IEEE-Press, Portland, Oregon, USA.

Van Den Bergh, F. & Engelbrecht, A. (2001). Effects of Swarm Size on Cooperative Particle Swarm Optimisers, *Proceedings of the Genetic and Evolutionary Computation Conference, GECCO 2001*, pp. 892-899, ISBN 1-55860-774-9, Holiday Inn Golden Gateway Hotel, July 2001, Morgan Kaufmann, San Francisco, California, USA.

Van Den Bergh, F. (2002). An Analysis of Particle Swarm Optimizers, PhD thesis, Department of Computer Science, University of Pretoria, Pretoria, South Africa.

Zhang, W.; Xie, X. & Bi, D., Handling Bloundary Constraints for Numerical Optimization by Particle Swarm Flying in Periodic Search Space, *Proceedings of the 2004 Congress on Evolutionary Computation*, pp. 2307–2311, ISBN 0-7803-8515-2, Portland Marriott Downtown, June 2004, IEEE-Press, Portland, Oregon, USA.

5

Using Crowding Distance to Improve Multi-Objective PSO with Local Search

Ching-Shih Tsou[1], Shih-Chia Chang[1] and Po-Wu Lai[2]
[1]*Department of Business Administration, National Taipei College of Business*
[2]*Department of Information Management, Shih Hsin University*
Taiwan

1. Introduction

Biology inspired algorithms have been gaining popularity in recent decades and beyond. These methods are based on biological metaphor such as Darwinian evolution and swarm intelligence. One of the most recent algorithms in this category is the Particle Swarm Optimization (PSO). PSO is a population-based approach using a set of candidate solutions, called particles, which move within the search space. The trajectory followed by each particle is guided by its own experience as well as by its interaction with other particles. Specific methods of adjusting the trajectory are motivated by the observations in birds, fishes, or other organisms that move in swarms.

Multi-objective optimization (MOO) is an important field to apply swarm intelligence meta-heuristics because there is not only one solution for MOO ingeneral. The solution of a MOO problem is generally referred as a non-dominated solution, which is different from the optimal solution of single-objective optimization problem. A solution is said to be non-dominated over another only if it has superior, at least no inferior, performance in all objectives. Hence, non-dominance means that the improvement of one objective could only be achieved at the expense of other objectives. This concept always gives not a single solution, but rather a set of solutions called the non-dominated set or non-dominated archive.

Generally speaking, there are two approaches to MOO: classical methods and evolutionary methods. Classical methods first convert separate objective functions into a single objective function by weighted sum method, utility function method, or goal programming method, and then solve them by traditional optimization techniques. Such modelling puts the original problem in an inadequate manner, using a surrogate variable with incomplete information. Subsequent optimization techniques also contradicts our intuition that single-objective optimization is a degenerate case of MOO (Deb, 2001). The result of classical approach is a compromise solution whose non-dominance can not be guaranteed (Liu et al., 2003). Lastly, but not the least, a single optimized solution could only be found in each simulation run of traditional optimization techniques such that it limits the choices available to the decision maker. Therefore, using a population of solutions to evolve towards several non-dominated solutions in each run makes evolutionary algorithms, such as swarm intelligence methods, popular in solving MOO problems.

One of the successful applications of PSO to MOO problems, named Multi-Objective PSO (MOPSO), is the seminal work of Coello-Coello and Lechuga (2002). In a subsequent study done by them, MOPSO is not only a viable alternative to solve MOO problems, but also the only one, compared with the Non-dominated Sorting Genetic Algorithm-II (NSGA-II) (Deb et al., 2002), the Pareto Archive Evolutionary Strategy (PAES) (Knowles and Corne, 2000), and the micro-Genetic Algorithm (microGA) (Coello-Coello and Pulido, 2001) for MOO, can cover the full Pareto-optimal front of all the test functions therein.

The goal of generating the non-dominated front is itself multi-objective. That is, designing a Pareto optimizer usually has two major goals - how to converge to the true Pareto-optimal front while achieving a well-distributed set of solutions (Zitzler et al., 2004). Tsou et al. (2006) proposed an improved MOPSO with local search and clustering procedure trying to attain to these goals. Although the best way to obtain a well-distributed set of solutions would be probably to use some clustering algorithm, this effort is usually computationally expensive (Kukkonen and Deb, 2006). This paper extends the research of Tsou et al. (2006), but the clustering algorithm is dropped out. A local search and flight mechanism based on crowding distance is incorporated into the MOPSO. The local search procedure intends to explore the less-crowded area in the current archive to possibly obtain more non-dominated solutions nearby. Besides this, the non-dominated solutions in the less-crowded area are used to guide the population fly over sparse area of the current archive. Such that a more uniform and diverse front might be formed by the optimizer. In a short, mechanisms based on the crowding distance not only implicitly maintain the diversity of the external archive, but also facilitate the convergence of MOPSO to the true Pareto-optimal front. Our approach seeks to reach a reasonable compromise between the computational simplicity and efficiency. Several test problems are employed to verify the performance of our approach.

The rest of this paper is organized as follows. Section 2 reviews the basic concept of MOO. MOPSO with a random line search is described in Section 3.1. Extensions based on crowding distance are presented in Section 3.2. Section 4 reports the experimental results against four test problems. Finally, conclusions and future research are drawn out in Section 5.

2. Multi-objective Optimization

Without loss of generality, a MOO problem (also known as a vector optimization problem) is the problem of simultaneously minimizing K objectives $f_k(\vec{\mathbf{x}})$, $k=1,2,\cdots,K$, of a vector $\vec{\mathbf{x}}$ in the feasible region Ω. That is,

$$\underset{\vec{\mathbf{x}}\in\Omega}{\text{Vector minimize}} \quad \vec{\mathbf{f}}(\vec{\mathbf{x}}) = [f_1(\vec{\mathbf{x}}), f_2(\vec{\mathbf{x}}), ..., f_K(\vec{\mathbf{x}})]^T \tag{1}$$

, where $\vec{\mathbf{x}} = [x_1, x_2, ..., x_D]^T$ is a D-dimensional vector and $f_k(\vec{\mathbf{x}})$ ($k = 1,2,...,K$) are linear or nonlinear functions. A decision vector $\vec{\mathbf{u}} = (u_1, u_2, ..., u_D)$ is said to strongly dominate $\vec{\mathbf{v}} = (v_1, v_2, ..., v_D)$ (denoted by $\vec{\mathbf{u}} \prec \vec{\mathbf{v}}$) if and only if $\forall i \in \{1,2,...,K\}$, $f_i(\vec{\mathbf{u}}) < f_i(\vec{\mathbf{v}})$. Less stringently, a decision vector $\vec{\mathbf{u}}$ weakly dominates $\vec{\mathbf{v}}$ (denoted by $\vec{\mathbf{u}} \preceq \vec{\mathbf{v}}$) if and only if $\forall i \in \{1,2,...,K\}$, $f_i(\vec{\mathbf{u}}) \le f_i(\vec{\mathbf{v}})$ and $\exists i \in \{1,2,...,K\}$, $f_i(\vec{\mathbf{u}}) < f_i(\vec{\mathbf{v}})$.

Certainly, we are not interested in solutions dominated by other solutions. A set of decision vectors is said to be a non-dominated set if no member of the set is dominated by any other member. The true Pareto-optimal front is the non-dominated set of solutions which are not dominated by any feasible solution. One way to solving a MOO problem is to approximate the Pareto-optimal front by the non-dominated solutions generating from the solution algorithm.

3. MOPSO with Local Search

To speak of MOPSO, let us start with the PSO. In PSO, a population is initialized with random solutions, called "particles". All particles have fitness values that are evaluated by the function to be optimized. Each particle flies through the problem space with a velocity, which is constantly updated by the particle's own experience and the experience of the particle's neighbors, to search for optima iterations by iterations. Compared to genetic algorithms, the advantages of PSO are that it is easy to implement and there are fewer parameters to adjust.

In every iteration, the velocity of each particle is updated by two best values. The first one is the best solution it has achieved so far. This value is called *pbest*. Another best value tracked by the optimizer is the best value obtained so far by the neighbourhood of each particle. This best value is a local best and is called *lbest*. If the neighbourhood is defined as the whole population, each particle will move towards its best previous position and towards the best position ever been in the whole swarm, this version is called *gbest* model. In this paper, we use the global version of PSO. The velocity and position of each particle are updated by the following equations.

$$v_d^{i(new)} = \omega \cdot v_d^{i(old)} + c_1 \cdot RAND \cdot (p_d^i - x_d^i) + c_2 \cdot RAND \cdot (g_d - x_d^i) \tag{2}$$

$$x_d^{i(new)} = x_d^i + v_d^{i(new)}, \tag{3}$$

where

$v_d^{i(old)}$ is the old velocity of particle i along dimension d,

$v_d^{i(new)}$ is the new velocity of particle i along dimension d,

ω is the inertia weight which is usually between 0.8 and 1.2,

c_1 and c_2 are the learning factors (or acceleration coefficients), usually between 1 and 4,

x_d^i is the current position of particle i along dimension d,

p_d^i is the personal best solution of particle i along dimension d,

g_d is the global best solution the whole population ever been along dimension d, and

$RAND$ is a random number between 0 and 1.

The difficulty in extending the PSO to MOO problems is how to select a global guide for each particle. Because there is not a single optimum in MOO, the non-dominated solutions found by MOPSO so far are all stored in an archive. Each particle can randomly select a non-dominated solution from the archive as the global guide of its next flight. Although this selection method is simple, it can promote convergence (Alvarez-Benitez et al., 2005). The pseudo-code of MOPSO is shown in Fig. 1.

```
MOPSO()
Initialize()
iter ← 1
while iter < MAXITER do
    Flight()
    CalculateObjVector()
    UpdateNondominatedSet()
    iter = iter + 1
end while
```

Figure 1. The pseudo-code of MOPSO

3.1 Local search

Local search plays a role in adding an exploitative component allows algorithms to make use of local information to guide the search towards better regions in the search space. This feature leads to faster convergence with less computational burden. One of the simplest local search algorithms is the random line search. It starts with calculating the maximum step length according to the parameter δ. For a non-dominated solution, improvement is sought coordinate by coordinate. The temporary D- dimensional vector, $\vec{\mathbf{z}}$, first holds the initial information of each particle. Next, two random numbers are generated to set moving direction and step length for each coordinate, respectively. If the vector $\vec{\mathbf{z}}$ observes a better non-dominated solution, the non-dominated set is updated and the local search for particle i ends. The local search procedure (shown in Fig. 2) incorporated into the MOPSO is so called MOPSO-LS.

```
LocalSearch(δ)
L = δ·( max_d {u^d − l^d} )
S̃ = random(10% of Ã)
for i = 1 to |S̃|
    z⃗ = x⃗^i
    for d = 1 to D do
        λ1 = RAND(0,1)
        λ2 = RAND(0,1)
        if λ1 > 0.5 then
            z^d = z^d + λ2 L
        else
            z^d = z^d − λ2 L
        end if
    end for
    CalculateObjVector(z⃗)
    if z⃗ ≺ x⃗^i or z⃗ ⊀⊁ x⃗^i then
        UpdateNondominatedSet(z⃗)
        x⃗^i = z⃗
    end if
end for
```

Figure 2. The pseudo-code of local search procedure

3.2 Enhancements from crowding distance

The crowding distance of a non-dominated solution provides an estimate of the density of solutions surrounding it (Deb et al., 2002). It is calculated by the size of the largest cuboid enclosing each particle without including any other point. After normalizing the crowding distance for each non-dominated solution, we sort them in ascending order (Line 01 in Fig. 4). As mentioned earlier, the selection of global guide is a critical step in MOPSO. It affects both the convergence to the true Pareto-optimal front and a well-distributed front. Instead of randomly choosing a global guide from the whole non-dominated archive, it is randomly selected from the top 10% less crowded area of the archive for each particle that is dominated by any solution located in this area. Global guides of other particles are randomly selected from the whole archive as usual. This is the flight procedure used in MOPSO-CDLS (Line 03 in Fig. 4). Raquel and Naval (2005) were the first ones to incorporate the crowding distance into the global best selection in MOPSO, however, each particle associated with its own global guide solely selected from the top 10% less crowded area of the archive. It is too restrictive for those particles far away from the less crowded area and could possibly perturb their happy flight.

Flight()
01: SortArchiveByCrowdingDistance()
02: for $i = 1$ to m do
03:     if $\vec{\mathbf{x}}^i$ is dominated by the top 10% less crowded area in $\tilde{A}$ then
04:         $\left(\vec{\mathbf{x}}^i\right)^{Gbest} = Random(top\ 10\%\ less\ crowded\ area\ in\ \tilde{A})$
05:     else
06:         $\left(\vec{\mathbf{x}}^i\right)^{Gbest} = Random(\tilde{A})$
07:     end if
08:     for $d = 1$ to D do
09:         $v_d^i \leftarrow \omega v_d^i + c_1 \cdot RAND \cdot (p_d^i - x_d^i) + c_2 \cdot RAND \cdot (g_d^i - x_d^i)$
10:         $x_d^i \leftarrow x_d^i + v_d^i$
11:     end for
12:     CalculateObjVector($\vec{\mathbf{x}}^i$)
13:     UpdateNondominatedSet($\vec{\mathbf{x}}^i$)
14: end for

Figure 4. The pseudo-code of flight procedure

Besides the flight mechanism based on crowding distance, the local search procedure is also modified to only be executed on the non-dominated solutions in the top 10% less crowded area of the archive. That is, Line 02 in Fig. 2 is modified as $\tilde{S} = top\ 10\%\ less\ crowded\ area\ of\ \tilde{A}$. It is expected that better solutions, at least non-dominated, could be found by the random line search around the less crowded area. Dual effects of pushing further towards the true Pareto-optimal front as well as maintaining a diverse and well-distributed archive might be arisen.

4. Experimental Results

The well-known ZDT test problems (Zitzler et al., 2000) were used to validate the MOPSO-CDLS. ZDT1 is an easy bi-objective problem and has a convex and continuous Pareto-optimal front. ZDT2 has a non-convex but still continuous front. The front of ZDT3 is convex, however, it is discontinuous. In other words, it has several disconnected Pareto-optimal front. The last test problem, ZDT4, is convex but has many local fronts.

The population size for MOPSO-LC and MOPSO-CDLC are set to 25 with a step size 25 till 75. The numbers of iterations are set to 30 with a step size 10 till 50. To compare all results in a quantitative way, we use the following performance measures: archive count $|\tilde{A}|$, set coverage metric $C(U,V)$, spacing (S), and maximum spread (D) (Okabe et al., 2002).

$$C(U,V) = \frac{\left|\{b \in V \mid \exists\, a \in U : a \preceq b\}\right|}{|V|} \tag{4}$$

, where $|\cdot|$ means the number of components in the set.

$$S = \sqrt{\frac{1}{|\tilde{A}|}\sum_{i=1}^{|\tilde{A}|}\left(d_i - \bar{d}\right)^2} \tag{5}$$

, where $d_i = \min_{j \in \tilde{A} \wedge j \neq i} \sum_{k=1}^{K} \left| f_k^i - f_k^j \right|$ and $\bar{d}$ is the mean value of the absolute distance measure

$$\bar{d} = \sum_{i=1}^{|\tilde{A}|} \frac{d_i}{|\tilde{A}|}.$$

$$D = \sqrt{\sum_{k=1}^{K}\left(\max_{i=1}^{|\tilde{A}|} f_k^i - \min_{i=1}^{|\tilde{A}|} f_k^i\right)^2} \tag{6}$$

Tables 1-4 are the results of four test problems for both algorithms. C and L in the parentheses of the first row stand for MOPSO-CDLS and MOPSO-LS, respectively. Some findings are explained in the following.

Iter.	Pop.	C(C,L)	C(L,C)	S(C)	S(L)	D(C)	D(L)	Count(C)	Count(L)	Time(C)	Time(L)
30	25	0.901639	0	0.170416	0.088285	1.417687	1.52305	61	55	0.89	0.843
30	50	0.785714	0	0.029987	0.086507	1.414402	1.519982	70	55	1.078	0.969
30	75	0.071429	0.114286	0.026999	0.033471	1.414214	1.414214	70	68	1.203	1.047
40	25	0.125	0.138889	0.045418	0.044254	1.41424	1.414214	72	73	1.313	1.188
40	50	0.811594	0	0.057449	0.064995	1.414903	1.519977	69	56	1.406	1.313
40	75	0.830986	0	0.059604	0.077409	1.414214	1.519981	71	59	1.672	1.391
50	25	0.876923	0	0.045133	0.08563	1.414563	1.519915	65	57	1.656	1.468
50	50	0.104478	0.044776	0.04486	0.063149	1.414214	1.414214	67	68	1.937	1.671
50	75	0.1	0.1125	0.046662	0.067414	1.414214	1.414214	80	72	2.125	1.797

Table 1. Computational results of ZDT1 problem

Iter.	Pop.	C(C,L)	C(L,C)	S(C)	S(L)	D(C)	D(L)	Count(C)	Count(L)	Time(C)	Time(L)
30	25	0.609756	0	0.074917	0.123052	1.414265	1.417507	41	34	0.921	0.843
30	50	0.885714	0	0.13882	0.087169	1.414214	1.3933	35	34	0.985	0.906
30	75	0.125	0.025	0.093266	0.116607	1.414214	1.414063	40	35	1.047	0.937
40	25	0.939394	0	0.108248	0.14694	1.413647	1.373224	33	31	1.25	1.109
40	50	0.228571	0.028571	0.123745	0.138773	1.414214	1.414332	35	34	1.344	1.25
40	75	0.222222	0.027778	0.052225	0.10615	1.414212	1.414	36	37	0.688	0.594
50	25	0.894737	0	0.05814	0.104946	1.412791	1.392065	38	36	1.593	1.453
50	50	0.27027	0.027027	0.047095	0.110726	1.414142	1.414255	37	35	1.015	0.797
50	75	0.228571	0	0.123088	0.138386	1.414227	1.414231	35	40	1.781	1.562

Table 2. Computational results of ZDT2 problem

Iter.	Pop.	C(C,L)	C(L,C)	S(C)	S(L)	D(C)	D(L)	Count(C)	Count(L)	Time(C)	Time(L)
30	25	0.473684	0	0.032093	0.291718	0.335081	1.864763	19	18	0.672	0.734
30	50	0.410256	0.025641	0.093437	0.337072	1.95883	1.884636	39	36	0.922	0.812
30	75	0.142857	0.119048	0.053984	0.107845	1.961352	1.927156	42	51	1.047	0.891
40	25	0.5	0.033333	0.122377	0.53802	1.934344	1.947032	30	20	1.094	0.969
40	50	0.2	0.228571	0.030287	0.159101	1.950184	1.94119	35	41	1.203	1.141
40	75	0.163265	0.204082	0.006431	0.008037	1.95511	1.949345	49	47	1.328	1.235
50	25	0.870968	0	0.37742	0.183748	1.953586	2.028031	31	27	1.438	1.313
50	50	0.266667	0.088889	0.097678	0.169007	1.931062	1.955391	45	43	1.609	1.453
50	75	0.148936	0.170213	0.16836	0.135811	1.958623	1.962591	47	53	1.688	1.531

Table 3. Computational results of ZDT3 problem

Iter.	Pop.	C(C,L)	C(L,C)	S(C)	S(L)	D(C)	D(L)	Count(C)	Count(L)	Time(C)	Time(L)
30	25	0.583333	0.027778	0.085428	0.120843	1.415008	1.431134	36	29	0.844	0.782
30	50	0.428571	0.071429	0.070559	0.070263	1.438755	1.429762	42	31	0.875	0.813
30	75	0.513514	0.162162	0.054137	0.11659	1.409016	1.430743	37	36	0.922	0.844
40	25	0.612903	0.032258	0.124403	0.212547	1.417124	1.453333	31	26	1.093	1.078
40	50	0.452381	0.214286	0.083199	0.076452	1.412184	1.410637	42	39	1.172	1.156
40	75	0.589286	0.142857	0.073391	0.101297	1.422002	1.416985	56	54	1.282	1.156
50	25	0.575758	0.212121	0.088226	0.082615	1.440936	1.437883	33	33	1.438	1.328
50	50	0.565217	0.173913	0.079993	0.097561	1.43185	1.429264	46	47	1.562	1.422
50	75	0.433333	0.1	0.037096	0.077393	1.42348	1.417994	60	59	1.656	1.516

Table 4. Computational results of ZDT4 problem

1. In view of the set coverage metric in Tables 1-4, MOPSO-CDLS exhibit better results than MOPSO-LS even in more difficult problem such as ZDT3 and ZDT4. That is, the non-dominated solutions generated by MOPSO-CDLS are closer to the Pareto-optimal front than those by MOPSO-LS.

2. For the maximum spread in Tables 1-4, there is no significant difference for both algorithms. However, MOPSO-CDLS outperforms MOPSO-LS in the spacing metric. This implies MOPSO-CDLS can generate well-distributed front than MOPSO-LS.
3. It is not surprising that particles flying towards sparse area and gathering local information around it make MOPSO-CDLS find more non-dominated solutions than MOPSO-LS on the average.
4. Certainly, crowding distance calculation need additional time to execute. Although the execution time (in second) of MOPSO-CDLS is a little bit longer than that of MOPSO-LS in all tables, MOPSO-CDLS is still a reasonable simple and efficient algorithm for MOO.

5. Conclusions

It is well known that local search, even in its simplest form, prevents search algorithms from premature convergence and, therefore, possibly drives the solution closer to true Pareto-optimal front. A local search procedure and a flight mechanism both based on crowding distance are incorporated into the MOPSO, so called MOPSO-CDLS, in this paper. Computational results against ZDT1-4 problems show that it did improve the MOPSO with random line search in all aspects except the execution time. Local search in less crowded area of the front not only reserves the exploitation capability, but also helps to achieve a well-distributed non-dominated set. Global guides randomly selected from the less crowded area help the particles dominated by the solutions in this area to explore more diverse solutions and in a hope to better approximate the true front.

This study intends to highlight a direction of combining more intelligent local search algorithms into a Pareto optimization scheme. Mechanisms based on crowding distance employed here did not explicitly maintain the diversity of non-dominated solutions which is its original intention, but they indeed facilitate the possibilities of flying towards the Pareto-optimal front and generating a well-distributed non-dominated set. Further researches include comparisons with other multi-objective evolutionary algorithms and accommodating constraints-handling mechanism in the Pareto optimizer.

6. References

Alvarez-Benitez, J.E., Everson, R.M. & Fieldsend, J.E. (2005). A MOPSO algorithm based exclusively on Pareto dominance concepts. *Lecture Notes in Computer Science*, 3410, 459-473.

Coello Coello, C.A. and Lechuga, M.S. (2002), MOPSO: A proposal for multiple objective particle swarm optimization, *Proceedings of the 2002 IEEE Congress on Evolutionary Computation*, pp. 12-17, Honolulu, U.S.A., May 2002, IEEE Press, New Jersey.

Coello Coello, C.A. & Pulido, G.T. (2001), Multiobjective optimization using a micro-genetic algorithm, *Proceedings of the 2001 Conference on Genetic and Evolutionary Computation Conference*, pp. 274-282, San Francisco, CA, July 2001, IEEE Press, New Jersey.

Deb, K. (2001). Multi-Objective Optimization using Evolutionary Algorithms, John Wiley & Sons, New York.

Deb, K.; Pratap, A.; Agarwal S. & Meyarivan, T. (2002). A fast and elitist multiobjective genetic algorithm: NSGA-II. *IEEE Transactions on Evolutionary Computation*, Vol. 6, 182-197.

Knowles, J.D. & Corne, D.W. (2000). Approximating the nondominated front using the Pareto archived evolution strategy. *Evolutionary Computation Journal*, Vol. 8, 149-172.

Kukkonen, S. And Deb, K. (2006). Improved pruning of non-dominated solutions based on crowding distance for bi-objective optimization problems, *Proceedings of the 2006 IEEE Congress on Evolutionary Computation*, pp.1179-1186, Vancouver, Canada, July 2006, IEEE Press, New Jersey.

Liu, G.P.; Yang, J.B. & Whidborne, J.F. (2003). *Multiobjective Optimisation and Control*, Research Studies Press, Hertfordshire.

Okabe, T.; Jin, Y. & Sendhoff, B. (2003). A critical survey of performance indices for multi-objective optimization, *Proceedings of the 2003 IEEE Congress on Evolutionary Computation*, pp. 878-885, December 2003, IEEE Press, New Jersey.

Raquel, C.R. & Naval, P.C. Jr. (2005). An effective use of crowing distance in multiobjective particle swarm optimization, *Proceedings of the 2005 Conference on Genetic and Evolutionary Computation*, pp. 257-264, Washington D.C., U.S.A., June 2005, ACM Press, New York.

Tsou, C.-S.; Fang, H.-H.; Chang, H.-H. & Kao, C.-H. (2006). An improved particle swarm Pareto optimizer with local search and clustering. *Lecture Notes in Computer Science*, 4247, 400-406.

Zitzler, E.; Deb, K. & Thiele, L. (2000). Comparison of multiobjective evolutionary algorithms : empirical results. *Evolutionary Computation Journal*, Vol. 8, No. 2, 125-148.

Zitzler, E.; Laumanns, M. & Bleuler, S. (2004). A tutorial on evolutionary multiobjective optimization, in Gandibleux, X.; Sevaux, M.; Sörensen, K. & T'kindt, V. (Ed.), *Metaheuristics for Multiobjective Optimisation*, Springer, Heidelberg, pp. 3-37.

6

Simulation Optimization Using Swarm Intelligence as Tool for Cooperation Strategy Design in 3D Predator-Prey Game

Emiliano G. Castro and Marcos S. G. Tsuzuki
Polytechnic School of University of São Paulo
Brazil

1. Introduction

It has long been established that simulation is a powerful tool for aiding decision making. This is due to a number of factor, such as the inherent ability to evaluate complex systems with large number of variables and interactions for which there is no analytical solution. It is considered as a tool to answer "what if" questions, not a solution generator technique. This scenario could be changed with the aid of optimization procedures, and so simulation could answer not only "what if" questions but also answers "how to" questions, providing the best set of input variables and maximize or minimize some performance measure. For the purposes of optimization, the simulation is simply a "black box" which computes a realization of the (stochastic) function value for a given combination of the parameter values (Magoulas et al., 2002).

Simulation optimization is the process of finding the best values of some decision variables for a system where the performance is evaluated based on the output of a simulation model of this system. The components of a typical optimization system are present in a simulation optimization system: decision variables, objective function and constraints. The decision variables must be contained in some feasible region defined by the constraints. The objective function is a real valued function defined on these variables, but due to the complexity and stochastic nature of the underlying system an analytical expression can not be determined and the value returned by the stochastic simulation must be used instead.

The predator-prey game is a multi-agent system, which originally came from the field of Artificial Intelligence (AI). At first, this field was called Distributed Artificial Intelligence (DAI); instead of reproducing the knowledge and reasoning of one intelligent agent as in AI, the objective became to reproduce the knowledge and reasoning of several heterogeneous agents that need to jointly solve planning problems. Some researchers have focused more on the agent and its autonomy (for instance, the definition of an agent proposed by Wooldridge and Jennings (1999): "an agent is a computer system that is situated in some environment, and that is capable of autonomous action in this environment in order to meet its design objectives"), while others, engaged in the field of multi-agent systems, have focused more on the organization of multiple agent interactions (Huhns & Stephens, 1999).

The aiming of this work is to propose a simulation optimization tool for solutions' synthesis to a problem involving a dynamic and complex system (to bring forth strategies for a

hunting game between predators and prey in a three-dimensional environment) whose solution involves their agents' emergent behavior (in this case, the predators'). Moreover, this simulation optimization uses the PSO as optimization algorithm which in turn, is also based on emergent behavior. That is, a tool that employs emergence to project emergence.
The organization of this work is as follows: Section 2 contains a review of the Particle Swarm Optimization (PSO). Section 3 describes the 3D predator-prey game: the predator and prey behaviors, the parameter of the hunting game and predator's model of strategy. Section 4 presents the developed tool. The results are presented in Section 5, and some concluding remarks are given in Section 6.

2. Particle Swarm Optimization (PSO)

PSO is based on the collective motion of a flock of particles: the particle swarm. Each member of the particle swarm is moved through a problem space by two elastic forces. One attracts it with random magnitude towards the best location so far encountered by any member of the swarm. The position and velocity of each particle are updated at each time step (possibly with the maximum velocity being bounded to maintain stability) until the swarm as a whole converges.
The update rule for PSO contains only two parameters: the relative importance of the influences on a particle of the particle best and the swarm best solutions, and the number of particles to be used as neighbor. A particle can use as reference the best result obtained by any particle of the swarm, or just for their neighbor particles. In that case, the analogy is in the topological mean, and not for the eventual momentary proximity in the parameter space. Thus, the size of this neighborhood to be considered is a variable in the algorithm.
Perhaps inspired by the original derivation of PSO (an abstract version of the factors involved in the feeding behavior of flocks of birds), early progress in PSO often took the form of adding terms based on biological or physical analogies. One of the most successful of these was the "inertia weight" (a friction coefficient added to the velocity update rule). It is employed to control the impact of the previous history of velocities on the current velocity. In this way, the "inertia weight" regulates the trade-off between the global and local exploration of the swarm. A large inertia weight facilitates global exploration, while a small one tends to facilitate local exploration, fine-tuning the current search space.
The PSO happens in accordance to the following formula:

$$\mathbf{v}_i(t) = w\,\mathbf{v}_i(t-1) + \varphi_1\,[\mathbf{p}_i - \mathbf{x}_i(t-1)] + \varphi_2\,[\mathbf{p}_g - \mathbf{x}_i(t-1)] \quad (1)$$

Where $\mathbf{p}_i$ is the best position found by the particle i so far, $\mathbf{p}_g$ is the best position among all particles, and φ_1 and φ_2 are positive random variables, evenly distributed in the intervals $[0, \varphi_{1max}]$ and $[0, \varphi_{2max}]$, calculated at each iteration for each particle. w is the inertia weight. The position of each particle is updated at every iteration using the vector of velocity (adopting the time unit as the iteration step):

$$\mathbf{x}_i(t) = \mathbf{x}_i(t-1) + \mathbf{v}_i(t) \quad (2)$$

PSO belongs to the class of the evolutionary algorithms based on population, as well as the genetic algorithms. However, unlike those, that uses as a metaphor the survival of the better-adapted ones, in PSO the motivation is the simulation of social behavior. Such as the other evolutionary algorithms, PSO is initialized with a population of random solutions. The main difference is that in PSO, each potential (individual) solution is also associated to a random velocity in the initialization process; the potential solutions, designated as particles, may therefore "fly" through the parameter space of the problem.

3. The Hunting Game

DAI is a field that has been quickly unfolded and diversified since its beginning in the second half of the 1970's decade. It still represents a promising research and application domain as well, characterized by its multi-disciplinary nature, gathering concepts from fields such as Computer Science, Sociology, Economy, Administration, Work Management and Philosophy.

DAI's primary focus is on the coordination as interaction form, particularly significant to reach the goal or to fulfill the tasks. And the two basic and contrasting standards of coordination are competition and cooperation. In the competition, several agents work against each others because their goals are conflicting. In the cooperation, the agents work together and they congregate their knowledge and capacities to reach a joint objective (Weiss, 2000). In this work, by the own nature of the application chosen (group hunting), only cooperative strategies will be considered.

The hunting's problem (or persecution's game) is a classical theme in AI. Just as originally proposed (Benda & Jagannathan, 1985), it is made of two classes of agents (predators and preys, classically four predators and a single prey) disposed in a rectilinear grid (plane and discrete domain), all at the same velocity. The predators' purpose is to catch the prey. To encircle it, each predator should occupy an adjacent "square" to the prey in the rectilinear grid. The prey, in turn, "wins" the game if it gets to escape away from the "board's" domain borders before being caught. In this classic version, the agents' movement is quite simple: at each "step" or simulation cycle, each agent can move a "square" in vertical or horizontal direction, since this square is not occupied yet. In general the prey is programmed with random movement, while the predators' strategy is the focus on the approaches of AI.

This kind of problem acts as an excellent benchmark for comparative evaluation on different approaches of artificial intelligence, using central, local or distributed control (Manela & Campbell, 1995). Given the nature of the problem, each individual influences and is influenced by the whole system and, since that the goal cannot be reached by a single agent separately, it is only natural the emergence of cooperative strategies. This work proposes an evolution in the game in its classical form, so that the hunt and the persecution extrapolate the discrete plane, expanding to a continuous and three-dimensional domain. Another evolution point consists of a more elaborated formulation for the behaviors and the strategies, for both predators and prey.

3.1 Behavior of Prey and Predators

In this section, the concepts for the three dimensional hunting are defined. Catching is the situation in which at least one of the predators reaches the prey. Technically speaking, it invades a kind of "vital bubble", a small sphere related to the prey's body volume and having it as the center. The prey, in its turn, has as a goal to avoid being caught by the predators for a determined period. Time limiting is due to a series of practical circumstances, among them all the fact that the performance in the game will serve, in the end, as a target function of the algorithm's optimization; and it should naturally have a foreseen stop criterion to the cases of which predators are unable to succeed in catching the prey. The prey's behavior in this 3D pursuing game in the continuous space also evolved in relation to its classical version. It is under the control of a Finite State Machine (FSM). The projected machine to describe the prey's behavior has three states:

- Free walk: Initial state of the game. In this state, the prey behaves as it does in the classical version, having random movement at a low velocity given by $\mathbf{v}_{yw}$.
- Escape: The prey, when noticing that is being hunted, because at least a predator is inside of its "perception bubble" with velocity above certain limit given by $\mathbf{v}_{dc}$ or had it settled whatever the velocity, in its "proximity bubble", begins to move in its maximum velocity given by $\mathbf{v}_{ye}$, to a calculated direction considering the two closest predators' standings. The perception and proximity bubbles are spheres centered in the prey with radius of R_{ye} and R_{yx}, respectively (Figure 1). If the conditions that determined to get into this state have dropped away, the prey turns in to the Free Walk state.
- Caught: In this state, at least one predator has already invaded the prey's "vital bubble". It is considered being caught and its action is ceased. The game is closed. The vital bubble is a sphere centered at the prey with radius of R_{yv} (Figure 1).

Predators' behavior is controlled by a FSM set by the following three states described below:

- Hunt: Initial state of the game. The predator moves with a velocity that has direction and module defined by its strategy. This strategy's synthesis what will be exactly the target of this work, the product of the synthesis' tool that involves a simulator and an optimization algorithm.
- Pursue: The predator sets itself in this state when the prey sets in escaping mode, perceiving the approach of this one or even another predator. When pursuing, the predator has its moving direction exclusively based on the prey's position, and it moves itself at maximum velocity given by $\mathbf{v}_{dp}$, thereon, having no more any kind of strategy.
- Capture: The predator invaded the prey's "vital bubble" and its catching proceeded. The game is over.

3.2 Hunting Game's Parameters

Given the general rules, the game of three-dimensional hunt still has certain versatility margin. Several combinations can be checked and compared, depending on how some free parameters are defined; this joined to some simulation parameters arranges the configuration's settings of the game: number of predators n_d, game time limit t_{max}, initial distance D_0 and coefficient of inertia C.

The predators have to capture the prey under the considered time limit; in case this time has passed, the prey is considered as the winner. The initial distance defines the distance between the prey and each one of the predators in the beginning of the game. The coefficient of inertia must be between 0 and 1, and it simulates the inertia effect, both for the predators and prey, at each simulation step. It is applied accordingly to the following expression:

$$v(t) \leftarrow C\ v(t-1) + (1 - C)\ v(t) \tag{3}$$

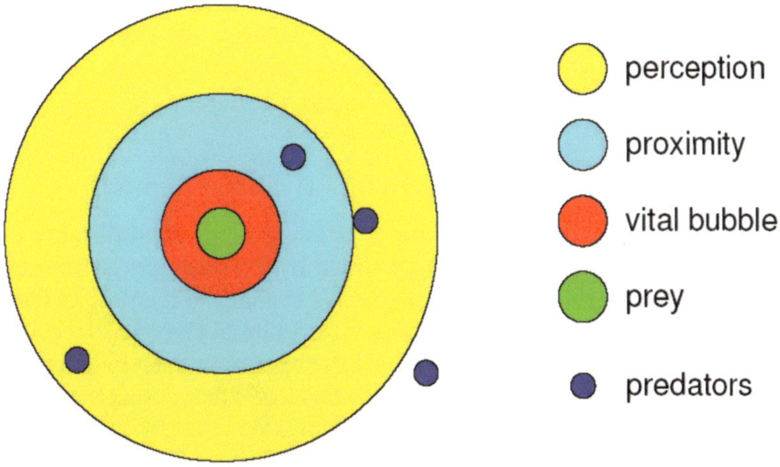

Figure 1. Perception, proximity and vital bubbles of the prey

It is natural to expect that, for each (coherent) group of free parameters, the strategies' synthesis tool presents a different result, since the circumstances aroused by these parameters in the hunt conditions be sufficiently distinct.

3.3 The Predators' Strategies

The predators do not need to move in-group, but to increase their survival chances they should be capable of self-organize in order to encircle and to capture a prey, thus guaranteeing their food. Evidently, without using any type of direct communication during the task. Police officers' teams use the radio to coordinate their encircling maneuvers, but wolves do not use walkie-talkies at the time they leave in pack for hunting a moose (Parunak, 1997). Through some rules based on visual tracks about the moose's grounding and of the other wolves, they must be able to encircle the moose without any explicit form of communication or negotiation (nothing such like “I'll go to the northward; why don't you go southward?”).

All of the predators should share (as part of the problem's definition) the same hunt strategy, which does not involve memory or direct communication among the agents. Taking as a base the predators' sensorial world at the hunting time, the strategy ought to, at most, take into consideration the following parameters: direction of the prey $\mathbf{q}_y$, direction of the closest predator (neighbor) $\mathbf{q}_n$ and distance of the prey D_y. As the kinematical reference for the predators are their own positions, the first two parameters should be calculated in the following way:

$$\mathbf{q}_y = (\mathbf{P}_y - \mathbf{P}_d)/(|\mathbf{P}_y - \mathbf{P}_d|) \tag{4}$$

$$\mathbf{q}_n = (\mathbf{P}_n - \mathbf{P}_d)/(|\mathbf{P}_n - \mathbf{P}_d|)$$

Where $\mathbf{P}_y$, $\mathbf{P}_d$ and $\mathbf{P}_n$ are the vectors of position (in relation to the center of the coordinate system) of the prey, the current predator and its closest neighbor, respectively. The only capacity of allowed decision to the predators in the game is to control its own moving, that is, dynamically change its vectorial velocity using the parameters provided by its sensorial system ($\mathbf{q}_y$, $\mathbf{q}_n$ and D_y). The strategy formulation developed for this work obeys to the following expression:

$$D = \min (D_y / D_0 , 1) \tag{5}$$

$$\mathbf{v}_d(d) = \mathbf{v}_{dp}\, d^{X1} (d^{X2}\, \mathbf{q}_y + X3\, d\, \mathbf{q}_n) / (|\, d^{X2}\, \mathbf{q}_y + X3\, d\, \mathbf{q}_n |)$$

Where $\mathbf{v}_d(d)$ is the velocity of the predator as a function of normalized distance to the prey; and X1, X2 and X3 are decision parameters (provided by the strategies' synthesis tool). The variable X1 is related to the influence of the predator's distance to the prey in the module of its velocity; X2 reflects the importance of the prey's direction in the vectorial composition of the velocity's direction, whilst X3 represents the influence of the closest neighbor's direction. The strategies are then defined by triple ordinates (X1, X2,X3) that define the behavior of the predators' movement. The presented formulation allows no-linearity and a wide range of possibilities both for the module and the vectorial composition of the velocity as a function of the predators' distance to the prey. Evidently, the same problem would hold other countless strategy formulations. Amplifying the sensorial capacity, for instance, the predators' velocity could also be a function of the distance to the closest neighbor. Or even maintaining the defined sensorial group in this work, quite diverse mathematical expressions could be formulated.

4. Synthesis of Strategies by the Particle Swarm

Simulation environments are important to evaluate the performance of strategies that could not be tested in any type of analytical expression. The same strategy is used by a predators' group, each influencing towards movement of another, in a chain reaction. The hunt can only be verified through the strategies' effects overtime. Based on this model, a simulation environment was implemented, and beside an optimization algorithm, it composes a synthesis tool that will provide, at the end of the process, a satisfactory solution for the initial problem. That tool was implemented in the program called PREDATOR. During the process of strategies' synthesis, the simulator changes information continuously with the optimizer. The optimizer, tracking its algorithm (particle swarm), defines some “points” in the space of solutions and it submits, one by one, these solution-candidates to the simulator, that receives and interprets them as the entry parameters for the simulation. At the end of the simulation, the outcomes of this are sent back to the optimizer, which interprets this information as the objective function of the solution-candidate that had been sent. It processes this information inside the algorithm routine and sends the next solution-candidate, restarting a cycle that only ends when the optimizer finds some of its stopping criteria. Figure 2 shows the optimization flow diagram.

To illustrate the simulation of the hunt game in the program PREDATOR, all agents were represented by fishes. These animals were chosen because, unlike humans, they are subject to huntings that can only be modeled in three-dimensional domains.

In the simulation, predators and prey's velocities possess a term of “momentum”, which emulates a kind of “inertia”, even without processing the dynamic equations that would necessarily involve forces and the agents' masses. This mechanism avoids that the agents (in this case the fishes) might be moved in an implausible way in the simulation setting, executing curves and maneuvers visibly out of the dynamic reality that should reign in a real situation.

The program PREDATOR was designed in a way to present a quite simple and intuitive interface (Figure 3). All of the buttons and displays were clustered in a control panel, in which their buttons allows the user to load a file containing one of the three types of possible configurations: simulation, optimization and animation (of the particles' movement resulting from an optimization process). In the illustrated example in Figure 3, the strategy used in the simulation is the correspondent to the particle of number 1 of the 40th iteration (40-01), the line right below exhibits their parameters' strategy (X1, X2 and X3) and the inferior line presents the predators' medium distance in pursuing (the number of predators in pursuing is presented between parenthesis). There are two chronometers to the right in the panel. The first indicates the hunting [1] time; and the second, which starts only when the first one stops, marks the pursuing [2] time. There is also a field indicating the prey's current state (in the example, in escape).

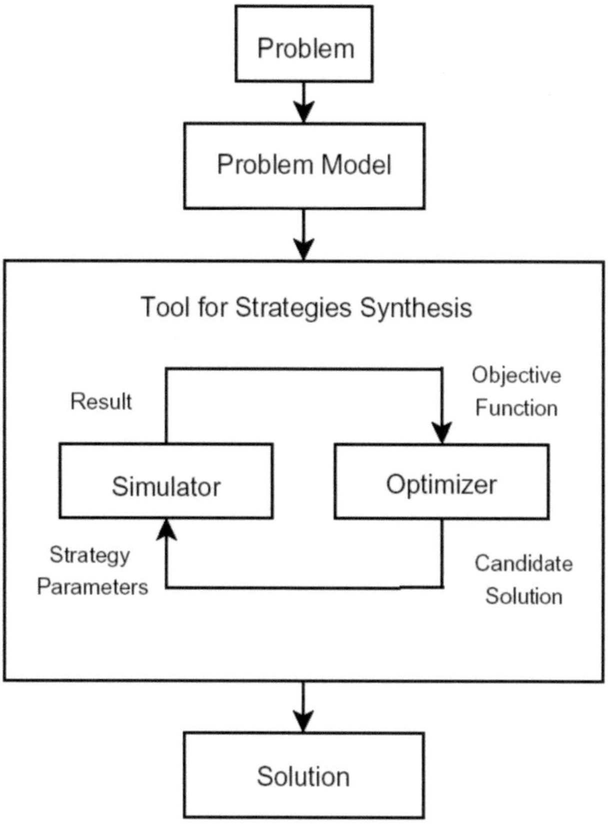

Figure 2. Optimization flow diagram

[1] All agents are in the first state of their FSMs.

[2] All agents are in the second state of their FSMs.

In spite of the interface's detailed information about positions and the fishes' velocities, to follow the simulation through the observation of tables is a superhuman task. To help the user to understand the simulation, the program PREDATOR provides four visualization windows, which exhibit the perspective projections of the tracking cameras (Figure 3). Even with all of the visualization resources implemented, it is not easy to process the visual information of the four (or even three) images in real time. Behind this difficulty there is probably a hidden evolutionary reason. The user (that is a human being) didn't have, unlike what probably happened with the fishes, his cognitive system adapted to process visual information coming from all directions. In an attempt to build a "bridge" among these differences in visual processing, a "3D radar" was implemented. This radar consists of two disks, being the superior used to represent the front part of the prey and the inferior the back part, working as if it was a rear-view mirror.

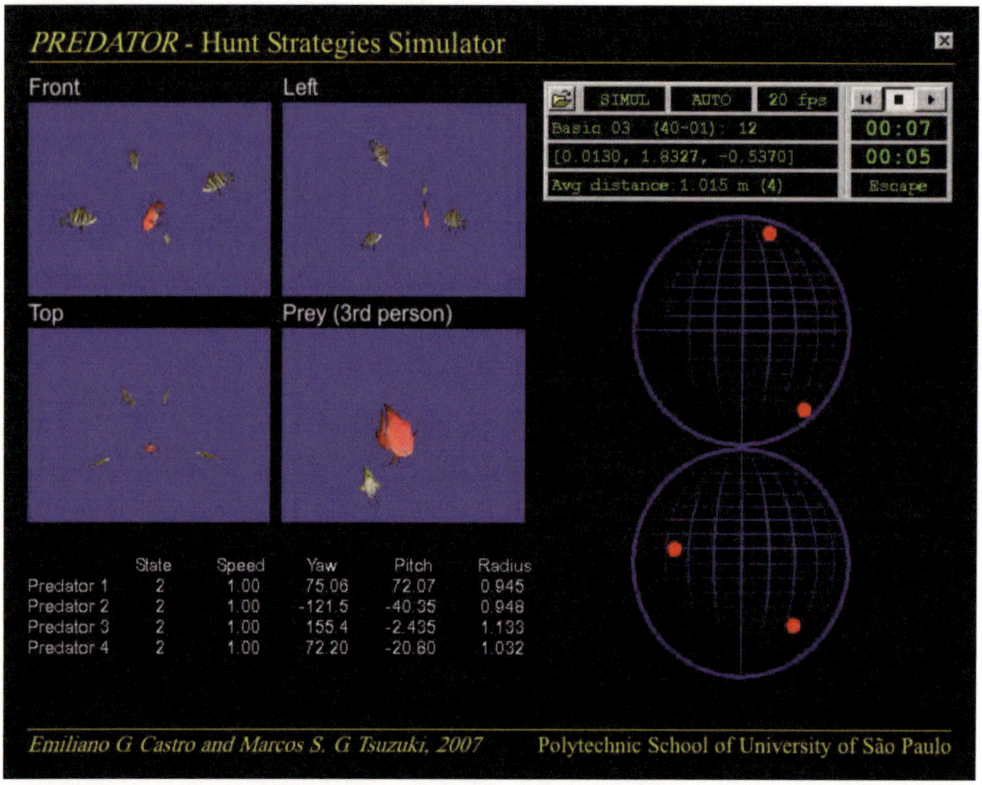

Figure 3. Window of the program PREDATOR

The optimization algorithm, "embedded" in the PREDATOR program, in order to evaluate the result of the simulation, uses the following rule that works as the objective function:

- For strategies that get to capture the prey in an available time (the free variable t_{max}), the result of the simulation is:

$$f(X1,X2,X3) = t_{hunt} + t_{purs} \tag{6}$$

  Where t_{hunt} is the time used in the hunt and t_{purs} the time spent in the pursuing (both in seconds), that are exhibited in the two chronometers of the control panel;

- For strategies that don't get to capture the prey inside of the available time, the result of the simulation is:

$$f(X1,X2,X3) = t_{max} (1 + D_{average} / D_0) \quad (7)$$

Where t_{max} is the time limit allowed for the simulation (in seconds), $D_{average}$ is the medium distance of the predators to the prey at the end of the simulation and D_0 the initial distance between the predators and the prey (both in meters).

Besides the simulations' configuring information, necessary for the simulating that will evaluate the strategies generated by PSO, the program also reads the adjustment parameters in the configuration file from PSO's algorithm itself. Moreover, besides the kinematics' variables of the particles, they comprise the maximum number of iterations, the number of particles, the number of simulations by particle and the size of the neighborhood (number of particles of the subset considered as each particle's "neighborhood", including itself, for the comparison among the best individual results obtained as yet).

5. Results

Dozens of optimization tests were accomplished, varying not only the simulation's configuration features, in order to analyze different "rules" for the three-dimensional hunting game, but also the optimizing configuration, to study the sensibility of the parameters of the PSO.

The parameter "number of simulations by particle" revealed itself, soon in the preliminary tests, of fundamental importance within the optimization process. In some tests considering just a single simulation run by particle, it was common that some particles presented performance of difficult reproduction, which were resultants from simulator initializations extremely advantageous (all of the predators already actually encircling the prey, for instance). As the initialization of the predators' positions is stochastic, that is a phenomenon hard to avoid. And, as a consequence, these results got registered in the algorithm and they "pulled", in a certain measure, the swarm for a solution often far from being the most appropriate, but only "lucky" when first (and only) evaluated.

Although the PSO's algorithm is strong enough to escape from these traps, its performance gets quite harmed, once several iterations are wasted while the influence of these exceptional results does not weaken. Increasing this parameter from 1 to 5, these situations were practically eliminated, and as the performance's average of the simulations is the one to be considered as the particles' objective function, this repetition ends up working as a type of filter against the results derived from extraordinary random conditions.

The optimization's amount of time, considering as stop criterion the maximum number of iterations, is certainly a function of a series of parameters, that might be divided in two groups: the simulation and optimization one. In the first group, the most evident is the simulation time limit (45 seconds to most tests). In the second, they are preponderantly the maximum number of iterations (50 or 100), the number of particles (tests were made with 10 and 20) and the number of simulations for particle (5 in most of the tests).

The parameter t_{max} limits the time for the simulation, and consequently affects the hunting. Its value is intrinsically related to the velocity of the fishes and the several bubbles radius.

The parameter t_{max} has a fundamental influence in the objective function. A t_{max} with a small value will not allow the development of some strategies which are not so interesting initially. However, these strategies can generate very interesting solutions at the end. A larger value of t_{max} can reduce the problem; however, values too large of t_{max} will increase exaggeratedly the computational time. Finally, it is suggested that before the optimization, a sequence of preliminary simulations must be done, so that it is possible to estimate the impact of the parameters in the hunting.

A basic simulation setting was made (see Table 1), for reference, and tested with a series of preliminary tests. Variations of this basic setting were elaborated with the purpose of detecting the sensibility of some parameters.

The simulations could be watched in the Predator's visualization windows, real time. The program also renders three views of the paths described by the agents during the pursue, condensing all the animation in a single picture. An example can be seen in Fig. 4, which shows the trajectories of all agents in a successful hunt. The sudden trajectory change made by all fishes (easily seen in the path of agent number 5 in the top view) is related to the moment the fishes stop moving to encircle the prey and start pursuing it.

n_p	= 6	(number of predators)
t_{max}	= 45 s	(time limit of the game)
v_{pw}	= 0,2 m/s	(prey's walk velocity)
v_{ye}	= 1,0 m/s	(prey's escape velocity)
D_0	= 10 m	(initial distance)
R_{pe}	= 5 m	(radius of the prey's bubble of perception)
R_{pr}	= 3 m	(radius of the prey's bubble of proximity)
R_v	= 0,3 m	(radius of the prey's vital bubble)
v_{dw}	= 1,0 m/s	(predators' pursuing velocity)
v_{dp}	= 0,6 m/s	(predators' critical approach velocity)
C	= 0,95	(inertia coefficient)

Table 1. Basic scenario configuration

Some optimizer configurations were tested to generate the best strategy for this basic simulation setting, taking as base values suggested by the literature of this area (Kennedy & Eberhart, 2001). Different PSO's adjustments took to strategy parameters with very much alike performances, all providing very fast hunts. These configurations (and results) are shown in Table 2. Figure 5 allows an analysis of the convergence from four different adjustment settings of used PSO.

Configuration A has a slower convergence as a consequence of the reduced number of simulations, while configurations B and C (with very similar adjusts) presented convergence curves very similar. Configuration D showed a faster convergence, which can be a consequence of the greater number of particles allowing an efficient exploration of the parameter space.

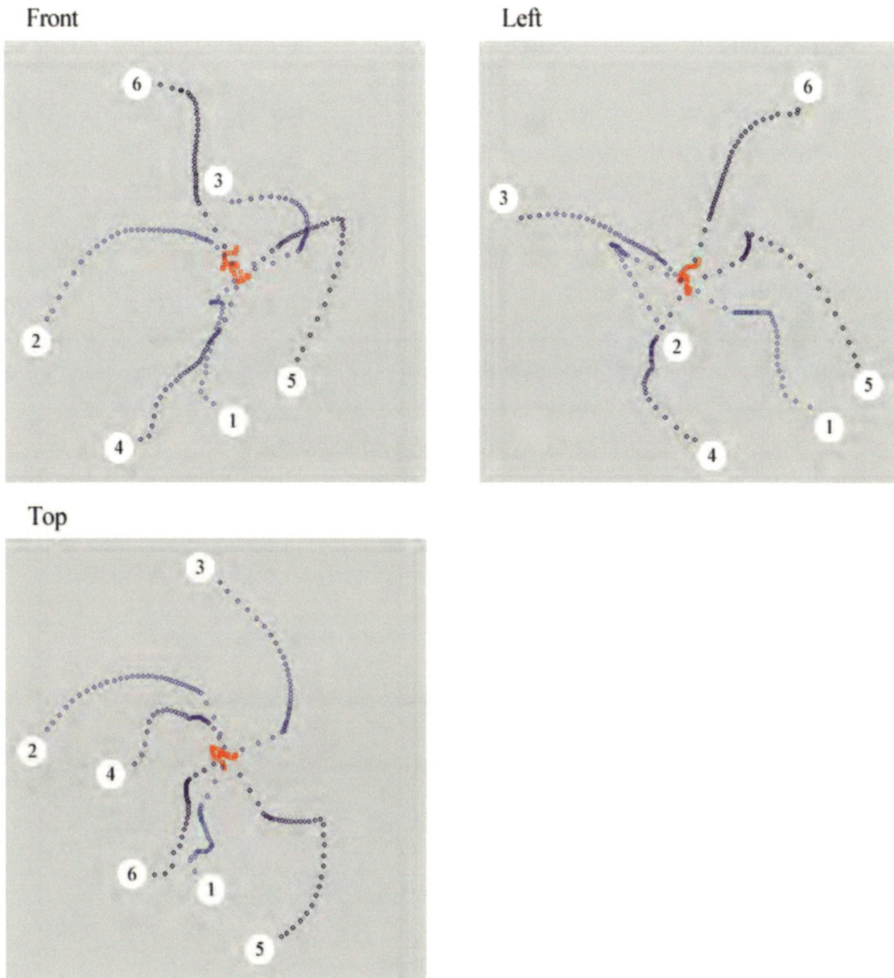

Figure 4. Trace of 6 predators (blue) hunting the prey (red)

The strategy parameters created in these tests are triple ordinates very similar, indicating "points" in the universe of solutions very close to one another. One of those tests, for instance, generated as the best strategy (for the particle number 14, in the 50th iteration) that one capable of capturing the prey after a hunt of, on average, 10.2 seconds, and defined by the parameters (X1, X2, X3) = (0.0753; 1.6763; -0.2653).

	CfgOtim A	CfgOtim B	CfgOtim C	CfgOtim D
Number of Particles	10	10	10	20
Number of Simulations/Particle	1	5	5	5
Neighborhood Size	5	5	5	5
Inertia weight (w)	1,0	1,0	1,0	1,0
φ_{1max}	0,5	0,5	0,4	0,7
φ_{2max}	0,2	0,2	0,2	0,4
V_{max}	1,0	2,0	2,0	2,0
Hunt time of the best generated strategy (s)	11,6[3]	10,4	11,4	10,2

Table 2. Generated strategies for the basic scenario

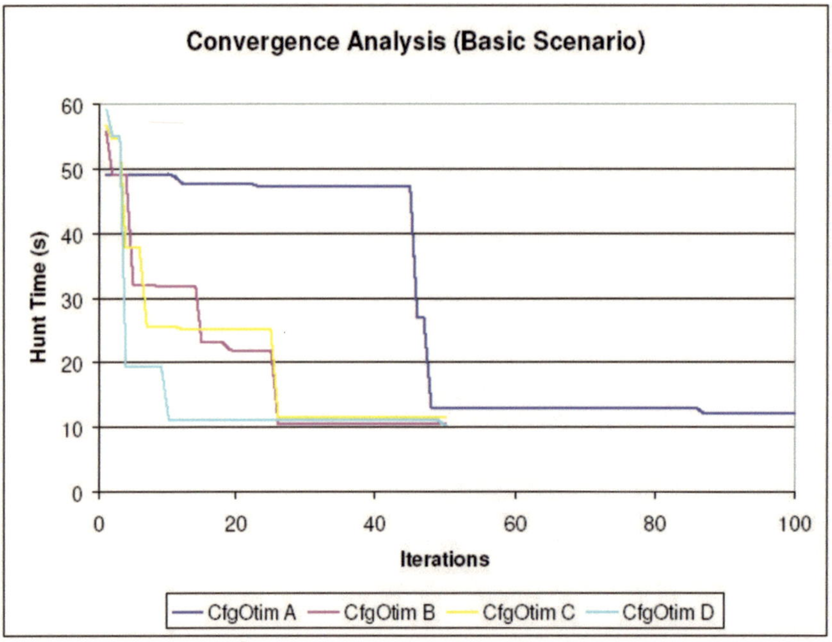

Figure 5. Convergence Analysis

Besides the results shown in Fig. 4, it is possible to visually observe the PSO optimization process through the animation mode of the PREDATOR program. Fig. 6 presents 4 frozen

[3] Value obtained at iteration number 163.

moments of an animation basic scenario, with PSO configured with 20 particles. Each frame contains three cameras illustrating the three views (top, front and rear) of the parameter space, represented as a gray box with dimensions defined by the constraints.

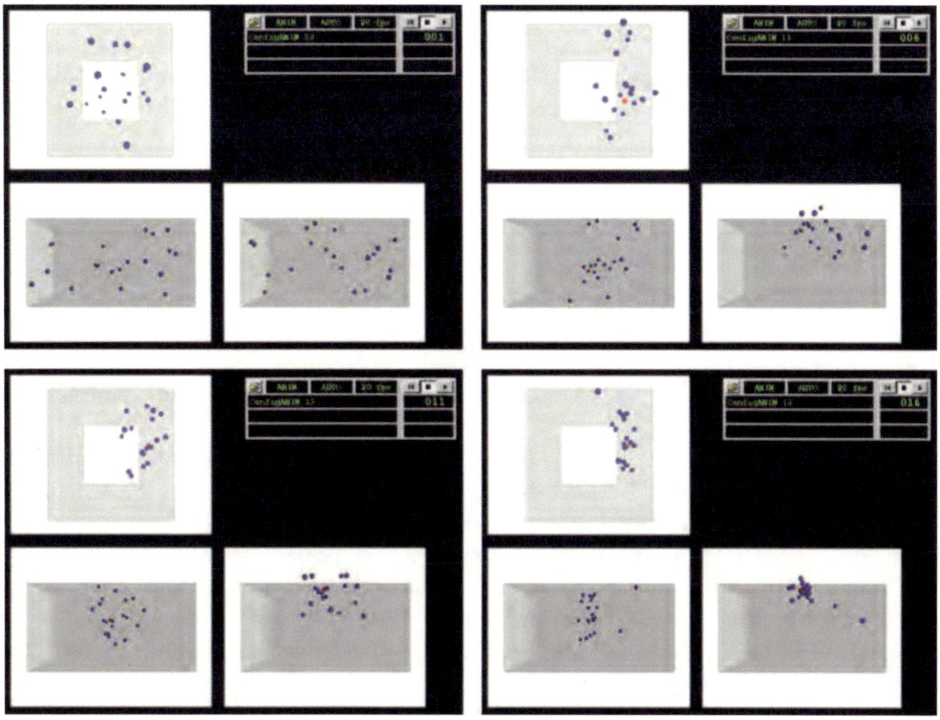

Figure 6. Twenty particles (PSO) searching for better strategies at four frozen moments: t=1 (upper left), t=6 (upper right), t=11 (lower left) and t=16 (lower right)

6. Conclusions

The problem solving capability of the multiagent systems using co-operative strategies expands the solution universe of some classes of problems to beyond some human limits of reasoning and intuition. The hard time we have trying to mentally process, in a parallel fashion, the several "instances" sensorial-cognitive-motor that represents the agents is the reason that makes invariably surprising the system's behavior as a whole. That is the emergent behavior.

In this work, we tried to demonstrate that it is possible to project these Distributed Artificial Intelligence systems knowing just how to model the problem. The "fine tuning" of the project details was accomplished by a synthesis tool, using an optimization systems that also takes advantage of the emergent behavior (of the PSO particles). Therefore, part of the problem's complexity was solved without any analytical approach, but using instead an intelligent and automatic solution searching process.

The results obtained in this work can attest that the tool of synthesis developed is really capable to provide, as long as working with well elaborated models, satisfactory solutions for problems of complex nature, of difficult resolution by analytical approaches.

Delegating the task of solving a problem for a tool in the moulds proposed in this work means, in a final analysis, to trust in the emergent properties of a complex system to produce solutions for another system (not coincidentally, also complex). These solutions are not pre-defined in the program. Neither are we capable to easily understand the solutions generated in terms of the program code. This tends to go in the opposite direction of the essence from traditional engineering. However, will eventually unveils a field still poorly explored in the area of project development.

7. References

Benda, R. D. M. & Jagannathan, V. (1985) On optimal cooperation of knowledge sources. In *Technical Report BCS-G2010-28*, Boeing AI Center, Boeing Computer Services, Bellevue. Washington.

Huhns, M. N. & Stephens, L. M. (1999) Exploiting expertise through knowledge networks. *IEEE Internet Computing*, Vol. 3, Number 6, pp. 89-90.

Kennedy, J. & Eberhart, R. C. (2001) *Swarm Intelligence*. Ed. Morgan Kaufmann, Sao Francisco.

Magoulas, G. D.; Eldabi, T.; Paul, R. J. (2002) Global search for simulation optimisation. *Proceedings of the 2002 Winter Simulation Conference*, Ed. Ycesan, E.; Chen, C. H.; Snowdon, J. L.; Charnes, J. M. pp. 1978-1985.

Manela, M. & Campbell, J. A. (1995) Designing good pursuit problems as testbeds for distributed AI: a novel application of genetic algorithms. In *Lecture Notes on Artificial Intelligence 957*, Springer Verlag.

Parunak, H. V. D. (1997) Go to the ant: Engineering principles from natural agent systems. In *Annals of Operations Research*.

Weiss, G. (2000) Multiagent *Systems: a modern approach to Distributed Artificial Intelligence*. Ed. MIT Press, Massachusetts.

Wooldridge, M. J. & Jennings, N. R. (1999) Software engineering with agents: Pitfalls and pratfalls. *IEEE Internet Computing*, Vol. 3, Number 3, pp. 20-27.

7

Differential Meta-model and Particle Swarm Optimization

Jianchao Zeng[1] and Zhihua Cui[2,1]
[1]*Division of System Simulation and Computer Application, Taiyuan University of Science and Technology*
[2]*State Key Laboratory for Manufacturing Systems Engineering, Xi'an Jiaotong University*
China

1. Introduction

Optimization has been an active area of research for several decades. As many real-world optimization problems become increasingly complex, better optimization algorithms are always needs. Without loss of generally, the unconstrained optimization problem is identified with the discovery of the global minimizer of a real valued objective function

$$f: \ S \rightarrow R \tag{1}$$

i.e. finding a point $x^* \in S$ such that

$$f(x^*) \leq f(x), \forall x \in S \tag{2}$$

Where $S \in R^D$ is a nonempty compact set.

There are two main categories for global optimization methods: deterministic and probabilistic methods. Traditionally, the deterministic methods need some information to determine the optima such as grads etc. However, for many real-world optimization problems, the optimization function may be discontinuous. Furthermore, the deterministic methods only can be applied into the problems with slow dimension because of the huge time-cost for large dimensionality. Therefore, from the 1960's, many researchers pay their attentions to the probabilistic methods. All of these rely on probabilistic judgements to determine whether or not search should depart from the neighbourhood of a local optimum (Forgo, 1988; Hansen, 1992; Rao, 1996).

Different from adaptive stochastic search algorithms, evolutionary computation (EC) is a new kind of probabilistic method. They exploit a ser of potential solutions (called population), and detect the optimal problem solution through cooperation and competition among the individuals of the population. The well-known EC methods are all inspired from the evolution of nature such as: genetic algorithm (GA) (Goldberg, 1989; Michalewica, 1994), evolution strategy (ES) (Back, 1996; Schwefel, 1975), evolutionary programming (EP) (Fogel, 1996), and artificial life methods.

Recently, particle swarm optimization (PSO) method (Kennedy and Eberhart, 1995) is proposed known as a member of the wide category of swarm intelligence methods

(Kennedy and Eberhart, 2001). It simulates the animal social behaviour such as birds flocking, fish schooling, and animal herding.
In this paper, the basic concept of particle swarm optimization is explained. Then, a new framework for PSO - differential meta-model is proposed. Thirdly, a new modified variants – differential evolutionary PSO with PID controller is designed. Finally, we provide a conclusion and some future search topic.

2. Particle Swarm Optimization

In a PSO system, multiple candidate solutions coexist and collaborate simultaneously. Each solution called a "particle", flies in the problem search space looking for the optimal position to land. A particle, as time passes through its quest, adjusts its position according to its own "experience" as well as the experience of neighbouring particles. Tracking and memorizing the best position encountered build particle's experience. For that reason, PSO possesses a memory (i.e. every particle remembers the best position it reached during the past). PSO system combines local search method (through self experience) with global search methods (through neighbouring experience), attempting to balance exploration and exploitation.
Each particle maintains two character items: velocity and position. Both of them are updated as follows:

$$v_j(t+1) = v_j(t) + c_1 r_1 (p_j - x_j(t)) + c_2 r_2 (p_g - x_j(t)) \tag{3}$$

$$x_j(t+1) = x_j(t) + v_j(t+1) \tag{4}$$

where $v_j\ (t)$ denotes the velocity vector of particle j at time t. $x_j\ (t)$ represents the position vector of particle j at time t . Vector p_j is the memory of particle j at current generation, and vector p_g *is* the best location found by the whole swarm. Cognitive coefficient c_1 and social coefficient c_2 are known as acceleration coefficients. r_1 and r_2 are two random number with uniform distribution. To reduce the likelihood, a threshold is introduced to limit the value of $v_{jk}\ (t+1)$ (k^{th} value of velocity vector) so that

$$| v_{jk}(t+1) | \le v_{\max} \tag{5}$$

The well-known earliest modification is the introduction of inertia weight w (Shi and Eberhart, 1998). The inertia weight is a scaling factor associated with the velocity during the previous time step, resulting a new velocity update equation, so that

$$v_j(t+1) = w v_j(t) + c_1 r_1 (p_j - x_j(t)) + c_2 r_2 (p_g - x_j(t)) \tag{6}$$

Therefore, the original PSO can be obtained by setting w =1. Empirical experiments have been performed with an inertia weight set to decrease linearly from 0.9 to 0.4 during the course of a simulation. There are still many other variants to improve the convergence speed, such as PSO with constriction factor (Clerc, 1999), Spatial neighbourhood (Suganthan, 1999), etc. The details please refer to the corresponding references.

3. Differential Meta-model Particle Swarm Optimization

In this section, a uniform model -differential meta-model (Zeng and Cui, 2005) is presented based on the analysis of the standard PSO and its several variants. Then, the convergence performance is analyzed with linear control theory, and the upper bound estimate of the convergence speed is given using Lyapunov function. Finally, an adaptive parameters adjusted algorithms is given to improve the global optimality of convergence.

3.1 Differential Meta-model

Consider the following differential equations:

$$\begin{cases} \frac{dv_i(t)}{dt} = \chi[(w - \frac{1}{\chi})v_i(t) + c_1 r_1 (p_i - x_i(t)) + c_2 r_2 (p_g - x_i(t))] \\ \frac{dx_i(t)}{dt} = v_i(t+1) \end{cases} \tag{7}$$

If Euler numeral integral method is used with step length one, we can obtain the following results:

1. When $w = 1$ and $\chi = 1$, the original PSO is obtained;
2. The standard PSO with inertia weight w is obtained with $w \neq 1$ and $\chi = 1$.

$$\chi = \frac{2}{|2 - \varphi_{12} - \sqrt{\varphi_{12}^2 - 4\varphi_{12}}|} (\varphi_{12} = c_1 r_1 + c_2 r_2)$$

3. When $w = 1$ and $\chi = \frac{2}{|2 - \varphi_{12} - \sqrt{\varphi_{12}^2 - 4\varphi_{12}}|} (\varphi_{12} = c_1 r_1 + c_2 r_2)$, the PSO with constriction factor is obtained.
4. When $w = 0$ and $\chi = 1$, the stochastic PSO is obtained (Cui and Zeng,2004).

Therefore, based on the choice of the parameters w and χ, the different PSO evolutionary model is represented by equation (7). In other words, equation (7) can be used to express the meta-model for PSO, called differential meta-model of PSO. For convenience, the following symbols are defined as:

$$a_0 = \chi(w - \frac{1}{\chi}) \tag{8}$$

$$\varphi_1' = \chi c_1 r_1, \varphi_2' = \chi c_2 r_2 \tag{9}$$

$$\varphi_{12} = \varphi_1' + \varphi_2' \tag{10}$$

$$\varphi_p' = \varphi_1' p_i + \varphi_2' p_g \tag{11}$$

Then, equation (7) can be expressed as

$$\begin{cases} \frac{dv(t)}{dt} = a_0 v(t) - \varphi_{12}' x(t) + \varphi_p' \\ \frac{dx(t)}{dt} = v(t+1) \end{cases} \tag{12}$$

which is the standard form of differentia meta-model of PSO.

3.2 Analysis of PSO Evolutionary Behavior

The first-order approximate for $v(t+1)$ is used to replace $v(t+1)$, i.e.,

$$v(t+1) = v(t) + \frac{dv(t)}{dt},$$

then resulting the following equation (12):

$$\begin{cases} \dfrac{dv(t)}{dt} = a_0 v(t) - \varphi'_{12} x(t) + \varphi'_p \\ \dfrac{dx(t)}{dt} = (a_0+1) v(t) - \varphi'_{12} x(t) + \varphi'_p \end{cases} \tag{13}$$

Define:

$$Y(t) = \begin{bmatrix} v(t) \\ x(t) \end{bmatrix}, U(t) = \begin{bmatrix} P_i \\ P_g \end{bmatrix}, A = \begin{bmatrix} a_0 & -\varphi'_{12} \\ 1+a_0 & -\varphi'_{12} \end{bmatrix}, B = \begin{bmatrix} \varphi'_1 & \varphi'_2 \\ \varphi'_1 & \varphi'_2 \end{bmatrix} \tag{14}$$

The standard state equation of linear system is obtained:

$$\dot{Y}(t) = AY(t) + BU(t) \tag{15}$$

and its solution is solved as follows:

$$Y(t) = e^{A(t-t_0)} Y(t_0) + \int_0^t e^{A(t-\tau)} BU(\tau) d\tau \tag{16}$$

From linear system theory, if all eigenvalues of matrix A have negative real part, equation (16) is convergence. The eigen-equation of matrix A is listed as follows:

$$|\lambda I - A| = \lambda^2 + (\varphi'_{12} - a_0)\lambda + \varphi'_{12} = 0 \tag{17}$$

and its eigenvalues are solved:

$$\lambda_{12} = \frac{a_0 - \varphi'_{12} \pm \sqrt{(\varphi'_{12} - a_0)^2 - \varphi'_{12}}}{2} \tag{18}$$

Therefore, both eigenvalues of matrix A have negative real part if $a_0 - \varphi'_{12} < 0$ is true. In other words, if $a_0 - \varphi'_{12} < 0$ is satisfied, the differential PSO evolutionary model described by equation (13) is convergent, and the limit is obtained by the follows.

$$\lim_{t\to+\infty} Y(t) = \lim_{t\to+\infty} e^{A(t-t_0)} Y(t_0) + \lim_{t\to+\infty} \int_0^t e^{A(t-\tau)} BU(\tau) d\tau = \begin{bmatrix} 0 \\ \dfrac{\varphi'_p}{\varphi'_{12}} \end{bmatrix} \tag{19}$$

that is:

$$\lim_{t \to +\infty} v(t) = 0 \tag{20}$$

$$\lim_{t \to +\infty} x(t) = \frac{\varphi_p'}{\varphi_{12}'} \tag{21}$$

Equation (21) implies that following conclusion is true:

$$\lim_{t \to +\infty} (\varphi_1' + \varphi_2')x(t) = \varphi_1' P_i + \varphi_2' P_g \tag{22}$$

Because of the randomness of φ_1' and φ_2', the above equation is satisfied if and only if $\lim_{t \to +\infty} x(t) = P_i = P_g$ is true.

It can be seen that all the particles according to the evolutionary equation (13) is convergent to the best position p_g discovered by any of the particles when $a_0 - \varphi_{12}' < 0$ is satisfied. In other words, if the best position p_g keeps constant within the test generation, the positions of all particles will converge to p_g.

Meanwhile, from equation (15) and $U(t) = \begin{bmatrix} P_i \\ P_g \end{bmatrix}$, the behavior of PSO is actually identical to the trajectory of a linear system under the step signal inputs with stochastic disturbance, and the amplitude of step signal inputs is increased or not decreased within the evolution of PSO.

In following section, the upper bound estimate of convergence speed for equation (15) is deduced. A Lyapunov function is defined as follows

$$V(Y) = Y^T PY \tag{23}$$

and

$$\dot{V}(Y) = -Y^T QY \tag{24}$$

where P is a positive definite matrix and Q is a positive definite symmetrical matrix, and following Lyapunov equation is satisfied:

$$A^T P + PA = -Q \tag{25}$$

From the view of linear system, the convergence performance of system can be evaluated by:

$$\eta = -\frac{\dot{V}(Y)}{V(Y)} \tag{26}$$

Evidently, the less is $V(Y)$ and the larger for absolute $\dot{V}(Y)$, the larger value η, the faster convergence speed, and vice versa.

Integrate equation (26) with t from 0 to t, resulting:

$$-\int_0^t \eta dt = \int_0^t \frac{\dot{V}(Y)}{V(Y)} dt = \ln \frac{V(Y)}{V(Y_0)} \tag{27}$$

Further,

$$V(Y) = V(Y_0)e^{-\int_0^t \eta dt} \tag{28}$$

Equation (28) is hard to solve, since then, we suppose

$$\eta_{\min} = \min_Y\{-\frac{\dot{V}(Y)}{V(Y)}\} = constant \tag{29}$$

η in equation (28) is replaced by $\eta_{\min}$, may result

$$V(Y) \le V(Y_0)e^{-\int_0^t \eta_{\min} dt} = V(Y_0)e^{-\eta_{\min}} \tag{30}$$

It can be seen that when $\eta_{\min}$ is determined, the upper bound estimate of $V(Y)$ convergent time can be evaluated. From equations (23) and (24), we have

$$\eta_{\min} = \min_Y\{-\frac{\dot{V}(Y)}{V(Y)}\} = \min_Y\{\frac{Y^T QY}{Y^T PY}\} = \min\{Y^T QY, Y^T PY = 1\} \tag{31}$$

Then, for linear constant system,

$$\eta_{\min} = \lambda_{\min}(QP^{-1}) \tag{32}$$

where, $\lambda_{\min}$ (•) is the minimum eigenvalue of (•).

3.3 Adaptive Parameter Adjustment Strategy

A differential form of PSO is given in equation (12), and the convergence condition is easy to satisfy. In order to improve the global convergence performance, an adaptive parameter adjustment strategy is discussed in this part.

From the conducted convergence condition $a_0 - \varphi_{12}' < 0$, we have the less value $a_0 - \varphi_{12}' < 0$, the faster convergence speed it is. By this way, we select the parameter values so that the convergence condition $a_0 - \varphi_{12}' < 0$ is always true in the evolutionary iteration. Further, we let $a_0 - \varphi_{12}' < 0$ has little absolute value in the earlier stage, while in the later stage of evolution, $a_0 - \varphi_{12}' < 0$ has a larger absolute value. In other words, there is a slow convergence speed and a powerful global exploration capacity in the earlier period of evolution, as well as in the later period of evolution, the local exploitation capacity is addressed and convergence speed is faster. In order to balance the ability of the global exploration and the local exploitation, an adaptive parameter adjustment strategy is proposed.

With the definition of φ_{12}',

$$\varphi_{12}' = \varphi_1' + \varphi_2' = r_1 c_1' + r_2 c_2' \tag{33}$$

The convergence condition implies $a_0 < c_1^{'} + c_2^{'}$. Evidently, the differential PSO algorithm has three parameters a_0, $c_1^{'}$ and $c_2^{'}$. From the experiment results, $c_1^{'} + c_2^{'} = 4$ can make a better performance. Therefore, the parameters are adjusted as follows:

$$c_1' = 1 + at \tag{34}$$

$$c_2' = 3 - at \tag{35}$$

$$a_0 = c_1' + c_2' - \beta \tag{36}$$

Where t is evolutionary generation, a and /? are two adjusted parameters to control the change rate. Generally, a=0.01~0.001, β=0.01~0.005.

4. Differential Evolutionary Particle Swarm Optimization with Controller (Zeng & Cui, 2005)

With the same model (7), we suppose $\varphi_0 = \chi(w - \frac{1}{\chi})$, $\varphi_1 = \chi c_1 r_1$, $\varphi_2 = \chi c_2 r_2$, then euation (7) can be changed as follows:

$$\begin{cases} \dfrac{dv_i(t)}{dt} = \varphi_0 v_i(t) + \varphi_1 \ (p_i - x_i(t)) + \varphi_2 (p_g - x_i(t)) \\ \dfrac{dx_i(t)}{dt} = v_i(t+1) \end{cases} \tag{37}$$

The PSO algorithm described by differential evolutionary equations (37) is called differential evolutionary PSO (DEPSO). The analysis of the evolutionary behavior of DEPSO is made by transfer function as follows. The first order difference approximation of $v_i\ (t + 1)$ is $v_i\ (t + 1)$ = $v_i(t) + \dfrac{dv_i(t)}{dt}$, then equation (37) will be

$$\begin{cases} \dfrac{dv_i(t)}{dt} = \varphi_0 v_i(t) + \varphi_1 \ (p_i - x_i(t)) + \varphi_2 (p_g - x_i(t)) \\ \dfrac{dv_i(t)}{dt} = (\varphi_0 + 1) v_i(t) + \varphi_1 (p_i - x_i(t)) + \varphi_2 (p_g - x_i(t)) \end{cases} \tag{38}$$

Laplace transformation is made on equation (38), and suppose the initial values of $v_i\ (t)$ and $x_i\ (t)$ are zero, we have

$$SV_i(s) = \varphi_0 V_i(s) + \varphi_1 (P_i(s) - X_{i(s)}) + \varphi_2 (P_{g(s)} - X_{i(s)}) \tag{39}$$

$$SX_i(s) = (\varphi_0 + 1) V_i(s) + \varphi_1 (P_i(s) - X_i(s)) + \varphi_2 (P_g(s) - X_i(s)) \tag{40}$$

From equation (39), it is known that

$$V_i(s) = \frac{\varphi_1}{s-\varphi_0}(P_i(s) - X_i(s) + \frac{\varphi_2}{s-\varphi_0}(P_g(s) - X_i(s)) \tag{41}$$

Substituting (41) into (40) yields

$$X_i(s) = \frac{\varphi_1(s+1)}{s(s-\varphi_0)}(P_i(s) - X_i(s) + \frac{\varphi_2(s+1)}{s(s-\varphi_0)}(P_g(s) - X_i(s)) \tag{42}$$

Suppose $P_i(s)$ and $P_g(s)$ are two input variables, $X_i(s)$ is output variable, then the system structure reflecting by equation (42) can be shown as in Fig.l.

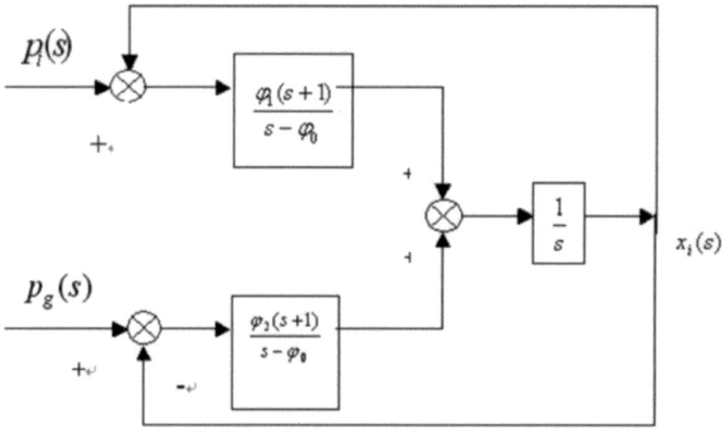

Figure 1. The System Diagram of DEPSO

The open-loop transfer function from $P_i(s)$ to $X_i(s)$ is

$$G_{K1}(s) = \frac{\varphi_1(s+1)}{s(s-\varphi_0)} \tag{43}$$

And the eigenequation is 1 + G_K (s) = 0, thus results in

$$s^2 + (\varphi_1 - \varphi_0)s + \varphi_1 = 0 \tag{44}$$

the two eigenvalues are

$$\lambda_{1,2} = \frac{\varphi_0 - \varphi_1 \pm \sqrt{(\varphi_1 - \varphi_0)^2 - 4\varphi_1}}{2} \tag{45}$$

DEPSO will converge when λ_1 and λ_2 have negative real parts. This is obtained with

$$(\varphi_1 - \varphi_0)^2 - 4\varphi_1 > 0 \text{ .and. } \sqrt{(\varphi_1 - \varphi_0)^2 - 4\varphi_1} < \varphi_1 - \varphi_0 \tag{46}$$

So, the convergence of DEPSO with $P_i(s)$ as input can be guaranteed if

$$\varphi_1 - \varphi_0 > 0 \tag{47}$$

By the same way, the convergence of DEPSO with $P_g(s)$ and $X_i(s)$ as input and output respectively can be guaranteed if $\varphi_2 - \varphi_0 > 0$. Therefore, the convergence condition of DEPSO is

$$\varphi_0 < \min(\varphi_1, \varphi_2) \tag{48}$$

From Fig.1, it is obvious that

$$X_i(s) = \frac{\varphi_1(s+1)P_i(s) + \varphi_2(s+1)P_g(s)}{s(s-\varphi_0) + \varphi_1(s+1) + \varphi_2(s+1)} \tag{49}$$

From (48), we have

$$\begin{aligned} \lim_{t\to\infty} x_i(t) = \lim_{s\to 0} sX_i(s) &= \lim_{s\to 0} \frac{\varphi_1(s+1)P_i(s) + \varphi_2(s+1)P_g(s)}{s(s-\varphi_0) + \varphi_1(s+1) + \varphi_2(s+1)} \\ &= \frac{\varphi_1 P_i + \varphi_2 P_g}{\varphi_1 + \varphi_2} \end{aligned} \tag{50}$$

it means

$$-(\varphi_1 + \varphi_2)\lim_{t\to\infty} x_i(t) + \varphi_1 p_i + \varphi_2 p_g = 0 \tag{51}$$

Since φ_1 and φ_2 are stochastic variables, it is obviously that the above equation is satisfied only if

$$\lim_{t\to\infty} x_i(t) = p_i = p_g \tag{52}$$

To improve the dynamic evolutionary behaviour of DEPSO, the evolutionary function of DEPSO is considered as a control plant and PID controller is introduced. The parameter of PID controller can be dynamically adjusted in the evolutionary process, and the new algorithm is called PID-DEPSO.
The system structure is showed in Fig.2.

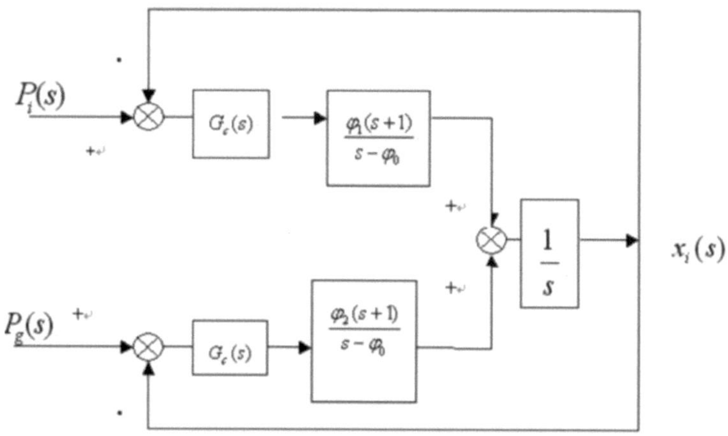

Figure 2. The System Diagram of PID-DEPSO

From Fig.2, we have

$$G_c(s) = K_p(1 + \frac{1}{T_I s} + T_D s) = K_p^{'}.\frac{T_D T_I s^2 + T_I s + 1}{s} \tag{53}$$

Where $K_p^{'} = \frac{K_p}{T_I}$.

The open-loop transfer function taking $P_i(s)$ as input is :

$$G_{Kc_1}(s) = G_c(s)\frac{\varphi_1(s+1)}{s(s-\varphi_0)} = \frac{\varphi_1 K_p^{'}(s+1)(T_D T_I s^2 + T_I s + 1)}{s^2(s-\varphi_0)} \tag{54}$$

its eigenequation is $1 + G_{Kc_1}(s) = 0$, then

$$\begin{aligned}&(K_p^{'}\varphi_1 T_D T_I + 1)s^3 \\ &= (K_p^{'}\varphi_1 T_I + K_p^{'}\varphi_1 T_D T_I - \varphi_0)s^2 + K_p^{'}\varphi_1(1 + T_I)s + K_p^{'}\varphi_1 = 0\end{aligned} \tag{55}$$

According to Routh's stability criteria, the stability condition of the system with $P_i(s)$ and $X_i(s)$ as input and output respectively are

$$K_p^{'}T_D(T_I + 1) > \frac{\varphi_0}{\varphi_1} \tag{56}$$

As a result, the stability of PID-DEPSO is stability if

$$K_p^{'}T_D(T_I + 1) > \max(\frac{\varphi_0}{\varphi_1}, \frac{\varphi_0}{\varphi_2}) \tag{57}$$

Similarly, if (57) is satisfied, $\lim_{t\to\infty} x_i(t) = \lim_{s\to 0} sX_i(s)$. From Fig.2, we have

$$X_i(s) = \frac{K_p^{'}(s+1)(T_D T_I s^2 + T_I s + 1)(\varphi_1 P_i(s) + \varphi_2 P_g(s))}{s^2(s-\varphi_0) + K_p^{'}(s+1)(T_D T_I s^2 + T_I s + 1)(\varphi_1 + \varphi_2)} \tag{58}$$

Thus

$$\lim_{t\to\infty} x_i(t) = \lim_{s\to 0} sX_i(s) = \frac{\varphi_1 p_i + \varphi_2 p_g}{\varphi_1 + \varphi_2} \tag{59}$$

The evolutionary equation of PID-DEPSO is deduced as follow:

$$\begin{aligned}&X_i(s) = G_{kc1}(s)(P_i(s) - X_i(s)) + G_{kc2}(s)(P_g(s) - X_i(s)) = \\ &\frac{(s+1)(T_D T_I s^2 + T_I s + 1)}{s^2(s-\varphi_0)}[K_p^{'}\varphi_1(P_i(s) - X_i(s)) + K_p^{'}\varphi_2(P_g(s) - X_i(s))]\end{aligned} \tag{60}$$

it means:

$$\frac{s^2(s-\varphi_0)}{(s+1)(T_DT_Is^2+T_Is+1)}X_i(s)=K_p^{'}\varphi_1(P_i(s)-X_i(s))+K_p^{'}\varphi_2(P_g(s)-X_i(s)) \tag{61}$$

Suppose

$$\frac{dx_i(t)}{dt}=v_t(t+1)=v_t(t)+\frac{dv_i(t)}{dt} \tag{62}$$

then $V_i(s)=\frac{s}{s+1}X_i(s)$, substituting it into (61), we have

$$\frac{s(s-\varphi_0)}{(s+1)(T_DT_Is^2+T_Is+1)}V_i(s)=K_p^{'}\varphi_1(P_i(s)-X_i(s))+K_p^{'}\varphi_2(P_g(s)-X_i(s)) \tag{63}$$

Let

$$\frac{dv_i(t)}{dt}=\varphi_0v_i(t)+a_i(t) \tag{64}$$

then $A_i(s)=(s-\varphi_0)V_i(s)$, substituting it into (63), we have

$$\frac{sA_i(s)}{(s+1)(T_DT_Is^2+T_Is+1)}=K_p^{'}\varphi_1(P_i(s)-X_i(s))+K_p^{'}\varphi_2(P_g(s)-X_i(s)) \tag{65}$$

Let $a=1+K_p^{'}T_DT_I(\varphi_1+\varphi_2),\beta=K_p^{'}T_I(\varphi_1+\varphi_2)(\varphi_0T_D+T_D+1)$, and the Laplace inverse transformation of $sP_i(s),s^2P_i(s),sP_g(s)$ are zero, then

$$\frac{da_i(t)}{at}=-\frac{{}_0\beta}{a}\cdot V_i(t)-\frac{\beta}{a}\cdot a_i(t)+K_p^{'}\cdot\frac{\varphi_1}{a}\cdot(P_i-X_i(t))+K_p^{'}\cdot\frac{\varphi_2}{a}\cdot(P_g-X_i(t)) \tag{66}$$

Let $\frac{\beta}{a}=\gamma,K_p^{'}\cdot\frac{\varphi_1}{a}=\varphi_1^{'},K_p^{'}\cdot\frac{\varphi_2}{a}=\varphi_2^{'}$, then the evolutionary equations of PID-DEPSO are

$$\frac{da_i(t)}{dt}=-\varphi_0\gamma v_i(t)-\gamma a_i(t)+\varphi_1^{'}(p_i-x_i(t))+\varphi_2^{'}(p_g-x_i(t)) \tag{67}$$

$$\frac{dv_i(t)}{dt}=\varphi_0v_i(t)+a_i(t) \tag{68}$$

$$\frac{dx_i(t)}{dt}=v_i(t+1)=v_i(t)+\frac{dv_i(t)}{dt}=(\varphi_0+1)v_i(t)+a_i(t) \tag{69}$$

5. Conclusion

This chapter introduces one uniform differential meta-model, and a new variant development for PSO combined with PID controller is proposed. The current results show it is an interesting area with the control theory to improve the performance. The future research includes incorporating some other controllers into the PSO methodology.

6. References

Back, T. (1996). Evolutionary Algorithms in Theory and Practice. Oxford University Press, New York.

Clerc, M. (1999). The Swarm and the Queen: Towards a Deterministic and Adaptive Particle Swarm Optimization. *Proceedings of the Congress on Evolutionary Computation*, pp.1951- 1957, Washington DC, USA, July 1999. IEEE Service Center, Piscataway, NJ.

Cui, Z.H. & Zeng, J.C. (2004). A New Particle Swarm Optimizer. *Proceedings of the 2004 Congress on Evolutionary Computation*, pp.316-319. IEEE Service Center, Piscataway, NJ.

Fogel, D. (1996). *Evolutionary Computation: Towards a New Philosophy of Machine Intelligence.* IEEE Press, Piscataway, NJ.

Forgo, F. (1988). *Nonconvex Programming*. Akademiai Kiado, Budapest.

Goldberg, D. (1989). *Genetic Algorithms in Search, Optimization, and Machine Learning.* Addison Wesley, Reading, MA.

Hansen, E.R. (1992). *Global Optimization Using Interval Analysis*. Marcel Dekker, New York.

Kennedy, J. & Eberhart, R.C. (1995). Particle Swarm Optimization. *Proceedings of IEEE International Conference on Neural Networks*, IV: pp. 1942-1948. IEEE Service Center, Piscataway, NJ.

Kennedy, J. & Eberhart, R.C. (2001). *Swarm Intelligence*. Morgan Kaufmann Publishers.

Michalewica, Z. (1994). *Genetic Algorithms + Data Structures = Evolution Programs*. Springer, Berlin.

Rao, S.S. (1996). *Engineering Optimization-Theory and Practice*. Wiley.

Schwefel, H.P. (1975). Evolutionsstrategie und numerische Optimierung. Technical University of Berlin, Department of Process Engineering, *Dr.-Ing.Thesis*.

Shi, Y. & Eberhart, R.C. (1998). A Modified Particle Swarm Optimizer. In: *Porto VW, Saravanan N, Waagen D and Eiben AE (eds) Evolutionary Programming* VII, pp. 611-616, Springer.

Suganthan, P.N. (1999). Particle Swarm Optimizer with Neighbourhood Operator. *Proceedings of the Congress on Evolutionary Computation*, pp.1958-1961, Washington DC, USA, July 1999. IEEE Service Center, Piscataway, NJ.

Zeng, J.C. & Cui, Z.H.(2005). A Differential Meta-model for Particle Swarm Optimization. *Progress in Intelligence Computation & Applications*, pp.159-164, Wuhan, China.

Zeng, J.C. & Cui, Z.H. (2005). A Differential Evolutionary Particle Swarm Optimization with Controller. In: Wang, L., Chen K. and Ong, Y.S. (eds) *Lecture Notes in Computer Science*, Vol.3612, pp.467-476, Changsha, China.

8

Artificial Bee Colony Algorithm and Its Application to Generalized Assignment Problem

Adil Baykasoğlu[1], Lale Özbakır[2] and Pınar Tapkan[2]
[1]*University of Gaziantep, Department of Industrial Engineering*
[2]*Erciyes University, Department of Industrial Engineering*
Turkey

1. Introduction

There is a trend in the scientific community to model and solve complex optimization problems by employing natural metaphors. This is mainly due to inefficiency of classical optimization algorithms in solving larger scale combinatorial and/or highly non-linear problems. The situation is not much different if integer and/or discrete decision variables are required in most of the linear optimization models as well. One of the main characteristics of the classical optimization algorithms is their inflexibility to adapt the solution algorithm to a given problem. Generally a given problem is modelled in such a way that a classical algorithm like simplex algorithm can handle it. This generally requires making several assumptions which might not be easy to validate in many situations. In order to overcome these limitations more flexible and adaptable general purpose algorithms are needed. It should be easy to tailor these algorithms to model a given problem as close as to reality. Based on this motivation many nature inspired algorithms were developed in the literature like genetic algorithms, simulated annealing and tabu search. It has also been shown that these algorithms can provide far better solutions in comparison to classical algorithms. A branch of nature inspired algorithms which are known as swarm intelligence is focused on insect behaviour in order to develop some meta-heuristics which can mimic insect's problem solution abilities. Ant colony optimization, particle swarm optimization, wasp nets etc. are some of the well known algorithms that mimic insect behaviour in problem modelling and solution. Artificial Bee Colony (ABC) is a relatively new member of swarm intelligence. ABC tries to model natural behaviour of real honey bees in food foraging. Honey bees use several mechanisms like waggle dance to optimally locate food sources and to search new ones. This makes them a good candidate for developing new intelligent search algorithms. In this chapter an extensive review of work on artificial bee algorithms is given. Afterwards, development of an ABC algorithm for solving generalized assignment problem which is known as NP-hard problem is presented in detail along with some comparisons.

It is a well known fact that classical optimization techniques impose several limitations on solving mathematical programming and operational research models. This is mainly due to inherent solution mechanisms of these techniques. Solution strategies of classical optimization algorithms are generally depended on the type of objective and constraint functions (linear, non-linear etc.) and the type of variables used in the problem modelling (integer, real etc.). Their efficiency is also very much dependent on the size of the solution space, number of variables and constraints used in the problem modelling, and the structure of the solution space (convex, non-convex, etc.). They also do not offer general solution strategies that can be applied to problem formulations where, different type of variables, objective and constraint functions are used. For example, simplex algorithm can be used to solve models with linear objective and constraint functions; geometric programming can be used to solve non-linear models with a posynomial or signomial objective function etc. (Baykasoğlu, 2001). However, most of the optimization problems require different types of variables, objective and constraint functions simultaneously in their formulation. Therefore, classic optimization procedures are generally not adequate or easy to use for their solution.

Researchers have spent a great deal of effort in order to adapt many optimization problems to the classic optimization procedures. It is generally not easy to formulate a real life problem that suits a specific solution procedure. In order to achieve this, it is necessary to make some modifications and/or assumptions on the original problem parameters (rounding variables, softening constraints etc.). This certainly affects the solution quality. A new set of problem and model independent nature inspired heuristic optimization algorithms were proposed by researchers to overcome drawbacks of the classical optimization procedures. These techniques are efficient and flexible. They can be modified and/or adapted to suit specific problem requirements (see Figure 1). Research on these techniques is still continuing all around the globe.

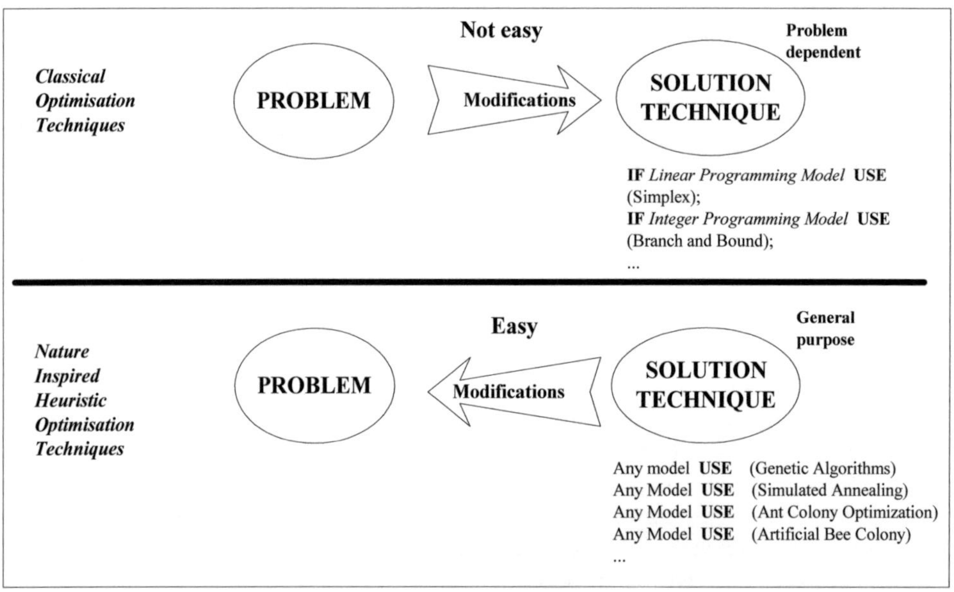

Figure 1. A pictorial comparison of classical and modern heuristic optimisation strategies (Adapted from Baykasoğlu, 2001)

A branch of nature inspired algorithms which are called as swarm intelligence is focused on insect behaviour in order to develop some meta-heuristics which can mimic insect's problem solution abilities. Interaction between insects contributes to the collective intelligence of the social insect colonies. These communication systems between insects have been adapted to

scientific problems for optimization. One of the examples of such interactive behaviour is the waggle dance of bees during the food procuring. By performing this dance, successful foragers share the information about the direction and distance to patches of flower and the amount of nectar within this flower with their hive mates. So this is a successful mechanism which foragers can recruit other bees in their colony to productive locations to collect various resources. Bee colony can quickly and precisely adjust its searching pattern in time and space according to changing nectar sources.
The information exchange among individual insects is the most important part of the collective knowledge. Communication among bees about the quality of food sources is being achieved in the dancing area by performing waggle dance (Figure 2).

Figure 2. Waggle dance of honey bees

The previous studies on dancing behaviour of bees show that while performing the waggle dance, the direction of bees indicates the direction of the food source in relation to the Sun, the intensity of the waggles indicates how far away it is and the duration of the dance indicates the amount of nectar on related food source. Waggle dancing bees that have been in the hive for an extended time adjust the angles of their dances to accommodate the changing direction of the sun. Therefore bees that follow the waggle run of the dance are still correctly led to the food source even though its angle relative to the sun has changed. So collective intelligence of bees based on the synergistic information exchange during waggle dance.
Observations and studies on honey bee behaviours resulted in a new generation of optimization algorithms. In this chapter a detailed review of bee colony based algorithms is given. Afterwards a bee based algorithm that we name as "artificial bee colony" is explained in detail along with an application to "generalized assignment problem" which is known as a NP-hard problem.

2. Description of the Behaviour of Bees in Nature

Social insect colonies can be considered as dynamical system gathering information from environment and adjusting its behaviour in accordance to it. While gathering information and adjustment processes, individual insects don't perform all the tasks because of their specializations. Generally, all social insect colonies behave according to their own division labours related to their morphology. Bee system consists of two essential components:

- **Food Sources**
  The value of a food source depends on different parameters such as its proximity to the nest, richness of energy and ease of extracting this energy.
- **Foragers**
  - *Unemployed foragers:* If it is assumed that a bee have no knowledge about the food sources in the search field, bee initializes its search as an unemployed forager. There are two possibilities for an unemployed forager:
    - *Scout Bee* (S in Figure 3): If the bee starts searching spontaneously without any knowledge, it will be a scout bee. The percentage of scout bees varies from 5% to 30% according to the information into the nest. The mean number of scouts averaged over conditions is about 10% (Seeley, 1995).
    - *Recruit* (R in Figure 3): If the unemployed forager attends to a waggle dance done by some other bee, the bee will start searching by using the knowledge from waggle dance.
  - *Employed foragers* (EF in Figure 3): When the recruit bee finds and exploits the food source, it will raise to be an employed forager who memorizes the location of the food source. After the employed foraging bee loads a portion of nectar from the food source, it returns to the hive and unloads the nectar to the food area in the hive. There are three possible options related to residual amount of nectar for the foraging bee.
    - If the nectar amount decreased to a low level or exhausted, foraging bee abandons the food source and become an unemployed bee.
    - If there are still sufficient amount of nectar in the food source, it can continue to forage without sharing the food source information with the nest mates
    - Or it can go to the dance area to perform waggle dance for informing the nest mates about the same food source. The probability values for these options highly related to the quality of the food source.
  - *Experienced foragers:* These types of forager use their historical memories for the location and quality of food sources.
    - It can be an inspector which controls the recent status of food source already discovered.
    - It can be a reactivated forager by using the information from waggle dance. It tries to explore the same food source discovered by itself if there are some other bees confirm the quality of same food source (RF in FigureS).
    - It can be scout bee to search new patches if the whole food source is exhausted (ES in Figure 3).
    - It can be a recruit bee which is searching a new food source declared in dancing area by another employed bee (ER in Figure 3).

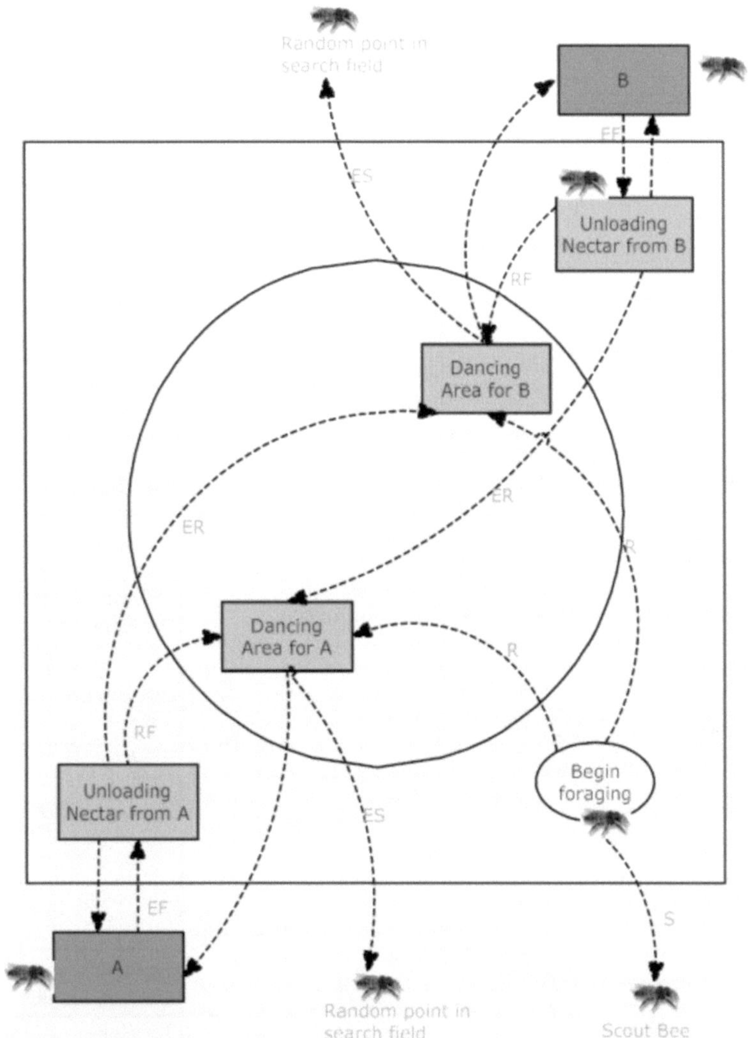

Figure 3. Typical behaviour of honey bee foraging

3. Review and Categorization of Studies on Artificial Bee Systems

The foraging behaviour, learning, memorizing and information sharing characteristics of bees have recently been one of the most interesting research areas in swarm intelligence. Studies on honey bees are in an increasing trend in the literature during the last few years. After a detailed literature survey, the previous algorithms are categorized in this work by concerning the behavioural characteristics of honey bees.

- Foraging behaviours
- Marriage behaviours
- Queen bee concept

The researches, their main contributions and applications are summarized as shown in Table 1.

Type	Honey Bee Literature	Algorithm	Application
Foraging Behaviour	Yonezawa and Kikuchi (1996) Seeley and Buhrman (1999) Schmickl et al. (2005) Lemmens (2006)		*Biological simulation*
	Sato and Hagiwara (1997)	Bee System	*Genetic Algorithm Improvement*
	Karaboga (2005)	Artificial Bee Colony Algorithm (ABC)	*Continuous Optimization*
	Yang (2005)	Virtual Bee Algorithm (VBA)	*Continuous Optimization*
	Basturk and Karaboga (2006)	ABC	*Continuous Optimization*
	Pham et al. (2006a)	Bees Algorithm (BA)	*Continuous Optimization*
	Lucic and Teodorovic (2001)	Bee System (BS)	*Travelling Salesman Problem(TSP)*
	Lucic (2002)	BS	*TSP and Stochastic Vehicle Routing Problem*
	Lucic and Teodorovic (2002)	BS	*TSP*
	Lucic and Teodorovic (2003a)	BS	*TSP*
	Lucic and Teodorovic (2003b)	BS + Fuzzy Logic	*Stochastic Vehicle Routing*
	Teodorovic and Dell'Orco (2005)	Bee Colony Optimization (BCO) + Fuzzy Bee System (FBS)	*Ride-Matching Problem*
	Nakrani and Tovey (2003)	A Honey Bee Algorithm	*Dynamic Allocation of Internet Service*
	Wedde et al. (2004)	BeeHive	*Telecommunication Network Routing*
	Bianco (2004)		*Large Scale Precise Navigation*
	Chong et al. (2006)		*Job Shop Scheduling*
	Drias et al. (2005)	Bees Swarm	*Max-W-Sat Problem*
	Pham et al. (2006b)	BA	*LVQ-Neural Network*
	Pham et al. (2006c)	BA	*MLP- Neural Network*
	Pham et al. (2006d)	BA	*Neural Network*
	Quijano and Passino (2007)		*Dynamic Resource*
	Markovic et al. (2007)	BCO Based	*Max-Routing and Wavelength Assignment*

Marriage Behaviour	Abbass (2001a,b,c)	Marriage in Honey-Bees Optimization (MBO)	*3-Sat Problem*
	Teo and Abbass (2001, 2003)	Modified MBO	*3-Sat Problem*
	Bozorg Haddad and Af shar (2004)	MBO	*Water Resources Management Problems*
	Bozorg Haddad et al. (2006)	Honey-Bees Mating Optimization -HBMO	*Nonlinear constrained and unconstrained optimization*
	Chang (2006)	MBO Based	*Stochastic Dynamic Programming*
	Afshar et al. (2007)	Improved HBMO	*Continuous Optimization*
	Fathian et al. (2007)	HBMO Based	*Data Mining -Clustering*
	Koudil et al. (2007)	MBO Based	*Integrated Partitioning/Scheduling*
	Benatchba et al. (2005)	MBO Based	*Data Mining*
Queen Bee	Sung (2003)	Queen-Bee Evolution Algorithm(QBE)	*Genetic Algorithm Improvement*
	Qin et al. (2004)	QBE Based	*Economic Power Dispatch*
	Kara (2004)	Bee Crossover	*Genetic Algorithm Improvement*
	Azeem and Saad (2004)	Modified QBE	*Genetic Algorithm Improvement*

Table 1. Categorization of literature and applications

In this section, contributions of these researches are explained in detailed to clarify the background of honey bees based optimization algorithms.

Yonezawa and Kikuchi (1996) examine the foraging behaviour of honey bees and construct an algorithm to indicate the importance of group intelligence principals. The algorithm is simulated with one and three foraging bees and the computational simulation results showed that three foraging bees are faster than the system with one foraging bee at decision making process. They also indicate that the honey bees have an adaptive foraging behaviour at complex environment.

Seeley and Buhrman (1999) investigated the nest site selection behaviour of honey bee colonies. The nest site selection process starts with several hundred scout bees that search for potential nest sites. The scouts then return to the cluster, report their findings by means of waggle dances, and decide the new nest site. The type of waggle dance depends on the quality of the site being advertised. The authors repeated the observations of Lindauer in 1955 by taking advantage of modern video-recording and bee-labelling techniques on three honey bee colonies. Many of the results confirmed with the previous study and some of the results provided new and important insights. They pointed out that a colony's strategy of decision making is a weighted additive strategy which is the most accurate but most information demanding one. This strategy evaluates each alternative according to the relative attributes, gives weights to each attribute according to its importance, sums the weighted attributes for each alternative, and finally chooses the alternative whose total valuation is the highest. Similarly, the bee colony considers a dozen or more alternative nest sites, evaluates each alternative nest site with respect to at least six distinct attributes with different weightings e.g. cavity volume, entrance height, entrance area, entrance direction etc. Consequently, the bee colony uses this strategy by distributing among many bees both the task of evaluating the alternative sites and the task of identifying the best of these sites.

Schmickl et al. (2005) evaluate the robustness of bees' foraging behaviour by using a multi-agent simulation platform. They investigate how the time-pattern of environmental fluctuations affects the foraging strategy and the efficiency of the foraging. They conclude that the collective foraging strategy of a honeybee colony is robust and adaptive, and that its emergent features allow the colony to find optimal solutions.

Lemmens (2006) investigated whether pheromone-based navigational algorithms (inspired by biological ant colony behaviour) are outperformed by non-pheromone-based navigational algorithms (inspired by biological bee colony behaviour) in the task of foraging. The results of the experiments showed that (i) pheromone-based navigational algorithms use less time per iteration step in small-sized worlds, (ii) non-pheromone-based algorithms are significantly faster when finding and collecting food and use fewer time steps to complete the task, and (iii) with growing world sizes, the non-pheromone-based algorithm eventually outperforms pheromone-based algorithms on a time per time step measure. In spite of all these profits it is mentioned that non-pheromone-based algorithms are less adaptive than pheromone-based algorithms.

Sato and Hagiwara (1997) proposed an improved genetic algorithm based on foraging behaviour of honey bees. In a honey bee colony, each bee looks for the feed individually. When a bee finds feed, then it notifies the information to the other many bees by dance and they engage in a job to carry the feed. When they finish the work, each bee tries to find new one individually again. Similarly in the proposed algorithm, named Bee System, global search is done first, and some chromosomes with pretty high fitness (superior chromosomes) are obtained using the simple genetic algorithm. Second, many chromosomes obtain the information of superior chromosomes by the concentrated crossover and they search intensively around there using multiple populations. In the conventional crossover each pair is made randomly, while in the concentrated crossover all of the chromosomes make pair with superior chromosome. Lastly, pseudo-simplex method is contributed to enhance the local search ability of the Bee System. If the solution found by one cycle is not satisfactory, the global search is repeated. As it is known genetic algorithms have good global search ability, however they lack the local search ability. On the other hand with Bee System probability of falling into a local optimum is low because of the combination of local and global search since the aim of the algorithm is to improve the local search ability of genetic algorithm without degrading the global search ability. In the experimental studies Bee System is compared with the conventional genetic algorithm and it is found that Bee System shows better performance than the conventional genetic algorithm especially for highly complex multivariate functions.

Karaboga (2005) analyzes the foraging behaviour of honey bee swarm and proposes a new algorithm simulating this behaviour for solving multi-dimensional and multi-modal optimization problems, called Artificial Bee Colony (ABC). The main steps of the algorithm are: 1) send the employed bees onto the food sources and determine their nectar amounts; 2) calculate the probability value of the sources with which they are preferred by the onlooker bees; 3) stop the exploitation process of the sources abandoned by the bees; 4) send the scouts into the search area for discovering new food sources, randomly; 5) memorize the best food source found so far. In the algorithm, an artificial bee colony consists of three groups of bees: employed bees, onlookers and scouts. Employed bees are associated with a particular food source which they are currently exploiting. They carry the information about this particular source and share this information with a certain probability by waggle dance. Unemployed bees seek a food source to exploit. There are two types of unemployed bees: scouts and onlookers. Scouts search the environment for new food sources without any guidance. Occasionally, the scouts can accidentally discover rich, entirely unknown food sources. On the other hand onlookers observe the waggle dance and so are placed on the food sources by using a probability based selection process. As the nectar amount of a food source increases, the probability value with which the food source is preferred by onlookers increases, too. In the ABC algorithm the first half of the colony consists of the employed bees and the second half includes the onlookers. For every food source, there is only one employed bee. Another issue that is considered in the algorithm is that the employed bee whose food source has been exhausted by the bees becomes a scout. In other words, if a solution representing a food source is not improved by a predetermined number of trials, then the food source is abandoned by its employed bee and the employed bee is converted to a scout. The algorithm is tested on three well known test functions. From the simulation results, it is concluded that the proposed algorithm can be used for solving uni-modal and multi-modal numerical optimization problems.

Yang (2005) presents a virtual bee algorithm (VBA) which is effective on function optimization problems. The main steps of the algorithm are: 1) create an initial population of virtual bees where each bee is associated with a memory; 2) encode the optimization function into virtual food; 3) define the criterion for communicating food location with others; 4) march all the virtual bees randomly to new positions for virtual food searching, find food and communicate with neighbouring bees by virtual waggle dance; 5) evaluate the encoded intensity /locations of bees; 6) decode the results to obtain the solution to the problem. However the proposed algorithm is similar with genetic algorithm, it is much more efficient due to the parallelism of the multiple independent bees. To realize this statement, the VBA algorithm is tested on two functions with two parameters, one is single-peaked and the other is multi-peaked. The results show that the new algorithm is much efficient than genetic algorithm.

Basturk and Karaboga (2006) presented another ABC algorithm and expanded the experimental results of Karaboga (2005). The performance of the algorithm is tested on five multi-dimensional benchmark functions and the results were compared with genetic algorithms. It is pointed out that ABC algorithm outperforms genetic algorithm for functions having multi-modality and uni-modality.

Pham et al. (2006a) proposed an optimization algorithm inspired by the natural foraging behaviour of honey bees, called Bees Algorithm. The proposed algorithm is also applicable to both combinatorial and functional optimization problems. In real life, foraging process begins by scout bees being sent to search for promising flower patches. When they return to the hive, unload their nectar and go to the dance floor to perform a dance known as the waggle dance which is essential for colony communication. After waggle dancing, the dancer goes back to the flower patch with follower bees that were waiting inside the hive. More follower bees are sent to more promising patches. This allows the colony to gather food quickly and efficiently.

Similarly Bees Algorithm starts with scout bees being placed randomly on the search space. The main steps of the algorithm are: 1) initialize population with random solutions; 2) evaluate fitness of the population; 3) determine a certain number of fittest bees and select their sites for neighbourhood search; 4) recruit a certain number of bees for selected sites, evaluate their fitness; 5) select the fittest bee from each site to form the new population; 6) assign remaining bees to search randomly and evaluate their fitness. The Bees Algorithm is applied to two standard functional optimization problems with two and six dimensions, respectively. The results showed that the Bees Algorithm is able to find solutions very close to the optimum. The algorithm is also applied to eight benchmark functions and the results were compared with deterministic simplex method, stochastic simulated annealing optimization procedure, genetic algorithm and ant colony system. Bees Algorithm generally outperformed other techniques in terms of speed of optimization and accuracy of results. On the other hand Bees Algorithm has too many tuneable parameters.

Luck and Teodorovic (2001) published the first study on Bee System based on the PhD thesis of Luck for 6 Travelling Salesman Problem (TSP) test problems. Luck (2002) aimed to explore the possible applications of collective bee intelligence in solving complex traffic and transportation engineering problems. In this context, (TSP) and stochastic vehicle routing problem (SVRP) were studied. TSP is an NP-hard problem that aims to find the minimum distance circuit passing through each node only once. The algorithm starts with locating the hive in one of the nodes on the graph that the bees are collecting nectar i.e. the graph in which the travelling salesman route should be discovered. The artificial bees collect the nectar during a certain prescribed time interval and the position of the hive is randomly changed. The bees start to collect the nectar from the new location and again the location of the hive is randomly changed. The iteration in the searching process represents one change of the hive's position and the iteration ends when one or more feasible solution is created. The artificial bees live in an environment characterized by discrete time and consequently each iteration is composed of a certain number of stages. During any stage, bees choose nodes to be visited in a random manner. By this probability function it is provided that the greater the distance between two nodes, the lower the probability that a bee chooses this link. The influence of the distance is lower at the beginning of the search process. The greater the number of iterations, the higher the influence of the distance. On the other hand the greater the total number of bees that visited by certain link in the past, the higher the probability is of choosing that link in the future. This represents the interaction between individual bees in the colony. During one stage the bee visits a certain number of nodes, create a partial travelling salesman tour, and return to the hive. In the hive the bee participates in a decision making process. The bee decides whether to recruit the nest mates by dancing before returning to the food source, to continue to forage at the food source without recruiting the nest mates, or to abandon the food source. The second alternative has very low probability since bees are social insects and communicate each other. The probability that a bee uses the same partial tour (or abandons it) depends on the length of the partial tour. The longer the tour that the bee has discovered, the smaller is the probability that the bee will fly again along the same tour. It is noted that the nectar quantity along a certain link is inversely proportional to the link length. At the beginning of any stage if a bee does not use the same partial travelling salesman tour, the bee goes to the dancing area and follows another bee according to a probability function. This function depends on the total length of the partial route and the number of bees that are advertising this route.

Additionally, before relocating the hive, 2-opt and 3-opt heuristic algorithms are applied to improve the solution obtained by the bees in the current iteration. On the other hand in nature, not all bees start foraging simultaneously and in the algorithm it is assumed that at the beginning of each iteration all bees are in the hive and the number of foraging bees in every subsequent stage is increased. The performance of the algorithm was tested on 10 benchmark problems. Experimental results showed that in all instances with less than 100 nodes, the Bee System produced the optimal solution and the times required to find the best solutions by the Bee System were low. At the second part of this thesis Bee System was integrated with fuzzy logic and this approach was applied to Vehicle Routing Problems (VRP). The procedure and the results were presented at Luck and Teodorovic (2003b). Luck and Teodorovic (2002, 2003a) published their second and third study on Bee System based on Luck's (2002) 8 and 10 TSP test problems.

Luck and Teodorovic (2003b) combined Bee System algorithm, which was first proposed by Luck and Teodorovic (2001), and fuzzy logic approach to obtain good solutions for stochastic VRP. The proposed approach contains two steps: 1) solve VRP as a TSP by using Bee System and obtain frequently an infeasible solution to the original problem; 2) decide when to finish one vehicle's route and when to start with the next vehicle's route by using the solution created at the previous step and fuzzy rule base generated by Wang-Mendel's algorithm. Stochastic VRP is to find a set of routes that would minimize transportation cost where the locations of the depot, nodes to be served and vehicle capacity are known, and demand at the nodes only approximated. Due to the uncertainty of demand at the nodes, a vehicle might not be able to service a node once it arrives there due to insufficient capacity. It is assumed in such situations that the vehicle returns to the depot, empties what it has picked up thus far, returns to the node where it had a failure, and continues service along the rest of the planned route. Consequently, demand at nodes is treated as a random variable and actual demand value is known only after the visit to the node. The developed model was tested on 10 TSP examples. In order to convert the original TSP problems into the corresponding VRPs, the first node was treated as a depot. The results were compared with the best solution obtained by the heuristic algorithm based on Bee System. The results were found to be very close to the best solution assuming that the future node demand pattern was known.

Teodorovic and Dell'Orco (2005) proposed Bee Colony Optimization (BCO) meta-heuristic which was the generalization of the Bee System presented by Luck (2002). The BCO was capable to solve deterministic combinatorial problems, as well as combinatorial problems characterized by uncertainty. The primary goal of their paper was to explore the possible applications of collective bee intelligence in solving combinatorial problems characterized by uncertainty. In this respect Fuzzy Bee System (FBS) was introduced where the agents use approximate reasoning and rules of fuzzy logic in their communication and acting. The performance of FBS algorithm was tested on ride-matching problem which aims to constitute routing and scheduling of the vehicles and passengers by minimizing the total distance travelled by all participants, minimizing the total delay, or equalizing vehicle utilization. There were no theoretical results that could support proposed approach but preliminary results were very promising.

Nakrani and Tovey (2003) proposed a honey bee algorithm for dynamic allocation of internet services. In the proposed algorithm, servers and HTTP request queues in an Internet server colony were modelled as foraging bees and flower patches respectively. The algorithm was compared with an omniscient algorithm that computes an optimal allocation policy, a greedy algorithm that uses past history to compute allocation policy, and an optimal-static algorithm that computes omnisciently the best among all possible static allocation policies. The experimental results showed that the algorithm performs better than static or greedy algorithms. On the other hand it was outperformed by greedy algorithm for some low variability access patterns.

Wedde et al. (2004) introduced a fault-tolerant, adaptive and robust routing protocol inspired from dance language and foraging behaviour of honey bees for routing in telecommunication network, called BeeHive. In order to evaluate the performance of the algorithm, it was tested on Japanese Internet Backbone and compared with AntNet, DGA and OSPF. The results showed that BeeHive achieves a similar or better performance as compared to the other algorithms.

Bianco (2004) presented a mapping paradigm for large scale precise navigation that takes inspiration from the bees' large scale navigation behaviour. Bees performed very long navigations when they feed, travelling for many kilometres but, at the same time, getting an excellent precision when they return to their small hives. Test results demonstrated that such capabilities were sufficient to get rather good precision.

Chong et al. (2006) presented a novel approach that uses the honey bees foraging model, inspired by Nakrani and Tovey (2004), to solve the job shop scheduling problem. Job shop scheduling is concerned with finding a sequential allocation of competing resources that optimizes a particular objective function. Each machine can process only one job and each job can be processed by only one machine at a time. The performance of the algorithm was tested on 82 job shop problem instances and compared with ant colony and tabu search algorithms. The experimental results conducted that tabu search outperforms other two heuristics according to solution quality and execution time. On the other hand bee algorithm performed slightly better than ant algorithm and the execution time for both heuristics was approximately equal.

Drias et al. (2005) introduced a new intelligent approach named Bees Swarm Optimization (BSO), which is inspired from the behaviour of real bees especially harvesting the nectar of the easiest sources of access while always privileging the richest. The proposed algorithm was adapted to the maximum weighted satisfiability problem (MAX-W-SAT) problem which was NP-Complete. MAX-W-SAT problem asks for the maximum weight which can be satisfied by any assignment, given a set of weighted clauses. The performance of the algorithm was compared with GRASP, SSAT and AGO and it was concluded that BSO outperformed the other evolutionary algorithms.

Pham et al. (2006b) presented the use of the Bees Algorithm, proposed by Pham et al. (2006a) to train the Learning Vector Quantization (LVQ) neural network for control chart pattern recognition. The training of a LVQ network can be regarded as the minimization of an error function. The error function defines the total difference between the actual output and the desired output of the network over a set of training patterns. In terms of the Bees Algorithm, each bee represents a LVQ network with a particular set of reference vectors. The aim of the algorithm was to find the bee with the set of reference vectors producing the smallest value of the error function. Despite the high dimensionality of the problem, the algorithm still succeeded to train more accurate classifiers than that produced by the standard LVQ training algorithm.

Pham et al. (2006c) presented the use of the Bees Algorithm, proposed by Pham et al. (2006a) to train the Multi-layered Perceptron (MLP) neural network for control chart pattern recognition. The training of a MLP network can be regarded as the minimization of an error function. The error function defines the total difference between the actual output and the desired output of the network over a set of training patterns. In terms of the Bees Algorithm, each bee represents a MLP network with a particular set of weight vectors. The aim of the algorithm was to find the bee with the set of weight vectors producing the smallest value of the error function. Despite the high dimensionality of the problem, the algorithm succeeded to train more accurate classifiers than back propagation algorithm.

Pham et al. (2006d) presented an application of the Bees Algorithm, proposed by Pham et al. (2006a) to the optimization of neural networks for the identification of defects in wood veneer sheets. The Bees Algorithm was used instead of a back propagation algorithm to optimize the weights of the neural network. The optimization using the Bees Algorithm involves the bees searching for the optimal values of the weights assigned to the connections between the neurons within the network where each bee represents a neural network with a particular set of weights. The aim of the Bees Algorithm was to find the bee producing the smallest value of the error function. The experimental results show that the Bees Algorithm was able to achieve an accuracy that was comparable to the back propagation method. However, the Bees Algorithm proved to be considerably faster.

Quijano and Passino (2007) developed an algorithm, based on the foraging behaviour of honey bees, to solve resource allocation problem. The primary sources for constructing components of the proposed model were: dance strength determination, dance threshold, unloading area, dance floor and recruitment rates, explorer allocation and its relation to recruitment. They also proposed an engineering application on dynamic resource allocation for multi-zone temperature control, to highlight the main features of the dynamical operation of the honey bee social foraging algorithm.

Markovic et al. (2007) used the BCO algorithm, which was introduced by Teodorovic and Dell'orco (2005) to solve Max-Routing and Wavelength Assignment (Max-RWA) problem in all-optical networks. The Max-RWA problem is to maximize the number of established lightpaths in a given optical network for a given traffic demand matrix and the given number of wavelengths. The proposed BCO-RWA algorithm was tested on European Optical Network and the results were compared with the results obtained by the LP relaxation approach and the tabu meta-heuristic algorithm. The BCO-RWA algorithm always outperformed the results of the compared algorithms and was able to produce very good solutions in a reasonable computation time.

Abbass (2001a) presented the first novel search algorithm inspired by the marriage process in honey bees. A honey bee colony consists of the queen(s), drones, worker(s), and broods. In this study the colony was assumed to have a single queen and a single worker. In real life a mating flight starts with a dance performed by the queens and the drones follow the queens to mate with them. In each mating, sperm reaches the spermatheca and accumulates there to form the genetic pool of the colony. Each time a queen lays fertilized eggs, she retrieves at random a mixture of the sperms accumulated in the spermatheca to fertilize the egg. Similarly at the MBO algorithm the mating flight can be visualized as a set of transitions in a state space where the queen moves between the different states in the space and mate with the drone encountered at each state probabilistically. The probability of mating is high when either the queen is still in the start of her mating flight and therefore her speed is high, or when the fitness of the drone is as good as the queen's. The algorithm starts with initializing the queen's genotype at random. After that a heuristic is used to improve the queen's genotype realized by workers. Afterwards, a set of mating flights is undertaken. In each mating flight, the queen's energy and speed are initialized randomly. The queen then moves between different states (solutions) in the space according to her speed and mates with the drone. If a drone is successfully mated with the queen (the drone passes the probabilistic decision rule), its sperm is added to the queen's spermatheca (list of partial solutions) and the queen's speed and energy are reduced. After the queen finishes her mating flight, she returns to the nest, selects a sperm randomly, performs crossover and mutation. The worker is then used to improve the resultant brood and the number of workers represents the number of heuristics encoded in the program. Afterwards, the queen is replaced with the fittest brood if the latter is better than the former. The remaining broods are then killed and a new mating flight starts. The MBO algorithm has three user-defined parameters: the queen's spermatheca size representing the maximum number of matings in a single mating flight, the number of broods that will be born by the queen, and the amount of time devoted to brood care signifying the depth of local search. A general constraint satisfaction problem (CSP) is the problem of finding an assignment to a set of variables that satisfies a set of constraints over the domains of those variables. The prepositional satisfiability problems (SAT) is a special case of CSP where the domain of each variable is either true or false. Also 3-SAT is a special case of SAT where each constraint contains three variables. The MBO algorithm was applied to a hundred different 3-SAT problems and the experimental results conducted that the algorithm was very successful. The heuristics that workers use was Greedy SAT (GSAT) and random walk. At the experimental studies GSAT, random walk, MBO with GSAT and MBO with random walk were compared and MBO-GSAT performed the best among the other three.

Abbass (2001b) presented a variation of the MBO algorithm which was first proposed by Abbass (2001a) where the colony contains a single queen with multiple workers. For the workers six different heuristics were used: GSAT, random walk, random flip, random new, 1-point and 2-point crossover. The algorithm was tested on a group of one-hundred hard 3-SAT problems. The best results were occurred with the smallest colony size and average spermatheca size. On the other hand, the fittest worker was GSAT, which was followed by random walk. It was also showed that MBO performed better than GSAT alone although GSAT was the heuristic with the highest fitness in MBO.

Abbass (2001c) analyzed the marriage behaviour of honey bees again as the continuation of the work (Abbass, 2001a). The difference between these studies was the number of queens and workers. Abbass (2001c) considered the honey bee colony with more than one queen in addition to a group of workers, where at the colony of Abbass (2001a) there was only one queen and one worker. In the paper MBO algorithm was applied to fifty different 3-SAT problems containing 50 variables and 215 constraints. The experimental results concluded that the largest spermatheca size, an average colony size, and the smallest number of queens gave the best performance. On the other hand the algorithm was compared with WalkSAT, one of the state-of-the-art algorithms for SAT, and MBO algorithm outperformed WalkSAT.

Teo and Abbass (2001) presented a modification of MBO algorithm which can be considered as an extension of Abbass (2001a) and Abbass (2001c). The purpose of this modification was to use a more conventional annealing approach during the trajectory acceptance decision to guide the search process towards a more optimal solution space. New trajectories were only be accepted as a potential drone for mating if it was a more optimal trajectory that was if the trajectory was fitter than the queen's genotype. Otherwise, if it was a trajectory that takes the search to a less optimal solution space, then it is only accepted probabilistically subject to the new annealing function. In other words, rather than accepting all the trajectories created during a queen's flight as in the original MBO algorithm, a new trajectory is accepted only if it is a move to a fitter solution space. Otherwise, the algorithm will accept a transition to a less optimal solution space probabilistically according to a function of the queen's fitness. On the other hand, five different heuristics were used for improving broods by workers: GSAT, random walk, probabilistic greedy, one point crossover, and WalkSAT. As in Abbass (2001a) Teo and Abbass again considered the honey bee colony with only one queen. Experimental studies were conducted in three manner: testing each of five different heuristics working alone without MBO, testing the performance of each heuristic with the original MBO and modified MBO, and lastly testing the proposed algorithm against the original MBO using the five different heuristics operating in combination as a committee of heuristics. For the test problems, ten different 3-SAT problems were generated each comprising of 1075 constraints and 250 variables. The heuristic performance's resulted with the following order for the first group of experiments: WalkSAT, GSAT, random walk, probabilistic greedy and one point crossover. At the second group of experiments both the original and proposed annealing functions used during the mating flight process were similarly efficient with all heuristics. However, the effectiveness of MBO with WalkSAT in finding solutions was improved slightly by the new annealing function as the proposed version of MBO found more solutions than the original version. Lastly at the third group of experiments both annealing strategies were again similarly efficient.

Teo and Abbass (2003) proposed another modification of MBO algorithm based on Teo and Abbass (2001). In both Abbass (2001a) and Teo and Abbass (2001), the annealing function used the queen's fitness as the basis for accepting/rejecting a transition in the drone's space, either during the spawning or mating stage. In a conventional simulated annealing approach, the previous state was used as the basis for the transition. Moreover, from a biological point of view, the drone's creation is independent of the queen as they usually come from another colony, although they might be related. Therefore, it is more natural to accept a transition based on the drone's own fitness. As a result the objective of their paper was to test a purely conventional annealing approach as the basis for determining the pool of drones. The performance of the modified algorithm was tested on ten different 3-SAT problems and compared with the previous versions of MBO. All heuristics were failed to find even a single solution when working alone whereas their performances were improved significantly when combined with MBO. On the other hand the proposed version of MBO dominated the previous studies and able to find solutions for problems where the previous versions cannot.

Bozorg Haddad and Afshar (2004) benefited from MBO algorithm based on the study of Abbass (2001c) and performed an application to water resources management problems. The algorithm was modelled to find good solutions for optimum management of a single reservoir. The results compared very well with similar heuristic methods as well as global optimal results.

Bozorg Haddad et al. (2006) proposed Honey-Bees Mating Optimization (HBMO) algorithm, based on Abbass (2001a, 2001c), to solve highly non-linear constrained and unconstrained real valued mathematical models. The performance of the HBMO was tested on several constrained and unconstrained mathematical optimization functions and compared with the results obtained by genetic algorithm. Results from the genetic algorithm and HBMO algorithm converge well with minor improvement in the HBMO solution. Moreover, to illustrate the model application and performance, the HBMO algorithm was also used for developing an optimum operation policy for a single reservoir. The HBMO again generated a significantly better solution.

Chang (2006) gave the first demonstration of the capability of the MBO approach in a theoretical perspective for solving combinatorial optimization problems and stochastic sequential decision making problems. The paper first concerned with MBO algorithm for solving non-stochastic combinatorial optimization problems and proved that MBO has the ability to converge to the global optimum value. MBO was then adapted into an algorithm called "Honey-Bees Policy Iteration" (HBPI) for solving infinite horizon discounted cost stochastic dynamic programming (SDP) problems, also known as markov decision processes (MDPs) and HBPI algorithm was also proved converging to the optimal value. Chang (2006) points out that MBO can be considered as a hybrid scheme of simulated annealing and genetic algorithm. Simulated annealing corresponds to the queen's mating flight to obtain the potential drone sperms in her spermatheca and genetic algorithm corresponds to broods generation and improvements step with some differences.

Afshar et al. (2007) presented an improved version of the HBMO algorithm for continuous optimization problems and its application to a nonlinear-constrained continuous single reservoir problem. By the comparison with global optimum values obtained from LINGO 8.0 NLP solver, it was observed that the convergence of the algorithm to the optimum was very rapid.

Fathian et al. (2007) presented an application of HBMO algorithm for clustering which is one of the attractive data mining techniques that is in use in many fields. To evaluate the performance of the algorithm in clustering, it was tested on several real datasets and compared with several typical stochastic algorithms including the ACO algorithm, the simulated annealing approach, the genetic algorithms, and the tabu search approach. The results illustrated that the proposed HBMO approach can be considered as a viable and an efficient heuristic to find optimal or near optimal solutions to clustering problems since the results were very encouraging in terms of the quality of solutions found, the average number of function evaluations and the processing time required.

Koudil et al. (2007) adapted MBO algorithm which was first presented by Abbass (2001) to solve integrated partitioning/scheduling problem in codesign. The proposed approach was tested on a benchmark problem and the results were compared with genetic algorithm. The test results showed that MBO achieves good results in terms of solution quality, and it gives better results than genetic algorithm in terms of execution times.

Benatchba et al. (2005) used the MBO algorithm which was first presented by Abbass (2001a, 2001b, 2001c) to solve a data mining problem expressed as a Max-Sat problem. For MBO, four different heuristics were used for improving broods by workers: a local search algorithm LS, GSAT, HSAT, and GWSAT. The training set used as benchmark was extracted from a medical one, aiming at analyzing the most revealing symptoms of the presence or not of a laparotomy of the principal bile duct. The best result obtained with MBO was the solution with 96% satisfaction by using GSAT as a worker.

Sung (2003) proposed queen-bee evolution to enhance the capability of genetic algorithms. In the queen-bee evolution algorithm the queen-bee crossbreeds with the other bees selected as parents by a different selection algorithm instead of known selection algorithms such as roulette wheel selection. This procedure increases the exploitation of genetic algorithms but on the other hand increases the probability of falling into premature convergence. To decrease this probability some individuals were strongly mutated instead of mutating all individuals with small mutation probability as in the normal evolution. The proposed algorithm was tested with one combinational and two typical function optimization problems. Experimental results demonstrated that the proposed algorithm enabled genetic algorithms to quickly approach to the global optimum.

Qin et al. (2004) applied queen bee evolution which was proposed by Sung (2003) into economic power dispatch problem (EPD). EPD problem is to minimize the overall cost rate and meet the load demand of a power system simultaneously and formulated as a nonlinear constrained complex optimization problem. The numerical results demonstrated that the proposed algorithm was faster and more robust than the conventional genetic algorithm.

Kara (2004) proposed a new crossover type, which is called Bee Crossover to improve the genetic algorithm's performance. The bee queen has the sexual intercourses with other male bees, and similarly a specified chromosome can be considered as bee queen for the first parent of crossover and the other parent is one of the remaining chromosomes in the colony. The author proposed three different crossover types. At the first type, the chromosome with the best fitness value is fixed parent and all the remaining chromosomes are crossed over with this fixed parent at least once in each generation. At the second type, the chromosome with the worst fitness value is a fixed parent and the remaining procedure is the same with the first type. At the third type, population is sorted with respect to the fitness values and the fixed parent in the first generation is determined by the first chromosome in this list. In the second generation, the fixed parent is the second chromosome in the list and so on. The performance of these crossover types were compared with uniform crossover. The results showed that in the most of time, honey bee crossovers obtained results in less number of iterations and the worst results were obtained by uniforms crossover. On the other hand, uniform crossover lost the diversity of population in a small range of time while honey bee crossovers lost the population diversity in the larger ranges of time.

Azeem and Saad (2004) proposed a modified queen bee evolution which was first presented by Sung (2003). In the proposed algorithm, if any solution has the fitness very close or above of the fitness of the queen bee, this solution is identified to a new pool as a queen bee where the original algorithm is limited to a single pool. Another difference between the original and proposed algorithm is on the crossover operator. The original algorithm utilizes uniform crossover where each gene is crossed with some probability. On the other hand proposed algorithm uses weighted uniform crossover where weights are assigned to each gene according to the similarity of the test patterns in the population. With this type of crossover, genetic algorithm will search more new state spaces. The algorithm was tested for tuning of scaling factor for the Fuzzy Knowledge Base Controller (FKBC) on two complex non-linear examples. Experiments showed that FKBC yielded superior results than conventional control algorithms in the complex situations where the system model or parameters were difficult to obtain. Moreover, the results were compared with roulettes wheel parent selection and obtained results were encouraging.

In the following sections of this work the first application of a nature inspired bee based algorithm (that we name as Artificial Bee Colony, ABC) to generalized assignment problem is presented.

4. Generalized Assignment Problem

The Generalized Assignment Problem (GAP) aims that assigning a set of tasks to a set of agents with minimum cost. Each agent represents a single resource with limited capacity. Each task must be assigned to only one agent and it requires a certain amount of the resource of the agent.

There are many application domains of GAP such as computer and communication networks, location problems, vehicle routing, group technology, scheduling etc. Extended review of this problem and its possible applications is presented in Martello and Toth (1981, 1990), Cattrysse (1990) and Cattrysse et al. (1994). Several exact algorithms for GAP have been proposed by Ross and Soland (1975), Fisher et al. (1986), Martello and Toth (1990) and recently Savelsberg (1997) and Nauss (2003). Also several heuristics have been proposed to solve GAP. Martello and Toth (1981, 1990) proposed a combination of local search and greedy method. Osman (1995) developed new Simulated Annealing and Tabu Search algorithms to investigate their performance on GAP. Chu and Beasley (1997) presented a Genetic Algorithm for GAP that tries to improve feasibility and optimality simultaneously. Different variable depth search algorithms (Racer and Amini (1994), Yagiura et al. (1998, 1999)), Ejection Chain based Tabu Search algorithms (Laguna et al. (1995), Diaz and Fernandez (2001), Yagiura et al. (2004)), Path Relinking approaches (Alfandari et al. (2001, 2002, 2004), Yagiura et al. (2001, 2002, 2006)) , Ant Colony Optimization (Randall (2004)), Max-Min Ant System Heuristic based on greedy randomized adaptive heuristic (Lourencp and Serra (2002)) can be mentioned as the other meta-heuristic approaches proposed for GAP in recent years.

The aim of this study is to present an artificial bee colony algorithm to solve GAP. Our main interest on this problem came from its NP-hard structure that was proved by Fisher et al. (1986). Moreover, Mortello and Toth (1990) presented the NP-completeness of proving that a solution is a feasible solution. GAP can be formulated as an integer programming model as follows;

$$\min \sum_{i=1}^{n}\sum_{j=1}^{m} c_{ij}x_{ij}$$

subject to

$$\sum_{i=1}^{n} a_{ij}x_{ij} \le b_j \qquad \forall j,\ 1 \le j \le m$$

$$\sum_{j=1}^{m} x_{ij} = 1 \qquad \forall i,\ 1 \le i \le n$$

$$x_{ij} \in \{0,1\} \qquad 1 \le i \le n \ \ \forall i,\ \ 1 \le j \le m \ \ \forall j$$

I is set of tasks (i=1,..,n); J is set of agents (j= 1,..,m); b_j = resource capacity of agent j; a_{ij} = resource needed if task i is assigned to agent j ; c_{ij} = cost of task i if assigned to agent j

x_{ij} = decision variable (x_{ij}=1, if task i is assigned to agent j; 0, otherwise)

The first constraint set is related to the resource capacity of agents. The second constraint set ensure that each task is assigned to only one agent.

5. Artificial Bee Colony Algorithm for GAP

In this section the general ABC framework and the principal algorithms for the initial solution and neighbour solutions generation for GAP are presented. The general steps of the proposed ABC algorithm are presented in Table 2.

1. *Initialize parameters*
2. *Construct initial Employed Bee Colony solutions by using Greedy Randomized Adaptive Search Heuristic (GRAH)*
3. *Evaluate fitness value for each bee*
4. *I=0*
5. *Repeat*
6. *N=0*
7. *repeat*
   a. *Apply Shift neighbourhood*
   b. *Apply DoubleShift neighbourhood*
   c. *Calculate probabilities related to fitness values*
   d. *Assign Onlooker Bees to Employed Bees according to probabilities*
   e. *For all Onlooker Bees*
      i. *Ejection -Chain Neighbourhood*
   f. *Find best Onlooker, replace with respective Employed Bee iffit(Best Onlooker)<fit(Employed)*
   g. *Find best Feasible Onlooker, replace with Best solution, if fit (BestFeas Onlooker)<fit(Best)*
   h. *N=N+1*
8. *Until (N=Employed Bee)*
9. *I=I+1*
10. *Until (I=MaxIteration)*

Table 2. ABC algorithm for GAP

Each step of the general ABC algorithm is detailed in Table 3.

0. *Parameter Initialization*

n = Number of employed bees
m = Number of onlooker bees (m>n)
Iteration : Maximum iteration number
α_j *: initial value of penalty parameter for* j^{th} *agent*
EC-Length : Length of ejection chain neighbourhood

1. *Initialize employed bees with GRAH algorithm*

σ^i *:* i^{th} *employed bee in the population*

2. *Evaluate employed bees*

Fitness Function (for minimization)

$$\sum_{j=1}^{m}\sum_{i=1}^{n} c_{ij}x_{ij} + \alpha\sum_{j=1}^{m}\max\left\{0, \sum_{i=1}^{n} b_{ij}x_{ij} - a_j\right\}$$

3. *Repeat*

Cycle = 1
1. *Number of Scout bees = 0,1*n*

2. *For each Employed Bee*
   a. *Apply SHIFT Neighbourhood*
      i. *If fit(ShiftNeighbour)<fit(EmployedBee) then*
         1. *Employed Bee = Shift Neighbour*
   b. *Apply DOUBLESHIFT Neighbourhood*
      i. *If fit(DoubleShiftNeighbour)<fit(EmployedBee) then*
         1. *Employed Bee = DoubleShift Neighbour*
   c. *Determine probabilities by using fitness function*

$$p_i = \frac{\sum \left(\frac{1}{fit_i} \right)^{-1}}{fit_i} \quad \text{(for minimization)}$$

   d. *Calculate the number of onlooker bees which will be sent to food sources of employed bees, according to previously determined probabilities*
   e. N_i*= Number of onlooker bees sent to* i^{th} *sites =* $p_i * m$
   f. O_{ij}: j^{th} *onlooker bee of* i^{th} *solution* $(j=1,\ldots,N_i)$
      $\{O_{i1}, O_{i2},\ldots,O_{iNi}\}=EjectionChain(\sigma^i)$
   g. *Calculate fitness values for each onlooker bee*
      If the best fitness value of onlooker bees is better than the fitness value of employed bee, employed bee solution is replaced with this onlooker solution.
      If $(\min(fit(O_{ij}))<fit(\sigma^i)$ *then* $\sigma^i = O_{ij}$
3. *Best Solution*
   If $fit(Best_{Cycle-1}) > Min(Fit(\sigma^i))_{i=1..n}$ *then* $Best_{Cycle} = \sigma^i$
   Else $Best_{Cycle} = Best_{Cycle-1}$

Until (i=n)

4. *Scout bees*
   a. *Initialize scout bees with GRAH algorithm*
   b. *The worst employed bees as many as the number of scout bees in the population are respectively compared with the scout solutions. If the scout solution is better than employed solution, employed solution is replaced with scout solution. Else employed solution is transferred to the next cycle without any change.*
5. *Cycle = Cycle+1*

Until (cycle =Iteration)

Table 3. Detailed ABC algorithm for GAP

Initial bee colony is constructed by using GRAH algorithm (Lourenço and Serra, 2001). The greedy heuristic constructs a solution as follows:

- At each step, a next task to be assigned is selected.
- The agent (the selected task is going to be assigned to) is determined.
- Repeat these two steps until all tasks have been assigned to an agent.

In GRAH procedure the choice is probabilistic bias to a probability function. This function is updated at each iteration in a reinforcement way by using the features of good solutions. The main execution steps of the GRAH algorithm is summarized as shown in Table 4.

1. *Let* $S_j = \emptyset \quad \forall j = 1,...,m$ *(S_j is the set of task assigned to agent j)*
2. *Construct a list of agents for each task, L_i, initially $Li=\{1,\ldots,m\}$ $\forall i$.*
3. *Consider any order of the tasks, i=1.*
4. *While (not all tasks have been assigned) repeat*
   - 4.1 *Choose randomly an agent j^* from L_i following the probability function that depends on the resource of agent j and the resource need by task i:*

$$p_{ij} = \frac{a/b_{ij}}{\sum_{l \in L_i} a_l / b_{il}}, \quad j \in L_i$$

   The agent with minimal cost has greater probability to be chosen.
   - 4.2 *Assign task i to agent* $j^* : S_{j^*} = S_{j^*} \cup \{i\}$. *Let i=i+1 and if* $\sum_{i \in S_{j^*}} b_{ij^*} > a_{j^*}$ *remove j^* from any list. Repeat step 4 (Note that the capacity constraint can be violated).*
5. *Let* $\sigma(i) = j$ *if* $i \in S_j$

Table 4. The GRAH Algorithm

6. Neighbourhood Structures

Shift Neighbourhood: This type of neighbour is obtained from original solution by changing the agent assignment of one task. The algorithm steps are summarized in Table 5. An example implementation of this algorithm is portrayed in Figure 4.

Double Shift Neighbourhood: This neighbourhood structure is the special case of the long chain neighbourhood. Since the two shift moves are performed in double shift, this is the (EC-Length=2) state of the long chain. Double shift neighbourhood contains the swap neighbourhood, which is the interchange of agents of two different tasks assigned to, within its scope. In the long chain neighbourhood, task for each shift move is selected from B list. In double shift neighbourhood, new shift move is determined by using the set of all tasks. Because, there is no restriction to achieve a new shift move. A simplified demonstration of the neighbourhood is shown in Figure 5.

Shift (σ)

1. *Let* $S = \{i \mid i \in \{1...n\}\}$, k=1, *ShiftNeighbour=* σ
2. *If* $S = \emptyset$ *then stop; otherwise i_k is ejected from* σ_k. $S = S - \{i_k\}$
3. *Let j^* be the agent j that minimizes*

$$c_{ikj} + \alpha_j \max\{0, \left(\sum_{i \in l, \sigma(i)=j} a_{ij}\right) + a_{ikj} - b_j\} \quad \text{among all agents } j \in J \setminus \{\sigma(\mathrm{i_k})\}.$$

4. *Assign i_k to j^*, output* σ', *calculate Fitness(*σ'*)*
5. *If Fitness(*σ'*)<Fitness (ShiftNeighbor) then ShiftNeighbour =* σ'
6. *k:= k+1, return to Step 2*
7. *Output ShiftNeighbour*

Table 5. Shift neighbourhood

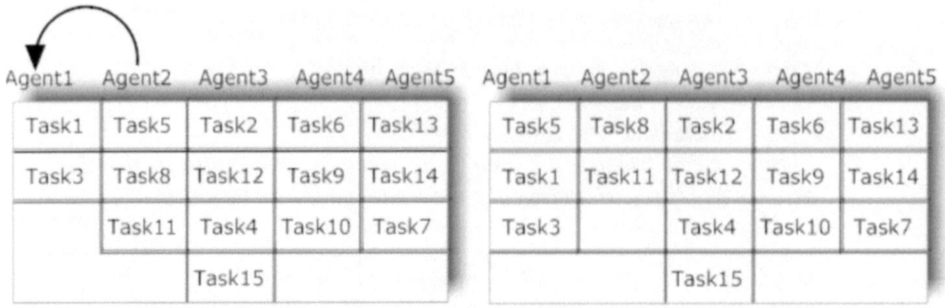

Figure 4. Shift neighbourhood structure

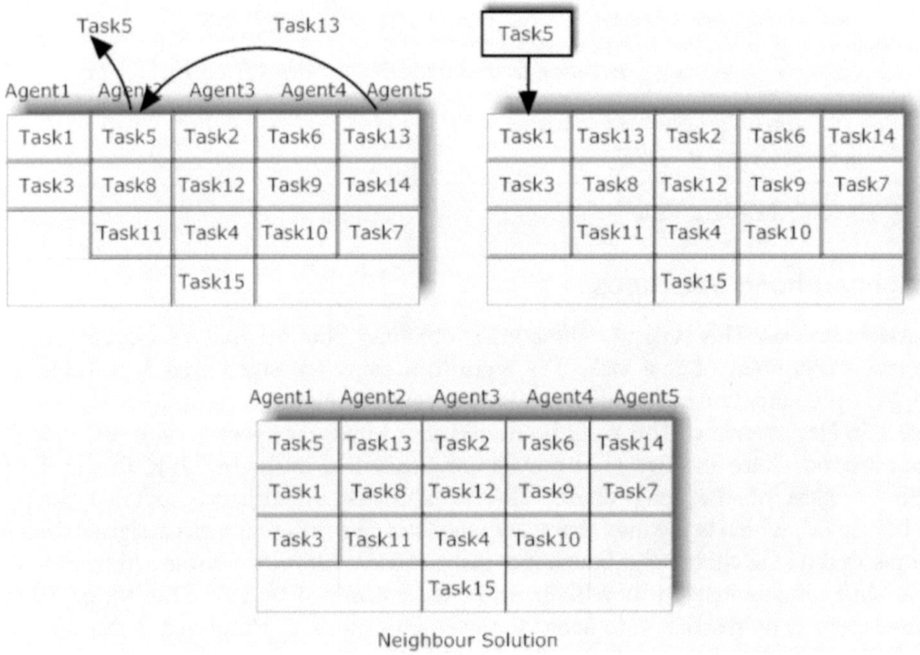

Figure 5. Double shift neighbourhood structure

Long Chain Neighbourhood: A neighbour is obtained by performing the multiple shift moves whose length is specified as chain length. A simple explanation of the neighbourhood structure and main steps of the algorithm are presented here, but detailed information can be obtained from Yagiura et al. (2004). Assume that task io is ejected from agent $\sigma(i_0)$ as a free task where $\sigma(i_0)$ denotes the agent that task i_0 is assigned to. The amount of resource of $\sigma(i_0)$ is increased by this ejection move. Avail is defined as the resulting amount of resource as shown in the following equation.

$$avail(i) = \begin{cases} a_{i,\sigma(i)} - p_{\sigma(i)}(\sigma) & \text{if} \quad a_{i,\sigma(i)} > p_{\sigma(i)}(\sigma) \\ a_{i,\sigma(i)} & \text{otherwise} \end{cases}$$

Assuming that task i_1 is the task whose shift into $\sigma(i_0)$ is most profitable among the tasks satisfying $a_{i1,\sigma(i_0)} \leq avail(i_0)$ Task i_1 is shifted into agent $\sigma(i_0)$. This is called as reference structure. After this first ejection move, the free task i_0 will be tried to assign into some other agents according to its effect on fitness function as shown in Table 6 (Step 4). This is called as the trial move. The next ejection move is applied to the previous reference structure, not to the solutions generated by the trial moves. Same steps are repeated until the stopping criterion is satisfied. The general mechanism of the long chain neighbourhood is presented in Table 6 and portrayed in Figure 6.

Long Chain (σ)

1. *Let* $S := \emptyset$.
2. *If* $S = I'$, *stop; otherwise randomly choose a* $i_0 \in I \setminus S'$,

   Let $S := S \cup \{i_0\}$, *and* $\sigma' := \sigma$. *(Job i_0 is ejected from* $\sigma(i_0)$.*)*
3. *Let j^* be the agent j that minimizes* $c_{i_0 j} + \alpha_j \max\{0, \left(\sum_{i \in l, \sigma(i)=j} a_{ij}\right) + a_{i_{01} j} - b_j\}$

   among all agents

   $j \in J / \{\sigma(i_0)\}$, *and let* l:=0.
4. *If* $B(i_l) \setminus \{i_k | k \le l\} = \emptyset$, *return to Step 2; otherwise let* l:=l+1 *and proceed to Step 5.*
5. *Randomly choose* $i_l \in B(i_{l-1}) \setminus \{i_k | k \le l-1\}$ *and let* $\sigma'(i_l) := \sigma(i_{l-1})$ *(an ejection move of job i_l).*

   Then execute the following Steps (a) and (b) (two trial moves).

   (a) *Let* $\sigma'(i_0) := \sigma(i_l)$ *(i_0 is inserted into* $\sigma(i_l)$*), and output* σ'.

   (b) *Let* $\sigma'(i_0) := j^*$ *(i_0 is inserted into i^*), and output* σ'.
6. *Return to Step 4.*

Table 6. Long chain neighbourhood structure

$$p_j(\sigma) = \max\left\{0, \left(\sum_{i \in l, \sigma(i)=j} a_{ij}\right) - b_j\right\}$$

$$score(i,j) = -c_{ij} + c_{i,\sigma(i)}$$

$$I' = \left\{k \in I \middle| \exists h \in I \text{ s.t. } a_{h,\sigma(k)} \le avail(k) \text{ and } \sigma(h) \ne \sigma(k)\right\}$$

$$bestscore(i) = \min\left\{score(k, \sigma(i)) \middle| k \in l \quad \sigma(k) \ne \sigma(i) \text{ and } a_{k,\sigma(i)} \le avail(i)\right\}$$

$$B(i) = \left\{k \in I' \middle| score(k, \sigma(i)) = bestscore(i), \quad \sigma(k) \ne \sigma(i) \text{ and } a_{k,\sigma(i)} \le avail(i)\right\}$$

As shown in Figure 6, Task 5 is selected as the free task and removed from Agent 2. After avail(TaskS) is updated, Task 13 is determined for the shift move which has the best score among the other tasks satisfying avail(Task5). Task 13 removed from Agent 5 and assigned to Agent 2. This is the reference structure for neighbourhood. In the next step, a trial move to assign the free task Task 5 to an agent is determined according to the assignment effect on fitness function value. Assuming that Agent 1 is determined, Task 5 is assigned to that agent to complete the trial move. The result of a trial move is the complete neighbour for the original solution. This neighbour is obtained by applying l=2 (two shift moves) which is also called as double shift neighbourhood. If the length of ejection chain > 2, then the same steps are repeated on the previous reference structure, which is in the case of the free task is not assigned to an agent. In Figure 6, avail(Task!3) is updated and Task 2 is determined for the next shift move. After Task 2 is assigned to Agent 5, a new trial move is performed to assign ejection task. Assuming that the most profitable agent is Agent 2, Task 5 is assigned to Agent 2 to obtain a complete neighbour solution. This is the long chain with length 3 (three shift moves). Same steps are repeated to complete the previously determined length of ejection.

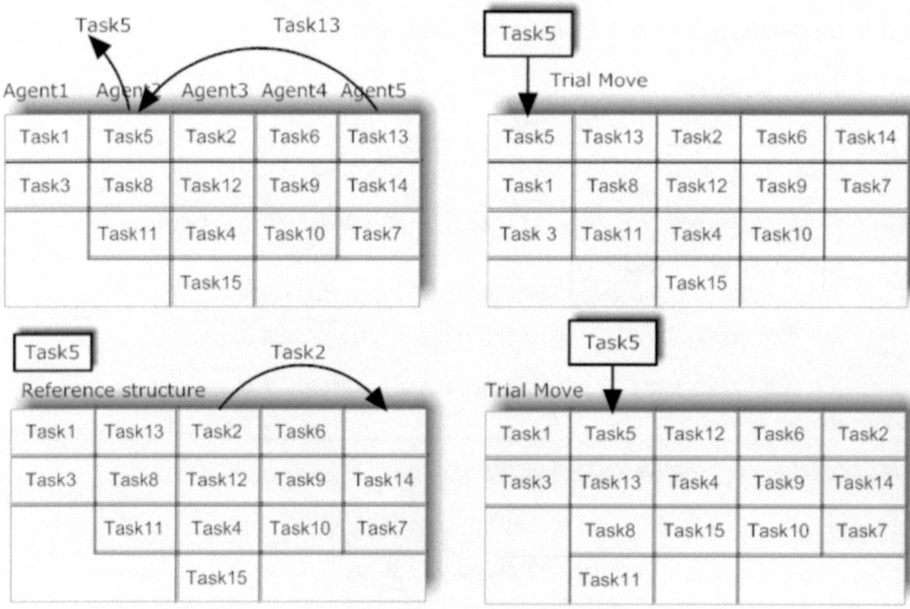

Figure 6. Long chain neighbourhood structure (l=3)

7. Computational Study

The proposed ABC algorithm is coded in C# and tested in a set of problems ranging from 5 agents-15 tasks to 10 agents-60 tasks. These test problems are publicly available from the www.OR-Library.com. The set of test problems can be divided into two groups: Gapl-Gap6/easy and Gap7-Gapl2/difficult. Each problem set consists of 5 different problems with the same size, so there are 12*5 =60 problems to solve. These set of problems are of maximization form of GAP and optimal values are known.

In this section, a simple GAP example is designed to explain the execution of one iteration of the proposed ABC algorithm. An example consisting of 3 agent and 6 task assignment problem is implemented to solve as a minimization problem. A bee solution is represented as an array of tasks which contains the assignment of agents.

There are 3 Employed Bees and 5 Onlooker Bees in the example. Initial solutions of bee colony are generated by using the GRAH algorithm. A shift neighbourhood structure is applied to each Employed Bee. For Bee 1, after shift neighbourhood, a better solution is obtained by changing the assignment of Task 1 from Agent 2 to Agent 1 and original Bee 1 solution is changed to neighbour solution as shown in Figure 7. In the second step, double shift neighbourhood is applied to new Bee 1. Since there is no solution better than Bee 1, employed bee solution is not changed by this neighbourhood. Shift and Double Shift steps are repeated for Bee 2 and Bee 3. After these steps, a transient bee colony is constituted to determine the probabilities. These probabilities are calculated by using the equation in Table 3 (3.2.c) to determine the number of onlooker bees assigned to each employed bee. As shown in Figure 7, the worst bee (Bee 3) retains the minimum number of onlooker bee. For each employed bee, ejection chain neighbourhood is applied and the quantity of neighbours generated is determined according to the number of onlooker assigned to employed bee. The fitness value of onlooker bees are compared with the original employed bee fitness and the best onlooker is selected as the winner. Updated bee colony for the next iteration is shown in Figure 7. In addition to this updating stage, the best feasible solution among the bee colony is compared to the best solution found so far. If the employed bee is better than the best, the best solution is updated.

Experimental Setup for GAP Problems

Parameters of proposed algorithm are defined as follows;

- Number of employed bees (n)
- Number of onlooker bees (m>n)
- Number of scout bees (0.1*n)
- Maximum iteration number (Iteration)
- Initial value of penalty coefficient (a_j)
- Length of ejection chain neighbourhood (EC-Length)

Penalty function is used to calculate the fitness function. While constructing initial solutions by using the GRAH algorithm and generating neighbours by using shift, double shift and ejection chain algorithms, proposed approach allows producing infeasible solutions. Consequently, there is an additional term in the objective function determined by penalizing the infeasible solutions with a_j coefficient ($a_j > 0$). Fitness function is computed by using the following equation.

$$fit(\sigma_i) = \sum_{j=1}^{m} \sum_{i=1}^{n} c_{ij} x_{ij} + \left(\sum_{j=1}^{m} \alpha_j \max\left\{ 0, \sum_{i=1}^{n} b_{ij} x_{ij} - a_j \right\} \right)$$

The first term in the equation denotes the total cost of assignment of tasks to agents. The second term is defined as an additional penalty function for minimization, a_j represents the cost of using one unit of overloaded capacity of jth agent. Initial values of a_j's are determined as user defined parameter. If a solution is not feasible the second term will be positive and therefore the search will be directed to feasible solution. If the capacity is not exceeded, this term will be 0 to ensure not penalized. The parameter a_j can be increased during the run to penalize infeasible solutions and drive the search to feasible ones which means the adaptive control of penalty costs.

Initial values of a_j's are designed as user defined (a_j>0). Updating stage is adapted from Yagiura et al. (2004) by using the following equations. After the generation of onlooker neighbours of each employed bee a_j values are updated.

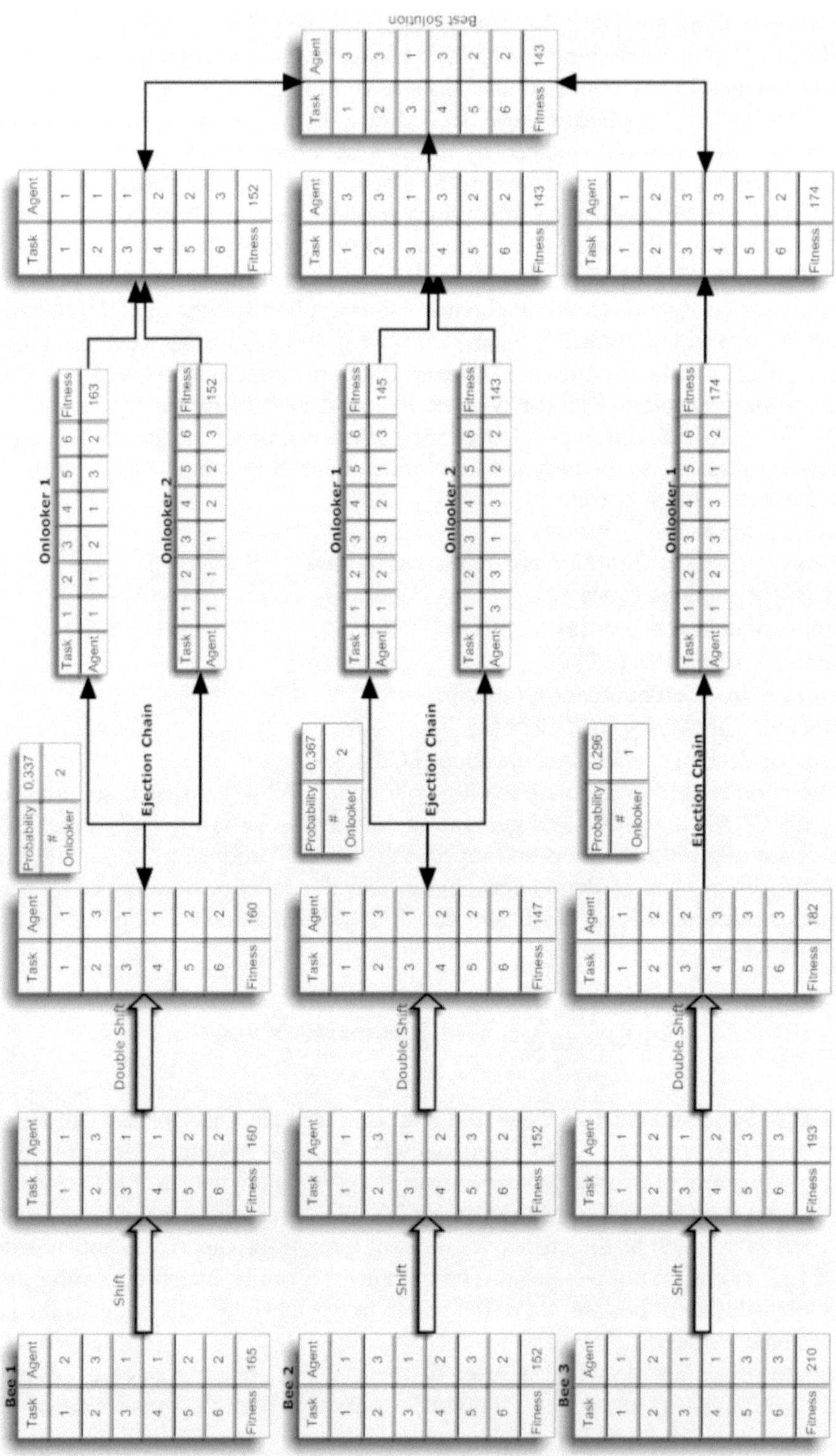

Figure 7. A sample execution of neighbourhood structure

1. If there is no feasible solution found in onlooker neighbours, a_j are increased for all $j \in J$ by

$$\alpha_j = \begin{cases} \alpha_j(1+\Delta q_j^{inc}(\sigma)), & \alpha_j > 0 \\ \Delta q_j^{inc}(\sigma) \min_{h \in J}\{b_h \alpha_h \mid b_h \alpha_h > 0\} / b_j, & otherwise \end{cases}$$

Where

$$\Delta = \begin{cases} \dfrac{stepsizeinc}{\max_{j \in J} \left| q_j^{inc}(\sigma) \right|}, & if \quad \max_{j \in J} \left| q_j^{inc}(\sigma) \right| > 0 \\ 0, & otherwise \end{cases}$$

2. (Otherwise) If at least one feasible solution found within onlooker neighbours, all a_j are decreased by using the same equations except that $q^{dec}(\sigma)$ instead of $q^{inc}(\sigma)$ and *stepsizedec* instead of *stepsizeinc.*

$$q_j^{inc}(\sigma) = p_j(\sigma) / b_j$$

$$q_j^{dec}(\sigma) = \begin{cases} -1, & if \quad p_j(\sigma) = 0 \\ 0, & otherwise \end{cases}$$

Parameter Setting

Parameters of algorithm are treated as two different sets. As mentioned before Gapl to Gap6 problem sets are specified as easy while Gap7 to Gapl2 as difficult. Accordingly, two different parameter sets are determined as shown in Table 7.

Parameter	Gapl-Gap6	Gap7-Gapl2
# of Iteration	100	250
# of Employed Bee	50	50
# of Onlooker Bee	100	500
# of Scout Bee	5	5
α	1	1
EC-Length	5	10

Table 7. Parameter setting

Five runs for each problem are evaluated. Different algorithms that solved Gapl-Gapl2 in the literature are determined for comparison. The values in Table 8 represent the mean deviation from the optimal value for each problem set. Proposed algorithm found the optimal solutions in all five runs for all problem sets with previously defined parameters. As compared to other 12 algorithms the proposed algorithm is unambiguously the best performer.

	ABC	*MTH*	*FJVBB*	FSA	*MTBB*	SPH	*LT1FA*	RSSA	*TS6*	TS1	*GAk*	GA,	ASH+LS +TS
Gapl	0.00	5.43	0.00	0.00	0.00	0.08	1.74	0.00	0.00	0.00	0.00	0.00	-
Gap2	0.00	5.02	0.00	0.19	0.00	0.11	0.89	0.00	0.24	0.10	0.00	0.01	-
Gap3	0.00	2.14	0.00	0.00	0.00	0.09	1.26	0.00	0.03	0.00	0.00	0.01	-
Gap4	0.00	2.35	0.83	0.06	0.18	0.04	0.72	0.00	0.03	0.03	0.00	0.03	-
Gap5	0.00	2.63	0.07	0.11	0.00	0.35	1.42	0.00	0.04	0.00	0.00	0.10	-
Gap6	0.00	1.67	0.58	0.85	0.52	0.15	0.82	0.05	0.00	0.03	0.01	0.08	-
Gap7	0.00	2.02	1.58	0.99	1.32	0.00	1.22	0.02	0.02	0.00	0.00	0.08	0.00
Gap8	0.00	2.45	2.48	0.41	1.32	0.23	1.13	0.10	0.14	0.09	0.05	0.33	0.042
Gap9	0.00	2.18	0.61	1.46	1.06	0.12	1.48	0.08	0.06	0.06	0.00	0.17	0.00
Gap10	0.00	1.75	1.29	1.72	1.15	0.25	1.19	0.14	0.15	0.08	0.04	0.27	0.013
Gap11	0.00	1.78	1.32	1.10	2.01	0.00	1.17	0.05	0.02	0.02	0.00	0.20	0.00
Gap12	0.00	1.37	1.37	1.68	1.55	0.10	0.81	0.11	0.07	0.04	0.01	0.17	0.00

ABC: The Proposed Algorithm, MTH: Martello and Toth (1981) constructive heuristic, FJVBB: Fisher et al. (1986) branch and bound procedure with and upper CPU limit, FSA: Cattrysse (1990) fixing simulated annealing algorithm, MTBB: Martello and Toth (1991) branch and bound procedure with an upper CPU limit, SPH: Cattrysse et al. (1994) set partitioning heuristic, LT1FA: Osman (1995) long term descent, 1-interchange mechanism and first admissible, RSSA: Osman (1995) hybrid SA/TS with different seed values, TS6: Osman (1995) long term TS, BA selection, Rl tabu restrictions and Al aspiration criterion, TS1: Osman (1995) long term TS, FA selection, Rl tabu restrictions and Al aspiration criterion, GAi>: Chu and Beasley (1997) genetic algorithm with heuristic operator, GAa: Chu and Beasley (1997) genetic algorithm without heuristic algorithm

Table 8. Comparison of results

8. Conclusion

In this study a relatively new member of swarm intelligence family that is named as "artificial bee colony" is explained in detail. Actually, different names were used in the literature for the algorithms inspired from natural honey bees. Here we prefer to use the name "artificial bee colony" to reflect population characteristic of the algorithm. A very detailed literature review along with a categorization is presented in this study. All accessible previous work on bee based optimization algorithms is tried to be reviewed. Most of the work in the literature is carried out in last two years and researchers mainly concentrated on continuous optimization and TSP problems. Previous work has presented that bee inspired algorithms have a very promising potential for modelling and solving complex optimization problems. But there is still a long way to go in order to fully utilise the potential of bee inspired algorithms. Such an attempt is also made in this study to present performance of a bee inspired algorithm, "artificial bee colony" on a NP-hard problem which is known as generalised assignment problem. The proposed bee algorithm is found very effective in solving small to medium sized generalized assignment problems. Actually, the proposed algorithm easily found all optimal solutions where the compared 12 algorithms were not able to find for most of the cases. Our research is still under progress and we are hoping to find effective solutions for large size and tightly constrained generalised assignment problems. These problems are over complex, therefore their solution can be considered as a very good indicator for the potential of the nature inspired algorithms including "artificial bee colony".

9. Acknowledgements

The first author is grateful to Turkish Academy of Sciences (TUBA) for supporting his scientific studies.

10. References

Abbass H.A., A Single Queen Single Worker Honey-Bees Approach to 3-SAT, *GECCO2001 The Genetic and Evolutionary Computation Conference*, San Francisco, USA, 2001a.

Abbass H.A., A Monogenous MBO Approach to Satisfiability, *CIMCA'2001 International Conference on Computational Intelligence for Modeling, Control and Automation*, Las Vegas, NV, USA, 2001b.

Abbass H.A., MBO: Marriage in Honey Bees Optimization A Haplometrosis Polygynous Swarming Approach, *CEC2001 Proceedings of the Congress on Evolutionary Computation*, Seoul, Korea, 207-214,2001c.

Afshar A., Bozorg Haddad O., Marino M.A., Adams B.J., Honey-Bee Mating Optimization (HBMO) Algorithm for Optimal Reservoir Operation, *Journal of the Franklin Institute*, In press.

Alfandari L., Plateau A., Tolla P., A Two-Phase Path Relinking Algorithm for the Generalized Assignment Problem, In *Proceedings of the Fourth Metaheuristics International Conference*, Porto, Portugal, 175-179,2001.

Alfandari L., Plateau A., Tolla P., A Two-Phase Path Relinking Algorithm for the Generalized Assignment Problem, *Technical Report* No: 378, CEDRIC, CNAM, 2002.

Alfandari L., Plateau A., Tolla P., A Path Relinking Algorithm for the Generalized Assignment Problem, In M.G.C. Resende, J.P. de Sousa (Eds.), *Metaheuristics: Computer Decision-Making*, Kluwer Academic Publishers, Boston, 1-17,2004

Azeem M.F., Saad A.M., Modified Queen Bee Evolution Based Genetic Algorithm for Tuning of Scaling Factors of Fuzzy Knowledge Base Controller, *IEEE INDICON 2004 Proceedings of the India Annual Conference*, 299-303,2004.

Basturk B., Karaboga D., An Artificial Bee Colony (ABC) Algorithm for Numeric Function Optimization, *IEEE Swarm Intelligence Symposium 2006*, Indianapolis, Indiana, USA, 2006.

Baykasoğlu A., Goal Programming using the Multiple Objective Tabu Search, *Journal of Operational Research Society*, 52(12), 1359-1369,2001.

Benatchba K., Admane L., Koudil M., Using Bees to Solve a Data Mining Problem Expressed as a Max-Sat One, In *Proceedings of IWINAC'2005, International Work Conference on the Interplay between Natural and Artificial Computation*, Canary Islands, Spain, 212-220,2005.

Bianco G.M., Getting Inspired from Bees to Perform Large Scale Visual Precise Navigation, *Proceedings of 2004 IEEE/RSJ International Conference on Intelligent Robots and Systems*, Sendai, Japan, 619-624,2004.

Bozorg Haddad O., Afshar A., MBO Algorithm, A New Heuristic Approach in Hydrosystems Design and Operation, *1st International Conference on Managing Rivers in the 21st Century*, 499-504,2004.

Bozorg Haddad O., Afshar A., Mariano M.A., Honey-Bees Mating Optimization (HBMO) Algorithm: A New Heuristic Approach for Water Resources Optimization, *Water Resources Management*, 20, 661-680,2006.

Cattrysse D., Set Partitioning Approaches to Combinatorial Optimization Problems, *Ph.D. Thesis*, Katholieke Universiteit Leuven, Centrum Industrieel Beleid, Belgium, 1990.

Cattrysse D., Salomon M., Van Wassenhove L.N., A Set Partitioning Heuristic for the Generalized Assignment Problem, *European Journal of Operational Research*, 72,167-174.1994.

Chang H.S., Converging Marriage in Honey-Bees Optimization and Application to Stochastic Dynamic Programming, *Journal of Global Optimization*, 35,423-441,2006.

Chong C.S., Low M.Y.H., Sivakumar A.I., Gay K.L., A Bee Colony Optimization Algorithm to Job Shop Scheduling, *Proceedings of the 37th Winter Simulation*, Monterey, California, 1954-1961,2006.

Chu P.C., Beasley J.E., A Genetic Algorithm for the Generalized Assignment Problem, *Computers Operations Research*, 24,17-23,1997.

Diaz J.A., Fernandez E., A Tabu Search Heuristic for the Generalized Assignment Problem, *European Journal Operational Research*, 132,22-38,2001.

Drias H., Sadeg S., Yahi S., Cooperative Bees Swarm for Solving the Maximum Weighted Satisfiability Problem, *IWAAN International Work Conference on Artificial and Natural Neural Networks*, Barcelona, Spain, 318-325,2005.

Fathian M., Amiri B., Maroosi A., *Application of Honey-Bee Mating Optimization Algorithm on Clustering*, In press.

Fisher M.L., Jaikumar R., Van Wassenhove L.N., A Multiplier Adjustment Method for the Generalized Assignment Problem, *Management Science*, 32,1095-1103,1986.

Karaboga D. An Idea Based on Honey Bee Swarm for Numerical Optimization, *Technical Report-TR06*, Erciyes University, Engineering Faculty, Computer Engineering Department, Turkey, 2005.

Kara A., Imitation of Bee Reproduction as a Crossover Operator in Genetic Algorithms, *PRICAI 2004*, LNAI 3157, C. Zhang, H.W. Guesgen, W.K. Yeap (Eds.), Springer-Verlag, Berlin Heidelberg, 1015-1016,2004.

Koudil M., Benatchba K., Tarabet A., Sahraoui E.B., Using Artificial Bees to Solve Partitioning and Scheduling Problems in Codesign, *Applied Mathematics and Computation*, 186(2), 1710-1722,2007.

Laguna M., Kelly J.P., Gonzalez-Velarde J.L., Glover P., Tabu Search for the Multilevel Generalized Assignment Problem, *European Journal of Operational Research*, 82,176-189.1995.

Lemmens N.P.P.M., To Bee or Not to Bee: A Comparative Study in Swarm Intelligence, *Master Thesis*, Maastricht University, Maastricht ICT Competence Centre, Institute for Knowledge and Agent Technology, Maastricht, Netherlands, 2006.

Lourengo H.R., Serra D., Adaptive Search Heuristics for the Generalized Assignment Problem, *Mathware and Soft Computing*, 9,209-234,2002.

Lucic P., Modeling Transportation Problems Using Concepts of Swarm Intelligence and Soft Computing, *PhD Thesis*, Civil Engineering, Faculty of the Virginia Polytechnic Institute and State University, 2002.

Lucic P., Teodorovic D., Bee system: Modeling Combinatorial Optimization Transportation Engineering Problems by Swarm Intelligence, *Preprints of the TRISTAN IV Triennial Symposium on Transportation Analysis*, Sao Miguel, Azores Islands, 441-445,2001.

Luckic P., Teodorovic D., Transportation Modeling: An Artificial Life Approach, *ICTAI'02 14th IEEE International Conference on Tools with Artificial Intelligence*, 216-223,2002.

Lucic P., Teodorovic D., Computing with Bees: Attacking Complex Transportation Engineering Problems, *International Journal on Artificial Intelligence Tools*, 12(3), 375-394,2003a.

Lucic P., Teodorovic D., Vehicle Routing Problem with Uncertain Demand at Nodes: The Bee System and Fuzzy Logic Approach, in *Fuzzy Sets in Optimization*, Editor J.L. Verdegay, Springer-Verlag, Berlin Heidelbelg, 67-82,2003b.

Markovic G.Z., Teodorovic D., Acimovic-Raspopovic V.S., Routing and Wavelength Assignment in All-Optical Networks Based on the Bee Colony Optimization, *AI Communications - The European Journal on Artificial Intelligence*, (in press).

Martello S., Toth P., An Algorithm for the Generalized Assignment Problems, *Operational Research*, ed. J.P. Brans. North-Holland, 589-603,1981.

Martello S., Toth P., *Knapsack Problems: Algorithms and Computer Implementations*, Wiley, New York, 1990.

Nakrani S., Tovey C, On Honey Bees and Dynamic Allocation in an Internet Server Colony, *Proceedings of 2nd International Workshop on the Mathematics and Algorithms of Social Insects*, Atlanta, Georgia, USA, 2003.

Nauss R.M., Solving the Generalized Assignment Problem: An Optimizing and Heuristic Approach, *INFORMS Journal of Computing*, 15,249-266,2003.

Osman I.H., Heuristics for the Generalized Assignment Problem: Simulated Annealing and Tabu Search Approaches, *OR Spektrum*, 17,211-225,1995.

Pham D.T., Kog E., Ghanbarzadeh A., Otri S., Rahim S., Zaidi M., The Bees Algorithm - A Novel Tool for Complex Optimisation Problems, *IPROMS 2006 Proceeding 2nd International Virtual Conference on Intelligent Production Machines and Systems*, Oxford, Elsevier, 2006a.

Pham D.T., Otri S., Ghanbarzadeh A., Kog E., Application of the Bees Algorithm to the Training of Learning Vector Quantisation Networks for Control Chart Pattern Recognition, *ICTTA'06 Information and Communication Technologies*, 1624-1629, 2006b.

Pham D.T., Koc E., Ghanbarzadeh A., Otri S., Optimisation of the Weights of Multi-Layered Perceptions Using the Bees Algorithm, *Proceedings of 5th International Symposium on Intelligent Manufacturing Systems*, Sakarya, Turkey, 38-46,2006c.

Pham D.T., Soroka A.J., Ghanbarzadeh A., Kog E., Otri S., Packianather M., Optimising Neural Networks for Identification of Wood Defects Using the Bees Algorithm, *IEEE International Conference on Industrial Informatics*, 8,1346-1351,2006d.

Qin L.D., Jiang Q.Y., Zou Z.Y., Cao Y.J., A Queen-Bee Evolution Based on Genetic Algorithm for Economic Power Dispatch, *UPEC 2004 39th International Universities Power Engineering Conference*, Bristol, UK, 453-456,2004.

Quijano N., Passino K.M., Honey Bee Social Foraging Algorithms for Resource Allocation Theory and Application, *American Control Conference*, New York City, USA, 2007.

Racer M., Amini M.M., A Robust Heuristic for the Generalized Assignment Problem, *Annals of Oper. Res.*, 50,487-503,1994.

Randall M., Heuristics for Ant Colony Optimisation Using the Generalised Assignment Problem, In *Proceedings of the IEEE Congress on Evolutionary Computation*, Portland, Oregon, 2,1916-1923,2004.

Ross G.T., Soland P.M., A Branch and Bound Based Algorithm for the Generalized Assignment Problem, *Mathematical Programming*, 8,91-103,1975.

Sato T., Hagiwara M., Bee System: Finding Solution by a Concentrated Search, *Proceedings of the IEEE International Conference on Systems, Man, and Cybernetics*, 4(C), 3954-3959,1997.

Savelsbergh M., A Branch-and-Price Algorithm for the Generalized Assignment Problem, *Operations Research*, 45,831-841,1997.

Schmickl T., Thenius R., Crailsheim K., Simulating Swarm Intelligence in Honey Bees: Foraging in Differently Fluctuating Environments, *GECCO'05*, Washington, DC, USA, 273-274,2005.

Seeley T.D., *The Wisdom of the Hive*, Harvard University Press, Cambridge, MA, 1995.

Seeley T.D., Buhrman S.C., Group Decision Making in Swarms of Honey Bees, *Behav. Ecol. Sociobiol.*, 45,19-31,1999.

Sung H.J., Queen-Bee Evolution for Genetic Algorithms, *Electronic Letters*, 39(6), 575-576, 2003.

Teo J., Abbass H.A., An Annealing Approach to the Mating-Flight Trajectories in the Marriage in Honey Bees Optimization Algorithm, *Technical Report CS04/01*, School of omputer Science, University of New South Wales at ADFA, 2001.

Teo J., Abbass H.A., A True Annealing Approach to the Marriage in Honey-Bees Optimization Algorithm, *International Journal of Computational Intelligence and Applications*, 3(2), 199-211,2003.

Teodorovic D., Dell'Orco M., Bee Colony Optimization - A Cooperative Learning Approach to Complex Transportation Problems, *Advanced OR and AI Methods in Transportation*, 51-60,2005.

Wedde H.F., Farooq M., Zhang Y., BeeHive: An Efficient Fault-Tolerant Routing Algorithm Inspired by Honey Bee Behavior, *Ant Colony, Optimization and Swarm Intelligence*, Eds. M. Dorigo, Lecture Notes in Computer Science 3172, Springer Berlin, 83-94,2004.

Yagiura M., Yamaguchi T., Ibaraki T., A Variable-Depth Search Algorithm with Branching Search for the Generalized Assignment Problem, *Optimization Methods and Software*, 10,419-441,1998.

Yagiura M., Yamaguchi T., Ibaraki T., A Variable-Depth Search Algorithm for the Generalized Assignment Problem, Vob S, Martello S., Osman I.H., Roucairol C, (Eds.), *Meta-Heuristics: Advances and Trends in Local Search Paradigms for Optimization*, Kluwer Academic Publishers, Boston, 459-471,1999.

Yagiura M., Ibaraki T., Glover P., An Effective Metaheuristic Algorithm for the Generalized Assignment Problem, In *2001 IEEE International Conference on Systems, Man and Cybernetics*, pg 242, Tucson, Arizona, 2001.

Yagiura M., Ibaraki T., Glover P., A Path Relinking Approach for the Generalized Assignment Problem, In *Proceedings of the International Symposium on Scheduling*, 105-108,2002.

Yagiura M., Ibaraki T., Glover P., An Ejection Chain Approach for the Generalized Assignment Problem, *Informs Journal of Computing*, 16(2), 131-151,2004.

Yagiura M., Ibaraki T., Glover E, A Path Relinking Approach with Ejection Chains for the Generalized Assignment Problem, *European Journal of Operational Research*, 169,548-569,2006.

Yang X.S., Engineering Optimizations via Nature-Inspired Virtual Bee Algorithms, *IWINAC 2005, LNCS 3562*, Yang, J. M. and J.R. Alvarez (Eds.), Springer-Verlag, Berlin Heidelberg, 317-323,2005.

Yonezawa Y., Kikuchi T., Ecological Algorithm for Optimal Ordering Used by Collective Honey Bee Behavior, *7th International Symposium on Micro Machine and Human Science*, 249-256,1996.

Finite Element Mesh Decomposition Using Evolving Ant Colony Optimization

Ardeshir Bahreininejad
Tarbiat Modares University
Iran

1. Introduction

Combinatorial optimization problems arise in many areas of science and engineering. Unfortunately, due to the NP (non-polynomial) nature of these problems, the computations increase with the size of the problem (Bahreininejad & Topping, 1996; Topping & Bahreininejad, 1997).

Finite Elements (FE) mesh decomposition (partitioning) is a well known NP-hard optimization problem and is used to split a computationally expensive FE mesh into smaller subdomains (parts) for parallel FE analysis. Partitioning must be performed to ensure:

- Load balancing: for a mesh idealized using a single element type, then the number of elements in each partition must be the same, and
- Inter-processor communication: the partitions must be performed so that the number of nodes or edges shared between the subdomains is minimized to ensure that the minimum inter-processor communication during the subsequent parallel FE analysis is achieved (Topping & Bahreininejad, 1997; Topping & Khan, 1996).

Numerous methods have been used to decompose FE meshes (Farhat, 1988; Simon, 1991; Toping & Khan, 1996; Topping & Bahreininejad, 1997).

For automatic partitioning of FE meshes, Farhat (1988) proposed a domain decomposition method which is based on a greedy algorithm. The method provides FE mesh partitions in relatively short duration of time. The division of a mesh with respect to assigning a certain number of mesh elements to a mesh partition may be accomplished with simple arithmetic. In this method, the partitions are created sequentially from an overall FE mesh until the number of partitions become equal to the desired number.

Each FE element node is assigned a weight factor which is equal to the number of elements connecting to that particular node. The inner boundary of a partition is defined as the common boundary between two partitions. Two elements are considered to be adjacent if they share a vertex (node). The number of elements per partitions is determined by the total number of elements in the mesh, the number of different type of elements used in the mesh (triangular, quadrilateral, etc.), and the number of required partitions. In the case of a single type of elements, it is equal to the ratio between the total number of elements within the mesh and the number of required partitions (Farhat, 1988).

Although Farhat's method provides quick partitioning of FE meshes, the optimality of the mesh partitions with respect to the number of interfaces between adjacent partitions is not guaranteed. In addition, the resulting partitions by this method are sensitive to the elements and node numbering of the FE mesh. Hence, for a given mesh topology, different solutions may be found if different node/element numbering of mesh elements are used.

Simon's method (1991) performs recursive bisection of FE mesh and uses eigenvector information to determine the partitions which have an equal number of elements on each side of the bisected mesh and have a minimum inner boundary. The rationale behind using recursive bisection instead of dividing the mesh into *N* number of partitions in a single step is based upon the following considerations:

- It is easier to bisect a graph rather than dividing it into more than two parts. The graph is bisected such that the requirements of load balancing and the minimization of the inner boundary nodes/edges between parts are effectively met for the two partitions.
- There is an aspect of parallelism within the recursive bisection. Initially a mesh may be divided into two parts and then each of these parts may be worked upon in parallel to form four partitions of the total mesh under consideration. Hence, the extent of parallelism that may be employed increase exponentially with the increase in the number of recursions.

The Simon's method provides efficient partitions, however the main drawback is the computational cost to reach a desired solution which increases nonlinearly with the increase in the size of the mesh.

The Subdomain Generation Methods (SGM) proposed by Topping and Khan (1996) and followed on by Topping and Bahreininejad (1997) presented a technique which incorporates an optimization algorithm (genetic algorithms or Hopfield-type neural network) and a trained multi-layered feedforward neural network based on the backpropagation algorithm (Rumelhart et al., 1986; Pao, 1989; Topping & Bahreininejad, 1997) to decompose FE meshes. The trained backpropagation neural network is used to estimate (predict) the number of elements which will be generated inside every individual element of the (initial) coarse mesh after mesh generation procedure is carried out. The estimated number of elements is incorporated into the optimization algorithm (module) to decompose a coarse FE domain rather than decomposing the fine mesh generated from the refinement of the initial mesh.

Ant Colony Optimization (ACO) is a type of algorithm that seeks to model the emergent behaviour observed in ant colonies and utilize this behaviour to solve combinatorial problems (Colorni, et al., 1991; Dorigo & Gambardella, 1997; Bonabeau, et al., 2000; Maniezzo & Carbonaro, 2001). This technique has been applied to several problems, most of which are graph related because the ant colony metaphor can be most easily applied to such types of problems.

A hybrid optimization approach is presented here to solve the FE mesh bisection problem. The algorithm incorporates several ACO features as well as local optimization techniques using a recursive bisection procedure. The algorithm was tested on a FE mesh with refined mesh sizes of 27155 triangular elements.

The chapter consists of an introduction to the ACO technique in Section 2. Section 3 describes how the ACO concept can be applied to FE mesh bisection. Local optimization techniques have been presented to improve the solution quality of the ACO for FE mesh bisection problem.

The predictive ACO bisection approach is described in Section 4 which uses a trained multi-layered feedforward neural network based on the backpropagation algorithm. The trained neural network is used to estimate the number of triangular elements that will be generated after FE mesh generation (refinement) is carried out. Section 5 presents a recursive mesh bisection case study using the proposed hybrid ACO and neural networks mesh recursive bisection procedure. This FE mesh is also partitioned using a greedy FE mesh decomposing algorithm proposed by Farhat (Farhat, 1988). The comparison between the obtained results from the proposed hybrid ACO method and Farhat's greedy algorithm is presented. Finally conclusions are given in Section 6.

2. The Ant Colony Optimization Method

The ACO is a heuristic technique that seeks to imitate the behaviour of a colony of ants and their ability to collectively solve a problem. It has been observed (Colorni, et al., 1991; Dorigo & Gambardella, 1997; Bonabeau, et al., 2000; Maniezzo & Carbonaro, 2001) that a colony of ants is able to find the shortest path to a food source. As an ant moves and searches for food, it lays down a chemical substance called *pheromone* along its path. As the ant travels, it looks for pheromone trails on its path and prefers to follow trails with higher levels of pheromone deposits.

If there are two possible paths to reach a food source, as shown in Fig 1, an ant will lay the same amount of pheromone at each step regardless of the path chosen (minor evaporation of pheromone occurs during time). However, it will return to its starting point quicker when it takes the shorter path which contains more pheromone. It is then able to return to the food source to collect more food.

Thus, in an equal amount of time, the ant would lay a higher concentration of pheromone over its path if it takes the shorter path, since it would complete more trips in the given time. The pheromone is then used by other ants to determine the shortest path to find food as described in (Dorigo & Gambardella, 1997; Bonabeau, et al., 2000).

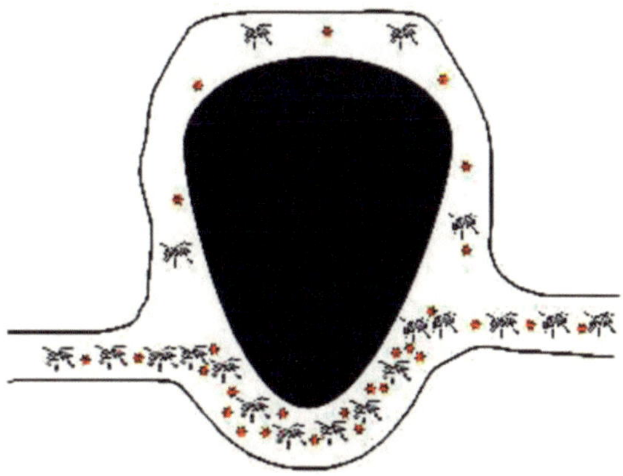

Figure 1. The pheromone deposition of ants (shown as dots) and their pursuing of the shortest path

The ACO technique has been successfully applied to the graph bisection problem by Bui and Strite (2002). They utilized the idea of finding shortest paths and the idea of territorial colonization and *swarm intelligence* in the ACO algorithms. Kuntz and Snyers (1994) and Kuntz, et al. (1997) applied these concepts to a graph clustering problem. Their algorithm combines the features of the ACO technique with swarm intelligence to form a model which is an artificial system designed to perform a certain task. Their model referred to the

organisms as *animats,* (ant agents), reflecting the fact that the system draws ideas from several sources and not just ant colonies. These ideas are important in the graph partitioning problem because the graph can be viewed as territory to be colonized (Bui & Strite, 2002; Bahreininejad, 2004; Bahreininejad & Hesamfar, 2006).
The combination of these two ideas of animats following paths and forming colonies is used to solve the FE mesh bisection problem using triangular elements. However, the proposed ACO method can be used for the decomposition any graph based problem.

3. ACO for FE Mesh Bisection

The basic foundation of the ACO algorithm is to consider each (triangular) element in the FE mesh as a location that can hold any number of animats. The animats can move around the FE mesh by moving across (triangular) *edges* shared between two elements to reach a new element. Each animat belongs to one of two species (e.g. species A and B). However, animats of both species follow the same rules.
To start the algorithm, an initial number of animats are placed on the FE mesh. Their species and location are chosen randomly. At any point throughout the algorithm, the configuration of animats on the FE mesh constitutes a bisection of the mesh in the following way (Bahreininejad, 2004; Bahreininejad & Hesamfar, 2006).
Each element is considered to be colonized by one species. At a given time, it is said to be colonized by whichever species that has the greater number of animats on it. Any ties are recorded and after the colonies of all other elements are calculated, the ties are broken in a random order by assigning the element to the species which results in a lower cut-size (inner boundary between bisections). The set of all elements colonized by species A constitutes A's colony and likewise the elements colonized by species B form B's colony.
In addition, each element can hold a quantity of pheromone. The two species produce separate types of pheromone, so an amount of A pheromone and/or B pheromone is left on each element. The idea of the algorithm is for each species of animats to form a colony consisting of a set of elements that are highly connected to each other while highly disconnected from the other colony. The result should be two sets of elements that are highly connected amongst themselves, but have few edges going between the two sets.
For an individual animat, the goal will be to lay down pheromone when the current element is a good position for animats of its own species and to move to new elements that it wants to add to its species' colony. If each animat follows these goals, the result will be a partitioning of the elements into two sets of similar size with few edges going between the two sets. A greedy algorithm is also formulated which fine tunes the bisection obtained from the ACO procedure.

3.1 ACO implementation

The ACO algorithm is an iterative procedure in which a percentage of animats are activated in each of the iterations. When an animat is activated, it adds an amount of pheromone to the element it is currently residing. It then may *die* with a certain probability or it may *reproduce* with a certain probability and it will move to a new element.
These operations involve only local information known by the animat. The animat is assumed to know the current time (i.e. iteration number), information about the element it is located at (such as the number and species of other animats on that element), and

information about the elements adjacent to its location. The mesh is updated with the new information after the completion every iteration.

The algorithm is divided up into S number of sets, each comprised of I number of iterations. After each set is carried out, the configuration of the mesh is forced into a bisection using a greedy algorithm (Bahreininejad, 2004; Bahreininejad & Hesamfar, 2006). During each set, the parameters corresponding to the probabilities for *activation, death* and *reproduction* are modified. The parameters are changed in such a way that at the beginning of a set, colonial changes are high and by the end of the set the colonies should converged to a stable configuration.

The next set begins at the state where the previous set ended. However, if the animats follow their usual rules too soon, they may not be able to move away from the local optimum that has been reached.

Therefore, for all, but the initial set, a *shake* is performed for a certain number of the first iterations to help move the configuration, or distribution, of animats on the elements away from the solution to which it had prematurely converged as described in (Bui & Strite, 2002; Bahreininejad, 2004; Bahreininejad & Hesamfar, 2006). The shake allows animats to select moves randomly instead of following the normal rules for movement. The *length of the shake* is changed during the algorithm. The first shake lasts for a fixed number of iterations and for the subsequent shakes, the length decreases linearly until the last set where no shaking occurs.

The bisection should come closer to the optimal bisection as the number of iterations increases and consequently shorter and shorter shakes are needed. The length of the shake is given by the following equation:

$$L_{shake} = \frac{L_{\max}(S_i - 2)}{2 - S_{total}} + L_{\max} \tag{1}$$

where L_{max} is the maximum shake length, S_i is the ith set and S_{total} is the total number of sets.

3.1.1 Iteration and activation of animats

An iteration of the algorithm consists of a percentage of the animats being activated and then performing the necessary operations in parallel. The probability of an animat being activated changes during the set.

During the early iterations of a set, more animats are activated. By the end of a set, only a small percentage of the animats are activated in all iterations. The more animats that are activated in a single iteration, the larger the possible change in the configuration will be. The actual probability of activation is a sigmoid-like function given as:

$$a_{(I_I)} = \frac{1}{1 + e^{\frac{\ln(4)(2I_i - (I_{total}+1))}{I_{total}-1}}} \tag{2}$$

where I_i is the iteration number, I_{total} is the total number of iterations. To prove the Equation 2, consider the sigmoid function for the backpropagation algorithm activation function (Pao, 1989) given as:

$$a_{(I_I)} = \frac{1}{1 + e^{\frac{I_i - b}{\theta}}} \tag{3}$$

where b corresponds to the bias of the neural network and θ is the shape factor.
Considering the maximum (0.8) and minimum (0.2) values of the activation probability for the first and the I_{total} iterations respectively, chosen by the user and replacing them for $a_{(I_i)}$ in Equation 3, therefore:

$$\frac{b-1}{\theta} = \ln(4) \tag{4}$$

$$\frac{I_{total} - b}{\theta} = \ln(4) \tag{5}$$

Using Equations 4 and 5, b and θ are given by:

$$b = \frac{I_{total} + 1}{2} \tag{6}$$

$$\theta = \frac{I_{total} - 1}{2(\ln(4))} \tag{7}$$

Replacing Equations 6 and 7 in Equation 3, hence Equation 2 will be obtained. The function starts at a maximum and ends at a minimum. The maximum and minimum values are defined values set by the user in an ACO configuration file.
After the activations of animats have been completed, a percentage of the pheromone on each element is evaporated. Bui and Strite (2002) explain that the evaporation prevents pheromone from building up too much and highly populated elements from being overemphasized which in turn prevents the algorithm from converging prematurely. When an animat is activated:

- It deposits pheromone on its current element,
- It dies or reproduces with a certain probability,
- It moves to another element.

These operations are performed by the animat using local information to make decisions.

3.1.2 Pheromone

The purpose of pheromone is to allow the algorithm to retain a *memory* of good configurations that have been found in the past. Members of each species deposit their pheromone on an element to indicate that this is a good configuration and more animats of their species should come to this element.
The effect of pheromone on the overall performance of the algorithm is to control the animats' movements prohibiting them to set astray over the optimization domain, In other words, pheromone is used a means to control animats' movements throughout the algorithm, thus enabling the optimization process to move towards a solution.
When an animat is activated, it determines the colonization percentage of its adjacent elements. If the FE mesh element is highly connected to elements colonized by the animat's species, then the animat knows that this element is a good candidate for being colonized by its own species. The animat then attempts to reinforce this element by depositing a larger amount of its pheromone.
However, if the animat determines that the element is not highly connected to elements colonized by its own species, it will lay down less pheromone to discourage more of its

species to come to this element. In addition, the animats place lesser amounts of pheromone in the early iterations and more pheromone in later iterations.
The reason for this is that, in early iterations more change is needed. This allows the animats to explore more of the search space in the beginning and to exploit more of their current configuration near the end.
There is also a limit to the amount of pheromone of each species that can be stored on an element. The limit for the amount of pheromone for an element is the product of the connectivity degree of that element to its adjacent elements and the pheromone limit parameter. This allows densely connected elements to accumulate more pheromone. The formula for the amount of pheromone to be deposited is given as:

$$ph(a, I_i) = \frac{a_{col}}{a_{total}} \frac{I_i}{I_{total}} \tag{8}$$

where a is the animat, a_{col} is the number of elements adjacent to the animat's current location which are colonized by the animat's species, and a_{total} is the total number of elements adjacent to the animat's current location.

3.1.3 Death

The animat will die with a death probability which is fixed throughout the algorithm. The main purpose of death is to avoid overpopulation of animats. Overpopulation may influence the speed of computations. In addition, death can manipulate the algorithm's configurations by adding changes to animat's species.
The activation probability changes throughout the set so that early in a set, more animats are activated and therefore more animats die early in the set. The purpose of this is to have shorter life spans in the beginning, which allows more changes in the configuration. Later in the set, the animats are allowed to live longer and thus, there is less change and the solution is able to converge. An animat is removed from the list if it is selected to die.

3.1.4 Reproduction

If an animat is not selected for death, the algorithm proceeds to the reproduction step. An animat is selected for reproduction with fixed reproduction probability. However, the number of new animats that are produced depends on time (iterations).
In the first iteration of a set, the average number of animats born is β_{init} and it decreases linearly over time to β_{final} in the last iteration of a set. The changing birth rate serves to allow more change in earlier iterations, in which animats live for shorter lengths of time. The number of animats born is defined by:

$$\beta = \frac{-(\beta_{final} - \beta_{init})(I_i - 1)}{(1 - I_{total})} + \beta_{init} \tag{9}$$

The actual number of animats born is selected uniformly at random over a range, centered on the average birth rate for the iteration. The number of animats born can be up to β_{range} more or less than the specified average. The β_{range} is usually taken as 50 percent (Pao, 1989, Bahreininejad, 2004; Bahreininejad & Hesamfar, 2006).
New animats are the same species as their parents. If the element on which the parent is located is colonized by its own species, the newly born animats are all placed on that

element. However, if the element is colonized by the opposite species, only β_{stay} percent of the offspring animats are placed there. The remaining new animats will be placed on the element to which the parent animat moves in the next step.

The justification for this is that, if the parent animat is already at an element populated by its own colony and moves to another element, it should leave its offspring behind to help maintain the majority on that element. If the parent's species is not in majority, it should take most of its children to the new element in which it is trying to create a colony. However, the parent leaves some of its offspring behind so that some of its species remain at that element (in case that element really should be part of their colony).

There are two other constraints on reproduction. First, there is a limit of β_{limit} to how many offspring an animat can produce during its lifetime. This value is fixed throughout the algorithm and is the same for each animat. Once the limit is reached, the animat can no longer reproduce. This serves to prevent one species from taking over the entire FE mesh and forcing the other species into extinction.

Another problem arises when an animat reproduces and places all of its children on its current element. Once one of the children is activated, it will in turn reproduce and deposit more children on the same element before moving.

This overemphasizes that element and does not allow the colonies to change much from their original starting configuration. Because of this, animats are not able to reproduce until they have made a fixed minimum number of moves. This ensures that the mesh is explored and that new configurations are created by the reproduction and movement rather than being inhibited by these operations.

Therefore, the main aim of reproduction is to encourage the species of animats which have colonized an element. This can influence the rate of convergence of the overall algorithm.

3.1.5 Movement

Movement is by far the most important operation the animats perform. The animats' movement is the main mechanism by which the solution is produced. The animat can move to any element which is connected to its current location by an edge. There are two factors used to select a move from the set of possible moves. For each element to which the animat could move, the connectivity to other elements is examined. The animat should move to an element that is highly connected to other elements colonized by its own species. In addition, the animat should learn from the past and take into account the pheromone that other animats have deposited.

Throughout the course of a set, these two factors are weighted differently. Initially, the pheromone is weighted at ω_{pmin} with the weight increasing linearly to ω_{pmax}. Conversely, the connectivity is weighted at ω_{cmax} to begin and decreases linearly to ω_{cmin}. In this way, the configuration of the colonies changes greatly in early iterations and over time, learning is incorporated into the algorithm.

These basic factors drive the animats to create colonies of highly connected elements which are highly disconnected from the elements colonized by the opposing species. These factors are the basis of move selection.

The probability of moving to an adjacent element is proportional to the two combined factors. Specifically, the factors are combined according to Equation 10 to create a probability of moving to a specific element *e*.

$$pr(e) = ce_c + pe_p + \varepsilon \tag{10}$$

where e_c is the number of elements adjacent to e that are colonized by the animat's own species, c is the connectivity weight where $\omega_{c\min} \le c \le \omega_{c\max}$, e_p is the amount of pheromone of the animat's species on element e, p is the pheromone weight where $\omega_{p\min} \le p \le \omega_{p\max}$, and ε is a fixed amount added to prevent any probabilities from being zero. The values of c and p are given by the following equations:

$$c = \frac{(\omega_{c\max} - \omega_{c\min})(I_i - 1)}{1 - I_{total}} + \omega_{c\max} \tag{11}$$

$$p = \frac{(\omega_{p\max} - \omega_{p\min})(I_i - 1)}{1 - I_{total}} + \omega_{p\max} \tag{12}$$

In order to encourage animats to explore more of the FE mesh, the probability of selecting the move which would result in the animat returning to its previous location is reduced. A factor is used and initialized by a defined value and decreases linearly after the completion of each set until it reaches zero in the final set.

Therefore, animats move in order to find suitable locations to colonize their species. The movement is aimed to find locations (elements) for colonization so that such locations are highly connected while highly disconnected from the locations of the colonization of other animat's species. This is the main purpose of the ACO algorithm for partitioning graphs.

3.1.6 Between the sets

After each set of iterations, several other operations are performed based on the history of animates activities.

First, the algorithm looks for *mistakes* the animats have made. The algorithm looks for individual elements with a high percentage of their adjacent elements colonized by the opposite species. Therefore an element colonized by spices A having a high percentage of it adjacent elements colonized by species B is swapped to the B colony.

Next the algorithm looks for any *discontinuities* which may be generated during each set. In each set the program swaps the smallest discontinuous colonization of each species. This is carried out using a recursive greedy optimization procedure (Bahreininejad, 2004; Bahreininejad & Hesamfar, 2006) which will be discussed further. As was discussed earlier, any given configuration of animats on the FE mesh does not necessarily induce bisection. Therefore, if one species is colonizing more elements than the other, some elements will be swapped to the other species. The elements to be swapped are selected from the set of *border elements*, that is, elements that are adjacent to an element of the opposite colony. By changing the colony of only border elements, the algorithm continues in the direction the animats were heading, rather than selecting elements in a region that is completely dominated by one species and creating an irregularity. Elements are selected to be swapped by making the greedy choice from amongst the border elements. This is carried out, for triangular elements, according to the pseudo code procedure shown in Table 1.

After each element is selected, the swap is performed and the subsequent choices are made based on the new configuration of the colonies. At this point, the two colonies form bisection and this information is recorded.

```
WHILE
      Number of elements in colony A is not equal to number of elements in colony B
DO
      BEGIN
        Swap border elements of colony with greater number of elements based on
        priority rules
        Priority Rules
           First, randomly swap elements with two edges in boundary and will result in
           one edge in boundary after swapping
           Second, randomly swap elements with one edge in boundary and will result
           in one edge in boundary after swapping
           Third, randomly swap elements with one edge in boundary and will result in
           two edges in boundary after swapping
END
```

Table 1. The pseudo rules for the element swap procedure

Now, if this was not the final set, the mesh and population is prepared to start a new set by performing two more manipulations. The number of animats on the mesh may differ from the initial number of animats of both species. Usually after a set, the number of animats is higher than the initial number. The problem with this is that, if it continues, the number of animats grows so large that the computations become prohibitively expensive (since a percentage of animats are activated in each of the iterations). To correct this, the number of animats is reduced to the initial number. This is carried out by randomly removing animats until the correct population size is reached. This disruption of the colonies is negligible since each new set begins with a shake anyway.

Finally, the number of animats in the two species is equalized. Normally the number of animats in each species is quite close, since the colonies have been forced into bisection. However, this may not always be the case. The bisection may not guarantee that the two species have the same number of animats. To improve this possible problem, animats are added to equalize the number of animats in each species. Usually this is a very small number and thus is not problematic in consideration of the previous operation (reducing the number of animats to the initial number). The new animats are added only to elements where their own species is already in majority. Thus, this operation does not significantly alter the configuration of the colonies; it merely gives added strength to the colonies in which animats are added.

Following this operation, a new set is begun. Again, the time (iteration) is initialized and all probabilities relating to time are reset. Therefore, as the animats have converged on a possible solution, starting a new set allows the animats to move away from that solution in expectation of finding a better solution in case this solution was a local optimum. After a total of specified sets have been completed, the solution should represent partitioning with minimum cut-size.

3.2 Greedy algorithm for partition enhancement

The ACO algorithm should ensure the minimum cut-size and balanced partitions. However, sometimes discontinuous partitions may be developed where *islands* of partitions are generated (e.g. a domain is bisected and three partitions are generated where one of the partitions is composed of two separate partitions). A recursive greedy algorithm is used to improve the partition solutions given by the ACO and will swap the smallest generated discontinuity in each set.

The algorithm consists of two major parts. Initially, it searches and identifies each discontinuity. This is carried out by means of a recursive procedure which calls itself in order to give an index to an element and all its adjacent elements with similar spices.

Therefore, when an element colonized by one of the spices has been given an index, all its adjacent elements with the same species will also get the same index. This scheme is illustrated according to the pseudo code procedure shown in Table 2. The procedure in Table 2 is used by another procedure to index all the mesh elements using different index for each partition. This scheme is shown in Table 3.

After that the algorithm will swap the colonization of the smallest generated discontinuity with the colonization of other species in each set. This is carried out according to the pseudo code procedure shown in Table 3. Table 4 presents the pseudo code procedure for the proposed ACO-based algorithm for FE mesh recursive bisection.

3.3 Flying ants

Another approach to deal with cases where discontinuous partitions may occur was to assume that ants (animats) are able to fly which agrees with flying ants present in nature. This is especially true when a colony of ants may become localized and surrounded by ants of other colony and ants in the localized colony will find it impossible to search for better places to colonize.

```
Procedure GiveIndex(i)
BEGIN
    index of element i = index
    FOR k = 1 to Number of adjacent
      elements of element i
    IF colonization of adjacent element k = colonization of element i
    THEN
      GiveIndex(adjacent element k)
END
```

Table 2. The pseudo code for indexing an element of a discontinuity and all its adjacent elements with the same colonization

```
FOR I = 1 to NumElements do
  IF index of Element i = 0
  THEN
    BEGIN
      index = index + 1
      GiveIndex(i)
    END
Determine the index which refers to a discontinuity with smallest number of elements
in each species.
Swap the colonization of elements correspond to that index.
```

Table 3. The pseudo rule for indexing all the mesh elements using different indexing scheme and swapping process of the smallest discontinuity

This brings the idea of using flying ants approach to *prevent* ants getting stuck in localizations. In this approach, all the animats are capable of flying from the beginning of the optimization. The moving probability is determined using Equation (3) except that all the elements in the mesh are considered.

The animats can fly to the element with the highest moving probability in the mesh. However, the animats which already exist in the element with the highest moving probability prior to the arrival of new animats will have to move to the element with the second highest moving probability. This process is carried out by both spices of animats. The animats continue searching for better elements to colonize.

4. Neural Network Predictor

The Subdomain Generation Methods (SGM) proposed by Topping and Khan (1996) and followed on by Topping and Bahreininejad (1997) presented a technique which incorporates an optimization algorithm (genetic algorithms or Hopfield-type neural network) and a trained multi-layered feedforward neural network based on backpropagation algorithm. The trained backpropagation neural network is used to estimate the number of elements which will be generated inside every individual element of the coarse mesh after mesh generation procedure is carried out.

The estimated number of elements is incorporated into the optimization algorithm to decompose a coarse FE domain rather than decomposing the fine mesh generated from the refinement of the initial mesh.

A backpropagation-based multi-layered network with 5-12-8-6-1 (five units in intput layer, 12 units in the first hidden layer, 8 units in the second hidden layer, 6 units in the third hidden layer and finally one unit in the output layer) topology was adopted and trained which is capable of estimating a number up to 1760 triangular elements corresponding to the generated elements after mesh refinement is carried out.

The inputs to this network are the three scaled side lengths of each triangular element and the two scaled mesh parameters of each element. The scaling was made using one of the three mesh parameters (Topping & Bahreininejad, 1997).

The predicted number of elements generated in each element of the coarse mesh after mesh refinement, is used after the last set is completed. This information is used in a greedy algorithm which forces the solution to a bisection considering the same priority rules presented in Section 3.2.

The original SGM method partitions a FE mesh based on the coarse mesh using genetic algorithms (Topping & Khan, 1996). The generated subdomains are then refined individually using adaptive mesh refinement procedure.

In most cases, it has been observed that the total number of elements generated by the refinement of individual subdomains may not be the same as the total number of elements generated after the mesh refinement of the initial coarse mesh.

The presented method partitions the coarse mesh based on ACO and the SGM neural predictor approach and the resulting subdomains are mapped onto the final refined mesh.

```
BEGIN
 Randomly add animats to the mesh
 FOR Set = 1 to S
 BEGIN
  FOR iteration = 1 to I
  BEGIN
   FOR animat = 1to N
   BEGIN
    Activate e(iteration)% of animats
    Determine degree of species in each element
    IF animat activated
    BEGIN
     Add ph(animat, iteration) pheromone to animat's location
     Kill r_d% of animats of elements
     IF animat is not chosen for death
     BEGIN
      IF animat meets reproduction criteria
      BEGIN
       r_r% of animats reproduce
      ENDIF
      IF iteration is in shake length
      BEGIN
        Move animats randomly
      ELSE
          Move based on pheromone and connectivity
      ENDIF
     ENDIF
    ENDIF
  ENDFOR
  Evaporate Y% of pheromone
  ENDFOR
  Look for mistakes and swap elements
  Run the greedy algorithm to reduce discontinuities
  Record the bisection solution
  Reduce total number of animats to the initial value
  Equalize the number of animats in each species
 ENDFOR
 Return the best solution
END
```

Table 4. The pseudo rules for the proposed ACO algorithm for FE mesh decomposition

5. ACO Partitioning Case Study

A case study is presented to illustrate the ACO-based optimization approach for recursive FE mesh bisection. The optimization procedure is based on flying ants ACO using the neural network predictor. This method was compared with a greedy algorithm for partitioning FE meshes by Farhat.

The case study was carried out on a PC with Intel Pentium III 500 MHz processor. Twenty simulation runs were conducted and Table 5 represents the ACO parameters adopted for the final solutions. The computation times were less than 20 seconds for the proposed method and 38 seconds for the Farhat's method.

In this case study, an inverted U-shaped domain shown in Fig 2 was used for partitioning the domain into eight subdomains.

Fig 3 represents the resulting partitioned mesh by recursively bisecting the coarse mesh into eight subdomains using the proposed method. Fig 4 represents the partitioning of the refined mesh into eight subdomains using Farhat's method.

Table 6 shows the cut-size and the number of elements in each partition after recursive bisection using the proposed approach.

Table 7 shows the result obtained from the mesh decomposition into eight subdomains using Farhat's method.

The imbalance between the actual and the desired number of elements in each generated subdomain using the ACO method is shown in Table 6.

Parameter	**Value**
Number of iterations per set	100
Number of sets	10
Maximum shake length	5
Initial number of animats	100
Number of moves needed before an animat can reproduce	2
Maximum number of offspring per animat	10
Average number of animats born in first iteration	4
Expected number of animats born in final iteration	2
Minimum pheromone weight	0
Maximum pheromone weight	1
Minimum connection weight	250
Maximum connection weight	500
Pheromone limit	1000
Percentage range from average number of animats born	0.5
Maximum activation probability	0.8
Minimum activation probability	0.2
Death probability	0.035
Reproduction probability	0.011
Minimum probability for moving to an element	0.1
Reduction factor for returning to previous location	0.9
Percentage of offspring that stay on old location when not colonized	0.2
Percentage of adjacent elements needed for swap	0.75
Percentage of animats needed for majority	0.9
Evaporation rate	0.2

Table 5. Ant colony optimization run-time parameters

The load imbalance problem may have occurred from the inaccuracy of the predictive neural network to closely estimate the number of elements which will be generated in a single element of the coarse mesh after mesh refinement is carried out. A better trained neural network may improve the quality of the solutions.

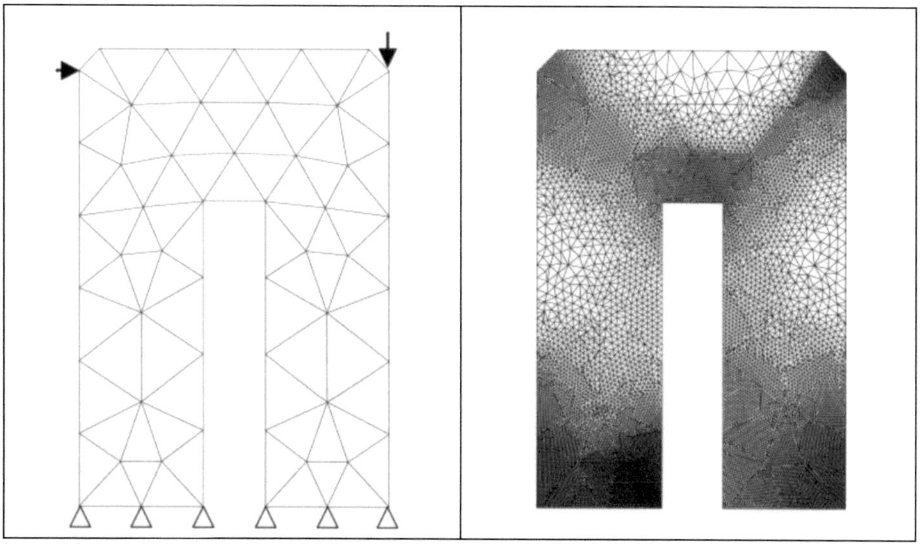

Figure 2. The initial mesh with 75 elements and the final refined mesh with 27155 elements

Figure 3. The initial coarse mesh and the final mesh devided into 8 subdomains using the proposed method

The imbalance of elements shown in Table 6 may not pose a serious threat. In fact, this may be used advantageously on coarse grained parallel networked computers where system architecture and the computational load among machines may differ (heterogeneous environment).

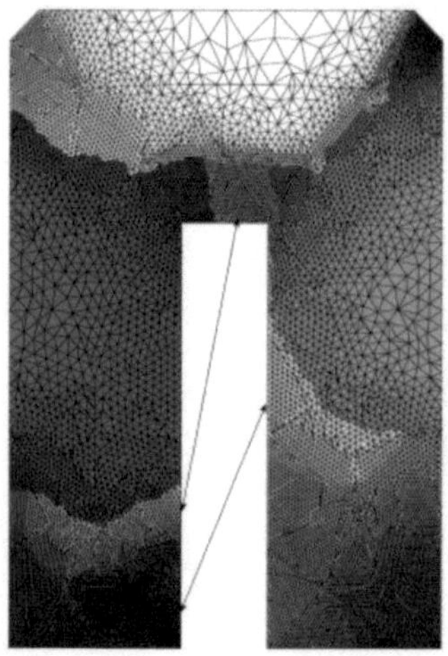

Figure 4. The the final mesh devided into 8 subdomains using the Farhat's method where the disjointed subdomains are shown with the arrows

On the other hand, Farhat's method offers the best load balancing results while producing a large number of interfacing edges. In parallel FE computations, the number of interfacing edges imposes a great deal of inter-processor communications. Thus the efficiency of parallel computations can greatly depend of lower cut-size (interfacing edges/nodes) between the subdomains. The proposed ACO method can produce much more appealing cut-sizes which reduces the inter-processor communications during parallel FE computations while producing satisfactory load balancing between partitions.

Subd. Number	**Num. of elements**	**Desired num. of elements**	**Diff.**
1	3266	3394.375	-128.375
2	3907	3394.375	512.625
3	3604	3394.375	209.625
4	3243	3394.375	-151.375
5	3881	3394.375	486.625
6	3400	3394.375	5.625
7	3153	3394.375	-241.375
8	2701	3394.375	-693.375
Total number of interfacing edges			370

Table 6. Comparison between the desired and the obtained number of elements in each subdomain and the number of interfacing edges using the proposed method

Subd. Number	Num. of elements	Desired num. of elements	Diff.
1	3395	3394.375	0.625
2	3395	3394.375	0.625
3	3395	3394.375	0.625
4	3395	3394.375	0.625
5	3395	3394.375	0.625
6	3395	3394.375	0.625
7	3395	3394.375	0.6255
8	3390	3394.375	-4.375
Total number of interfacing edges			1234

Table 7. Comparison between the desired and the obtained number of elements in each subdomain and the number of interfacing edges using Farhat's method

6. Conclusions

The application of ant colony optimization using swarm intelligence concepts, in combination with a trained feedforward neural network predictor which estimates the number of elements which will be generated within each element of the (initial) coarse mesh after mesh refinement is carried out, to the recursive bisection of finite elements meshes was described. This algorithm combines the features of the classical ant colony optimization technique with swarm intelligence to form a model which is an artificial system designed to perform a certain task. This model is used to solve the finite elements mesh recursive bisection problem which should ensure the minimum cut-size between bisections while maintaining balanced bisections.

A recursive greedy algorithm is also presented to improve the partition solutions given by the ant colony optimization algorithm and will swap the smallest generated discontinuity in each set of partitions.

A trained feedforward neural network predictor is used to estimate the number of elements which will be generated within each element of the coarse mesh after mesh refinement is carried out. This information is used to partition a coarse mesh using the proposed method based on the estimated number of elements after mesh refinement is conducted (i.e. partitioning is not carried out on the final refined mesh. The optimization method uses the estimated number of elements which will be generated after mesh generation is carried out and partitions the coarse mesh.)

The presented case study demonstrates the efficiency of the proposed method in comparison with a well known mesh decomposing algorithm. The predictive ant colony optimization technique produced good-quality solutions in short period of time.

7. References

Bahreininejad, A. & Topping, BHV. (1996). Finite element mesh partitioning using neural networks. *Advances in Engineering Software*, 27, 103-115

Bahreininejad, A. (2004). A hybrid ant colony optimization approach for finite elements mesh decomposition. *Structural and Multidisciplinary Optimization,* 28, 5, 307-316

Bahreininejad, A. & Hesamfar, P. (2006). Subdomain generation using emergent ant colony optimization. *Computers & Structures*, 84, 1719-1728

Bonabeau, E.; Dorigo, M. & Theraulaz, G. (2000). Inspiration for optimization from social insect behavior. *Nature*, 406, 39–42

Bui, TN. & Strite, LC. (2002). An ant system algorithm for graph bisection. *GECCO 2002: Proceedings of the Genetic and Evolutionary Computation Conference,* USA, Morgan Kaufmann, 43-51

Colorni, A.; Dorigo, M. & Maniezzo, V. (1991). Distributed optimization by ant colonies. *Proceedings of the first European Conference on Artificial Life,* USA, 134–142

Dorigo, M. & Gambardella, L. (1997). Ant colony system: a cooperative learning approach to the traveling salesman problem. *IEEE Transactions on Evolutionary Computation.* 1, 1, 53–66

Farhat, C. (1988). A simple and efficient automatic FEM domain decomposer. *Computers and Structures*, 28, 5, 579-602

Kuntz, P. & Snyers, D. (1994). Emergent colonization and graph partitioning. *Proceedings of the Third International Conference on Simulation of Adaptive Behavior: From Animals to Animats*, 494–500

Kuntz, P.; Layzell, P. & Snyers, D. (1997). A colony of ant-like agents for partitioning in VLSI technology. *In: Proceedings of the Fourth European Conference on Artificial Life*, 417-424

Maniezzo, V. & Carbonaro, A. (2001). Ant colony optimization: an overview. *Essays and surveys in metaheuristics*, Kluwer Academic Publishers, 21–44

Pao, YH. (1989). Adaptive Pattern Recognition and Neural Networks, Addison-Wesley, USA

Rumelhart, DE.; Hinton, GE. & Williams, RJ. (1986). Learning internal representation by error propagation. *Parallel distributed processing: explorations in the microstructure of cognition*, Rumelhart, DE. & McClelland, JL. (Eds.), MIT Press, USA, 1, 318-362

Simon, H.D. (1991). Partitioning of unstructured problems for parallel processing. *Computing Systems in Engineering,* 2, 2-3, 135-138

Topping, BHV. & Bahreininejad, A. (1997). *Neural Computing for Structural Mechanics*, Saxe-Coburg, UK

Topping, BHV. & Khan, AI. (1996). *Parallel Finite Element Computations,* Saxe-Coburg, UK

10

Swarm Intelligence and Image Segmentation

Sara Saatchi and Chih-Cheng Hung
Southern Polytechnic State University
USA

1. Introduction

Image segmentation plays an essential role in the interpretation of various kinds of images. Image segmentation techniques can be grouped into several categories such as edge-based segmentation, region-oriented segmentation, histogram thresholding, and clustering algorithms (Gonzalez & Woods, 1992). The aim of a clustering algorithm is to aggregate data into groups such that the data in each group share similar features while the data clusters are being distinct from each other.

The K-means algorithm is a widely used method used for finding the structure of data (Tou & Gonzalez 1974). This unsupervised clustering technique has a strong tendency to get stuck into local minima when finding an optimal solution. Therefore, clustering results are heavily dependent on the initial cluster centers distribution. Hence, the search for good initial parameters is a challenging issue and the clustering algorithms require a great deal of experimentation to determine the input parameters for the optimal or suboptimal clustering results.

Competitive learning model introduced in (Rumelhart & Zipser, 1986) is an interesting and powerful learning algorithm which can be used in unsupervised training for image classification (Hung, 1993). Simple Competitive Learning (SCL), shows stability over different run trials but this stable result is not always the global optima. In fact, in some cases the SCL converges to local optima over all run trials and the learning rate needs to be adjusted in the course of experimentation so that the global optimization can be achieved.

There are a number of techniques, developed for optimization, inspired by the behaviours of natural systems (Pham & Karaboga, 2000). Swarm intelligence (SI) including Ant Colony Optimization (ACO) introduced in (Dorigo et al., 1996) and Particle Swarm Optimization (PSO) introduced in (Kennedy & Eberhart, 1995) has been introduced in the literature as an optimization technique. There are several SI approaches for data clustering in the literature which use clustering techniques such as K-means algorithm. In most of these approaches ACO or PSO are used to obtain the initial cluster centers for the K-means algorithm. We propose a hybrid algorithm which combines SI with K-means. We also use the same method to combine SI with SCL.

Our aim is to make segmentation results of both K-means and SCL less dependent on the initial cluster centers and learning rate respectively. Hence, their results are more accurate and stabilized by employing the ACO and PSO optimization techniques. This improvement is due to the larger search space provided by these techniques. In addition, our methodology of considering both spatial and spectral features of the image helps to produce results with improved accuracy.

We have integrated the K-means and simple competitive learning algorithms with ACO in (Saatchi & Hung, 2005) and (Saatchi & Hung, 2006) respectively. In this paper we will study the hybridization of PSO with each of the K-means and the SCL algorithms. A thorough comparison study on ACO-K-means, PSO-K-means, ACO-SCL, PSO-SCL, K-means and SCL algorithms will also be provided.

2. Clustering Algorithms

2.1 K-means

The K-means algorithm, first introduced in (McQueen, 1967), is an is an unsupervised clustering algorithm which partitions a data set into a certain number of clusters. The K-means algorithm is based on the minimization of a performance index which is defined as the sum of the squared distances from all points in a cluster domain to the cluster center (Tou & Gonzalez, 1974). First K random initial cluster centers are chosen. Then, each sample is assigned to a cluster based on the minimum distance to the cluster centers. Finally cluster centers are updated to the average of the values in each cluster. This is repeated until cluster centers no longer change. Steps in the K-Means algorithm are:

Step 1: Initialize K initial cluster centers randomly.

Step 2: For each pixel, calculate the distance to the cluster centers and assign the pixel to a cluster which has the minimum distance to its center.

Step 3: Calculate the average of the pixel values in each cluster and take them as new cluster centers.

Step 4: Repeat steps 2 and 3 until new cluster centers converge to the previous ones.

The K-means algorithm tends to find the local minima rather than the global minima. Therefore, it is heavily influenced by the choice of initial cluster centers and the distribution of data. Most of the time the results become more acceptable when initial cluster centers are chosen relatively far apart since the main clusters in a given data are usually distinguished in such a way. If the main clusters in a given data are too close to one another in the feature space, the K-means algorithm fails to recognize these clusters. For its improvement the K-means algorithm needs to be enhanced with the optimization technique in order to be less dependent on a given data set and initial cluster centers.

2.2 Simple Competitive Learning

Competitive learning model introduced by Rumelhart and Zipser in (Rumelhart & Zipser, 1986) is an interesting and powerful learning algorithm which can be used in unsupervised training for image classification (Hung, 1993). Several different competitive learning algorithms have been proposed by neural network researchers. These algorithms are capable of detecting various features represented in input signals. They have been applied in several different areas such as graph bipartitioning, vector quantization, etc (Hertz & Krogh, 1991). In this section the unsupervised simple competitive learning will be briefly presented.

The neural network models are characterized by the topology, activation function and learning rules. The topology of the simple competitive learning algorithm can be represented as a one-layered output neural net. Each input node is connected to each output node. The number of input nodes is determined by the dimension of the training patterns. Unlike the output nodes in the Kohonen's feature map, there is no particular geometrical relationship between the output nodes in the simple competitive learning. In the following development, a 2-D one-layered output neural net will be used. During the process of training, the input vectors are fed into the network sequentially in time. The "trained" classes are represented by the output nodes and the center of each class is stored in the connection weights between input and output nodes.

The following algorithm outlines the operation of the simple competitive learning as applied to unsupervised training in (Hung, 1993); Let L denote the dimension of the input vectors, which for us is the number of spectral bands. We assume that a 2-D (N x N) output layer is defined for the algorithm, where N is chosen so that the expected number of the classes is less than or equal to N^2.

Step 1: Initialize weights $w_{ij}(t)$ ($i = 1, \ldots, L$ and $j = 1, \ldots, N \times N$) to small random values.

Steps 2 to 5 are repeated for each pixel in the training data set for each iteration.

Step 2: Present an input pixel $X(t) = (x_1, \ldots, x_L)$ at time t.

Step 3: Compute the distance d_j between x_i and each output node using

$$d_j = \sum_{i=1}^{L} (x_i - w_{ij}(t))^2 \tag{1}$$

where i, j, L, w_{ij} and x_i are similarly defined as in steps 1 and 2.

Step 4: Select an output node j^* which has the minimum distance. This node is called the best matching unit (BMU) or the winning node.

Step 5: Update weights of the winning node j^* using

$$w_{ij^*}(t+1) = w_{ij^*}(t) + \Delta(t)(x_i - w_{ij^*}(t)),\ i = 1, \ldots, L \ and\ 1 \le j^* \le N\ x\ N \tag{2}$$

where $\Delta(t)$ is a monotonically slowly decreasing function of t and its value is between 0 and 1.

Step 6: Select a subset of these N^2 output nodes as classes.

SCL shows stability over different run trials but this stable result is not always the global optima. In fact, in some cases the SCL converges to local optima over all run trials and the learning rate needs to be adjusted in the course of experimentation so that the global optimization can be achieved.

3. Swarm Intelligence

There are a number of techniques, developed for optimization, inspired by the behaviours of natural systems (Pham & Karaboga, 2000). In this study, we employ swarm intelligence, a natural optimization technique for optimizing both K-means and SCL algorithms.

3.1 Ant Colony Optimization

The ACO heuristic is inspired by the foraging behaviour of a real ant colony in finding the shortest path between the nest and the food. This is achieved by a deposited and accumulated chemical substance called *pheromone* by the passing ant which moves towards the food. In its searching the ant uses its own knowledge of where the smell of the food comes from (we call it as *heuristic information*) and the other ants' decision of the path toward the food (*pheromone information*). After it decides its own path, it confirms the path by depositing its own pheromone making the pheromone trail denser and more probable to be chosen by other ants. This is a learning mechanism ants possess besides their own recognition of the path. As a result of t this consultation with the ants' behaviors already shown in searching for the food and returning to the nest, the best path which is the shortest is marked between the location of the nest and the location of the food.

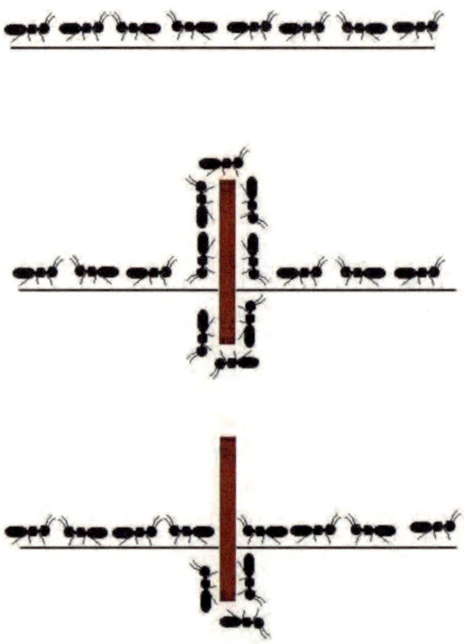

Figure 1. Ants finding the shortest path around an obstacle as a result of pheromone concentration

It was reported in the literature (Dorigo et al, 1996) that the experiments show when the ants have two or more fixed paths with the same length available from a nest to the food, they eventually concentrate on one of the paths and when the available paths are different in length they often concentrate on the shortest path. This is shown in Figure 1, when an obstacle is placed on the established path of ants, they first wander around the obstacle randomly. The ants going on a shorter path reach the food and return back to the nest more quickly. After a certain amount of time, the shorter path will be reinforced by pheromone. This path eventually becomes the preferred path of the ants (Zheng et al., 2003).

ACO uses this learning mechanism for the optimization. Furthermore, in the ACO algorithm, the pheromone level is updated based on the best solution obtained by a number of ants. The pheromone amount that is deposited by the succeeding ant is defined to be proportional to the quality of the solution it produces. For the real ants as shown in Figure 1, the best solution is the shortest path and it is marked with a strong pheromone trail. In the shortest path problem using the ACO algorithm, the pheromone amount deposited is inversely proportional to the length of the path.

In their research, Dorigo et al (1996) took the ant system as a colony of cooperating agents for solving the traveling salesman problem (TSP). Considering the short path problem, suppose for any pair of nodes V_i and V_j on the graph G, there is a connection cost attached to the edge (V_i, V_j) and the pheromone trail and heuristic information are stored on the edge.

The goal of an ACO heuristic is then to find the shortest path on graph G. In ACO heuristic, m artificial ants are normally used to find the best solution. Suppose an ant k is in vertex V_i at certain step i during its search process. This ant selects the connection with the probability (Dorigo et al., 1996):

$$P_{ij}^{k} = \begin{cases} \dfrac{\tau_{ij}^{\alpha}\eta_{ij}^{\beta}}{\sum_{h \in allowed_k(t,I)} \tau_{ih}^{\alpha}\eta_{ih}^{\beta}}, & j \in allowed_k(t,I) \\ 0, & otherwise \end{cases} \tag{3}$$

where P^k_{ij} is the probability of ant k choosing the path (V_i, V_j) from V_i. Parameters τ_{ij} and η_{ij} are the pheromone and heuristic information assigned to the edge (V_i, V_j) respectively, α and β are constants that determine the relative influence of the pheromone and heuristic information, and $allowed_k(t, I)$ is the set of vertices which is allowed to be visited according to problem constraints.

Then ant k moves and deposits a pheromone on the trail, which is defined below:

$$\Delta\tau_{ij}^{k} = \begin{cases} \dfrac{Q}{L_k}, & \text{if ant } k \text{ uses connection} (V_i, V_j) \text{ in its solution} \\ 0, & otherwise \end{cases} \tag{4}$$

where Q is a positive constant and L_k is the cost of the path used by ant k. After all m ants completed their path finding, the pheromone on each edge is updated according to the following formula:

$$(1-\rho)\tau_{ij} + \sum_{k=1}^{m} \Delta\tau_{ij}^{k} \Rightarrow \tau_{ij} \tag{5}$$

where ρ is the evaporation factor ($0 \le \rho \le 1$) which causes the earlier pheromones vanish over the iterations. Therefore, as the solution becomes better, the corresponding pheromone have more effect on the next solution rather than the earlier pheromones which correspond to the initial undesired solutions found.

This pheromone information will be a guide for the new set of ants. Each time, the current best solution is saved, and this process will be repeated until a termination criterion is met.

3.2 Particle Swarm Optimization

The PSO algorithm is inspired by the group behavior of schools of fish, flocks of birds and swarms of insects. As an example, birds are likely to find food in flocks, without knowing its location in advance. It seems that members of the flock buildup their intuition in order to find their nutriment. As sociobiologist E. O. Wilson (Wilson, 1975) has written, in reference to fish schooling, "In theory at least, individual members of the school can profit from the discoveries and previous experience of all other members of the school during the search for food. This advantage can become decisive, outweighing the disadvantages of competition for food items, whenever the resource is unpredictably distributed in patches." (p. 209)

The PSO algorithm consists of a swarm of particles flying through the search space (Kaewkamnerdpong & Bentley, 2005). Each particle's position is a potential solution to the problem. Each particle's velocity is modified based on its distance from its personal best

position and the global best position. In other words the particles move according to their experience and that of their neighbors which yields to the best fitness value.
Each particle *i* maintains the following information (van der Merwe & Engelbrecht, 2003):

- x_i, the current position of the particle,
- v_i, the current velocity of the particle,
- y_i, the personal best position of the particle (*pbest*); the best position visited so far by the particle, and
- $\hat{y}$, the global best position of the swarm (*gbest*); the best position visited so far by the entire swarm.

The objective function evaluates the positions of the particles. Personal best position (*pbest*) is then obtained as follows (van der Merwe & Engelbrecht, 2003):

$$y_i(t+1) = \begin{cases} y_i(t) & \text{if } f(x_i(t+1)) \geq f(y_i(t)) \\ x_i(t+1) & \text{if } f(x_i(t+1)) < f(y_i(t)) \end{cases} \tag{6}$$

where *f* is the objective function. The global best position (*gbest*) is obtained as follows (van der Merwe & Engelbrecht, 2003):

$$\hat{y}(t) \in \{y_0, y_1, ..., y_s\} = \min\{f(y_0(t)), f(y_1(t)), ..., f(y_s(t))\} \tag{7}$$

For each iteration of a PSO algorithm, v_i and x_i are updated as follows (van der Merwe & Engelbrecht, 2003):

$$v_i(t+1) = \omega v_i(t) + c_1 r_1(t)(y_i(t) - x_i) + c_2 r_2(t)(\hat{y}(t) - x_i(t)) \tag{8}$$

$$x_i(t+1) = x_i(t) + v_i(t+1) \tag{9}$$

where ω is the inertia weight which serves as a memory of previous velocities. The inertia weight controls the impact of the previous velocity. The cognitive component, $y_i(t)$–x_i represents the particle's own experience as to where the best solution is. The social component, $\hat{y}(t) - x_i$ represents the belief of the entire swarm as to where the best solution is. c_1 and c_2 are acceleration constants and $r_1(t)$, $r_2(t) \sim U(0,1)$,where $U(0,1)$ is a random number between 0 and 1.
The PSO algorithm is repeated until a termination criterion is reached or the changes in velocity get near to zero. A fitness function is used to evaluate the optimality of the solution. The following algorithm outlines a PSO based image classification (Omran et al., 2002). In this algorithm, a single particle x_i represents N cluster means such that $x_i=(m_{i1},...,m_{ij},...,m_{iN})$ where m_{ij} represents the *j*-th cluster centroid vector of the *i*-th particle. Therefore, a swarm represents a number of candidate cluster centers. The fitness of each set of cluster is measured using:

$$f(x_i, Z_i) = \omega_1 \bar{d}_{\max}(Z_i, x_i) + \omega_2(z_{\max} - d_{\min}(x_i)) \tag{10}$$

where z_{max}=2*s* -1 for an s-bit image; Z is a matrix representing the assignment of pixels to clusters of particle *i*. Each element z_{ijp} indicates if pixel z_p belongs to cluster C_{ij} of particle *i*. The constants w_1 and w_2 are user defined constants. Also,

$$\bar{d}_{\max}(Z_i, x_i) = \max_{j=1,\dots,N_c} \{ \sum_{\forall z_p \in C_{ij}} d(z_p, m_{ij}) / |C_{ij}| \} \tag{11}$$

is the maximum average Euclidean distance of particles to their associated clusters and

$$d_{\min}(x_i) = \min_{\forall j_1, j_2, j_1 \neq j_2} \{ d(m_{ij_1}, m_{ij_2}) \} \tag{12}$$

is the minimum Euclidean distance between any pair of clusters. The algorithm is as follows:

Step 1: Initialize cluster centers for each particle randomly.
Step 2: For each particle, assign each pixel to a cluster that has the minimum distance to its cluster center.
Step 3: Calculate the fitness function for each particle and find the global best solution.
Step 4: Update the cluster centers using Eqs. (8) and (9).
Step 5: Repeat the procedure until the stopping criterion is reached.

4. Swarm Intelligence and K-means

4.1 The Hybrid ACO-K-means Algorithm

We propose a hybrid ACO-K-means algorithm which uses the ACO to improve the performance of the K-means algorithm for clustering. The proposed algorithm starts by choosing the number of clusters and a random initial cluster center for each cluster. ACO plays its part in assigning each pixel to a cluster. This is done according to a probability which is inversely proportional to the distance (similarity) between the pixel and cluster centers and a variable, τ, representing the pheromone level. We define pheromone to be proportional to minimum distance between each pair of cluster centers and inversely proportional to the distances between each pixel and its cluster center. So the pheromone gets larger when the cluster centers are far apart and clusters are more compact (our criterion for best solution), making the probability of assigning a pixel to that cluster high. Pheromone evaporation is considered to weaken the influence of the previously chosen solutions, which are less likely to be desired. Similar to the K-means algorithm, at this stage new cluster centers are updated by calculating the average of the pixels in each cluster and this will be repeated until cluster centers no longer change. But unlike K-means, this algorithm doesn't stop here. We assume that the clustering job is performed by an ant and there are m ants repeating this job, each with their own random initialization, and they all will end up with a solution. A criterion is defined to find the best solution and the pheromone level is updated accordingly for the next set of m ants as a leading guide. If the termination criterion is satisfied, the algorithm will be terminated. Hence, an optimal solution is obtained.

The algorithm starts by assigning a pheromone level τ and a heuristic information η to each pixel. Then each ant will assign each pixel to a cluster with the probability distribution P derived from Eq. (13), (Dorigo et al., 1996):

$$P_i(X_n) = \frac{[\tau_i(X_n)]^{\alpha}[\eta_i(X_n)]^{\beta}}{\sum_{j=0}^{K}[\tau_j(X_n)]^{\alpha}[\eta_j(X_n)]^{\beta}} \tag{13}$$

where $P_i(X_n)$ is the probability of assigning pixel X_n to cluster i, $\tau_i(X_n)$ and $\eta_i(X_n)$ are the pheromone and heuristic information assigned to pixel X_n in cluster i respectively, α and β are constant parameters that determines the relative influence of the pheromone and heuristic information, and K is the number of clusters. Heuristic information $\eta_i(X_n)$ is obtained from:

$$\eta_i(X_n) = \frac{\kappa}{CDist(X_n, CC_i) * PDist(X_n, PC_i)} \tag{14}$$

where X_n is the nth pixel, CC_i is the ith spectral cluster center and PC_i is the ith spatial cluster center. $CDist\ (X_n, CC_i)$ is the Euclidean distance between X_n and CC_i, considering the color features of the pixels and $PDist\ (X_n, PC_i)$ is the Euclidean distance between X_n and PC_i, considering the position of the pixels on the image. Constant κ is used to balance the value of η with τ.

The value for the pheromone level τ assigned to each pixel is initialized to 1 so that it does not have any effect on the probability at the beginning. This pheromone gets larger over the iterations which we describe later.

Suppose m number of ants is chosen for clustering an image. Each ant is giving its own clustering solution. After m ants have done their clustering, the current best solution is chosen and the assigned pheromone to this solution is incremented. All the cluster centers are updated using the cluster centers of the current best solution. The next set of ants is inspired from the previous set. In each of the iterations, each one of the m ants search for a solution based on its own heuristic knowledge and the best solution found by the previous m ants. This is repeated a certain amount of times until the overall best solution is obtained.

The best solution of the m solutions found in each of iterations is selected according to two factors; Euclidean distance between cluster centers in terms of spectral values (separateness of clusters), and sum of the Euclidean distances between each pixel and its cluster center, in terms of spectral and spatial values (similarity and compactness of each cluster). To choose the best solution: 1) the Euclidean distance between cluster centers in terms of spectral signatures should be large so the clusters are more distinct, 2) the sum of the Euclidean distances between each pixel and its cluster center in terms of spectral signatures should be small so that each cluster becomes more homogeneous, and 3) the sum of the Euclidean distances between each pixel and its cluster center in terms of spatial signatures should be small so that each cluster becomes more compact. To achieve the first one, for each clustering performed by ant k ($k = 1,\dots,m$), we compute the distances between every pair of cluster centers and sort these distances. Then we select the minimum distance $Min(k)$. Now we compare all these minimums performed by all the ants, and select the maximum of them [$MinMax(k)$]. To achieve the second and third, for each clustering performed by ant k we compute the sum of the distances between each pixel and its cluster center, and sort these sums of the distances. Then we select the maximum and compare all these maximums performed by all ants, and select the minimum of them. The second maximum and third maximum of the solutions are compared in the same way and the minimum is selected. Each time a solution is selected it gets an additional vote. The solution with the largest vote is selected as the best solution.

After the best solution is found, the pheromone value is updated according to Eq. (15) (Li & Xu, 2003):

$$\tau_i(X_n) \leftarrow (1-\rho)\,\tau_i(X_n) + \Sigma_i\, \Delta\tau_i(X_n) \tag{15}$$

where ρ is the evaporation factor ($0 \le \rho \le 1$) which causes the earlier pheromones vanish over the iterations. Therefore as the solution becomes better, the corresponding pheromone have more effect on the next solution rather than the earlier pheromones which correspond to the initial undesired solutions found. The parameter $\Delta\tau_i(X_n)$ in Eq. (15) is the amount of pheromone added to previous pheromone by the succeeded ant, which is obtained from:

$$\Delta\tau_i(X_n) = \begin{cases} \dfrac{Q * Min(k')}{AvgCDist(k',i) * AvgPDist(k',i)} & \text{if } X_n \text{ is a member of cluster i.} \\ 0 & \text{otherwise.} \end{cases} \quad (16)$$

In Eq. (16), Q is a positive constant which is related to the quantity of the added pheromone by ants. $Min(k')$ is the minimum distance between every two cluster centers obtained by ant k' (the winner ant) in spectral feature space. $AvgCDist(k',i)$ is the average of the spectral Euclidean distances and $AvgPDist(k',i)$ is the average of the spatial Euclidean distances between all pixels in cluster i and their spectral cluster center and spatial cluster center obtained by ant k', respectively. $Min(k')$ causes the pheromone become larger when clusters get more far apart and hence raise the probability. $AvgCDist(k',i)$ and $AvgPDist(k',i)$ cause the pheromone become larger when the cluster has more similar pixels and is more compact respectively. In other words, the more the $Min(k')$ is, the more far apart our clusters are which is desired and the larger the pheromone is. The less the $AvgCDist(k',i)$ and $AvgPDist(k',i)$ are, the more similar and compact our clusters are which is desired and the larger the pheromone is.

Next, cluster centers are updated using the cluster centers of the best solution. This algorithm is repeated a certain amount of times until the very best solution is obtained.

The Hybrid ACO-K-means algorithm is described below:

Step 1: Initialize pheromone level assigned to each pixel to 1, the number of clusters to K and number of ants to m.

Step 2: Initialize m sets of K random cluster centers to be used by m ants.

Step 3: Let each ant, assign each pixel X_n to one of the clusters (i), randomly, with the probability distribution $P_i(X_n)$ given in Eq. (13).

Step 4: Calculate new cluster centers; If the new cluster centers are approximately equal to the old ones, go to next step. Otherwise, go to Step 3.

Step 5: Save the best solution among the m solutions found.

Step 6 Update the pheromone level for each pixel according to the best solution using Eqs. (15) and (16).

Step 7: Assign cluster center values of the best clustering solution to the clusters centers of all ants.

Step 8: If the termination criterion is satisfied go to the next step. Otherwise, go to Step 3.

Step 9: Output the optimal solution.

4.2 The Hybrid PSO-K-means Algorithm

As discussed in section 3.2, in the PSO based clustering presented in (Omran et al., 2002) the cluster centers assigned to particles were initialized randomly. Each pixel was distributed to a cluster with minimal Euclidean distance. Then PSO was used to refine the cluster centers using a fitness function. In (van der Merwe & Engelbrecht, 2003) the K-means algorithm was applied to feed one particle of the initial swarm and the rest of the swarm were initialized randomly. Then the same algorithm described above is employed. We propose a new hybridization of PSO-K-means algorithm where the K-means is applied to all particles and solutions are evaluated in a way similar to the evaluation used in the proposed ACO-K-means algorithm.

The proposed PSO-K-means algorithm is presented as follows:

Step 1: Initialize the number of clusters to K and number of particles to m.

Step 2: Initialize m sets of K random cluster centers to be used by m particles.

Step 3: For each particle, let each pixel x belong to a cluster in which it has the smallest Euclidean distance to the centroid.

Step 4: Calculate new cluster centers; If the new cluster centers converge to the old ones, go to the next step. Otherwise, go to Step 3.

Step 5: Save the best solution found so far performed by each particle. Call it *pbest* or personal best solution.

Step 6: Save the best solution among the m personal best solutions found. Call it *gbest* or global best solution.

Step 7: Update cluster centers of each particle according to the cluster center values of the *pbest* and *gbest* solution, using Eqs. (8) and (9).

Step 8: If the termination criterion is satisfied go to next step. Otherwise, go to Step 3.

Step 9: Output the optimal solution.

5. Swarm Intelligence and Simple Competitive Learning

5.1 The Hybrid ACO-SCL Algorithm

We apply the ACO to simple competitive learning algorithm and investigate its performance. Similar to our previous hybrid algorithms described in section 4, the pheromone and heuristic information are defined to satisfy the clustering criteria which include the similarity of data in each cluster, distinction of the clusters and compactness of each cluster. At the end of all iterations, the best solution is selected in the same way as what we used for the ACO-K-means algorithm.

The ACO-SCL algorithm is described as follows. Let L denote the dimension of the input vectors, which for us is the number of spectral bands. We assume that a 2-D ($N \times N$) output layer is defined for the algorithm, where N is chosen so that the expected number of the classes is less than or equal to N^2. Here weights of the nodes contain cluster center values.

Step 1: Initialize the number of clusters to K and the number of ants to m. Initialize pheromone level assigned to each pixel to 1 so that it does not have any effect on the probability using later at the beginning.

Step 2: Initialize m sets of K different random cluster centers to be used by m ants.

Step 3: Let each ant, assign each pixel X_n to one of the clusters (i), randomly, with the probability distribution $P_i(X_n)$ given in Eq. (13) where heuristic information $\eta_i(X_n)$ is obtained from Eq. (14).

Step 4: For each input pixel the cluster center of the cluster which it belongs to is considered as the BMU. Calculate new cluster centers using:

$$C_i(t+1) \leftarrow C_i(t) + \Delta(t)(x_i - C_i(t)),\ i = 1, \ldots, L \qquad (17)$$

where Δ(t) is a monotonically slowly decreasing function of t and its value is between 0 and 1. *L* is the number of spectral bands.
Step 5: Save the best solution among the *m* solutions found.
Step 6: Update the pheromone level for each pixel according to the best solution. The pheromone value is updated according to Eq. (15).
Step 7: Assign cluster center values of the best clustering solution to the clusters centers of all ants.
Step 8: If the termination criterion is satisfied go to next step. Otherwise, go to Step3.
Step 9: Output the optimal solution.

5.2 The Hybrid PSO-SCL Algorithm

The PSO-SCL algorithm which combines the PSO and SCL, is described as follows. Let *L* denote the dimension of the input vectors, which for us is the number of spectral bands. We assume that a 2-D ($N \times N$) output layer is defined for the algorithm, where *N* is chosen so that the expected number of the classes is less than or equal to N^2. Here weights of the nodes contain cluster center values.
Step 1: Initialize the number of clusters to *K* and the number of particles to *m*.
Step 2: Initialize *m* sets of *K* different random cluster centers to be used by *m* particles.
Step 3: For each particle, let each pixel *x* belong to a cluster in which it has the smallest Euclidean distance to the centroid.
Step 4: For each input pixel the cluster center of the cluster which it belongs to is considered as the BMU. Calculate new cluster centers using Eq. (17).
Step 5: Save the best solution found so far performed by each particle. Call it *pbest* or personal best solution.
Step 6: Save the best solution among the *m* personal best solutions found. Call it *gbest* or global best solution.
Step 7: Update cluster centers of each particle according to the cluster center values of the *pbest* and *gbest* solution, using Eq. (8).
Step 8: If the termination criterion is satisfied go to next step. Otherwise, go to Step 3.
Step 9: Output the optimal solution.

6. Simulation Results

Experimental results from our proposed hybrid algorithms were compared with those of the K-means and the SCL algorithms, and discussed in this section. Since the SCL is very dependent on the learning rate, i.e. $\Delta(t)$ in Eq. (17), we performed some experiments on choosing a value for $\Delta(t)$. Considering that $\Delta(t)$ is a monotonically slowly decreasing function of *t* and its value is between 0 and 1, we suggest the following formula:

$$\Delta(\mathrm{t}) = \frac{0.2}{t^r + 1} \tag{18}$$

where *t* and *r* denote iteration and a rate which is a constant that we obtained by experiments, respectively. The experiments were performed over 20 run trials on several different images, for *r* from 10 to 50 incrementing by 10. Two of them reported in this chapter. Experiments showed better results for $r = 10$. Therefore, the experiment was repeated similarly but this time for r from 1 to 10 incrementing by 1. This experiment showed better results for r between 1 and 5. In our experiments r is chosen to be 2.

The ACO-K-means and ACO-SCL algorithms were shown to be dependant on parameterization as well. Parameters used in these algorithms, other than r include κ, Q, ρ, α, and β. Parameters α, β and κ are used to keep the values of τ and η in the same order. Parameter Q controls the added amount of pheromone and ρ eliminates the influence of the earlier added pheromone. Considering that r should be between 1 and 5 from the previous experiment, r was chosen to be 2. Evaporation factor was set to be $\rho = 0.8$. According to the performance of the experiments, parameters κ and Q were shown to have little influence on the results, while α and β were more influential. The parameter values tested were as follows: κ =1000 and 10000, Q =10 and 100, α =0.1 to 50 incrementing by 10, and β =0.1 to 50 incrementing by 10. Each experiment was performed for 20 run trials on each image. There were unacceptable results when β =0.1. There were good results when α =0.1, for images shown here but they were unstable. There were some sets of parameters that still did well for one of the images but not for the other. Knowing that α should be small while β should not be small, we set up another experiment: κ =1000 and 10000, Q =10 and 100, α =0.1 to 2 incrementing by 0.1, β =50 to 5 decrementing by 5. All the results were acceptable but not all of them were stable. So in this experiment stability of the results was examined. Experimental results show that β should not be very large, otherwise it becomes unstable. When β is chosen to be 5 and α is between 0.1 and 2, the result showed to be more stabled. From these sets of experiments, the chosen parameters are as follows: $r = 2$, $\rho = 0.8$, $\alpha = 2$, $\beta = 5$, $\kappa = 1000$, and $Q = 10$. The number of ants was chosen to be $m = 5$.

The PSO-K-means and PSO-SCL algorithms also include a set of parameters to be determined empirically. The parameters were chosen as suggested by (van der Merwe and Engelbrecht, 2003) which resulted in good convergence. Parameters were set as follows: c_1, $c_2 = 1.49$ and $\omega = 0.72$. The number of ants was chosen to be $m = 10$.

We examined the proposed hybrid algorithms and compared the results with those of the K-means and the SCL algorithms in Figs. 2 to 5. Images used include flamingo, cubes, aurora and river. The number of clusters to be found in all images is 3 except for cubes which is 4. The most dominant results of the algorithms over 20 different run trials are presented. The improvement of the ACO and PSO on the K-means algorithm is obvious in all of the images tested. In cubes, flamingo and Aurora images it can be seen that the K-means algorithm has unstable results and in some cases it misses some clusters while the ACO-K-means and PSO-K-means algorithms are more stable and they clearly recognize the clusters. In the river image the results show that the K-means algorithm can generate stable results and the ACO-K-means algorithm seems to be less stable, but it is apparent that even for this image, the ACO-K-means algorithm can improve the classification results. This is also the case with the ACO-SCL and PSO-SCL algorithms as opposed to SCL in Aurora image. Results on Aurora image clearly show that the ACO and PSO algorithms can improve the SCL in cases where the SCL algorithm is trapped into local optima. To further investigate the behavior of the algorithms described, we obtained the classification accuracy percentage of the results on the river image. Each algorithm is run 30 times on the river image, shown in Fig. 5 (a). Then , by comparing the classification results with the ground truth data, shown in Fig. 5 (h), the error matrix for each classified image is calculated. The best, worst and average cases are shown in Fig. 6. The stability of the SCL algorithm over the ACO-SCL and the PSO-SCL algorithms can be inferred from this figure. But, as it was stated before in the aurora image this stable result is not always a global optima. Similarly, it can be inferred from Fig. 6 that the K-means algorithm is more stable than the ACO-K-means algorithm in the case of river image. Nevertheless, results of the ACO-K-means algorithm include some very good results with much higher classification accuracy percentage than those of the K-means algorithm.

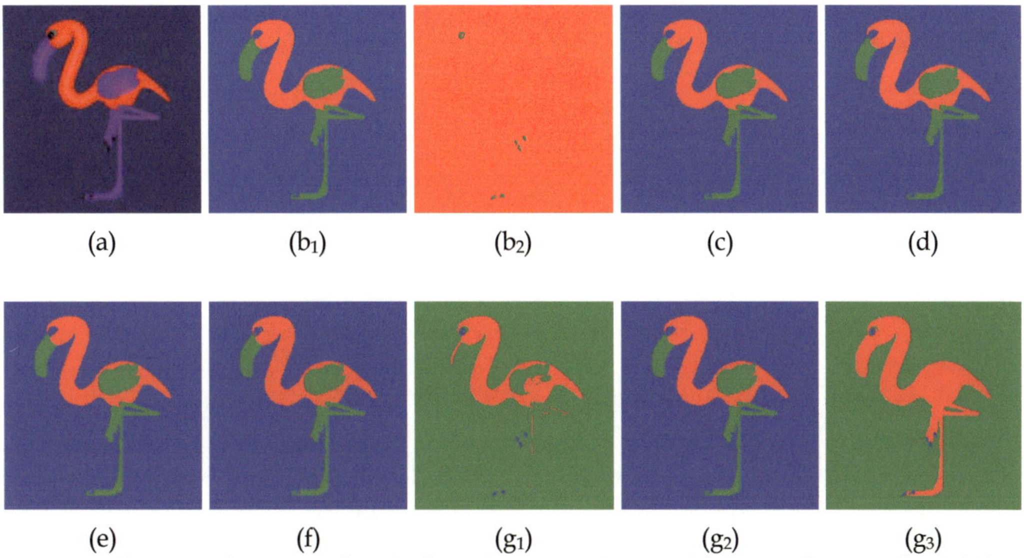

Figure 2. The most dominant classified results among 20 runs (a) Original image, (b1 & b2) K-means (c) Hybrid ACO-K-means, (d) Hybrid PSO-K-means, (e) SCL, (f) Hybrid ACO-SCL, (g1, g2, & g3) Hybrid PSO-SCL

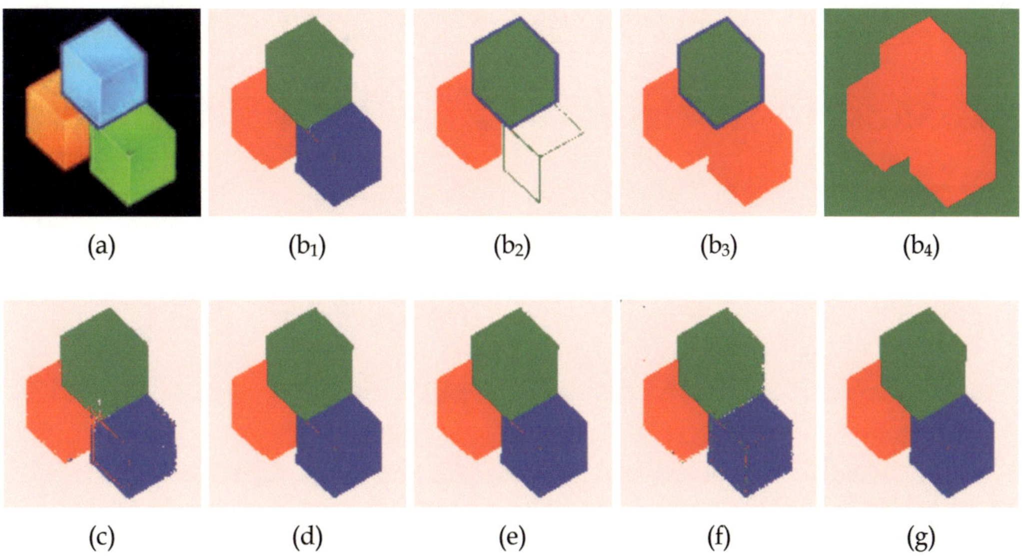

Figure 3. The most dominant classified results among 20 runs (a) Original image, (b_1, b_2, b_3 & b_4) K-means, (c) Hybrid ACO-K-means, (d) Hybrid PSO-K-means, (e) SCL, (f) Hybrid ACO-SCL, (g) Hybrid PSO-SCL

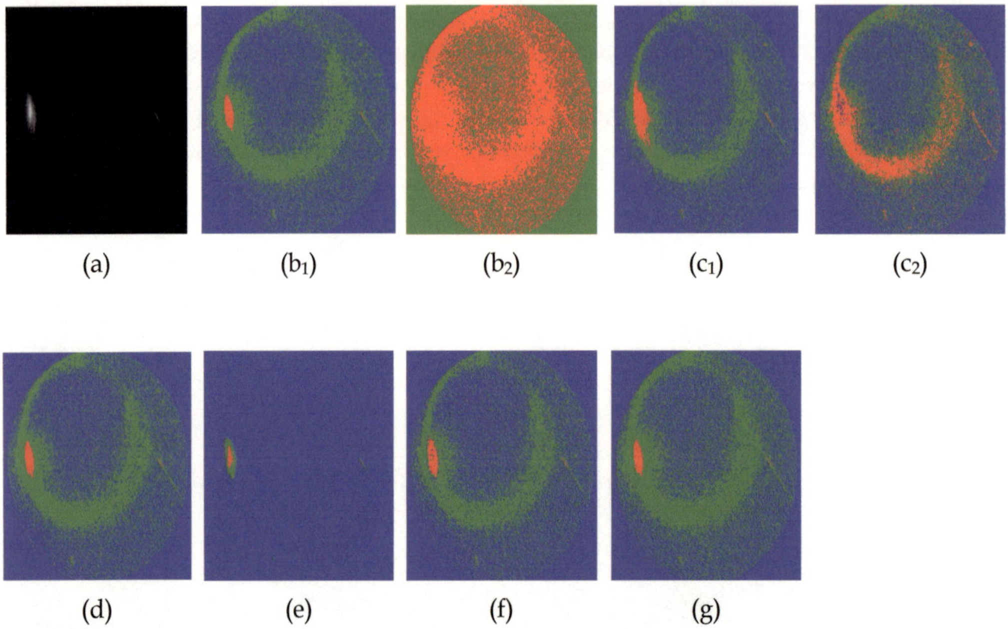

Figure 4. The most dominant classified results among 20 runs (a) Original image, (b_1 & b_2) K-means, (c_1 & c_2) Hybrid ACO-K-means, (d) Hybrid PSO-K-means, (e) SCL, (f) Hybrid ACO-SCL, (g) Hybrid PSO-SCL

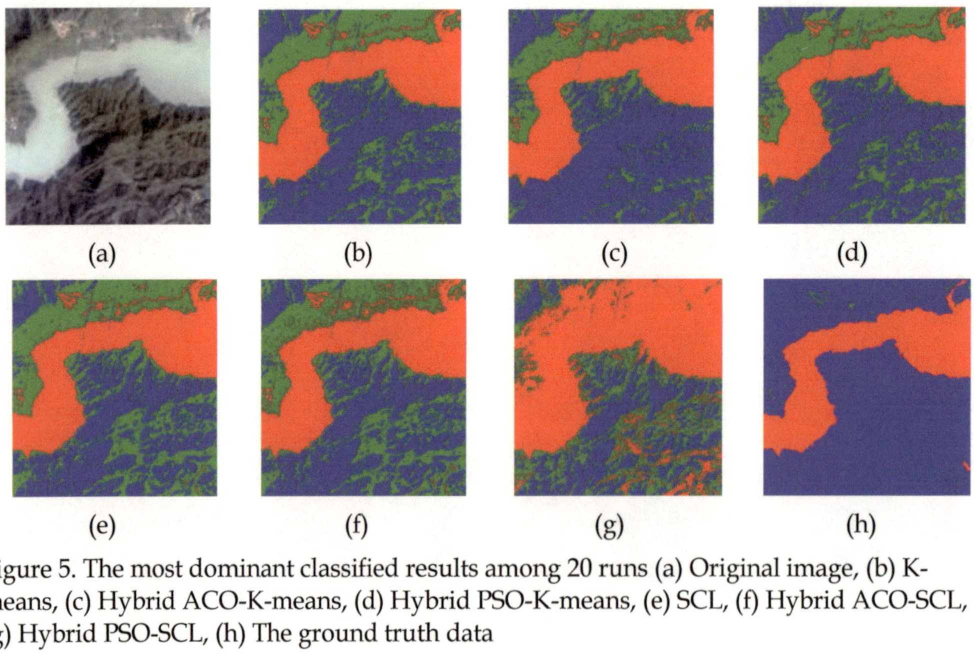

Figure 5. The most dominant classified results among 20 runs (a) Original image, (b) K-means, (c) Hybrid ACO-K-means, (d) Hybrid PSO-K-means, (e) SCL, (f) Hybrid ACO-SCL, (g) Hybrid PSO-SCL, (h) The ground truth data

Besides, the stability of the K-means algorithm over the ACO-K-means algorithm inferred from fig. 6, is a particular case, i.e. for the river image. The K-means algorithm is not stable in general. In fact in the case of flamingo and cubes, ACO-K-means algorithm produced more stabled results compared to K-means algorithm.

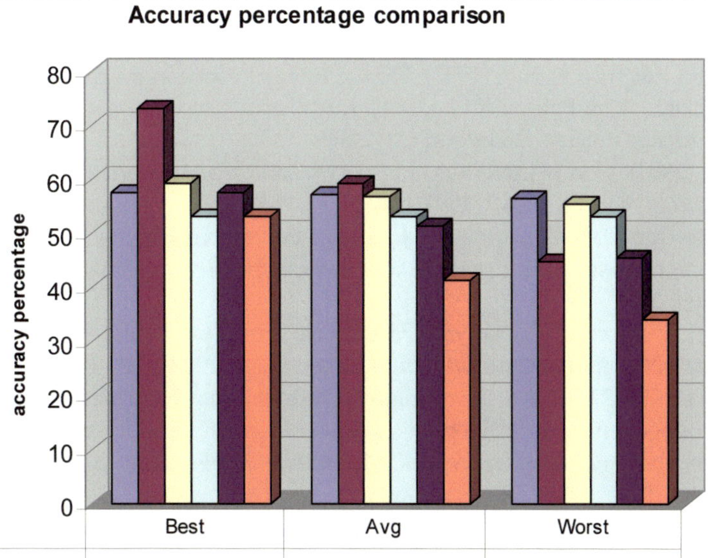

	Best	Avg	Worst
K-means	57.6714	57.16168276	56.5216
ACO-K-means	73.1819	59.32477586	44.8396
PSO-K-means	59.3386	56.73025862	55.3813
SCL	53.0684	53.0684	53.0684
ACO-SCL	57.4838	51.25234483	45.3872
PSO-SCL	53.0472	41.3774069	34.1707

Figure 6. Comparison of the results generated by algorithms using error matrix evaluation on the river image

7. Conclusion

Experimental results showed that SI techniques can improve the K-means and the SCL algorithms in recognizing the clusters. The K-means algorithm often fails to realize clusters since it is heavily dependent on the initial cluster centers. The ACO-K-means and PSO-K-means algorithms provides a larger search space compared to the K-means algorithm. By employing these algorithms for clustering, the influence of the improperly chosen initial cluster centers will be diminished over a number of iterations. Therefore, these algorithms are less dependent on randomly chosen initial seeds and is more likely to find the global optimal solution.

We have also shown that SI can be beneficial to the SCL algorithm. SI can help SCL find the global optima using the same parameter set and learning rate as those used in the SCL and recognize the clusters where the SCL fails to do, in some cases. This can be advantageous since for SCL to find the global optima the learning rate should be adjusted in the course of experimentation.

8. References

Dorigo, M.; Maniezzo, V. & Colorni, A. (1996). Ant system: optimization by a colony of cooperating agents, In: *IEEE Transactions on Systems, Man and Cybernetics*, Part B, Vol. 26, 1996, pp. 29-41

Gonzalez, R.C. & Woods, R.E. (1992). Digital Image Processing. Addison-Wesley, 1992

Hertz, J.; Krogh, A. & Palmer R.G. (1991). Introduction to the theory of neural computation, Addison-Wesley, Redwood City, 1991

Hung C.C. (1993). Competitive learning networks for unsupervised training, *INT. J. Remote Sensing*, vol. 14, no. 12, 1993, pp. 2411-2415

Kaewkamnerdpong, B. & Bentley, P.J. (2005). Perceptive Particle Swarm Optimisation: an Investigation, *IEEE Swarm Intelligence Symposium*, pp. 169-176, Pasadena, CA, USA, June, 2005

Kennedy, J. & Eberhart, R. (1995). Particle Swarm Optimization, In: *Proceedings of IEEE International Conference on Neural Networks*, pp.1942-1948, 1995

Li, Y. & Xu, Z. (2003). An Ant Colony Optimization Heuristic for Solving Maximum Independent Set Problems, In: *Proceedings of the 5th International Conference on Computational Intelligence and Multimedia Applications*, pp. 206-211, Xi'an, China, Sept. 2003

McQueen, J.B. (1967). Some Methods of Classification and Analysis of Multivariate Observations, In L. M. LeCam and J. Neyman, editors, *Proceedings of the Fifth Berkeley Symposium on Mathematical Statistic and Probability*, pp. 281-297, University of California Press, Berkley, CA, 1967

Omran, M.; Salman, A. & Engelbrecht, A.P. (2002). Image Classification Using Particle Swarm Optimization, 2002

Pham, D.T. & Karaboga, D. (2000). Intelligent Optimization Techniques: Genetic Algorithms, Tabu Search, *Simulated Annealing and Neural Networks*, Springer, 2000

Rumelhart, D.E. & Zipser, D. (1986). Feature discovery by competitive learning, In *Parallel Distributed Processing: Explorations in the Microstructure of Cognition*, eds. J.L. McClelland & D.E. Rumelhart, MIT Press, Cambridge, M.A., 1986, pp. 151-193

Saatchi, S. & Hung, C.C. (2005). Hybridization of the Ant Colony Optimization with the K-means Algorithm for Clustering, Image Analysis, *Proceedings Lecture Notes in Computer Science* 3540, 2005, pp. 511- 520

Saatchi, S.; Hung, C.C. & Kuo, B.C. (2006). A comparison of the improvement of k-means and simple competitive learning algorithms using ant colony optimization, In *Proceedings of the 7th International Conference on Intelligent Technology*, Taipei, Taiwan, December, 2006

Tou, J.T. & Gonzalez, R.C. (1974). Pattern Recognition Principles, Addison-Wesley, 1974

van der Merwe, D.W. & Engelbrecht A.P. (2003). Data Clustering Using Particle Swarm Optimization, 2003 *Congress on Evolutionary Computation*, 2003, pt. 1, Vol.1, pp. 215-220

Wilson, E.O. (1975). Sociobiology: the new synthesis, Belk Press, Cambridge, MA, 1975

Zheng, H.; Zheng, Z. & Xiang Y. (2003). The application of ant colony system to image textute classification [textute read texture], In: *Proceedings of the 2nd International Conference on Machine Learning and Cybernetics*, vol. 3, pp. 1491-1495, Xi'an, China, Nov. 2003

11

Particle Swarm Optimization – Stochastic Trajectory Analysis and Parameter Selection

M. Jiang, Y. P. Luo and S. Y. Yang
Tsinghua University
China

1. Introduction

Two important topics in Particle Swarm Optimization (PSO) research filed are trajectory analysis of particles and parameter selection method. Trajectory analysis is important because it can help to determine where the position of each particle is at each evolutionary step, and consequently it can help to clarify the running mechanism of PSO algorithm, so as to explain why and when PSO algorithm can be successful to solve optimization problems. Parameter selection of PSO algorithm is important because the performance of PSO algorithm is sensitive to the chosen parameters.

Till now, some research works have been published in literatures to investigate both of these two topics, but unfortunately, the trajectory analysis is based on simplified deterministic algorithms, regardless of the randomness in real PSO algorithm; and the parameter selection is based on experimental results instead of theoretical results.

This chapter is proposed to investigate both of these two important topics. In this chapter, the trajectory of particle in a general PSO algorithm is theoretically investigated, considering the randomness thoroughly. For arbitrary dimension d of an arbitrary particle i in the general particle swarm system, the update equations investigated in this chapter are given in Eqs. (1) and (2), where t is the evolutionary step, V is the velocity of particle i, X is the position of particle i, P_i is the history best position found by particle i, and P_g is the history best position found by the total swarm.

$$V_i^d(t+1) = \omega V_i^d(t) + c_1 r_{1,i}^d(t)(P_i^d(t) - X_i^d(t)) + c_2 r_{2,i}^d(t)(P_g^d(t) - X_i^d(t)) \tag{1}$$

$$X_i^d(t+1) = aX_i^d(t) + bV_i^d(t+1) \tag{2}$$

By regarding each particle's position on each evolutionary step as a stochastic vector, the general PSO algorithm determined by five-dimensional parameter tuple $\{\omega, c_1, c_2, a, b\}$ is formally analyzed using stochastic process theory. Because the position of particle at each step is stochastic and can not be determined directly, its expected value and variance are investigated instead of the position itself. To make the analysis possible, the particle swarm is supposed to be in stagnation phase.

At the same time, the relationship between convergent speed of particle's trajectory and parameter sets is studied. Those results give some hints on how the chosen parameters can influence the performance of PSO algorithm, and thus parameter selection guideline is given. According to the analysis result, it is believed that parameters {a, b} would only increase the complexity of PSO algorithm without enhancing performance of PSO algorithm, thus it is suggested to fix both of them to be 1 in PSO algorithm. For more details, see Section 4.

Then, a set of suggested parameter {ω=0.715, c_1=c_2=1.7} is given, which is compared against three sets of parameters which are proposed in literatures.

The structure of this chapter is as follows. Section 2 overviews related works. Stochastic convergence analysis of the general PSO algorithm is investigated in Section 3. Some parameter selection guidelines are given in Section 4; and a set of parameters is suggested. In Section 5, experiments are conducted to compare different parameter sets. Section 6 concludes this chapter.

2. Related Works

Ozcan and Mohan published the first theoretical studies of particle trajectories (Ozcan & Mohan, 1998; Ozcan & Mohan, 1999). In their first study (Ozcan & Mohan, 1998), a simplified PSO system was considered with

- one partcle in the swarm,
- one-dimensional particles,
- P_i=P_g=P keeps constant,
- no inertia weight, i.e. $\omega = 1$,
- no stochastic component, i.e. $\phi_1(t) = \phi_1 = c_1, \phi_2(t) = \phi_2 = c_2$ for all t.

Later, Ozcan and Mohan generalized their findings to a PSO system with multiple, multi-dimensional particles with P_i and P_g not necessarily the same point (Ozcan & Mohan, 1999). For the more general system, Ozcan and Mohan derived the following particle position update equation (Ozcan & Mohan, 1999):

$$X_{ij}(t) - (2 - \phi_1 - \phi_2)X_{ij}(t-1) + X_{ij}(t-2) = \phi_1 P_{ij} + \phi_2 P_{gj} \tag{3}$$

From Eq. (3), when $0 < \phi_1 + \phi_2 < 4$, the following closed form can be easily obtained:

$$X_{ij}(t) = \Lambda_{ij}\sin(\theta_{ij}t) + \Gamma_{ij}\cos(\theta_{ij}t) + \kappa_{ij} \tag{4}$$

where Λ_{ij}, Γ_{ij}, θ_{ij} and κ_{ij} are constants derived from the initial conditions and the value of ϕ_1 and ϕ_2:

$$\delta_{ij} = i\sqrt{4 - (2 - \phi_1 - \phi_2)^2} \tag{5}$$

$$\Lambda_{ij} = \frac{2V_{ij}(0) - (\phi_1 + \phi_2)X_{ij}(0) + \phi_1 P_{ij} + \phi_2 P_{gj}}{\|\delta_{ij}\|} \tag{6}$$

$$k_{ij} = \frac{\phi_1 P_{ij} + \phi_2 P_{gj}}{\phi_1 + \phi_2} \tag{7}$$

$$\Gamma_{ij} = X_{ij}(0) - k_{ij} \tag{8}$$

$$\theta_{ij} = \text{atan}(\frac{\|\delta_{ij}\|}{2-\phi_1-\phi_2}) \tag{9}$$

The main conclusion from their work is that particle trajectories follow periodic sinusoidal waves. An optimum is searched by randomly 'catching' another wave, and manipulating its frequency and amplitude. In addition to this general finding, Ozcan and Mohan studied the trajectories of particles under a number of special cases.

For the same simple PSO system as given above, Clerc and Kennedy provided a theoretical analysis of particle trajectories to ensure convergence to a stable point (Clerc & Kennedy, 2002),

$$P = \frac{\phi_1 P_i + \phi_2 P_g}{\phi_1 + \phi_2} \tag{10}$$

the main result of this work is the introduction of the constriction coefficient, which is derived to prevent the velocity to grow out of bounds, with the advantage that, theoretically, velocity clamping is no longer required. In addition, Clerc and Kennedy also studied several different classes of constriction models. As a result of this study, the velocity update equation changes to (Clerc & Kennedy, 2002)

$$V_{ij}(t+1) = \chi[V_{ij}(t) + \phi_{1j}(t)(P_{ij}(t) - X_{ij}(t)) + \phi_{2j}(t)(P_{gj}(t) - X_{ij}(t))] \tag{11}$$

where χ is the constriction coefficient calculated as

$$\chi = \frac{2\kappa}{2-\phi-\sqrt{\phi^2-4\phi}} \tag{12}$$

with $\phi = \phi_1 + \phi_2 \geq 4$ and κ□[0, 1]. The constant κ controls the speed of convergence. For κ≈0, fast convergence to a stable points is obtained, while a κ≈1 results in slow convergence.

Both above two studies consider a simplified PSO system without an inertia weight, i.e. only the simple situation with $\omega = 1$ is studied. van den Bergh analyzed the convergence of the PSO algorithm with inertia weight (van den Bergh, 2001). Considering the velocity and position of a particle at discrete time steps, the following non-homogeneous recurrence relation is obtained:

$$X_{t+1} = (1+\omega-\phi_1-\phi_2)X_t - \omega X_{t-1} + \phi_1 P_i + \phi_2 P_g \tag{13}$$

The characteristic equation corresponding to the recurrence relation is

$$\lambda^2 - (1+\omega-\phi_1-\phi_2)\lambda + \omega = 0 \tag{14}$$

The solutions to this equation gives the eigenvalues

$$\lambda_1 = \frac{1+\omega-\phi_1-\phi_2+\gamma}{2} \tag{15}$$

$$\lambda_2 = \frac{1+\omega-\phi_1-\phi_2-\gamma}{2} \tag{16}$$

where

$$\gamma = \sqrt{(1+\omega-\phi_1-\phi_2)^2 - 4\omega} \tag{17}$$

For initial conditions $X(0) = X_0$ and $X(1) = X_1$, the explicit closed form of the recurrence relation is then given by

$$X_t = k_1 + k_2\lambda_1^t + k_3\lambda_2^t \tag{18}$$

where

$$k_1 = \frac{\phi_1 P_i + \phi_2 P_g}{\phi_1 + \phi_2} \tag{19}$$

$$k_2 = \frac{\lambda_2(X_0 - X_1) - X_1 + X_2}{\gamma(\lambda_1 - 1)} \tag{20}$$

$$k_3 = \frac{\lambda_1(X_1 - X_0) + X_1 - X_2}{\gamma(\lambda_2 - 1)} \tag{21}$$

and $X_2 = (1+\omega-\phi_1-\phi_2)X_1 - \omega X_0 + \phi_1 P_i + \phi_2 P_g$.

Note that the above equation assumes that $P_i(t) = P_i$ and $P_g(t) = P_g$ for all t. The closed form representation in Eq. (18) therefore remains valid until a better position X (and thus P_i and P_g) is discovered. When a better position is discovered, the above equations can be used again after recalculating the coefficients k_1, k_2 and k_3.

van den Bergh only discussed the situation with imaginary eigenvalues, i.e. $(1+\omega-\phi_1-\phi_2)^2 < 4\omega$. He obtained the conclusion that when $\max\{\|\lambda_1\|,\|\lambda_2\|\} < 1$, the particle's position sequence will converge and

$$\lim_{t\to+\infty} X_t = k_1 = \frac{\phi_1 P_i + \phi_2 P_g}{\phi_1 + \phi_2} \tag{22}$$

That means, under the condition that $\max\{\|\lambda_1\|,\|\lambda_2\|\} < 1$, a particle converges to a weighted average of its individual best and global best positions.

In the case that ϕ_1 and ϕ_2 are stochastic, the average behavior of the system can then be observed by considering the expected values of ϕ_1 and ϕ_2 (assuming uniform distribution): $E[\phi_1] = c_1/2$, $E[\phi_2] = c_2/2$. Using the expected values, the limit becomes

$$\lim_{t\to+\infty} X_t = \frac{c_1 P_i + c_2 P_g}{c_1 + c_2} = (1-a)P_i + aP_g \tag{23}$$

where $a = c_2/(c_1+c_2) \in [0,1]$.

Furthermore, with experimental analysis, van den Bergh proposed parameter range to satisfy the condition of $\max\{\|\lambda_1\|,\|\lambda_2\|\} < 1$, i.e., $\omega > (c_1+c_2)/2 - 1$. van den Bergh also discussed on convergence of particle trajectory with certain parameters, but the

experimental results did not conform to his conjecture. This disagreement was informally explained by stochastic probability.
Some other similar results were proposed by Yasuda (Yasuda et al, 2003) and Trelea (Trelea, 2003). Although those results provide insights into how particle swarm system works, all those analysis discard the randomness in the PSO algorithm, and are all based on a simplified deterministic algorithm. Obviously, those analytical results more or less deviate from the real particle swarm system due to the loss of randomness. Recently, researchers have begun to make progress in the analysis of randomness in PSO algorithm. Clerc (Clerc, 2006) mathematically analyzed the stochastic behavior of the particles when the swarm is in stagnation, but he only discussed properties of stochastic coefficients and did not regard the velocity (and position) as stochastic variable, and thus he seemed unaware of the dependent relationship between velocity and the stochastic coefficients. Later, Jiang (Jiang et al, 2007a) extended Clerc's results by regarding each particle's position on each evolutionary step as a stochastic vector. Then the PSO algorithm was analyzed using stochastic process theory. Some stochastic characteristics (including expected value, variance, and auto-variance) of particle's position are obtained, both in explicit and implicit representations, and corresponding properties are analyzed.
Jiang (Jiang et al, 2007b) present the first formal stochastic convergence analysis of the standard particle swarm optimization (PSO) algorithm, which involves with randomness. By regarding each particle's position on each evolutionary step as a stochastic vector, the standard PSO algorithm determined by non-negative real parameter tuple $\{\omega, c_1, c_2\}$ was analyzed using stochastic process theory. The stochastic convergent condition of the particle swarm system and corresponding parameter selection guidelines were also derived.

3. Stochastic Convergence Analysis of PSO in Stagnation

In this section, stochastic convergence analysis of the particle swarm system is conducted, assuming the particle swarm is in stagnation. The particle swarm system is thought to be in stagnation, if arbitrary particle i's history best position P_i and the total swarm's history best position P_g keep constant over some time steps.
There exist many factors that would influence the convergence property and performance of PSO algorithm, including selection of parameter tuple $\{\omega, c_1, c_2, a, b\}$; velocity clamping; position clamping; topology of neighborhood; etc. This chapter focuses on analyzing how the selection of parameter tuple $\{\omega, c_1, c_2, a, b\}$ would influence the trajectories of particles in the PSO algorithm. Factors such as velocity clamping, position clamping, topology of neighborhood may influence the trajectories of particles, but the discussion of those factors is beyond the scope of this chapter. At the same time, the situation with variable parameter values during evolution is also not discussed here. That means, the PSO algorithm studied here is only determined by fixed real-value parameter set $\{\omega, c_1, c_2, a, b\}$. Velocity and position clamping are not considered, and the neighborhood of any particle is the whole swarm.
When the particle swarm system is in stagnation, arbitrary P_i and P_g would keep constant over some time steps, then it's easy to find out that all particles would evolve independently. Thus, only particle i needs to be studied. For i is chosen arbitrarily, the result can be applied to all other particles. At the same time, it appears from Eqs. (1) and (2) that each dimension is updated independently. Thus, without loss of generality, the algorithm

description can be reduced to the one-dimensional case. By omitting particle and dimension notations, and considering discrete time situation, update equations become:

$$V_{t+1} = \omega V_t + c_1 r_{1,t}(P_i - X_t) + c_2 r_{2,t}(P_g - X_t) \tag{24}$$

$$X_{t+1} = aX_t + bV_{t+1} \tag{25}$$

It's obviously that the velocity is only an auxiliary variable, and the position is the real significant variable. By substituting Eq. (24) into Eq. (25), the following non-homogeneous recurrence relation is obtained:

$$X_{t+1} = (a + \omega - c_1 b r_{1,t} - c_2 b r_{2,t})X_t - a\omega X_{t-1} + c_1 b r_{1,t} P_i + c_2 b r_{2,t} P_g \tag{26}$$

From Eq. (26), it's easy to know that single value of coefficients c_1 and b is not important at all. The important factor is the multiple $c_1 b$. Coefficient c_2 and b share the same relationship. Thus, without loss of generality, we can choose $b \equiv 1$ if $b \neq 0$. As a matter of fact, when $b = 0$, it's easy to get $X_i^d(t+1) = a^{t+1} X_i^d(0)$ from Eq. (2), whose convergence condition is $a \le 1$. This case is not an interesting one, thus it is supposed that $b \neq 0$ in following analysis. Thus we can suppose $b \equiv 1$, and the iteration equation becomes

$$X_{t+1} = (a + \omega - c_1 r_{1,t} - c_2 r_{2,t})X_t - a\omega X_{t-1} + c_1 r_{1,t} P_i + c_2 r_{2,t} P_g \tag{27}$$

Notice that there exist random numbers in Eq. (27), and that X_0, X_1 are also random numbers, thus each X_t should be regarded as a random variable, and the iterative process $\{X_t\}$ should be regarded as a stochastic process. The expectation and variance of each random variable X_t can then be calculated, and the convergence property of the iterative process can be analyzed.

3.1 Convergence analysis of the expectation of particle's position

In this subsection, the iteration equation of EX_t is obtained, where EX_t is the expectation of random variable X_t. Based on the iteration equation, the convergent condition of sequence $\{EX_t\}$ is analyzed.

According to Eq. (27), iteration equation of sequence $\{EX_t\}$ can be easily obtained.

$$EX_{t+1} = (a + \omega - \frac{c_1 + c_2}{2})EX_t - a\omega EX_{t-1} + \frac{c_1 P_i + c_2 P_g}{2} \tag{28}$$

The characteristic equation of the iterative process shown in Eq. (28) is

$$\lambda^2 - (a + \omega - \frac{c_1 + c_2}{2})\lambda + a\omega = 0 \tag{29}$$

Theorem 1. If and only if conditions $-1 < a\omega < 1$ and $2(1-\omega)(a-1) < c_1 + c_2 < 2(1+\omega)(1+a)$ are satisfied together, iterative process $\{EX_t\}$ is guaranteed to converge to $EX = (c_1 P_i + c_2 P_g)/[2(1-\omega)(1-a) + c_1 + c_2]$.

Proof: Let $\psi = a + \omega - (c_1 + c_2)/2$, the convergent condition of iterative process {EX$_t$} is that the absolute values (or complex modulus) of both eigenvalues λ_{E1}, λ_{E2} are less than 1. That is, $\left\| \psi \pm \sqrt{\psi^2 - 4a\omega} \right\| / 2 < 1$. Consider two cases:

1. $\psi^2 < 4a\omega$

Here, both eigenvalues are complex numbers, $\|\lambda_{E1}\|^2 = \|\lambda_{E2}\|^2 = (\psi^2 + 4a\omega - \psi^2)/4 = a\omega$, so $\max\{\|\lambda_1\|, \|\lambda_2\|\} < 1$ requires only $a\omega < 1$. Condition (1) itself requires $a\omega > 0$ and $2(a + \omega - 2\sqrt{a\omega}) < c_1 + c_2 < 2(a + \omega + 2\sqrt{a\omega})$.

2. $\psi^2 \geq 4a\omega$

Here, both eigenvalues are real numbers. Condition (2) is satisfied if

$a\omega \leq 0$;

or

$a\omega > 0$, and $c_1 + c_2 \geq 2(a + \omega + 2\sqrt{a\omega})$ or $c_1 + c_2 \leq 2(a + \omega - 2\sqrt{a\omega})$. Consider two more cases.

$\psi < 0$

Here $\max\{\|\lambda_{E1}\|, \|\lambda_{E2}\|\} < 1$ requires $c_1 + c_2 < \min\{2(2 + a + \omega), 2(1 + \omega)(1 + \mathrm{a})\}$. Conditions (2) and (2.1) together lead to

$0 < a\omega < 1$ and $2(a + \omega + 2\sqrt{a\omega}) \leq c_1 + c_2 < 2(1 + \omega)(1 + a)$;

or

$-1 < a\omega \leq 0$ and $2(a + \omega) \leq c_1 + c_2 < 2(1 + \omega)(1 + a)$;

$\psi \geq 0$

Here $\max\{\|\lambda_{E1}\|, \|\lambda_{E2}\|\} < 1$ requires $c_1 + c_2 > \max\{2(\omega + a - 2), 2(1 - \omega)(\mathrm{a} - 1)\}$. Conditions (2) and (2.2) together lead to

$0 < a\omega < 1$ and $2(1 - \omega)(\mathrm{a} - 1) \leq c_1 + c_2 < 2(a + \omega - 2\sqrt{a\omega})$;

or

$-1 < a\omega \leq 0$ and $2(1 - \omega)(a - 1) \leq c_1 + c_2 < 2(a + \omega)$;

Synthesize case (1) and case (2), the guaranteed convergent condition of iterative process {EX$_t$} is

$-1 < a\omega < 1$ and $2(1 - \omega)(a - 1) < c_1 + c_2 < 2(1 + \omega)(1 + a)$.

When iterative process {EX$_t$} is convergent, the convergent value EX can be calculated using $EX = (a + \omega - (c_1 + c_2)/2)EX - a\omega EX + (c_1 P_i + c_2 P_g)/2$. That gets

$EX = (c_1 P_i + c_2 P_g)/[2(1 - \omega)(1 - a) + c_1 + c_2]$.

It's easy to know that, even if sequence $\{EX_t\}$ can converge, generally speaking, $EX \neq P_g$ is always true.

3.2 Convergence analysis of the variance of particle's position

To further study the convergence property of particle swarm, the variance sequence should be studied. In this subsection, the iteration equation of DX$_t$ is obtained, where DX$_t$ is the variance of random variable X_t. Based on the iteration equation, the convergent condition of sequence $\{DX_t\}$ is analyzed.

In order to make the procedure of calculating DX_t clear, some symbols should be introduced firstly. Let $\varpi = a\omega$, $\upsilon = (c_1 + c_2)/2$, $\psi = a + \omega - \upsilon$, $R_t = c_1 r_{1,t} + c_2 r_{2,t} - \upsilon$, $Q_t = c_1 r_{1,t} P_i + c_2 r_{2,t} P_g$, from Eq. (27), it is easy to ontain that

$$X_{t+1} = (\psi - R_t)X_t - \varpi X_{t-1} + Q_t \tag{30}$$

Since $r_{1,t}$, $r_{2,t}$ are two independent uniform random number ranged in [0,1], it's obvious that $ER_t = 0$, $EQ_t = (c_1 P_i + c_2 P_g)/2$, $DR_t = (c_1^2 + c_2^2)/12$, $DQ_t = (c_1^2 P_i^2 + c_2^2 P_g^2)/12$, and $E(R_t Q_t) = (c_1^2 P_i + c_2^2 P_g)/12$. Notice that EQ_t, DR_t, DQ_t, and $E(R_t Q_t)$ are all constants, let $Q_E = EQ_t$, $R = DR_t$, $Q_D = DQ_t$, $T = E(R_t Q_t)$.

If $R = 0$, that means $c_1 = c_2 = 0$, which is not an interesting case. Thus we suppose $R > 0$ in all following discussions .

Notice that X_t and X_{t-1} are both independent on R_t and Q_t, but X_t and X_{t-1} are dependent. Thus the following expectation can be obtained.

$$\begin{aligned} EX_{t+1}^2 = (\psi^2 + R)EX_t^2 + \varpi^2 EX_{t-1}^2 + Q_D + Q_E^2 - 2\varpi\psi E(X_t X_{t-1}) \\ + 2(\psi Q_E - T)EX_t - 2\varpi Q_E \cdot EX_{t-1} \end{aligned} \tag{31}$$

$$\begin{aligned} EX_{t+2}^2 = (\psi^2 + R)EX_{t+1}^2 + \varpi^2 EX_t^2 + Q_D + Q_E^2 - 2\varpi\psi E(X_{t+1} X_t) \\ + 2(\psi Q_E - T)EX_{t+1} - 2\varpi Q_E \cdot EX_t \end{aligned} \tag{32}$$

$$E(X_{t+1}X_t) = \psi EX_t^2 - \varpi E(X_t X_{t-1}) + Q_E \cdot EX_t \tag{33}$$

From Eqs. (31)-(33), eliminating $E(X_{t+1}X_t)$ and $E(X_t X_{t-1})$, get

$$\begin{aligned} EX_{t+2}^2 + \varpi EX_{t+1}^2 = (\psi^2 + R)(EX_{t+1}^2 + \varpi EX_t^2) + \varpi^2(EX_t^2 + \varpi EX_{t-1}^2) \\ + (Q_D + Q_E^2)(1 + \varpi) - 2\varpi\psi(\psi EX_t^2 + Q_E EX_t) \\ + 2(\psi Q_E - T)(EX_{t+1} + \varpi EX_t) - 2\omega Q_E(EX_t + \varpi EX_{t-1}) \end{aligned} \tag{34}$$

Substitute $EX_{t+2} = \psi EX_{t+1} - \varpi EX_t + Q_E$, $\varpi EX_{t-1} = \psi EX_t - EX_{t+1} + Q_E$ and $DX_t = EX_t^2 - (EX_t)^2$ into Eq. (34), obtain

$$\begin{aligned} DX_{t+2} = (\psi^2 + R - \varpi)DX_{t+1} - \varpi(\psi^2 - R - \varpi)DX_t + \varpi^3 DX_{t-1} \\ + R \cdot [(EX_{t+1})^2 + \varpi(EX_t)^2] - 2T \cdot (EX_{t+1} + \varpi EX_t) + Q_D(1 + \varpi) \end{aligned} \tag{35}$$

The characteristic equation of the iterative process shown in Eq. (35) is

$$\lambda^3 - (\psi^2 + R - \varpi)\lambda^2 + \varpi(\psi^2 - R - \varpi)\lambda - \varpi^3 = 0 \tag{36}$$

The iteration equation and characteristic equation of iterative process $\{DX_t\}$ are both quite complex, and it is hard to analyze these two equations directly. Fortunately, the convergent condition of the iterative process $\{DX_t\}$ defined in Eq. (35) is comparatively simple. Before discussing convergence property of iterative process {DX$_t$}, we can firstly determine the intervals in which the three eigenvalues of the characteristic equation are located. Let

$$f(\lambda)=\lambda^3-(\psi^2+R-\varpi)\lambda^2+\varpi(\psi^2-R-\varpi)\lambda-\varpi^3 \quad (37)$$

First of all, consider two special cases.

If $\varpi=0$, then two among three eigenvalues are zeros. Without loss of generality, let $\lambda_{D2}=\lambda_{D3}=0$, then $\lambda_{D1}=\psi^2+R>0$.

If $\psi=0$, then $\lambda_{D3}=-\varpi$ and λ_{D1}, λ_{D2} are roots of equation $\lambda^2-R\lambda-\varpi^2=0$. Since $R>0$, get $\max\{\|\lambda_{D1}\|,\|\lambda_{D2}\|\}=(R+\sqrt{R^2+4\varpi^2})/2>|\varpi|$. Then $\min\{\|\lambda_{D1}\|,\|\lambda_{D2}\|\}<|\varpi|$ must be satisfied due to $\lambda_{D1}\lambda_{D2}\lambda_{D3}=\varpi^3$.

Next consider two general cases.

When $R>0$, $\psi\neq0$ and $\varpi>0$, it is easily verified that

$$f(0)=-\varpi^3<0\ ;\ f(\varpi)=-2\varpi^2R<0;\ f(-\varpi)=-2\psi^2\varpi^2<0.$$

According to conclusions in elementary mathematics, because $f(-\varpi)$, $f(0)$ and $f(\varpi)$ have the same sign, the number of roots in the interval $(-\varpi,0)$ and $(0,\varpi)$ must both be even. Thus there must be at least one root located in interval (ϖ,∞) to satisfy $\lambda_{D1}\lambda_{D2}\lambda_{D3}=\varpi^3>0$.

When $R>0$, $\psi\neq0$ and $\varpi<0$, it is easily verified that

$$f(0)=-\varpi^3>0\ ;\ f(\varpi)=-2\varpi^2R<0;\ f(-\varpi)=-2\psi^2\varpi^2<0.$$

Likely, according to conclusions in elementary mathematics, there must be one root located in the interval $(\varpi,0)$ and one root located in the interval $(0,-\varpi)$. The third root must be located in the interval $(-\varpi,\infty)$ to satisfy $\lambda_{D1}\lambda_{D2}\lambda_{D3}=\varpi^3<0$.

Without loss of generality, suppose $\|\lambda_{D1}\|\ge\|\lambda_{D2}\|\ge\|\lambda_{D3}\|$, then it is clear that relationship $\lambda_{\max D}=\lambda_{D1}>|\varpi|\ge\|\lambda_{D2}\|\ge\|\lambda_{D3}\|$ exists, and λ_{D1} must be a positive real number.

Theorem 2. Given $R>0$, if and only if $-1<\varpi<1$ and $f(1)>0$ are satisfied together, it is guaranteed that $\lambda_{\max D}=\max\{\|\lambda_{D1}\|,\|\lambda_{D2}\|,\|\lambda_{D3}\|\}<1$.

Proof: Obviously, If $|\varpi|\ge1$, then $\lambda_{\max D}>|\varpi|\ge1$, which violate $\max\{\|\lambda_{D1}\|,\|\lambda_{D2}\|,\|\lambda_{D3}\|\}<1$. Thus only cases with $-1<\varpi<1$ needs to be discussed. At this point, if and only if $f(1)>0$, it is guaranteed that $\lambda_{\max D}$ is located in the interval $(|\varpi|,1)$. □

As a matter of fact, conditions $-1<\varpi<1$ and $f(1)>0$ satisfied together implies that $2(1-\omega)(a-1)<c_1+c_2<2(1+\omega)(1+a)$. Because $f(1)=(1+\varpi)^2(1-\varpi)-R(1+\varpi)-(1-\varpi)\psi^2$, then $-1<\varpi<1$ and $f(1)>0$ lead to $\psi^2<(1+\varpi)^2-(1+\varpi)R/(1-\varpi)<(1+\varpi)^2$, that is $2(1-\omega)(a-1)<c_1+c_2<2(1+\omega)(1+a)$.

Theorem 3. Given $R>0$, if and only if $-1<\varpi<1$ and $f(1)>0$ are satisfied together, iterative process {DX$_t$} is guaranteed to converge to

$$DX = \frac{\frac{1}{12}(1+\varpi)}{f(1)\cdot[2(1-a)(1-\omega)+c_1+c_2]^2}\{2c_1^2c_2^2(P_g-P_i)^2+4(1-a)(1-\omega)c_1c_2(c_2P_g-c_1P_i)(P_g-P_i) + (c_1^2P_i^2+c_2^2P_g^2)[2(1-a)(1-\omega)]^2\}$$

where $f(1)$ is defined in Eq. (37).

Proof: The iteration equation of DX_t, Eq. (35), contains items related to EX_t, thus the condition shown in Theorem 1 should be satisfied firstly to make DX_t convergent. As stated above, $-1<\varpi<1$ and $f(1)>0$ implies that $2(1-\omega)(a-1)<c_1+c_2<2(1+\omega)(1+a)$. Thus conditions $-1<\varpi<1$ and $f(1)>0$ together make sure that the conditions stated in Theorem 1 are satisfied.

After EX_t is convergent, the convergent condition of iterative process $\{DX_t\}$ is that the absolute values(or complex modulus) of the three eigenvalues λ_{D1}, λ_{D2}, λ_{D3} are all less than 1. Theorem 2 proves that, $-1<\varpi<1$ and $f(1)>0$ are the necessary and sufficient condition of $\max\{\|\lambda_{D1}\|,\|\lambda_{D2}\|,\|\lambda_{D3}\|\}<1$.

Thus, $-1<\varpi<1$ and $f(1)>0$ together give the necessary and sufficient conditions to guarantee iterative process $\{DX_t\}$ convergent. If iterative process $\{DX_t\}$ is convergent, the convergent value can be easily calculated to be

$$DX = \frac{\frac{1}{12}(1+\varpi)}{f(1)\cdot[2(1-a)(1-\omega)+c_1+c_2]^2}\{2c_1^2c_2^2(P_g-P_i)^2+4(1-a)(1-\omega)c_1c_2(c_2P_g-c_1P_i)(P_g-P_i) + (c_1^2P_i^2+c_2^2P_g^2)[2(1-a)(1-\omega)]^2\}$$

It's easy to know that, even if sequence $\{DX_t\}$ can converge, generally speaking, the convergent value can not reach zero.

4. Parameter Selection Guidelines

Holland discussed the balance between *exploration* and *exploitation* that an algorithm must maintain (Holland, 1975). Exploration ability is related to the algorithm's tendency to explore new regions of the search space, while exploitation is the tendency to search a smaller region more thoroughly.

Researchers in PSO community used to believe that inertia weight ω balances exploration and exploitation in PSO algorithm, but new theoretical results give a different new explanation (Jiang et al, 2007a). It is believed that inertia weight can not balance exploration and exploitation by itself in PSO algorithm. The factor to balance exploration and exploitation should be the value of $\lambda_{\max D}$. The larger $\lambda_{\max D}$ is, the stronger is the exploration ability of the PSO algorithm. An empirical evidence can be found in (Xie et al, 2004), which shows that the relationship between exploration ability of PSO algorithm and inertia weight ω is not monotone. For more explanation about this matter, please refer to (Jiang et al, 2007a).

It is widely accepted that PSO algorithm have a good global search ability, while its fine-tune ability is relatively weak. That is to say, PSO algorithm can easily locate the good area of the solution space in which good solutions are located, while the procedure to find the good solutions is not equally easy for PSO algorithm. Thus it is quite important for PSO algorithm to enhance local search ability. While in PSO algorithm determined by five-dimensional parameter tuple {ω, c_1, c_2, a, b}, generally speaking, the expectation of each particle's position can never reach P_g, and the variance of particle's position can never drop to zero. This is not a desired property for PSO algorithm, for this will make the fine-tune ability of PSO algorithm even worse.

If $(1-a)(1-\omega)=0$, then when P_i is equal to P_g, the expectation of particle's position will converge to P_g, and the variance of particle's position will converge to zero. This may help PSO algorithm to enhance fine-tune ability. Without loss of generality, suppose a=1. Then the PSO algorithm reduces to a simpler version totally determined by three-dimensional parameter tuple {ω, c_1, c_2}. For this simpler version, the following two corollaries apply.

Corollary 1. For PSO algorithm determined by three-dimensional parameter tuple, if and only if conditions $-1<\omega<1$ and $0<c_1+c_2<4(1+\omega)$ are satisfied together, iterative process {EX_t} is guaranteed to converge to $EX=(c_1P_i+c_2P_g)/(c_1+c_2)$.

Corollary 2. For PSO algorithm determined by three-dimensional parameter tuple, given $R>0$, if and only if $-1<\omega<1$ and $f(1)>0$ are satisfied together, iterative process {DX_t} is guaranteed to converge to $DX=(c_1c_2)^2(P_g-P_i)^2(1+\omega)/(c_1+c_2)^2/f(1)/6$.

It is easily verified that, in the simpler PSO version, when P_i is equal to P_g, the expectation of particle's position will gradually converge to P_g, and the variance will gradually converge to zero. This means that the PSO algorithm can thoroughly search around the best position found so far. If the convergent speed of variance is slow, it is more likely to find good solutions in the good area.

Below is the graphical illustrations of parameter ranges, which are determined by conditions shown in above two corollaries.

The parameter range to guarantee the convergence of iterative process {EX_t} is illustrated in Fig. 1. The cyan(light) area in Fig. 1 corresponds to case (1) discussed in Theorem 1, and the blue(dark) area in Fig. 1 corresponds to case (2) discussed in Theorem 1.

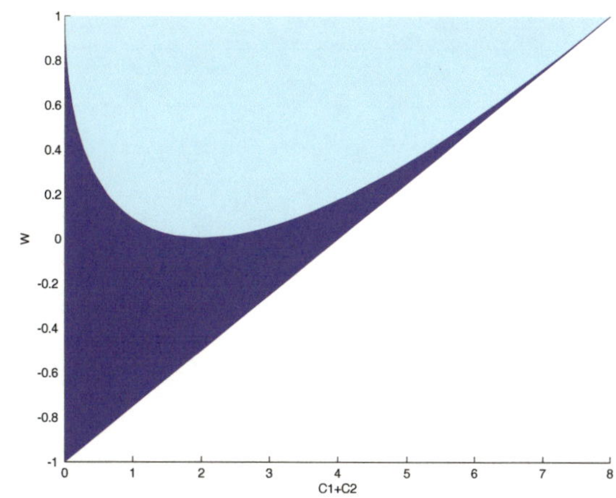

Figure 1 Parameter range to guarantee the convergence of iterative process {EX_t}. The cyan(light) area corresponds to case with complex eigenvalues, the blue(dark) area corresponds to case with real eigenvalues

The parameter ranges to guarantee the convergence of iterative process $\{DX_t\}$ are illustrated in Fig. 2-3. In Fig. 2, the relationship between c_1 and c_2 is illustrated. The relationship between lower and higher range of ω and c_1, c_2 are illustrated in Fig. 3.
The parameter selection of PSO algorithm in literatures favors $c_1=c_2=c$, so more detailed discussion on this condition is given. The relationship between ω and c is illustrated in Fig. 4, in which blue(dark) area is the parameter range to guarantee the convergence of expectation sequence of particle's position, and the cyan(light) area is the parameter range to guarantee the convergence of variance sequence of particle's position.

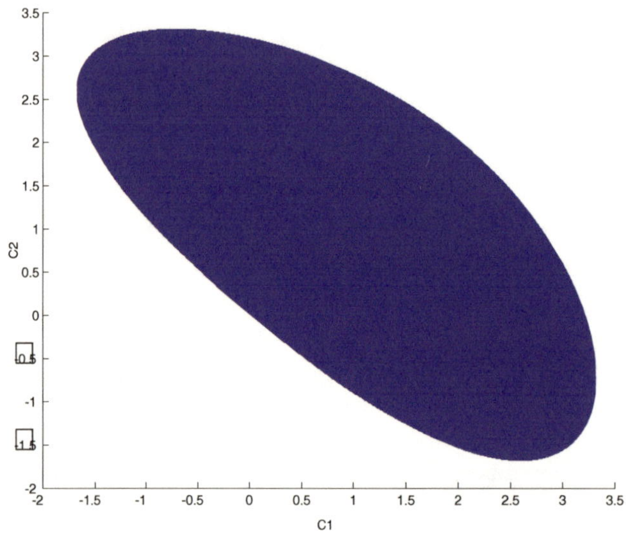

Figure 2 Relationship between c_1 and c_2 to guarantee the convergence of iterative process $\{DX_t\}$

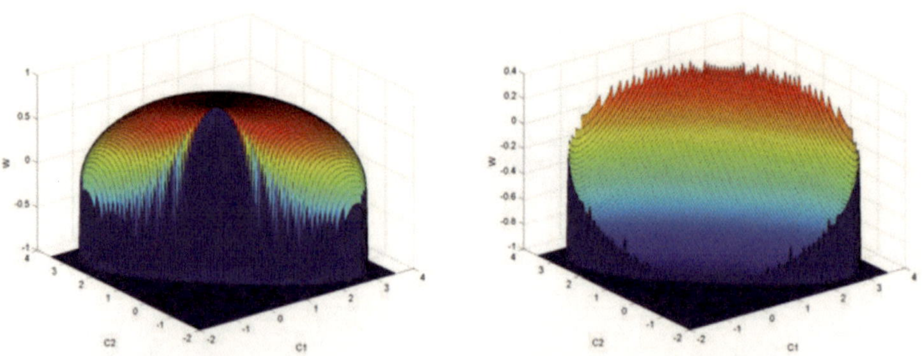

Figure 3 Relationship between lower(left) and higher(right) range of ω and c_1, c_2 to guarantee the convergence of iterative process $\{DX_t\}$

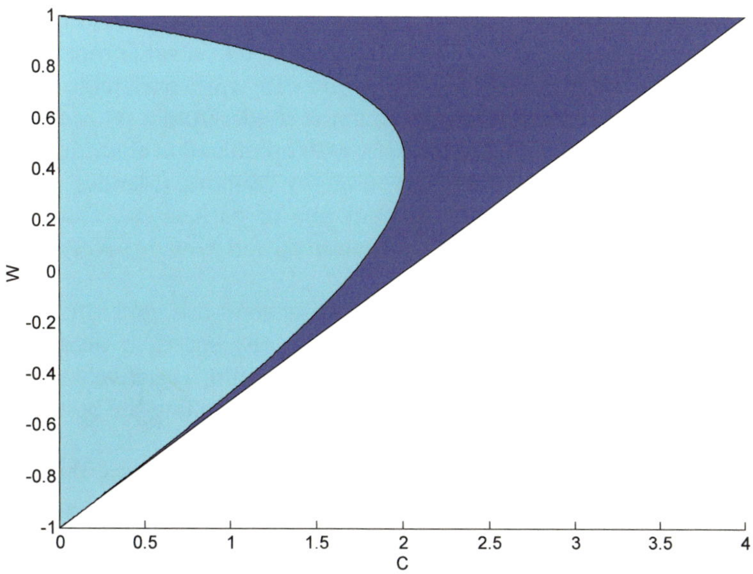

Figure 4 Relationship between ω and c when $c_1=c_2=c$ to simultaneously guarantee the convergence of iterative processes $\{EX_t\}$ and $\{DX_t\}$

Based on the theoretical analysis results obtained above and related experimental results, in order to help PSO algorithm to search the solution space more thoroughly, it is necessary to determine parameters to make $\lambda_{\max D} \approx 1$. Thus we propose a new set of parameters: $\{\omega=0.715, c_1=c_2=1.7\}$. This set of parameters can help PSO algorithm to search the solution space thoroughly, slowly converge to the best position found so far, so as to find the optima with higher probability. In next section, the PSO algorithm using our suggested parameters will be compared against PSO algorithms using parameters suggested in literatures.

5. Performance Comparison

Parameter selection of PSO algorithm is quite important and have drawn attention from many researchers. Different researchers have proposed many different sets of parameters, such as $\omega=0.729$, $c_1=c_2=1.494$ (Clerc & Kennedy, 2002); $\omega=0.6$, $c_1=c_2=1.7$ (Trelea, 2003); $\omega=0.729$, $c_1=2.041$, $c_2=0.948$ (Carlisle & Dozier, 2001). For those parameters, corresponding $\lambda_{\max D}$ can be calculated. When $\omega=0.729$ and $c_1=c_2=1.494$, $\lambda_{\max D}=0.942$; when $\omega=0.6$ and $c_1=c_2=1.7$, $\lambda_{\max D}=0.889$; and when $\omega=0.729$, $c_1=2.041$, $c_2=0.948$, $\lambda_{\max D}=0.975$. Obviously, $\lambda_{\max D}$ corresponding to all those three sets of parameters are all around 1, this may help to explain why the performance of PSO algorithm using those sets of parameters are promising. But it is easy to find out that $\lambda_{\max D}$ corresponding to those parameters is still not large enough to enhance the exploration ability of PSO algorithm, so that the algorithm is often trapped in local optima. For above reasons, we propose a new set of parameters: $\omega=0.715$, $c_1=c_2=1.7$ (corresponding to $\lambda_{\max D}=0.995$), and performance comparison is conducted.

No Free Lunch theorem (Wolpert & Macready, 1997) asserts that no algorithm can be better than any other, over all possible functions. Thus it does not seem interesting to demonstrate that the PSO algorithm with suggested parameters is good on some functions and not on others. What we hope for is a problem-solver that can work well with a wide range of problems. Thus, in the current exercises we combine results from a set of test functions, all of which are commonly used in experimentation with optimization algorithms.

Based on three performance measures proposed by Mendes (Mendes et al, 2004), we compare several PSO algorithms with different sets of parameters. Those measures are average standardized optima, average success iterations and average success rate.

1. Standardized Optima

The first measure is simply the best function result after some arbitrary number of iterations; here we use 2,000. Basically this is a measure of sloppy speed. It does not necessarily indicate whether the algorithm is close to the global optimum; a relatively high score can be obtained on some of these multimodal functions simply by finding the best part of a locally optimal region.

It is not possible to combine raw results from different functions, as they are all scaled differently. For instance, almost any decent algorithm will find a function result less than 0.01 on the sphere function, but a result of 40.0 on Rosenbrock is considered good. In order to combine the function outputs, we standardized the results of each function to a mean of 0.0 and standard deviation of 1.0. All results of all trials for a single function are standardized to the same scale; as all of these problems involve minimization, a lower result is better, and after standardization a negative result means to be better than average. After standardizing each function separately, we can combine them and find the average for each single condition.

2. Success Iterations

The second measure is the number of iterations required to reach a criterion. This is also a measure of speed, but in this case the criteria are intended to indicate that the searcher has arrived in the region of the global optimum.

There is, however, a problem with this measure, too. That is, some trials might never reach the criteria. Many hours have been lost waiting, trying to give each version a fair chance to find the global optimum, often in vain. Trials where the criteria are not met after a reasonable time – here we use 10,000 iterations – must be coded as infinite, which means among other things that the mean is meaningless.

The proper measure of central tendency for such a data set is the median. If the majority of trials are coded as infinite, then the median is represented as infinity, shown in the results tables with the lemniscus. In order to combine iteration data, mean of the medians is used, with the caveat that if any median were infinite, the mean would be infinite, too.

It is obviously that the first measure is different from the second one. The first measure determines whether the algorithm can get a good solution fast, e.g., after only 2,000 iterations, while the second measure determines how long it takes to find the global optimum if left to run, or whether it can find it at all. Generally speaking, iterations to calculate the second performance should be much larger than iterations to calculate the first measure.

3. Success Rate

The third measure is perhaps the most important one. This is a simple binary code indicating whether the criteria were met within 10,000 iterations or not. Averaged over all function trials, this gives the proportion of trials that successfully found the global optimum. There is no trick to this one; the mean of the ones and zeroes, where one indicates success and zero failure, gives the proportion of successes. Iteration used for this measure is the same as that used for the second measure, i.e., 10,000 iterations.

Function	Formula	Optima	Optimal Position
Ackley	$f_1(x) = 20 + e - 20e^{-0.2\sqrt{\frac{1}{n}\sum_{i=1}^{n} x_i^2}} - e^{\frac{1}{n}\sum_{i=1}^{n}\cos(2\pi x_i)}$	0	(0,…,0)
Griewank	$f_2(\vec{x}) = \frac{1}{4000}\sum_{i=1}^{n} x_i^2 - \prod_{i=1}^{n}\cos(\frac{x_i}{\sqrt{i}}) + 1$	0	(0,…,0)
Rastrigin	$f_3(\vec{x}) = \sum_{i=1}^{n}(x_i^2 - 10\cos(2\pi x_i) + 10)$	0	(0,…,0)
Rosenbrock	$f_4(\vec{x}) = \sum_{i=1}^{n-1}\left(100(x_{i+1} - x_i^2)^2 + (x_i - 1)^2\right)$	0	(1,…,1)
Sphere	$f_5(\vec{x}) = \sum_{i=1}^{n} x_i^2$	0	(0,…,0)

Table 1 Benchmark functions

Function	Dimension n	Value Range $[X_{min}, X_{max}]$	Criteria
Ackley	10	$[-32,32]^{10}$	1
	30	$[-32,32]^{30}$	2
	50	$[-32,32]^{50}$	2
Griewank	10	$[-600,600]^{10}$	0.1
	30	$[-600,600]^{30}$	0.05
	50	$[-600,600]^{50}$	0.05
Rastrigin	10	$[-5.12,5.12]^{10}$	10
	30	$[-5.12,5.12]^{30}$	60
	50	$[-5.12,5.12]^{50}$	100
Rosenbrock	10	$[-30,30]^{10}$	5
	30	$[-30,30]^{30}$	20
	50	$[-30,30]^{50}$	50
Sphere	10	$[-100,100]^{10}$	1e-5
	30	$[-100,100]^{30}$	1e-5
	50	$[-100,100]^{50}$	1e-5

Table 2 Value range and criteria of benchmark functions

Based on those three measures, we conduct experiments on five benchmark problems, which are commonly used in literature. Those five benchmark functions are Ackley, Griewank, Rastrigin, Rosenbrock and Sphere. Corresponding function formula, optima and optimal positions are shown in Table 1; value range and criteria are listed in Table 2.
Features of those five functions are: Sphere is a simple unimodal function; Rosenbrock is also an unimodal function, but Rosenbrock's variables are strongly dependent and gradient information often misleads algorithms; Ackley, Griewank and Rastrigin are multimodal functions with many local optima. Griewank is strongly multi-modal with significant interaction between its variables, caused by the product term. This function has the interesting property that the number of local minima increases with dimensionality.
The four sets of parameters used to be compared are listed as follows:
Set A (Clerc & Kennedy, 2002): $\omega = 0.729$, $c_1 = c_2 = 1.494$;
Set B (Carlisle & Dozier, 2001): $\omega = 0.729$, $c_1 = 2.041$, $c_2 = 0.948$;
Set C (Trelea, 2003): $\omega = 0.6$, $c_1 = c_2 = 1.7$;
Set D: $\omega = 0.715$, $c_1 = c_2 = 1.7$.

		Set A	Set B	Set C	Set D
Mean (Deviation)	Ackley	0.1139 (0.4041)	0.1155 (0.3483)	0.1765 (0.4460)	0.0511 (0.2553)
	Griewank	0.0944 (0.0583)	0.0606 (0.0357)	0.0876 (0.0457)	0.0803 (0.0411)
	Rastrigin	8.7357 (4.5793)	4.7758 (2.2978)	8.6263 (4.0645)	6.0593 (3.4700)
	Rosenbrock	2.4308 (9.2956)	3.2329 (11.1348)	2.0431 (9.2136)	8.5559 (25.0940)
	Sphere	0 (0)	0 (0)	0 (0)	0 (0)
Success Rate	Ackley	0.92	0.90	0.86	0.96
	Griewank	0.64	0.90	0.67	0.72
	Rastrigin	0.68	1.00	0.69	0.88
	Rosenbrock	1.00	0.99	1.00	1.00
	Sphere	1.00	1.00	1.00	1.00
Success Iteration	Ackley	84	72.5	63	108
	Griewank	265	192	160.5	426
	Rastrigin	179	161	141	201
	Rosenbrock	333.5	319.5	280.5	538.5
	Sphere	186	162	139	259

Table 3. Experimental results on 10-dimensional functions

Experiments are conducted on all five benchmark functions, considered dimensions are 10, 30 and 50, corresponding particle swarm sizes are separately 20, 40 and 100. Each algorithm with each set of parameter is run 100 times, and the final result is the statistical result of all 100 runs.

The intermediate experimental results include mean function value (deviation), success rate and success iteration. Experimental results related to 10-dimensional functions are listed in Table 3. Experimental results related to 30-dimensional functions are listed in Table 4. And experimental results related to 50-dimensional functions are listed in Table 5. Although we don't want to compare the PSO algorithm using different parameters on each single function, it is clearly shown in Table 3-5 that the performance of PSO algorithm using our suggested parameters is promising.

		Set A	Set B	Set C	Set D
Mean (Deviation)	Ackley	1.2639 (0.9417)	1.3589 (0.8030)	1.3556 (0.9833)	0.0250 (0.1761)
	Griewank	0.0155 (0.0196)	0.0208 (0.0242)	0.0160 (0.0199)	0.0113 (0.0144)
	Rastrigin	59.0109 (18.2530)	41.0719 (10.1841)	57.5682 (15.3826)	42.9026 (11.8995)
	Rosenbrock	28.8497 (28.7922)	33.1788 (39.6960)	31.9139 (34.7045)	58.6477 (51.5653)
	Sphere	0 (0)	0 (0)	0 (0)	0 (0)
Success Rate	Ackley	0.82	0.78	0.70	1.00
	Griewank	0.91	0.86	0.90	0.98
	Rastrigin	0.61	0.94	0.59	0.94
	Rosenbrock	0.99	0.90	0.97	0.84
	Sphere	1.00	1.00	1.00	1.00
Success Iteration	Ackley	190	142.5	150.5	280
	Griewank	285	197	237	503.5
	Rastrigin	287.5	182.5	179.5	345.5
	Rosenbrock	1832	2051	1689	5323
	Sphere	435.5	295	363	772

Table 4. Experimental results on 30-dimensional functions

The final synthesized results are listed in Table 6. Experimental data shown in Table 6 clearly indicates that the PSO algorithm using parameter set D outperforms other algorithm in the measures of standardized optima and average success rate, and is outperformed by other algorithms in the measure of success iteration. Both two phenomena can be explained by $\lambda_{\max D}$ corresponding to each set of parameters.

		Set A	Set B	Set C	Set D
Mean (Deviation)	Ackley	1.2454 (0.9683)	1.8311 (0.5866)	1.2278 (0.8901)	0 (0)
	Griewank	0.0130 (0.0229)	0.0108 (0.0200)	0.0140 (0.0219)	0.0079 (0.0118)
	Rastrigin	118.1610 (24.7108)	87.0787 (16.8852)	113.8330 (23.4990)	70.3967 (15.1534)
	Rosenbrock	71.0803 (41.1463)	70.3772 (40.7945)	67.8099 (33.8612)	87.6412 (42.7683)
	Sphere	0 (0)	0 (0)	0 (0)	0 (0)
Success Rate	Ackley	0.77	0.60	0.82	1.00
	Griewank	0.94	0.94	0.93	0.98
	Rastrigin	0.25	0.80	0.27	0.97
	Rosenbrock	0.80	0.60	0.91	0.61
	Sphere	1.00	1.00	1.00	1.00
Success Iteration	Ackley	257	214	214	471
	Griewank	383	214	338	789
	Rastrigin	∞	262	∞	597
	Rosenbrock	2188	3981	2205	5474
	Sphere	603	332	531	1281

Table 5. Experimental results on 50-dimensional functions

	Dimension	Set A	Set B	Set C	Set D
Standardized Optima	10	0.1193	**-0.2070**	0.1137	-0.0260
	30	0.1134	-0.0121	0.1337	**-0.2350**
	50	0.1286	0.0032	0.0882	**-0.2199**
Average Success Rate	10	0.848	**0.958**	0.844	0.912
	30	0.866	0.896	0.832	**0.952**
	50	0.752	0.788	0.786	**0.912**
Average Success Iteration	10	209.5	181.4	**156.8**	306.5
	30	606	573.6	**523.8**	1444.8
	50	∞	**1000.3**	∞	1722.3

Table 6 Synthesized performance comparison results

Parameter set D corresponds to a largest $\lambda_{\max D}$ among all four set of parameters, thus PSO algorithm using parameter set D has the strongest exploration ability, so it is not easy to be trapped into local optima. When the dimension increase, the solution space get more complex, and PSO algorithm gets more likely to be trapped into local optima. At this time, the influence of exploration ability to the performance of algorithm would be more significant. This is why PSO algorithm using parameter set D can outperform other algorithm in the measures of standardized optima and average success rate, and this advantage gets more significant when the dimension increases.

Also due to the strong exploration ability that PSO algorithm using parameter set D has, the algorithm has to waste a lot of time in exploring new search area, so as to influence the speed.

6. Conclusion

The stochastic process theory is applied to analyze the particle swarm optimization algorithm determined by five-dimensional real-value parameter tuple {ω, c_1, c_2, a, b}, considering the randomness thoroughly. Specifically speaking, stochastic convergence analysis is conducted on PSO algorithm when it is in stagnation phase, and the convergent properties of expectation and variance sequence of particle's position are studied. The analysis results determines corresponding parameter ranges, both in formular and graphical form. This result is helpful to understand the mechanism of PSO algorithm and select appropriate parameters to make PSO algorithm more powerful.

After the theoretical stochastic convergence analysis of PSO algorithm in stagnation phase, parameter selection guidelines are discussed, and a set of suggested parameters {ω=0.715, c_1=c_2=1.7} is given, which is compared against other three sets of parameters which are proposed in literatures. Experimental result shows that the PSO algorithm using our suggested parameters can achieve robust performance, but the time expires before reaching optimal area is longer than PSO algorithm using other suggested parameters.

7. References

Carlisle, A. & Dozier, G. (2001). An off-the-shelf pso. *Proceedings of the Workshop on Particle Swarm Optimization*. Indianapolis, USA. 2001.

Clerc, M. & Kennedy, J. (2002). The particle swarm-explosion, stability and convergence in a multidimensional complex space. *IEEE Trans. Evol. Comput.*, Vol. 6, No. 2, April 2002, 58–73.

Clerc M. (2006). *Stagnation analysis in particle swarm optimisation or what happens when nothing happens*. Technical Report CSM-460, Department of Computer Science, University of Essex. August 2006. ISSN: 1744-8050.

Holland, J. (1975). *Adaption in natural and artificial systems*, University of Michigan Press, Ann Arbor, MI, 1975.

Jiang, M.; Luo, Y. P. & Yang, S. Y. (2007a). Stagnation Analysis in Particle Swarm Optimization, *Proceedings of IEEE Swarm Intelligence Symposium 2007*, pp. 14-17, Hawaii, USA. 1-5 April 2007.

Jiang, M.; Luo, Y. P. & Yang, S. Y. (2007b). Stochastic convergence analysis and parameter selection of the standard particle swarm optimization algorithm. *Information Processing Letters*, Vol. 102, No. 1, April 2007, 8-16

Mendes, R.; Kennedy, J. & Neves, J. (2004). The fully informed particle swarm: Simpler, maybe better. *IEEE Trans. Evol. Comput.*, Vol. 8, No. 3, June 2004, 204–210.

Ozcan, E. & Mohan, C. (1998). Analysis of a simple particle swarm optimization system, *Intelligent Engineering Systems Through Artificial Neural Networks*, 1998. 253-258.

Ozcan, E. & Mohan, C. K. (1999). Particle swarm optimization: Surfing the waves. *Proc. IEEE Congr. Evol. Comput.*, Washington, DC. Jul. 1999. 1939–1944.

Trelea, I. C. (2003). The particle swarm optimization algorithm: Convergence analysis and parameter selection. *Inf. Process. Lett.*, Vol. 85, 2003, 317–325.

van den Bergh, F. (2001). *An analysis of particle swarm optimizers*: [Ph.D. dissertation]. University of Pretoria, Pretoria, South Africa, 2001.

Wolpert, D. H. & Macready, W. G. (1997). No free lunch theorems for optimization. *IEEE Trans. Evol. Comput.*, Vol. 1, No. 2, April 1997, 67–82.

Xie, X-F. ; Zhang, W-J. & Bi, D-C. (2004). Optimizing semiconductor devices by self-organizing particle swarm. *Congress on Evolutionary Computation (CEC)*, pp. 2017-2022, Oregon, USA, 2004.

Yasuda, K.; Ide, A. & Iwasaki, N. (2003). Adaptive particle swarm optimization. *Proceedings of the IEEE International Conference on Systems, Man, and Cybernetics.* 2003. 1554-1559.

12

Stochastic Metaheuristics as Sampling Techniques using Swarm Intelligence

Johann Dreo and Patrick Siarry
Universite Paris 12, Laboratoire Images, Signaux et Systemes Intelligents
France

1. Introduction

Optimization problems appear in many fields, as various as identification problems, supervised learning of neural networks, shortest path problems, *etc.* Metaheuristics [22] are a family of optimization algorithms, often applied to "hard" combinatorial problems for which no more efficient method is known. They have the advantage of being generic methods, thus do not require a complex tuning for each problem, and can be used as a kind of "black boxes". Recall that, generally, optimization algorithms search for a *point* into the *search space,* so as to optimize *(i.e.,* minimize or maximize) the *objective function* (also called fitness or goal function). Metaheuristics are often divided into two sets:

1. Algorithms handling a *single point,* making it evolve towards a solution.
2. Algorithms handling a *population, i.e.,* a finite set of points, and computing a new population at each iteration.

An essential observation is that the population of the second category is a stochastic *sampling* of the objective function. Although those classes are not disjoint (an algorithm can belong to both classes, according to the point of view), we only consider population metaheuristics, which are simply referred as *metaheuristics* hereafter.

An important contribution in this domain comes from the theory of self-organization [10, p.8], which allows to analyze the properties of several metaheuristics stemming from real-world metaphors, often biological ones. This theory (notably studied except the biology [47]) describes the conditions of appearance of complex phenomena from distributed systems, the agents of which are the object of simple, but numerous interactions. The theory puts in front concepts such as communication, feedback, amplification of fluctuations and emergence. In the metaheuristics field, swarm intelligence was so explicitely used on two main fronts: via an approach "self-organized systems" (having given place to ant colony algorithms) and via an approach "socio-cognitive systems" (having led to the particle swarm optimization).

We suggest putting the theory of the swarm intelligence in connection with the concept of adaptive learning search, which tries to describe key points of modern metaheuristics, notably by insisting on the role of the learning and the mechanisms of intensification and diversification. More generally, we think that the theory of self-organization combined with the adaptive learning search gives keys to design the basic components of metaheuristics, recovering from swarm intelligence.

2. Fundamental concepts

2.1 Adaptive Memory Programming

Adaptive Memory Programming (AMP) is a common framework to metaheuristics [53], described in Algorithm 1.. It stresses out the concepts of *memory, intensification,* and *diversification.* In the literature of evolutionary algorithms, these two last notions are often replaced by the words *exploitation* and *exploration,* which have a similar meaning.

1. Memorization of a set of solutions, or of a data structure containing the characteristics of the solutions produced by the search.
2. Construction of a temporary solution based on the data memorized.
3. Improvement of the solution by an algorithm of local search.
4. Memorization of the new solution, or of the data structure associated.

Algorithm 1. AMP framework

We briefly detail each element of the AMP framework:

- *Memory* stands for the information collected by the algorithm on the objective function distribution. It can be represented either as a simple set of points, or as more complex structures, like pheromone tracks in ant colony algorithms. Memory can be defined as global (compared to the problem as a whole) or inter-individual (a solution relative to another one).
- *Intensification* exploits the information obtained, in order to improve the current solutions. This is typically a local search algorithm (for instance with the Nelder-Mead algorithm [45] or a taboo search).
- *Diversification* aims at collecting new information, by exploring the search space.

The three components presented are not always clearly distinct, and are strongly interdependent in an algorithm. An example of metaheuristic that fits well the AMP model is the method GRASP [50].

2.2 Objective Function Sampling and AMP

Metaheuristics share a certain number of properties. An essential one is that they handle a sampling of the objective function, via common processes.

The probabilistic sampling should ideally pick the best solutions with higher probability. However, in an optimization problem, the effective goal is not to sample the objective function, but to find the distribution's optimum. Thus, sampling must concentrate on the areas of interest, while converging gradually towards the optimum by means of "learning" algorithms. From the point of view of sampling, this convergence is carried out by a progressive fall of dispersion in these areas.

In the majority of metaheuristics, the sampling of the objective function is probabilistic (diversification, also named exploration, synonym used almost indifferently [51, p.292])). Ideally, this sampling should be performed with respect to an approximation of the distribution of the points, so as to locate an area of interest, and then converge towards the optimum (intensification, or exploitation).

Most of the metaheuristics do not have any *a priori* information on the distribution, thus *implicitely* learn it by diversification and intensification, such as ant colony algorithms, and "classical" metaheuristics. Conversely, some methods use an approximation of the distribution, and are called *explicit* methods (see [3]).

2.3 General Scopes

We assisted to several attempts of structuration in the scope of distribution sampling. For instance, Monmarche *et al.* proposed the model Probabilistic Search Metaheuristic [42, 43] (PSM), based on the comparison of the algorithms PBIL [2, 4], BSC [52], and the ant system algorithm [13]. The general principle of a PSM method is presented in Algorithm 2.. Notice the relation of this approach with the estimation of distribution algorithms. However, the PSM approach is limited to the use of probability vectors, while specifying an essential update rule for these vectors.

Initialize a probability vector $p_0(x)$

Until stopping criteria:

  Build m individuals $x_1^l, \ldots, x_m^l$ using $p_l(x)$

  Evaluate $f(x_1^l), \ldots, f(x_m^l)$

  Rebuild a probability vector $p_{l+1}(x)$ while considering $x_1^l, \ldots, x_m^l$ and $f(x_1^l), \ldots, f(x_m^l)$

End

Algorithm 2. The scope of the *PSM* method

Initialize a population P_0 of n points

Until stopping criteria:

  Memorize the worst point θ

  Search an appropriate distribution $D_i(X)$ from the population P_{i-1}

  Build a population O_i of m points according to $D_i(X)$, with $\forall O_i^j \in O_i$: $f\left(O_i^j\right) < f(\theta)$

  Create a population P_i from a part of P_{i-1} and a part of O_i

  Evaluate P_i

End

Algorithm 3. The IDEA approach

The EDA's were presented as evolutionary algorithms, with an explicit diversification [44]. They are undoubtedly the algorithms closest to a general scope. The Iterated Density Evolutionary Algorithms [7, 8, 9] (IDEA) are a generalization of those, presented in Algorithm 3..

IDEA uses a more general diversification than PSM, while not being limited to a probability vector as model, but specifying that the search for the best probability distribution forms an integral part of the algorithm. However, the fall of dispersion is carried out by selecting the best individuals, no precision on the use of different intensification principles is given.

2.4 I&D frame

A classical problem when designing metaheuristics is the difficulty to achieve the balance between intensification and diversification. This has lead Blum and Roli to propose the *I&D frame* [51], which emphasizes the fact that the different components of a metaheuristic cannot be categorized as performing *strict* intensification or diversification. They propose to consider that components could be spaced out between three poles, determined upon the origin of the information comes from:

- the objective function,
- a random process,
- other functions.

Furthermore, each component can be considered as *intrinsic* or *strategic,* depending whether the component is defined by the basic idea of the metaheuristic, or added to it to improve its performances.

However, this framework does not give precise indication on the algorithms design, nor on the relation between components and probabilistic sampling aspects.

2.5 Self-organization and swarm intelligence

As a field of research, swarm intelligence deals with the study of self-organization in natural and artificial swarm systems. The *self-organization* is a phenomenon described in many disciplines, notably in the fields of physics and biology. A formal definition has been proposed in [10, p.8]:

> Self-organization is a process in which *pattern* at the global level of a system *emerges* solely from numerous interactions among *lower-level* components of the system. Moreover, the rules specifying interactions among the system's components are executed using only local information, without reference to the *global* pattern.

Two terms need clarification for a better understanding, "pattern" and "to emerge". Generally, the first one applies to an "organized arrangement of objects in space or time". Additionally, an *emerging* property of a system is a characteristic which appears unforeseen (not being *explicitly* determined), from the interactions among the components of this system.

Thus, the crucial question is to understand how the components of a system interact with each other to produce a complex pattern (in relative sense of the term, i.e. *more* complex than the components themselves). A certain number of necessary phenomena have been identified: these are the processes *of feedback* and the management of the *information flow.*

The *positive feedbacks* are processes which result in reinforcing the action, for example by amplification, facilitation, self-catalysis, etc. Positive feedbacks are able to amplify the *fluctuations of* the system, permitting the updating of even imperceptible informations. Such

processes can easily lead to an explosion of the system, if they are not controlled by applying *negative feedbacks*. Hence negative feedbacks act as stabilizers for the system. When they are coupled, such feedback processes can generate powerful models.
Within the framework of biological behavior, it is easy to understand that the interactions among the components of a system will very often give rise to *communications* processes i.e. transfer of information between individuals. Generally, individuals can communicate, either by means of signals, i.e. by using a specific means to carry information, or by means of indices, where information is carried accidentally. In a similar manner, information can come directly from other individuals, or pass via the state of a work in progress. This second possibility of exchanging information, by means of modifying the environment, is called the *stigmergy*.
Generally, all these processes are more or less inter-connected, allowing a system consisting of a large number of individuals to act together to solve problems that are too complex for a single individual.
Certain characteristics of the self-organized systems are very interesting, in particular their *dynamism*, or their capacity to generate *stable* patterns. Within the framework of the study of the behavior of the social insects, certain concepts related to the principle of self-organization deserve to be underlined: the intrinsic *decentralisation* of these systems, their organization in *dense heterarchy* and the recurring use of the *stigmergy*. Indeed, these concepts are sometimes used to view the same problem from different angles and partially cover the principles of self-organization.
In a swarm intelligence system, there is no decision-making at a given level, in a specified order and no predetermined actions. In fact, in a decentralized system, each individual has a *local* vision of his environment, and thus does not know the problem as a whole. The literature of the multi-agent systems (see [24] for an initial approach) often employs this term or that of "distributed artificial intelligence" [34]. However, generally this discipline tends to study more complex behaviors patterns, founded in particular in cognitive sciences.
To be precise, the advantages of decentralized control are the *robustness* and the *flexibility* [6]. Robust systems are desired because of their ability to continue to function in the event of breakdown of one of their components; flexible devices are welcome, because they can be useful for dynamic problems.

2.6 Adaptive Learning Search

Adaptive Learning Search (ALS) is a framework for considering the structure of metaheuristics [21], relying on the AMP, the I&D frame and the notion of objective function sampling.
Instead of considering only a memorization process, as in AMP, we propose to consider a *learning* phase. Indeed, the memory concept is quite static and passive; in a sampling approach, it suggests that the sample is simply stored, and that the metaheuristic only takes into account the previous iteration, without considering the whole optimization process. We emphasize on the fact that the memorized data is not only a raw input, but provides *information* on the distribution, and thus on the solutions.
Thereby, we propose to consider three terms to describe the characteristic processes in a population metaheuristic: learning, diversification and intensification. Metaheuristics progress in an iterative way, archetypally by alternating phases of intensification, diversification and learning, or mixing these notions in a more narrow way. The state of

departure is often randomly chosen, the algorithm running until a criterion of stop is reached. A simple ALS algorithm could thus be organized as presented in Algorithm 4.

Initialize a sample;

Iterate until stopping criteria:

> **Sampling:** either explicit, implicit or direct,
>
> **Learning:** the algorithm extracts information from the sample,
>
> **Diversification:** it searches for new solutions,
>
> **Intensification:** it searches to improve the existing sample,
>
> **Replace** the previous sample with the new one.

End

Algorithm 4. ALS algorithm

The diversification indicates the processes harvesting information about the optimized problem. The intensification aims at using the information already harvested to define how much an area is interesting. The memory is the support of the learning, which allows the algorithm to take into account only zones where the global optimum may be, so avoiding the local optima. The notions of intensification and diversification are important in the design of metaheuristics, which have to reach a delicate balance between these two dynamics of search. Both notions are not thus contradictory, but additional, and there are numerous strategies mixing at the same moment both of the aspects.

We use here a terminology similar to the one used for the I&D frame, but slightly modified to be easier to comprehend and manipulate. Notably, we have chosen to assign the terms to archetypal processes:

Intensification: the sampling only uses informations from the objective function (local search, determinist selection operators, etc.),

Diversification: the sampling is purely random (noise, uniform mutation operator),

Learning: use of a distribution constructed from the whole set of solutions sampled from the start of the algorithm.

Moreover, in ALS, we proposed to split up metaheuristics in three categories, according to the way the sampling is managed:

Implicit: an implicit probability density function (PDF) is used to draw the sample (e.g. evolutionary algorithms),

Explicit: a specific PDF is used (e.g. estimation of distribution algorithms),

Direct: an approximation of the objective function is used as a PDF (e.g. simulated annealing).

The implicit methods permit to avoid the hard choice of the PDF model to use, but are difficult to control and understand. Explicit methods permit to control their components almost independently, but are pledged to the choice of a model. The direct algorithms use the "ideal" model (the objective function itself), but make the intensification difficult.

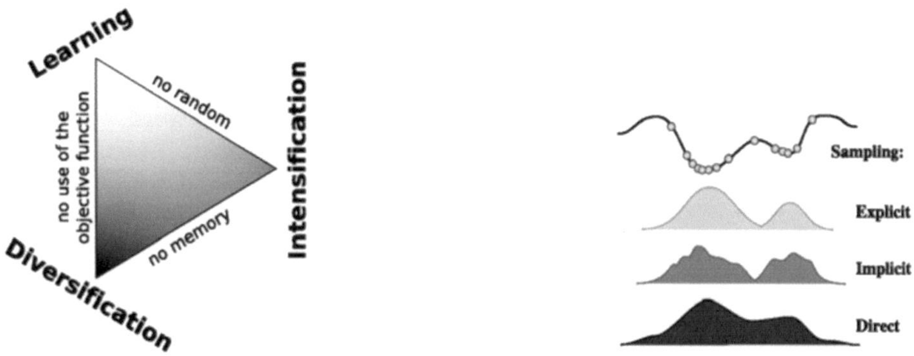

Figure 1. The three classes of metaheuristics proposed in adaptive learning search are defined according to the sampling of the objective function. They combine themselves with the three archetypal components, that form the set of possible behaviours

3. Metaheuristics

Metaheuristics form a wide class of methods, among which the more interesting are often stochastic algorithms manipulating a sample of points (also called a "population" of "individuals"). In this section, we will briefly introduce some of the best known metaheuristics, from the simulated annealing (which does not use swarm intelligence) to ant colony algorithms (a method well known for using swarm intelligence). Each metaheuristic is here described along with its position regarding adaptive learning search and swarm intelligence.

3.1 Simulated Annealing

The simulated annealing [37, 11] was created from the analogy between a physical process (the annealing) and an optimization problem. As a metaheuristic, it is based on works simulating the evolution of a solid towards its minimal energetic state [41, 30].
The classic description of simulated annealing presents it as a probabilistic algorithm, where a point evolves in the search space. The method uses the Metropolis algorithm, recalled in Algorithm 5., inducing a markovian process [1, 38]. The simulated annealing, in its usual version ("homogeneous"), calls this method at each iteration.

Initialize a starting point x_0 and a *temperature* T

For $i = 1$ to n:

  Until x_i accepted

    If $f(x_i) \leq f(x_{i-1})$: accept x_i

    If $f(x_i) > f(x_{i-1})$: accept x_i with a probability $e^{-\frac{f(x_i)-f(x_{i-1})}{T}}$

  End

End

Algorithm 5. Sampling with the Metropolis method

It is possible to see the simulated annealing as a population algorithm. Indeed, the Metropolis algorithm directly samples the objective function using a degenerated parametric Boltzmann distribution (of parameter T). Hence, one of the essential parameters is the temperature decrease, for which many laws were proposed [54]. There also exist some versions of the simulated annealing more centred on the handling of a points population [32, 55, 40, 33].
Here, the Metropolis method represents the diversification (coupled with the learning), while the temperature decrease is controlling the intensification process. Note that other methods than Metropolis' may be used [14, 48].
Algorithm 6. presents a synthesis of the simulated annealing. The learning step is not present in basic versions, but many existing variants have tried to link the temperature to certain characteristics of the sampling obtained through the Metropolis method [25, 46, 19].

Sampling: direct.

Learning: relational mechanisms between the set of points and the temperature.

Diversification: sampling of the objective function through the Metropolis method.

Intensification: temperature decrease.

Algorithm 6. ALS model for the simulated annealing

Simulated annealing cannot be considered as a metaheuristic using swarm intelligence operators. Indeed, the behavior of the system is defined by a global rule (the Metropolis method), without any use of local interactions. Finally, the simulated annealing is mainly characterized by its direct sampling of the objective function. The mechanism behind this algorithm is one of the most common to all the metaheuristics and should thus be underlined.

3.2 Estimation of Distribution Algorithms

Estimation of Distribution Algorithms (EDA) were first created as an alternative to evolutionary algorithms [44]: the main difference is that crossover and mutation steps are replaced by the choice of random individuals with respect to an estimated distribution obtained from the previous populations. The general process is presented in Algorithm 7.
The main difficulty is how to estimate the distribution; the algorithms used for this are based on an evaluation of the dependency of the variables, and can belong to three different categories:

1. Models without any dependency: the probability distribution is factorized from univariant independent distributions, over each dimension. That choice has the defect not to be realistic in case of hard optimization, where a dependency between variables is often the rule.
2. Models with *bivariant* dependency: the probability distribution is factorized from bivariant distributions. In this case, the learning of distribution can be extended to the notion of *structure*.

3. Models with *multiple* dependencies: the factorization of the probability distribution is obtained from statistics with an order *higher* than two.

$D_0 \leftarrow$ Randomly generate M individuals.

$i = 0$

While stopping criteria:

$i = i + 1$

$D_{i-1}^{S_e} \leftarrow$ Select $N \leq M$ individuals in D_{i-1} using the selection method.

$p_i(x) = p\left(x \mid D_{i-1}^{S_e}\right) \leftarrow$ Estimate the probability distribution of the selected individuals.

$D_i \leftarrow$ Sample M individuals from $p_i(x)$

End

Algorithm 7. Estimation of distribution algorithm

For continuous problems, the distribution model is often based on a normal distribution. Some important variants were proposed, using for example "data clustering" for multimodal optimization, parallel variants for discrete problems (see [39]). Convergence theorems were also formulated, in particular with modeling by Markov chains, or dynamic systems.
EDA algorithms in the ALS scope are modelled in Algorithm 8.

Using an *explicit* sampling.

Learning: extraction of the parameters of an explicit distribution;

Diversification: sampling of the distribution;

Intensification: selection (or dispersion reduction techniques).

Algorithm 8. ALS model for estimation of distribution algorithms

3.3 Particle Swarm Optimization

The particle swarm optimization ("Particle Swarm Optimization", *PSO)* [35, 36] evolved from an analogy drawn with the collective behavior of the animal displacements (in fact, the metaphor was largely derived from socio-psychology). Indeed, for certain groups of animals, e.g. the fish schools, the dynamic behavior in relatively complex displacements can be observed, where the individuals themselves have access only to limited information, like the position and the speed of their closer neighbors. For example, it can be observed that a fish school is able to avoid a predator in the following manner: initially it gets divided into two groups, then the original school is reformed, while maintaining the cohesion among the school.

The authors, who proposed the method of particle swarm optimization, drew their original inspiration by first comparing the behaviors in accordance with the theory of socio-psychology for data processing and the decision-making in social groups, side by side. It is an exceptional and remarkable achievement that this metaheuristic was originally conceived for the continuous domain, and, till date, majority of its applications are in this domain. The method conceives a large group *of particles,* in the form of vectors, moving in the search space. Each particle *i* is characterized by its *position* $\vec{x}_i$ and a vector of change in position (called *velocity)* $\vec{v}_i$. In each iteration, the movement of the particle can be characterized as: $\vec{x}_i(t) = \vec{x}_i(t-1) + \vec{v}_i(t-1)$. The core of the method consists in the manner in which $\vec{v}_i$ is chosen, after each iteration. Socio-psychology suggests that the movements of the individuals (in a socio-cognitive chart) are influenced by their last behavior and that of their neighbors (closely placed in the social network and not necessarily in space). Hence, the updating of the position of the particles is dependent on the direction of their movement, their speed, the best preceding position $\vec{p}_i$ and the best position $\vec{p}_g$ among the neighbors:

$$\vec{x}_i(t) = f\left(\vec{x}_i(t-1), \vec{v}_i(t-1), \vec{p}_i, \vec{p}_g\right)$$

The change in position, in each iteration, is thus implemented according to the following relation:

$$\begin{cases} \vec{v}_i(t) = \vec{v}_i(t-1) + \varphi_1\left(\vec{p}_i - \vec{x}_i(t-1)\right) + \varphi_2\left(\vec{p}_g - \vec{x}_i(t-1)\right) \\ \vec{x}_i(t) = \vec{x}_i(t-1) + \vec{v}_i(t-1) \end{cases}$$

where the φ_n parameters are drawn randomly from the discourse $U_{[0,\varphi_{max}]}$ and are influential in striking a balance between the relative roles of the *individual experience* (governed by φ_1) and of the *social communication* (governed by φ_2). Uniform random selection of these two parameters is justified from the fact that it does not give any a priori importance to any of the two sources of information. The algorithm also employs another parameter, V_{max}, to limit the rapidity of movement in each dimension, so that it can prevent any "explosion" of the system, in case there are too large amplifications of the oscillations.

The algorithm could implement an effective compromise between intensification and diversification. The only problem arises when the points p_i and p_g move apart, in that case the particles will continue to oscillate between these two points without converging. An interesting characteristic of this algorithm is that, if a new optimum is discovered after the algorithm converged (i.e., after a phase of intensification), the particles will explore the search space around the new point (i.e. a phase of diversification).

The ALS modelling of this generic scheme is presented in Algorithm 13.

Sampling: implicit.

Learning: weight accorded to the best solutions and spreading of this information in the swarm.

Diversification: expansion of the swarm.

Intensification: contraction of the swarm around a point.

Algorithm 9. ALS model for particle swarm optimization

In this algorithm, the positive feedbacks are situated at the level of the particles attraction. The moves limitations of each particle form the negative feedbacks. There is a memory situated at the local level, between neighbor particles, as each one does only move according to the state of its closest neighbors, and not according to the whole system.
The readers are redirected to read [36] to obtain a detailed, state of the art, understanding of the particle swarm optimization and the concepts associated with it and [12] for a synthesis.

3.4 Evolutionary Algorithms

Evolutionary algorithms [23] are inspired from the biological process of the adaptation of alive beings to their environment. The analogy between an optimization problem and this biological phenomenon has been formalized by several approaches [31, 26, 49], leading for example to the famous family of genetic algorithms [27]. The term *population* metaheuristics fits particularly well; following the metaphor, the successive populations are called *generations*. A new generation is computed in three stages, detailed below.

1. Selection: improves the reproduction ability of the best adapted individuals.
2. Crossover: produces one or two new individuals from their two parents, while recombining their characteristics.
3. Mutation: randomly modifies the characteristics of an individual.

One clearly identifies the third step with the diversification stage, while the first one stands for the intensification. We interpret the crossover as a learning from the previous information (*i.e.* from the ancesters). Several methods [52, 29, 28, 5] were designed for the diversification operators, which emphasize the implicit process of distribution sampling.
The ALS modelling of this generic scheme is presented in Algorithm 13.

Sampling: implicit.

Learning: crossover.

Diversification: mutation.

Intensification: selection.

Algorithm 10. ALS model for evolutionary algorithms

In this family of metaheuristics, feedback processes are sometimes difficult to figure out, as there are many variants. Generally speaking, the positive feedbacks are situated on selection operators, whereas negative feedbacks are typically implemented in mutation operators. There is a form of local memory, as the evolution of each individual at each iteration is linked to the evolution of its neighbors.

3.5 Immune Systems

The term "artificial immune systems" *(AIS)* is applicable for a vast range of different systems, in particular for metaheuristic optimization, inspired by the operation of the immune system of the vertebrates. A great number of systems have been conceived in several varied fields e.g. robotics, the detection of anomalies or optimization (see [18] for a detailed exploration of various applications) .

The immune system is responsible for the protection of the organism against the "aggressions" of external organisms. The metaphor from which the *AIS* algorithms originate harps on the aspects of *training* and *memory* of the immune system known as *adaptive* (in opposition to the system known as *innate),* in particular by discriminating between *self* and *non-self.*

1. Generate a collection of solutions P composed of an entire collection of cell memories P_M added to the present population P_r: $P = P_M + P_r$;
2. Determine the n best cells P_n from the population P, which is based on the measure of affinity;
3. Clone n individuals to form a population C. The number of clones produced for each cell is a function of affinity;
4. Implement a hyper-mutation process for the clones, which thus generates a population C^*. The mutation is proportional to affinity;
5. Select the individuals C^* to form the memory population P_M;
6. Replace the worst individuals in P to form P_r;
7. If a termination criterion is not reached, return to 1.

Algorithm 11. A simple example of the algorithm of *artificial immune system*

The principal ideas used for the design of this metaheuristic are the selections operated on the lymphocytes accompanied by the positive feedback, allowing the multiplication and the implementation of memory by the system. Indeed, these are the chief characteristics to maintain the self-organized characteristics of the system.

The approach used in the *AIS* algorithms is very similar to that of the evolutionary algorithms but was also compared with that of the neural networks. Within the framework of difficult optimization, the *AIS* can be regarded to take the shape of evolutionary algorithm, introducing particular operators. To operate the selection, it has to be based, for example, on a measurement of affinity (i.e. between the receiver of a lymphocyte and an antigen). The process of mutation takes place through an operator of hyper-mutation, resulting directly from the metaphor. In the final analysis, the algorithm developed is very close to a genetic algorithm (see algorithm 11.).

The ALS modelling of this generic scheme is presented in Algorithm 12.

Sampling: implicit.

Learning: memory.

Diversification: mutation.

Intensification: selection.

Algorithm 12. ALS model for immune systems

A description of the basic theory and many applications of the artificial immune systems can be found in [17], [18] and in [16], and also in a book of reference [15].

3.6 Ant Colony Algorithms

An elegant description of ant colony algorithms was proposed in [20], which can be applied to the (combinatorial) problems where a partial construction of the solution is possible. This description, although restrictive, makes it possible to highlight the original contributions of these metaheuristics (called *ACO*, for "Ant Colony Optimization", by the authors).

> Artificial ants used in ACO are stochastic solution construction procedures that probabilistically build a solution by iteratively adding solution components to partial solutions by taking into account (i) heuristic information on the problem instance being solved, if available, and (ii) (artificial) pheromone trails which change dynamically at run-time to reflect the agents' acquired search experience.

A more precise formalization exists [20]. It develops a *representation* of the problem on the basis of a basic *behavior* of the ants and a general *organization* of the metaheuristic under consideration. Several concepts have also been laid down to facilitate the understanding of the principles of these algorithms, in particular the definition of the trails of pheromone as an *adaptive memory*, the need for an adjustment of *intensification /diversification* and finally, the use of a *local search.*

The problem is represented by a *set of solutions*, an *objective function* assigning a value for each solution and a *set of constraints.* The objective is to find the global optimum satisfying the constraints. The various states of the problem are characterized similarly to a sequence of components. It should be noted that, in certain cases, a cost can be associated to the states which do not belong to the set of solutions. In this representation, the ants build solutions while moving on a graph $G = (C,L)$, where the nodes are the components of C and the set L connects the components of C'. The constraints of the problem are implemented directly in the rules of displacement of the ants (either by preventing the movements which violate the constraints, or by penalizing such solutions).

The movements of the ants can be characterized like a stochastic procedure of *building* constructive solutions on the graph $G = (C, L)$. In general, the ants try to work out feasible solutions, but if necessary, they can produce unfeasible solutions. The components and the connections can be associated with the trails of pheromone τ (establishing an adaptive memory describing the state of the system) and a heuristic value η (representing a priori information about the problem, or originating from a source other than that of the ants; it is very often the cost of the state in progress). The trails of pheromone and the value of the heuristics can be associated either with the components, or with the connections.

Each ant has a memory to store the path traversed, an initial state and the stopping conditions. The ants move according to a probabilistic rule of decision function of the local *trails* of pheromone, *state* of the ant and *constraints* of the problem. At the time of addition of a component to the solution in progress, the ants can update the trail associated with the component or the corresponding connection. Once the solution is built, they can update the trail of pheromone components or connections used. Lastly, an ant has the capacity of at least building a solution for the problem.

In addition to the rules governing the behavior of the ants, another major process is activated: the *evaporation* of the trails of pheromone. In fact, with each iteration, the value of the trails of pheromone is *decreased.* The goal of this reduction is to avoid a too fast

convergence and the trapping of the algorithm in local minima. This causes a gradual lapse in memory which helps in exploration of new areas.
According to the authors of the *AGO* formalism, it is possible to implement other processes requiring a *centralized* control (and thus not being able to be directly controlled by some ants), as additional processes. In our opinion, this is not desirable; in fact, one then loses the decentralized characteristic of the system. Moreover, the implementation of the *additional* processes with rigorous formalization becomes difficult, because one should be able to view any process there.
The use of the *stigmergy* is a crucial factor for the ant colony algorithms. Hence, the choice of the method for implementation of the trails of pheromone is significant to obtain the best results. This choice is mainly related to the possibilities of *representation* of the search space, each representation being able to bring a different way to implement the trails. For example, for the traveling salesman problem, an effective implementation consists in using a trail τ_{ij} between two cities *i* and *j* like a representation of the *interest* to visit the city *j* after the city *i*. Another possible representation, less effective in practice, consists in considering τ_{ij} as a representation of the interest to visit *i* as the *j*th city. In fact, the trails of pheromone describe the state of the search for the solution by the system in each iteration and the agents modify the way in which the problem will be *represented* and perceived by the other agents. This information is shared by the ants by means of modifications of the *environment,* in form of an indirect communication: the stigmergy.
The structure of ant colony metaheuristics comprises of an *intrinsic parallelism*. Generally, the good quality solutions emerge as a result of the indirect *interactions* taking place inside the system, not of an explicit implementation of exchanges. Here each ant takes only the local information about its environment (the trails of pheromones) into account; it is thus very easy to parallel such an algorithm. It is interesting to note that the various processes in progress in the metaheuristic (i.e. the behavior of the ants, evaporation and the additional processes) can also be implemented independently, the user has the liberty to decide the manner in which they will interact.

Sampling: implicit.

Learning: memory, construction of the model.

Diversification: random search for new solution components.

Intensification: evaporation, heuristics.

Algorithm 13. ALS model for ant colony algorithms

4. Conclusion

Population metaheuristics can be viewed as algorithms handling a probabilistic sampling of a probability distribution, representing the objective function of an optimization problem. These algorithms can be described either as implicit, explicit or direct, according to their way of sampling the objective function. These algorithms are iteratively manipulating the sample thanks to components that can be classified among three tendencies: learning,

intensification and diversification. These metaheuristics can thus be viewed as adaptive learning search algorithms.
A lot of the stochastic metaheuristics make use of swarm intelligence to design efficient components that can solve a large scale of different hard optimization problems. Among them, implicit metaheuristics like evolutionary computation or particle swarm optimization are the most known for their self-organized aspects.
These two theories are thus complementary and, from the point of view of the design of metaheuristics, there is a simple relation between them: the ALS describes the "goal" to be reached, and the theory of the swarm intelligence a "means" to reach this goal. So, an effective metaheuristic should, according to the adaptive learning search, set up mechanisms of learning, intensification and diversification, stays the question of the means to be used to set up these mechanisms. The swarm intelligence proposes a model of implementation: an algorithm on base of population defining simple interactions at the local level, allowing the emergence of a complex behavior at the global level.
Both presented theories should allow to better understand the functioning of existing metaheuristics and to direct the design of new ones. The concepts important to retain are the use by modern metaheuristics of learning, intensification and diversification, as well as the distributed aspect and the flexible hose of the swarm intelligence. However it is necessary to underline the difficulty to design a swarm intelligence system, what explains that the inspiration comes from the biology, where such systems are relatively common. The main difficulties are the following ones:

- Design sampling operators from which it is easy to extract the relevant information to direct the search,
- Set the balance between techniques of intensification, diversification and learning,
- Maintain the flexibility of the algorithm, so that it adapts itself to the problem.

5. Bibliography

E. H. L. Aarts and P. J. M. Van Laarhoven. Statistical cooling : a general approach to combinatorial optimisation problems. *Philips J. of Research,* 40:193-226, 1985. [1]

S. Baluja. Population-based Incremental Learning: A Method for Integrating Genetic Search Based Function Optimization and Competitive Learning. *Technical Report* CMU-CS-94-163, Carnegie Mellon University, 1994. [2]

S. Baluja. Genetic Algorithms and Explicit Search Statistics. *Advances in Neural Information Processing Systems,* 9:319-325, 1997. [3]

S. Baluja and R. Caruana. Removing the Genetics from the Standard Genetic Algorithm. In A. Prieditis and S. Russel, editors, *International Conference on Machine Learning,* pages 38-46, Lake Tahoe, California, 1995. Morgan Kaufmann. [4]

S. Baluja and S. Davies. Fast probabilistic modeling for combinatorial optimization. In *Fifteenth National Conference on Artificial Intelligence, Tenth Conference on Innovative Applications of Artificial Intelligence,* Madison, Wisconsin, 1998. [5]

E. Bonabeau, M. Dorigo, and G. Theraulaz. *Swarm Intelligence, From Natural to Artificial Systems.* Oxford University Press, 1999. [6]

P. A. N. Bosnian and D. Thierens. An algorithmic framework for density estimation based evolutionary algorithm. Technical Report UU-CS-1999-46, Utrech University, 1999. [7]

P.A.N. Bosnian and D. Thierens. Continuous iterated density estimation evolutionary algorithms within the IDEA framework. In M. Muehlenbein and A.O. Rodriguez, editors, *Proceedings of the Optimization by Building and Using Probabilistic Models OBUPM Workshop at the Genetic and Evolutionary Computation Conference GECCO-2000,* pages 197—200, San Francisco, California, 2000. Morgan Kauffmann. [8]

P.A.N. Bosnian and D. Thierens. IDEAs based on the normal kernels probability density function. Technical Report UU-CS-2000-11, Utrecht University, 2000. [9]

S. Camazine, J.L. Deneubourg, N. Franks, J. Sneyd, G. Theraulaz, and E. Bonabeau. *Self-Organization in Biological Systems.* Princeton University Press, 2000. [10]

V. Cerny. Thermodynamical approach to the traveling salesman problem : an efficient simulation algorithm. *J. of Optimization Theory and Applications,* 45(1):41-51, 1985. [11]

M. Clerc. L'optimisation par essaim particulaire : principes, modeles et usages. *Technique et Science Informatiques,* 21:941—964, 2002. [12]

A. Colorni, M. Dorigo, and V. Maniezzo. Distributed Optimization by Ant Colonies. In F. Varela and P. Bourgine, editors, *Proceedings of ECAL'91 -First European Conference on Artificial Life,* pages 134-142, Paris, France, 1992. Elsevier Publishing. [13]

M. Creutz. Microcanonical Monte Carlo simulation. *Physical Review Letters,* 50(19):1411-1414, May 1983. [14]

D. Dasgupta. *Artificial Immune Systems and their applications.* Springer Verlag, 1999. [15]

D. Dasgupta and N. Attoh-Okine. Immune-based systems: A survey. In *Proceedings of the IEEE International Conference on Systems, Man and Cybernetics,* volume 1, pages 369—374, Orlando, October 1997. IEEE Press. [16]

L.N. De Castro and F. Von Zuben. Artificial Immune Systems: Part I: Basic Theory and Applications. Technical Report TR-DCA 01/99, Department of Computer Engineering and Industrial Automation, School of Electrical and Computer Engineering, State University of Campinas, Brazil, December 1999. [17]

L.N. De Castro and F. Von Zuben. Artificial Immune Systems: Part II -A Survey of Applications. Technical Report DCA-RT 02/00, Department of Computer Engineering and Industrial Automation, School of Electrical and Computer Engineering, State University of Campinas, Brazil, February 2000. [18]

P. M. C. De Oliveira. Broad Histogram : An Overview, *arxiv :cond-mat/0003300vl,* 2000. [19]

M. Dorigo and T. Stiitzle. *Handbook of Metaheuristics,* volume 57 of *International series in operations research and management science,* chapter The Ant Colony Optimization Metaheuristics: Algorithms, Applications and Advances. Kluwer Academic Publishers, Boston Hardbound, January 2003. [20]

J. Dreo, J.-P. Aumasson, W. Tfaili, and P. Siarry. Adaptive learning search, a new tool to help comprehending metaheuristics. *International Journal on Artificial Intelligence Tools,* 16(3), June 2007. [21]

J. Dreo, A. Petrowski, P. Siarry, and E. D. Taillard. *Metaheuristics for hard optimization.* Springer, 2006. [22]

J. E. Eiben, A. E. Smith. *Introduction to Evolutionary Computing.* Springer Verlag, 2003. [23]

J. Ferber. *Les systemes multi-agents. Vers une intelligence collective.* In-terEditions, 1997. [24]

A. M. Ferrenberg and R. H. Swendsen. Optimized Monte Carlo Data Analysis. *Phys. Rev. Lett,* 63:1195, 1989. [25]

L. J. Fogel, A. J. Owens, and M. J. Walsh. *Artifical Intelligence through Simulated Evolution.* Wiley, 1966. [26]

D. E. Goldberg. *Genetic Algorithms in Search, Optimization and Machine learning.* Addison-Wesley, 1989. [27]

G. Harik. Linkage learning in via probabilistic modeling in the EcGA. *Technical Report* 99010, IlliGAL, 1999. [28]

G. Harik, F. G. Lobo, and D. E. Goldberg. The compact genetic algorithm. In *IEEE Conference on Evolutionary Computation,* pages 523-528, 1998. [29]

W. K. Hastings. Monte Carlo sampling method using Markov chains and their applications. *Biometrika,* 57, 1970. [30]

J. H. Holland. Outline for logical theory of adaptive systems. *J. Assoc. Comput. Mach.,* 3:297-314, 1962. [31]

K. Hukushima and K Nemoto. Exchange Monte Carlo method and application to spin glass simulations. *J. Phys. Soc. Jpn.,* 65:1604-1608, 1996. [32]

Y. Iba. Population Annealing: An approach to finite-temperature calculation. In *Joint Workshop of Hayashibara Foundation and SMAPIP.* Hayashibara Forum, 2003. [33]

N. R. Jennings. Coordination Techniques for Distributed Artificial Intelligence. In G. M. P. O'Hare and N. R. Jennings, editor, *Foundations of Distributed Artificial Intelligence,* pages 187-210. John Wiley & Sons, 1996. [34]

J. Kennedy and R. C. Eberhart. Particle swarm optimization. In *Proc. IEEE Int. Conf. on Neural Networks,* volume IV, pages 1942-1948, Piscat-away, NJ: IEEE Service Center, 1995. [35]

J. Kennedy, R.C. Eberhart, and Y. Shi. *Swarm Intelligence.* Evolutionary Computation. Morgan Kaufmann, April 2001. [36]

S. Kirkpatrick, C.D. Gelatt, and M.P. Vecchi. Optimization by simulated annealing. *Science,* 220(4598):671-680, 1983. [37]

W. Krauth. *Advances in Computer Simulation,* chapter Introduction To Monte Carlo Algorithms. Springer-Verlag, 1998. [38]

P. Larranaga and J.A. Lozano. *Estimation of Distribution Algorithms, A New Tool for Evolutionary Computation.* Genetic Algorithms and Evolutionary Computation. Kluwer Academic Publishers, 2002. [39]

F. Liang and W. H. Wong. Evolutionary Monte Carlo: Application to C_p Model Sampling and Change Point Theorem. *Statistica Sinica,* 10, 2000. [40]

N. Metropolis, A. W. Rosenbluth, M. N. Rosenbluth, A. H. Teller, and E. Teller. Equation of state calculations by fast computing machines. *Journal of Chemical Physics,* 21:1087-1092, 1953. [41]

N. Monmarche, E. Ramat, G. Dromel, M. Slimane, and G. Venturini. On the similarities between AS, BSC and PBIL: toward the birth of a new meta-heuristics. E3i 215, Universite de Tours, 1999. [42]

N. Monmarche, N. Ramat, L. Desbarat, and G. Venturini. Probabilistic search with genetic algorithms and ant colonies. In A.S. Wu, editor, *Proceedings of the 2000 Genetic and Evolutionary Computation Conference Workshop,* pages 209-211, 2000. [43]

H. Miihlenbein and G. Paa/3. From recombination of genes to the estimation of distributions I. Binary parameters. *Lecture Notes in Computer Science 1411: Parallel Problem Solving from Nature,* PPSN IV:178-187, 1996. [44]

J. A. Nelder and R. Mead. A simplex method for function minimization. *Computer Journal,* 7:308 — 313, 1965. [45]

M. E. J. Newman and R. G. Palmer. Error estimation in the histogram Monte Carlo method. *arxiv:cond-mat/98043006,* 1998. [46]

G. Nicolis and I. Prigogine. *Self-organization in Non-equilibrium Systems.* New York, 1977. [47]

Y Okamoto and U. H. E. Hansmann. Thermodynamics of helix-coil transitions studied by multicanonical algorithms. *J. Phys. Chem.,* 99:11276— 11287, 1995. [48]

I. Rechenberg. *Cybernetic Solution Path of an Experimental Problem.* Royal Aircraft Establishment Library Translation, 1965. [49]

M.G.C. Resende. Greedy randomized adaptive search procedures (GRASP). Technical Report TR 98.41.1, AT&T Labs-Research, 2000. [50]

Christian Blum Andrea Roli. Metaheuristics in combinatorial optimization: Overview and conceptual comparison. *ACM Computing Surveys,* 35(3):268-308, September 2003. [51]

G. Syswerda. Simulated Crossover in Genetic Algorithms. In L. D. Whitley, editor, *Second workshop on Foundations of Genetic Algorithms,* pages 239-255, San Mateo, California, 1993. Morgan Kaufmann. [52]

E. D. Taillard, L. M. Gambardella, M. Gendreau, and J.-Y. Potvin. Adaptive Memory Programming: A Unified View of Meta-Heuristics. *European Journal of Operational Research,* 135(1): 1—16, 1998. [53]

E. Triki, Y. Collette, and P. Siarry. A theoretical study on the behavior of simulated annealing leading to a new cooling schedule. *European Journal of Operational Research,* 166:77-92, 2005. [54]

O. Wendt and W. Konig. Cooperative Simulated Annealing: How Much Cooperation is Enough ? Technical Report 97-19, Institute of Information Systems, Goethe University, Frankfurt, 1997. [55]

13

Artificial Ants in the Real World: Solving On-line Problems Using Ant Colony Optimization

Bruno R. Nery[1], Rodrigo F. de Mello[1], André P. L. F. de Carvalho[1] and Laurence T. Yang[2]

[1]*Universidade de São Paulo,* [2]*St. Francis Xavier University*
[1]*Brazil,* [2]*Canada*

1. Introduction

In the last years, there has been a large growth in the research of computational techniques inspired in nature. This area, named Bioinspired Computing, has provided biologically motivated solutions for several real world problems. Among Bioinspired Computing techniques, one can mention Artificial Neural Networks (ANN), Evolutionary Algorithms (EA), Artificial Immune Systems (AIS) and Ant Colony Optimization (ACO).

ACO is a meta-heuristic based on the structure and behavior of ant colonies. It has been successfully applied to several optimization problems. Several real world optimization problems may change the configuration of its search space with time. These problems are known as dynamic optimization problems. This chapter presents the main concepts of ACO and show how it can be applied to solve real optimization problems on dynamic environments. As a case study, it will be illustrated how ACO can be applied to process scheduling problems.

The chapter starts describing how real ants forage for food, environmental modifications related to this activity (for example, the blockage of a path) and the effects of these modifications in the colony. After, a brief review of previous works on Ant Colony Optimization is presented.

For computer simulations, the activities of an ant colony may be modeled as a graph. After modeling the problem of foraging for food (as a graph), the goal (finding the shortest path at a given moment) is defined and the mechanism to solve the problem is presented.

The need to model an on-line problem as a graph, the goal of finding the shortest path and the mechanisms adopted for solving the problem (an adapted version of the AntSystem) are detailed.

Before ACO is applied to the process scheduling problem, the problem is analyzed and modeled using a graph representation. Next, simulation results obtained in a set of experiments are presented, which are validated by results obtained in a real implementation. Important issues related with the use of ACO for process scheduling, like parameter adjustments, are discussed.

In the conclusion of this chapter, we point out a few future directions for ACO researches.

The use of computational techniques inspired in nature has become very frequent in the last years. This area, named Bioinspired Computing, provides efficient biologically motivated solutions for several real world problems. Among the most popular bioinspired techniques, we may cite Artificial Neural Networks (ANN), Evolutionary Algorithms (EA), Artificial Immune Systems (AIS) and Ant Colony Optimization (ACO).

ACO [DMC96], a meta-heuristic based on the structure and behavior of ant colonies, has been successfully applied to several optimization problems [FMS05, PB05, BN06, SF06, PLF02, WGDK06, CF06, HND05]. For such, it has attracted a large deal of attention lately. Next, we will briefly describe key recent works using ACO to solve real world problems.

Foong et al. [FMS05] proposed a power plant maintenance scheduling optimization considering ant colony optimization algorithms. In this work,the performance of two ACO algorithms were compared: Best Ant System (BAS) and Max-Min Ant System (MMAS). Experimental results suggested that the performance of the studied algorithms can be significantly better than those obtained by other meta-heuristics, such as genetic algorithms and simulated annealing, in this particular application. The work considered as case study a 21-unit power plant maintenance problem investigated in previous researches. In this study, parameters like the number of ants, initial pheromone level, reward factor and others were varied to investigate the ACO search sensitivity.

Pinto and Baran [PB05] presented two multiobjective algorithms for the Multicast Traffic Engineering problem considering new versions of the Multi-Objective Ant Colony System (MOACS) and the Max-Min Ant System (MMAS). These ACO algorithms simultaneously optimize the maximum link usage, the cost of a multicast routing tree, the average delay and maximum end-to-end delay. Results showed a promising performance of the proposed algorithms for a multicast traffic engineering optimization.

Bui and Nguyen [BN06] proposed an algorithm to solve the graph coloring problem. The algorithm employed a set of agents, called ants, to color the graph. The ants were distributed on the vertices of the input graph based on the conflicts. Each ant colored a portion of the graph. Although based on traditional ACO algorithms, each ant solved part of the problem, making it suitable for distributed problems.

Smaldon and Freitas [SF06] investigated a new version of the Ant-Miner algorithm [PLF02], named Unordered Rule Set Ant-Miner, which produces an unordered set of classification rules. The proposed version was compared to the original Ant-Miner algorithm in six public-domain datasets, presenting similar accuracy. However, it discovered more modular rules, which could be interpreted independently from others, supporting its application for interpreting discovered knowledge in data mining systems.

Wang *et al.* [WGDK06] proposed a design exploration method to exploit the duality between the time and resource constrained scheduling problems. The proposed approach used the Max-Min Ant Colony Optimization to solve both the time and the resource constrained scheduling problems. Compared to using force directed scheduling exhaustively at every time step, the proposed algorithm provided relevant solution quality savings with similar execution time.

Chan and Freitas [CF06] proposed a new ant colony algorithm for multi-label classification, named MuLAM (Multi-Label Ant-Miner). This algorithm is a major extension of Ant-Miner, the first ant colony algorithm for discovering classification rules. According to experimental results, MuLAM presented a better predictive accuracy than other classification techniques investigated.

Hijazi *et al.* [HND05] used an ant colony algorithm in the wireless communication domain. The problem investigated was how to detect users in a multi-user environment in synchronous MC-CDMA (Multi-Carrier Code Division Multiple Access) systems, minimizing the interference noise. The optimization solutions found by the ACO reduced the execution time requirements by as much as 98% when compared to an exhaustive search method.

All previous works found biological inspired motivations to solve real world problems. We believe that the approach followed by ant colonies to find the shortest path between their nest and a food source can provide an efficient solution to the process scheduling problem. For such, this chapter presents concepts on Ant Colony Optimization and how it can be applied to optimize process scheduling. This chapter is organized as follows: the section 2 presents ant colony optimization concepts; the problem of foraging for food and how ants solve it is presented in section 3; examples of Ant Colony Optimization algorithms are shown in section 4; the section 5 presents how Ant Colony Optimization can be used for a real class problem, in this case the process scheduling; the section 6 shows the conclusions and future directions, finally the references.

2. How real ants work

Apparently simple organisms, ants can deal with complex tasks by acting collectively. This collective behavior is supported by the release of a chemical substance, named pheromone. During their movement, ants deposit pheromone in their followed paths. The presence of pheromone in a path attracts other ants. In this way, pheromone plays a key role in the information exchange between ants, allowing the accomplishment of several important tasks. A classical example is the selection of the shortest path between their nest and a food source.

For instance, consider four ants and two possible paths, P_1 and P_2 (Figure 1), which link a nest N_E to a food source F_S, such that $P_1 > P_2$. Initially, all the ants (A_1, A_2, A_3 and A_4) are in N_E and must choose between the paths P_1 and P_2 to arrive to F_S.

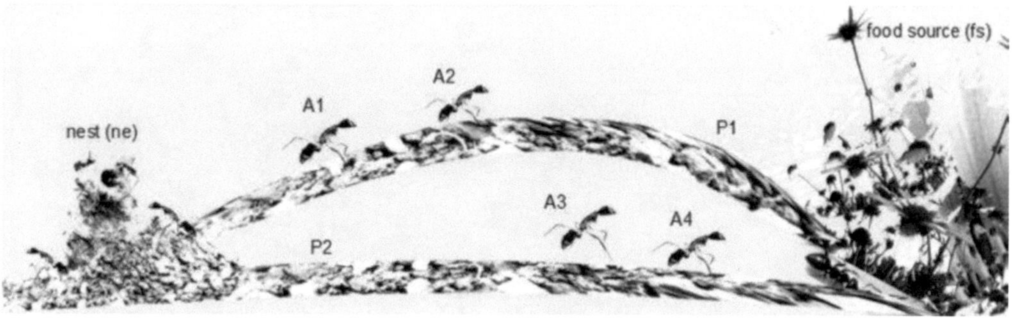

Figure 1. Ants foraging for food

1. In N_E, the ants (A_1, A_2, A_3 and A_4) do not know the localization of the food source (F_S). Thus, they randomly choose between P_1 and P_2, with the same probability. Assume that ants A_1 and A_2 choose P_1, and ants A_3 and A_4 choose P_2.
2. While the ants pass by P_1 and P_2, they leave a certain amount of pheromone on the paths, τ_{C1} and τ_{C2}, respectively.
3. As $P_1 < P_2$, A_3 and A_4 arrive to F_S before A_1 and A_2. In this moment, $\tau_{C2} = 2$. Since A_1 and A_2 have not arrived to F_S, $\tau_{C1} = 0$. In order to come back to N_E, A_3 and A_4 must choose

again between P_1 and P_2. As in F_S, $\tau_{C2} > \tau_{C1}$, the probability of these ants choosing P_2 is higher. Assume that A_3 and A_4 choose P_2.

4. When A_3 and A_4 arrive to N_E again, τ_{C2} arrives to 4. This increase in τ_{C2} and consolidates the rank of P_2 as the shortest path. When A_1 and A_2 arrive to F_S, $\tau_{C2} = 4$ and $\tau_{C1} = 2$. Thus, the probability of A_1 and A_2 coming back to N_E through P_2 becomes higher.

In the previous example, at the beginning, when there is no pheromone, an ant looking for food randomly chooses between P_1 and P_2 with a probability of 0.5 (50% of possibility for each path). When there is pheromone on at least one of the paths, the probability of selecting a given path is proportional to the amount of pheromone on it. Thus, paths with a higher concentration of pheromone have a higher chance of being selected.

However, this simple approach leads to the problem of stagnation. Suppose, for example, that ants get addicted to a particular path. Sometimes in near future, that path may become congested, becoming non-optimal. Another problem arises when a favorite path is obstructed and can no longer be used by the ants. In the case of real ants, the environment solves this problem by evaporation[1], i.e., reducing the pheromone values to prevent high concentration in optimal paths (which avoid the exploration of possible - new or better - alternatives).

3. Solving problems using ACO

In order to understand how ant colonies may be used to solve problems, we have to understand the problem of foraging for food and how ants solve it. Suppose that each location (nest, food source, etc.) is represent by a node and each path by an edge in a graph, as shown in Figure 2.

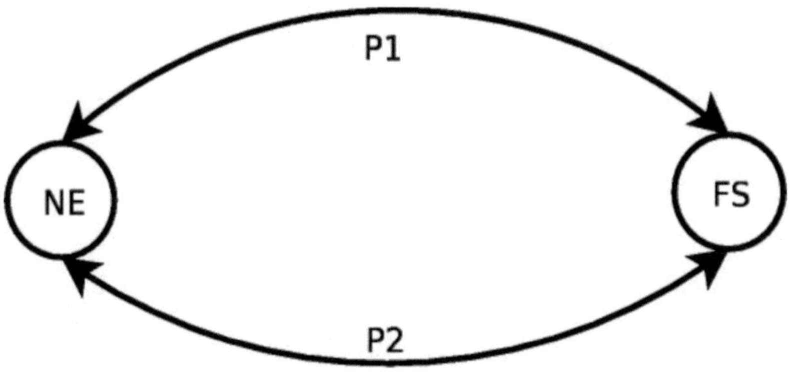

Figure 2: The forage problem modeled as a graph

Thus, to solve a problem using ant colony optimization we have to represent its domain as a graph and its goal as finding a good path. Assume the problem of the traveling salesman [FS91] where, given a set of n towns, it is necessary to find a minimal length closed tour that visits each town once. The towns are easily represented as the graph nodes and the paths, as the graph edges.

---

1 When applying ant colonies to solve real problems, this approach may be used together with an heuristic one, combining the pheromone concentration with another information to take decisions.

Another example is the problem of graph coloring: consider a graph $G = (V, E)$ where V is a set of vertices and E is a set of edges. The goal is to assign colors to the vertices in such a way that connected vertices do not have the same color. This must me done using as few different colors as possible.

4. Algorithms for Ant Colony Optimization

Based on the representation presented in the previous section, Dorigo *et al.* [DMC96] proposed an algorithm called ant-cycle which mimics the ants behavior. Dorigo showed how this algorithm can be used to solve the traveling salesman problem.

In Dorigo's algorithm, n ants are distributed in the n towns, one ant at each town. Each ant chooses among the linked towns the next visited town. The probability of each town being selected is a function of the next town distance and the amount of pheromone on the link between the current and the next towns. Ants can visit each town only once (this is achieved using a tabu list [BR03]). After completing a path, each ant leaves an amount of pheromone on the visited links. The shortest path found by an ant or set of ants is usually followed by the remaining ants, defining an optimal or suboptimal path. A pheromone evaporation process is frequently used to avoid the selection of the first tours and stagnation. A generic version of the ACO algorithm may be seen in Algorithm 1.

```
Set parameters, initialize pheromone trails
loop
        while termination conditions not met do
                Construct AntSolutions
                ApplyLocalSearch (optional)
                UpdatePheromones
        end while
end loop
Choose best solution
```

Algorithm 1 Dorigo's algorithm (ACO heuristic)

The same approach (Ant Colony Optimization) was used by Negara [G.N06] to solve the coloring graph problem (Algorithm 2). The author considered an adjacent matrix A to represent the graph $G = (V,E)$ where: $a_{uv} = 1$, if the edge $(u, v) \in E$ $a_{uv} \leq 0$, otherwise (considering $u, v \in V$). Such work considers the parallel solution of the problem where agents cope among themselves sharing experiences. It also considers elitism where the good agents can modify the mutual knowledge.

5. Applying on the real world: process scheduling

The increasing availability of low cost microprocessors and the evolution of computing networks have made economically feasible the construction of sophisticated distributed systems. In such systems, processes execute on computers and communicate to each other to perform a collaborative computing task. A load balancing algorithm is frequently adopted to distribute processes among available computers.

```
read matrix A
for iteration do
        for ant a in Ants do
                a colors the graph based on previous experience using one of the specific
                coloring algorithms
                if a is elitist then
                        a modifies the matrix A
                end if
        end for
end for
Use results
```

Algorithm 2. Negara's algorithm

A load balancing algorithm is responsible to equally distribute the processes load among the computers of a distributed environment [SKS92]. Krueger and Livny [KL87] demonstrate that such algorithms reduce the mean and standard deviation of process response times. Lower response times result in higher performance.

The load balancing algorithms involve four policies: transference, selection, location and information [SKS92]. The transference policy determines whether a computer is in a suitable state to participate in a task transfer, either as a server or as a process receiver. The selection policy defines the process to be transferred from the busiest computer to the idlest one. The location policy is responsible to find a suitable transfer partner (sender or receiver) for a computer, once the transfer policy has decided about its state. A serving computer distributes processes, when it is overloaded; a receiving computer requests processes, when it is idle. The information policy defines when and how the information regarding the computer availability is updated in the system. Several works related to load balancing can be found in the literature [ZF87, TL89, SKS92, MTPY04, SdMS+05].

Zhou and Ferrari [ZF87] evaluated five server-initiated load balancing algorithms, i.e. initiated by the most overloaded computer: Disted, Global, Central, Random and Lowest. In Disted, when a computer suffers any modification in its load, it emits messages to the other computers to inform its current load. In Global, one computer centralizes all the computer load information and sends broadcast messages in order to keep the other computers updated. In Central, as in Global, a central computer receives all the load information related to the system; however, it does not update the other computers with this information. This central computer decides the resources allocation in the environment. In Random, no information about the environment load is handled. Now, a computer is selected by random in order to receive a process to be initiated. In Lowest, the load information is sent when demanded. When a computer starts a process, it requests information and analyzes the loads of a small set of computers and submit the processes to the idlest one, the computer with the shortest process queue.

Theimer and Lantz [TL89] implemented algorithms similar to Central, Disted and Lowest. They analyzed these algorithms for systems composed of a larger number of computers (about 70). For the Disted and Lowest algorithms, a few process receiver and sender groups were created. The communication within these groups was handled by using a multicast protocol, in order to minimize the message exchange among the computers. Computers

with load lower than a inferior limit participate of the process receiver group, whilst those with load higher than a superior limit participate of the process sender group.
Theimer and Lantz recommend decentralized algorithms, such as Lowest and Disted, as they do not generate single points of failure, as Central does. Central presents the highest performance for small and medium size networks, but its performance decreases in larger environments. They concluded that algorithms like Lowest work with the probability of a computer being idle [TL89]. They assume system homogeneity, as they use the size of the CPU waiting queue as the load index. The process behavior is not analyzed; therefore, the actual load of each computer is not measured.
Shivaratri, Krueger and Singhal [SKS92] analyzed the server-initiated, receiver-initiated, symmetrically initiated, adaptive symmetrically initiated and stable symmetrically initiated algorithms. In their studies, the length of the process waiting queue at the CPU was considered as the load index. This measure was chosen because it's simple and, therefore, can be obtained with fewer resources. They concluded that the receiver-initiated algorithms present a higher performance than the server-initiated ones. In their conclusions, the algorithm with the highest final performance was the stable symmetrically initiated. This algorithm preserves the history of the load information exchanged in the system and takes actions to transfer the processes by using this information.
Mello *et al.* [MTPY04] proposed a load balancing algorithm for distributing processes on heterogeneous capacity computers. This algorithm, named TLBA (Tree Load Balancing Algorithm), organizes computers in a virtual tree topology and starts delivering processes from the root to the leaves. In their experiments, this algorithm presented a very good performance, with low mean response time.
Senger *et al.* [SdMS+05] proposed GAS, a genetic scheduling algorithm which uses information regarding the capacity of the processing elements, applications' communication and processing load, in order to allocate resources on heterogeneous and distributed environments. GAS uses Genetic Algorithms to find out the most appropriate computing resource subset to support applications.
Motivated by all the previous ACO presented works (section 1) and the scheduling problem, Nery *et al.* [NMdCYOB] proposed an algorithm inspired in ant colonies to schedule processes on heterogeneous capacity computer clusters, which can be considered as an alternative approach for load balancing systems. Such algorithm is named Ant Scheduler and is based in ant colony optimization techniques. The next sections describe the algorithm and compare its results with others found in literature.

5.1 The Ant Scheduler

The problem of process allocation in heterogeneous multicomputing environments can be modeled by using graphs, as illustrated in Figure 3 [AAB+00]. In this case, each process is a request for execution that has the nodes *S* and *T* as origin and destination, respectively. *S* and *T* are connected by *N* different paths, each corresponding to a computer in a cluster. This graph is employed to improve the general performance of the system by minimizing the mean congestion of the paths.
The good results obtained by ACO in graph-based problems favor the use of ACO for the optimization of process allocation on heterogeneous cluster computing environments. For such, each initiated process can be seen as an ant looking for the best path starting in the

nest in order to arrive as fast as possible to the food source. In this search, each computer can be seen as a path and the conclusion of the program execution as the food source.

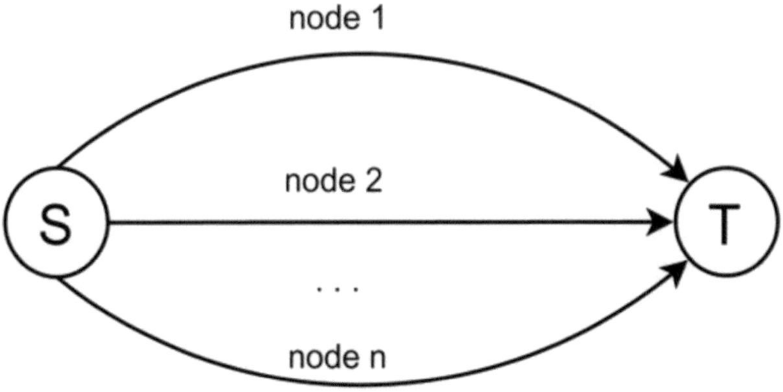

Figure 3. A cluster modeled as a graph of resources

The Ant Scheduler algorithm is based on the ant-cycle proposed by Dorigo *et al.* [DMC96]. When the computer responsible for the distribution of processes (master) in the cluster is started, each edge in the graph has its pheromone intensity initiated with a value $\tau_i = c$. When a process is launched, it is seen as an ant able to move. Thus, this process must select one of the paths (the computers of the cluster) to its destination (complete execution). The probability of an ant choosing a path *i* is given by Equation 1, where τ_i is the pheromone level on path *i*, η_i is a value associated to the computer i by a heuristic function, and the parameters α and β control the relevance of τ_i and η_i.

$$p_i = \frac{\tau_i^{\alpha} \cdot \eta_i^{\beta}}{\sum_{j=1}^{N} \tau_j^{\alpha} \cdot \eta_j^{\beta}} \tag{1}$$

This heuristic function is proportional to the load of the ith computer. The denominator is the sum of the pheromone levels weighted by the heuristic function and controlled by the parameters α and β. When an ant arrives to its destination (when a process finishes), it deposits a Δ amount of pheromone in the covered path (equation 2: where Q is a constant and T is the time spent by the ant to arrive at its destination (the process running time)).

$$\Delta_i = \Delta_i + \frac{Q}{T} \tag{2}$$

In order to prevent an addiction to a particular computer, the paths face continuous pheromone evaporation. Thus, in regular time intervals, the amount of pheromones changes according to the rule of equation 3, where ρ is a coefficient such that $(1 - \rho)$ represents the pheromone evaporation between t and $t + 1$. Additionally, Δ_i is reseted ($\Delta_i = 0$) in regular time intervals.

$$\tau_i(t+1) = \rho \cdot \tau_i(t) + \Delta_i \tag{3}$$

One problem with this approach is the possibility of a poor performance due to the different range of values for τ_i and η_i. In order to overcome this problem, these values are normalized using a logarithmic scale, modifying the equation 1 and originating the equation 4.

$$p_i = \frac{(\log \tau_i)^\alpha \cdot (\log \eta_i)^\beta}{\sum_{j=1}^{N} (\log \tau_j)^\alpha \cdot (\log \eta_j)^\beta} \tag{4}$$

Another problem found was the frequent allocation of a low value, between 0 and 1, to τ_i, making $\log \tau_i < 0$, leading to unrealistic values for the probability function. This problem was solved by using $\log \epsilon + \tau_i$ instead of $\log \tau_i$, where $\epsilon = 1$. This resulted in the equation 5.

$$p_i = \frac{(\log \epsilon + \tau_i)^\alpha \cdot (\log \epsilon + \eta_i)^\beta}{\sum_{j=1}^{N} (\log \epsilon + \tau_j)^\alpha \cdot (\epsilon + \log \eta_j)^\beta} \tag{5}$$

The Ant Scheduler is composed of the Algorithms 3, 4 and 5. The first algorithm is executed when a new process, with possibility of migration, is initiated. When a process completes its execution, the second algorithm starts its execution. The third algorithm is periodically executed, in order to perform the pheromone evaporation.

Choose a computer with probability p_i, calculated using equation 5
Schedule process on chosen computer

Algorithm 3. Ant Scheduler: process started

Update the amount of pheromone Δ_i using equation 2

Algorithm 4. Ant Scheduler: process finished

```
loop
    for all i such that i is a cluster node do
        Update the amount of pheromone τ_i using equation 3
        Reset the amount of pheromone Δ_i (Δ_i = 0)
    end for
end loop
```

Algorithm 5. Ant Scheduler: pheromone evaporation

5.2 Simulation

Several experiments have been carried out on environments with 32 computers for the evaluation of the Ant Scheduler algorithm behavior. The Ant Scheduler parameters used were $\alpha = 1$, $\beta = 1$, $\rho = 0.8$ and $Q = 0.1$. Parallel applications of up to 8, 64 and 128 tasks have been evaluated. This configuration allows the evaluation of the algorithm in situations where there are many tasks synchronized with others, that is, tasks that communicate among themselves to solve the same computing problem.

The workload imposed by such applications follows the workload model by Feitelson [2][FJ97j. This model is based on the analysis of six execution traces of the following production environments: 128-node iPSC/860 at NASA Ames; 128-node IBM SP1 at

---

[2] http://www. cs.huji.ac.il/labs/parallel/workload/models. html

Argonne; 400-node Paragon at SDSC; 126-node Butterfly at LLNL; 512-node IBM SP2 at CTC; 96-node Paragon at ETH.
According to this model, the arrival of processes is derived from an exponential probability distribution function (**pdf**) with mean equal to 1,500 seconds. This model was adopted to simulate and allow a comparative evaluation of Ant Scheduler and other algorithms found in the literature.
In order to carry out the experiments and evaluate the scheduling algorithm proposed in this study, the authors used the model for creation of heterogeneous distributed environments and evaluation of the parallel applications response time - UniMPP (Unified Modeling for Predicting Performance) [dMS06]. The adopted model is able to generate the mean execution time of the processes submitted to the system. The mean response time is generated after reaching the confidence interval of 95%.
In this model, every processing element (PE), PE_i, is composed of the sextuple $\{pc_i, mm_i, vm_i, dr_i, dw_i, lo_i\}$, where pc_i is the total computing capacity of each computer measured in instructions per time unit, mm_i is the main memory total capacity, vm_i is the virtual memory total capacity, dr_i is the hard disk reading throughput, dw_i is the hard disk writing throughput, and lo_i is the time between sending and receiving a message.
In this model, every process is represented by the sextuple $\{mp_j, sm_j, pdf\ dm_j, pdf\ dr_j, pdf\ dw_j, pdf\ net_j\}$, where mp_j represents the processing consumption, sm_j is the amount of static memory allocated by the process, $pdf\ dm_j$ is the probability distribution for the memory dynamic occupation, $pdf\ dr_j$ is the probability distribution for file reading, $pdf\ dw_j$ is the probability distribution for file writing, and $pdf\ net_j$ is the probability distribution for messages sending and receiving.
In order to evaluate the Ant Scheduler algorithm, a class was included in the object-oriented simulator[3] [dMS06j. This class implements the functionalities of Ant Scheduler and has been aggregated to the UniMPP model simulator to generate the mean response times of an application execution. These results were used to evaluate the performance of Ant Scheduler and to allow comparisons with other algorithms.

5.2.1 Environment parameters

Experiments were conduced in environments composed of 32 computers. In these experiments, each PE_i for the UniMPP model was probabilistically defined. The parameters pc_i, mm_i, vm_i, dr_i, dw_i were set by using an uniform probability distribution function with the mean of 1,500 Mips (millions of instructions per second), 1,024 MBytes (main memory), 1,024 MBytes (virtual memory), 40 MBytes (file reading transference rate from hard disk) and 30 MBytes (file writing transference rate to hard disk). These measures were based on the actual values obtained using a group of machines from our research laboratory (Distributed Systems and Concurrent Programming Laboratory). These measures followed the benchmark proposed by Mello and Senger [dMS06][4]. These parameter values and the use of probability distributions allow the creation of heterogeneous environments to evaluate the Ant Scheduler algorithm.
The Feitelson's workload model was used to define the occupation parameter (in Mips) of the processes (or tasks) that take part of the parallel application. The remaining parameters

[3] SchedSim - available at website http://www.icmc.usp.br/~mello.

[4] available at http://www.icmc.usp.br/~mello/

required for the UniMPP to represent a process were defined as: sm_j, the amount of static memory used by the process, based on an exponential distribution with a mean of 300 KBytes; *pdf* dm_j, the amount of memory dynamically allocated, defined by an exponential distribution with a mean of 1, 000 KBytes; *pdf* dr_j, the file reading probability, defined by an exponential distribution with a mean of one read at each 1, 000 clock ticks, same value used to parameterize the writing in files (*pdf* dw_j); *pdf* net_j, the receiving and sending of network messages, parameterized by an exponential distribution with a mean of one message at each 1,000 clock ticks.

During the experiments, all computers were located at the same network, as an ordinary cluster. Within the network, the computers present a delay (RTT - Round-Trip Time according to the model by Hockey [Hoc96]) of 0.0001 seconds (mean value extracted by the *net* benchmark by Mello and Senger [dMS06] for a Gigabit Ethernet network).

5.2.2 Algorithms simulated

The performance of Ant Scheduler is compared with 5 other scheduling and load balancing algorithms proposed in literature: **DPWP** [ASSS99], **Random**, **Central**, **Lowest** [ZF87], **TLBA** [MTPY04] and **GAS** [SdMS+05].

The **DPWP** (Dynamic Policy Without Preemption) algorithm performs the parallel applications scheduling taking into account a distributed and heterogeneous execution scenario [ASSS99]. This algorithm allows the scheduling of the applications developed on PVM, MPI and CORBA. The details involved in the task attributions are supervised by the scheduling software, AMIGO [SouOO][5].

The load index used in this algorithm is the queue size of each PE (processing element). Through this index, the load of a PE is based on the ratio between its number of tasks being executed and its processing capacity. The processing capacity is measured by specific benchmarks [SouOO, SSSSOlj. The **DPWP** scheduling algorithm uses load indexes to create an ordered list of PEs. The parallel application tasks are attributed to the PEs of this list, in a circular structure.

The **Lowest**, **Central** and **Random** algorithms were investigated for load balancing in [ZF87]. These algorithms are defined by two main components: LIM (Load information manager) and LBM (Load balance manager). The first component is responsible for the information policy and for monitoring the computers' load in order to calculate the load indexes. The latter defines how to use the collected information to find out the most appropriate computer to schedule processes. The approach followed by these components to perform their tasks allows the definition of distinct algorithms. These algorithms differ from the scheduling algorithms by being designed to perform the load balance, thus there is no global scheduling software to which the applications are submitted. In fact, each PE should locally manage the application tasks that reach it, initiating them locally or defining how another PE will be selected to execute tasks.

[5] We have compared our results to this work, because it was also developed in our laboratory.

The **Lowest** algorithm aims to achieve the load balance by minimizing the number of messages exchanged among its components. When a task is submitted to the environment, the LIM receiving the request defines a limited set of remote LIMs. The loads of the PEs of this set are received and the idlest PE is selected to receive the task.
The **Central** algorithm employs a master LBM and a master LIM. Both of them centralize the decision making related to the load balance. The master LIM receives the load indexes sent by the slave LIMs. The master LBM receives the requests to allocate processes to the system and uses the information provided by the master LIM to make these allocations.
The **Random** algorithm does not use information regarding the system load to make decisions. When a task is submitted to the execution environment, the algorithm randomly selects a PE. The load index used by the **Lowest** and **Central** algorithms is calculated based on the number of processes in the execution queue. Zhou and Ferrari [ZF87] have observed that the **Lowest** and **Central** algorithms present similar performance and that the **Random** algorithms present the worst results of all. They also suggested the **Lowest** algorithm for distributed scenarios, because it's not centralized.
The **TLBA** (Tree Load Balancing Algorithm) algorithm aims at balancing loads in scalable heterogeneous distributed systems [MTPY04]. This algorithm creates a logical interconnection topology with all PEs, in a tree format, and performs the migration of tasks in order to improve the system load balance.
The **GAS** (Genetic Algorithm for Scheduling) algorithm uses Genetic Algorithms to propose optimized scheduling solutions [SdMS+05j. The algorithm considers knowledge about the execution time and applications' behavior to define the most adequate set of computing resources to support a parallel application on a distributed environment composed of heterogeneous capacity computers. **GAS** uses the crossover and mutation operators to optimize the probabilistic search for the best solution for a problem. Based on Genetics and Evolution, Genetic Algorithms are very suitable for global search and can be efficiently implemented in parallel machines.

5.2.3 Experimental results

For the validation of the Ant Scheduler algorithm, its performance was compared with results obtained by the five algorithms previously described. For such, the authors carried out simulations where all these algorithms were evaluated running parallel applications composed of different numbers of tasks. Figures 4 and 5 show the process mean response times for parallel applications with up to 64 and 128 tasks, respectively.
Random had the worst results, while Ant Scheduler presented the best performance. The poor performance obtained by GAS can be explained by the fact that its execution time increases according to the number of computers. This occurs due to the use of larger chromosomes (this approach is based on Genetic Algorithms), which have to be evaluated by the fitness function. This evaluation requires a long time, which is added to the scheduling cost, jeopardizing the process execution time. It is hard to observe the curve for Ant Scheduler in Figure 4 due to the small mean response times in comparison with the other algorithms.
These results show that, in all the scenarios investigated, the Ant Scheduler presented the best performance.

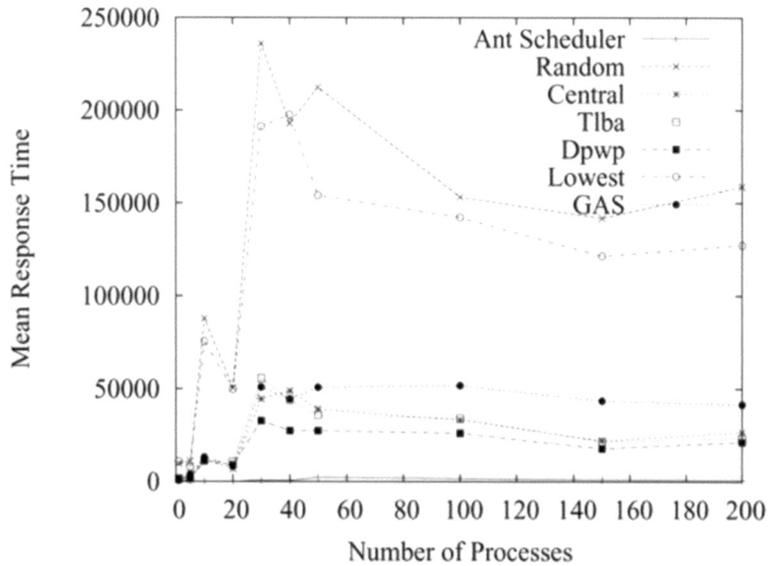

Figure 4. Simulation results: 64 tasks

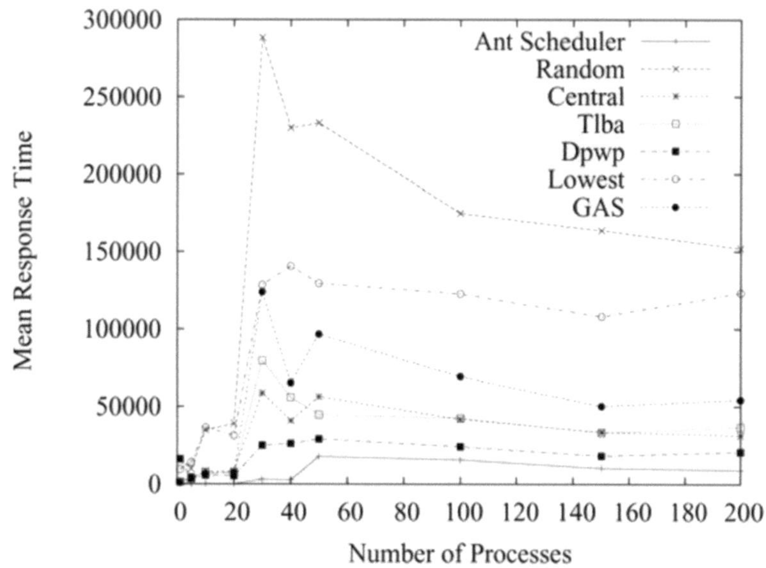

Figure 5. Simulation results: 128 tasks

5.3 Implementation

In order to allow real experiments, Ant Scheduler was implemented using the Linux kernel 2.4.24. This implementation uses the process migration service of the openMosix[6] patch. openMosix is a software designed to balance the load of clusters by distributing processes.

---

[6] openMosix is a Linux kernel patch developed by Moshe Bar which allows automatic process migration in a cluster environment — Available at http://openmosix.sourceforge.net/

The implementation was performed by adding a set of traps inside the Linux kernel. The first trap was implemented in the system call do_fork. Whenever a new process is started, do_fork is called. This system call executes the first trap of Ant Scheduler, which chooses the node where the new process will run. This phase is based on the pheromone level and the computing capacity of each node. Similarly, when a process finishes, the system call do_exit is made. This system call executes the second trap of Ant Scheduler, which updates the amount of pheromone in the computer (ant's path) where the process was running.
These traps were implemented in a kernel module by using function pointers, allowing simple changes to use another process scheduling algorithm. When the module is loaded, it registers its functions (traps). This module also starts a thread that periodically updates the pheromone level of each computer applying the equation 3.
Experiments were carried out to evaluate the process execution time for an environment using Ant Scheduler and openMosix on a set of five Dual Xeon 2.4 Ghz computers. Table 1 presents the results in process mean execution time (in seconds) for a load of 10 low-load, 10 mean-load and 10 high-load applications executing simultaneously. According to these results, the use of Ant Scheduler reduced the mean response time.

Experiment	without Ant Scheduler	with Ant Scheduler
1	351.00	327.00
2	351.00	336.00
3	351.00	318.00
4	354.00	321.00
5	351.00	318.00
6	351.00	333.00
7	351.00	321.00
8	351.00	336.00
9	348.00	309.00
10	348.00	315.00
Mean	350.70	323.40
Std Dev	1.615	8.777

Table 1. Experimental Results

In order to evaluate the statistical significance of the results obtained, the authors applied the Student's t-test. In this analysis, the authors used the standard error s_x for small data samples [W.C88], given by equation 6, where s is the standard deviation and n is the number of samples. Applying the equation, the standard errors of 0.51 and 2.775 were obtained without Ant Scheduler and with Ant Scheduler, respectively.

$$s_x = \frac{s}{\sqrt{n}} \tag{6}$$

In the test, the null hypothesis proposed is H_0: $\mu_{with} = \mu_{without}$, with the alternative hypothesis H_A: $\mu_{with} < \mu_{without}$ to evaluate whether the results are statistically equivalent. The hypothesis

H_0 considers the results of the Ant Scheduler and the standard openMosix to be similar. If the test is rejected, the alternative hypothesis H_A is accepted. This hypothesis considers the process mean response time for the environment adopted. Such mean response time is lower when the processes are distributed using the Ant Scheduler, what confirms its superiority.
The significance level used for one-tailed test is $\alpha = 0.0005$. μ_{with} is the process mean response time with Ant Scheduler; $\mu_{without}$ is the process mean response time with the standard openMosix. For the adopted significance level α, the data sets have to present a difference of at least 4.781 in the t-test to reject the hypothesis. This value is found in tables of critical values for the *t*-student distribution.
Applying the equation 7, the value 9.83 is found, confirming that the results present statistic differences with $p < 0.005$, rejecting the hypothesis H_0. In this way the hypothesis H_A is valid and the system with Ant Scheduler presents better results than standard openMosix.

$$t = \frac{\mu_{without} - \mu_{with}}{s_x} \qquad (7)$$

By applying statistic tools[7] over the data sets, it's possible to find the most precise $\alpha = 0.0000018$ for a one-tailed test. This value shows how many times the alternative hypothesis is true. In this case, H_A can be considered true in 9,999,982 out of 10,000,000 executions, showing that Ant Scheduler reduces the response time. Only in 18 of these executions the results of Ant Scheduler and openMosix would not present significant statistical differences.

6. Conclusions and future directions

The behavior of real ants motivated Dorigo *et al.* [DMC96] to propose the Ant Colony Optimization (ACO) technique, which can be used to solve problems in dynamic environments. This technique has been successfully applied to several optimization problems [FMS05, PB05, BN06, SF06, PLF02, WGDK06, CF06, HND05]. Such results have motivated this chapter which presents ACO concepts, case studies and also a complete example on process scheduling optimization.
Besides the successful adoption of ACO, it presents some relevant questions which have been motivating future directions such as: how to adjust parameters which depend on the optimization problem [SocOSj; how to reduce the execution time [G.N06, MBSD06]; the optimization improvement by using incremental local search [BBSD06]; and the aggregation of different and new concepts to ACO [RL04]. Those works confirm ACO is an important optimization technique and also that is has been improved and present a promising future.

7. Acknowledgments

We would like thank Ines Tristao Silva for the ant figure composition. This paper is based upon work supported by CAPES - Brazil under grant no. 032506-6 and FAPESP - Brazil. Any opinions, findings, and conclusions or recommendations expressed in this material are those of the authors and do not necessarily reflect the views of the CAPES or FAPESP.

---

7 The authors applied the Gnumeric tool in this analysis – a free software tool licensed under GNU/GPL terms.

8. References

Yair Amir, Baruch Awerbuch, R. Sean Borgstrom, Amnon Barak, and Arie Keren. An opportunity cost approach for job assignment and reassignment in a scalable computing cluster. *IEEE Transactions on Parallel and Distributed Systems*, 11:760,768, October 2000. [AAB+OO]

A. P. F. Araujo, M. J. Santana, R. H. C. Santana, and P. S. L. Souza. DPWP: A new load balancing algorithm. In *ISAS'99*, Orlando, U.S.A., 1999. [ASSS99]

Prasanna Balaprakash, Mauro Birattari, Thomas Stiitzle, and Marco Dorigo. Incremental local search in ant colony optimization: Why it fails for the quadratic assignment problem. In *ANTS Workshop*, pages 156-166, 2006. [BBSD06]

Thang N. Bui and ThanhVu H. Nguyen. An agent-based algorithm for generalized graph colorings. In *GECCO '06: Proceedings of the 8th annual conference on Genetic and evolutionary computation*, pages 19-26, New York, NY, USA, 2006. ACM Press. [BN06]

Christian Blum and Andrea Roll. Metaheuristics in combinatorial optimization: Overview and conceptual comparison. *ACM Comput. Surv.*, 35(3):268-308, 2003. [BROS]

Allen Chan and Alex A. Freitas. A new ant colony algorithm for multi-label classification with applications in bioinfomatics. In *GECCO '06: Proceedings of the 8th annual conference on Genetic and evolutionary computation*, pages 27-34, New York, NY, USA, 2006. ACM Press. [CF06]

Marco Dorigo, Vittorio Maniezzo, and Alberto Colorni. The ant system: Optimization by a colony of cooperating agents. *IEEE Transactions on Systems, Man, and Cybernetics-* Part B, 26:1,13, 1996. [DMC96]

R. F. de Mello and L. J. Senger. Model for simulation of heterogeneous high-performance computing environments. In *7th International Conference on High Performance Computing in Computational Sciences - VECPAR 2006*, page 11. Springer-Verlag, 2006. [dMS06]

D. G. Feitelson and M. A. Jette. Improved utilization and responsiveness with gang scheduling. In Dror G. Feitelson and Larry Rudolph, editors, Job Scheduling Strategies for Parallel Processing, pages 238-261. Springer, 1997. *Lect. Notes Comput. Sci.* vol. 1291. [FJ97]

Wai Kuan Foong, Holger R. Maier, and Angus R. Simpson. Ant colony optimization for power plant maintenance scheduling optimization. In *GECCO '05: Proceedings of the 2005 conference on Genetic and evolutionary computation*, pages 249-256, New York, NY, USA, 2005. ACM Press. [FMS05]

J. A. Freeman and D. M. Skapura. Neural networks: algorithms, applications, and programming techniques. Addison Wesley Longman Publishing Co., Inc., Redwood City, CA, USA, 1991. [FS91]

G.Negara. Parallel experience-based ant coloring. *Adaptation in Artificial and Biological Systems*, 2:166-173, 2006. [G.N06]

Samer L. Hijazi, Balasubramaniam Natarajan, and Sanjoy Das. An ant colony algorithm for multi-user detection in wireless communication systems. In *GECCO '05: Proceedings of the 2005 conference on Genetic and evolutionary computation*, pages 2121-2126, New York, NY, USA, 2005. ACM Press. [HND05]

Roger W. Hockney. The Science of Computer Benchmarking. *Soc for Industrial fc Applied Math*, 1996. [Hoc96]

P. Krueger and M. Livny. The diverse objectives of distributed scheduling policies. In *Seventh Int. Conf. Distributed Computing Systems*, pages 242-249, Los Alamitos, California, 1987. IEEE CS Press. [KL87]

Max Manfrin, Mauro Birattari, Thomas Stiitzle, and Marco Dorigo. Parallel ant colony optimization for the traveling salesman problem. In *ANTS Workshop*, pages 224-234, 2006. [MBSD06]

R. F. Mello, L. C. Trevelin, M. S. Paiva, and L. T. Yang. Comparative analysis of the prototype and the simulator of a new load balancing algorithm for heterogeneous computing environments. In *International Journal of High Performance Computing and Networking*, volume 1, No.1/2/3, pages 64-74. Interscience, 2004. [MTPY04]

Bruno R. Nery, Rodrigo F. Mello, Andre C. P. L. F. de Carvalho, and Laurence T. Yang. *Process scheduling using ant colony optimization techniques. ISPA,* pages 304-316, 2006. [NMdCY06]

Diego Pinto and Benjamin Baran. Solving multiobjective multicast routing problem with a new ant colony optimization approach. In *LANG '05: Proceedings of the 3rd international IFIP/ACM Latin American conference on Networking,* pages 11-19, New York, NY, USA, 2005. ACM Press. [PB05]

RS Parpinelli, HS Lopes, and AA Freitas. Data Mining with an Ant Colony Optimization Algorithm. *IEEE Trans on Evolutionary Computation, special issue on Ant Colony Algorithms,* 6(4):321-332, August 2002. [PLF02]

Marc Reimann and Marco Laumanns. A hybrid aco algorithm for the capacitated minimum spanning tree problem. In *Hybrid Metaheuristics,* pages 1-10, 2004. [RL04]

L. J. Senger, R. F. de Mello, M. J. Santana, R. H. C. Santana, and L. T. Yang. Improving scheduling decisions by using knowledge about parallel applications resource usage. In *Proceedings of the 2005 International Conference on High Performance Computing and Communications (HPCC-05),* pages 487-498, Sorrento, Naples, Italy, September 21-23, 2005. [SdMS+05]

James Smaldon and Alex A. Freitas. A new version of the ant-miner algorithm discovering unordered rule sets. In *GECCO '06: Proceedings of the 8th annual conference on Genetic and evolutionary computation,* pages 43-50, New York, NY, USA, 2006. ACM Press. [SF06]

N. G. Shivaratri, P. Krueger, and M. Singhal. Load distributing for locally distributed systems. *IEEE Computer,* 25(12):33-44, 1992. [SKS92]

Krzysztof Socha. The influence of run-time limits on choosing ant system parameters. In E. Cantu-Paz et al., editor, *Proceedings of GECCO 2003 -Genetic and Evolutionary Computation Conference,* LNCS. Springer-Verlag, Berlin, Germany, July 2003. [Soc03]

P. S. L. Souza. AMIGO: Uma Contribuigao para a Convergencia na Area de Escalonamento de Processes. *PhD thesis,* IFSC-USP, Jun. 2000. [SouOO]

R. R. Santos, P. S. L. Souza, M. J. Santana, and R. H. C. Santana. Performance evaluation of distributed applications development tools from interprocess communication point of view. In *Proceedings of the 2001 International Conference on Parallel and Distributed Processing Techniques and Applications,* Las Vegas, USA, Jun. 2001. [SSSS01]

M. M. Theimer and K. A. Lantz. Finding idle machines in a workstation-based distributed system. *IEEE Transactions on Software Engineering,* 15(11):1444-1458, Nov. 1989. [TL89]

W.C.Shefler. Statistics: Concepts and Applications. The Benjamin/Cummings, 1988. [W.C88]

Gang Wang, Wenrui Gong, Brian DeRenzi, and Ryan Kastner. Design space exploration using time and resource duality with the ant colony optimization. In *DAC '06: Proceedings of the 43rd annual conference on Design automation*, pages 451-454, New York, NY, USA, 2006. ACM Press. [WGDK06]

S. Zhou and D. Ferrari. An experimental study of load balancing performance. *Technical Report UCB/CSD 87/336*, PROGRES Report N.o 86.8, Computer Science Division (EECS), Universidade da California, Berkeley, California 94720, Jan. 1987. [ZF87]

14

Application of PSO to design UPFC-based stabilizers

Ali T. Al-Awami[1], Mohammed A. Abido[1] and Youssef L. Abdel-Magid[2]
[1]*King Fahd University of Petroleum & Minerals,* [2]*The Petroleum Institute*
[1]*Saudi Arabia,* [2]*United Arab Emirates*

1. Introduction

Today, power demand grows rapidly and expansion in transmission and generation is restricted with the limited availability of resources and the strict environmental constraints. Consequently, power systems are today much more loaded than before. In addition, interconnection between remotely located power systems turned out to be a common practice. These give rise to low frequency oscillations in the range of 0.1-3.0 Hz. If not well damped, these oscillations may keep growing in magnitude until loss of synchronism results.

Power system stabilizers (PSSs) have been used in the last few decades to serve the purpose of enhancing power system damping to low frequency oscillations. PSSs have proved to be efficient in performing their assigned tasks. A wide spectrum of PSS tuning approaches has been proposed. These approaches have included pole placement (Chen & Hsu, 1987), damping torque concepts (Gibbard, 1988), H_∞ (Klein et al, 1995), variable structure (Samarasinghe & Pahalawaththa, 1997), and the different optimization and artificial intelligence techniques (Abdel-Magid et al, 1999; Abido, 2001; Abido & Abdel-Magid, 1997). However, PSS may adversely affect voltage profile and may not be able to suppress oscillations resulting from severe disturbances, such as three-phase faults at generator terminals (Mehran et al, 1992).

On the other hand, Flexible AC Transmission Systems (FACTS) have shown very promising results when used to improve power system steady-state performance. In addition, because of the extremely fast control action associated with FACTS-device operations, they have been very promising candidates for utilization in power system damping enhancement.

A unified power flow controller (UPFC) is the most promising device in the FACTS concept. It has the ability to adjust the three control parameters, i.e. the bus voltage, transmission line reactance, and phase angle between two buses. A major function of the UPFC is to redistribute power flow among transmission lines during steady state. During transients, it can be used to improve the damping of low frequency oscillations. To perform these tasks, the UPFC needs to be equipped with a power flow controller, a DC voltage regulator, and a supplementary damping controller.

Till now, not much research has been devoted to the analysis and control of UPFCs. Several trials have been reported in the literature to model a UPFC for steady-state and transient studies. Based on Nabavi-Iravani model (Nabavi-Niaki & Iravani, 1996), Wang developed a linearized UPFC model (Wang, 1999a & b) which has been incorporated into the Heffron-

Phillips model (Heffron & Phillips, 1952). Only a single operating point has been considered in the design process presented in (Wang, 1999a), which does not guarantee robust performance.

A number of control schemes have been suggested to perform the oscillation-damping task. Huang et al. (2000) attempted to design a conventional fixed-parameter lead-lag controller for a UPFC installed in the tie line of a two-area system to damp the interarea mode of oscillation. Mok et al. (2000) considered the design of an adaptive fuzzy logic controller for the same purpose. Dash et al. (2000) suggested the use of a radial basis function NN for a UPFC to enhance system damping performance. Robust control schemes, such as $H\infty$ and singular value analysis, have also been explored (Vilathgamuwa et al, 2000; Pal, 2002). To avoid pole-zero cancellation associated with the $H\infty$ approach, the structured singular value analysis have been utilized in (Seo et al, 2001) to select the parameters of the UPFC controller to have the robust stability against model uncertainties. However, the adaptive and robust control schemes proposed in (Mok et al, 2000; Dash et al, 2000; Vilathgamuwa et al, 2000; Pal, 2002; Seo et al, 2001) are still not widely implemented in power systems. In addition, the work cited proposed different techniques to design the damping controller without considering the power flow controller and the DC voltage regulator, or to design the three controllers sequentially, i.e. one at a time. To the best of the authors' knowledge, there has been no attempt till now to design the three controllers simultaneously.

1.1 Objectives

The objective of this chapter is to investigate the potential of particle swarm optimization as a tool in designing UPFC-based stabilizers to improve power system transient stability. To estimate the controllability of each of the UPFC control signals on the electromechanical modes, singular value decomposition is employed. The problem of designing all the UPFC-based stabilizers individually is formulated as an optimization problem. Particle swarm optimizer is utilized to search for the optimum stabilizer parameter settings that optimize a given objective function. Coordinated design of the different stabilizers is also carried out by finding the best parameter settings for more than one stabilizer at a given operating condition in a coordinated manner.

To further illustrate the potential of PSO in handling complex design problems, robust controller design using simultaneous stabilization is also explored. That is, to ensure the robustness of the proposed control schemes, the design procedure is repeated considering a wide range of operating conditions simultaneously in the design stage. To assess the effectiveness of the proposed designs, eigenvalue analysis as well as nonlinear time-domain simulations are carried out.

Two different objective functions will be considered. The first objective is eigenvalue-based while the other is time-domain-based. It will be shown that using a time-domain-based objective function has two advantages:

- Nonlinear models of the power system can be used in the design stage without the need for linearization.
- Coordinated designs of several controllers with different objectives can be achieved. (Abido et al, 2006b)

This chapter aims to demonstrate the potential of PSO in:

- Designing an individual UPFC-based stabilizer considering a single operating condition.

- Designing an individual UPFC-based stabilizer considering a wide range of operating conditions, i.e. robust control.
- Designing multiple UPFC-based stabilizers in a coordinated manner considering a wide range of operating conditions.
- Designing multiple UPFC-based stabilizers with different objectives in a coordinated manner using a time-domain objective function.

1.2 Definitions

At this point, it is worth emphasizing the meaning of the following terms:
Individual and coordinated designs: Individual design refers to the process of designing a single controller in the absence of any other controllers. Coordinated design, however, refers to the process of designing more than one controller concurrently so that coordination among the different controllers is achieved.
Single-point and robust tuning: Single-point tuning refers to the situation where a single operating condition is considered in the design stage. Robust tuning refers to the situation where multiple operating conditions are considered in the design stage to achieve robustness.
Simultaneous stabilization: Simultaneous stabilization refers to the technique used to design a controller taking into account several operating conditions. This technique guarantees the stability of the system at all the operating conditions considered in the design stage. The way simultaneous stabilization is implemented in this work, for the case of the eigenvalue-based objective function, is:

1. Declare a vector J
2. Pick an operating condition.
3. Linearize the system model around that operating condition.
4. Find the system complex eigenvalues and stack them in the vector J.
5. Repeat the same process (steps 2-4) until all operating conditions are covered. That is, vector J will contain all complex eigenvalues corresponding to all the considered operating conditions.
6. Search for the optimum controller's parameters that will push all those complex eigenvalues of J furthest to the left of the complex s-plane.

2. Problem Statement

Figure 1 shows a SMIB system equipped with a UPFC. The UPFC consists of an excitation transformer (ET), a boosting transformer (BT), two three-phase GTO based voltage source converters (VSCs), and a DC link capacitors. The four input control signals to the UPFC are m_E, m_B, δ_E, and δ_B, where

m_E is the excitation amplitude modulation ratio,
m_B is the boosting amplitude modulation ratio,
δ_E is the excitation phase angle, and
δ_B is the boosting phase angle.

2.1 Power System Nonlinear Model

By applying Park's transformation and neglecting the resistance and transients of the ET and BT transformers, the UPFC can be modeled as (Wang 1999a); Abido et al, 2006b):

:
$$\begin{bmatrix} v_{Etd} \\ v_{Etq} \end{bmatrix} = \begin{bmatrix} 0 & -x_E \\ x_E & 0 \end{bmatrix} \begin{bmatrix} i_{Ed} \\ i_{Eq} \end{bmatrix} + \begin{bmatrix} \dfrac{m_E \cos\delta_E v_{dc}}{2} \\ \dfrac{m_E \sin\delta_E v_{dc}}{2} \end{bmatrix} \tag{1}$$

$$\begin{bmatrix} v_{Btd} \\ v_{Btq} \end{bmatrix} = \begin{bmatrix} 0 & -x_B \\ x_B & 0 \end{bmatrix} \begin{bmatrix} i_{Bd} \\ i_{Bq} \end{bmatrix} + \begin{bmatrix} \dfrac{m_B \cos\delta_B v_{dc}}{2} \\ \dfrac{m_B \sin\delta_B v_{dc}}{2} \end{bmatrix} \tag{2}$$

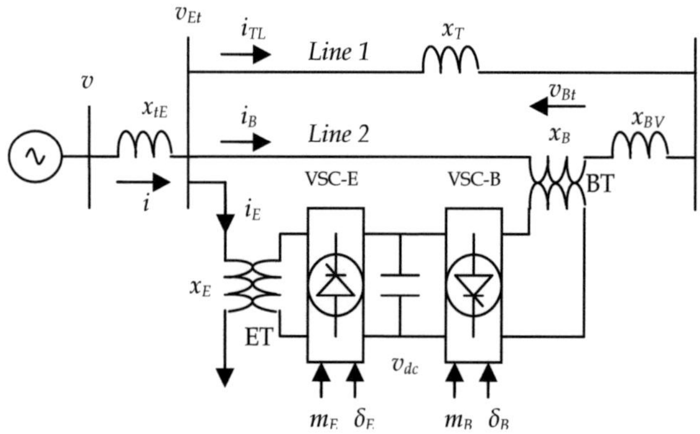

Figure 1. SMIB power system equipped with UPFC

$$\dot{v}_{dc} = \frac{3m_E}{4C_{dc}} \begin{bmatrix} \cos\delta_E & \sin\delta_E \end{bmatrix} \begin{bmatrix} i_{Ed} \\ i_{Eq} \end{bmatrix} + \frac{3m_B}{4C_{dc}} \begin{bmatrix} \cos\delta_B & \sin\delta_B \end{bmatrix} \begin{bmatrix} i_{Bd} \\ i_{Bq} \end{bmatrix} \tag{3}$$

where v_{Et}, i_E, v_{Bt}, and i_B are the excitation voltage, excitation current, boosting voltage, and boosting current, respectively; C_{dc} and v_{dc} are the DC link capacitance and voltage, respectively.

The ET, BT and line 2 currents can be stated as:

$$i_{TLd} = \frac{1}{x_T}\left(x_E i_{Ed} + \frac{m_E \sin\delta_E v_{dc}}{2} - v_b \cos\delta\right) \tag{4}$$

$$i_{TLq} = \frac{1}{x_T}\left(x_E i_{Eq} - \frac{m_E \cos\delta_E v_{dc}}{2} + v_b \sin\delta\right) \tag{5}$$

$$i_{Ed} = \frac{x_{BB}}{x_{d2}} E_q' + x_{d7} \frac{m_B \sin\delta_B v_{dc}}{2} + x_{d5} v_b \cos\delta + x_{d6} \frac{m_E \sin\delta_E v_{dc}}{2} \tag{6}$$

$$i_{Eq} = x_{q7} \frac{m_B \cos\delta_B v_{dc}}{2} + x_{q5} v_b \sin\delta + x_{q6} \frac{m_E \cos\delta_E v_{dc}}{2} \tag{7}$$

$$i_{Bd} = \frac{x_E}{x_{d2}} E_q' - \frac{x_{d1}}{x_{d2}} \frac{m_B \sin\delta_B v_{dc}}{2} + x_{d3} v_b \cos\delta + x_{d4} \frac{m_E \sin\delta_E v_{dc}}{2} \tag{8}$$

$$i_{Bd} = \frac{x_{q1}}{x_{q2}} \frac{m_B \cos\delta_B v_{dc}}{2} + x_{q3} v_b \sin\delta + x_{q4} \frac{m_E \cos\delta_E v_{dc}}{2} \tag{9}$$

where x_E and x_B are the ET and BT reactances, respectively; the reactances x_{qE}, x_{dE}, x_{BB}, x_{d1}-x_{d7}, and x_{q1}- x_{q7} are as shown in (Abido et al, 2006b).
The non-linear model of the SMIB system of Figure 1 is:

$$\dot{\delta} = \omega_b(\omega - 1) \tag{10}$$

$$\dot{\omega} = (P_m - P_e - D(\omega - 1)) / M \tag{11}$$

$$\dot{E}_q' = (E_{fd} - (x_d - x_d')i_d - E_q') / T_{do}' \tag{12}$$

$$\dot{E}_{fd} = (K_A(V_{ref} - v + u_{PSS}) - E_{fd}) / T_A \tag{13}$$

where $P_e = v_d i_d + v_q i_q, v = (v_d^2 + v_q^2)^{1/2}, v_d = x_q i_q,\ v_q = E_q' - x_d' i_d, i_d = i_{Ed} + i_{Bd}, i_q = i_{Eq} + i_{Bq}$

P_m and P_e are the input and output power, respectively; M and D the inertia constant and damping coefficient, respectively; ω_b the synchronous speed; δ and ω the rotor angle and speed, respectively; E_q', E'_{fd}, and v the generator internal, field and terminal voltages, respectively; T'_{do} the open circuit field time constant; x_d, x'_d, and x_q the d-axis reactance, d-axis transient reactance, and q-axis reactance, respectively; K_A and T_A the exciter gain and time constant, respectively; V_{ref} the reference voltage; and u_{PSS} the PSS control signal.

2.2 Power System Linearized Model

The non-linear dynamic equations can be linearized around a given operating point to have the linear model given by:

$$\dot{x} = Ax + Bu \tag{14}$$

where the state vector x, control vector u, and matrices A and B are

$$x = \begin{bmatrix} \Delta\delta & \Delta\omega & \Delta E_q' & \Delta E_{fd} & \Delta v_{dc} \end{bmatrix}^T \tag{15}$$

$$u = \begin{bmatrix} \Delta u_{pss} & \Delta m_E & \Delta\delta_E & \Delta m_b & \Delta\delta_b \end{bmatrix}^T \tag{16}$$

$$A = \begin{bmatrix} 0 & \omega_b & 0 & 0 & 0 \\ -\frac{K_1}{M} & -\frac{D}{M} & -\frac{K_2}{M} & 0 & -\frac{K_{pd}}{M} \\ -\frac{K_4}{T_{do}'} & 0 & -\frac{K_3}{T_{do}'} & \frac{1}{T_{do}'} & -\frac{K_{qd}}{T_{do}'} \\ -\frac{K_A K_5}{T_A} & 0 & -\frac{K_A K_6}{T_A} & -\frac{1}{T_A} & -\frac{K_A K_{vd}}{T_A} \\ K_7 & 0 & K_8 & 0 & -K_9 \end{bmatrix} \tag{17}$$

$$B=\begin{bmatrix} 0 & 0 & 0 & 0 & 0 \\ 0 & -\frac{K_{pe}}{M} & -\frac{K_{p\delta e}}{M} & -\frac{K_{pb}}{M} & -\frac{K_{p\delta b}}{M} \\ 0 & -\frac{K_{qe}}{T'_{do}} & -\frac{K_{q\delta e}}{T'_{do}} & -\frac{K_{qb}}{T'_{do}} & -\frac{K_{q\delta b}}{T'_{do}} \\ \frac{K_A}{T_A} & -\frac{K_A K_{ve}}{T_A} & -\frac{K_A K_{v\delta e}}{T_A} & -\frac{K_A K_{vb}}{T_A} & -\frac{K_A K_{v\delta b}}{T_A} \\ 0 & K_{ce} & K_{c\delta e} & K_{cb} & K_{c\delta b} \end{bmatrix} \tag{18}$$

where K_1 – K_9, K_{pu}, K_{qu}, and K_{vu} are linearization constants.

2.3 Structures of UPFC Controllers

The UPFC damping controllers are of the structure shown in Figure 2, where u can be m_E, δ_E, m_B, or δ_B.

In order to maintain the power balance between the series and shunt converters, a DC voltage regulator must be incorporated. The DC voltage is controlled through modulating the phase angle of the ET voltage, δ_E. In addition, to dispatch the power flow among transmission lines, a power flow controller is included. The power flow is controlled through modulation the amplitude of the BT voltage, m_B. Therefore, the δ_E and m_B damping controllers to be considered are those shown in Figure 3 and Figure 4, where the DC voltage regulator and the power flow controller are PI-controllers.

2.4 Objective Functions and Stabilizers' Design

To select the best stabilizer parameters that enhance most the power system transient performance, two objective functions are considered, one is eigenvalue-based and the other is time-domain-based. The eigenvalue-based objective function is:

$$J_e = \max[\sigma] \tag{19}$$

where σ is a vector of the real parts of all the complex eigenvalues (the damping factors) of the system at all loading conditions considered.

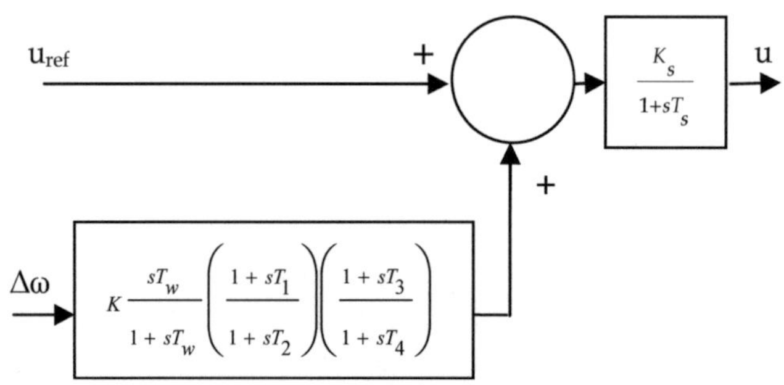

Figure 2. UPFC with lead-lag damping controllers

The objective function J_e identifies the maximum value of the damping factors, i.e. the real parts of the eigenvalues, among all the system complex modes of all loading conditions considered in the design process. Hence, the goal is to Minimize J_e to shift the poorly damped eigenvalues to the left in the s-plane improving the system response settling time and enhancing the system relative stability. It is worth emphasizing that by minimizing J_e, all the operating conditions considered in the design stage are damped simultaneously. It is noteworthy that J_e is used to design the damping controllers only. That is, the UPFC DC voltage regulator and power flow controller must be designed beforehand.

In order to be able to design the damping controller, DC voltage regulator, and power flow controller in a coordinated manner, a time-domain-based objective function is used. This objective function is called the integral of time multiplied by absolute error (ITAE) and is defined as

$$J_t = \alpha \int t\,|\Delta\omega|\,dt + \beta \int t\,|\Delta P_{e2}|\,dt + \gamma \int t\,|\Delta V_{dc}|\ \ dt \tag{20}$$

where $\Delta\omega$, ΔP_{e2}, and ΔV_{dc} are the deviations in system speed, real power flow of line 2, and DC voltage of the capacitor link, α, β, and γ are weighting factors.

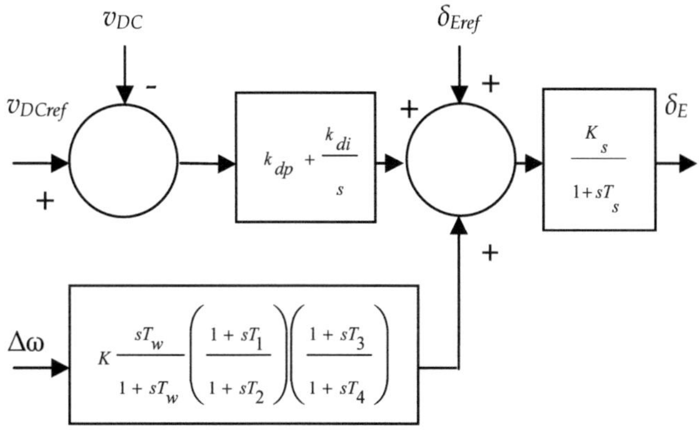

Figure 3. UPFC with lead-lag damping controller and DC voltage regulator

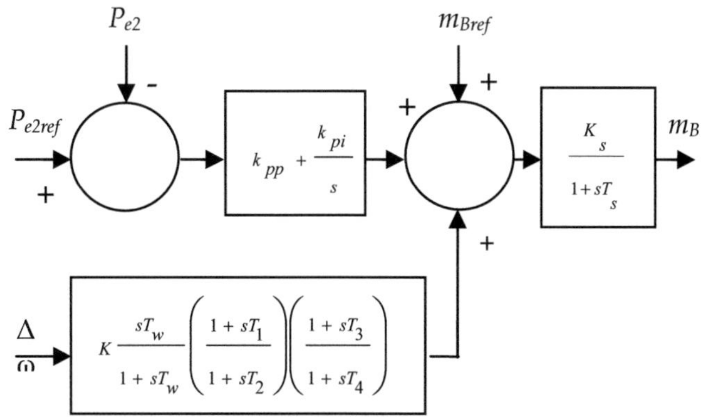

Figure 4. UPFC with lead-lag damping controller and power flow controller

Hence, the design problem can be formulated as:

$$\text{minimize } J$$

Subject to

$$K_j^{\min} \le K_j \le K_j^{\max}$$

$$T_{ji}^{\min} \le T_{ji} \le T_{ji}^{\max}$$

where i = 1, 2, 3, or 4, and K_j and T_{ji} are the gain and time constants of the jth damping controllers.
The proposed approach employs PSO to search for the optimum parameter settings of the given controllers.

3. Controllability Measure

To measure the controllability of the EM mode by a given input (control signal), the singular value decomposition (SVD) is employed. The matrix B can be written as $B = [b_1\ b_2\ b_3\ b_4\ b_5]$ where b_i is a column vector corresponding to the ith input.
The minimum singular value, σmin, of the matrix $[\lambda I\text{-}A\ b_i]$ indicates the capability of the ith input to control the mode associated with the eigenvalue λ. Actually, the higher the σ_{min}, the higher the controllability of this mode by the input considered. As such, the controllability of the EM mode can be examined with all inputs in order to identify the most effective one to control the mode. (Hamdan, 1999; Al-Awami et al, 2005)

4. Particle Swarm Optimization

Particle Swarm Optimization (PSO) was introduced first in (Kennedy & Eberhart, 1995). PSO approach features many advantages; it is simple, fast and can be coded in few lines. Also, its storage requirement is minimal.
Moreover, this approach is advantageous over evolutionary and genetic algorithms in many ways. First, PSO has memory. That is, every particle remembers its best solution (personal best - *pbest*) as well as the group best solution (global best - *gbest*). Another advantage of PSO is that the initial population of the PSO is maintained, and so there is no need for applying operators to the population, a process that is time- and memory-storage consuming. (Kennedy & Eberhart, 1995; Eberhart & Kennedy, 1995; Shi & Eberhart, 1998)
PSO starts with a population of random solutions "particles" in a D-dimension space. The ith particle is represented by $X_i=(x_{i1}, x_{i2}, \ldots, x_{iD})$. PSO consists of, at each step, changing the velocity of each particle toward its *pbest* and *gbest* according to equation (21). The velocity of particle i is represented as $V_i=(v_{i1}, v_{i2}, \ldots, v_{iD})$. The position of the ith particle is then updated according to equation (22) (Kennedy & Eberhart, 1995; Eberhart & Kennedy, 1995; Shi & Eberhart, 1998).

$$v_{id} = wv_{id} + c_1 r_1 (p_{id} - x_{id}) + c_2 r_2 (p_{gd} - x_{gd}) \tag{21}$$

$$x_{id} = x_{id} + v_{id} \tag{22}$$

where, $p_{id} = pbest$ and $p_{gd} = gbest$

An excellent simplified description of the PSO algorithm can be found in (Abido, 2001).
Figure 5 shows a flow chart of the PSO algorithm that is adopted for this specific problem. It is described as follows:
Step 1: Define the problem space and set the boundaries, i.e. the acceptable limits of the controller parameters.
Step 2: Initialize an array of particles with random positions and their associated velocities inside the problem space. These particle positions represent the initial set of solutions.

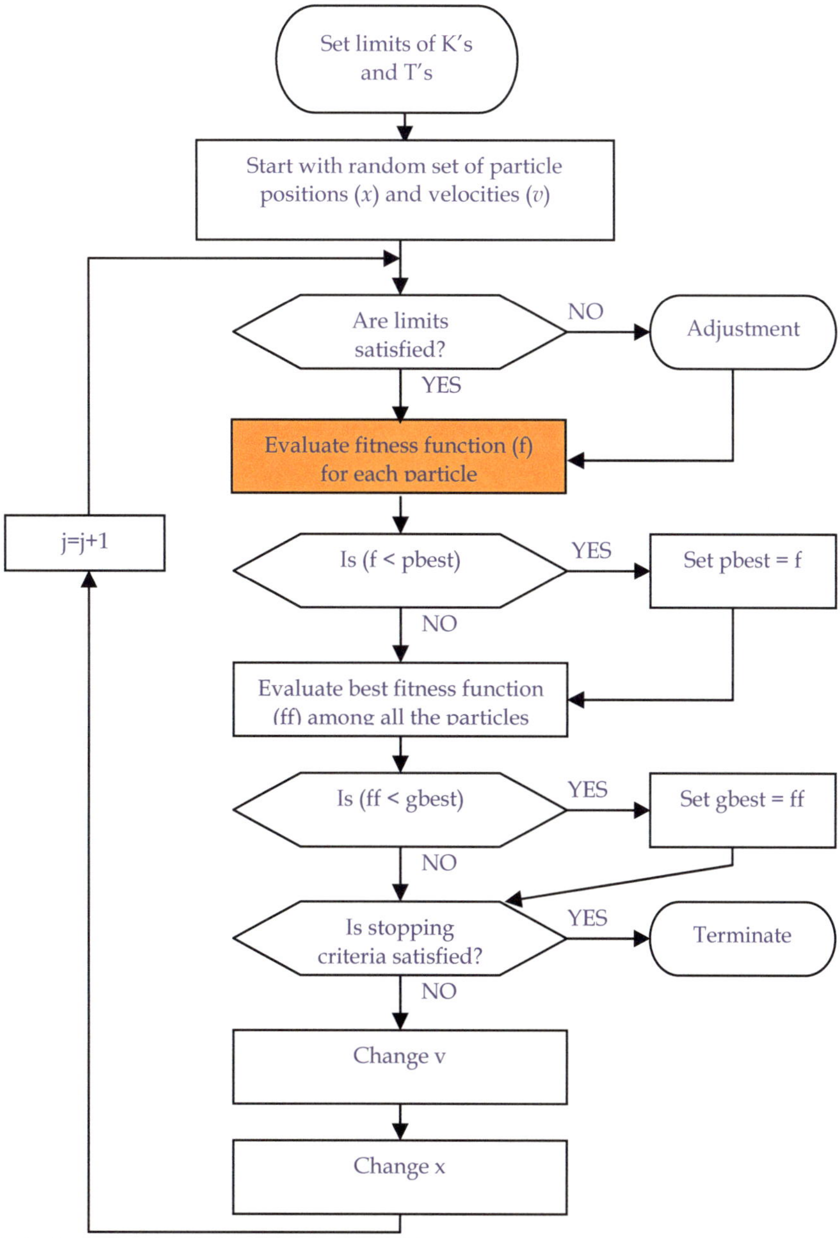

Figure 5. Particle Swarm Optimization algorithm

Step 3: Check if the current position is inside the problem space or not. If not, adjust the positions so as to be inside the problem space.
Step 4: Evaluate the fitness value of each particle.
Step 5: Compare the current fitness value with the particles' previous best value ($pbest_i$). If the current fitness value is better, then assign the current fitness value to $pbest_i$ and assign the current coordinates to $pbestx_i$ coordinates.
Step 6: Determine the current global minimum among particle's best position.

Step 7: If the current global minimum is better than *gbest*, then assign the current global minimum to *gbest* and assign the current coordinates to *gbestx* coordinates.
Step 8: Change the velocities according to (21).
Step 9: Move each particle to the new position according to (22) and return to Step 3.
Step 10: Repeat **Step 3- Step 9** until a stopping criteria is satisfied.
To adopt the PSO algorithm so that simultaneous stabilization is achieved, i.e. several operating points are considered simultaneously, the fitness function evaluation process contains an inner loop, see Figure 6. That is, for every operating point i, the objective J_i is computed. Then, $J = \max(J_1, J_2, ..., J_{N_{op}})$, where N_{op} is the number of operating points considered, is evaluated. (Al-Awami et al, 2006a; Al-Awami et al, 2007; Abido et al, 2006b)
The proposed PSO-based approach was implemented using a MATLAB library built by the authors. In all implementations, the inertia weight, w, is linearly decreasing from 0.9 to 0.4, c_1 and c_2 are selected as 2, and the maximum number of iterations is 400.

5. Simulation Results

5.1 Electromechanical Mode Controllability Measure

Singular value decomposition (SVD) is employed to measure the controllability of the electromechanical mode (EM) from each of the four UPFC inputs: m_E, δ_E, m_B, and δ_B. For comparison, the power system stabilizer input, u_{pss}, is also included. The minimum singular value, σ_{min}, is estimated over a wide range of operating conditions. For SVD analysis, P_e ranges from 0.05 to 1.4 pu and Q_e= [-0.4, 0, 0.4]. At each loading condition, the system model is linearized, the EM mode is identified, and the SVD-based controllability measure is implemented. (Al-Awami et al, 2007)

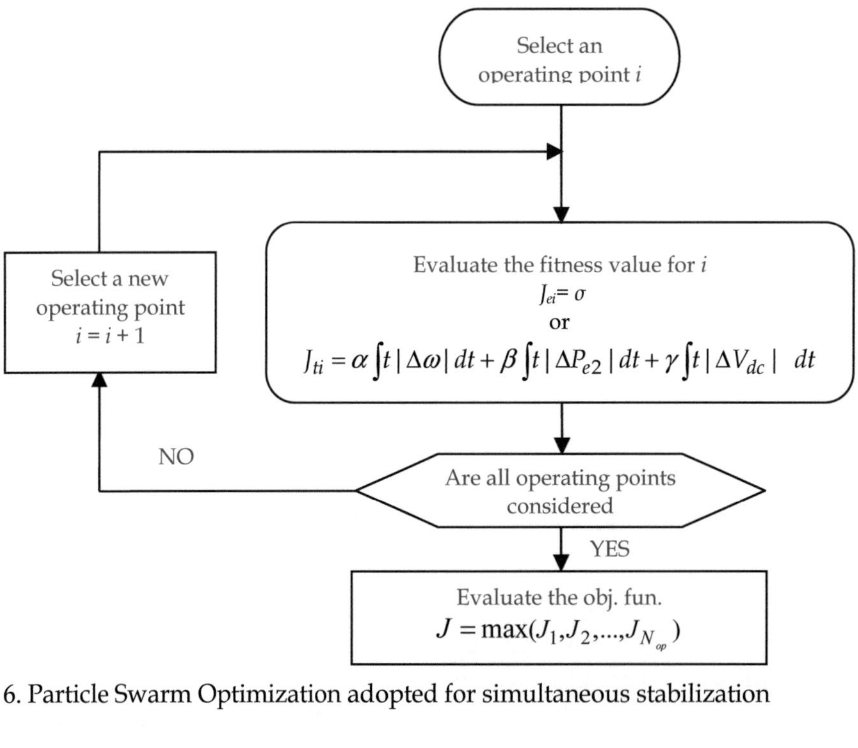

Figure 6. Particle Swarm Optimization adopted for simultaneous stabilization

For comparison purposes, the minimum singular value for all inputs at Qe = - 0.4, 0.0 and 0.4 pu is shown in Figures 7, 8, and 9, respectively. From these figures, the following can be noticed:

- EM mode controllability via δ_E is always higher than that of any other input.
- The capabilities of δ_E and m_B to control the EM mode is higher than that of PSS.
- The EM mode is more controllable with PSS than with either m_E or δ_B.
- All control signals except m_B at $Q_e = 0$ and δ_E suffer from low controllability to EM mode at low loading conditions.

5.2 Design and Analysis Using Eigenvalue-based Objective Function J_e

In this section, stabilizer design is carried out using the eigenvalue-based objective function, J_e, given by (19). Both single-point tuning and robust tuning using simultaneous stabilization are presented. A coordinated design of stabilizers is also demonstrated. The system used is that shown in Figure 1 and the system data used is given in the Appendix. (Al-Awami et al, 2007; Al-Awami et al, 2005; Al-Awami et al, 2006)

To assess the effectiveness of the proposed controllers, four different loading conditions are considered for eigenvalue analysis, see Table 1.

Moreover, the nominal and light loading conditions with 6-cycle three-phase fault disturbances are considered for nonlinear time-domain simulations.

Loading Condition	(P_e, Q_e) pu
Nominal	(1.0, 0.015)
Light	(0.3, 0.015)
Heavy	(1.1, 0.400)
Leading Pf	(0.7, -0.30)

Table 1. Loading conditions

5.2.1 Single-point Tuning Using J_e

The PSS, m_E-, δ_E-, m_B-, and δ_B-based stabilizers are designed individually considering the nominal loading condition. PSO is used to search for the optimum parameter settings of each controller individually so as to minimize the maximum damping factor of all the system complex eigenvalues at nominal loading condition. The final settings of the optimized parameters for the proposed stabilizers and the minimum damping factors achieved are given in Table 2.

The system electromechanical mode without and with the proposed stabilizers at the four operating points, nominal, light, heavy, and leading Pf, are given in Table 3. Table 3 clearly demonstrate the effectiveness of the δ_E- and m_B-based stabilizers in enhancing system stability. Again, It can be observed that, in most cases, the EM mode is either unstable or poorly damped when driven by m_E- or δ_B-based stabilizers. This conclusion is in line with those already drawn from SVD analysis. Because of their poor performance, the m_E- and δ_B-based stabilizers will be excluded from the analysis hereafter.

The system behaviour due to the utilization of the proposed controllers under transient conditions has been tested by applying a 6-cycle 3-phase fault at the infinite bus at t = 1s. The system response at nominal loading is shown in Figures 10 and 11, and the response at light loading is shown in Figures 12 and 13. From these figures, the following can be observed:

- The three stabilizers designed with the proposed PSO-based technique effectively improve the stability of the power system under study.

- As expected from SVD analysis, the δ_E-based stabilizer is robust to operating point variations.
- Both UPFC-based stabilizer outperform the PSS in terms of their effect on voltage profile.

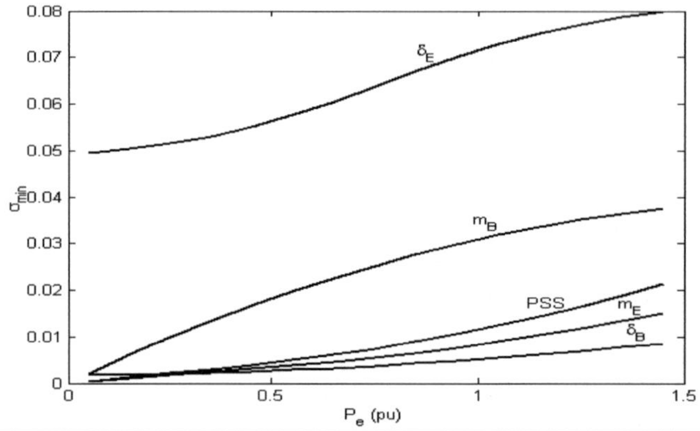

Figure 7. Minimum singular value with all stabilizers at Q_e = – 0.4

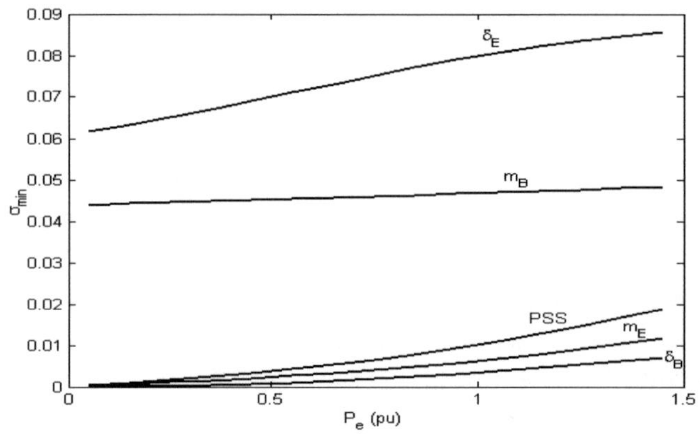

Figure 8. Minimum singular value with all stabilizers at Q_e=0.0

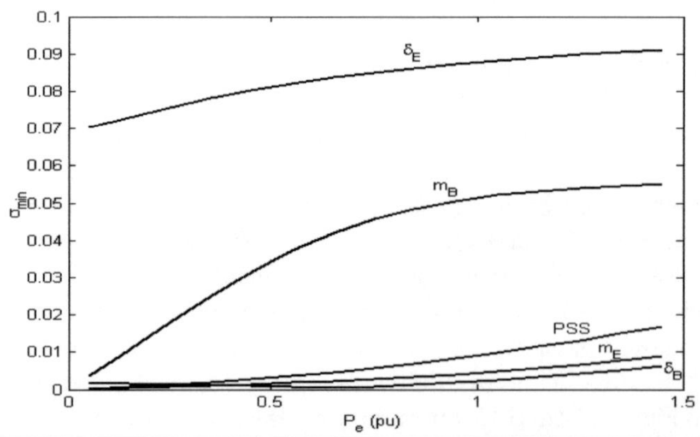

Figure 9. Minimum singular value with all stabilizers at Q_e=0.4

	PSS	m_E	δ_E	m_B	δ_B
K	29.26	-29.83	-100.00	100.00	-72.89
T_1	2.92	0.25	5.00	0.11	2.02
T_2	1.19	2.46	1.08	0.01	0.13
T_3	0.13	2.95	0.06	2.18	2.94
T_4	0.01	0.01	1.44	2.35	2.42
J_e	-5.44	-1.69	-4.63	-4.15	-1.39

Table 2. Optimal parameter settings with J_e, single-point tuning, individual design

	No Control	PSS	m_E	δ_E	m_B	δ_B
N	$1.50 \pm 5.33i$	$-5.44 \pm 0.18i$	$-1.69 \pm 7.62i$	$-4.62 \pm 5.88i$	$-4.15 \pm 6.06i$	$-1.39 \pm 6.02i$
L	$1.39 \pm 5.08i$	$-1.10 \pm 4.67i$	$0.90 \pm 5.37i$	$-3.17 \pm 5.88i$	$-3.24 \pm 6.88i$	$1.30 \pm 5.12i$
H	$1.41 \pm 5.00i$	$-1.71 \pm 2.00i$	$0.08 \pm 7.05i$	$-1.81 \pm 1.74i$	$-4.62 \pm 3.75i$	$-1.79 \pm 5.48i$
L_{pf}	$1.45 \pm 5.35i$	$-5.70 \pm 16.79i$	$-0.81 \pm 6.34i$	$-1.97 \pm 5.48i$	$-1.37 \pm 6.07i$	$-0.26 \pm 5.58i$

Table 3. System electromechanical modes at all loading conditions with no parameter uncertainties with J_e settings, single-point tuning, individual design (N: Nominal, L: Light, H: Heavy, L_{pf}: Leading power factor)

5.2.2 Robust Tuning with Simultaneous Stabilization Using J_e

In this situation, the objective is to design robust stabilizers to ensure their effectiveness over a wide range of operating conditions. Both individual and coordinated designs are considered. The design process takes into account several loading conditions including nominal, light, heavy, and leading Pf conditions. These conditions are considered without and with system parameter uncertainties, such as machine inertia, line impedance, and field time constant. The total number of 16 operating conditions is considered during the design process as given in Table 4.

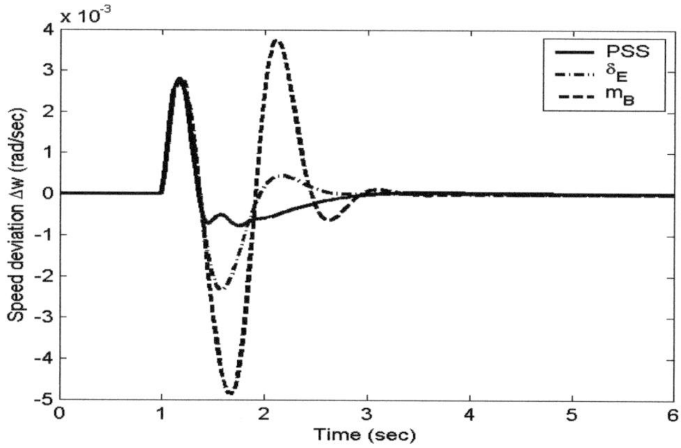

Figure 10. Speed response for 6-cycle fault with nominal loading, J_e settings, single-point tuning, individual design

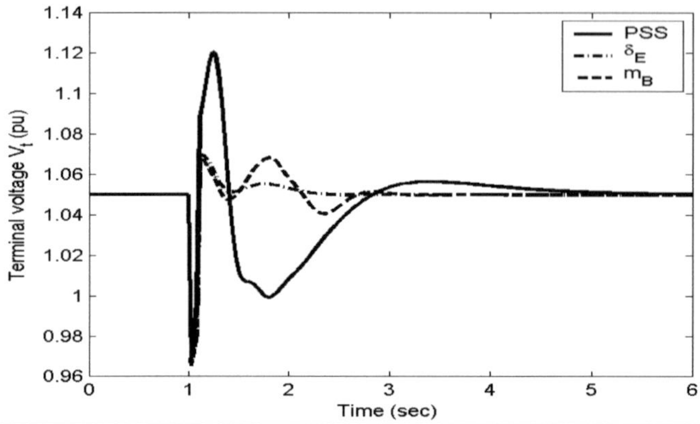

Figure 11. Terminal voltage response for 6-cycle fault with nominal loading, J_e settings, single-point tuning, individual design

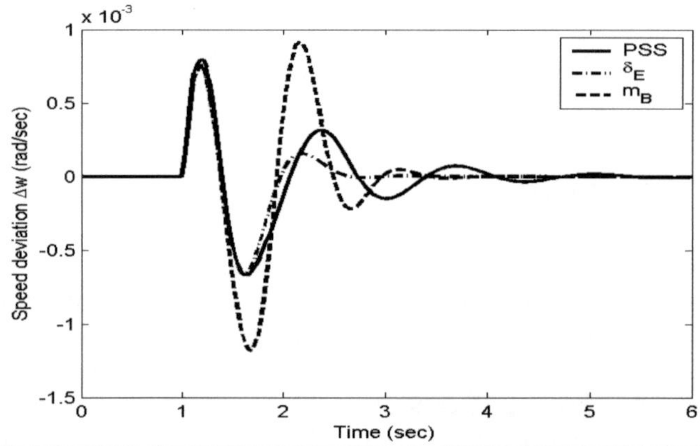

Figure 12. Speed response for 6-cycle fault with light loading, J_e settings, single-point tuning, individual design

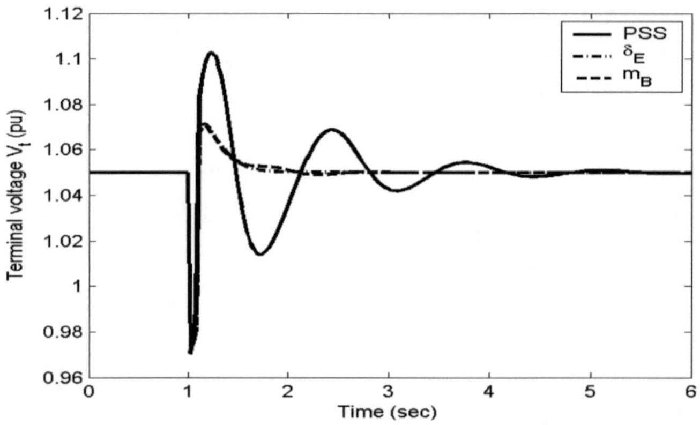

Figure 13. Terminal voltage response for 6-cycle fault with light loading, J_e settings, single-point tuning, individual design

Loading Condition	(P_e, Q_e) pu	Parameter Uncertainties
N	(1.0, 0.015)	No parameter uncertainties
L	(0.3, 0.100)	30% increase of line reactance X_{BV}
H	(1.1, 0.100)	25% decrease of machine inertia M
L_{pf}	(0.7, -0.30)	30% decrease of field time constant T'_{do}

Table 4. Loading conditions and parameter uncertainties considered in the design stage

Table 5 lists the open-loop eigenvalues associated with the electromechanical modes of all the 16 operating points considered in the robust design process, respectively. It is evident that all these modes are unstable.

In the individual design, the PSS, δ_E-, and m_B--based stabilizers are designed individually considering all the operating points mentioned above. PSO is used to optimize the parameters of each controller that minimize the maximum damping factor of all the complex eigenvalues associated with the 16 operating points simultaneously. The final settings of the optimized parameters for the proposed stabilizers and the minimum damping factors achieved are given in Table 6.

The system electromechanical mode without and with the proposed stabilizers at the four operating points, nominal, light, heavy, and leading Pf, are given in Table 7. Table 7 clearly demonstrate the effectiveness of the proposed stabilizers in enhancing system stability. Comparing Table 7 with Table 3, the effectiveness of robust tuning with simultaneous stabilization can be observed. For example, the maximum damping factor of the system electromechanical modes using single-point tuning for PSS is -1.10. However, the maximum damping factor using robust tuning with simultaneous stabilization is -2.58.

The system behaviour due to the utilization of the proposed stabilizers under transient conditions has been tested by applying a 6-cycle 3-phase fault at the infinite bus at t = 1s. The system response at nominal loading is shown in Figures 14 and 15, and the response at light loading is shown in Figures 16 and 17. These simulation results prove the effectiveness of the proposed technique in designing robust stabilizers. It can be observed by comparing Figure 12 with Figure 16 that including the light loading condition in the robust tuning technique helped improve PSS response to transients in the system. In addition, it can be readily seed again that both UPFC-based stabilizer outperform the PSS in terms of their effect on voltage profile.

	No parameter uncertainties	30% increase of line reactance X	25% decrease of machine inertia M	30% decrease of field time constant T'_{do}
N	$1.50 \pm 5.33i$	$1.41 \pm 4.99i$	$1.80 \pm 5.94i$	$1.5034 \pm 5.40i$
L	$1.39 \pm 5.08i$	$1.32 \pm 4.74i$	$1.67 \pm 5.66i$	$1.3951 \pm 5.09i$
H	$1.41 \pm 5.00i$	$1.25 \pm 4.52i$	$1.70 \pm 5.57i$	$1.4038 \pm 5.08i$
L_{pf}	$1.45 \pm 5.35i$	$1.40 \pm 5.08i$	$1.74 \pm 5.97i$	$1.4498 \pm 5.39i$

Table 5. Open-loop eigenvalues associated with the EM modes of all the 16 points considered in the robust design process

Although the controllability measure analysis based on the singular value decomposition and the nonlinear time-domain simulation show the relative robustness of the δ_E-based stabilizer in damping the EM mode oscillation, there is still room for more improvement through coordination with the m_B-based stabilizer. In the following, the coordinated design of δ_E- and m_B-based stabilizers is considered at all the 16 operating points described earlier. PSO is used to simultaneously search for the optimum parameter settings of both controllers that minimize the maximum damping factor of all the system complex eigenvalues at all the 16 operating points concurrently. The final settings of the optimized parameters for the proposed stabilizers are given in Table 8.

	PSS	δ_E	m_B
K	95.58	-100.00	96.8
T_1	4.34	5.00	4.99
T_2	0.01	1.03	2.57
T_3	0.07	0.06	0.12
T_4	3.51	1.54	0.01
J_e	-1.95	-1.77	-3.54

Table 6. Optimal parameter settings with J_e, multiple-point tuning, individual design

	No Control	PSS	δ_E	m_B
N	$1.50 \pm 5.33i$	$-2.58 \pm 17.5i$	$-3.52 \pm 5.32i$	$-3.91 \pm 12.7i$
L	$1.39 \pm 5.08i$	$-3.91 \pm 3.62i$	$-2.93 \pm 5.65i$	$-3.71 \pm 12.1i$
H	$1.41 \pm 5.00i$	$-2.80 \pm 17.0i$	$-1.92 \pm 1.76i$	$-3.56 \pm 13.1i$
L_{pf}	$1.45 \pm 5.35i$	$-2.72 \pm 16.2i$	$-1.82 \pm 5.47i$	$-3.53 \pm 2.61i$

Table 7. System electromechanical modes at all loading conditions with no parameter uncertainties with J_e settings, robust tuning, individual design

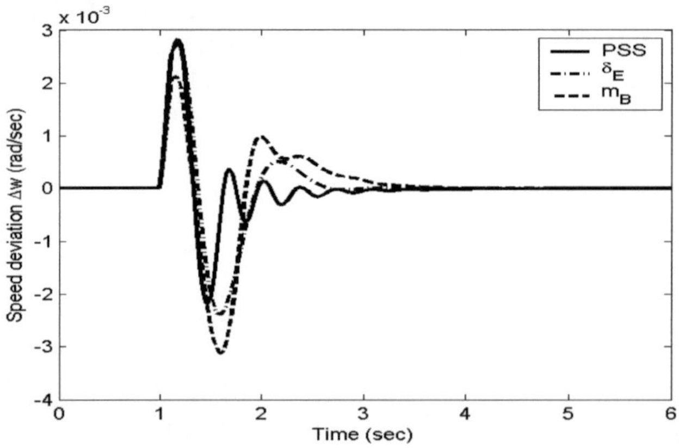

Figure 14. Speed response for 6-cycle fault with nominal loading, J_e settings, robust tuning, individual design

The system electromechanical modes without and with the proposed δ_E- and m_B-based controllers when applied individually and through coordinated design at the four loading conditions; nominal, light, heavy, and leading Pf, are given in Table 9. It is evident that the damping factor of the EM mode is greatly enhanced using the proposed coordinated stabilizers design.

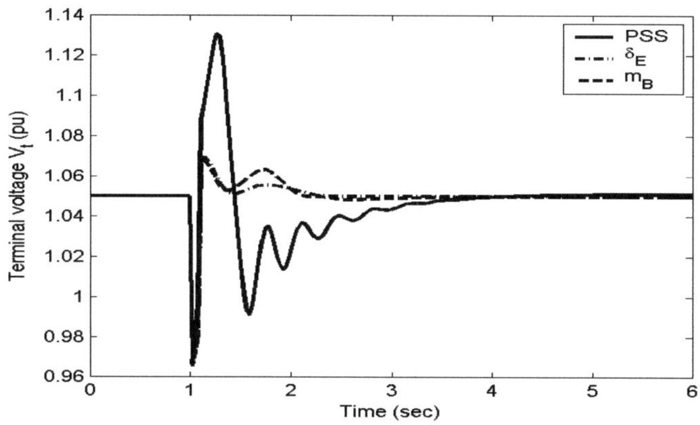

Figure 15. Terminal voltage response for 6-cycle fault with nominal loading, J_e settings, robust tuning, individual design

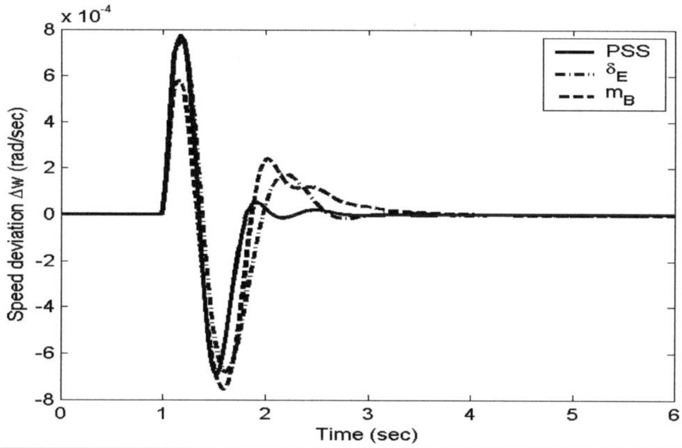

Figure 16. Speed response for 6-cycle fault with light loading, J_e settings, robust tuning, individual design

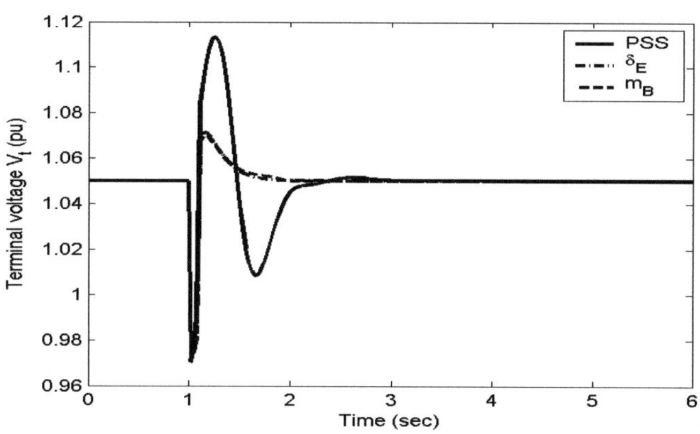

Figure 17. Terminal voltage response for 6-cycle fault with light loading, J_e settings, robust tuning, individual design

Moreover, the nonlinear time-domain simulations are carried out at the nominal and light loading conditions specified previously. The speed deviations, DC voltage, electrical power, and δ_E and m_B control signals for a 6-cycle three-phase fault at nominal loading conditions are shown in Figures 18-22, respectively. The simulation results indicate a clear enhancement of the proposed coordinated δ_E-m_B design over both individual designs. This enhancement can be easily recognized from the sound reduction in overshoot and settling time of the speed, electrical power and DC voltage responses as well as the reduction in the control efforts of the coordinated design as compared with the control efforts of the two individual designs. Similar conclusions can be drawn from light loading results. Due to limitation in space, only speed deviations at light loading conditions are shown, see Figure 23. It is noteworthy that using coordination, the problem of low effectiveness of the m_B-based stabilizer individual designs at light loading level has been solved.

	Individual		Coordinated	
	δ_E	m_B	δ_E	m_B
K	-100.00	96.8	-66.18	100.00
T_1	5.00	4.99	1.53	5.00
T_2	1.03	2.57	1.61	3.09
T_3	0.06	0.12	4.42	5.00
T_4	1.54	0.01	3.95	3.32

Table 8. Optimal parameter settings with J_e, multiple-point tuning, coordinated design

Loading	δ_E	m_B	δ_E & m_B
N	$-3.52 \pm 5.32i$	$-3.91 \pm 12.72i$	$-7.51 \pm 10.64i$
L	$-2.93 \pm 5.65i$	$-3.71 \pm 12.19i$	$-5.81 \pm 11.04i$
H	$-1.92 \pm 1.76i$	$-3.56 \pm 13.12i$	$-7.21 \pm 11.65i$
L_{pf}	$-1.82 \pm 5.47i$	$-3.53 \pm 2.61i$	$-5.86 \pm 6.46i$

Table 9 System eigenvalues with all the stabilizers at different loading conditions

5.3 Coordinated Design of Damping Stabilizers and Internal Controllers Using Time-domain-based Objective Function J_t

In this section, stabilizer design is carried out using the time-domain-based objective function, J_t, given by (20). Using J_t, the need for linearizing the nonlinear power system model is eliminated. That is, the nature of the objective function makes it suitable for both linear and nonlinear systems (Al-Awami et al, 2006b; Abido et al, 2006b). Moreover, it is possible to design several controllers with different objectives in a coordinated manner (Abido et al, 2006b). As will be shown, using the time-domain-based objective function, it is possible to design the UPFC damping controller, DC voltage regulator, and power flow controller, each of which has a different objective, in a coordinated manner. In this section, a coordinated design of UPFC damping stabilizers and internal controllers at nominal loading conditions is demonstrated. The effectiveness of the proposed controllers in damping low frequency oscillations is verified through eigenvalue analysis and non-linear time simulation. A comparison with a sequential design of the controllers under study is also included. The system used is that shown in Figure 1 and the system data used is given in the Appendix. (Abido et al, 2006b)

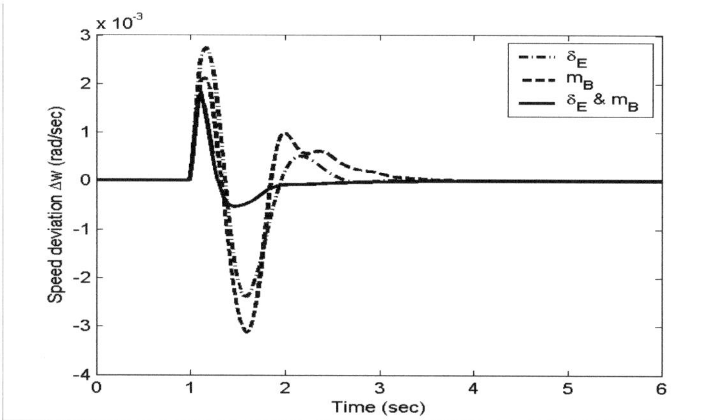

Figure 18. Speed response for 6-cycle fault with nominal loading, J_t settings, robust tuning, coordinated design

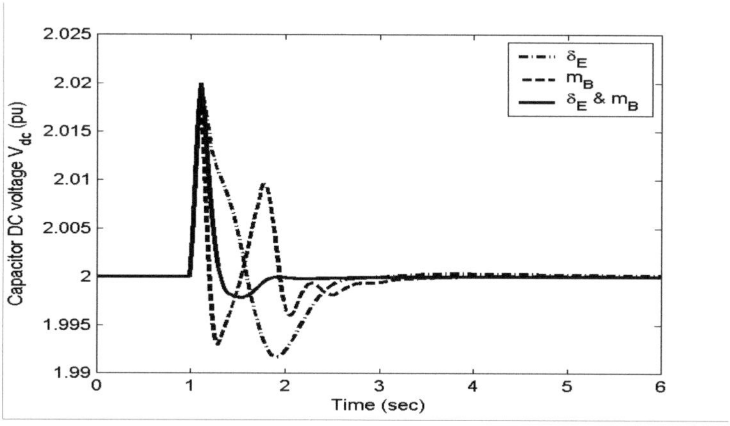

Figure 19. UPFC DC voltage response for 6-cycle fault with nominal loading, J_t settings, robust tuning, coordinated design

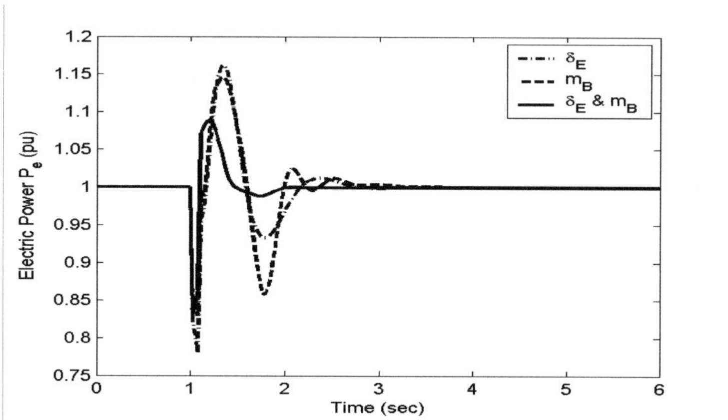

Figure 20. Electrical Power response for 6-cycle fault with nominal loading, J_t settings, robust tuning, coordinated design

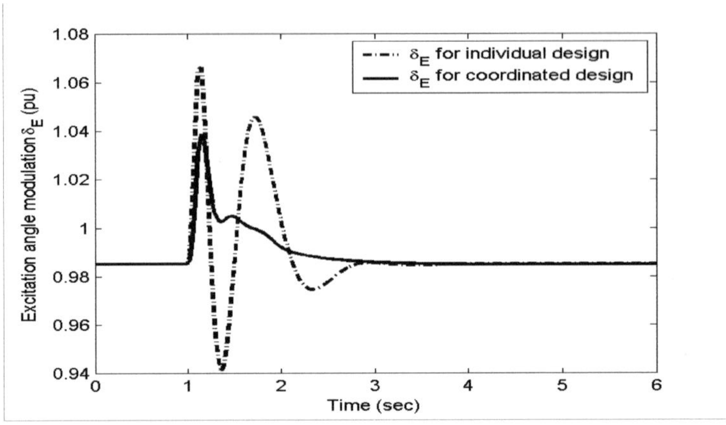

Figure 21. δ_E control signal response for 6-cycle fault with nominal loading, J_t settings, robust tuning, coordinated design

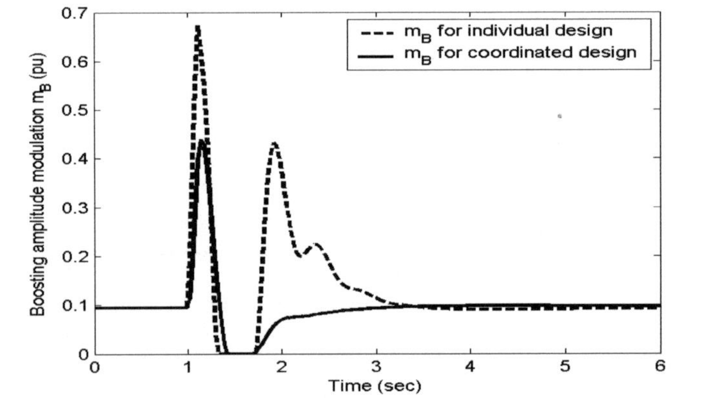

Figure 22. m_B control signal response for 6-cycle fault with nominal loading, J_t settings, robust tuning, coordinated design

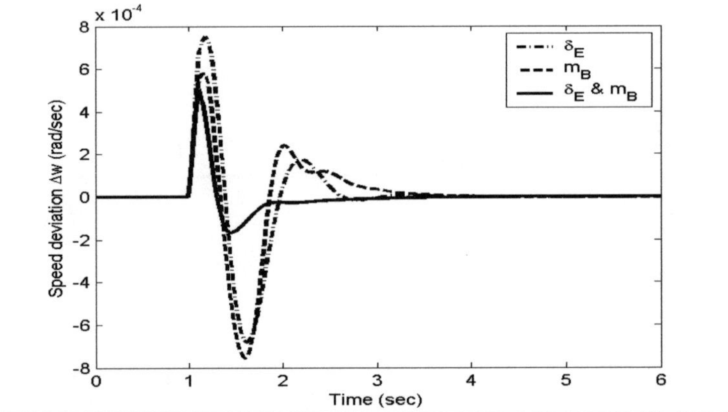

Figure 23. Speed signal response for 6-cycle fault with light loading, J_t settings, robust tuning, coordinated design

5.3.1 Sequential Controller Design

In this stage, the three controllers are designed sequentially (Abido et al, 2006b). That is, (1) the DC voltage regulator (VR) is designed first, then (2) the power flow controller (PFC) is designed in the presence of the regulator, and finally (3) the damping controllers (DC) are designed, one at a time, in the presence of the other two controllers (VR and PFC). In each step, PSO has been used to find the optimum parameters of each controller that optimize the objective function defined by (20). A nominal loading condition has been considered in the design stage, see Table 10.

Since each of the three controllers has a different function, the objective function weights and the disturbances used in the design stage are different. Table 11 shows the details of each step in the sequential design. Step (1) resulted in the following optimum parameters for the DC voltage regulator: k_{dp} = - 4.56, k_{di} = - 19.98. Step (2) resulted in the following optimum parameters for the power flow controller: k_{pp} = 0.0005, k_{pi} = - 0.0047. The final settings of the optimized parameters for the proposed damping controllers are given in Table 12.

To test the performance of these stabilizers, eigenvalue analysis and nonlinear time-domain simulations are carried out. The system data is given in the Appendix The system EM modes and their corresponding damping ratios with the PSS and UPFC-based controllers when tested at nominal loading are given in Table 13. Moreover, the speed deviations for a 6-cycle three-phase fault at nominal loading conditions are shown in Figure 24. It is evident that the sequential designs give rise to poorly damped or even unstable responses.

Loading Condition	P_e (pu)	Q_e (pu)
Nominal	1.000	0.015
Light	0.300	0.100

Table 10. Loading Conditions

Controller	Weights of J			Disturbance
	α	β	γ	
VR	0	0	1	step change in V_{DCref}
PFC	0	1	0	step change in P_{e2ref}
DC	1	0	0	Impulse change in P_m

Table 11. Objective Function Weights and Disturbances Used in Steps (1)-(3) for the Sequential Design

	δ_E	m_B	PSS
K	83.94	92.31	71.37
T_1	1.18	0.40	0.27
T_2	1.01	0.63	0.69
T_3	1.50	1.49	0.34
T_4	0.57	0.72	0.05
J	36.21	139.88	0.29

Table 12. The Optimal Parameter Settings of the Individual Controllers - Sequential Design

	δ_E	m_B	PSS
EM	1.30 ± 3.10*i*	1.79 ± 7.39*i*	-0.80 ± 5.04*i*
ζ	-0.39	-0.24	0.16

Table 13. System Eigenvalues of the Individual Controllers at Nominal Loading - Sequential Design

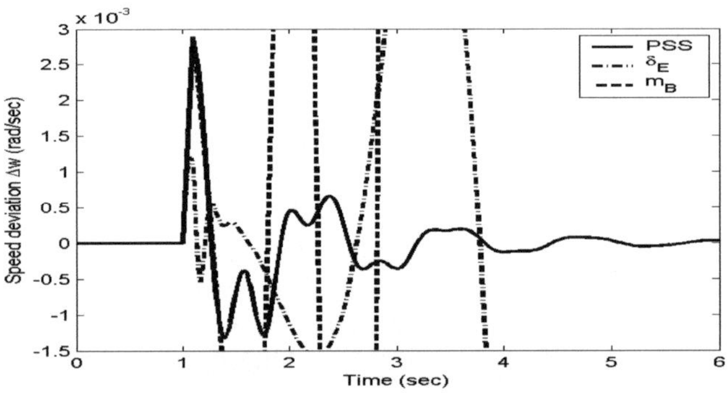

Figure 24. Speed response for a 6-cycle fault with nominal loading - sequential design

5.3.2 Coordinated Controller Design

In this stage, the three controllers are designed in a coordinated manner (Abido et al, 2006b). That is, PSO is used to concurrently find the optimum parameters of the VR, PFC, and DC minimizing the error objective function defined in (20). In order to end up with the optimum controllers, the objective function weights and the disturbances have to be selected carefully. Table 14 shows the objective function weights used in every case. In all cases, the following two disturbances have been used:

1. An impulse change in P_m
2. A step change in P_{e2ref}.

The final settings of the optimized parameters for the proposed controllers are given in Table 15.

To test the performance of the proposed stabilizers, eigenvalue analysis and nonlinear time-domain simulations are carried out.

The system EM modes and their corresponding damping ratios with the proposed PSS and UPFC-based controllers when tested at nominal and light loading conditions are given in Table 16. It is evident that system stability is greatly enhanced by the proposed coordinated designs.

Damping Controller	Weights of J		
	α	β	γ
δ_E	100	1	30
m_B	120	1	10
PSS	100	1	10

Table 14. Objective Function Weights and Disturbances Used in the Simultaneous Design

	δ_E	m_B	PSS
K	100.00	100.00	1.64
T_1	1.28	1.50	0.62
T_2	0.76	0.49	0.17
T_3	0.05	1.50	1.01
T_4	0.57	0.49	0.05
k_{pp}	0.51	-13.21	-19.93
k_{pi}	-0.92	-14.60	-17.44
k_{dp}	-7.69	-20.00	-13.77
k_{di}	-2.19	-15.46	-5.41
J	124.9	35.0	27.0

Table 15. The Optimal Parameter Settings of the Individual Controllers - Simultaneous Design

		δ_E	m_B	PSS
N	EM	$-2.15 \pm 6.97i$	$-2.37 \pm 6.49i$	$-1.97 \pm 5.25i$
	ζ	0.30	0.34	0.35
L	EM	$-2.18 \pm 6.59i$	$-2.44 \pm 6.30i$	$-1.80 \pm 8.72i$
	ζ	0.31	0.36	0.20

Table 16. System Eigenvalues of the Individual Controllers at Nominal (N) and Light (L) Loading - Simultaneous Design

Moreover, the nonlinear time-domain simulations are carried out at nominal and light loading conditions. The deviations in speed, power flow of line 2, and DC voltage for a 6-cycle three-phase fault at nominal loading condition are shown in Figures 25-27, respectively. From these figures, it is observed that:

- The proposed coordinated designs give rise to superior responses.
- After the fault, the three signals shown in Figures 25-27 have settled with no steady-state error, excellent settling time, and reasonably good overshoot.
- The δ_E-based controller outperforms the m_B-based controller and PSS, especially in terms of overshoot.

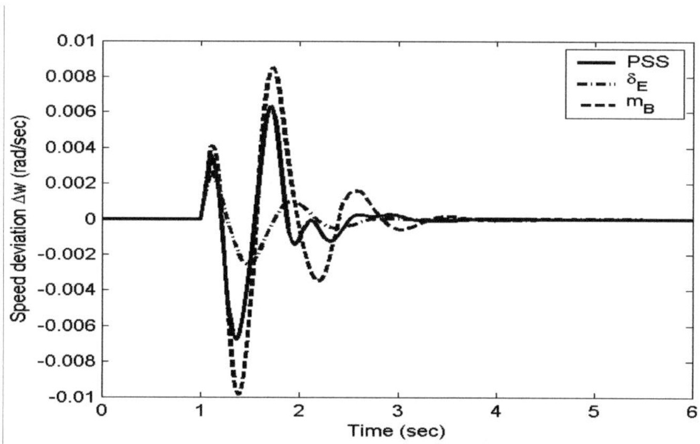

Figure 25. Speed response for a 6-cycle fault with nominal loading - Coordinated design

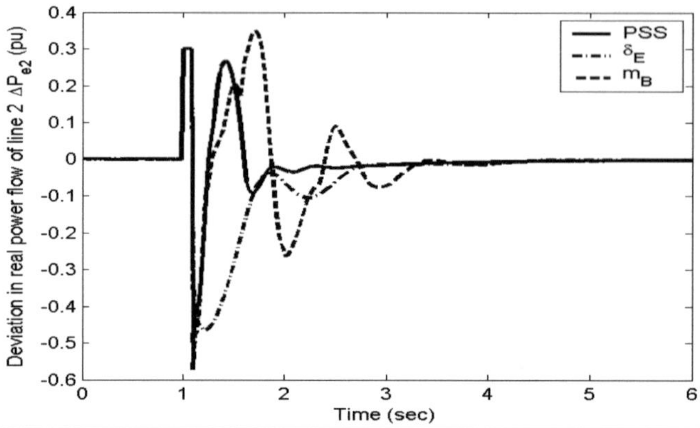

Figure 26. Power flow response of line 2 for a 6-cycle fault with nominal loading - Coordinated design

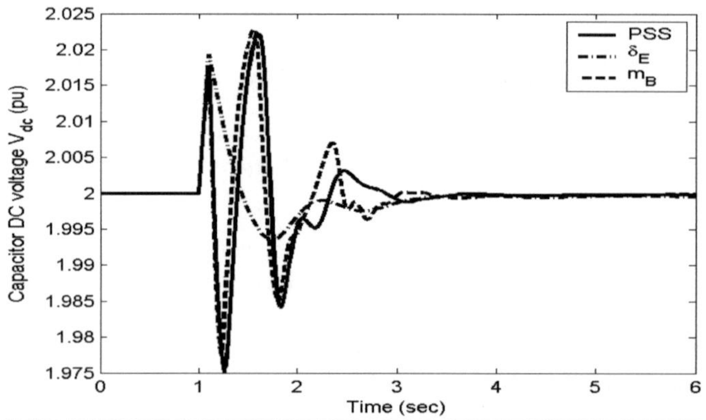

Figure 27. DC voltage response for a 6-cycle fault with nominal loading - Coordinated design

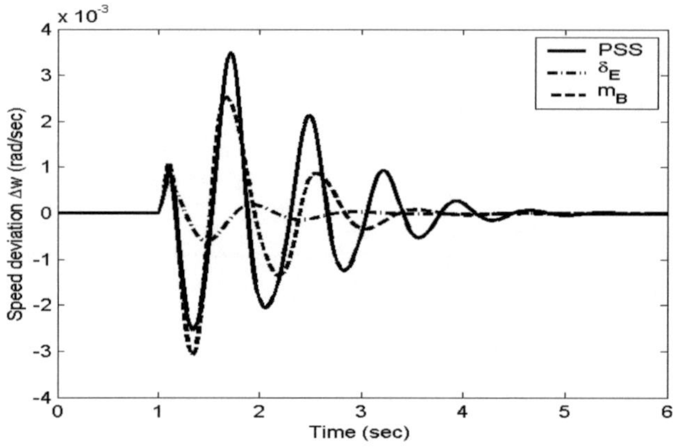

Figure 28. Speed response for a 6-cycle fault with light loading - coordinated design

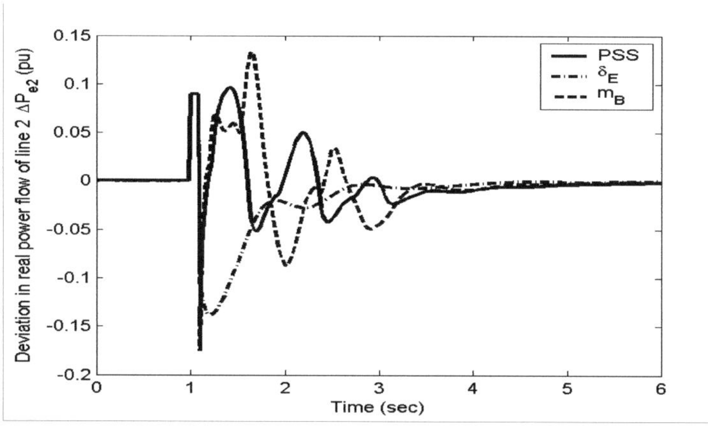

Figure 29. Power flow response of line 2 for a 6-cycle fault with light loading - simultaneous design

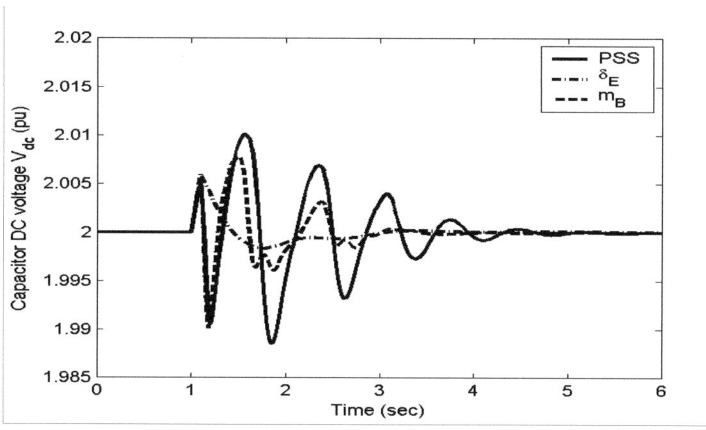

Figure 30. DC voltage response for a 6-cycle fault with light loading - simultaneous design

In addition, the deviations in torque angle, power flow of line 2, and DC voltage for a 6-cycle three-phase fault at light loading conditions are shown in Figures 28-30, respectively. From these figures it can be concluded that the δ_E-based controller is the most effective controller in terms of overshoot, settling time, and steady-state error. This shows that the performance of δ_E-based controller is almost unaffected with the loading level. The performance of m_B-based controller and PSS, however, is degraded at this loading condition.

6. Conclusion

In this work, the problem of enhancing the power system dynamic stability through individual and coordinated design of UPFC-based damping stabilizers has been investigated. The controllability of the electromechanical mode over a wide range of operating conditions by a given control input has been measured using a singular value decomposition-based approach. Such a study is very important as it laid the foundations of the requirements of the coordinated design problem. The stabilizer design problem has been formulated as an optimization problem with an eigenvalue-based as well as a time domain-based objective functions, which was then solved by particle swarm optimization. The use of the first objective function results in placing the electromechanical modes of oscillations furthest to the left of the complex s-plane, thus improving the damping of these modes. The use of the second objective function results in improving the time domain specifications of the system performance in terms of overshoot and settling time.

Individual design as well as coordinated design of the proposed stabilizers with and without system parameter uncertainties have been investigated and discussed. It has been concluded that the eigenvalue-based objective function can be used to design efficient individual as well as coordinated stabilizers. However, the time-domain-based objective function has the advantage of designing several controllers with different objectives in a coordinated manner. This feature has been utilized to design the UPFC damping stabilizers and internal controllers in a coordinated manner.

In all cases, the damping characteristics of the proposed control schemes to low frequency oscillations over a wide range of operating conditions have been evaluated using the eigenvalue analysis. The effectiveness of the proposed control schemes in enhancing the power system dynamic stability has been verified through comprehensive nonlinear time-domain simulations for a variety of loading conditions. It was clearly shown that the coordinated design approach outperforms the individual designs.

7. Appendix

$M = 8.0s$;	$T'_{do} = 5.044$;	$D = 0.0$;	$x_d = 1.0$;
$x'_d = 0.3$;	$x_q = 0.6$;	$X_T = 0.6$;	$\lvert u_{PSS} \rvert \leq 0.2$ pu;
$K_A = 50$;	$T_A = 0.05$;	$T_w = 5.0$;	$\lvert E_{fd} \rvert \leq 7.3$ pu;
$v = 1.05$ pu;	$x_{tE} = 0.1$;	$x_{BV} = 0.6$;	$K_s = 1.0$;
$T_s = 0.05$;	$x_E = 0.1$;	$x_B = 0.1$;	$C_{dc} = 3$;
$V_{dc}=2$;			

All resistances and reactances are in pu and time constants are in seconds.

Notes:

1. All simulations using the eigenvalue-based objective function J_e are carried out assuming line 1 open, i.e. $x_T = \infty$.
2. All simulations using the eigenvalue-based objective function J_e are carried out assuming $k_{dp} = -10$ and $k_{di} = 0$.

8. References

Abdel-Magid, Y.L.; Abido, M.A.; Al-Baiyat, S. & Mantawy, A.H. (1999). Simultaneous Stabilization of Multimachine Power Systems via Genetic Algorithms, *IEEE Trans. on Power Sys.*, Vol. 14, No. 4, November 1999, pp. 1428-1439.

Abido, M.A. & Abdel-Magid, Y.L. (1997). Radial basis function network based power system stabilizers for multimachine power systems, *Intl. Conf. Neural Networks*, Vol. 2, 9-12 June 1997, pp. 622 -626

Abido, M.A. (2001). Particle swarm optimization for multimachine power system stabilizer design, *IEEE Power Eng. Society Summer Meeting*, Vol. 3, 15-19 July 2001, pp. 1346 - 1351

Abido, M.A.; Al-Awami, A.T. & Abdel-Magid, Y.L. (2006a). Analysis and design of UPFC damping stabilizers for power system stability enhancement, *IEEE Symposium on Industrial Electronics* ISIE'2006, Vol. 3, July 2006, pp. 2040-2045

Abido, M.A.; Al-Awami, A.T. & Abdel-Magid, Y.L. (2006b). Power system stability enhancement using simultaneous design of damping controllers and internal controllers of a unified power flow controller, the 2006 IEEE *PES General Meeting*, June 2006, pages: 8

Al-Awami, A.T.; Abdel-Magid, Y.L. & Abido, M.A. (2005). Simultaneous stabilization of power systems equipped with unified power flow controller using particle swarm, *The 15th Power Systems Computation Conference*, Session 12, Paper 2, Aug. 2005, pp. 1-7

Al-Awami, A.T.; Abdel-Magid, Y.L. & Abido, M.A. (2006a). Simultaneous stabilization of power system using UPFC-based controllers, *Electric Power Components and Systems*, Vol. 34, No. 9, Sept 2006. pp. 941 - 959

Al-Awami, A.T.; Abido, M.A. & Abdel-Magid, Y.L. (2006b) Power system stability enhancement using unified power flow controllers,' *The 3nd Industrial Electrical and Electronics GCC Conference*, IEEE-GCC3, March 2006

Al-Awami, A.T.; Abdel-Magid, Y.L. & Abido, M.A. (2007). A particle-swarm-based approach of power system stability enhancement with unified power flow controller, *Int'l J. Electrical Power & Energy Syst.*,Vol. 29, 3, March 2007, pp. 251-259

Chen, C.L. & Hsu, Y.Y. (1987). Coordinated synthesis of multimachine power system stabilizer using an efficient decentralized modal control (DMC) algorithm, IEEE *Trans. on Power Systems*, Vol. 9, No. 3, pp. 543-551

Dash, P.K.; Mishra, S. & Panda, G. (2000). A radial basis function neural network controller for UPFC, *IEEE Trans.Power Systems*, Vol. 15, No. 4, Nov. 2000, pp. 1293 -1299

Eberhart, R. & Kennedy J. (1995). A new optimizer using particle swarm theory, *Proc. the Sixth Intl. Symposium on Micro Machine and Human Science*, 4-6 Oct 1995, pp. 39 -43

Gibbard, M.J. (1988). Co-ordinated design of multimachine power system stabilisers based on damping torque concepts, *IEE Proc. Pt. C*, Vol. 135, No. 4, pp. 276-284.

Hamdan, A.M.A. (1999). An investigation of the significance of singular value decomposition in power system dynamics, *Int. Journal Electrical Power and Energy Systems*, 21, pp. 417-424

Heffron, W.G. & Phillips, R.A. (1952). Effect of modern amplidyne voltage regulators on under-excited operation of large turbine generator, *AIEE Trans. Power Apparatus and Systems*, Aug 1952, pp. 692-697.

Huang, Z.; Yinxin, N.; Shen, C.M.; Wu, F.F.; Chen, S. & Zhang, B. (2000). Application of unified power flow controller in interconnected power systems-modeling, interface, control strategy, and case study, *IEEE Trans. Power Systems*, Vol. 15, No. 2 , May 2000, pp. 817 -824

Kennedy, J. & Eberhart, R. (1995). Particle swarm optimization, *Proc. IEEE Intl. Conf. Neural Networks*, 4, Nov/Dec 1995, pp. 1942 -1948.

Klein, M.; Le, L.X.; Rogers, G.J.; Farrokhpay, S. & Balu, N.J. (1995). $H\infty$ damping controller design in large power systems, *IEEE Trans. on Power Systems*, Vol. 10, no. 1, Feb. 1995, pp. 158 -166

Mahran, A.R.; Hogg, B.W. & El-Sayed, M.L. (1992). Co-ordinated control of synchronous generator excitation and static VAR compensator, *IEEE Trans. Energy Conversion*, Vol. 7, Issue 4, Dec. 1992, pp. 615 -622.

Mok, T.K.; Ni, Y. & Wu, F.F. (2000). Design of fuzzy damping controller of UPFC through genetic algorithm, *IEEE Power Eng. Society Summer Meeting*, Vol. 3, 16-20 July 2000, pp. 1889 - 1894

Nabavi-Niaki, A. & Iravani, M.R. (1996). Steady-state and dynamic models of unified power flow controller (UPFC) for power system studies, *IEEE Trans. Power Systems*, Vol. 11, No. 4, Nov. 1996, pp. 1937-1943

Pal, B.C. (2002). Robust damping of interarea oscillations with unified power flow controller, *IEE Proc. Gen. Trans. and Distrib.*, Vol. 149, No. 6, pp. 733-738.

Samarasinghe, V.G.D.C. & Pahalawaththa, N.C. (1997). Damping of multimodal oscillations in power systems using variable structure control techniques, *IEE Proc. Gen. Trans. and Distrib.*, Vol. 144, No. 3, pp. 323-331.

Seo, J.C.; Moon, S.; Park, J.K. & Choe, J.W. (2001). Design of a robust UPFC controller for enhancing the small signal stability in the multi-machine power systems, IEEE *Power Eng. Society Winter Meeting*, Vol. 3 , 28 Jan.-1 Feb. 2001, pp. 1197 -1202

Shi, Y. & Eberhart, R. (1998). A modified particle swarm optimizer, *The 1998 IEEE Intl. Conf. on Evolutionary Computation Proc.*, IEEE World Congress on Computational Intelligence., 4-9 May 1998, pp. 69 – 73.

Vilathgamuwa, M.; Zhu, X. & Choi, S.S. (2000). A robust control method to improve the performance of a unified power flow controller, *Electric Power System Research*, 55, pp. 103-111.

Wang, H.F. (1999a). Damping function of unified power flow controller, *IEE Proc. Gen. Trans. and Distrib.*, Vol. 146, No. 1, pp. 81-87.

Wang, H.F. (1999b). Application of modeling UPFC into multi-machine power systems, *IEE Proc. Gen. Trans. and Distrib.*, Vol. 146, No. 3, pp. 306-312.

15

CSV-PSO and Its Application in Geotechnical Engineering

Bing-Rui Chen and Xia-Ting Feng
State Key Laboratory of Geomechanics and Geotechnical Engineering, Institute of Rock and Soil Mechanics, Chinese Academy of Sciences
China

1. Introduction

Since the particle swarm optimization (PSO), being a stochastic global optimization technique,was proposed by Kennedy and Eberhart in 1995(Kennedy & Eberhart, 1995; Eberhart & Kennedy, 1995), it has attracted interests of many researchers worldwide and has found many applications in various fields such as autocontrol, machinofacture, geotechnical engineering et al. (Mark & Feng, 2002; Dong et al, 2003; Su & Feng, 2005). There are two main reasons: one is the preferable performance of PSO, the other is its simplicity in operation. In order to avoid the premature and divergence phenomena often occurring in optimization process by using the PSO, especially for multi-dimension and multi-extremum complex problems, as well as to improve the convergence velocity and precision of the PSO to a maximum extent, many kinds of schemes were introduced to enhance the PSO. The following are some representative schemes: inertia weight (Shi & Eberhart, 1998), constriction factor (Eberhart & Shi, 2000), crossover operation (Lovbjerg et al, 2001) and self-adaptation (Lü & Hou, 2004). The PSO modified by introducing the inertia weight or crossover operation or self-adaptation technique has an excellent convergence capability with a decreased velocity of convergence. The PSO with a constriction factor can reach the global goal quickly, but the divergence phenomenon sporadically occurs in the optimized solutions.

So we proposed an improved PSO, named CSV-PSO, in which flight velocity limit and flight space of particles are constricted dynamically with flying of particles (Chen & Feng, 2005). A great deal of numerical calculation indicates CSV-PSO has a faster convergence velocity, greater convergence probability and is a more stable. But this algorithm with a random number generator having time as its random seed may obtain different goal values at different running time. It is difficult to determine uniqueness of solution, especially for complicated engineering problem. So a random number generator with mixed congruential method is introduced to solve uncertainty of solution, and its random seed can be set artificially. To indicate advantage of the proposed algorithm, it is compared with other modified vertions and sensitivity analysis is carried out for its several important parameters, which the five benchmark functions are as examples. The results show CSV-PSO with a new random number generator is excellent. Back analysis which is based on monitoring information with numerical method is a very time-consuming job in geotechnical engineering field. It is necessary to introduce a scheme for improving calculation efficiency. A parallel strategy is adopted, and a parallel CSV-PSO with master-slave mode, called PCSV-PSO, is proposed. Finally, rheological parameters of soft and weak rock mass, as an engineering practical example, are identified using back analysis of displacement based on PCSV-PSO, at the No. 72 experimental tunnel, left bank of Longtan hydropower station, China. The results show that the proposed method is feasible, efficient and robust in multi-parameter optimization and is a new analysis tool for engineering application.

2. PSO

In PSO algorithm, the birds are abstractly represented as particles which are mass-less and volume-less and extended to D dimensional space. The position of the particle i in the D dimensional space is represented by a vector $\overrightarrow{X_i}=(X_{i1},X_{i2},\cdots,X_{iD})$, and the flying velocity is represented by a vector $\overrightarrow{V_i}=(V_{i1},V_{i2},\cdots,V_{iD})$. The vectors $\overrightarrow{P_i}=(P_{i1},P_{i2},\cdots,P_{iD})$ and $\overrightarrow{P_g}=(P_{g1},P_{g2},\cdots,P_{gD})$ are the optimal position of the particle i recognized so far and the optimal position of the entire particle swarms recognized so far, respectively. The position of each particle in the D dimensional space, $\overrightarrow{X_i}$, is a tentative solution in the problem space. The fitness of the model, representing applicability of the $\overrightarrow{X_i}$, can be obtained by substituting $\overrightarrow{X_i}$ to the target function. Therefore, the search procedure of PSO algorithm depends on interaction among particles. The position and velocity of the particle i can be updated as Eq.(1) and (2) (Kennedy & Eberhart,1995; Shi & Eberhart,1998) .

$$V_{id}=wV_{id}+c_1r_1(P_{id}-X_{id})+c_2r_2(P_{gd}-X_{id}) \quad (1)$$

$$X_{id}=X_{id}+V_{id} \quad (2)$$

In which, w is inertia weight; c_1 and c_2 are constants for learning, $c_1>0$, $c_2>0$; r_1 and r_2 are random numbers in [0,1]; $d=1,2,\cdots,D$.

The basic PSO algorithm has advantages of simple operation and convenient application. However, as other optimization algorithms such as genetic algorithms, the basic PSO algorithm has also the problems of premature and slow convergence, therefore, an improvement in accuracy is needed.

3. CSV-PSO

In order to improve the convergence velocity and precision of the PSO algorithm, the CSV-PSO algorithm which can adjust inertia weight, flight velocity limit and flight space of particles dynamically and nonlinearly was proposed. This Algorithm has been documented in our early paper (Chen & Feng, 2005). Random Number Generator and parallel CSV-PSO algorithm (PCSV-PSO) are described in detail and CSV-PSO algorithm is briefly introduced in this section.

3.1 Random Number Generator

Random number is the crucial factor for the performance of swarm intelligence algorithms, and a good random number generator can always get twice the result with half the effort. A algorithm with random number generator that time is as its random seed always tends to give different results in different runtime, which brings troubles for the final determination of solving proposal of engineering problems. To resolve this problem, a random number generator with the mixed congruential method is proposed in the paper. This generator can generate random numbers of uniform distribution in the interval of (0, 1) and random seed can be set artificially. A great deal numerical results show that this technique is excellent. The process of the generation of random seeds is as following.

The iterative formulae of the mixed congruential method are:

$$x_{i+1} = (\lambda x_i + c)(\mathrm{mod} M) \tag{3}$$

$$r_{i+1} = x_{i+1} / M \tag{4}$$

Where λ、x_0、c and M are constants and can set beforehand, x_{i+1} is the remainder of M divided by $\lambda x_i + c$ and r_{i+1} is a random number within the interval of (0, 1). Each random number generated by the mixed congruential method in accordance with an index number and is stored in an internal array after random number generator is initialized. If random number is needed, the random number generator will firstly call the computing function of the mixed congruential method to generate random integer used as index, then the random number is picked up from internal array in terms of the index, finally the random number generator carries out the mixed congruential method again to update the internal array. The random number sequences obtained by this method are much better than those obtained by common mixed congruential methods. The C language codes which are used to describe the above mentioned method are as follows:

```
double CRandom::ran(long *idum)
{
// idum is random seed
const long M1=259200l;
const long IA1=7141l;
const long IC1=54773l;
const double RM1 = (1.0/M1);
const long M3=243000l;
const long IA3=4561l;
const long IC3=51349l;
static long ix1,ix2,ix3;
static double r[98];
double temp;
static int iff=0;
long j; //int j;
if (*idum < 0 || iff == 0) {
ff=1;
x1=(IC1-(*idum)) % M1;
ix1=(IA1*ix1+IC1) % M1;
```

```
ix3=ix1 % M3;
for (j=0;j<=97;j++) {
 ix1=(IA1*ix1+IC1) % M1;
 r[j]=ix1*RM1;
}
*idum=1;
}
ix1=(IA1*ix1+IC1) % M1;
ix3=(IA3*ix3+IC3) % M3;
j=(97*ix3)/M3;
if (j > 97 || j < 0) cout<<"RAN: This cannot happen."<<endl;
temp=r[j];
r[j]=ix1*RM1;
return (double)temp;
}
```

3.2 CSV-PSO

3.2.1 Inertia Weight

The notion of inertia weight parameter is introduced by Shi and Eherhart (Shi & Eberhart, 1998) to control the impact of the previous history of velocities on current velocity. This enables to influence the tradeoff between global and local exploration abilities of the particles. A larger inertia weight facilitates global optimization, while smaller inertia weight facilitates local optimization.A decreasing inertia weight with iteration was introduced in terms of a linear formulation by Shi and Eherhart. A equation for ineria weight modification is proposed by a great deal numerical simulations here as following:

$$w = w_0 \left(1 - \left(\frac{k-1}{k} \right)^n \right) \tag{5}$$

Where w_0 is a constant given; k is number of fly; n is a constant determined for fitness function in global optimum problem.

3.2.2 Limit of the Flying Velocity

The limit of the flying velocity of the particles is an important factor that affects velocity of convergence of the PSO (Eberhart & Shi, 2000).In fact, a good limitation is of advantage to both velocity and precision of convergence.Here we adopt Eq. (6) and (7) to determine limit of the flying velocity of the particles.

In which, $Up_{\max d}$, $Down_{\min d}$, $V_{\max d}$, $V_{\min d}$ are the upper limit and the lower limit of the position and the upper limit and lower limit of the velocity at d dimensional space, respectively, $d = 1,2,\cdots,D$. The parameter α can be determined using Eq. (8).

$$V_{\max d} = \alpha (Up_{\max d} - Down_{\min d}) \tag{6}$$

$$V_{\min d} = \alpha (Down_{\min d} - Up_{\max d}) \tag{7}$$

$$\alpha = \alpha_0 \left(1 - \left(\frac{k-1}{k} \right)^n \right) \tag{8}$$

Where α_0 is a given constant; k is number of fly; m is a constant determined for fitness function in optimum problem.

3.2.3 Compression of Search Space

Particles approach excellent domain step by step with the "flying" of particles continuously. If domain for searching global goal is compressed properly in the "flying" process, convergence of PSO will be accelerated. So the equations for compressing search space are introduced as following:

$$Up'_{\max d} = \beta_0 (Up'_{\max d} - G_{cd}) + G_{cd} \tag{9}$$

$$Down'_{\min d} = \beta_0 (Down'_{\min d} - G_{cd}) + G_{cd} \tag{10}$$

Where $0 < \beta_0 < 1$; $Up'_{\max d}$, $Down'_{\min d}$ and G_{cd} are the upper limit, the lower limit and the geometrical center of gravity of particle swarm in the d dimensional direction of the compressed space, respectively; G_{cd} can be calculated using Eq. (11) (Clerc, 1999) as

$$G_{cd} = \sum_{i=1}^{N_{pop}} x_{id} \Big/ N_{pop} \tag{11}$$

Where N_{pop} is the population of the particles; x_{id} is position of the No. i particle in the d dimensional direction.

3.2.4 CSV-PSO Algorithm

In process of space compressing, on the one hand the global optimum probably is out of searching ranges so that the global goal is unable to be found, on the other hand flying velocity of particles is decreased, which can be obviously by Eq. (6) and (7), and the performance of the algorithm jumpting out local solution is reduced. Therefore, searching space and flying velocity limit can't be compressed without limitations. The compression should is finished when limit of flying velocity is less a small given value. Particles may fly to the same local value with "flying" of particles continuouly. Therefore, stagnancy phenominon may occur in PSO (The so called stagnancy phenominon is that best particle doesn't move toward any direction during "flying" of particles). If no measure is taken, the PSO may need a long time to get rid of the particle stagnancy or traps into local goal forever. Initializing partial particles' position and flying velocity is an efficient method again when the present best particle is not move to global goal within some "flying" times. The particles are divided into two parts: one part are given new position and flying velocity in compressed space, the other is initialized in original space. These ensure that the algorithm have a better convergence precision and a faster convergence velocity. The whole optimized process of CSV-PSO is as following:

Step 1: Initialize the inertia weight w_0, learning factors c_1 and c_2, the population of group N_{pop}, number of stagnancy generation N_s, constants α_0 and β_0, and end remark of evolutionary process N_g and ε_0, go to Step 2.

Step 2: The positions of the particles are randomly generated in $\left[\overrightarrow{Down_{\min}}, \overrightarrow{Up_{\max}}\right]$. The limitations of flying velocity of the particles, $\overrightarrow{V_{\min}}$ and $\overrightarrow{V_{\max}}$, are calculated using Eqs. (6) and (7). And then, the flying velocity of the particles is initialized randomly in $\left[\overrightarrow{V_{\min}}, \overrightarrow{V_{\max}}\right]$. Set up $n = 0$, go to Step 3.

Step 3: Substitute X_i to goal function to calculate the fitness of the No. i particle $f(X_i)$. The global optimal position of the particle swarm group $\overrightarrow{X_g^b}$ and the best position of particle individual during the fly $\overrightarrow{X_i^b}$ are determined according to the fitness $f(X_i)$, go to Step 4.

Step 4: Substitute $\overrightarrow{X_g^b}$ to goal function to calculate the best fitness of this flying f_g^b. If f_g^b is obviously better than that of the former flying, go to Step 5. Otherwise, go to Step 6.

Step 5: If $f_g^b < \varepsilon_0$ or $n > N_g$, then the optimization process ends. Otherwise, let $n = n+1$, the position and flying velocity of the particles are updated by using Eqs. (1) and (2) and insured in $\left[\overrightarrow{Down_{\min}}, \overrightarrow{Up_{\max}}\right]$ and $\left[\overrightarrow{V_{\min}}, \overrightarrow{V_{\max}}\right]$, go to Step 3.

Step 6: Use Eq.(5) to dynamically update w. If f_g^b is not changed in all N_s continuously, go to Step 7. Otherwise, go to Step 5 ;

Step 7: Use Eq.(6) and (7) to modify dynamically the limit of flying velocity of the particles, and use Eqs. (9) and (10) to compress the search space of the particles, go to Step 8.

Step 8: The particles are divided into two parts. One part is initialized in the compressed space $\left[\overrightarrow{Down'_{\min}}, \overrightarrow{Up'_{\max}}\right]$ and another part is renewedly initialized in the original space $\left[\overrightarrow{Down_{\min}}, \overrightarrow{Up_{\max}}\right]$, go to Step 5.

3.3 Performance Analysis of CSV-PSO

To test performance of the CSV-PSO with random numbers generated by the mixed congruential method, five nonlinear benchmark functions, whose basic characteristics and properties are listed as table 1, are used. To facilitate the description of the two CSV-PSO algorithms: one uses time as random seed, the other utilizes mixed congruential method to produce random numbers and random seed can be set artificially, the former is called CSV-PSO1 and the latter is named CSV-PSO2.

3.3.1 Convergence Velocity

For comparison, in all cases and all improved PSO algorithms, the population size was set to 30; the maximum number of iteration was set to 10,000; the factors for learning c_1 and c_2 are both set to 2.0 and five benchmark functions are set as shown in table 1. Inertia weights of CSV-PSO1 and CSV-PSO2 are set to 1.0 at the beginning of the run, different from that of Eberhart and Shi (Eberhart & Shi, 2000) and they can be decreased to a very small positive value by Eq. (5) .Newly introduced parameters N_s, α_0 and β_0 are 50,0.9 and 0.8 respectively and the α calculated by Eq. (8) can't be less 0.1. It is special for function *Schaffer's* f_6 that

α_0 was set to 0.5 in CSV-PSO1. Each version of PSO is run 20 times for each test function, among them the first four are run randomly and the last are run with random seed from 5 to 950 by an increment 50 for each run. Average number of iteration and ranges of iteration number for five functions are listed in table 2 where each method is convergent by 20 runs. The result of the former three versions is gained by Eberhart and Shi (Eberhart & Shi, 2000), and the fourth was from our reference (Chen & Feng, 2005).

Name	Expression	Dimension	Ranges	Optimum	Goal
Sphere	$f_0(x)=\sum_{i=1}^{n} x_i^2$	30	$[-100,100]^n$	0	0.01
Rosenbrock	$f_1(x)=\sum_{i=1}^{n-1}(100(x_{i+1}-x_i^2)^2+(x_i-1)^2)$	30	$[-30,30]^n$	0	100
Rastrigrin	$f_2(x)=\sum_{i=1}^{n}(x_i^2-10\cos(2\pi x_i)+10)$	30	$[-5.12,5.12]^n$	0	100
Griewank	$f_3(x)=\frac{1}{4000}\sum_{i=1}^{n} x_i^2-\prod_{i=1}^{n}\cos(\frac{x_i}{\sqrt{i}})+1$	30	$[-600,600]^n$	0	0.1
Schaffer's f_6	$f_6(x)=0.5+\frac{(\sin\sqrt{x_1^2+x_2^2})^2-0.5}{(1+0.001(x_1^2+x_2^2))^2}$	2	$[-100,100]^n$	0	10^{-5}

Table 1. Five benchmark functions for testing

		Inertia Weight	Constriction Factor (V_{max}=100000)	Constriction Factor (V_{max}=X_{max})	CSV-PSO1	CSV-PSO2
Sphere	N_{aver}	1537.8	552.05	529.65	680.15	599.45
	N_r	1485-1615	503-599	495-573	456-935	473-842
Rosen-brock	N_{aver}	3517.35	1424.1	992	203.2	297.05
	N_r	2866-4506	475-4793	402-1394	108-545	130-732
Rastr-igrin	N_{aver}	1320.9	6823	213.45	215.45	707.05
	N_r	743-1704	233-7056	161-336	86-726	100-2060
Griew-ank	N_{aver}	2757.7	437	312.6	510.45	622.26
	N_r	2638-3035	384-663	282-366	385-707	318-3647
Schaf-fer's f_6	N_{aver}	512.35	430.55	532.4	111.9	466.65
	N_r	339-748	105-899	94-2046	3-332	41-1981

Table 2. Convergence velocity of several versions of PSO for the five test functions

N_{aver} and N_r are average value and ranges of convergent iteration number among 20 runs respectively in the table 2. For example, N_{aver} and N_r are average value and ranges of iteration number of 17 runs separately when there are 3 divergent runs in 20 runs. If one run doesn't reach the goal in 10000 iterations, this run is regarded as divergence. Where constriction factor version (V_{max}=100000) and improved constriction factor version (V_{max}=X_{max}) have one divergence of 20 runs for function *Rastrigrin* for respectively; Constriction factor version (V_{max}=100000) has 3 divergences, improved constriction factor version ($V_{max}=X_{max}$) has one divergence, and CSV-PSO2 has one divergence for function *Griewank* among 20 runs. In comparison with other versions, CSV-PSO has a better convergence velocity, and is more stable. Performance of CSV-PSO2 is a bit worse than that of CSV-PSO1, but it is better than other versions, its random seed can be set artificially and unique solution can be obtained at each run using CSV-PSO2.

3.3.2 Precision of Convergence

A 30-dimension function *Rosenbrock*, whose variables are in interval of [-10, 10], is taken as an example for analyzing convergence precision of several improved versions of PSO. For comparison, in all versions of PSO, the population size was set to 20; the maximum number of iteration was set to 2000; the factors for learning c_1 and c_2 are both set to 2.0; Initial inertia weights of CSV-PSO1 and CSV-PSO2 are 1.0, which are different from that of other versions. Newly introduced parameters N_s , α_0 and β_0 are 50, 0.9 and 0.8 respectively. Each version of PSO is run 20 times for test function, the first five are run randomly and the last is run with random seed from 5 to 950 by an increment 50 for each run. Average value of 20 runs for each version is listed in table 3. The result of the former two columns is gained by Clerc and Kennedy (Clerc and Kennedy, 2002), the third and the fourth are from the literature (Ke et al., 2003), the fifth and the last are obtained by CSV-PSO1 and CSV-PSO2 respectively. In fact, when the goal of 0.4 is obtained using the proposed method in the paper, average iteration number of 20 runs is just 913.24. So the proposed method has a better velocity and precision of convergence for function *Rosenbrock*.

Constriction factor1	Constriction factor2	Inertia weight	MPSO	CSV-PSO1	CSV-PSO2
50.193877	39.118488	40.602026	30.316998	0.048169	0.001070

Table 3. Optimal precision of several versions of PSO for function *Rosenbrock*

3.4 Sensitivity Analysis of Parameters

Sensitivity analysis of parameters, on the one hand, can make algorithm do its better, and on the another hand, can offer reasonable basis for parameter selection. There has been a lot of research about basic parameter analysis of the PSO algorithm, and now we just analyze the sensitivity of several parameters used by the CSV-PSO algorithm. The five benchmark functions are selected as testing examples, whose characteristics and properties are shown in table 1.

3.4.1 Random Seeds

The initial population of PSO algorithm is generated randomly, and the main operations (such as the updating of the position and velocity of particles etc.) of PSO contain random factors. So, random seed must have some effect on algorithm performance. But how does it affect and are there any lows to follow? Effect of Random seed on CSV-PSO is analyzed and discussed based on five benchmark function in table 1 as following.

Parameters setting of CSV-PSO: the population size was set to 20; the maximum number of flight is 2000 times; the factors for learning c_1 and c_2 are both set to 2.0; initial inertia weights is 1.0; number of stagnancy iteration is 10; constant α_0 and β_0 is set to 0.9 and 0.8 respectively the α obtained by Eq. (8) can't be less 0.1; random seed is from 0 to 1000 by an increment 50 for each scheme; goal values of five functions are listed as table 1 and number of maximum iteration is the terminating condition of algorithm.

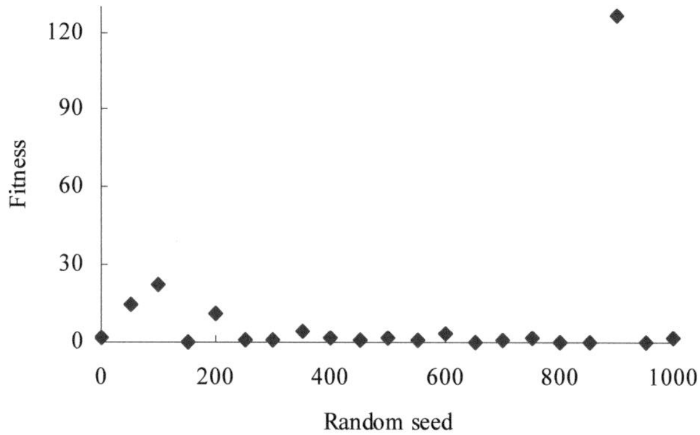

Figure 1. Effect of different random seed on precision of function *Sphere*

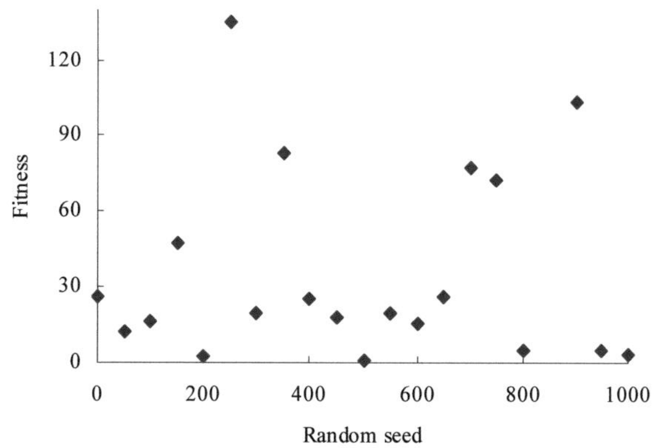

Figure 2. Effect of different random seed on precision of function *Rosenbrock*

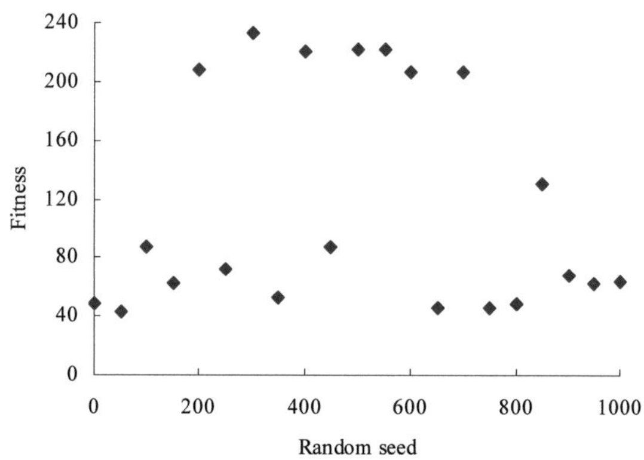

Figure 3. Effect of different random seed on precision of function *Rastrigrin*

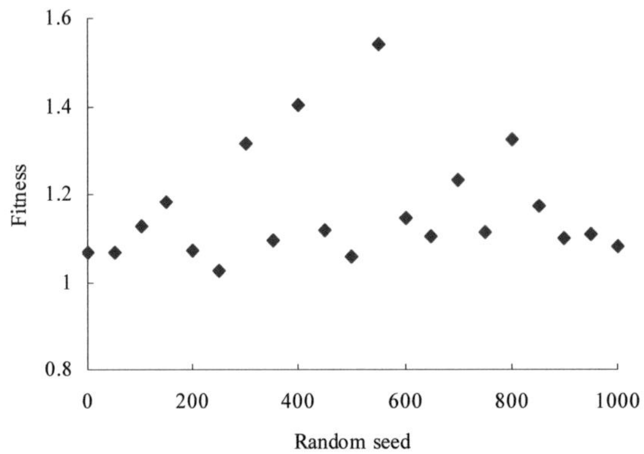

Figure 4. Effect of different random seed on precision of function *Griewank*

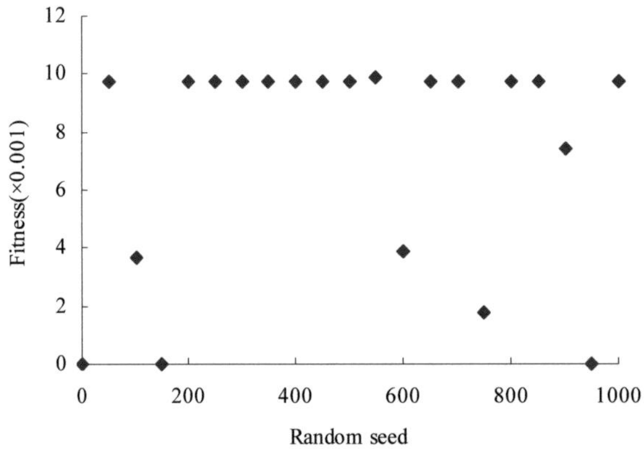

Figure 5. Effect of different random seed on precision of function *Schaffer'*f_6

The effects of random seeds on performance of algorithm for five functions are shown in Fig. 1 to Fig. 5. It is obviously that random seed greatly affects the convergence velocity and precision of the CSV-PSO. If random seed is appropriate, convergence velocity of CSV-PSO is quite fast; otherwise, convergence is slower and divergence is also probable. However, this effect is random and doesn't comply with any distinctive laws.

3.4.2 Stagnancy Number N_s

In process of optimization, the best particle may not move toward any direction during a short-term flying before goal value is obtained. This is named stagnancy phenomenon. To obtained the global goal value quickly, it is necessary to initialize part of the particles once more to break this temporary stagnation. But no final conclusion about the how many the stagnancy number is has yet been reached. How to determine stagnancy number N_s will be discussed in this section by taking the functions in table 1 as examples.

	Sphere	Rosenbrock	Rastrigrin	Griewank	Schaffer's f_6
Optimal value	13982.13	123073.22	264.40	126.83	9.71E-3

Table 4. Optimal value of 5 functions when stagnancy number is 1

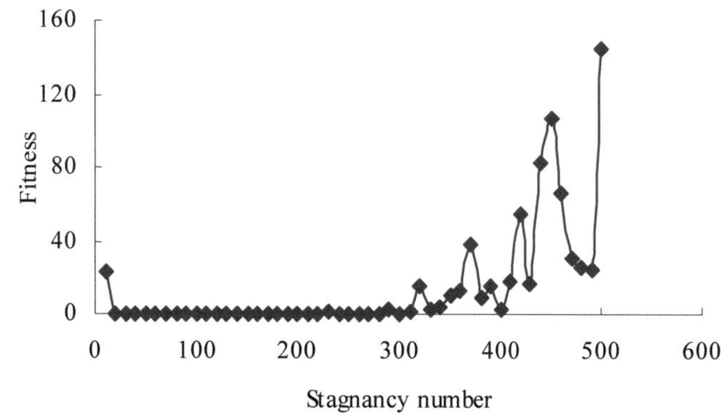

Figure 6. Effect of different stagnancy number on precision of function *Sphere*

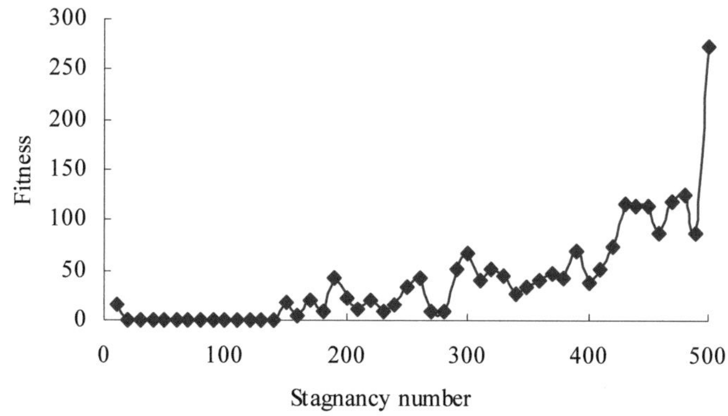

Figure 7. Effect of different stagnancy number on precision of function *Rosenbrock*

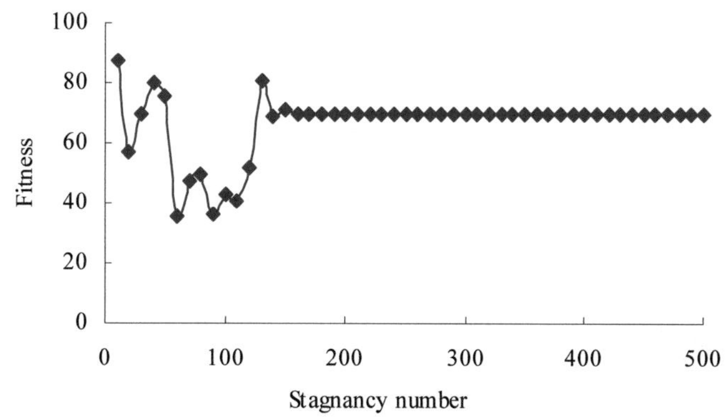

Figure 8. Effect of different stagnancy number on precision of function *Rastrigrin*

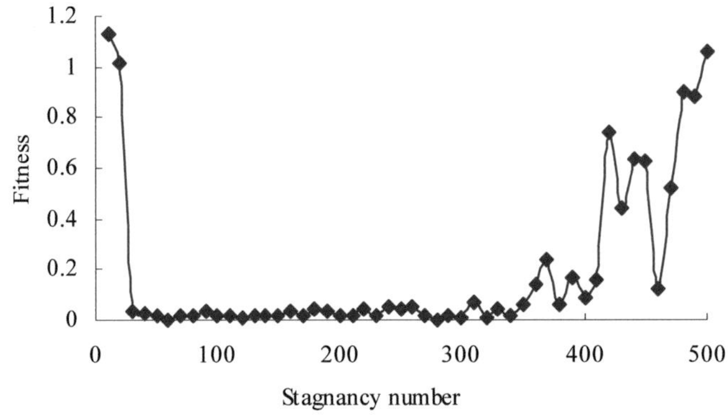

Figure 9. Effect of different stagnancy number on precision of function *Griewank*

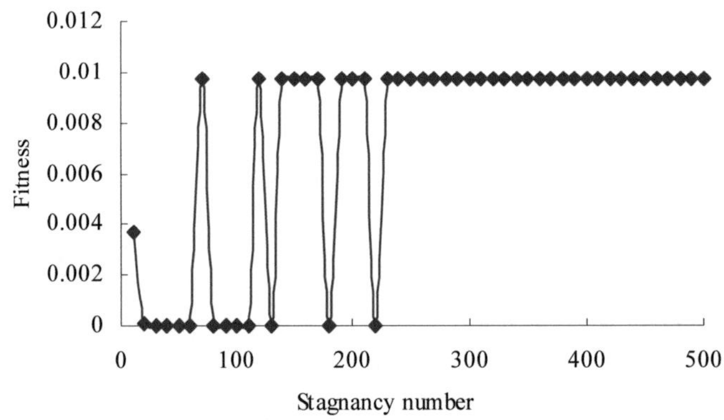

Figure 10. Effect of different stagnancy number on precision of function *Schaffer'*f_6

Most of the parameters in this section are set to be the same value as section 3.4.1 except for random seed and stagnancy number. Random seed is set to 100 and stagnancy number is set to be from 1 to 501 by an increment 10 for each solution. How the stagnancy number affects the convergence precision is indicated in Fig. 6 to Fig. 10. Because when the stagnancy number is 1, the optimal value is still very large at reaching end conditions, so these values are listed in table 4 separately.

Much numerical simulation has shown that there is stagnancy during the flight of particles. It is concluded that it is very important what time initializing part of particles is. If part of particles are initialized again when stagnancy just now happens (e.g. stagnancy number is 1.) during flight of particles, performance of CSV-PSO is least desirable and the algorithm is hard to converge. However, if the initializing is too late (e.g. stagnancy number is 500), the algorithm is also not stable and easily divergent, which are seen from table 4 and Fig. 6 to Fig. 10. The whole range can be divided into three intervals [1, 30), [30,120] and (120,501].The proposed algorithm is not easy to converge at intervals [1, 30) and (120,501] and has a trend that convergence becomes more and more difficult along with the increasing of stagnancy number at interval (120,501]. So it is suggested that initializing part of particles once again with stagnancy number between 30 and 120 will achieve better convergence.

3.4.3 Constant α_0

Constant α_0 is a parameter that determines limit of flying velocity of particles, which is shown by Eq. (6), (7) and (8). Many numerical tests show that different α_0 result in different velocity and precision of convergence in CSV-PSO. Parameters of CSV-PSO different from section 3.4.2 are stagnancy number and constant α_0 which are set to 20 and from 0 to 3.0 by an increment 0.1 for each scheme separately. And the α can be decreased without limitation by Eq. (8). The optimal values of each function vary with increasing of constant α_0 as shown in Fig. 11 to Fig. 15. As being comparatively large when constant α_0 is 0, optimal values for five functions are listed separately in table 5.

	Sphere	Rosenbrock	Rastrigrin	Griewank	Schaffer's f_6
Optimal value	51773.71	1690084.40	373.47	466.96	5.04 E-2

Table 5. Optimal value of 5 functions at α_0 =0

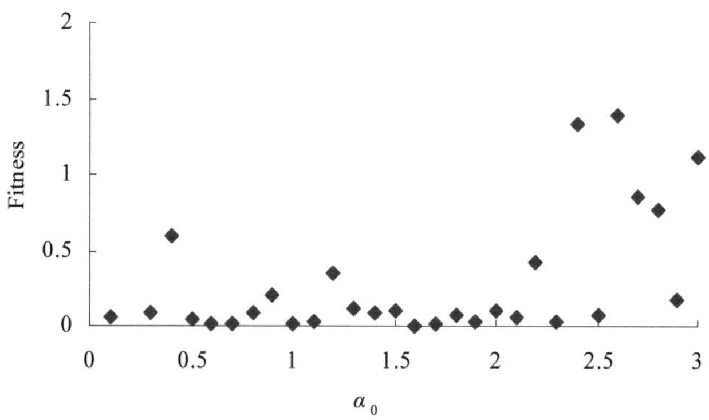

Figure 11. Effect of different constant α_0 on precision of function *Sphere*

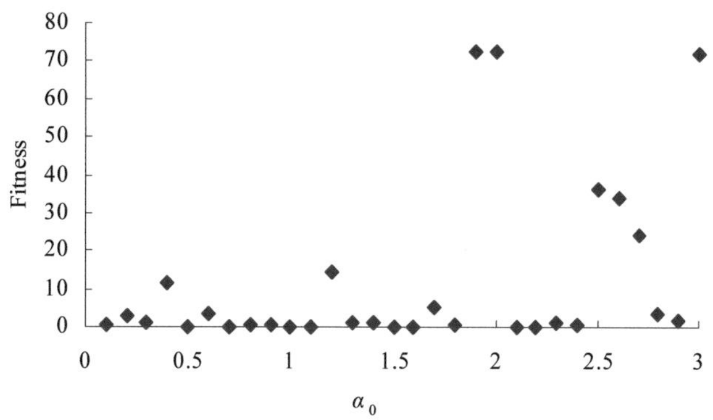

Figure 12. Effect of different constant α_0 on precision of function *Rosenbrock*

It is concluded that convergence precision of CSV-PSO for each function is very poor at meeting end condition of iteration when α_0 is 0 from table 5. If iteration continues, given goal value is also obtained hardly. This is because PSO has had no optimizing capacity when α_0 is 0, which is in accordance with the principle of the algorithm. Particles move toward an object by mainly interaction among particles. When α_0 is 0, the upper and lower limits of particles' velocity are both zero indicated by formula (6), (7) and (8), further the velocity of flying is also zero, and locations and velocities of particles can't both be updated. So that the whole population are stagnant and the PSO finally loses optimizing capacity.

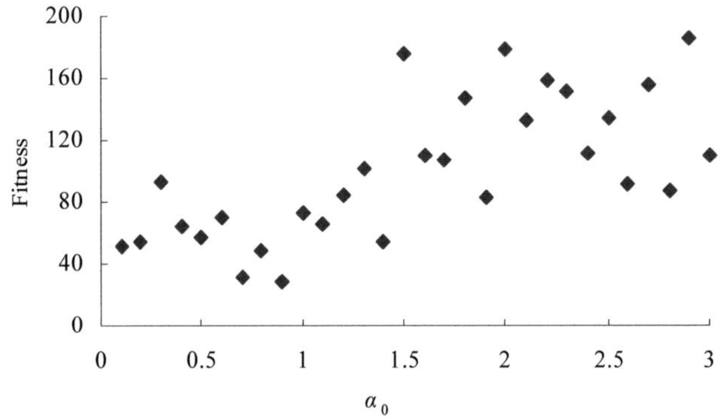

Figure 13. Effect of different constant α_0 on precision of function *Rastrigrin*

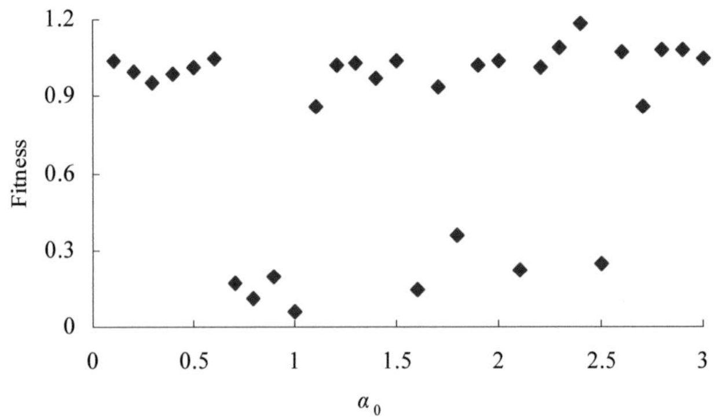

Figure 14. Effect of different constant α_0 on precision of function *Griewank*

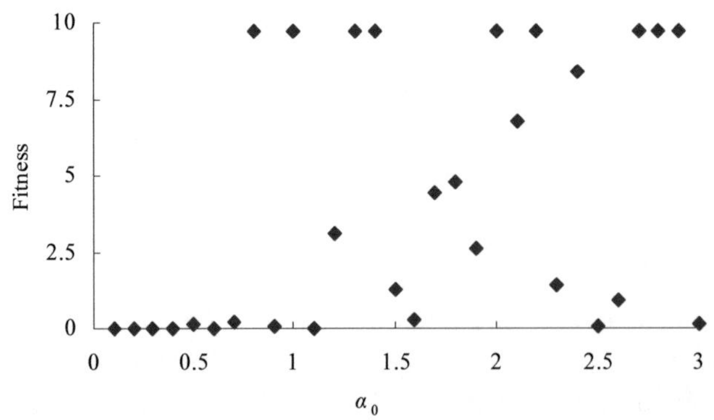

Figure 15. Effect of different constant α_0 on precision of function *Schaffer'f_6*

It is shown that the convergence capability of CSV-PSO undergoes three stages approximately along with the increasing of α_0 by Fig. 11 to Fig. 15. The first stage is at interval [0, 0.5) and convergence of the algorithm is unstable. Some functions can converge quickly to goal value while others will not in this stage. CSV-PSO has more stable convergence at interval [0.5, 1] for five testing functions. Convergent capability of the algorithm becomes much more poor and unstable when α_0 is more than 1. So interval [0.5, 1.0] is proposed.
In addition, numerical calculation indicates that if population scale is too small, algorithms may converge difficultly and the precision is bad, so enlarging the population can improve the convergence capability and enhance the precision of the algorithm; increasing iteration number can also improve the precision of the algorithm to some degree.

4. PCSV-PSO

Although the convergence speed and precision of the CSV-PSO have been are further improved, it is necessary to further improve calculation efficiency for some practical engineering application consuming a large amount of calculation time (such as rheology parameters back analysis, seepage simulation, etc.). Therefore, a parallel CSV-PSO algorithm based on MPI(Message Passing Interface, named PCSV-PSO), is proposed in the paper. As the calculations for parameter recgnition are mainly consumed in evaluation of particles' fitness, global parallel strategies (master-slave mode) is adopted in CSV-PSO algorithm in the paper. MPI is one of the most popular parallel techniques based on message passing mechanism (Du, 2001). It offers a criterion of message passing programming, which has nothing with languages and platforms, and can be widely accepted. In addition, it codes are practical, transplantable, high-efficiency and flexible.
Operation procedure can be simply introduced as following:
Firstly, the host computer allocates assignments for each process according to formula (12):

$$N' = \frac{N}{m} \tag{12}$$

Where N is the total number of assignments produced by CSV-PSO (namely N groups of schemes for problems to be solved), m is the number of personal computers(PC) participating in parallel calculation, N' is the number of assignments of each process.
Secondly, each process executes its assignments separately, and the calculation result will be evaluated by formula (13) (That is evaluation of solutions of problem.).

$$F(x) = \sum_{i=1}^{n} \left[f_i(X) - u_i\right]^2 \tag{13}$$

In which, $f_i(X)$ and u_t are calculation value and observed object value respectively; n is the total number of observed object value.
Then, the calculating result of each process is taken back, and position, velocity, velocity limit and searching space of particles and inertia weight are updated according to Eq. (1),(2) and (5) to (10) on master PC.

Finally, determine whether the result can meet the requirement of calculation. If so, terminate the parallel calculation; otherwise, allocate new assignments to slave computers, and begin new iteration.Repeat the above processes until the requried optimization solution is obtained.

By using the above proposed method, fitness calculation of particles (one group of solved schemes for problems) is independent in each PC, wherears evaluation of all particles and all operation(such as updating of position, velocity, velocity limit and search space of particles and inertia weight, etc) are executed only by master PC. The host PC communicates with slave PCs only when allocating assignments and taking back result. Thus reduces the communication overhead prominently. Hence, the efficiency of parallel calculation is high.

5. Application of PCSV-PSO in Geotechnical Engineering

Rock is a typical complex anisotropic natural geological material including all kind of fissures, joints and defects, so mechanical characteristic and physical property are obviously different for different rocks, even if for the same rock. Hard brittle rock buried deeply under high ground stress has a greater chance of rockburst when surrounding condition of rock is changed by excavation, artificial blasting or other factors. While soft and weak rock shows another mechanics property, which deformation increases under constant stress condition or stress decreases under constant deformation condition gradually with time in long-term run of rock engineering, named time dependant characteristic. For accurate describing physical and mechanical property and learning deformation laws *in situ* of studied rock, back analysis based on measured information *in situ* is used widely in geotechnical field and many achievements have been obtained (Wang & Yang, 1987; Gavrus et al., 1996; Deng et al., 2001; Liu et al., 2005). Measured displacement regarded as the goal, back analysis method for rheological parameters of rockmass based on FLAC^{3D} codes using PCSV-PSO is introduced firstly. Then this method is used for inversing rheological parameters of argillite at the No. 72 testing tunnel of left bank slope, Longtan Hydropower station, China.

5.1 Back Analysis of Rheologcial Parameters of Rockmass Based on PCSV-PSO

It is essential for inversing analysis method that searching a set of parameters makes calculated response accord with actual response in the whole space using an optimal technique. So for time dependant engineering problem, goal function used as back analysis can be written as following:

$$F(x) = \sum_{i=1}^{n} \sum_{t=0}^{T} [f_{it}(X) - u_{it}]^2 \tag{14}$$

Where X is a set of parameters required for inversing analysis; $f_{it}(X)$ and u_{it} are calculated displacement and measured displacement of the No. i monitoring site at t time respectively; n is total number of monitoring sites and T is total time for monitoring.

The back analysis method which is based on FLAC^{3D} solver with PCSV-PSO can be described as following (also seen from Fig. 16):

Step 1: Initializing parameters of PCSV-PSO and ranges of parameters requiring to be analyzed inversely;

Step 2: Initializing position and velocity of particles, population size *N*, namely *N* sets of parameters requiring to be analyzed inversely;
Step 3: Host PC allocates missions to *m*-1 slave PC and itself. *N*/*m* missions are allocated to each PC;
Step 4: Invoking FLAC^{3D} solver and calculating displacement of key points;
Step 5: Calculating fitness of particles by formula (14), and return the result to host PC;
Step 6: If the fitness is less than given value or iteration number is larger than maximum iteration number given, a set of optimal parameters is selected out by rheology mechanics characteristic of rock and some engineering experiences and back analysis is finished; otherwise, go to step 7;
Step 7: Updating limit of velocity, searching space and position and velocity of each particle inertia weight and so on, then go to step 3.

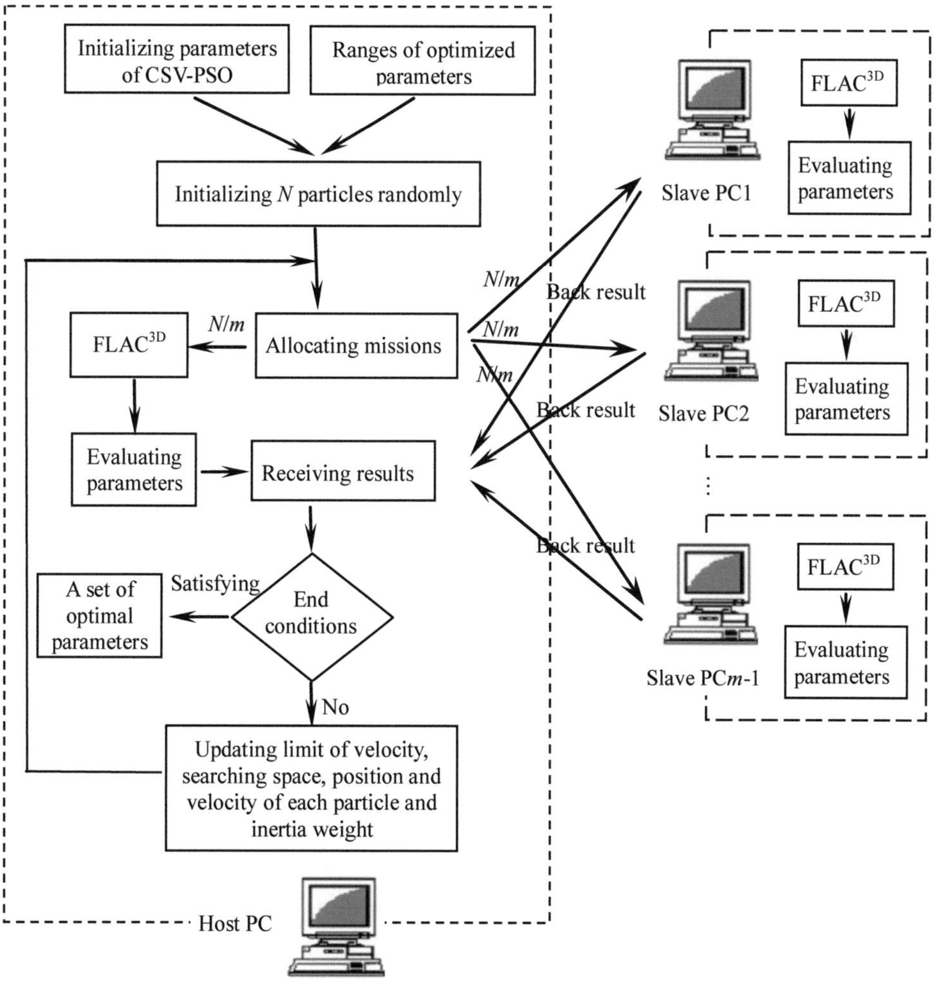

Figure 16. Flow chart of back analysis of parameters based on FLAC^{3D} using PCSV-PSO

5.2 An application in Geotechnical Engineering

5.2.1 Introduction of Longtan Hydropower Project

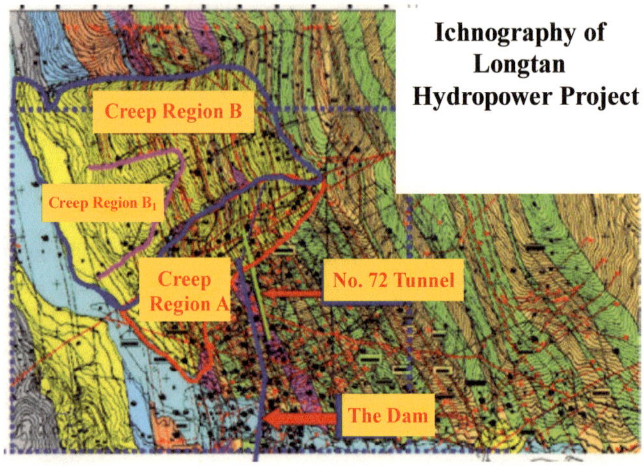

Figure 17. Distributing of creep regions of left slope at Longtan Hydropower Project

Longtan Hydropower Project, which is an important one in the implementation of national Great Western Development and the Power Transmission Project from West to East, is located in Tian'e county of Guangxi Autonomous Region, upstream of Hongshui River. It is the second largest hydropower project under construction in China, next to Three Gorges Project. The height of mountains is about 600m at both sides of the dam site. Slope on the left bank is 420m high and the slope angle is between 28 to 37 degrees, with a thickness of residual diluvial layer between 0.5 and 2m and locally from 8 to 25m. More than 500 faults are exposed in the Dam Area and about 50 ones of them are bigger. There are two big creep regions with sandstone and shale of Middle-lower Triassic Formation near dam site in the left of whole reservoir region, named creep regions A and B, which is shown as Fig. 17.

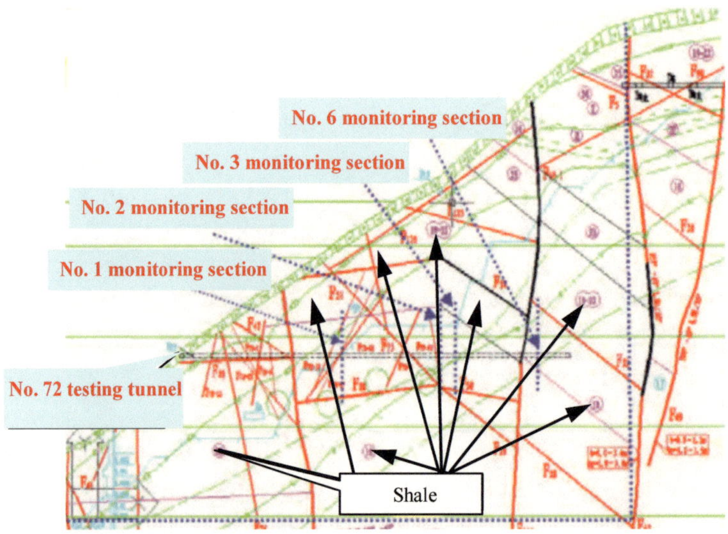

Figure 18. Engineering geological profile at location of No.72 testing tunnel

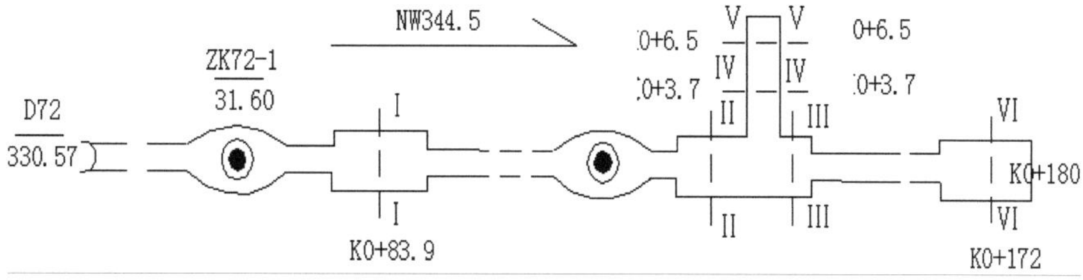

Figure 19. Disposal of monitoring sections at No.72 testing tunnel

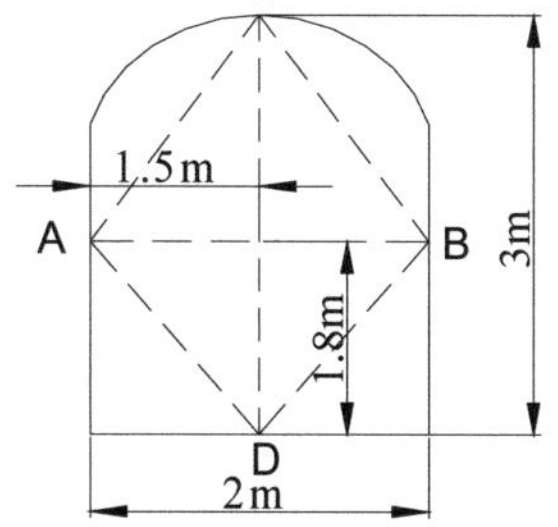

Figure 20. Disposal of survey lines at each monitoring section

As the geological conditions are quite complicated in this region, in order to know the geological conditions, rockmass physical and mechanical property, deformation characteristics and strike variation, the No.72 exploratory testing tunnel was excavated in one of the two creep regions on the left bank. Its location is shown in Fig. 17 and the main faults and strata which it passes through are shown in Fig. 18.

The No.72 test tunnel locates in the core of the left bank high slope, which is surrounded by shale and all of its 6 monitoring sections are also surrounded by shale mainly. The main tunnel is 180m long, and the branch tunnel is 136m far from the opening. The monitoring sections Ⅰ, Ⅱ, Ⅲ and Ⅵ, whose size is 2m width and 3m height, are located at 83.9, 132.4, 139.4 and 172m far from the opening of main tunnel and the monitoring sectionsⅣ and Ⅴ, having 2 m×2m sizes, are 3.7 and 6.5m far away from the opening of branch tunnel as shown as Fig. 19. The shape of all profiles is city gate. The measuring method is that the six convergent survey lines are fixed on four points of each profile. The survey lines are disposed as Fig. 20.

5.2.2 Numerical Calculation Model

To eliminate the boundary effect as much as possible, calculation ranges in which width is 100m at X direction, length is 280m at Y direction and height is from 240m yellow sea height to slope surface at Z direction is determined. The calculation region is shown in Fig. 21 in horizontal plane. 3D Meshes are generated in terms of the calculation region determined above, which contain 37343 elements and 8601 nodes of meshes. Local mesh refinement technique is used near six monitoring sections. Solid elements are used to simulate faults having some thickness. The model of calculation mesh of the whole ranges is shown in Fig. 22. Distribution of faults and test tunnels in calculation range is displayed in Fig. 23.

Initial stress fields adopt 3D initial stress fields regressed by Hu et al. (Hu et al., 2005). Bottom surface, planes vertical to X-axis and Y-axis are all constrained at normal direction and natural slope surface is free. According to deformation monitoring data *in situ*, testing tunnels go through instant elastic, attenuation and relatively stable deformation three stages. Therefore, the combined model of Kelvin-Voigt model for viscoelastic property of rock and Mohr-Coulomb model which is used to express plastic characteristic of material is adopted to describe viscoelastic plastic property of shale as Fig. 24.

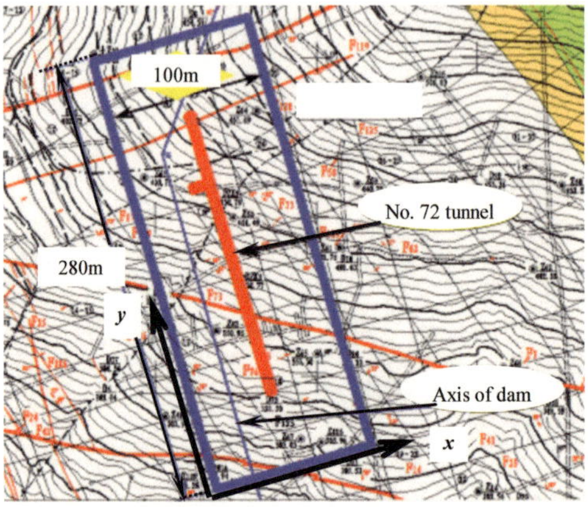

Figure 21. Calculation region for numerical model of the No.72 testing tunnel

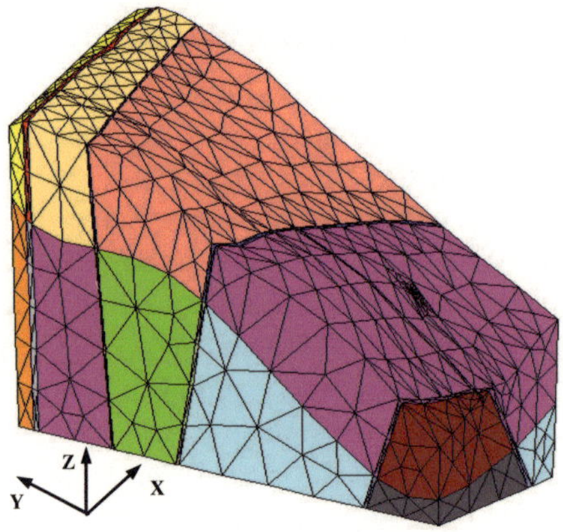

Figure 22. Three-dimension mesh model for calculation

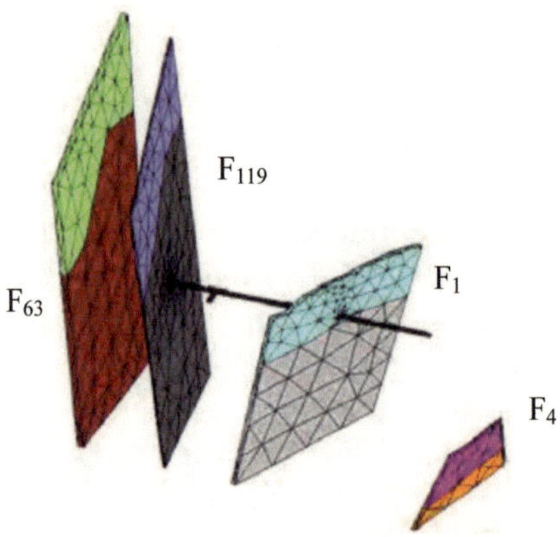

Figure 23. Distribution of faultages and testing tunnels

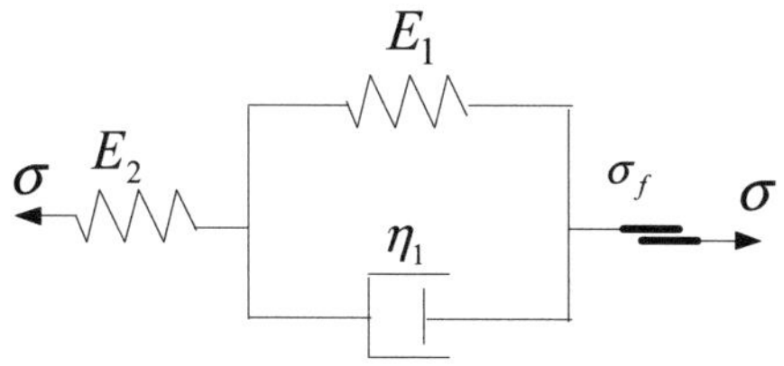

Figure 24. Combined model for describing viscoelastic-plastic characteristic

According to excavation schemes, monitoring data and the feasibility of numerical simulation, 180m-long NO.72 testing tunnel is excavated by 13 stages and each stage is finished once. As displacement monitoring is later than excavation and instant deformation of surrounding rock can't be reflected in displacement monitoring, proper measure must be taken to make process of numerical simulation agree with that of monitoring *in situ*.

FLAC^{3D} of the *ITASCA* company is used as a solver when numerical simulation starts. For each excavation, elastic and plastic analysis is carried out at first followed by rheological calculation. Strong weathered, weak weathered, slightly weathered shale and fresh sandstone interbedded with fresh shale four kinds material are considered for elastic and plastic calculation. Fully weathered and strong weathered shale are regarded as the same material and weak weathered and fresh shale are regarded with the same property in viscoelastic plastic numerical simulation. Several large faults F_1、F_4、F_{63} and F_{119} crossed by the No.72 testing tunnel are taken into concern in elasticplastic and viscoelastic plastic simulations.

5.2.3 The goal of back analysis

As excavation and all kind of artificial factors, monitoring data are not full and have big variations in profiles II and IV. In addition, the distance of profiles II and III and location of profiles IV and V are very close and profiles IV and V are in the branch tunnel, therefore, only monitoring data of profiles I ,III, V and VI are selected as the goal of back analysis, where only suvey lines AD,BD and CD of the first profile, suvey lines AC,CD and BD of the third profile, suvey lines AB,CD,AC and BC of the fifth profile and suvey lines AD and CD of the sixth profile are used as effective survey lines. The goal function of back analysis is described by formula (14).

5.2.4 Identification of Parameters of Constitutive Model

For Mohr-Coulomb model, mechanical property parameters of strong weathered, weak weathered, slightly weathered shale, fresh sandstone interbedded with fresh shale and the four faults are determined as listed in table 6 based on geological conditions and mechanical testing, in which elastic modulus are the same as elastic modulus of each rock in series branch of viscoelastic model and is gained by latter inversing analysis.

For Kelvin-Voigt model, its parameters are recognized using displacement back analysis method with PCSV-PSO as mentioned in section 5.1. Total eight PCs which are equipped with 2.8GHz CPU, 512MB memory, 10MBps/100MBps net card and 80GB hard disk participate in this parallel calculation of inversing analysis. Other equipments include a HUB with 16 interfaces, a 17 inch terminal, a manual control switch and some net wires, etc.

Sorts of rockmass	Unit	Tensile	Shear strength	Poisson's

	weight (kN m-3)	strength (Mpa)	Friction angle(°)	C(Mpa)	ratio
Strong weathered shale	25.5	0.08	36.9	0.49	0.34
weak weathered shale	26.5	0.8	50.2	1.18	0.28
slightly weathered shale	26.8	0.8	47.7	1.48	0.26
fresh sandstone with fresh shale	26.9	1.3	52.4	1.96	0.25
Faults F_1、F_4、F_{63} and F_{119}	21	0	18	0.04	0.34

Table 6. Property of several rockmass for Mohr-Coulomb model

Before the parameters are identified using swarm intelligence method, they must have ranges themselves. The ranges of parameters of Kelvin-Voigt model are determined by engineering experience, geology investigation, rock testing in laboratory and in field and a small amount of numerical calculation, as shown in table 7.

Fully and strong weathered shale			Weak weathered and new shale		
E_1(GPa)	η_1 (GPa.d)	E_2 (GPa)	E_1(GPa)	η_1 (GPa.d)	E_2 (GPa)
20-40	5-20	1-15	80-110	5-20	5-20

Table 7. Ranges of parameters of Kelvin-Voigt model for the two rockmass

The parameters of PCSV-PSO are set as follows: the maximum number of iteration is 20, the population size is 16, learning factors c_1 and c_2 are both 2.0, initial inertia weight is 1.0, constants α_0 and β_0 are set to be 0.9 and 0.8 respectively, random seed is set to be 100 and the maximum stagnancy number is 10.

Fully and strong weathered shale			Weak weathered and new shale		
E_1(GPa)	η_1 (GPa.d)	E_2 (GPa)	E_1(GPa)	η_1 (GPa.d)	E_2 (GPa)
31.90	9.02	5.82	92.52	78.41	12.98

Table 8. Recognized parameters of Kelvin-Voigt model for the two rockmass

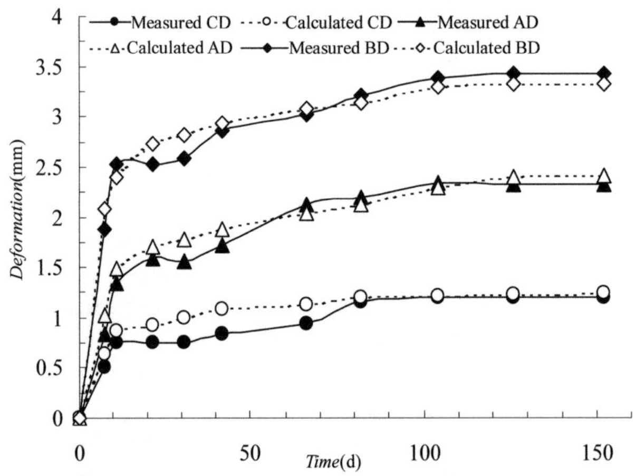

Figure 25. Comparison calculated deformation with monitored it at profile I

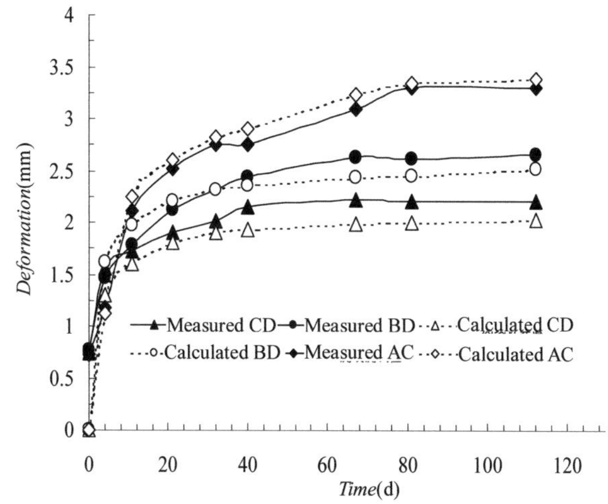

Figure 26. Comparison calculated deformation with monitored it at profile Ⅲ

As numerical simulation of rock rheology is a time-consuming job, although maximum number of iteration and the population size are set to smaller values, it still consumes almost two days until the final parameters of the two rocks are obtained using the proposed method in section 5.1. If finishing a scheme needs 50 minutes averagely, it will consume about 10 days that parameters are identified in single PC. So efficiency is improved highly using the PCSV-PSO algorithm. When iteration is executed 20 times, the final identified parameters are obtained in table 8 and the residual sum of squares of the calculated deformation and actual deformation is 9.36×10^{-5} m^2. The calculated deformation is compared with actual deformation, as shown in the Fig. 25 to Fig. 28. It is concluded that the calculation result of all survey lines of the four profiles is acceptable for practical engineering, the simulating trend of deformation with the above identified parameters accords with that recorded in the field from Fig. 25 to Fig. 28 and the proposed algorithm is a faster and more efficiency back analysis method for identifying parameters.

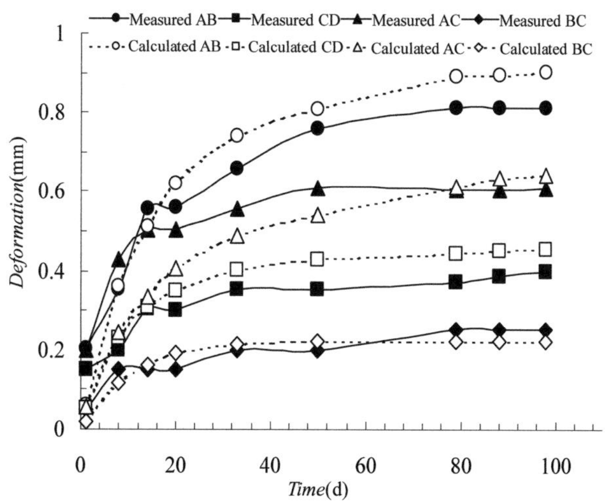

Figure 27. Comparison calculated deformation with monitored it at profile V

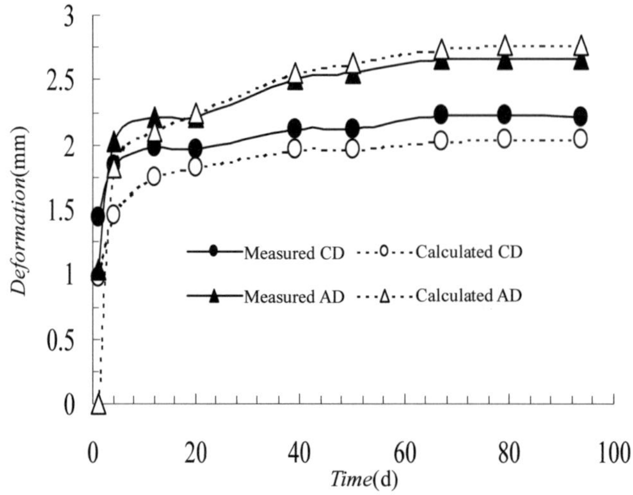

Figure 28. Comparison calculated deformation with monitored it at profile VI

6. Conclusion

Two modified versions of PSO are introduced: one is CSV-PSO algorithm in which random numbers are generated by the mixed congruential method, and another is PCSV-PSO algorithm for recognizing rheological parameters of rockmass. A great deal of numerical simulations show that the CSV-PSO algorithm has better convergence performance and more accurate convergence precision, its run is more stable and it can provide certainty solution in different runtime. Sensitivity analysis of the CSV-PSO algorithm indicates that random seed, stagnancy number and constant α_0 determining flying velocity of particles have a great effect on performance of the algorithm. Proper random seed can accelerate convergence of the algorithm; while bad random seed can not only slow convergence velocity but also possibly result in divergence. However, no obvious law can be followed. If the stagnancy number is too small or too large, the algorithm is hard to converge and unstable. The interval in which the algorithm converges more easily is [30,120]. If the constant α_0 is smaller in interval [0, 0.5], the optimizing capability of the algorithm is poorer and if the constant α_0 is zero, the algorithm loses optimizing capability. However, if constant α_0 is too large, the velocity of particles will be large so that the algorithm can't also unstably converge. That interval [0.5, 1.0] is suggested is proper for convergence of the algorithm. Based on monitoring information in situ, identifying mechanical parameters of rockmass using back analysis technique is a time-consuming task. Rheological parameters of the two rocks at the No.72 testing tunnel of left bank slope, Longtan Hydropower Station, China, as an example, are identified using the PCSV-PSO algorithm. The results indicate PCSV-PSO algorithm is a new feasible and high efficient analytical tool for solving geotechnical engineering problem.

7. Acknowledgement

Financial supports from the Hi_Tech Research and Development Program of China (863 Program) under Grant No. 2006AA06Z117, the National Science and Technology Support Program for the 10th five years of China under Grant No. 2006BAB04A06 and the National Nature Science Foundation of China under Grant no. 50539090 are gratefully acknowledged. The authors would like to give their acknowledgement to Professor Yongjia Wang and Mr. Tianbing Xiang for their helpful suggestions to improve the manuscript, to Assistant Professor Bin Hu for his mesh modelling and significant suggestions and to Longtan Hydropower Development Company and Mid-South Design and Research Institute, CHEGC for their experimental results and monitoring data *in situ*.

8. References

Chen B R, Feng X T (2005). Particle swarm optimization with contracted ranges of both search space and velocity. *Journal of Northeastern University (Natural Science)*, Vol.26, No.5,pp.488-491.

Clerc M (1999). The swarm and the queen: towards a deterministic and adaptive particle swarm optimization, *Proc. 1999 Congress Evolutionary Computation*,pp. 1951-1957, Piscataway,1999, NJ: IEEE Press.

Clerc M, Kennedy J (2002). The particle swarm: explosion, stability, and convergence in a multidimensional complex space. *IEEE Transations on Evolutionary Computation*,Vol.6, No.1, pp. 58-73.

Deng J, Lee C F, Ge X (2001). Disturbed Zones and Displacement Back Analysis for Rock Slopes. *Chinese Journal of Rock Mechanics and Engineering*, Vol.20, No.2, pp. 171-174.

Dong Y, Tang J, Xu B, et al. (2003). Application of Particle Swarm Optimization to Nonlinear Constrained Programming. *Journal of Northeastern University (Natural Science)*, Vol.24, No.12, pp. 1141-1144.

Du Z (2001). MPI Parallel Programming : High Performance Computation and Parallel Program Technique. Tsinghua University Press, Beijing.

Eberhart R C, Kennedy J. P.(1995). A New Optimizer Using Particle Swarm Theory.In: *Proc. of the Sixth International Symposium on Micro Machine and Human Science*,pp.39-43, Nagoya,Japan.

Eberhart R C, Shi Y (2000). Comparing inertia weights and constriction factors in particle swarm optimization. *Proc. 2000 Congress Evolutionary Computation*, pp.84-88, Piscataway, 2000,NJ: IEEE Press.

Gavrus A., Massoni E. and Chenot J. L. (1996). An inverse analysis using a finite element model for identification of rheological parameters. *Journal of Materials Processing Technology*, Vol.60, No.1-4,pp. 447-454.

Hu B, Feng X T, et al. (2005). Regression Analysis of Initial Geostress Field for Left Bank High Slope Region At Longtan Hydropower Station. *Chinese Journal of Rock Mechanics and Engineering*, Vol.24, No.22, pp.4055-4064.

Ke J, Qian J X, Qiao Y Z (2003). A Modified Particle Swarm Optimization Algorithm. *Journal of Circuits and Systems*, Vol.8, No.5, pp. 87-91.

Kennedy J, Eberhart R C (1995). Particle Swarm Optimization. *Proc. IEEE Int. Conf. Neural Networks*, pp.1942-1948, Piscataway, 1995, NJ: IEEE Press.

Liu Q J, Yang L D, Cao W G (2005). Statistical Damage Constitutive Model For Rock and Back Analysis of Its Parameters. *Chinese Journal of Rock Mechanics and Engineering*, Vol.24, No.4, pp.616-621

Lovbjerg M, Rasmussen T K, Krink T (2001). Hybrid Particle Swarm Optimizer With Breeding and Subpopulations. In: *Proc. of the third Genetic and Evolutionary Computation Conference*, pp.469-476, San Francisco.

Lü Z S, Hou Z R (2004). Particle Swarm Optimization with Adaptive Mutation. *Acta Electronica Sinica*, Vol.32, No.3, pp.416-420.

Mark S V, Feng X (2002). ARMA model selection using particle swarm optimization and AIC criteria. *15th Triennial World Congress*, pp.117-129, Barcelona, 2002, Spain: IFAC.

Wang S, Yang Z (1987). The back analysis method from displacement for viscoelastic rock mass. In: *Proc 2nd Int Symp on FMGM'87*,pp.1059-1068.

Su G, Feng X (2005). Parameter Identification Of Constitutive Model For Hard Rock Under High In-Situ Stress Condition Using Particle Swarm Optimization Algorithm. *Chinese Journal of Rock Mechanics and Engineering*,Vol.24,No.17, pp.3029-3034.

Shi Y, Eberhart R C(1998). A Modified Particle Swarm Optimizer. In: *IEEE World Congress on Computational Intelligence*, pp.69-73,Anchorage, Alaska.

16

Power Plant Maintenance Scheduling Using Ant Colony Optimization

Wai Kuan Foong, Holger Robert Maier and Angus Ross Simpson
School of Civil & Environmental Engineering, University of Adelaide
Australia

1. Introduction

Under the pressure of rapid development around the globe, power demand has drastically increased during the past decade. To meet this demand, the development of power system technology has become increasingly important in order to maintain a reliable and economic electric power supply (Lin *et al.*, 1992). One major concern of such development is the optimization of power plant maintenance scheduling. Maintenance is aimed at extending the lifetime of power generating facilities, or at least extending the mean time to the next failure for which repair costs may be significant. In addition, an effective maintenance policy can reduce the frequency of service interruptions and the consequences of these interruptions (Endrenyi *et al.*, 2001). In other words, having an effective maintenance schedule is very important for a power system to operate economically and with high reliability.

Determination of an optimum maintenance schedule is not an easy process. The difficulty lies in the high degree of interaction between several subsystems, such as commitment of generating units, economical planning and asset management. Often, an iterative negotiation is carried out between asset managers, production managers and schedule planners until a satisfactory maintenance schedule is obtained. In addition, power plant maintenance scheduling is required to be optimized with regard to a number of uncertainties, including power demand, forced outage of generating units, hydrological considerations in the case of hydropower systems and trading value forecasts in a deregulated electricity market. Consequently, the number of potential maintenance schedules is generally extremely large, requiring a systematic approach in order to ensure that optimal or near-optimal maintenance schedules are obtained within an acceptable timeframe.

Over the past two decades, many studies have focused on the development of methods for optimizing maintenance schedules for power plants. Traditionally, mathematical programming approaches have been used, including dynamic programming (Yamayee *et al.*, 1983), integer programming (Dopazo & Merrill, 1975), mixed-integer programming (Ahmad & Kothari, 2000) and the implicit enumeration algorithm (Escudero *et al.*, 1980). More recently, metaheuristics have been favored, including genetic algorithms (GAs) (Aldridge *et al.*, 1999), simulated annealing (SA) (Satoh & Nara, 1991) and tabu search (TS) (El-Amin *et al.*, 2000). These methods have generally been shown to outperform mathematical programming methods and other conventional approaches in terms of the

quality of the solutions found, as well as computational efficiency (Aldridge *et al.*, 1999; Satoh & Nara, 1991).
Ant Colony Optimization is a relatively new metaheuristic for combinatorial optimization problems that is based on the foraging behavior of ant colonies (Dorigo & Stützle, 2004). Compared to other optimization methods, such as GA, ACO has been found to produce better solutions in terms of computational efficiency and quality when applied to a number of combinatorial optimization problems, such as the Traveling Salesman Problem (TSP) (Dorigo & Gambardella, 1997a). Recently, ACO has also been successfully applied to scheduling, including the job-shop, flow-shop and resource-constrained project scheduling problems (Bauer *et al.*, 1999; Colorni *et al.*, 1994; Merkle *et al.*, 2002; Stützle, 1998). Recently, a formulation that enables ACO to be applied to the power plant maintenance scheduling optimization (PPMSO) problem has been introduced by the authors of this chapter (Foong *et al.*, 2005). The formulation was tested on a 21-unit case study and shown to outperform other metaheuristic methods previously applied to the same case study (Foong *et al.*, 2005). In Foong *et al.* (Accepted for publication), the formulation was further tested on a simplified version of a real hydro PPMSO problem, which was solved again using an improved version of the formulation (Foong *et al.*, 2008).
The overall aim of this chapter is to formalize the ACO-PPMSO formulation presented in Foong *et al.* (2005) and to extend the testing of the formulation by applying it to three additional case studies. In addition, the utility of a local search strategy and a heuristic formulation when adopting ACO-PPMSO are examined. In section 2, the general formulation of the PPMSO problem is introduced, are the proposed approach for using ACO to solve this problem (ACO-PPMSO) is introduced in section 3. The four problem instances on which the proposed approach has been tested are described in section 4 and the experimental procedures, results and discussion are presented in section 5. In section 6, a summary and conclusions are given.

2. Power Plant Maintenance Scheduling Optimization

PPMSO is generally considered as a minimization problem (S, f, Ω), where S is the set of all maintenance schedules, f is the objective function which assigns an objective function value $f(s)$ to each trial maintenance schedule $s \in S$, and Ω is a set of constraints. Mathematically, PPMSO can be defined as the determination of a set of globally optimal maintenance schedules $S^* \subset S$, such that the objective function is minimized $f(s^* \in S^*) \leq f(s \in S)$ (for a minimization problem) subject to a set of constraints Ω. Specifically, PPMSO has the following characteristics:

- It consists of a finite set of decision points $D = \{d_1, d_2, ..., d_N\}$ comprised of N maintenance tasks to be scheduled;
- Each maintenance task $d_n \in D$ has a normal (default) duration $NormDur_n$ and is carried out during a planning horizon T_{plan}.

Two decision variables need to be defined for each task d_n, including:

1. The start time for the maintenance task, $start_n$, with the associated set of options: $T_{n,chdur_n} = \{ t \in T_{plan};\ chdur_n \in K_n\!: ear_n \leq t \leq lat_n - chdur_n + 1\}$ where the terms in brackets denote the set of time periods when maintenance of unit d_n may start; ear_n is the earliest time for maintenance task d_n to begin; lat_n is the latest time for maintenance task d_n to end and $chdur_n$ is the chosen maintenance duration for task d_n.

2. The duration of the maintenance task, $chdur_n$, with the associated finite set of decision paths: $K_n = \{0, s_n, 2s_n, \ldots, NormDur_n - s_n, NormDur_n\}$, where the terms in brackets denote the set of optional maintenance durations for task d_n, and s_n is the time step considered for maintenance duration shortening.

A trial maintenance schedule, $s \in S = \langle(start_1, chdur_1), (start_2, chdur_2), \ldots, (start_N, chdur_N)\rangle$ is comprised of maintenance commencement times, $start_n$, and durations, $chdur_n$, for all N maintenance tasks that are required to be scheduled.

Binary variables, which can take on values 0 or 1, are used to represent the state of a task in a given time period in the mathematical equations of the PPMSO problem formulation. $X_{n,t}$ is set to 1 to indicate that task $d_n \in D$ is scheduled to be carried out during period $t \in T_{plan}$. Otherwise, $X_{n,t}$ is set to a value of 0, as given by:

$$X_{n,t} = \begin{cases} 1 & \text{if task } d_n \text{ is being maintained in period } t \\ 0 & \textit{otherwise} \end{cases} \quad (1)$$

In addition, the following sets of variables are defined:

- $S_{n,t} = \{k \in T_{n,chdur_n}, chdur_n \in K_n: t - chdur_n + 1 \leq k \leq t\}$ is the set of start times k, such that if maintenance task d_n starts at time k for a duration of $chdur_n$, that task will be in progress during time t;
- $D_t = \{d_n: t \in T_n\}$ is the set of maintenance tasks that is considered for period t.

Objectives and constraints

Traditionally, cost minimization and maximization of reliability have been the two objectives commonly used when optimizing power plant maintenance schedules. Two examples of reliability objectives are evening out the system reserve capacity throughout the planning horizon, and maximizing the total reservoir storage water volumes at the end of the planning horizon, in the case of a hydropower system. An additional objective associated with the more generalized definition of PPMSO is the minimization of the total maintenance duration shortened/deferred (Foong *et al.*, 2008). The rationale behind this objective is that shortening of maintenance duration (i.e. speeding up the completion of maintenance tasks) requires additional personnel and equipment, whereas deferral of maintenance tasks might result in unexpected breakdown of generating units, and in both events, additional costs are incurred by the power utility operator.

Constraints specified in PPMSO problems are also power plant specific. The formulation of some common constraints include the allowable maintenance window, continuity, load, availability of resources, precedence of maintenance tasks, reliability and the minimum maintenance duration required, which are presented in Eqs. 2 to 6.

The timeframes within which individual tasks in the system are required to start and finish maintenance form maintenance window constraints, which can be formulated as:

$$ear_n \leq start_n \leq lat_n - chdur_n + 1 \qquad \text{for all } d_n \in D. \quad (2)$$

where $start_n$ and $chdur_n$ are the start time and maintenance duration, respectively, chosen for task d_n.

Load constraints (Eq. 3) are usually rigid/hard constraints in PPMSO problems, which ensure that feasible maintenance schedules that do not cause demand shortfalls throughout the whole planning horizon are obtained:

$$\sum_{d_n \in D} P_{n,t} - \sum_{d_n \in D_t} \sum_{k \in S_{n,t}} X_{n,k} P_n \geq L_t \quad \text{for all } t \in T_{plan}. \tag{3}$$

where L_t is the anticipated load for period t and P_n is the loss of generating capacity associated with maintenance task d_n.

Resource constraints are specified in the case where the availability of certain resources, such as highly skilled technicians, is limited. In general, resources of all types assigned to maintenance tasks should not exceed the associated resource capacity at any time period, as given by:

$$\sum_{d_n \in D_t} \sum_{k \in S_{n,t}} X_{n,k} Res_{n,k}^r \leq ResAvai_t^r \quad \text{for all } t \in T_{plan}, r \in R. \tag{4}$$

where $Res_{n,k}^r$ is the amount of resource of type r available that is required by task d_n at period k; $ResAvai_t^r$ is the associated capacity of resource of type r available at period t and R is the set of all resource types.

Precedence constraints that reflect the relationships between the order of maintenance of generating units in a power system are usually specified in PPMSO problems. An example of such a constraint is a case where task 2 should not commence before task 1 is completed, as given by:

$$start_2 > start_1 + chdur_1 - 1. \tag{5}$$

where $start_n$ is the start time chosen for task d_n.

In the case of maintenance duration shortening, there is usually a practical limit to the extent that the duration can be shortened. Due to the different characteristics of maintenance tasks, minimum maintenance durations may vary with individual tasks:

$$NormDur_n \geq chdur_n \geq MinDur_n, \text{ for all } d_n \in D. \tag{6}$$

where $chdur_n$ is the maintenance duration of task d_n; $MinDur_n$ is the minimum shortened outage duration for task d_n; $NormDur_n$ is the normal duration of maintenance task d_n.

3. ACO for Power Plant Maintenance Scheduling Optimization (ACO-PPMSO)

Ant Colony Optimization (ACO) is a metaheuristic inspired by the foraging behavior of ant colonies (Dorigo & Stützle, 2004). By marking the paths they have followed with pheromone trails, ants are able to communicate indirectly and find the shortest distance between their nest and a food source when foraging for food. When adapting this search metaphor of ants to solve discrete combinatorial optimization problems, artificial ants are considered to explore the search space of all possible solutions. The ACO search begins with a random solution (possibly biased by heuristic information) within the decision space of the problem. As the search progresses over discrete time intervals, ants deposit pheromone on the components of promising solutions. In this way, the environment of a decision space is iteratively modified and the ACO search is gradually biased towards more desirable regions of the search space, where optimal or near-optimal solutions can be found. Readers are referred to Dorigo & Stützle (2004) for a detailed discussion of ACO metaheuristics and the benchmark combinatorial optimization problems to which ACO has been applied. Due to its robustness in solving these problems, ACO has recently been applied to, and obtained some encouraging results for, real-world engineering problems, such as the design of optimal water distribution systems (Maier *et al.*, 2003) and in the area of power systems (Gomez *et al.*, 2004; Huang, 2001; Kannan *et al.*, 2005; Su *et al.*, 2005).

As is the case with other metaheuristics, ACO can be linked with existing simulation models of power systems, regardless of their complexity, when solving a PPMSO problem. In addition, the unique way in which ACO problems are represented by using a graph makes ACO inherently suitable for handling various constraints that are commonly encountered in PPMSO problems. In this section, the novel formulation that enables ACO to be applied to PPMSO problems (herein referred to as ACO-PPMSO) introduced by Foong *et al.* (2005) is formalized.

3.1 Problem representation

Before the PPMSO problem can be optimized using ACO, it has to be mapped onto a graph shown in Fig. 1, which is expressed in terms of a set of decision points consisting of the N maintenance tasks that need to be scheduled $D = \{d_1, d_2, d_3, \ldots, d_N\}$.

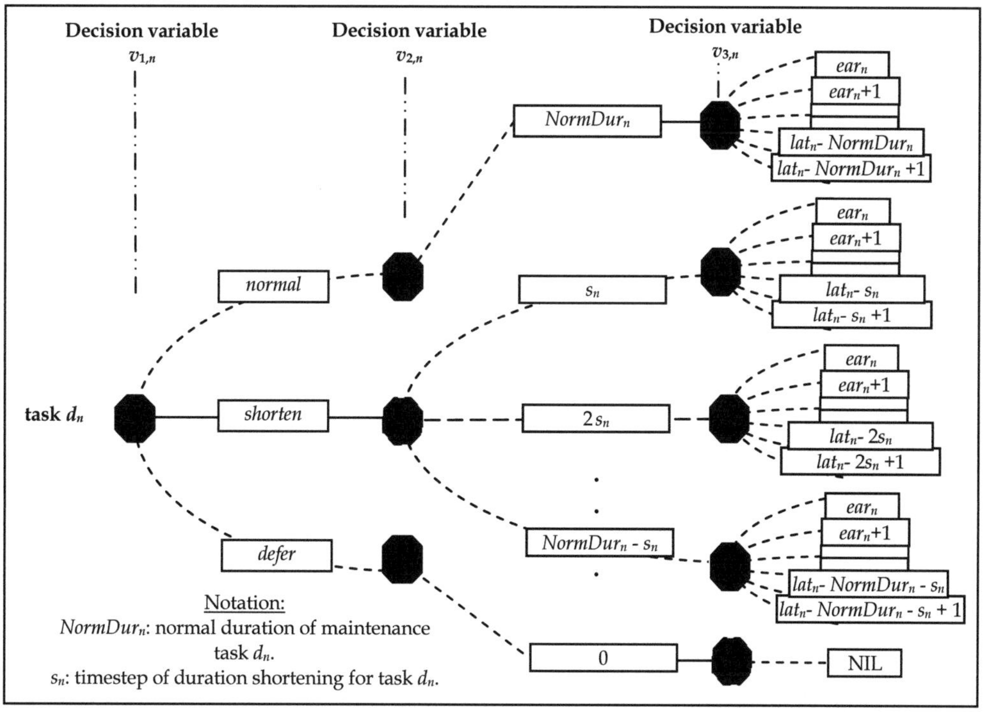

Figure 1. Proposed ACO-PPMSO graph

In accordance with the formulation introduced, there are three variables that need to be defined $V = \{v_1, v_2, v_3\}$ for each maintenance task:

- Variable 1, v_1: the overall state of the maintenance task under consideration (i.e. if maintenance currently being carried out or not),
- Variable 2, v_2: the duration of the maintenance is task, and
- Variable 3, v_3: the commencement time for the maintenance task.

For maintenance task d_n, a set of decision paths $DP_{c,n}$ is associated with decision variable $v_{c,n}$ (where subscript c = 1, 2 or 3) (shown as dashed lines in Fig. 1). For decision variable $v_{1,n}$, these correspond to the options of carrying out the maintenance tasks d_n at normal duration, shortening the maintenance duration and deferring maintenance tasks. For decision variable $v_{2,n}$, these correspond to the optional shortened durations available for the maintenance tasks. For decision variable $v_{3,n}$, these correspond to the optional start times for maintenance tasks d_n. It should be noted that, as the latest finishing time of maintenance tasks is usually fixed, there are different sets of start time decision paths, each corresponding to a maintenance duration decision path (Fig. 1). This graph can then be utilized to construct trial solutions using the ACO-PPMSO algorithm introduced in section 3.2.2.

3.2 ACO-PPMSO Algorithm

The new formulation proposed for power plant maintenance scheduling using Ant Colony Optimisation is implemented via an ACO-PPMSO algorithm, represented by the flowchart given in Fig. 2. The mechanisms involved in each procedure of the proposed ACO-PPMSO algorithm are detailed in sections 3.2.1 to 3.2.6.

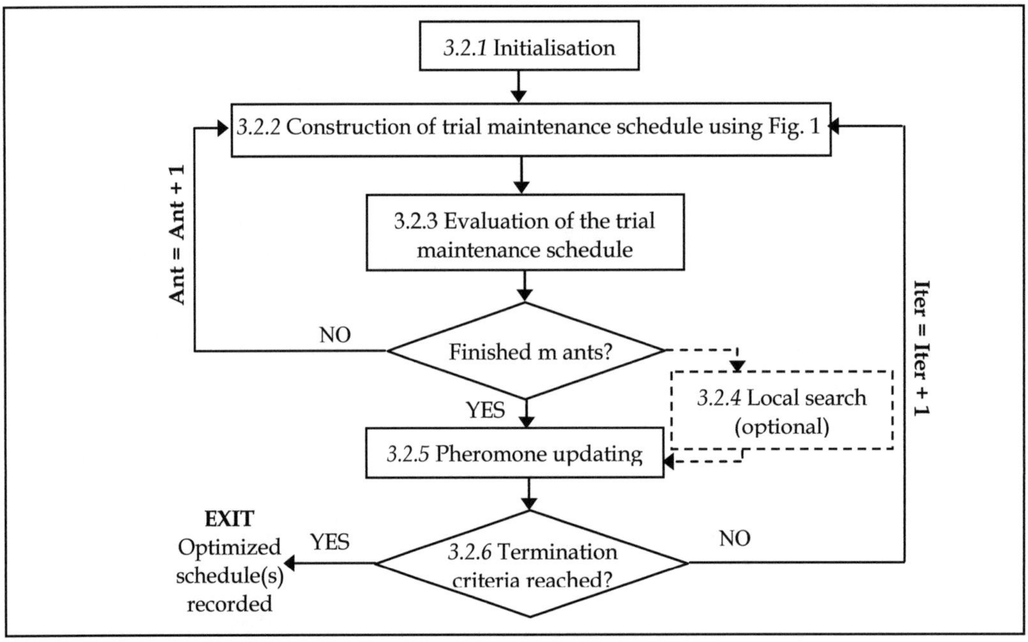

Figure 2. ACO-PPMSO algorithm

3.2.1 Initialization

The optimisation process starts by reading details of the power system under consideration (eg. generating capacity of each unit, daily system demands, time step for duration shortening etc.). In addition, various ACO parameters (eg. initial pheromone trail concentrations (τ_0), number of ants, pheromone evaporation rate etc.) need to be defined.

3.2.2 Construction of a trial maintenance schedule

A trial maintenance schedule is constructed using the ACO-PPMSO graph shown in Fig. 1. In order to generate one trial maintenance schedule, an ant travels to one of the decision points (maintenance tasks) at a time. At each decision point, d_n, a three-stage selection process that corresponds to the three decision variables, $v_{1,n}$, $v_{2,n}$ and $v_{3,n}$, is performed.

At each stage, the probability that decision path *opt* is chosen for maintenance of task d_n in iteration t is given by:

$$p_{n,opt}(t) = \frac{[\tau_{n,opt}(t)]^{\alpha} \cdot [\eta_{n,opt}]^{\beta}}{\sum_{y \in DP_{c,n}} [\tau_{n,y}(t)]^{\alpha} \cdot [\eta_{n,y}]^{\beta}}. \quad (7)$$

subscripts c = 1, 2 and 3 refer to the three decision variables, $v_{1,n}$, $v_{2,n}$ and $v_{3,n}$; $\tau_{n,opt}(t)$ is the pheromone intensity deposited on the decision path *opt* for task d_n in iteration t; $\eta_{n,opt}$ is the heuristic value of decision path *opt* for task d_n; α and β are the relative importance of pheromone intensity and the heuristic, respectively.

It should be noted that the term *opt* in Eq. 7 represents the decision path under consideration, of all decision paths contained in set $DP_{c,n}$. When used for stages 1, 2 and 3, respectively, the terms *opt* and $DP_{c,n}$ are substituted with those associated with the decision variable considered at the corresponding stage (Table 1). The pheromone level associated with a particular decision path (e.g. deferral of a particular maintenance task) is a reflection of the quality of the maintenance schedules that have been generated previously that contain this particular option. The heuristic associated with a particular decision path is related to the likely quality of a solution that contains this option, based on user-defined heuristic information. The following paragraphs detail the three-stage selection process for decision point (maintenance task) d_n, including the adaptations required when using Eq. 7 for each stage.

	Stage 1	Stage 2	Stage 3
c	1	2	3
opt	$stat \in DP_{1,n}$	$dur \in DP_{2,n}$	$day \in DP_{3,n,chdur_n}$
$DP_{c,n}$	$DP_{1,n}$={*normal, shorten, defer*}	$DP_{2,n} = \{0, s_n, 2s_n, \ldots, NormDur_n\}$	$DP_{3,n,chdur_n} = \{chdur_n \in DP_{2,n}: ear_n, ear_n+1, \ldots, lat_n - chdur_n + 1\}$
$\tau_{n,opt}$	$\tau_{n,stat}$	$\tau_{n,dur}$	$\tau_{n,chdur_n,day}$
$\eta_{n,opt}$	$\eta_{n,defer} < \eta_{n,shorten} < \eta_{n,normal}$	$\eta_{n,dur_n} \propto dur$	$\eta_{n,chdur_n,day} = \left(\eta^{Res}_{n,chdur_n,day}\right)^{w} \cdot \eta^{Load}_{n,chdur_n,day}$

Table 1. Adaptations for Eq. 7 in stages 1, 2 and 3 of the selection process

Stage 1: In stage 1, a decision needs to be made whether to perform the maintenance task under consideration at normal or shortened duration, or to defer it (decision variable $v_{1,n}$ in Fig. 1). In this case, c = 1 and $opt = stat \in DP_{1,n}$={*normal, shorten, defer*} is the set of decision paths associated with decision variable $v_{1,n}$ for task d_n. The probability of each of these options being chosen is a function of the strength of the pheromone trails and heuristic value associated with the option (Eq. 7). For the PPMSO problem, the heuristic formulation should generally be defined such that normal maintenance durations are preferred over duration shortening, and deferral is the least favored option (Eq. 8). However, real costs associated with duration shortening and deferral options can be used if the extra costs incurred associated with these options are quantifiable and available. The adaptations required for Eq. 7 to be used at the stage 1 selection process are summarized in Table 1. It is suggested that values of the heuristics should be selected such that:

$$\eta_{n,defer} < \eta_{n,shorten} < \eta_{n,normal} \,. \tag{8}$$

Stage 2: Once a decision has been made at stage 1, the selection process proceeds to stage 2 (decision variable $v_{2,n}$ in Fig. 1), where the duration of the maintenance task under consideration, d_n, is required to be selected from a set of available decision paths $DP_{2,n} = \{0, s_n, 2s_n, \ldots, NormDur_n\}$. The symbols s_n and $NormDur_n$ denote the time step for maintenance duration shortening, and the normal maintenance duration, respectively. For Eq. 7 to be used at stage 2, the terms c and opt in the equation are substituted by the values 2 and $dur \in DP_{2,n}$, respectively. It should be noted that if the 'normal' or 'defer' options were chosen at stage 1, the normal duration of the maintenance task, or a duration of 0, respectively, are automatically chosen for the task. In the case of duration shortening, a constraint is normally specified where each maintenance task has a minimum duration at which the completion of the task cannot be further accelerated due to limitations, such as the availability of highly specialized technicians. This constraint can be addressed at this stage such that only feasible trial maintenance schedules (with regard to this constraint) are constructed (see section 3.3 for details of such constraint-handling techniques). The pheromone trails and heuristic values associated with optional durations are used to determine the probability that these durations are chosen. In order to favor longer maintenance durations (i.e. the smallest amount of shortening compared with the normal maintenance duration), it is suggested that the heuristic value associated with a decision path should be directly proportional to the maintenance duration (Eq. 9).

$$\eta_{n,dur} \propto dur \,. \tag{9}$$

The substitutions for the various terms in Eq. 7 when used in stage 2 are summarized in Table 1.

Stage 3: Once a maintenance duration has been selected, the solution construction process enters stage 3 (decision variable $v_{3,n}$ in Fig. 1), where a start time for the maintenance task is selected from the set of optional start times available $DP_{3,n,chdur_n} = \{chdur_n \in DP_{2,n}: ear_n, ear_n+1, \ldots, lat_n - chdur_n + 1\}$, given a chosen duration of $chdur_n$. In order to utilize Eq. 7 at stage 3, adjustments are made such that $c = 3$ and $opt = day \in DP_{3,n,chdur_n}$. It should be noted that this stage is skipped if the 'defer' option is chosen at stage 1. The probability that a particular start day is chosen is a function of the associated pheromone trail and heuristic value. The suggested heuristic formulation for selection of the maintenance start day is given by Eqs. 10 to 15.

$$\eta_{n,chdur_n,day} = \left(\eta^{Res}_{n,chdur_n,day}\right)^{w} \cdot \eta^{Load}_{n,chdur_n,day} \,. \tag{10}$$

$$\eta^{Res}_{n,chdur_n,day} = \frac{\sum_{k \in J_{n,chdur_n,day}} Y_{ResV(k)=0} \cdot R_{n,chdur_n,day}(k)}{\sum_{k \in J_{n,chdur_n,day}} (Y_{ResV(k)=0} - 1) \cdot R_{n,chdur_n,day}(k)}. \quad (11)$$

$$\eta^{Load}_{n,chdur_n,day} = \frac{\sum_{k \in J_{n,chdur_n,day}} Y_{LoadV(k)=0} \cdot C_{n,chdur_n,day}(k)}{\sum_{k \in J_{n,chdur_n,day}} (Y_{LoadV(k)=0} - 1) \cdot C_{n,chdur_n,day}(k)}. \quad (12)$$

$$Y_{ResV(k)=0} = \begin{cases} 1 & \text{if no violation of resource constraints in time period } k \\ 0 & \text{otherwise} \end{cases} \quad (13)$$

$$Y_{LoadV(k)=0} = \begin{cases} 1 & \text{if no violation of load constraints in time period } k \\ 0 & \text{otherwise} \end{cases} \quad (14)$$

$$w = \begin{cases} 1 & \text{if resource constraints are considered} \\ 0 & \text{otherwise} \end{cases} \quad (15)$$

where $\eta_{n,chdur_n,day}(t)$ is the heuristic for start time $day \in DP_{3,n,chdur_n}$ for task d_n, given a chosen duration $chdur_n$; $R_{n,chdur_n,day}(k)$ represents the prospective resources available in reserve in time period k if task d_n is to commence at start time day and takes $chdur_n$ to complete (less than 0 in the case of resource deficits); $C_{n,chdur_n,day}(k)$ is the prospective power generation capacity available in reserve in time period k if task d_n is to commence at start time day and takes $chdur_n$ to complete (less than 0 in the case of power generation reserve deficits); $J_{n,chdur_n,day} = \{day \in DP_{3,n,chdur_n} : day \le k \le day + chdur_n - 1\}$ is the set of time periods k such that if task d_n starts at start time day, that task will be in maintenance during period k.

As mentioned above, the heuristic formulation in Eq. 10 includes a resource-related term, $\eta^{Res}_{n,chdur_n,day}$, and a load-related term, $\eta^{Load}_{n,chdur_n day}$. These two terms are expected to evenly distribute maintenance tasks over the entire planning horizon, which potentially maximizes the overall reliability of a power system. For PPMSO problem instances that do not consider resource constraints, the value of w in Eq. 10 can be set to 0 (Eq. 15). In order to implement the heuristic, each ant is provided with a memory matrix on resource reserves and another matrix on generation capacity reserves prior to construction of a trial solution. This is updated every time a unit maintenance commencement time is added to the partially completed schedule.

The three-stage selection process is then repeated for another maintenance task (decision point). A complete maintenance schedule is obtained once all maintenance tasks have been considered.

3.2.3 Evaluation of trial maintenance schedule

Once a complete trial maintenance schedule, $s \in S$, has been constructed by choosing a maintenance commencement time and duration at each decision point (i.e. for each maintenance task to be scheduled), an ant-cycle has been completed. The trial schedule's objective function cost (*OFC*) can then be determined by an evaluation function, which is a function of the values of objectives and constraint violations:

$$OFC(s) = f\left(obj_1(s), obj_2(s), ..., obj_{Z_T}(s), vio_1(s), vio_2(s), ..., vio_{C_T}(s)\right). \tag{16}$$

where *OFC*(*s*) is the objective function cost associated with a trial maintenance schedule, *s*; $obj_1(s)$ is the value of the first objective; $vio_1(s)$ is the degree of violation of the first constraint; Z_T is the total number of objectives; C_T is the total number of constraints that cannot be satisfied during the construction of trial solutions.

It should be noted that not all constraints specified in a problem are accounted for using Eq. 16. Maintenance windows, precedence and minimum duration constraints, just to name a few, can be satisfied during the construction of a trial solution and would not appear in Eq. 16. In other words, a complete trial solution would have satisfied these constraints already before the evaluation process is carried out. On the other hand, load constraints can only be checked upon completion of a complete trial solution and therefore the violations of these constraints, if there are any, can only be reflected through penalty terms in the objective function (Eq. 16). Detailed categorizations of constraints commonly encountered in PPMSO problems, as well as the appropriate methods of handling them, are presented in section 3.3. In general, the trial schedule has to be run through a simulation model in order to calculate some elements of the objective function and whether certain constraints (those accounted for through penalty terms) have been violated.

After *m* ants have performed procedures 3.2.2 and 3.2.3, where *m* (the number of ants) is predefined in procedure 3.2.1, an iteration cycle has been completed. At this stage, a total of *m* maintenance schedules have been generated for this iteration. It should be noted that all ants in an iteration can generate their trial solutions concurrently, as they are working on the same set of pheromone trail distributions in decision space.

3.2.4 Local search

Recently, local search has been utilized to improve the optimisation ability of ACO. While it has been found to result in significant improvements in some applications (den Besten *et al.*, 2000; Dorigo & Gambardella, 1997b), little success has been obtained in others (Merkle *et al.*, 2002). Local search has also been found useful for some problems (Foong *et al.*, 2008) where the formulation of heuristics is difficult (Dorigo & Stützle, 2004).

In this formulation, local search is coupled with ACO to solve the PPMSO problem. The local search operator proposed in this chapter is called PPMSO-2-opt, which is a modification of the 2-opt strategy used when solving the Travelling Salesman Problem (TSP) (Stützle *et al.*, 1997), where two edges of connected cities are exchanged. In PPMSO-2-opt, 'neighbor maintenance schedules' are generated by exchanging the maintenance start times of a pair of randomly selected tasks of the 'target maintenance schedule'. It should be noted that the maximum number of possible 'neighbor maintenance schedules' formed based on a 'target maintenance schedule' ($^NC_2 = \frac{N!}{2! \cdot (N-2)!}$) can be specified as the termination criterion of the local search. Otherwise, a smaller number of local solutions can be defined as the stopping criterion.

3.2.5 Pheromone updating

Two mechanisms, namely pheromone evaporation and pheromone rewarding, are involved in the pheromone updating process. Pheromone evaporation reduces all pheromone trails by a factor. In this way, exploration of the search space is encouraged by preventing a rapid increase in pheromone on frequently-chosen paths. Pheromone rewarding is performed in a way that reinforces good solutions.

Despite its original inspiration from the foraging behaviour of ant colonies, various ACO algorithms have evolved, such as Elitist-Ant System (EAS) (Dorigo (1992); Dorigo *et al.* (1996)) and Max-Min Ant System (MMAS) (Stützle & Hoos, 1997; Stützle & Hoos, 2000). These algorithms are distinguished from each other in the way pheromone updating is performed. In the ACO-PPMSO formulation, pheromone updating is performed on the pheromone matrices used for the three-stage selection process. A general pheromone updating formulation (regardless of the ACO algorithm adopted) is introduced for this purpose:

$$\tau_*(t+1)=\rho\cdot\tau_*(t)+\Delta\tau_*(t). \tag{17}$$

$$\Delta\tau_*(t)=\sum_{s\in Sol_{update}} q=\begin{cases}\dfrac{Q}{OFC(s_{update})} & \text{if } *\in s_{update}\\ 0 & \text{otherwise}\end{cases} \tag{18}$$

where t is the index of iteration; $(1 - \rho)$ is the pheromone evaporation rate; the subscript asterisk * of τ_* denotes the element of the pheromone matrix under consideration ($\tau_{n,opt}$, $\tau_{n,dur}$ and $\tau_{n,dur,day}$ for decision variables v_1, v_2 and v_3, respectively); s_{update} is any trial schedule contained in $Sol_{update}(t)$, which is the set of trial schedules chosen to be rewarded in iteration t; $\Delta\tau_*(t)$ is the amount of pheromone rewarded to pheromone trail τ_* at the end of iteration t; $OFC(s_{update})$ is the objective function cost associated with the trial schedule s_{update} that contains element *; Q is the reward factor (a user-defined parameter).

As EAS and MMAS are utilized in solving the PPMSO case study systems presented in section 4, the following additional specifications are made according to the general pheromone updating rules:

(A) Elitist-Ant System (EAS)

In EAS, only the least-OFC schedule(s) in every iteration is/are rewarded (Eq. 19).

$$Sol_{update}(t)=s_{iter-best}(t). \tag{19}$$

where $s_{iter-best}(t)$ is the best maintenance schedule evaluated in iteration t.

(B) Max-Min Ant System (MMAS)

Similarly to EAS, MMAS only rewards iteration-best trial solution(s) (Eq. 19). Additionally, upper and lower bounds are imposed on the pheromone trails in order to prevent premature convergence and greater exploration of the solution surface. These bounds are given by:

$$\tau_{max}(t+1)=\frac{1}{1-\rho}\cdot\frac{Q}{OFC_{iter-best}(t)}. \tag{20}$$

$$\tau_{c,min}(t+1) = \frac{\tau_{max}(t+1)(1-\sqrt[n_c]{p_{best}})}{(avg_c - 1)\sqrt[n_c]{p_{best}}}. \tag{21}$$

where n_c is the number of decision points for decision variable v_c; avg_c is the average number of decision paths available at each decision point for decision variable v_c; subscript c = 1, 2 and 3 refers to the three decision variables considered in procedure 3.2.2; p_{best} is the probability that the paths of the current iteration-best-solution, $s_{iter\text{-}best}(t)$, will be selected, given that non-iteration best-options have a pheromone level of $\tau_{min}(t)$ and all iteration-best options have a pheromone level of $\tau_{max}(t)$.
The lower and upper bound of pheromone are applied to all decision paths in the search space:

$$\tau_{c,min}(t) \leq \tau_{n,opt}(t) \leq \tau_{max}(t)\,;\, opt \in DP_{c,n} \;\; c = 1,2,3 \; for \; all \; t,n. \tag{22}$$

3.2.6 Termination of run

Procedures 3.2.2 to 3.2.5 are repeated until the termination criterion of an ACO run is met, e.g. either the maximum number of evaluations allowed has been reached or stagnation of the objective function cost has occurred. A set of maintenance schedules resulting in the minimum OFC is the final outcome of the optimisation run.

3.3 Constraints Handling

ACO is an unconstrained optimisation metaheuristic. As constraints are inevitable in PPMSO problems, there is a need to find ways of incorporating constraints during optimisation. In this research, two different constraint handling techniques are adopted. In order to decide which of the two techniques should be used, constraints encountered in PPMSO problems have been characterized using the following classification scheme:
Direct vs. indirect constraints: Constraints can be characterized based on the earliest stage at which they can be addressed during optimisation. The maintenance window (Eq. 2), precedence (Eq. 5) and minimum maintenance duration (Eq. 6) constraints can be addressed when trial solutions are being generated during ant cycles (procedure described in section 3.2.2). On the other hand, the violation of load (Eq. 3) and resource (Eq. 4) constraints often cannot be identified from a partially built trial maintenance schedule. As part of the classification scheme introduced in this paper, the former constraints are referred to as direct constraints and the latter as indirect constraints.
Rigid vs. soft constraints: Constraints can also be classified based on their "rigidity". For rigid constraints, such as maintenance windows, minimum maintenance duration, precedence and load constraints, even the slightest violations are generally intolerable. On the other hand, constraints, such as resource constraints, may be able to be violated to a degree specified by decision makers and are therefore referred to as "soft" constraints.
The two constraint handling techniques used in the ACO-PPMSO formulation and the constraint types they are able to accommodate include:
Graph-based technique: This technique utilizes candidate lists during ant cycles when trial solutions are being constructed (Fig. 1). Given a partially built trial schedule, a candidate list consists of the optional start times that are available for a maintenance task, such that the constraints under consideration are not violated. Direct and some rigid constraints, such as the maintenance window, precedence and minimum duration constraints, can be accounted

for using this technique. During the construction of a trial maintenance schedule, an ant incrementally adds start times to a partially built schedule. By dynamically updating the candidate lists of 'unvisited units', only start times that would result in solutions that satisfy the maintenance window and precedence constraints are considered.

Penalty-based technique: In ACO-PPMSO, penalty functions, which transform a constrained optimisation problem into an unconstrained problem by adding or subtracting a value to/from the objective function cost based on the degree of constraint violation (Coello Coello, 2002), are used to address indirect or potentially soft constraints, such as the availability of personpower to perform the maintenance and load constraints. When dealing with soft constraints, penalty factors may be varied to reflect the amount of constraint violation that may be tolerated. Penalty costs also have to be used to account for indirect constraints, as the degree of constraint violation is not known until a complete trial solution has been constructed, as discussed earlier. In such cases, the degree of violation generally has to be obtained with the aid of a simulation model.

The ability to implement direct and some rigid constraints using the graph-based technique is one of the attractive features of using ACO for PPMSO. Firstly, by preventing the generation of infeasible solutions, the number of simulation model runs required is reduced. This is advantageous for real-world PPMSO problems, as the number of times the simulation model has to be run is a major source of computational overhead. Moreover, there are difficulties associated with the use of penalty-based techniques that remain unresolved at the time of writing, in spite of extensive research into this area (Coello Coello, 2002). For example, hand tuning is required for assigning appropriate penalty factors to each constraint and objective term in the objective function.

4. Problem Instances

In order to test the utility of the proposed ACO-PPMSO formulation, it is applied to 4 problem instances, including 21- and 22-unit benchmark case studies from the literature and modified versions of these case studies. The 21- and 22-unit case studies have been chosen as they enable comparisons to be made with results obtained in previous studies. However, as these case studies can be solved without the need for maintenance shortening and deferral, modifications to the case studies are introduced in this chapter to test this feature of the proposed formulation. Details of the four problem instances are given below.

4.1 21-unit system

The first case study considered in this research is the 21-unit power plant maintenance problem investigated by Aldridge *et al.* (1999) and Dahal *et al.* (1999; , 2000) using a number of metaheuristics. This case study is a modified version of the 21-unit problem introduced by Yamayee *et al.* (1983), and consists of 21 generating facilities, of which 20 units are thermal and one is hydropower. Due to space constraints, system details are not presented here but can be found in Aldridge *et al.* (1999). All of the machines are to be scheduled for maintenance either in the first or second half of a year's planning horizon, which results in a combinatorial optimisation problem with approximately 5.18 x 10^{28} total possible solutions. The objective of the problem is to even out reserve generation capacity over the planning horizon, which can be achieved by minimizing the sum of squares of the reserve (SSR) generation capacity in each week.

Constraints to be satisfied include:

1. Maintenance window constraints: The earliest start time and latest finish time of maintenance tasks for each machine are detailed in Aldridge *et al.* (1999).
2. Resource constraints: A limit of 20 maintenance personpower is available each week.
3. Demand constraints: A single peak load of 4739 MW has to be met.

Problem formulation

Mathematically, this optimisation problem can be defined as the determination of maintenance schedule(s) such that SSR, which is defined as the sum of square of reserve generation capacity within the planning horizon, is minimized:

$$Min\left\{ SSR = \sum_{t\in T_{plan}} \left(\sum_{n=1}^{N} P_n - \sum_{d_n \in D_t} \sum_{k \in S_{n,t}} X_{n,k} P_n - L_t \right)^2 \right\}. \tag{23}$$

where P_n is the generating capacity of unit d_n; L_t is the anticipated load for period t, *subject to* the maintenance window, load and personpower constraints, as given by:

$$ear_n \le start_n \le lat_n - NormDur_n + 1 \quad \text{for all } d_n \in D. \tag{24}$$

$$\sum_{d_n \in D_t} \sum_{k \in S_{n,t}} X_{n,k} Res_{n,k} \le ResAvai_t \quad \text{for all } t \in T_{plan}. \tag{25}$$

$$\left(\sum_{n} P_n - \sum_{d_n \in D_t} \sum_{k \in S_{n,t}} X_{n,k} P_n \right) \ge L_t \quad \text{for all } t \in T_{plan}. \tag{26}$$

where ear_n is the earliest start time for unit d_n; lat_n is the latest start time for unit d_n; $NormDur_n$ is the outage duration (week) for unit d_n; $start_n$ is the maintenance start time for unit d_n and $ResAvai_t$ is the personpower available at period t.

It should be noted that personpower is considered as a type of resource constraint. The maintenance window constraints are taken into account by the construction graph-based technique (section 3.3), whereas both load and personpower constraints are indirect and are therefore taken into account by using penalty-based techniques (section 3.3).

When applying the ACO-PPMSO formulation to this case study, the heuristic developed as part of this research (Eqs. 10 to 15) was used together with pheromone for selection of start times when generating trial maintenance schedules. It should be noted that the value of w in Eq. 10 was set to 1, as utilization of resource (personpower) constraints is considered in this case. Upon completion of a trial maintenance schedule, a simulation model was used to calculate the SSR value and any violations of personpower or load constraints associated with schedule s. The quality of individual maintenance schedules in this problem is given by an objective function cost (OFC), which is a function of the value of SSR and the total violation of personpower and load constraints (Eq. 27).

$$OFC(s) = SSR(s) \cdot \left(ManVio_{tot}(s) + 1\right) \cdot \left(LoadVio_{tot}(s) + 1\right). \tag{27}$$

where $OFC(s)$ is the objective function cost ($) associated with schedule s; $SSR(s)$ is the sum of squares of reserve generation capacity (MW^2) associated with schedule s; $ManVio_{tot}(s)$ is the total personpower shortfall (person) associated with schedule s; $LoadVio_{tot}(s)$ is the total demand shortfall (MW) associated with schedule s.

The calculation of constraint violations is given in Eqs. 28 to 31. For a trial maintenance schedule, the total personpower shortfall associated with schedule s, $ManVio_{tot}(s)$, is given by summation of the personpower shortage in all periods within the planning horizon:

$$ManVio_{tot}(s) = \sum_{t \in T_{MV}} \left(\sum_{d_n \in D_t} \sum_{k \in S_{n,t}} X_{n,k} Res_{n,k} - ResAvai_t \right). \quad (28)$$

where T_{MV} is the period where personpower constraints are violated, and is given by:

$$T_{MV} = \left(t : \sum_{d_n \in D_t} \sum_{k \in S_{n,t}} X_{n,k} Res_{n,k} > ResAvai_t \right). \quad (29)$$

The total demand shortfall associated with schedule s, $LoadVio_{tot}(s)$, is the summation of demand shortfall in all periods within the planning horizon. The calculation of this value may be represented by the following equation.

$$LoadVio_{tot}(s) = \sum_{t \in T_{LV}} \left(\sum_{n} P_n - \sum_{d_n \in D_t} \sum_{k \in S_{n,t}} X_{n,k} P_n \right). \quad (30)$$

where T_{LV} is the period where load constraints are violated, and is given by:

$$T_{LV} = (t : \sum_{n} P_n - \sum_{d_n \in D_t} \sum_{k \in S_{n,t}} X_{n,k} P_n < L_t). \quad (31)$$

The *OFC* can be viewed as the virtual cost associated with a maintenance schedule.

4.2 22-unit system

The 22-unit power plant maintenance scheduling optimisation problem was first solved by Escudero *et al.* (1980) using an implicit enumeration algorithm and later by El-Amin *et al.* (2000) using tabu search. In this problem, each generating unit is required to be scheduled for maintenance once within a planning horizon of 52 weeks. Details of the system can be found in Escudero *et al.* (1980). The objective when scheduling for maintenance is to even out reserve generation capacity over the planning horizon subject to the following constraints:

1. The maintenance window constraints specify that all units can be maintained anytime within the planning horizon and have to finish maintenance by week 52, except for unit 10, which can only be taken offline between weeks 6 and 22.
2. Load constraints require peak demands (see Escudero et al., 1980) to be met.
3. The reliability constraint requires a minimum reserve of 20% of the peak demand throughout the planning horizon.
4. The two precedence constraints specify that maintenance of units 2 and 5 has to be carried out before that of units 3 and 6, respectively.
5. Units 15 and 16, as well as units 21 and 22, cannot be maintained simultaneously due to personpower constraints.

Problem formulation

In order to even out reserve generation capacity, the formulation used in both Escudero *et al.* (1980) and El-Amin *et al.* (2000) for the 22-unit problem was designed to minimize the summed deviation of generation reserve from the average reserve over the entire planning horizon, LVL. Mathematically, the optimisation of this case study can be described as the minimization of the sum of the deviation of generation reserve from the average reserve over the planning horizon (Eqs. 32 to 34):

$$Min\left\{ LVL = \sum_{t \in T_{plan}} \left| Res_{avg} - Res_t \right| \right\}. \tag{32}$$

where the generation reserve (Res_t) and average reserve (Res_{avg}) are given by:

$$Res_t = \sum_{n=1}^{N} P_n - \sum_{n \in D_t} \sum_{k \in S_{n,t}} X_{n,k} P_n - L_t . \tag{33}$$

$$Res_{avg} = \frac{\sum_{t \in T_{plan}} Res_t}{T} . \tag{34}$$

where L_t is the anticipated load demand for period t; P_n is the generating capacity of unit d_n; T is the total number of time indices, *subject to* the following constraints:

$$ear_n \le start_n \le lat_n - NormDur_n + 1 \quad \text{for all } d_n \in D. \tag{35}$$

$$\left(\sum_n P_n - \sum_{d_n \in D_t} \sum_{k \in S_{n,t}} X_{n,k} P_n \right) \ge L_t \quad \text{for all } t \in T_{plan}. \tag{36}$$

$$\left(\sum_n P_n - \sum_{d_n \in D_t} \sum_{k \in S_{n,t}} X_{n,k} P_n \right) \ge 1.2 L_t \quad \text{for all } t \in T_{plan}. \tag{37}$$

$$\begin{cases} start_3 > start_2 + NormDur_2 - 1 \\ start_6 > start_5 + NormDur_5 - 1 \end{cases} \tag{38}$$

$$\begin{cases} X_{15,k} = 0 \text{ for } k = [start_{16}, ..., start_{16} + NormDur_{16} - 1] \\ X_{16,k} = 0 \text{ for } k = [start_{15}, ..., start_{15} + NormDur_{15} - 1] \\ X_{21,k} = 0 \text{ for } k = [start_{22}, ..., start_{22} + NormDur_{22} - 1] \\ X_{22,k} = 0 \text{ for } k = [start_{21}, ..., start_{21} + NormDur_{21} - 1] \end{cases} \tag{39}$$

It is interesting to note that, given the same objective, the objective functiom formulations used by Escudero *et al.* (1980) and El-Amin *et al.* (2000) are quite different from that of Aldridge *et al.* (1999).

As there is no resource utilization throughout the planning horizon, there is no need for the inclusion of the resources term in the heuristic formulation (Eq. 10) for this case study (thus w may be set to 0). The precedence and maintenance window constraints of this system are direct and rigid constraints, which can be incorporated by using the graph-based technique, whereas the load and reliability constraints need to be taken into account using penalty functions. The objective function cost (OFC) used in this case study is a function of the reserve generation capacity LVL value and the total violation of load and reliability constraints (Eq. 40).

$$OFC(s) = LVL(s) \cdot \left(LoadResVio_{tot}(s) + 1\right). \tag{40}$$

where $OFC(s)$ is the objective function cost ($) associated with schedule s; $LVL(s)$ is the level of reserve generation capacity (MW) associated with schedule s; $LoadResVio_{tot}(s)$ is the total demand and reserve shortfall (MW) associated with schedule s.

It should be noted that the inclusion of a load constraint violation term in Eq. 40 is not necessary because violation of load constraints would be reflected as violation of reserve constraints. The calculation of constraint violations is given by Eqs. 41 and 42. The total load and reserve shortfall associated with schedule s, $LoadResVio_{tot}(s)$, is the summation of load and reserve shortfall in all periods within the planning horizon:

$$LoadResVio_{tot}(s) = \sum_{t \in T_{LV}} \left(\sum_{n} P_n - \sum_{d_n \in D_t} \sum_{k \in S_{n,t}} X_{n,k} P_n \right). \tag{41}$$

where T_{LV} is the period where load and reserve constraints are violated, and is given by:

$$T_{LV} = (t : \sum_{n} P_n - \sum_{d_n \in D_t} \sum_{k \in S_{n,t}} X_{n,k} P_n < 1.2 L_t). \tag{42}$$

4.3 Modified 21-unit system

The 21-unit case study system described in section 4.1 was modified in the following ways in order to ensure that maintenance task shortening and/or deferral are required to satisfy load constraints:

1. The original system load (4739MW) is increased by 5% throughout the whole planning horizon, and another 5% increment for weeks 15 to 25.
2. While all maintenance tasks have the option of being deferred, some maintenance tasks can be carried out in durations shorter than the original outage duration (shown in Table 2). The personpower requirements for shortened durations are also detailed in Table 2.

Unit No., n	**Optional Outage Duration, (weeks)**	**Personpower required for each week, $Res_{n,wk(wk=1,2,\ldots,NormDur_n)}$ (person)**
1	5	10, 10, 10, 8, 5
	3	15, 14, 14
2	3	15, 15, 10
5	3	17, 17, 16
8	4	13, 13, 13, 6
9	8	3, 3, 3, 2, 2, 3, 3, 3
	6	4, 4, 3, 3, 4, 4
	4	6, 5, 5, 6
	2	11, 11
10	2	15, 15
14	2	20, 20
20	2	20, 20

Table 2. Personpower utilization for the modified 21-unit case study system

Problem formulation

Despite the possibility of shortening and deferral options in this case study, they are unfavorable from both an economic and operations point of view. Therefore, the objective function used for the original version of this case study (Eq. 27) has been modified to:

$$OFC(s) = SSR(s) \cdot (ManVio_{tot}(s) + 1) \cdot (LoadVio_{tot}(s) + 1) \cdot (DurCut_{tot}(s) + 1). \tag{43}$$

where $OFC(s)$ is the objective function cost ($) associated with schedule s; $SSR(s)$ is the sum of squares of reserve generation capacity (MW^2) associated with schedule s; $ManVio_{tot}(s)$ is the total personpower shortfall (person) associated with schedule s; $LoadVio_{tot}(s)$ is the total demand shortfall (MW) associated with schedule s; $DurCut_{tot}(s)$ is the total reduction in maintenance duration (weeks) due to shortening and deferral associated with schedule s.
While the calculation of total demand shortfall associated with schedule s, $LoadVio_{tot}(s)$, total personpower shortfall associated with schedule s, $ManVio_{tot}(s)$, and the sum of squares of reserve generation capacity associated with schedule s, $SSR(s)$, are detailed in section 4.1, the value of $DurCut_{tot}(s)$ is given by:

$$DurCut_{tot}(s) = \sum_{n=1}^{21} (NormDur_n - chdur_n(s)). \tag{44}$$

where $NormDur_n$ is the normal duration of maintenance task d_n, and $chdur_n(s)$ is the maintenance duration (week) of task d_n associated with schedule s.
It should be noted that by using Eq. 43 to direct the search during an ACO run, a trial maintenance schedule that includes shortened and/or deferred maintenance tasks is being assigned a higher OFC, which represent an unfavorable solution to ACO during pheromone update.
As part of the modified case study, the minimum-duration constraints can be addressed during the stage-2 selection process when a trial solution is being constructed (section 3.2.2) by allowing only optional durations that are greater than the minimum duration for each maintenance task. In this way, trial solutions constructed will not violate the minimum duration constraints. For example, machine unit 1 that normally requires 7 days to be maintained, can be shortened to 5 or 3 days, or be deferred altogether (Table 2).

4.4 Modified 22-unit system

The 22-unit case study detailed in section 4.2 was modified as follows in order to ensure that maintenance task shortening and/or deferral are required to satisfy load constraints:

1. The weekly loads for the modified 22-unit case study system are increased by 60%.
2. Maintenance tasks 1 to 13 are allowed to be performed within the first half of the planning horizon, while the remainder of the tasks have to be performed in the second half (except for unit 10 as in original case study).
3. While all maintenance tasks can be deferred, the maintenance tasks listed in Table 3 can be shortened to the optional duration(s) specified.

Unit No., *n*	1	5	6	8	9	10	11	12	14	15	16	17	18	22
Optional shortened durations (weeks)	4, 2	4, 2	2	2	3	10, 8, 6, 4	2	6, 4	4	3	4	3	3	3

Table 3. Details of the modified 22-unit system

Problem formulation

The objective function used for the original 22-unit case study (Eq. 40) has been modified to accommodate the options of shortening and deferral, and is given by:

$$OFC(s) = LVL(s) \cdot \left(LoadResVio_{tot}(s) + 1\right) \cdot (DurCut_{tot}(s) + 1) . \qquad (45)$$

where $OFC(s)$ is the objective function cost ($) associated with schedule s; $LVL(s)$ is the level of reserve generation capacity (MW) associated with schedule s; $LoadResVio_{tot}(s)$ is the total load constraint violation (MW) associated with schedule s; $DurCut_{tot}(s)$ is the total reduction in maintenance duration (weeks) due to shortening and deferral associated with schedule s.

The calculation of the total load constraint violation associated with schedule s, $LoadResVio_{tot}(s)$, and the level of reserve generation capacity associated with schedule s, $LVL(s)$ have been detailed previously in section 4.2, whereas the value of the total duration shortened and deferred associated with schedule s, $DurCut_{tot}(s)$, is given by:

$$DurCut_{tot}(s) = \sum_{n=1}^{22} (NormDur_n - chdur_n(s)) . \qquad (46)$$

where $NormDur_n$ is the normal duration (weeks) of maintenance task d_n, and $chdur_n(s)$ is the maintenance duration (weeks) of task d_n associated with schedule s.

5. Experimental Procedure, Results and Analysis

5.1 Experimental procedure

Experiments have been conducted on both the original and modified versions of the 21-unit and 22-unit case studies to assess the utility of the proposed ACO-PPMSO formulation. Particular emphasis was given to assessing the usefulness of the heuristics developed, the impact of the local search operator and the overall performance of the proposed ACO-PPMSO formulation.

A. Usefulness of heuristic formulation

The effectiveness of the new heuristic formulations for general PPMSO problems (Eqs. 10 to 15) introduced in section 3.2.2 was examined by conducting optimisation runs with and without the heuristics (the latter was achieved by setting the relative weight of the heuristic, β, in Eq. 7 to 0). In addition, the sensitivity of optimisation results to increasing values of β was checked. It should be noted that, as a control, the value of α in Eq. 7 was fixed at 1.

B. Impact of local search operator

The impact of local search on the performance of the ACO-PPMSO algorithm was also investigated, both with and without heuristic. The total number of trial solutions evaluated in the ACO runs with local search was identical to those without local search.

C. Overall performance of ACO-PPMSO

In order to check the overall utility of the ACO-PPMSO formulation, the results obtained for the two original case studies were compared with those obtained using other optimisation methods in previous studies and the ability to account for maintenance shortening and deferral was assessed on the two modified case studies.

In order to achieve the objectives outlined above, the testing procedure shown in Fig. 3 was implemented separately for each of the four case studies. Items A, B and C mentioned above were investigated at Stages A, B and C in the testing procedure, respectively.

To minimize the impact the ACO algorithms and parameters used have on the evaluation of the effectiveness of the heuristic, local search and overall performance of the ACO-PPMSO algorithm, two ACO algorithms, namely Elitist-Ant System and MMAS, and a range of parameters (shown in the dashed box in Fig. 3) were used to solve the problem instance under consideration. In addition, each run was repeated 50 times with different random number seeds in order to minimize the influence of random starting values in the solution space on the results obtained and to enable Student's t-test to be conducted to determine whether any differences in the results obtained were significant. In total, 3,024 different combinations of parameters, each with 50 different starting random number seeds, were evaluated as part of this study. In order to facilitate fair comparisons, the same number of evaluations per optimisation run were used as in previous studies that investigated the 21-unit case problem (30,000 evaluations). In this research, 'one ACO run' is defined as the use of an ACO algorithm with or without using heuristic information, with or without local search and with a defined set of parameters to solve a PPMSO instance. An example of an ACO run is the use of EAS to solve the modified 21-unit case study with heuristic information and local search and a defined parameter set of m = 200; ρ = 0.9; τ_0 = 0.1; Q = 500,000; α = 1, β = 11, repeated for 50 random number seeds. The overall performance of a parameter set is then assessed based on the objective function cost (OFC) averaged over the 50 simulations using different random number seeds. An analysis of the results obtained with the testing procedure outlined in Fig. 3 is given in section 5.2.

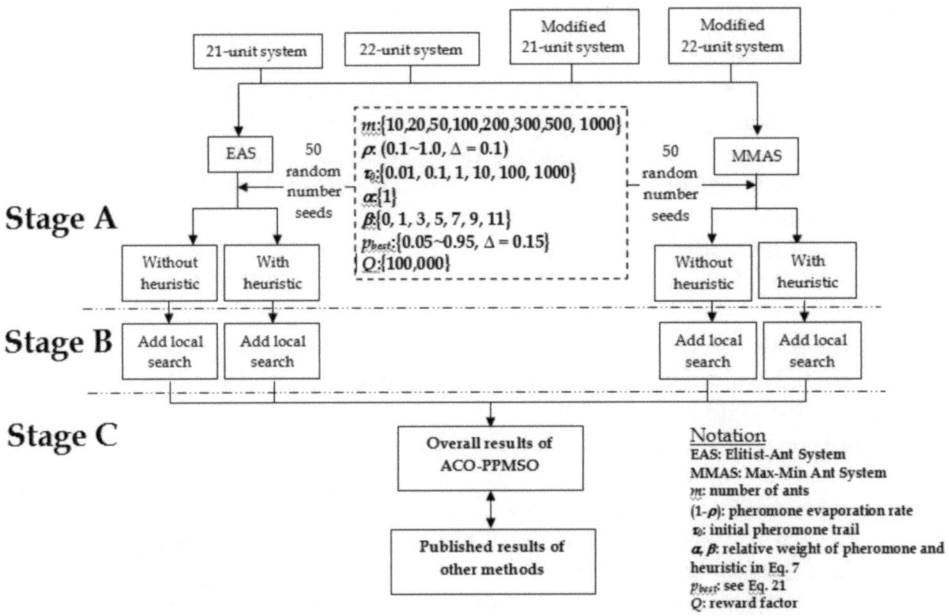

Figure 3. Expermental procedure

5.2 Results and analysis

The experimental results obtained for the original 21- and 22-unit case studies are summarized in Tables 4 to 7, while those for the modified case studies are presented in Tables 8 to 11.

Heu-ristic	Local search	Best OFC ($M)	Average OFC ($M)	Worst OFC ($M)	Std dev. ($M)	Average evaluations[a]	Best parameter settings {m; ρ; τ_0; β}[b]
✗	✗	14.84 [8.64%]	140.49 [928.48%]	365.13 [2572.99%]	86.00	28,841	{300; 0.9; 0.01; 0}
✓	✗	13.68 [0.15%]	13.71 [0.37%]	13.85 [1.39%]	0.03	20,692	{200; 0.9; 0.01; 9}
✗	✓	13.74 [0.59%]	51.62 [277.89%]	138.80 [916.11%]	33.72	25,494	{300; 0.8; 0.1; 0}
✓	✓	13.66 [0%]	13.70 [0.29%]	13.82 [1.17%]	0.03	22,434	{200; 0.9; 0.01; 9}

[a] Number of evaluations to reach the best solution in one run averaged over 50 runs with different random starting positions.

[b] m: number of ants; $(1-\rho)$: pheromone evaporation rate; τ_0: initial pheromone trail; β: relative weight of heuristic in Eq. 7

Table 4. Results for the 21-unit unit problem instance given by Elitist-Ant System (EAS) [deviation from best-known OFC of $13.66M]

Heu-ristic	Local search	Best OFC ($M)	Average OFC ($M)	Worst OFC ($M)	Std dev. ($M)	Average evaluations[c]	Best parameter settings {m; ρ; p_{best}; β}[d]
✗	✗	13.86 [1.46%]	16.11 [17.94%]	43.35 [217.35%]	5.95	16,480	{10; 0.3; 0.2; 0}
✓	✗	13.66 [0%]	13.68 [0.15%]	13.72 [0.44%]	0.01	13,593	{20; 0.4; 0.35; 5}
✗	✓	13.80 [1.02%]	17.90 [31.04%]	69.04 [405.42%]	10.51	18,089	{50; 0.2; 0.05; 0}
✓	✓	13.66 [0%]	13.69 [0.22%]	13.78 [0.88%]	0.02	15,867	{50; 0.5; 0.5; 11}

[a] Number of evaluations to reach the best solution in one run averaged over 50 runs with different random starting positions.

[d] m: number of ants; $(1-\rho)$: pheromone evaporation rate; p_{best}: refer to Eq. 21; β: relative weight of heuristic in Eq. 7.

Table 5. Results for the 21-unit unit problem instance given by Max-Min Ant System (MMAS) [deviation from best-known OFC of $13.66M]

Heur-istic	Local search	Best OFC ($M)	Average OFC ($M)	Worst OFC ($M)	Std dev. ($M)	Average evaluations[a]	Best parameter settings {m; ρ; τ_0; β}[b]
✗	✗	63.41 [21.80%]	72.27 [38.82%]	81.15 [55.88%]	4.17	29,294	{200; 0.9; 100; 0}
✓	✗	58.41 [12.20%]	64.31 [23.53%]	73.25 [40.70%]	3.21	28,384	{300; 0.9; 1; 11}
✗	✓	58.91 [13.16%]	67.03 [28.76%]	79.99 [53.65%]	4.70	25,858	{300; 0.8; 1; 0}
✓	✓	55.67 [6.93%]	60.55 [16.31%]	67.97 [30.56%]	2.90	26,931	{300; 0.8; 10; 11}

[a] Number of evaluations to reach the best solution in one run averaged over 50 runs with different random starting positions.

[b] m: number of ants; $(1-\rho)$: pheromone evaporation rate; τ_0: initial pheromone trail; β: relative weight of heuristic in Eq. 7.

Table 6. Results for the 22-unit unit problem instance given by Elitist-Ant System (EAS) [deviation from best-known OFC of $52.06]

Heur-istic	Local search	Best OFC ($M)	Average OFC ($M)	Worst OFC ($M)	Std dev. ($M)	Average evaluations	Best parameter settings {m; ρ; p_{best}; β}[d]
✗	✗	59.91 [15.08%]	66.90 [28.51%]	76.17 [46.31%]	3.67	24,597	{100; 0.9; 0.5; 0}
✓	✗	55.72 [7.03%]	62.22 [19.52%]	68.65 [31.87%]	2.97	28,433	{200; 0.9; 0.2; 11}
✗	✓	57.64 [10.72%]	64.81 [24.49%]	76.65 [47.23%]	4.27	27,455	{200; 0.8; 0.5; 0}
✓	✓	54.56 [4.80%]	59.42 [14.14%]	66.56 [27.85%]	2.87	24,537	{200; 0.8; 0.35; 11}

[a] Number of evaluations to reach the best solution in one run averaged over 50 runs with different random starting positions.

[d] m: number of ants; $(1-\rho)$: pheromone evaporation rate; p_{best}: refer to Eq. 21; β: relative weight of heuristic in Eq. 7.

Table 7. Results for the 22-unit unit problem instance given by Max-Min Ant System (MMAS) [deviation from best-known OFC of $52.06M]

Heu-ristic	Local search	Best OFC ($M)	Average OFC ($M)	Worst OFC ($M)	Std dev. ($M)	Average *DurCut*$_{tot}$ (wks)	Average evaluations[a]	Best parameter settings {*m*; ρ; τ_0; β}[b]
✗	✗	65.61 [317.63%]	120.39 [666.33%]	209.05 [1230.68%]	39.16	17.6	27,538	{300; 0.9; 0.01; 0}
✓	✗	16.15 [2.80%]	24.42 [55.44%]	31.06 [97.71%]	5.16	6.4	29,029	{500; 0.9; 0.01; 1}
✗	✓	68.42 [335.52%]	135.13 [760.15%]	219.07 [1294.46%]	36.67	19.3	28,784	{300; 0.9; 0.01; 0}
✓	✓	16.12 [2.61%]	26.87 [71.04%]	41.24 [162.51%]	5.17	6.9	28,213	{500; 0.9; 0.01; 1}

[a] Number of evaluations to reach the best solution in one run averaged over 50 runs with different random starting positions.
[b] *m*: number of ants; (1- *ρ*): pheromone evaporation rate; τ_0: initial pheromone trail; *β*: relative weight of heuristic in Eq. 7.

Table 8. Results for the Modified 21-unit unit problem instance given by Elitist-Ant System (EAS) [deviation from best-known OFC of $15.71M]

Heu-ristic	Local search	Best *OFC* ($M)	Average OFC ($M)	Worst OFC ($M)	Std dev. ($M)	Average *DurCut*$_{tot}$ (wks)	Average evaluations[c]	Best parameter settings {*m*; ρ; p_{best}; β}[d]
✗	✗	28.69 [82.62%]	61.32 [290.32%]	119.15 [658.43%]	19.54	11.8	16,934	{20; 0.2; 0.2; 0}
✓	✗	15.97 [1.65%]	19.69 [25.33%]	29.03 [84.79%]	4.02	5.6	18,551	{50; 0.2; 0.05; 1}
✗	✓	33.64 [114.13%]	71.67 [356.21%]	132.10 [740.87%]	24.64	12.6	24,898	{500; 0.1; 0.05; 0}
✓	✓	15.71 [0%]	22.04 [40.29%]	29.66 [88.80%]	4.86	6.1	23,713	{500; 0.7; 0.05; 1}

[a] Number of evaluations to reach the best solution in one run averaged over 50 runs with different random starting positions.
[d] *m*: number of ants; (1- *ρ*): pheromone evaporation rate; p_{best}: refer to Eq. 21; *β*: relative weight of heuristic in Eq. 7.

Table 9. Results for the Modified 21-unit problem instance given by Max-Min Ant System (MMAS) [deviation from best-known OFC of $15.71M]

Heu-ristic	Local search	Best OFC ($)	Average OFC ($)	Worst OFC ($)	Std dev. ($)	Average *DurCut*$_{tot}$ (wks)	Average evaluations[a]	Best parameter settings {*m*; ρ; τ_0; β}[b]
✗	✗	2186.22 [138.64%]	2797.85 [205.40%]	4267.31 [365.80%]	410.33	21.9	27,896	{300; 0.9; 0.01; 0}
		1365.60 [49.06%]	1756.34 [91.72%]	2153.97 [135.12%]	175.55	13.8	28,648	{500; 0.9; 0.01; 11}
✗	✓	2331.92 [154.54%]	2876.16 [213.95%]	4357.14 [375.61%]	501.14	23.2	26,187	{300; 0.9; 0.01; 0}
✓	✓	1174.10 [28.16%]	1724.37 [88.23%]	2238.34 [144.33%]	172.63	13.7	21,718	{300; 0.9; 0.01; 11}

[a] Number of evaluations to reach the best solution in one run averaged over 50 runs with different random starting positions.
[b] *m*: number of ants; (1- *ρ*): pheromone evaporation rate; τ_0: initial pheromone trail; *β*: relative weight of heuristic in Eq. 7.

Table 10. Results for the Modified 22-unit unit problem instance given by Elitist-Ant System (EAS) [deviation from best-known OFC of $916.12]

Heu-ristic	Local search	Best *OFC* ($)	Average *OFC* ($)	Worst *OFC* ($)	Std dev. ($)	Average $DurCut_{tot}$ (wks)	Average evaluations	Best parameter settings $\{m; \rho; p_{best}; \beta\}$[d]
✗	✗	1439.33 [57.11%]	2076.43 [126.65%]	3998.67 [336.78%]	440.16	15.6	26,219	{300; 0.6; 0.2; 0}
✓	✗	1008.13 [10.04%]	1489.54 [62.59%]	2017.44 [120.22%]	280.45	12.1	23,329	{20; 0.3; 0.35; 11}
✗	✓	1614.39 [76.22%]	2068.8 [125.82%]	3936.71 [329.72%]	425.87	15.0	20,767	{20; 0.3; 0.2; 0}
✓	✓	1001.12 [9.28%]	1513.86 [65.25%]	2084.59 [127.55%]	306.26	12.4	21,347	{50; 0.1; 0.35; 11}

[a] Number of evaluations to reach the best solution in one run averaged over 50 runs with different random starting positions.
[d] m: number of ants; (1- ρ): pheromone evaporation rate; p_{best}: refer to Eq. 21; β: relative weight of heuristic in Eq. 7.

Table 11. Results for the Modified 22-unit unit problem instance given by Max-Min Ant System (MMAS) [deviation from best-known OFC of $916.12]

Stage A: Impact of heuristic

Overall, the new heuristic formulation for applying ACO to PPMSO problems significantly improved the results obtained for all four case studies, with and without the use of a local search operator and for both ACO algorithms (using a Student's *t*-test at a 95% significance level). It can be seen that when the heuristic was used, not only were the average OFCs improved, but the standard deviations of the OFCs were also significantly smaller for all case studies (Tables 4 to 11), indicating that use of the new heuristic formulation enables good solutions to be found consistently.

In order to gain a better understanding of the searching behavior of the ACO algorithms in solving each of the four case studies with and without heuristic, the optimisation process of the ACO runs was examined. The investigation is facilitated by utilizing the following terms to describe a given ACO-PPMSO run:

- Objective function values (SSR, LVL and $DurCut_{tot}$) associated with iteration-best schedules (referred to as IB-SSR, IB-LVL and IB-$DurCut_{tot}$ hereafter)
- Violation of various constraints (demand and personpower shortfall) associated with iteration-best schedules (referred to as IB-$LoadVio_{tot}$, IB-$ManVio_{tot}$ and IB-$LoadResVio_{tot}$ hereafter)

The optimization process of only one ACO-PPMSO run for the modified 21-unit case system is used for discussion purposes (Fig. 4). Figs. 4a and 4b compare the behaviour of the ACO-PPMSO in solving the case system with and without heuristic. Overall, the ACO-PPMSO algorithm is found to explore the problem search space effectively by minimizing the objective function values (SSR, LVL and $DurCut_{tot}$) for the four case studies investigated. This is illustrated by the decreasing trends of the IB-SSR and IB-$DurCut_{tot}$ curves in Figs. 4a and 4b.

For all case studies, it is found that when the heuristic is used, the IB-SSR and IB-LVL obtained during the early stages of the optimisation runs were substantially lower (compare IB-SSR curves in Figs. 4a and 4b). In addition, it is observed that during the early stages of the ACO runs, fewer trial solutions that violated constraints were constructed when the heuristic was utilized (lower IB-$LoadVio_{tot}$, IB-$ManVio_{tot}$ and IB-$LoadResVio_{tot}$). It is also found that the improvement in OFCs obtained when the heuristic is used for the modified 21- and 22-unit case studies is partly attributed to a significant reduction in duration shortened. This is clearly shown in the comparison between Figs. 4a and 4b by the fact that the IB-$DurCut_{tot}$ curve is consistently lower throughout an ACO run when the heuristic formulation is used.

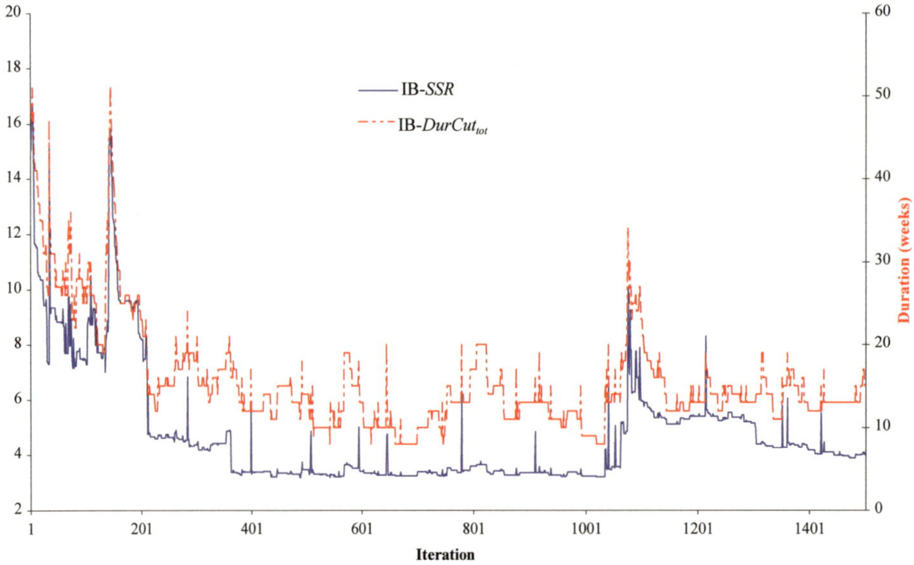

(a) Without heuristic‡

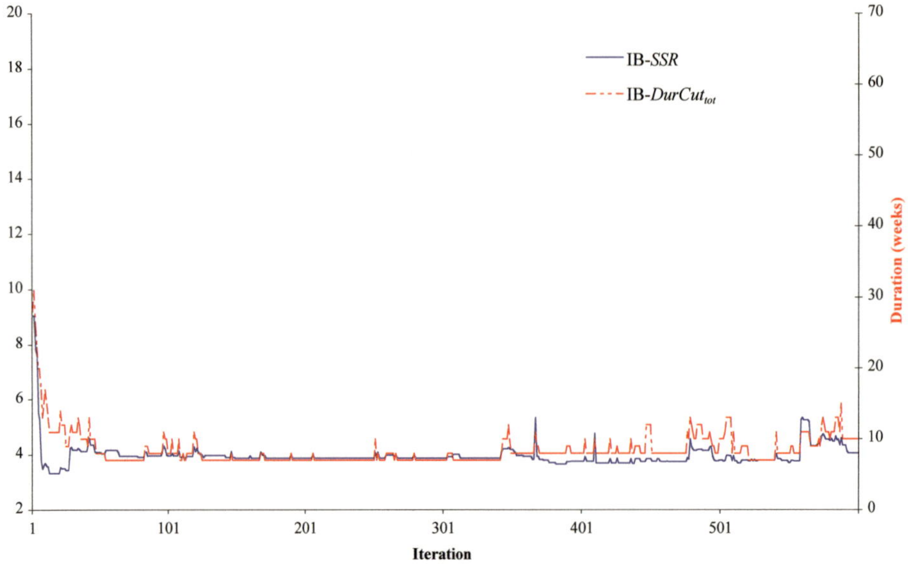

(b) With heuristic‡‡

‡ Parameter settings used shown in the first row, last column of Table 9 (random number seed = 655)
‡‡ Parameter settings used shown in the second row, last column of Table 9 (random number seed = 655)
IB-SSR: Sum of squares of reserve associated with iteration-best schedules;
IB-$DurCut_{tot}$: Total reduction in outage duration due to shortening and deferral associated with iteration-best schedules

Figure 4. Modified 21-unit case system - Comparison of the SSR- and total duration shortened values associated with iteration-best schedules during optimisation run (Best-known SSR = 2.62×10^6 MW^2 with 5-week deferral)

In view of the experimental results, the heuristic formulation is useful for ACO-PPMSO in three ways. Firstly, as the distribution of pheromone intensity within the search space of a problem is uniform at the beginning of an ACO run (assuming a single initial pheromone value is used), the optimisation process initially resembles a random search. During this period, the heuristic formulation can guide the algorithm to search in regions where feasible solutions are located with a higher probability. In this way, the number of infeasible solutions being constructed and rewarded with pheromone can be reduced. Secondly, even if a heuristic is not essential for constructing feasible/near feasible trial solutions (as is the case when the PPMSO problem is not highly constrained), the heuristic can assist with constructing trial solutions that consist of fewer overlapping tasks. In this way, the generation capacities throughout the planning horizon associated with trial maintenance schedules being constructed are more evenly distributed, which is one of the common objectives of PPMSO problems. Thirdly, when shortening and deferral options are allowed, use of the heuristic increases the probabilities that longer outage durations are chosen throughout an entire ACO run. This is particularly useful when shortening and deferral options are frequently chosen at random during the early stage of an ACO run.

In relation to the two ACO algorithms investigated (EAS and MMAS), the results obtained indicate that the heuristic has a significant positive impact on both EAS and MMAS. This is probably due to the ability of heuristic information to identify regions of the search space where high-quality initial solutions lie, reducing the number of low-quality trial solutions being reinforced at the beginning of an optimisation run. In addition, the results indicate that the ACO-PPMSO heuristic has a bigger positive impact on EAS compared to MMAS. EAS tends to stagnate after a number of iterations, which increases the impact of the quality of the initial solutions. The importance of the regions where the ants initially search using EAS is also highlighted by the relatively larger number of ants found for the best parameter settings than those for MMAS (Tables 4, 6, 8 and 10), implying that a search with more ants in each iteration (resulting in a smaller number of iterations during an optimisation run, as the total number of function evaluations is fixed) works better than one with fewer ants (resulting in a larger number of iterations during an optimisation run, as the total number of function evaluations is fixed). On the other hand, relatively smaller ant populations are found to perform best for MMAS (Tables 5, 7, 9 and 11), which might be attributed to the continuous exploration during an MMAS run (Fig. 4b) as a result of the lower and upper bound for pheromone values. It is interesting to observe that despite the expected overall downward trends throughout an optimisation run, the IB-*SSR* and IB-*LVL* curves spike occasionally throughout a run when a small population of ants is used (Fig. 4b). This phenomenon is found to be caused by the choice of non-best solutions after a short convergence (stagnation in OFC), which altered the distribution of pheromone over the problem search space. It should be noted that the possibility of having an iteration-best solution that is not the best-so-far solution is higher when a smaller population of ants is used.

B. Impact of local search

The optimisation results obtained by coupling the *PPMSO-2-opt* local search operator with the ACO algorithms investigated (Stage B of the testing procedure in Fig. 3) are tabulated in Tables 4 to 11. The unpaired Student's *t*-test was used to check the significance of the impact of the local search operator in solving the four case studies with and without heuristic (Tables 12 and 13).

Overall, the impact of the *PPMSO-2-opt* local search operator ranges from being insignificant, to significantly improving or degrading the performance of the ACO algorithm investigated. While having a positive impact on solving the original 22-unit case study, regardless of which of the two ACO algorithms was used, the *PPMSO-2-opt* local search operator was found to improve only the performance of EAS when the heuristic was not used for solving the original 21-unit case study. As for the modified case studies, the performance of ACO in solving the modified 21-unit case study was reduced significantly when the *PPMSO-2-opt* local search operator was adopted, while the impact of the local search was not significant when applied to the modified 22-unit case study.

	21-unit system		*22-unit system*		*Modified 21-unit system*		*Modified 22-unit system*	
Heuristic	**EAS**	**MMAS**	**EAS**	**MMAS**	**EAS**	**MMAS**	**EAS**	**MMAS**
✗	+	NIL	+	+	–	–	NIL	NIL
✓	NIL	NIL	+	+	–	–	NIL	NIL

Notation:
+: Significant positive impact; –: Significant negative impact; NIL: Insignificant impact.

Table 12. Impact of *PPMSO-2-opt* local search operator with and without heuristic

From the results of the Stage B testing, it is interesting to observe that despite the similarity in the number of generating units for the 21- and 22-unit case study systems, the impact of the *PPMSO-2-opt* local search algorithm on the optimisation results of these case studies was quite different, which is likely to be caused by the difference in the problem characteristics of the two systems.
In order to better understand the results obtained, a series of tests were conducted to investigate the mechanism of *PPMSO-2-opt* in detail. The satisfaction of constraints associated with iteration-best solutions (target solutions) used for the local search operation and the % of infeasible local solutions generated when using MMAS were examined. It should be noted that the results were obtained using the proposed heuristic formulation.

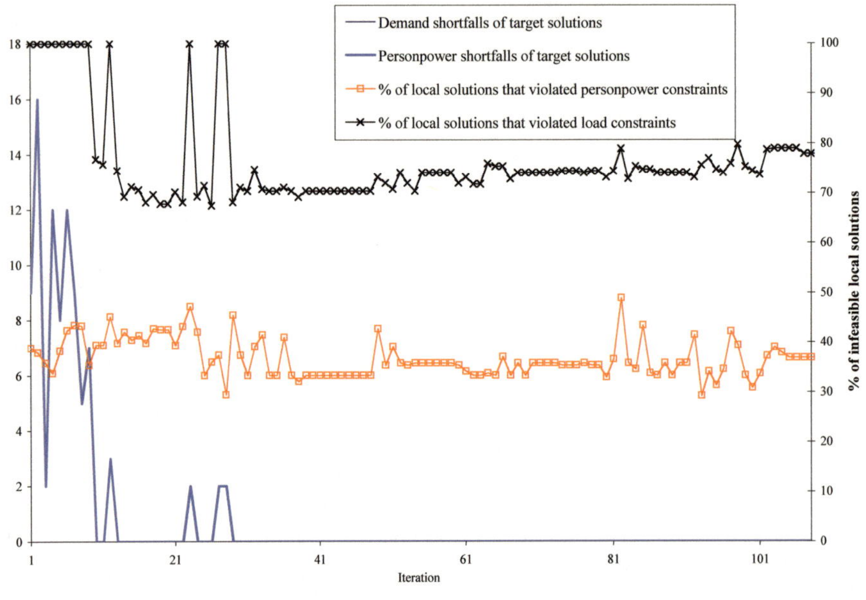

Figure 5. Infeasible local solutions obtained using *PPMSO-2-opt* (original 21-unit case study using MMAS)

It can be seen that for the original 21-unit case study (Fig. 5), a large number of infeasible local solutions were generated by *PPMSO-2-opt* in every iteration, even with feasible iteration-best solutions (target maintenance schedules). A local solution generated by simply exchanging the maintenance start time of two randomly chosen generating units without any guidelines is likely to result in infeasible solutions in such a highly constrained search space. As a result, *PPMSO-2-opt* seems to have an insignificant or even detrimental impact when coupled with ACO for solving the aforementioned case studies. This is particularly evident for the modified 21-unit case study, where as many as 50% to 80% of the local solutions generated by *PPMSO-2-opt* in every iteration are infeasible with regard to both load and personpower constraints, which is responsible for the significant decrease in ACO performance. These results suggest that the *PPMSO-2-opt* local search operator is not well suited to problems with highly constrained search spaces.

On the other hand, the local solutions generated by *PPMSO-2-opt* in solving the original 22-unit case study are all feasible, as the iteration-best solutions are also feasible. In fact, this is the only case study for which *PPMSO-2-opt* is found to be effective in improving the optimisation ability of ACO. Compared to the other three case systems, the original 22-unit case system is less constrained. Therefore, the results obtained indicate that *PPMSO-2-opt* can be useful for solving problems that are not highly constrained.

C. Overall performance of ACO-PPMSO

<u>Original 21-unit and 22-unit case studies</u>

By using the ACO-PPMSO algorithm, a new best-known objective value has been found for both the original 21-unit case study (SSR = 13.66 x 10^6 MW^2) and the original 22-unit case study (LVL = 52.06 MW).

A comparison of the results obtained by ACO-PPMSO with those obtained by various metaheuristics in other studies for the 21-unit case study, including those by Aldridge *et al.* (1999), who used a simple genetic algorithm (GA), a generational GA (GNGA) and a steady state GA (SSGA), and Dahal *et al.* (2000), who applied Simulated Annealing (SA) and an Inoculated GA to this problem, is shown in Fig. 6. As mentioned previously, the number of evaluations (trial solutions) allowed in the ACO runs and those of the other metaheuristics was identical. In particular, the best and average results of the metaheuristics were compared. While the best and average results given by the simple GA, SSGA, GNGA, inoculated GA and SA were obtained by 10 runs with different starting positions (Aldridge *et al.*, 1999; Dahal *et al.*, 1999; Dahal *et al.*, 2000), those of EAS and MMAS were obtained using 50 runs.

It can be seen that the EAS and MMAS algorithms have outperformed the algorithms that have been applied to this case study previously. It should be noted that a new best-found solution (SSR = 13.66 x 10^6 MW^2) for the 21-unit case study has been found by EAS and MMAS using the new ACO-PPMSO formulation. In addition, it can be seen that the differences between the average and best results of the ACO algorithms are much smaller than those for other metaheuristics (Fig. 6), which indicates a consistent performance of the ACO-PPMSO formulation.

Among the metaheuristics previously used for solving the 21-unit case study, the inoculated GA, where the initial population is generated using a heuristic that ranks the generating units in order of decreasing capacity, was found to perform best in terms of the average results obtained. This highlights the potential benefit of a heuristic in solving PPMSO problems.

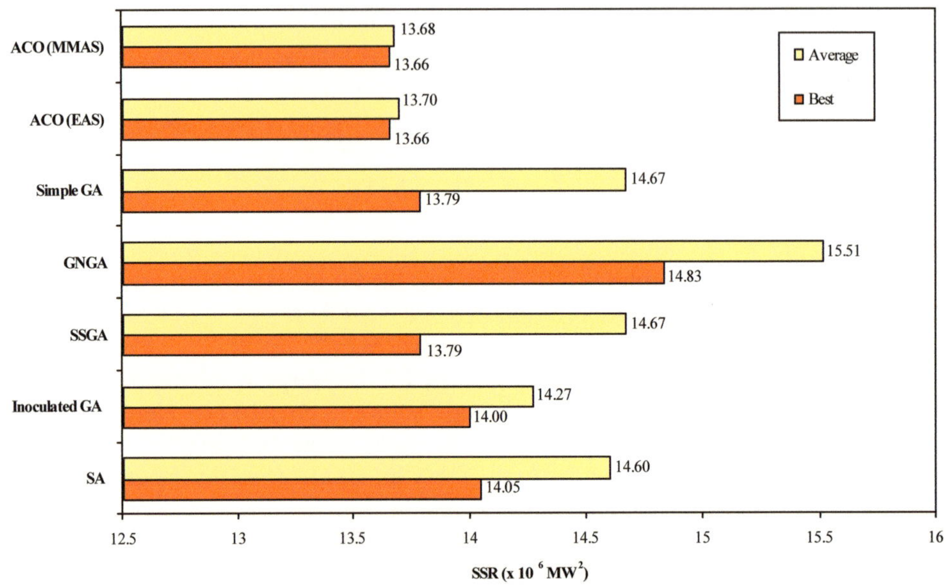

Figure 6. Comparison between results obtained using other optimisation methods (Aldridge *et al.*, 1999; Dahal *et al.*, 1999; Dahal *et al.*, 2000) and the ACO algorithms

As mentioned previously, a new best-found solution (SSR = 13.66 x 10^6 MW^2) has been found by the ACO-PPMSO formulation proposed in this chapter. An examination of the solutions obtained for the 21-unit case study found that different maintenance schedules are associated with the new best-found SSR solution. In other words, there is more than one optimal solution in the problem search space.

In Fig. 7, the reserve level across the planning horizon associated with the best-known schedule found by ACO-PPMSO for the original 22-unit case study is compared with those obtained by implicit enumeration (Escudero *et al.*, 1980) and tabu search (El-Amin *et al.*, 2000). It can be seen that the reserve level given by the ACO schedule is more evenly spread out (summed deviation of generation reserve from the average reserve, LVL = 52.06 MW) than those obtained with implicit enumeration (LVL = 118.81 MW) and tabu search (LVL = 256.93 MW). It should be noted that due to insufficient information about the optimum solution in El-Amin *et al.* (2000), the LVL value of tabu search shown in Fig. 7 was calculated using the best available published information.

Modified 21-unit and 22-unit case studies

As the modified versions of the 21- and 22-unit case studies have been introduced in this chapter to test the developed ACO-PPMSO formulation, there are no previous results available for comparison purposes. As can be seen in Tables 7 to 10, the optimized maintenance schedules of both the modified 21- and 22-unit case studies include the shortening and/or deferral of maintenance tasks (average duration shortened/deferred > 0). The best-found objective function costs (OFCs) found for the modified 21-unit case study is $15.71M and $916.12 for the modified 22-unit case study. In the maintenance schedules associated with the best-found OFC for the modified 21-unit case study, the maintenance tasks for generating units 11 and 21 are deferred, while all other tasks are carried out as normal. For the modified 22-unit case study, maintenance tasks for generating units 10, 16

and 17 are shortened by 2, 4 and 2 weeks, respectively. It should be noted that all constraints are satisfied by the best-found schedules.
The results for the modified versions of the 21-unit and 22-unit case studies indicate that the ACO-PPMSO formulation introduced in this chapter is able to identify maintenance schedules that satisfy hard system constraints (eg. system demands) by shortening and deferring maintenance tasks. More importantly, the shortening and deferral options were only used if necessary, as only a few, but not all, maintenance tasks were shortened/deferred.

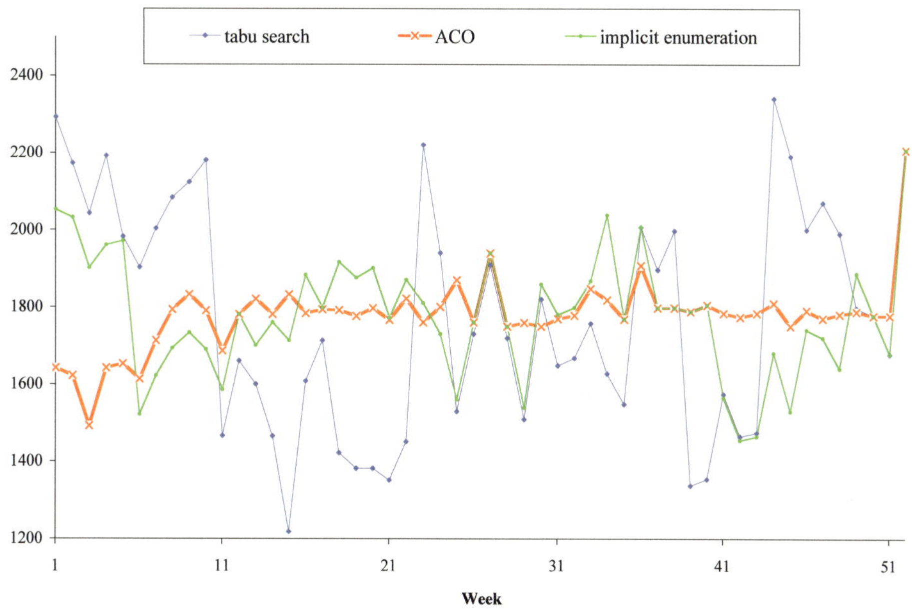

Figure 7. Comparison of reserve levels obtained using ACO, implicit enumeration (Escudero *et al.*, 1980) and tabu search (El-Amin *et al.*, 2000)

5. Summary and Conclusions

In this chapter, a formulation for applying Ant Colony Optimization (ACO) to power plant maintenance scheduling optimization (PPMSO) has been developed and successfully tested using four case studies (original and modified versions of two benchmark case studies from the literature). In particular, the performance of the heuristic formulation developed, the two local search algorithms introduced and the overall utility of the ACO-PPMSO formulation were investigated. The results obtained have shown that the heuristic formulation improves the performance of the ACO-PPMSO algorithm significantly when applied to the four case studies investigated. It was found that while the *PPMSO-2-opt* local search operator seems to work well for unconstrained problems, it is not suitable for highly-constrained PPMSO problems. Lastly, the results obtained by ACO-PPMSO for the two original case studies were better than those obtained by other optimisation methods, such as various genetic algorithm (GAs) formulations and simulated annealing (SA). For the 21-unit and 22-unit case studies, a new optimal solution has been found by the ACO-PPMSO formulation. In addition, the results given by ACO-PPMSO were more consistent compared with those obtained using other metaheuristics previously applied to the two benchmark case studies. The maintenance schedules found for the modified case studies have also been examined and it was found that the ACO-PPMSO formulation is able to meet hard system constraints by shortening and deferring maintenance. The results of experiments carried out using the original and modified versions of the 21-unit and 22-unit case studies indicate that the ACO-PPMSO formulation presented in this chapter has potential for solving real-world PPMSO problems.

6. References

Ahmad, A. and D. P. Kothari (2000). A practical model for generator maintenance scheduling with transmission constraints. *Electric Machines and Power Systems* 28: 501-513.

Aldridge, C. J., K. P. Dahal and J. R. McDonald (1999). Genetic algorithms for scheduling generation and maintenance in power systems. *Modern Optimisation Techniques in Power Systems*. Y.-H. Song. Dordrecht ; Boston, Kluwer Academic Publishers: 63-89.

Bauer, A., B. Bullnheimer, R. F. Hartl and C. Strauss (1999). An ant colony optimization approach for the single machine total tardiness problem. *Congr. Evolutionary Computation*.

Coello Coello, C. A. (2002). Theoretical and numerical constraint-handling techniques used with evolutionary algorithms: a survey of the state of the art. *Comput. Methods Appl. Mech. Engrg*(191): 1245-1287.

Colorni, A., M. Dorigo, V. Maniezzo and M. Trubian (1994). Ant system for job-shop scheduling. *Belg. J. oper. Res. Stat. Comp. Sci.* 34(1): 39-53.

Dahal, K. P., C. J. Aldridge and J. R. McDonald (1999). Generator Maintenance Scheduling Using A Genetic Algorithm With A Fuzzy Evaluation Function. *Fuzzy Sets and Systems* 102: 21-29.

Dahal, K. P., J. R. McDonald and G. M. Burt (2000). Modern Heuristic Techniques For Scheduling Generator Maintenance In Power Systems. *Transactions of the Institute of Measurement and Control* 22(2): 179-194.

den Besten, M., T. Stützle and M. Dorigo (2000). Ant Colony Optimization for the total weighted tardiness problem. *Proceedings of Parallel Problem Solving from Nature (PPSN-VI)*, Springer Verlag.

Dopazo, J. F. and H. M. Merrill (1975). Optimal Generator Maintenance Scheduling Using Integer Programming. *IEEE Transactions on Power Apparatus and Systems* PAS-94(5): 1537-1545.

Dorigo, M. (1992). Optimization, Learning and Natural Algorithms. Dipartimento di Elettronica. Italy, Politechnico di Milano: 140.

Dorigo, M. and L. M. Gambardella (1997a). Ant colonies for the travelling salesman problem. *BioSystems* 43: 73-81.

Dorigo, M. and L. M. Gambardella (1997b). Ant Colony System: A cooperative learning approach to the traveling salesman problem. *IEEE Transactions on Evolutionary Computation* 1: 53-66.

Dorigo, M., V. Maniezzo and A. Colorni (1996). Ant system: optimization by a colony of cooperating ants. *IEEE Transactions on Systems, Man, and Cybernetics. Part B, Cybernetics* 26: 29-42.

Dorigo, M. and T. Stützle (2004). *Ant Colony Optimization*. Cambridge, MA, MIT Press.

El-Amin, I., S. Duffuaa and M. Abbas (2000). A tabu search algorithm for maintenance scheduling of generating units. *Electric Power Systems Research* 54: 91-99.

Endrenyi, J., S. Aboresheid, R. N. Allan, G. J. Anders, S. Asgarpoor, R. Billinton, N. Chowdhury, E. N. Dialynas, M. Fipper, R. H. Fletcher, C. Grigg, J. McCalley, S. Meliopoulos, T. C. Mielnik, P. Nitu, N. Rau, N. D. Reppen, L. Salvaderi, A. Schneider and C. Singh (2001). The Present Status of Maintenance Strategies and the Impact of Maintenance on Reliability. *IEEE Transactions on Power Systems* 16(4): 636-646.

Escudero, L. F., J. W. Horton and J. E. Scheiderich (1980). On maintenance scheduling for energy generators. *IEEE Winter Power Meeting*, New York.

Foong, W. K., H. R. Maier and A. R. Simpson (2005). Ant Colony Optimization (ACO) for Power Plant Maintenance Scheduling Optimization (PPMSO). *GECCO 2005: Proceedings of the Genetic and Evolutionary Computation Conference*, Washington D.C., USA.

Foong, W. K., H. R. Maier and A. R. Simpson (2008). Ant colony optimisation for power plant maintenance scheduling - An improved formulation. *Engineering Optimization*, In Press, 1st quarter, 2008.

Foong, W. K., A. R. Simpson and H. R. Maier (Accepted for publication). Ant colony optimisation for power plant maintenance scheduling - A five-station hydropower system. *Annals of Operations Research.*

Gomez, J. F., H. A. Khodr, P. A. De Oliveira, L. Ocque, J. A. Yusta, R. Villasana and A. J. Urdaneta (2004). Ant colony system algorithm for the planning of primary distribution circuits. *IEEE Transactions on Power Systems* 19(2): 996-1004.

Huang, S. J. (2001). Enhancement of hydroelectric generation scheduling using Ant Colony System based optimization approaches. *IEEE Transactions on Energy Conversion* 16(3): 296-301.

Kannan, S., S. M. R. Slochanal and N. P. Padhy (2005). Application and comparison of metaheuristic techniques to generation expansion planning problem. *IEEE Transactions on Power Systems* 20(1): 466-475.

Lin, C. E., C. J. Huang, C. L. Huang, C. C. Liang and S. Y. Lee (1992). An Expert System for Generator Maintenance Scheduling Using Operation Index. *IEEE Transactions on Power Systems* 7(3): 1141-1148.

Maier, H. R., A. R. Simpson, A. Zecchin, C., W. K. Foong, K. Y. Phang, H. Y. Seah and C. L. Tan (2003). Ant colony optimisation for Design of Water Distribution Systems. *Journal of Water Resources Planning and Management* 129(3): 200-209.

Merkle, D., M. Middendorf and H. Schmeck (2002). Ant colony optimisation for Resource-Constrained Project Scheduling. *IEEE Transactions on Evolutionary Computation* 6(4): 333-346.

Satoh, T. and K. Nara (1991). Maintenance Scheduling By Using Simulated Annealing Method. *IEEE Transactions on Power Systems* 6(2): 850-857.

Stützle, T. (1998). An ant approach for the flow shop problem. *Proc. 6th Eur. Congr. Intelligent Techniques and Soft Computing*, Aachen, Germany.

Stützle, T. and H. Hoos (1997). Improvements on the Ant System: Introducing MAX-MIN Ant System. *Proc. Int. Conf. Artificial Neural Networks and Genetic Algorithms*, Springer Verlag, Wien.

Stützle, T. and H. H. Hoos (2000). MAX-MIN Ant System. *Future Generation Computer Systems* 16: 889-914.

Su, C. T., C. T. Chang and J. P. Chiou (2005). Optimal capacitor placement in distribution systems employing ant colony search algorithm. *Electric Power Components and Systems* 33(8).

Yamayee, Z., K. Sidenblad and M. Yoshimura (1983). A computational efficient optimal maintenance scheduling method. *IEEE Transactions on Power Apparatus and Systems* PAS-102(2): 330-338.

Particle Swarm Optimization for Simultaneous Optimization of Design and Machining Tolerances

Liang Gao, Chi Zhou and Kun Zan
Department of Industrial & Manufacturing System Engineering,
Huazhong Univ. of Sci. & Tech.
China

1. Introduction

Tolerance assignment in product design and process planning (machining) affects both the quality and the cost of the overall product cycle. It is a crucial issue to determine how much the tolerance should be relaxed during the assignment process, since a tight tolerance implies a high manufacturing cost and a loose tolerance results in low manufacturing cost. Hence, during tolerance assignment, a balance between a reduction in quality loss and a reduction in manufacturing cost must be considered. Traditionally, in the two stages (product design and process planning) tolerances (Ngoi & Teck, 1997) are often conducted separately. This is probably due to the fact that they deal with different type of tolerances. Product design is concerned with related component tolerances, whereas process designing focus on the process tolerance according to the process specification. However, this separated approach in tolerance design always suffers from several drawbacks. First of all, it is difficult to obtain optimal design tolerance because the designer can not determine the exact manufacturing cost without the specified manufacturing information. Therefore, the manufacturing engineer must frequently communicate with the designer to adjust the design tolerances and obtain the appropriate process planning. However, this task is time-consuming and painstaking. In addition, design tolerances are further distributed for machining tolerances. Nevertheless, the machining tolerances commonly can not occupy the design tolerances space. Thus the final tolerance distribution is suboptimal and accordingly, the actual cost will be inevitably higher than the desired cost. Moreover, due to the specified procedure, the manufacturing engineer is not informed the design details and does not have the overview of the whole product.

To overcome the above drawbacks, we need to develop a simultaneous tolerance design. Zhang (Zhang, 1996) presented the concept of simultaneous tolerance, proposed a general mathematical model for tolerance optimization in concurrent engineering context, and then introduced a new concept of interim tolerances that help determine appropriate manufacturing processes. Singh (Singh et al., 2003) utilized genetic algorithms and penalty function approach to solve the problem of simultaneous selection of design and manufacturing tolerances based on the minimization of the total manufacturing cost. Gao and Huang (Gao & Huang, 2003) utilized a nonlinear programming model for optimal process tolerance simultaneously based on the objective of total manufacturing cost with different weighting factors. (Huang et al., 2006) proposed a robust optimum tolerance design method in a concurrent environment to balance the conflict design targets between manufacturing tolerances and product satisfaction. A nonlinear optimal model was also established to minimize the summation of manufacturing costs and product quality loss.

Doubtlessly, the tremendous achievement has been obtained in the simultaneous tolerance optimization in the concurrent engineering context. However, this problem is characterized by nonlinear objective, multiple independent variables, and tight constraints which will turn the search space into a noisy solution surface. Even worse, most of the real world problems become more and more complex with the higher requirement of accuracy and the critical function of product. Traditional operational research algorithms are successful in locating the optimal solution, but they are usually problem dependent and lack of generality. Some modern heuristic methods are relatively more robust and flexible to solve these complex problems, but they may risk being trapped to a local optimum and are usually slow in convergence and require heavy computational cost. In view of the above problems and the past successful applications of PSO in nonlinear optimization, maybe PSO is a potential remedy to these drawbacks.

PSO is a novel population based heuristic, which utilizes the swarm intelligence generated by the cooperation and competition between the particles in a swarm (Kennedy & Eberhart, 1995, Shi & Eberhart, 1998). Compared with evolutionary algorithms (genetic algorithm, evolutionary programming, evolutionary strategy, and genetic programming), PSO still maintains the population based global search strategy but adopts the velocity-displacement model with more efficient information flow and easier implementing procedures. It has been used successfully to address problems such as complex nonlinear function optimization (Shi & Eberhart, 1999), task assignment (Salman & Ahmad, 2002) and optimum design of PID controller (Gaing, 2004). (Noorul et al., 2006) utilized PSO to achieve the multiple objective of minimum quality loss function and manufacturing cost for the machining tolerance allocation of the over running clutch assembly. The presented method outperforms other methods such as GP and GA, but it considered only two dimensional tolerance allocation of clutch assembly consisting of three components. Besides, the constraints are too loose and can not satisfy the practical requirement. This paper attempts to solve more complex tolerance assignment problems by PSO with a sophisticated constraints handling strategy.

This paper is organized as follows. In section 2, the problem of simultaneous design was described. The basic PSO algorithm was reviewed and the new sophisticated constraints handling strategy corresponding to PSO was presented in Section 3. Section 4 gave an example and the evaluation of the proposed technique is carried out on the example. Some conclusions and further discussion are offered in Section 5.

2. Simultaneous design

As mentioned before, design processes are commonly divided into two main stages: product design and process design. Dimensional tolerance analysis is very important in both product and process design. In product design stage, the functional and assembly tolerances should be appropriately distributed among the constituent dimensions, this kind of tolerances are called design tolerances. In the meantime, each design tolerance for the single dimension should be subsequently refined to satisfy the requirement for process plans in machining a part. Such tolerances for the specified machining operation are called manufacturing tolerance. However, the traditional process of design and machining tolerance allocations based on experiences can not guarantee optimum tolerance for minimum production cost. This work aimed at selecting the optimal tolerances sequences to achieve the minimum manufacturing cost considering the two types of tolerances simultaneously by a powerful global optimization tool. This problem is formulated as follows.

2.1 Objective Function

We take the manufacturing cost as the objective function. Generally, the processing of mechanical product is conducted in a series of process plans. Different process consumes different expense because different process is associated with different machining methods. Therefore, the cost of manufacture of the product is the summation of all operation cost. The machining operation can be modeled with many mathematical models for the cost-tolerance relationship. In this work, a modified form of the exponential cost (Singh et al., 2003) function will be adopted. The manufacturing cost of the machining tolerance is formulated as equation (1).

$$c_{ij}(\delta_{ij}) = a_0 e^{-a_1(\delta - a_2)} + a_3 \quad i = 1, \cdots, n \tag{1}$$

The total manufacturing cost of a product will be C, where:

$$C = \sum_{i=1}^{n} \sum_{j=1}^{m_i} c_{ij} \tag{2}$$

Where $c_{ij}(\delta_{ij})$ and δ_{ij} is the manufacturing cost and the tolerance of the jth manufacturing operation associated with the ith dimension respectively. n is the number of the dimensions and m_i is number of operations corresponding to dimension i. The constants a_0, a_1, a_2, a_3 sever as control parameters.

2.2 Constraints

Apart from the constraint of economical manufacturing ranges (process limits), the above objective is subjected to both the design and manufacturing tolerances.

(1) The design tolerances are those on the principal design dimensions (usually assembly dimensions) that relate to the functionality of the components. The principal design usually in turn relies on the other related dimensions which form a dimension chain. This results in a set of constraints on the principal design tolerances that should be suit for the optimal solution of the tolerance assignment. The aim of these constraints is to guarantee that the synthesized tolerance in the dimension chain does not exceed the desired tolerance of the principal dimension. There are many approaches available to formulate the synthesized tolerance. They are different tradeoff between the tolerances and the manufacturing cost. Four commonly used approaches (Singh et al., 2003) were adopted in this work.

(2) Manufacturing tolerances constraints are equivalent to stock allowance constraints. Stock allowance is associated with the stock removal, the layer to be removed from the surface in the machining process. Due to the tolerances of the dimensions, the stock removal is also not

fixed. This gives rise to another kind of tolerances, manufacturing tolerances, which can be formulated as follows:

$$\delta_{ij} + \delta_{i(j-1)} \leq \Delta A_{ij} \tag{3}$$

where δ_{ij} and $\delta_{i(j-1)}$ are the machining tolerances of process j and j-1 for part i respectively. ΔA_{ij} is the difference between the nominal and the minimum machining allowances for machining process j.

3. Particle Swarm Optimization

3.1 Background

The investigation and analysis on the biologic colony demonstrated that intelligence generated from complex activities such as cooperation and competition among individuals can provide efficient solutions for specific optimization problems (Kennedy et al., 2001). Inspired by the social behavior of animals such as fish schooling and bird flocking, Kennedy and Eberhart designed the Particle Swarm Optimization (PSO) in 1995 (Kennedy & Eberhart, 1995).

This method is a kind of evolutionary computing technology based on swarm intelligence. The basic idea of bird flocking can be depicted as follows: In a bird colony, each bird looks for its own food and in the meantime they cooperate with each other by sharing information among them. Therefore, each bird will explore next promising area by its own experience and experience from the others. Due to these attractive characteristics, i.e. memory and cooperation, PSO is widely applied in many research area and real-world engineering fields as a powerful optimization tool.

3.2 Drawbacks of Traditional Constraints Handling Strategy

Although PSO has successfully solved many research problems, the applications are mainly focused on unconstrained optimization problems. Some researchers attempt to solve the constrained problem by optimizing constrained problems indirectly using the traditional penalty function strategy.

Penalty function is an effective auxiliary tool to deal with simple constrained problems and has been the most popular approach because of their simplicity and ease of implementation. Nevertheless, since the penalty function approach is generic and applicable to any type of constraint, their performance is not always satisfactory, especially when the problems become more difficult and the imposed constrained conditions become more complex, this method usually fails to generate the best solution, sometimes even cannot achieve a feasible one. The underlying limitation is that unfair competition exists in the population. Thus to deal with this problem, the dynamic and adaptive penalty coefficients should be introduced, which are highly dependent on the specific problem.

When combined with PSO, the above problem is more severe in that PSO has an inherent mechanism based on memory information. This mechanism can produce high efficiency and effectiveness, but also low the flexibility for constrained optimization simultaneously. That is, the penalty factors cannot be changed during the iteration. In fact, the most difficult aspect of the penalty function strategy is to find appropriate penalty parameters to guide the search towards the constrained optimum. It is desirable to design a new constraint handling scheme suit for PSO to effectively solve numerous engineering problems and maintain high efficiency.

3.3 Constraints Handling Strategy for PSO

Taking account of the memory mechanism of PSO and penalty strategy, a new constraint-handling strategy is presented in Figure.1.

The core characteristics of the proposed strategy can be described as follows:

1. Corresponding to the memory mechanism of PSO, a special notation-Particle has been Feasible (PF) is introduced, which is used to record whether the current particle has ever satisfied all the constraint conditions. This notation preserves historical constrain status for each particle.
2. Each particle updates its individual best and neighborhood best according to the historical constraint information PF, the current constrain status (Current particle is Feasible, CF) and the objective function with the penalty term.
3. The algorithm selects the velocity updating strategy according to the historical information PF.
4. When updating the personal and neighborhood best, the algorithm adopts the static penalty strategy instead of the dynamic and the adaptive ones to guarantee the fairness. The detailed procedure for updating the personal and neighborhood best values based on the above constrain handling strategy is presented in Figure.1.

```
For Each Particle {
  If PF = true Then
    If f(x_i) ≤ f(p_i) and CF= true Then
      p_i = x_i
      If f(p_i) ≤ f(l_i) Then
        p_i = l_i
      End if
    End if
  Else if PF = false Then
    If CF = true Then
      p_i = x_i
      PF = true
      If f(p_i) ≤ f(l_i) Then
        p_i = l_i
      End if
    Else if f(x_i) ≤ f(p_i) Then
      p_i = x_i
    End if
  End if
```

Figure 1. The proposed constraint handling strategy for PSO

Special attention should be paid that the PSO algorithm based on the proposed constraint handling strategy does not have to guarantee the existence of feasible solutions in the initial population. With the randomized initial velocity, the PSO itself has the ability to explore the feasible space. In addition, the penalty function imposed on the violated particles also direct the search of PSO towards the feasible region. Therefore once feasible solutions emerge in the neighborhood population, the neighborhood best will be preserved in the subsequent iteration procedure. According to the velocity updating formula, each particle will obtain updating information from its neighborhood best particle, so the corresponding particle would return to the feasible solution space immediately.

4. Design Example

To validate the effectiveness of the new proposed strategy and illustrate the application of the concurrent design, the cylinder-piston assembly (Singh et al., 2003) (shown in Figure.2) is described. In this example, the piston diameter is 50.8mm, the cylinder bore diameter is 50.856mm, and the clearance is 0.056 ± 0.025 mm. The machining process plan is: (1) for the piston: rough turning, finish turning, rough grinding, and finally finish grinding. (2) for the cylinder bore: drilling, boring, semi-finish boring, and finally grinding. The ranges of the principal machining tolerances for the piston and cylinder bore were the same as in the (Singh et al., 2003).

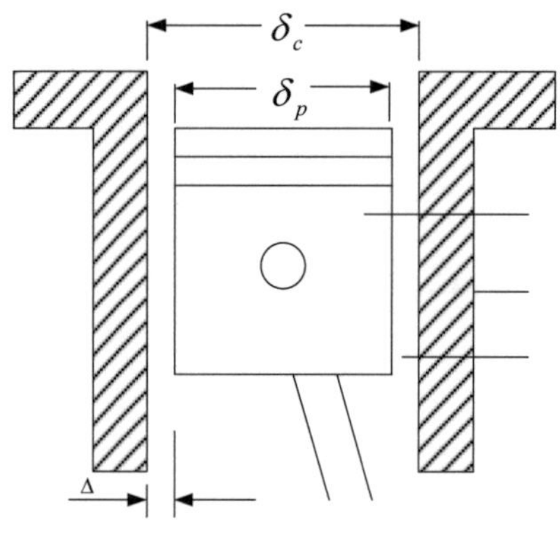

Figure 2. Cylinder-piston assembly

To formulate this problem, the objective and the constraints should be determined. In this problem, the principal tolerances are the design tolerances and the machining tolerances for the piston and the cylinder bore. So there are only two design tolerance parameters, for the piston diameter and cylinder bore diameter respectively. In the meantime, we have four machining tolerances for the piston diameter and four machining tolerances for the cylinder bore diameter. Therefore we have to consider totally 10 tolerances for the piston-cylinder bore assembly as follows. (1)The design tolerance parameters: δ_{11d} for the piston and δ_{21d} for the cylinder bore. Four stack-up conditions (Singh et al., 2003) (worst case, RSS, Spotts' modified method and estimated mean shift criteria) are employed to formulate the corresponding constraints. (2)The machining tolerance parameters are: δ_{ij} where i=1,2 and j=1,2,3,4. Here, the first subscript 1 refer to piston and 2 refer to the cylinder bore. The second subscript refers to the four machining processes. Usually, the process tolerance for the final finishing operation is same as the design tolerance, i.e. $\delta_{11d} = \delta_{14}$ and $\delta_{12d} = \delta_{24}$. Thus, there are actually 8 tolerance parameters to be considerd. The machining tolerance constraints are formulated based on Equation 3. The manufacturing decision is the total machining cost and is determined by summing the machining cost-tolerance model as Equation 1 and Equation 2 subjecting to the constraints and ranges of the principal design and machining tolerances. The constant parameters are the same as in (Singh et al., 2003).

GA				PSO					
Piston	Cylinder	Cost	Time (s)	Piston	Cylinder	Min	Ave	Max	Time (s)
0.0162	0.0162	66.85	350	0.0163	0.0163	66.74	66.74	66.74	83
0.0037	0.0038			0.0037	0.0037				
0.0013	0.0012			0.0013	0.0013				
0.0005	0.0005			0.0005	0.0005				

(a) Based on the worst case criteria

GA				PSO					
Piston	Cylinder	Cost	Time (s)	Piston	Cylinder	Min	Ave	Max	Time (s)
0.0161	0.0161	65.92	330	0.0161	0.0162	66.82	66.82	66.82	80
0.0039	0.0038			0.0039	0.0038				
0.0011	0.0012			0.0011	0.0012				
0.0007	0.0006			0.0007	0.0006				

(b) Based on the worst RSS criteria

GA				PSO					
Piston	Cylinder	Cost	Time (s)	Piston	Cylinder	Min	Ave	Max	Time (s)
0.0160	0.0159	66.23	330	0.0162	0.0162	65.93	65.93	65.93	78
0.0038	0.0038			0.0038	0.0038				
0.0012	0.0012			0.0012	0.0012				
0.0006	0.0005			0.0006	0.0006				

(c) Based on the worst Spotts' criteria

GA				PSO					
Piston	Cylinder	Cost	Time (s)	Piston	Cylinder	Min	Ave	Max	Time (s)
0.0162	0.0151	66.26	350	0.0161	0.0162	65.82	65.82	65.82	82
0.0037	0.0038			0.0039	0.0038				
0.0012	0.0011			0.0011	0.0012				
0.0006	0.0006			0.0006	0.0006				

(d) Based on the worst mean shift or Greenwood and Chase's unified criteria

Table 1. Optimal tolerances allocation using GA and PSO

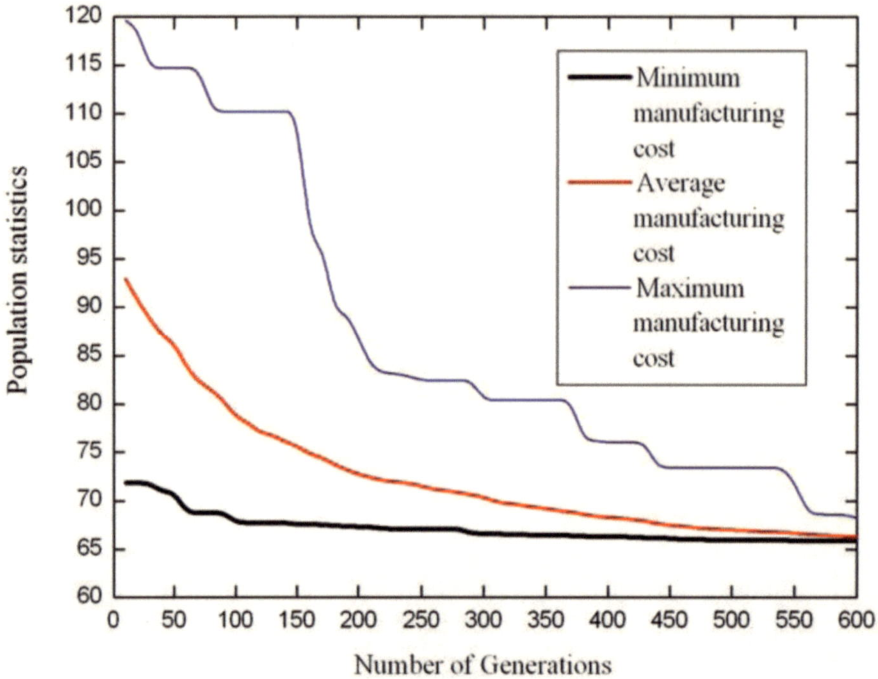

Figure 3. Variation of the minimum, maximum and average of the manufacturing costs with progress of the algorithm (Greenwood and Chase's unified, or estimated mean shift criteria)

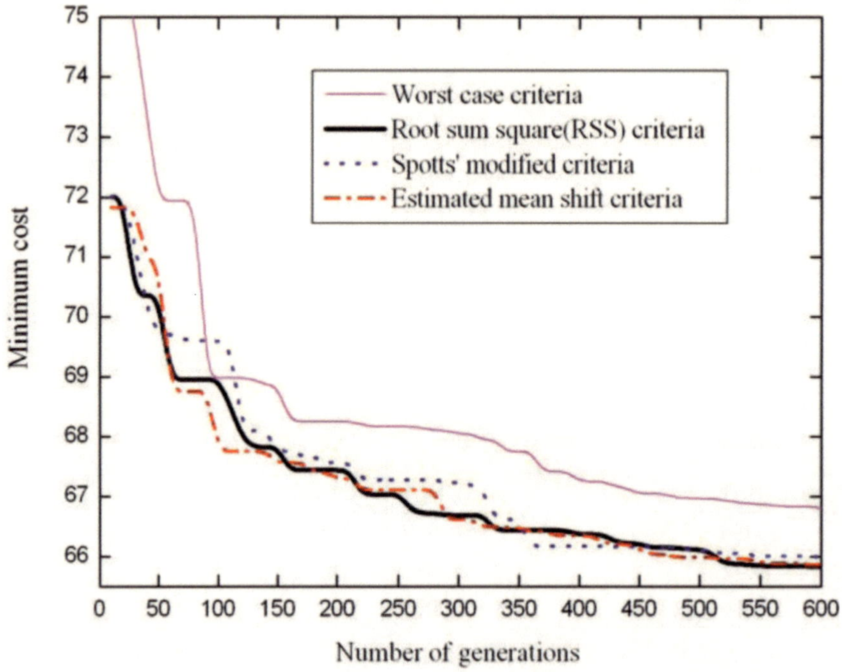

Figure 4. Minimum manufacturing cost in a given number of generations

The proposed PSO algorithm with special constraints handling strategy was used to solve this problem. To validate its efficiency, this new approach was compared with GA in (Singh et al., 2003). In the optimization process of HPSO, we set the population size *popsize*=80, the maximum iteration number *itermax*=600. These two parameters are the same as those in GA. The other parameters are set as the common used method. The inertial weight decreases from 0.9 to 0.4 linearly and the accelerated parameters $c_1=c_2=2$.

The optimal tolerance allocated using HPSO and GA based on the above four criteria and the corresponding CPU time are listed in Table 1. The computational results clearly indicate that HPSO outperformed GA in the terms of solution quality as well as computational expense. In addition, HPSO is able to find the optimum in each trial, that is, it has significantly larger probability of converging to optimal solutions. It is necessary to point out that one important merit of PSO algorithm is the high precision of the solutions. However, due to the limitation of display capacity of the tables, the entire data are rounded.

The statistical results obtained under the Greenwood and Chase's estimated mean shift criteria are demonstrated in Figure.3. Similar curves can be obtained for other cases. Improvement in the fitness function causes reduction in the assembly manufacturing cost and the amount of infeasibility in subsequent generations. Figure.3 reflects the general behavior about convergence of PSO algorithm. Sharply contrast with GA, the PSO algorithm has consistent convergence. The average and worst fitness are not fluctuant as in GA. Figure.4 demonstrates the minimum manufacturing cost under all four stack-up conditions. The different tendency and position of the curve reveals the difference of the fitness (manufacturing cost).

5. Conclusion

Tolerance assignment is very important in product design and machining. The conventional sequentially tolerance allocation suffers from several drawbacks. Therefore, a simultaneous tolerance assignment approach is adopted to overcome these drawbacks. However, the optimization task is usually difficult to tackle due to the nonlinear, multi-variable and high constrained characteristics. In trying to solve such constrained optimization problem, penalty function based methods have been the most popular approach. However, since the penalty function approach is generic and applicable to any type of constraint, their performance is not always satisfactory and consistent. In view of the memory characteristics of PSO, a new constraints handling strategy suit for PSO is designed. This new strategy can adequately utilize the historical information in PSO algorithm. The application on a cylinder-piston assembly example demonstrates its high efficiency and effectiveness.

However, when we attempt to extend the proposed approach to the constrained optimization with large number of complex equality constraints, subtle drawbacks emerged, as the constrained range is so narrow that the equality constraints are hard to satisfy. This problem reveals the new research direction, which is the effective equality constraint handling strategy desirable to develop for PSO based nonlinear programming. Furthermore, powerful local search methods should be introduced to combine with PSO to improve the ability of refined search. In view of its successful application in the above problems especially those engineering ones, PSO can be considered as a general nonlinear constrained optimization tool, and thus could be applied to more engineering optimization problems that can be modeled as nonlinear programming problems.

6. References

Gaing, Z.L. (2004). A Particle swarm optimization approach for optimum design of PID controller in AVR system. *IEEE Transaction on Energy Conversion*, Vol.19, 384-391

Gao, Y. & Huang, M. (2003). Optimal process tolerance balancing based on process capabilities. *International Journal of Advanced Manufacturing Technology*, Vol.21, 501–507

Huang, M.F. ; Zhong, Y.R. & Xu, Z.G.(2004). Concurrent process tolerance design based on minimum product manufacturing cost and quality loss. *International Journal of Advanced Manufacturing Technology*, Vol.25, 714-722

Kennedy, J. & Eberhart, R.C.(1995). Particle swarm optimization. *Proceedings of IEEE International Conference on Neutral Networks*, pp. 1942-1948, Perth, Australia

Kennedy, J. ; Eberhart, R.C. & Shi, Y. (2001) Swarm Intelligence. Morgan Kaufman, San Francisco

Ngoi, B.K.A. & Teck, O.C. (1997). A tolerancing optimization method for product design. *International Journal of Advanced Manufacturing Technology*, Vol. 13, 290-299

Noorul Hap, A. ; Sivakumar, K. ; Saravanan, R. & Karthikeyan, K. (2005). Particle swarm optimiza-tion (PSO) algorithm for optimal machining allocation of clutch assembly. *Interna-tional Journal of Advanced Manufacturing Technology*, Vol.27, 865-869

Salman, A. & Ahmad, I.(2002). Particle swarm optimization for task assignment problem. *Microprocessors and Microsystems*, Vol.26, 363-371

Shi, Y.H. ; & Eberhart, R.C.(1998). A modified particle swarm optimizer. *Proceedings of IEEE Conference on Evolutionary Computation*, pp. 69-73

Shi, Y.H. & Eberhart, R.C. (1999). Empirical study of particle swarm optimization. *IEEE Congress on Evolutionary Computation*

Singh, P.K. ; Jain, P.K. & Jain, S.C. (2003). Simultaneous optimal selection of design and manufactur-ing tolerances with different stack-up conditions using genetic algorithms. *International Journal of Production Research*, Vol.41 , 2411-2429

Zhang, G.(1996). Simultaneous tolerancing for design and manufacturing. *International Journal of Production Research*, Vol.34, 3361-3382

18

Hybrid optimisation method for the facility layout problem

Yasmina Hani, Lionel Amodeo, Farouk Yalaoui and Haoxun Chen
University of Technology of Troyes (ICD FRE CNRS 2848)
France

1. Introduction

Due to increased competition, the manufacturers are brought to quickly respond to the needs of customers for on-time delivery of high quality products. Many studies have been made to realize these objectives such as he studies on the facility layout problem (FLP).
It is to find a good configuration of the machines, equipments or other resources in a given facility in order to optimize the production flows while minimizing the total cost. The FLP arises in many industry cases, such as facility reorganization, construction of new production units, or equipment assignment.
To solve this problem, we develop an ant colony optimization algorithm combined with a local search method. This chapter presents the algorithm, its performance evaluation et application to an industrial case.
The remainder of this chapter is organised as follows: In section 2, the layout problem is described. In section 3, we present the general framework of the ACO algorithm and its enhancement by guided local search. Computational results on the performance evaluation of the algorithm using a set of benchmark instances are presented in section 4, and the application of the algorithm to an industrial case is reported in section 5. In section 6, we conclude this chapter with some remarks.

2. The layout problem

The layout problem is commonly met in the industry. A full description of the problem can be found in (Kusiak & Heragu, 1987). Layout problem is known to be NP-Hard (Sahni & Gonzales, 1976).
There are many cases where FLP is considered in facility reorganization, construction of new production units, or equipment assignment. Layout problem could be also found in many classical and theoretical studies. However, only few layout industrial cases are treated in the literature. Hicks (2004), developed a genetic algorithm for minimizing material movement in a manufacturing cell with application to practical problems related to the capital good industry. Lee *et al.* (2002) proposed a genetic algorithm for solving multi-floor facility layout problems with the facility's inner structure consisting of walls and passages. A study related to the fashion industry was presented by Martens (2004).

The FLP has been formulated as a Quadratic Assignment Problem (QAP). Other formulations also exist such as mixed integer programming (Meller et al., 1999) and graph theoretic model (Caccetta & Kusumah, 2001).
Many methods are used to solve the layout problem and they are essentially based on meta-heuristics such as Genetic Algorithms (GA) (Lee et al., 2002), Tabu Search (Chiang & Chiang, 1998), Simulated Annealing (SA) (Baykasoglu & Gindy, 2001), Ant Colony (Solimanpur et al., 2004). In our study, we consider a layout problem modelled as a QAP.

3. Hybrid Ant Colony Optimization

3.1 Ant colony optimization (ACO)

The principle of ACO algorithms (Corne & Dorigo, 1999; Dorigo et al., 2000) is based on the way ants search for food. Each ant takes into consideration (probabilistic choice) pheromone trails left by all other ant colony members which preceded its course, the pheromone trail being a trace, a smell left by every ant on its way. This pheromone evaporates with time, and therefore the probabilistic choice for each ant changes with time. After many ant courses, the path to the food will be characterized by higher pheromone traces and thus all ants will follow the same path. This collective behaviour, based upon a shared memory among all colony ants could be adapted and used for solving combinatorial optimization problems with the following analogies:

- The real ant search space becomes the space of the combinatorial problem solutions.
- The amount of food inside a source becomes the evaluation of the objective function for the corresponding solution.
- The pheromone trails become an adaptive shared memory.

Ant colony optimization (ACO) problems could therefore be encoded as finding the shortest path in a graph. One of the first applications of ACO was the travelling salesman problem.
In the general case, the ant colony algorithm applies the artificial ants' concept; it is represented by the following steps:

Step 1: Initialization of parameters
Step 2: Construction of solutions
Step 3: Local search algorithm
Step 4: Pheromone updating rule
Step 5: Return to 2 until a given stopping criterion satisfied

Ant colony optimization (ACO) is a method widely used for solving quadratic assignment problem. The first application was proposed by Maniezzo et al. in 1994. Since that, many applications were proposed, and the differences were in the generation of solutions, the local search method and the pheromone updating. Stutzle & Dorigo (1997) reviewed the ant algorithm applied to solve QAP and reported that the ACO algorithms are among the well performing methods to solve QAP. The MAX-MIN ant system algorithm (MMAS) proposed by Stutzle & Hoos (2000) allows only the best solution to add pheromone trail during the pheromone trail update. A bound is used for trail levels to avoid premature convergence of the search. Gambardella et al (1997) proposed a hybrid ant system HAS-QAP to solve QAP. The originality of their approach is in that the pheromone trail was not used to construct solutions but to modify them in the local search.
Most of the proposed metaheuristics for the FLP problem are effective for small instances. Their performances become worse with the increase of the problem size (i.e. number of resources). Solimanpur et al. (2004) proposed an ACO algorithm for the inter-cell layout

problem formulated as QAP. They proposed a technique based on the partial contribution of each assignment for the calculation of a lower bound used in (Maniezzo, 1999). It was limited to only 30 departments because of the complexity of the problem. In a previous study, ANTabu (Stützle & Dorigo, 1999) using an ant colony optimization with a tabu local search procedure, was successfully applied to the QAP for large instances (i.e. 256 resources).

The ant colony algorithm adapted to the layout problem is composed of the following elements:

1. Construction of solutions

In the proposed algorithm, it is assumed that each ant initially assigns a task i to location j noted (i,j), then another task to another location k, and so on until a complete solution is obtained. A tabu list represents the set of tasks that the ants has already assigned, the list of the couples (i,j). This list ensures that all the tasks are assigned to locations. The criterion of the tasks assignment takes into account the probability of assignment with a given site, and depends on two terms, one relating to each ant (visibility) and the other relating to the quantity of pheromones deposited by the whole of the ants.

2. Heuristic information

The ants are not completely blind, they calculate the cost relating to the assignment of a task to a given site. This cost takes into account the flow and distances matrix. Heuristic information, called *visibility* is a function of the assignment cost. Several formulas were used in the literature and each one is adapted to a given problem. Concerning QAP, the assignment of a task i to the site l depends on the tasks assigned before. We define the cost associated with the assignment (i,l) as:

$$C(i,l) = \sum_{s=1}^{l-1} (f_{r(s)i} \times d_{sl} + f_{ir(s)} \times d_{ls}) \tag{1}$$

where, r denotes a permutation of resources under construction. The visibility which represents the desirability of move is defined as:

$$\eta_{il} = \frac{1}{1 + \sum_{s=1}^{l-1} (f_{r(s)i} \times d_{sl} + f_{ir(s)} \times d_{ls})} \tag{2}$$

The reason for which number 1 is added to the denominator of the fraction in (2) is for avoiding division by 0. This formula means that the assignments with smaller contribution to the objective function would be more desirable for selection.

3. Pheromone updating

The pheromone updating mechanism is represented by the following equation

$$\tau_{il}(t) = \lambda \tau_{il}(t-1) + \sum_{k} \Delta \tau_{il}^{k} \tag{3}$$

where, $\tau_{il}(t)$ is the quantity of pheromone associated with the assignment of the task i to location l for each ant k for the iteration t. As an ant chooses this assignment, the quantity $\tau_{il}(t)$ increases. The parameter λ is a scaling factor. A large λ results in quick convergence to a local optima solution.

Finally,

$$\Delta\tau_{il}^{k} = \sum_{k} \frac{Bestfit}{fit[k]} \tag{4}$$

denotes the magnitude of change in the trail level of an assignment through ant. As seen, the smaller is the fitness solution *fit[k]* obtained by ant *k*, the more would be the increment in trail levels selected by ant *k*.

4. Selection probability

An ant k chooses task i to assign to location l by the following probability:

$$p_{il}^{k} = \frac{\alpha \times \tau_{il} + (1-\alpha) \times \eta_{il}}{\sum_{i \neq Tabu_k} (\alpha \times \tau_{il} + (1-\alpha) \times \eta_{il})}, \tag{5}$$

where, α contributes to make a balance between the choice adopted by the whole of the ants (α near to 1) and the choice of each ant based on its own visibility (α near to 0). We note that a task is assigned to a location if the relative quantity of pheromones is significant or if the associated cost is weak. Finally, the task having the largest probability is assigned to location *l*.

5. Local search

We choose local search method 2-opt which is simple and well adapted to QAP (Solimanpur et al., 2004). This method applies to a given solution all possible permutations of pairs of tasks. The permutation giving the minimal cost is selected as a local minimum next to the starting solution. This process is repeated until no improvement is observed.

In order to limit computation time during the exchanges, we made the following simplification; if the exchange is done between the elements π_i and π_j of the permutation π, the difference in the objective function value will be then:

$$\begin{aligned}\Delta(\pi,i,j) = &(d_{ii} - d_{jj})(f_{\pi_j\pi_j} - f_{\pi_j\pi_j}) + (d_{ij} - d_{ji})(f_{\pi_j\pi_i} - f_{\pi_i\pi_j}) + \\ &\sum_{k \neq i,j} (d_{ki} - d_{kj})(f_{\pi_k\pi_j} - f_{\pi_k\pi_i}) + (d_{ik} - d_{jk})(f_{\pi_j\pi_k} - f_{\pi_i\pi_k})\end{aligned} \tag{6}$$

This algebric simplification was used by Gambardella et al. in 1997 when they propose HAS-QAP, a hybrid ant colony system applied to the quadratic assignment problem.

The local search does not necessarily lead to a global minimum. In most cases, it converges to a local minimum. For this, a guided local search (GLS) method is used to "penalize" the local minimum found in order to converge to the global minimum. GLS will be explained in detail later.

6. Diversification

Used by Gambardella in 1997, the diversification mechanism is activated if during a number of iterations *max_iter*, no improvement to the best generated solution is detected. Diversification consists of erasing all the information contained in the pheromone trail by a re-initialization of the pheromone trail matrix and of generating randomly a new current solution for all the ants but one that receives the best solution produced by the search so far. Another possibility is to erase all pheromone trails except for the best solution.

Ant colony algorithm

We propose the following general ant colony optimization algorithm with 2-opt.

Step 1: initialization of parameters for all the tasks and locations
Step 2: for each ant
Assign tasks to locations with a probability p
Update the pheromones
If the best solution is not improved until max_iter iterations, $\tau_{il} = 0$, *except for the best solution.*
Step 3: Return to Step2 until stopping criterion is satisfied.

3.2 Enhancement of ACO by Guided Local Search (GLS)

Guided Local Search (GLS) (Mills and Tsang, 2002) is a metaheuristic which sits as a good local search algorithm. When the given local search algorithm settles in a local optimum, GLS changes the objective function, by increasing penalties in an augmented objective function, associated with *features* contained in the local optimum. The local search then continues to search using the augmented objective function.
The choice of solution features depends on the problem type, and each feature f_i defined must have the following components:

1. An indicator function $I_i(s)$ indicating whether the feature is present in the current solution or not. It is equal to 1 if the feature f_i is present in the solution s and 0 otherwise.
2. A cost function $c_i(s)$ which gives the cost of having f_i in s.
3. A penalty p_i initially set to 0, used to penalize the occurrence of f_i in local minima.

When the local search returns a local minimum s, GLS increases the penalty of the features of s which have maximum utility $util(s,f_i)$ defined as follow :

$$util(s, f_i) = I_i(s)\frac{c_i(s)}{1+p_i} \tag{7}$$

The idea is to penalise the features, which have highest costs first. GLS uses an augmented cost function (8) in order to guide the local search out of a local optimum. The idea is to make the local minimum more costly than the solutions in the surrounding search space, where the same features are not present.

$$h(s) = g(s) + \lambda' \sum_{i=1}^{n} I_i(s).p_i \tag{8}$$

where, $g(s)$ is the cost function and λ' a parameter used to alter the diversification of the search for solutions. A higher value for λ' will result in more diverse search.

The application of GLS for the QAP problem is realised with the following analogies:

- The feature $f_{i,\pi i}$ of a solution s corresponds to the assignment of task i to the location π_i.
- The cost related to feature $f_{i,\pi i}$ depends on the interaction of the task i with all other tasks of the solution s. This cost is given by

$$C(i,\pi_i) = \sum_{j=1}^{n} f_{ij} D_{\pi_i \pi_j} \tag{9}$$

- The value λ' well adapted to the QAP is given by

$$\lambda' = \frac{\sum_{i=1}^{n}\sum_{j=1}^{n} f_{ij} \times \sum_{i=1}^{n}\sum_{j=1}^{n} D_{ij}}{n^4} \tag{10}$$

The application of GLS technique to the QAP problem could be summarized in the following: Starting from the current solution, a local search method (2-opt for example) is used to find a local minimum, with respect to the augmented cost function. If this minimum has a cost (not augmented) lower than the lowest cost ever found, it is saved as the best ever found solution. Finally, the assignment having the maximum utility would have its corresponding penalty increased.

The GLSQAP algorithm could be summarized as follows:

Step 1: Calculation of λ'

Step 2: The best solution s' = initial solution s

Step 3: Perform a local search 2-opt with respect to the augmented cost function, s is found as the solution having the lower augmented cost.*

If cost (s) < cost (s'), replace s' by s*.*

Find the assignment (feature) of s having the maximum utility, let it be* $f_{i,\pi i}$ *for example.*

Increase the corresponding penalty: $p_{i,\pi i} = p_{i,\pi i} + 1$.

Step 4: Return to step 3 until a given stopping criterion is satisfied.

Step 5: s' is the best solution found for the original problem.

Finally, the algorithm procedure of ant colony optimization with GLS is given as follows:

Step 1: initialization of parameters

Step 2: for all ants

a. *Assign tasks to locations with the given assignment probability*
b. *Perform the guided local search GLSQAP*
c. *Update the pheromones*
d. *If the best solution is not improved until max_iter iterations,* $\tau_{il} = 0$, *except for the best solution.*

Step 3 : Return to step2 until a stopping criterion is satisfied.

4. Computational results

The algorithm was implemented using Visual C++ 6.0. on a Pentium 3 with 1.8 Ghz CPU speed. In the proposed algorithm four parameters: *ant number AN, alpha, max_iter and* τ_0 affect the performance of the algorithm. To find the appropriate parameters for our problem, pilot runs were performed. Ant number *AN* was tested between 5 and 60, and a compromise between the quality of the results and the convergence time was found for *AN* = 20. When *AN* was fixed, the best convergence was found for *max_iter* = 10 and *alpha* = 0.6.

Usually, *alpha* is close to 0.5. In our case the value 0.6 indicates that the construction of the solutions more supports the pheromone trails than the individual ant investigation. This value was found to be well adapted with the GLS procedure. Table 1 lists the appropriate values:

Parameter	Value
AN	20
Alpha	0.6
max_iter	10
τ_0	0

Table 1. Parameter values

The performance of this algorithm was tested on instances from the library QAPLIB (Burkard et al., 1991). We first compare our algorithm with the HAS-QAP (Gambardella et al., 1997) method based on ant colonies. We then compare it with ANTabu (Talbi et al., 2001) which is compared with other methods based on genetic algorithms, simulated annealing, tabu search or ant colony and with a recent ant colony optimization algorithm proposed by Solimanpur et al. (2004), which is adapted for problems with a small number of locations. Table 2 compares the results of all the cited algorithms for small instances with a number of locations falling between 19 and 30.
The instances we chose include the regular and irregular problems of QAPLIB. The difference relative to the QAPLIB best known solution is given as a percentage gap. It is almost impossible to have the same experimental settings as for previous studies, but in order to give an idea on the computation time, the mean execution time over 10 runs is shown in table 2.

	Best known value	**HAS_QAP**	**ANTabu**	**ACO Solimanpur**	**ACO_GLS**	**Time (s)**
Els 19	17212548	0.923	**0**	**0**	**0**	4
Tai 20b	122455319	0.243	**0**	**0**	**0**	5
Chr 25a	3796	3.0822	0.8957	**0**	**0**	3
Bur 26a	5426670	**0**	**0**	**0**	**0**	35
Bur 26b	3817852	**0**	0.0169	**0**	**0**	34
Bur 26c	5426795	**0**	**0**	**0**	**0**	34
Bur 26d	3821225	**0**	**0**	**0**	**0**	35
Bur 26e	5386859	**0**	**0**	**0**	**0**	34
Bur 26f	3782044	**0**	**0**	**0**	**0**	34
Bur 26g	10117172	**0**	**0**	**0**	**0**	33
Kra30a	88900	0.6299	0.2677	**0**	**0**	35
Kra 30b	91420	0.0711	**0**	0.0153	**0**	19
Nug30	6124	0.098	**0**	0.013	**0**	3

[a]Values indicate the average gap between solution value and best known value in percent

Table 2. Compare results on QAP instances selected from QAPLIB (best results are in boldface)[a]

Table 3 proves that for the instances with up to 30 tasks, ACO_GLS performs better than all other algorithms in comparison.
In order to generalize the application of our algorithm, large instances from the QAPLIB were studied with different classes of problems. Results are shown in Table 3. We have compared those algorithms on a set of 12 instances, ranging from 35 to 128 locations.
For larger instances, the results given by ANTabu are a little bit better, so we may have to perform more complicated local search in order to escape local minima in the problems with large instances. It is shown (table 3) that our algorithm ACO_GLS performs better than HAS-QAP. However, our algorithm can still obtain satisfactory solutions for large instance.
The proposed ACO-GLS algorithm proved to converge perfectly for instances up to 40 locations as shown in tables 2 and 3. This performance is quite satisfactory for industrial problems because real life problems usually do not exceed 30 to 40 locations. Therefore, this algorithm will be a very useful tool for layout optimization in the real life industrial case explained in this paper.

	Best known value	HAS_QAP	ANTabu	ACO_GLS	Time (s)
Tai 35a	2422002	1.762	0.215	**0**	109
Tai 35b	283315445	0.343	0.0408	**0**	112
Tai 40a	3139370	1.989	0.442	**0**	204
Tai 50a	4941410	2.800	**0.781**	1,28	228
Tai 60a	7208572	3.070	**0.919**	1.25	342
Tai 80a	13557864	**0.663**	**0.663**	1.53	1524
Wil 50	48816	0.061	**0.008**	0.01	1197
Sko42	15812	0.076	**0**	**0**	82
Sko49	23410	0.141	**0.038**	0.10	105
Sko56	34524	0.101	**0.002**	0.19	294
Sko64	48498	0.129	**0.001**	0.008	522
Esc 128	64	-	**0**	**0**	1292

Table 3. Compare results on QAP instances selected from QAPLIB (best results are in boldface)

5. Application to an industrial case

Our study (Hani et al., 2006; Hani et al., 2007) concerns an industrial layout problem for a train maintenance facility of the French railway system (SNCF).
The train maintenance facility is composed of buildings established on parallel rail tracks [15]. The cars to be treated arrive in batches and travel in the various buildings according to the sequence of their operations. They may travel transversally carried from one building to another by a transport which moves on a fixed trajectory. An on-rail transport permits movement along the rails. Some tasks require long processing, which would occupy their locations for a long time. These tasks represent bottlenecks for the facility.

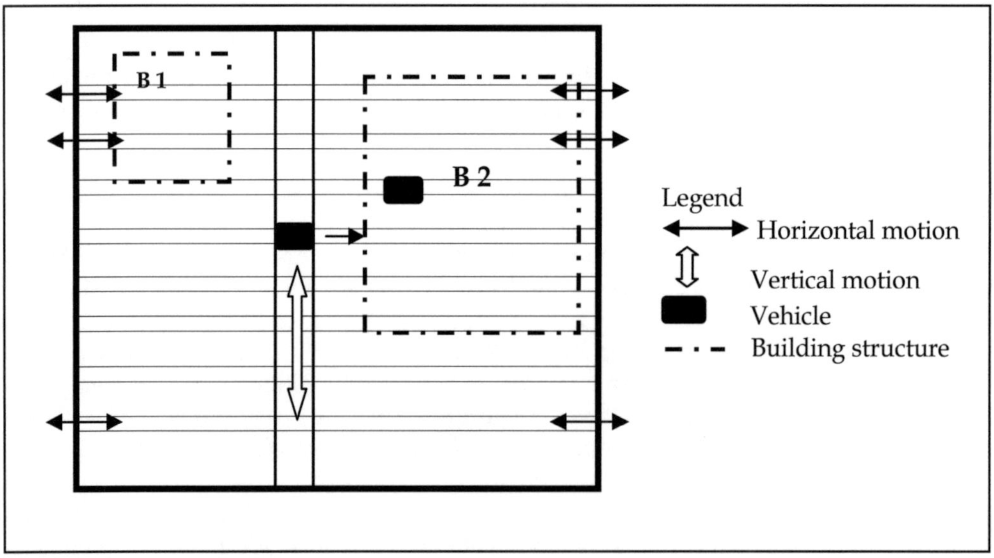

Figure 1. One example structure

In the current application, and due to the paucity of locations, some cars must be moved out of its building in order to give access to other cars in need of repair. The current facility layout has proved to be quite constraining for the production planning of the repair line. The problem is to find a layout of the resources in individual buildings in order to optimize the flow of cars between the buildings.
Figure 2 shows an example of a building composed of two parallel tracks and 6 locations. Access to the building is possible only via the lateral side. Suppose a car needs to pass from outside to location 2, and then to location 6. Then it is necessary to move the car which occupies location 1 or location 3 in order to let the new car access location 2. Then, in order to go to location 6, it is necessary to move the car on location 3 or that on location 1.
In other words, the problem is to find a new configuration of the resources in one of the buildings (figure 1) in order to optimize (minimize) the flow among all resources (facilities).

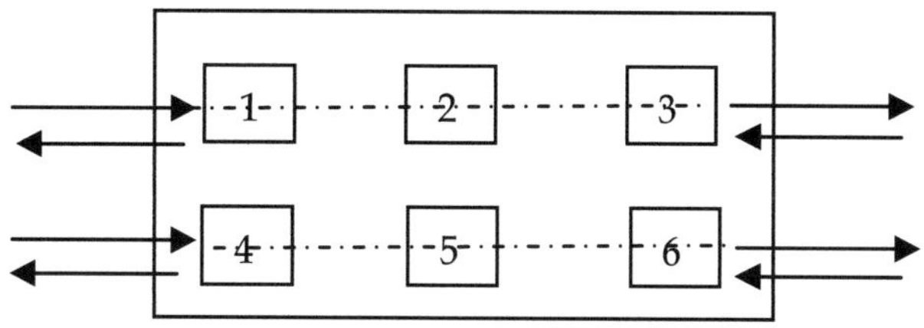

Figure 2. One building example

In order to model our problem, each rail is decomposed into zones called *car locations* where the maintenance tasks are performed.
The car locations can be categorized into three types:

- If a location is cluttered (e.g., stocks, workbench, etc.), then it is called *unusable.*
- If a location is occupied by a fixed resource (such as big machines for electric tests), it is called *specialized* since theses resources cannot be moved.
- If a location is neither *unusable* nor *specialized*, it is said to be *standardized.*

Note that when unusable locations exist, access becomes even more difficult, as for example having location 6 as unusable in figure 2.
Outside the building, there exists a transport system which carries cars from one side to another of the facility. There are three transporters: two transversal and one on-rail transport that effects the movement of the cars on the rails.
In other words, the problem is to find a new resource configuration in one of the buildings (figure 2) in order to optimize (minimize) the production flow between all resources (facilities).
We consider N resources to be assigned to N sites or car locations in the building. Given a distance matrix D, where each element $d_{k,w}$ denotes a distance between location k and w, for $k,w = 1, 2, \ldots N$, a flow matrix F, where each element $f_{i,j}$ denotes a flow cost between resource i and j , for $i, j = 1, 2, \ldots N$.
The flow cost depends on the number of trips between two resources in a given time horizon. In the problem considered, the matrix flow is not symmetric because of precedence constraints.
The distance matrix is symmetric. The distance calculation is related to the minimum vehicle number to move inside a building in order to make an exchange. As an example in figure 1, $d(2,3) = 0$, $d(1,5) = 1$ (by crossing position 4) et $d(2,5) = 2$ (by crossing position 1 and 4).

Our problem is modeled as a QAP. The flow cost depends on the number of trips between two resources in a given time horizon. In the problem considered, the matrix flow is not symmetric because of precedence constraints.
The distance matrix is symmetric. The distance calculation is related to the minimum number of vehicles to move inside a building in order to make an exchange.
Model parameters:

N: total number of locations

r_{ij} : Resource j assigned to task i

$D_{k,w}$: Distance between locations k and w. This distance is defined as the number of usable locations between both resources.

$f_{r_{ij},r_{i'j'}}$: Production flow between the resources r_{ij} and $r_{i'j'}$. This flow is evaluated as the number of cars passing between the two resources.

$$p_{r_{ij},k} = \begin{cases} 1 \text{ if } r_{ij} \text{ is assigned to the location k} \\ 0 \text{ else} \end{cases} \tag{11}$$

$$TE_k = \begin{cases} 1 \text{ if location k is standardized} \\ 0 \text{ else} \end{cases} \tag{12}$$

$$TES_k = \begin{cases} 1 \text{ if locationk is specialized} \\ 0 \text{ else} \end{cases} \tag{13}$$

In order to optimize the production flow, we define a quadratic function Z to minimize:

$$Z = \sum_i \sum_j \sum_{i'} \sum_{j'} \sum_k \sum_w f_{r_{ij},r_{i'j'}} \times D_{k,w} \times P_{r_{ij},k} \times P_{r_{i'j'},w} \tag{14}$$

If the unusable locations are excluded, the following constraints should be added:

$$\forall k: \sum_i \sum_j p_{r_{ij},k} = 1 \tag{15}$$

$$\forall i,j: \sum_k p_{r_{ij},k} = 1 \tag{16}$$

$$TE_k + TES_k = 1 \tag{17}$$

Constraints (15) and (16) are the standard constraints for the regular assignment problem. Constraint (17) implies that all occupied locations are either specialized or standardized.
The industrial problem consists of 72 locations with 27 unusable, 39 specialized and 6 standardized locations. 15 tasks with total of 27 resources had to be assigned. The actual resources assignment was taken as an initial condition for the algorithm. All calculations were done based upon data for one year planning.
As previously stated, the application of the hybrid GA algorithm to the industrial case has to exclude unusable and specialized locations from the locations choice; only standardized locations are considered.

The actual layout in the workshop produces a cost of 425, however, our algorithm ACO_GLS produces a solution with an improvement of 19.6% with respect to the actual layout. This means that it converges to a better solution, which proves its ability to solve an industrial layout problem.

We also found the exact solution of the problem by using an enumeration method since only six tasks needed to be assigned. The solution is the same as what was found by the algorithm. This implies that the algorithm converges to the optimal solution for this industrial problem.

The proposed application may be useful for the industrial case in the future. In fact, as stated above in the problem description, the industry is trying to increase its performance which means solving other facility problems. In addition, other vehicle sequences will be added, and many locations need to become free in order to accept new tasks. As it can be imagined, the future problem in the industry is to layout a greater number of locations which may reach 30 to 40 locations. The proposed ACO-GLS needs to be tested for large instance problems and its performance has to be evaluated with respect to other known algorithms. For this purpose, public sequences were tested and results were compared with other studies.

6. Conclusion

We have proposed a robust meta-heuristic algorithm for the layout problem modelled as a QAP. The algorithm is based on ant colony algorithm combined with a guided local search, and it uses an augmented cost function in order to guide the local search out of a local optimum. The performance of the proposed algorithm was also evaluated on a number of benchmark problems selected from the literature and compared with other heuristics developed for the facility layout problem as well as other algorithms recently developed for the QAP. The experimental results reveal that the proposed algorithm is effective and efficient for the facility layout problem considered. Other heuristic algorithms for the FLP shall be devised, tested, and compared with our algorithm in future studies.

7. References

Baykasoğlu A., Gindy N.N.Z. (2001). A simulated annealing algorithm for dynamic layout Problem, *Computers & Operations research 28,* 1403-1426.

Burkard R. E., Karisch S. & Rendel F. (1991). QAPLIB - A Quadratic Assignment Problem Library, *European Journal of Operational Research 55,* 115-119. Electronic update: http//fmtbhpl.tu-graz.ac.at/~karisch/qaplib.

Caccetta L. & Kusumah Y.S. (2001). Computational aspects of the facility layout design problem, *Non-Linear Analysis 47,* 5599-5610.

Chiang W.C. & Chiang C. (1998). Intelligent local search strategies for solving facility layout problems with the quadratic assignment problem formulation, *European Journal of Operational Research 106,* 457-488.

D. Corne, M. Dorigo & F. Glover (1999). New Ideas in Optimization, *Mac Graw Hill* .

M. Dorigo, E. Bonabeau & G. Theraulaz (2000) Ant algorithms and stimergy, *Future Generation Computer Systems* 2000; 16; 851-871.

L. M. Gambardella, E. D. Taillard & M. Dorigo (1997) Ant colonies for the QAP, *Technical report IDISIA;* 4-97.

Hani Y., Amodeo L., Yalaoui F. & Chen H. (2006). A hybrid genetic algorithm for solving an industrial layout problem, *Journal of Operation and Logistics,* 1, 4.1-4.11.

Hani Y., Amodeo L., Yalaoui F. & Chen H. (2007) « Ant colony optimization for solving an industrial layout problem» *EJOR European Journal of Operational Research 183, Issue 2,* 633-642.

Hicks C. (2004). A genetic algorithm tool designing manufacturing facilities in the capital goods industry, *International Journal of Production Economics 90 (2),* 199-211.

Kusiak, S. & Heragu, S. (1987). The facility layout problem, *European Journal of Operational research,* 29, 229-251.

Lee Y.H. & Lee M.H (2002): A shape-based block layout approach to facility layout problems using hybrid genetic algorithm, *Computers & Industriel engineering* 42, 237-248.

V. Maniezzo, A. Colorni, & M. Dorigo (1994), The ant system applied to the quadratic assignment problem. *Technical report IRIDIA/, Université Libre de Bruxelles,* 94-28.

V. Maniezzo, (1999) Exact and approximate nondeterministic tree-search procedures for the quadratic assignment problem, *INFORMS Journal on Computing*;11; 358–369.

Martens J. (2004) Two genetic algorithmes to solve a layout problem in fashion industry. *European Journal of Operational Research* 154 (1), 304-322.

Meller R. D., Narayanan V., Vance P.H. (1999) Optimal facility layout design, *Operations Research Letters 23,* 117-127.

Mills P., Tsang E., Ford J. (2003). Applying an extended Guided Local Search to the Quadratic Assignment Problem, *Annals of Operational Research,* 118, 121-135.

Sahni S. & Gonzales T. (1976) P-complete approximation problems, *Journal of Associated computer Machinery 23 (5),* 555-565.

Solimanpur M, Vrat P. & Shankar R. (2004) Ant Colony optimization algorithm to the inter-cell layout problem in cellular manufacturing, *European Journal of Operational Research 157,* 592-606.

T. Stützle, & M. Dorigo, (1999) Aco algorithm for the quadratic assignment problem, *Technical report IRIDIA/, Université Libre de Bruxelles,* 99-2.

T. Stützle, & H. Hoos, (2000) MAX-MIN ant system, *Future Generation Computer Systems* 16 889-914.

E. G. Talbi, O.Roux, C. Fonlupt & D. Robillard, (2001) Parallel Ant Colonies for the quadratic assignment problem, *Future Generation Computer Systems* 17, 441-449.

19

Selection of Best Alternative Process Plan in Automated Manufacturing Environment: An Approach Based on Particle Swarm Optimization

F.T.S. Chan[1], M.K. Tiwari[2] and Y. Dashora[2]
[1]*Department of Industrial and Manufacturing Systems Engineering, University of Hong Kong*
[2]*Department of Industrial Engineering and Management, Indian Institute of Technology, Kharagpur*
[1]*Hong Kong,* [2]*India*

1. Introduction

In the present flexible and automated manufacturing environment, selection of optimal process plan is a crucial decision making problem. The systematic determination of processing steps for the transformation of raw material to its finished product is identified as process planning. The real world dynamic shop floor is characterized by the availability of several machines, tools, fixtures/jigs etc., and demands the completion of several design tasks before the commencement of manufacturing actual manufacturing of a part type. Different geometrical and tolerance relationships among several features of the part types necessitate the arrangement of different setups to carry out various and hence, diverse alternative process plans to manufacture a part come into existence. Any of these feasible process plans can be used to produce the particular part type from its raw material [1], [2]. Due to the incorporation of dynamic shop floor situations such as bottleneck machines, non availability of tools, machine breakdown, etc., the process plan selection problem becomes non linear and NP hard in nature. The proliferation of Computer Aided Process Planning (CAPP) systems has made it easy and more efficient to tackle these types of non linear process planning systems. The scheduling complexity in the manufacturing systems was discussed in [2] and it was proposed that this can be reduced with the limited number of tools and auxiliary devices. The three reasons given by [2] to solve the process plan selection problem are: production cost, tool magazine capacity limitation, and reduction of auxiliary devices. Later, the process plan selection problem was attempted in [1] considering three objectives such as to minimize total time, minimize number of setups and to minimize dissimilarity among process plans. Reference [3] contributed in solving process plan selection problem using fuzzy approach to deal with the imprecise information. Reference [4] incorporated the factors such as similarity index within a process plan and degree of similarity among various process plans. They used fuzzy approach to take care of the part type processing sequence. PPS problem has also been attempted using Hybrid Hopfield Neural network and Genetic Algorithm Approach [13].

However, in this paper an attempt has been made to solve the PPS problem by giving a more rational view to part type processing sequence. Here, in addition to fuzzy membership vector a new feature called Similarity Attribute (λ) has been introduced that takes care of the similarity among different part types. Based on the consolidated approach incorporating fuzzy membership vector and similarity attribute, the part type processing sequence is evaluated. To ease the solution strategy, the undertaken PPS problem is modeled as a Traveling Salesman Problem (TSP) that helps to do away the problem complexity and ensures the easy application of various Artificial intelligence (AI) tools. The PPS problem is mapped as a TSP considering the distance of the tour in the terms of the objective function. Due to its NP-hard nature [5] and wide range applicability, TSP has been one of the most studied combinatorial optimization problem. This paper proposes a new Intelligent Particle Swarm Optimization algorithm with the modified concept of Local Repeller (IPSO-LR) to solve the aforementioned PPS problem.

Particle Swarm Optimization (PSO) is a new population based evolutionary computation technique that proceed via self adaptive search. In general, the evolutionary algorithms are based on population of individuals simulating some biological phenomenon. Particle Swarm Optimization is one of the recent developments of evolutionary systems first introduced by Kennedy and Eberhart in 1995 [6]. Unlike other evolutionary systems, no direct recombination of genetic material is incorporated in PSO while the search is in progress. The most important and distinctive feature of PSO is its working that is based on social behavior of particles or individuals in the swarm. The algorithm develops the search strategy by adjusting the trajectory of each particle towards own previous best location and best position of neighboring particles within the search space. Since its introduction, PSO has been tested invariably on several computationally complex NP hard problems [7]. The recent challenges are to employ the algorithm to the real world problems of various complexities than those on which initial versions of it have been applied. Most of the recent developments in the PSO are based on improving its ability to come out of local optima, as it is recognized as common problem encountered by swarms. In this paper, a new improved swarm algorithm is used that has enhanced capability to come out of local minima.

The application of IPSO-LR algorithm has been demonstrated considering one illustrative example. To assess the robustness of IPSO-LR based solution strategy, five well known test parts from the literature have been considered and five new parts have been developed. Rest of the paper has been organized as follows: The Process Plan Selection problem and its TSP formulation have been discussed in section 2. Section 3 gives an overview of PSO and details IPSO-LR algorithm. Section 4 illustrates the application of IPSO-LR to solve PPS problem with the help of an illustrative example. Computational experiments and the discussion of the results are provided in section 5. Section 6 concludes the paper.

2. Problem Environment

The PPS problem is concerned to the problem of making optimal choices among several alternatives and is featured by the selection of machines, cutting tools, fixtures, setups, etc. The problem is to select exactly one process plan for each part type from a number of accessible and feasible process plans and to provide optimal processing sequence for the manufacturing of part types. The problem formulation adopted in this paper is the extended and modified version of the formulation proposed by [4] and [8]. This paper aims to select a process plan for each part type, keeping in view the wider range of objectives as minimization of batch size, time remaining from due dates and number of machinable features, as well as calculating the part type processing sequence, that determine the processing cost and optimum utilization of resources, in a much more justifiable way. The various parameters involved in the process plan selection (PPS) problem can be summarized as:

1. A seven digit code to denote the machines, operations, tools, fixtures, etc., for each step of a process plan.
2. Material handling time for a process plan and the machining time on different machines for a process plan.
3. Batch size, due dates remaining and other manufacturing related features of a part type.

Minimization of batch size, total time remaining from due dates, number of machinable features and process plan execution time, as well as calculating part type processing sequence along with optimum utilization of resources are considered as main objectives targeted in the paper. To pursue these objectives, an integrated objective function is formulated that incorporates the parameters defined in [4] along with addition of a new parameter λ. These parameters warrants due attention because of their immense impact on the solution strategy and objective function formulation, and can be summed up as follows:

1. Similarity Index (SI) of a process plan of a part type.
2. Degree of Similarity (DS) among various process plans of a part type.
3. Membership vector (μ) of a part type.
4. Similarity attribute (λ) of different part types.

The details about the calculations and authenticity of first three parameters can be referred in [4]. This paper adds a new dimension to the solution of the PPS problem by the incorporation of a new parameter termed as Similarity Attribute. The formulation proposed by [4] did not take into account the similarity among the processing of part types that is a crucial parameter affecting the dynamics and cost efficiency of the shop floor. Hence, Similarity attribute (λ) has been incorporated in the objective function to make it more authentic. Its calculation strategy has been provided in section 4, where solution strategy for the underlying problem has been illustrated. Minimization of the aforementioned first two parameters provides cost efficiency and the values of rest two determine the part type processing sequence. Thus, to accomplish objectives highlighted in this paper, they have been integrated into single sub objective that is a trade-off between all the aforementioned features (detailed in section 3). To develop the solution strategy for the PPS problem, it is formulated as a Traveling Salesman Problem (TSP). It's basic TSP formulation is described in the following discussion:

2.1 TSP Formulation of the PPS Problem

In a TSP with one salesman, the salesman has to visit each city in his/her designated area and then come back to the home town [5]. Here, each process plan is considered as a city (*i.e. a* node) and a salesman is restricted to move through only one node among the nodes characterizing a part type. A tour is considered to be complete when the particle has moved through a node of each part type. In the TSP model of the problem, the value of objective function represents the total distance covered by the salesman in a tour. The criterion to move from one node to another depends upon the solution strategy; in the context of the PPS problem, it is based on the probability to choose, thus, not based on the integer model.

Hence the formulation can be considered as TSP with Mixed Integer Programming (MIP). The details are provided in the next section that provides an insight to the basics of PSO as well as details IPSO-LR algorithm.

3. Proposed IPSO-LR Algorithm

PSO belongs to a broad class of population based optimization technique that is guided by the social behavior of flocking organisms, like birds, honeybees, etc. The fundamental rules adhered by the individuals comprising a flock may be outlined as to match velocities with nearest neighbors, and to be closer with the others in the swarm. Thus mutation with conscience has been claimed for PSO [9]-[12]. In this case, each particle tends to accelerate towards its own previous best position and towards the best position of neighbor particles encountered, with the usual result being clustering of individuals in optimal regions of space. Since the advent of PSO, the challenge has been to apply PSO to the problems of various domains. In this paper, a new Intelligent Particle Swarm Optimization Algorithm (IPSO-LR) with the modified concept of local repeller has been developed to efficiently model the problem in the algorithmic context as well as to avoid the problem of entrapment in local optima.

At each position, the velocity and position of each particle is being updated using some basic equations and rules. The velocity of particle at each position is updated utilizing the aforementioned characteristics and the relation detailed in the following subsection:

3.1 Velocity Evaluation

The model for velocity and position updating signifies the intelligence of the swarm and can be mathematically formulated as:

$$\forall i \in N, \; v_{i\,next} = \chi [v_i + c_c \times \text{rand}(.) \times (\Delta x_{ci}) + c_s \times \text{rand}(.) \times (\Delta x_{ni})] \quad (1)$$

where, v_i is the current velocity of the particle; N is the number of particles; χ is the constriction coefficient, and is mathematically expressed as:

$$\chi = \frac{2\kappa}{[2-\beta-\sqrt{\beta^2-4\beta}]} \quad (2)$$

s.t. $\beta = c_1 + c_2 \quad , \beta > 4, \quad \kappa \in]0,1]$

Further, rand (.) is a random function with a range [0, 1]; c_c and c_s are positive constant parameters, called acceleration coefficients (which control the maxi-mum step size the particle can do). c_c and c_s controls the impact of previous values of particle positions and velocities on its current one. Suitable selection of acceleration coefficients can provide a balance between the global and the local search. The constriction factor χ helps to ensure convergence [9], whereas the factors such as c_c and c_s along with rand (.) guarantee the thorough search in the region near to o_i and n_i. Different configurations of χ as well as their theoretical analysis can be found in [9].

In the velocity relation, Δx_{ci} and Δx_{ni} are self best positional differences and neighborhood best positional difference. In the equation (2), Δx_{ci} and Δx_{ni} are calculated by the following relations:

$$\Delta x_{ci} = o_i - x_{ni}\,;\, and\,,\ \ \Delta x_{ni} = n_i - x_{ni}\,, \tag{3}$$

where,

o_i : Position of previous best position of particle.

x_{ni} : Position of nth feasible node. Here, $n \in N_{fi}$ (*i.e.* set denoting feasible nodes to move, for particle *i*.)

n_i : Previous best position of neighboring particles.

In the above discussion, the position of a particle is characterized by the set of variables characterizing a node. The velocity of ith particle to each feasible node is calculated as per the aforementioned equation that is followed by the position updating according to the relation:

$$\forall i \in N\,,\, x_i = x_{i\,vmax\,f}\,, \tag{4}$$

where, x_i denotes the position of the particle; $x_{i\,vmax\,f}$ is the position of the node for which the velocity found is maximum. The self previous best position of each particle is updated using the following relation:

$$\forall i \in N\,,\, o_i = \begin{cases} o_i & if\ f(x_i) \geq f(o_i) \\ x_i & if\ f(x_i) < f(o_i) \end{cases} \tag{5}$$

where, $f\,(x_i)$ denotes the respective objective function value considered in the problem. The previous best position of neighboring particles is updated according to the following relation:

$$\forall i \in N_i\,,\, n_i = \min_{o_i} f(o_i) \tag{6}$$

where, N_i is the set denoting neighbors of particle *i*.

to reduce the probability of leaving the search space, the velocity of particles is restricted to the range of [$-V_{max}$, $+V_{max}$], where,

$$V_{max} = \upsilon \times x_{max}\,; \quad 0.1 \leq \upsilon \leq 10 \tag{7}$$

3.2 Sociometry of IPSO-LR

Neighborhood is the most decisive criterion that directs the search procedure of swarms. It signifies how the movement a particle is influenced by the information carried by the other particles. The neighborhood is exploited for the mutual sharing of crucial information among particles that helps them in further movement and diversify search technique. The topological structure of population controls its propensity of exploration versus exploitation [11]. The initial versions of particle swarm select a particle from the specified neighbors as a source of influence and ignore others. This type of strategy only provides a choice of

choosing a particle from the neighborhood; the more is its size, the more is the likeliness of choosing the better one.
In this paper, a cluster type of network topology is adopted as it produces promising results as compared to that of other neighborhood topologies like ring, all, pyramid, triangular, frame, etc. [12]. In the proposed strategy, various process plans of a part type are in neighborhood with each other as they characterize same attributes of a part type. Thus, various process plans (particles) of a part type form a cluster that shares information among the members. In this case, the number of clusters formed is equal to the number of process plans. As evident from Figure 1, each cluster is in further interaction with other clusters through the arcs joining the two closest nodes of each pair of clusters.

3.3 Modified Strategy to Avoid Local Optima

Entrapment in the local optima is the situation where the algorithm sticks to some premature solutions and does not show any improvement. To alleviate this problem, the concept of local repeller [12] with some modifications to suit the problem structure has been utilized. The most alluring trait of this technique is its simplicity and efficacy to avoid local optima. As and when the path corresponding to local optima is encountered, the sequence of process plans that is identified to be constituent of local optimum is made 'repelling' *i.e* .the particles are compelled to explore the search space more thoroughly and hence, the search is directed towards global optimum. This strategy guarantees the escape from the local optima and thus is very effective.

4. Implementation of IPSO-LR Algorithm on the PPS Problem (Illustrative Example)

4.1 Problem Characteristics

This paper adopts the formulation of PPS problem from [4] and [8]. To denote the machines, operations, tools, fixtures etc. a seven-digit code has been used. The data related to alternative process plans, processing time on different machines, material handling time for the different process plans, the batch size, due dates remaining and features of each part type are adopted from [8].
In the undertaken problem, the objectives considered are minimization of batch size, time remaining from due dates and number of machinable features, as well as calculating part type processing sequence along with optimum utilization of resources. The objectives like maximization of batch size, minimization of time remaining from due dates and minimization of number of machinable features are incorporated in the definition of membership vector μ [4]. The parameter Similarity attribute (λ) quantifies the similarity among the part types that is based on the number of machines, fixtures, tools and operations performed to produce these. Its formulation is given as follows:

$$\lambda_{im} = \frac{C_{im}}{C_m}; \quad \lambda_{io} = \frac{C_{io}}{C_o}; \quad \lambda_i = \frac{C_{it}}{C_t}; \quad \lambda_{im} = \frac{C_{if}}{C_f}; \Rightarrow \lambda_i = \frac{\lambda_{im} + \lambda_i + \lambda_{im} + \lambda_{im}}{4}; \qquad (8)$$

where, $\lambda_{im}, \lambda_i, \lambda_{im}, \lambda_{im}$ are the constants denoting contribution of attributes related to machines, operations, tools and fixtures, respectively, to the calculation of similarity attribute; C_{im} , C_{io} , C_{it}, C_{if} are the cardinalities of the sets denoting number of machines, operations, tools and fixtures, respectively, utilized by the process plans of part type i ; C_m , C_o , C_t , C_f are the cardinalities of sets denoting the total number of machines, operations, tools and fixtures, respectively, used to manufacture all the part types from all the possible alternatives.

The parameter DS is a measure of accounting for the similarity among the several process plans of the different part types. It results from the comparison of their constituent elements, namely the operation codes. The parameter SI defines the similarity contained in a process plan itself. It denotes the ease with which a part can be made from the particular process plan. The details about the calculation of DS and SI can be referred from [4].

4.2 IPSO-LR Algorithm Based Solution Strategy

To initialize the process, all the particles are randomly distributed over the nodes. Here, the number of particles equals the number of nodes present in the TSP formulation. The most critical step in the application of IPSO-LR to solve the PPS problem is the characterization of the parameters that represents position. In the formulation used in the proposed paper, a node (*i.e. a process plan*) characterizes the position of the particle. In this case, the velocity to each feasible node j from the particle on node i is calculated as per the following equation:

$$v_{ij} = \chi [v_i + c_c \times \text{rand}(.) \times (\Delta x_{cij}) + c_s \times \text{rand}(.) \times (\Delta x_{nij})] \quad (9)$$

Here, Δx_{cij} and Δx_{nij} are the positional differences that needs to be defined in the problem context. In the scenario of PPS problem, these can be evaluated using the following relations:

$$\Delta x_{cij} = A \times [1 - DS_{o_i, x_{ji}} \times (SI_{o_i} + SI_{x_{ji}}) \times \mu_{x_{ji}} + \lambda_{x_{ji}}] + B \times t$$

$$\Delta x_{cij} = A \times [1 - DS_{n_i, x_{ji}} \times (SI_{n_i} + SI_{x_{ji}}) \times \mu_{x_{ji}} + \lambda_{x_{ji}}] + B \times t \quad (10)$$

Having updated the velocity, the position of particle is updated as per equation 9. Another major difference in the application of IPSO-LR from the traditional PSO lies in the definition of previous best position of the particle, o_i, and neighbor's previous best position, n_i. Because of the TSP structure of the problem the particles cannot be always in the constant motion and hence, after completing the tour, particles are again randomly distributed over the nodes and set to move. The updated previous best position and neighborhood best position guide the particles in the consecutive generations to choose the better alternatives. The pseudo code for the IPSO-LR algorithm applied to the PPS problem is given below:

Create the initial population P and set $iter_{max}$, and $iter_{LRmax}$ (*i.e.* number of iterations for which if solution is not improved, then local optimum is considered to be encountered)
iter = 0;
$iter_{LR}$ = 0;
for each particle $i \in$ P:
initialize the x_i , v_i , o_{ij} ,n_{ij} ,neighborhood N_i , global best position g_{ij} and value of overall

```
    global best tour g_j ( of all the particles). //Here, o_ij, n_ij, g_ij, g_j are the arrays containing the
     values of respective positions in each part type.
repeat:
    for (j=1:N)                    // Here, N is the
                                   number of part types.
      repeat:
          for each particle i ∈ P:
              if f (x_ij) < f (o_ij)
            then o_ij = x_ij;
              endif
              if f (o_ij) < f (g_ij)
                  then g_ij = o_ij;
              endif
          endfor
          if sum of the tour < (g_j)
              then g_j = sum of the tour;
                   iter_LR = 0;
          else iter_LR = iter_LR + 1;
          endif
          if iter_LR = iter_LRmax
              then mark the tour as repelling ( i.e. any
                   particle trying to complete this
                   tour is randomly thrown away.
          Update x_i and v_i accordingly.
    endfor
    iter = iter + 1;
until iter = iter_max;
```

5. Computational Experience

This section aims to provide the summary of numerical simulation of the proposed algorithm along with the comparative results with other established techniques from the literature in a condensed form. The number of alternative solutions increases exponentially as the number of part types and their alternative process plans increase. The complexity of the undertaken problem can be gauged by the fact that aforementioned 10 parts and their 52 alternative process plans give rise to a total of 1.28×10^{13} feasible solutions. By the application of IPSO-LR the best alternative process plans and their sequence obtained is listed in Table 1.

Application of the ACO strategy [8] also renders similar results. The applicability and efficacy of the proposed algorithm is evident from the fact that IPSO-LR outperforms other established techniques from the literature to solve the complex process plan selection problem with various formulations. In fact, due to its less computational complexity, the proposed IPSO-LR algorithm gains an edge over other techniques when the problems pertaining to real size data sets (like the undertaken data set) are concerned. The proposed algorithm is characterized by faster convergence along with the better and logical escape from the local optima.

Part type processing sequence	Part type	Process plan selected	Route of the plan
1	3	5	M011103,L020201,L070501,L080601,L120101,L100801,L050301
2	2	3	M011103,L020201,L030201,M151304,L080601
3	9	3	M011103, L020201,L080601,L090701,L110901
4	7	3	M011103, L02021,L030201,L080601,L070501,L060401,L120101
5	8	2	M011103, L020201,L030201,L060401,L070501,L080601
6	10	11	M011108,L020201,L030201,L040202,L080601,L090701,L110901
7	6	5	M011103, L020201,L040201,L060401,M100804
8	1	6	M011103,L020201,L030201,M100704
9	5	2	L010101,L020201,L030201,L040202,M151304,M100804
10	4	1	L010101,L020201,L060401,L120101,M171504

Table 1. Optimal Process Plan Selected

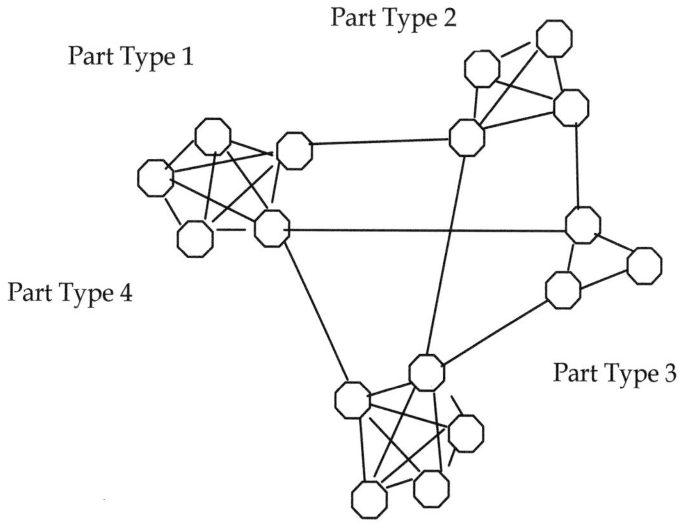

Figure 1. Graphical representation of PPS problem

Figure 2 provides a comparative plot between the fitness index of particles and the number of generations for the proposed strategy and ACO based strategy [8]. Here, the fitness index is defined as:

$$fi = \frac{Obj_{best} - Obj_{worst}}{Obj_{worst}}; \tag{11}$$

Where, Obj_{best} *and* Obj_{worst} are the objective function values of the particles covering shortest tour and longest tour respectively.

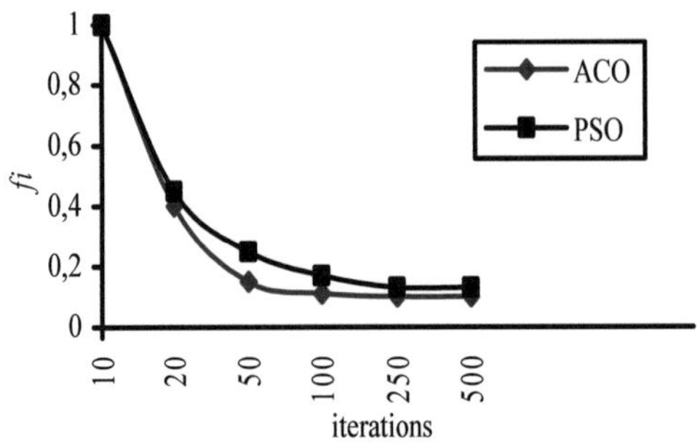

Figure 2. Comparative convergence with ACO [8]

The comparative convergence trend of the algorithm with ACO based approach proves the compatibility of the proposed algorithm, as shown in the Figure 2. Figure 3 plots the CPU time vs number of iterations. From the plot (Figure 2), it can be visualized that the value of fitness index decreases as the number of generations increase that in turn proves the clustering of particles around best solution. This clustering is further proved by the Figure 4 that provides the plot between the percentages of particles that deviates from the best particle by not more than 5%.

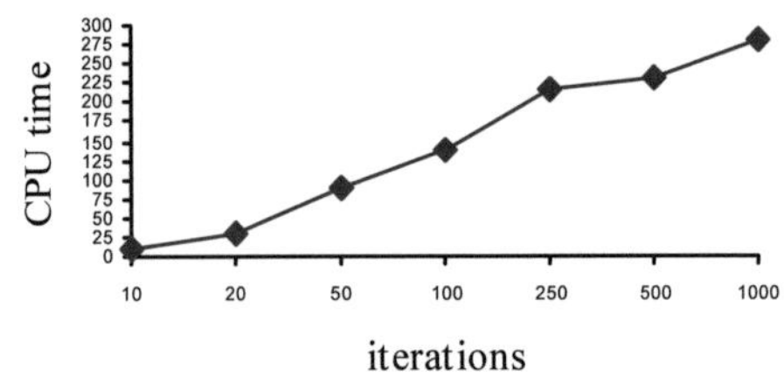

Figure 3. Variation of CPU time (ms) with number of iterations

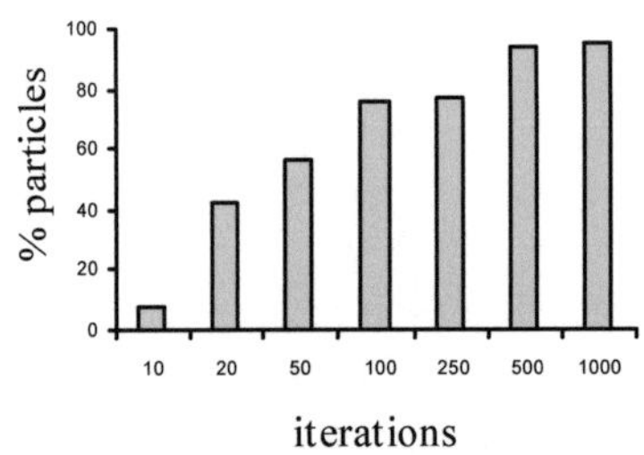

Figure 4. Percentage of deviating particles

In order to illustrate further the effectiveness of the proposed IPSO-LR algorithm, various problems taken from the literature [2], [3], [14] have been tested with the same formulation of objective functions and parameter as is proposed in them. As a matter of fact, the proposed approach obtains the best solutions for different process plan selection examples, the comparative results of which are provided in Table 2.

	Example of [1]		Example of [2]		Example of [3]	
Applied methodology ↓	Objective function value	Process plan selected	Objective function value	Process plan selected	Objective function value	Process plan selected
Reference [1]	33.1	1, 3, 7	30.8	1,4,7,9	61	3, 5, 7
Reference [2]	34.5	1, 3, 5	30.8	1,4,7,9	59	3, 4, 6
Reference [3]	32.5	1, 4, 5	30.8	1,4,7,9	61	3, 5, 6
ACO approach [8]	32.5	1, 4, 5	30.8	1,4,7,9	59	3, 4, 6
Proposed IPSO-LR approach	32.5	1, 4, 5	30.8	1,4,7,9	59	3, 4, 6

Table 2. Comparative results of various methodologies from the literature

In nutshell, the aforementioned computational results not only prove the efficacy and supremacy of the proposed strategy but also provide a new dimension to the solution of complex PPS problems in the practical environment.

6. Conclusive Remarks

Ever so changing competitive manufacturing structure is challenged by the issue to properly optimize resource allocation and their uses in order to get the best out of available alternatives. The PPS problem (amidst unpredictable disruptions observed in shop floor), is of substantial importance in flexible and automated manufacturing systems and needs much attention to be paid. The performance of flexible manufacturing systems is greatly influenced by the selection of viable and economic process plans among the other competing plans. This paper presents a new IPSO-LR algorithm to solve a complex real time PPS problem with the objectives like minimization of batch size, time remaining from due dates and number of machinable features, as well as calculating part type processing sequence along with optimum utilization of resources. The algorithm is characterized by the enhanced capability to come of local optima in a logical manner and has knack to handle the problems pertaining to large alternatives. The proposed work provides a new and broader dimension to the solution of PPS problem by consolidating a new parameter Similarity Attribute 'λ', that formulates the objective function in a more justifiable way. The real strength of swarms is derived from the interaction among particles while exploring the search space collaboratively. The terms of positional difference introduced in the velocity formula leads the particle to be successful regarding reaching towards optima and guides it by the previous successes of itself and other particles.

This paper finds its contribution in the expanding area of research of intelligent automation in industries as well as in the broad field of interdependent evolutionary computation. The computational experience establishes the fact that the proposed algorithm is effective to model and solve PPS problems of varying complexities. Experimental results have shown the robustness of the algorithm and its outperforming behaviour over established techniques in the process planning field. Also, based on these results, the use of IPSO-LR algorithm seems to be encouraging in supporting the premise of automated and dynamic and intelligent process planning. Future work includes the development of web enabled intelligent Process Planning System with embedded features of e-Manufacturing and application of various tools and techniques related to Data Mining to refine the search algorithms.

7. References:

Bhaskaran, K., 1990, Process plan selection .*International Journal of Production Research*, 28 (8), 1527-1539. [1]

Kusiak, A., and Finke, G., 1988,Selection of process plans in automated manufacturing systems. *IEEE Transactions of Robotics and Automation*, 4(4), 397 - 402[2]

Zhang, H.C., and Huang, S.H., 1994, A fuzzy approach to process plan selection . *International Journal of Production Research*, 32(6), 1265-1279. [3]

Tiwari, M.K., and Vidyarthi, N.K., 1998, An integrated approach to solving the process plan selection problem in an automated manufacturing system, *International Journal of Production Research*, 36(8), 2167-2184. [4]

Onwubolu, G. C. and Clerc, M., 2004. Optimal path for automated operations by a new heuristic approach using particle swarm optimization. *International Journal of Production and Research*, 42, 473-491. [5]

J. Kennedy and R. C. Eberhart, Particle swarm optimization, in *Proc. IEEE Int. Conf. Neural Networks*, vol. 4, Perth, Australia, Dec. 1995, pp. 1942–1948. [6]

Juang, C. F., 2004, A hybrid of Genetic Algorithm and Particle Swarm Optimization for Recurrent Network design, *IEEE Transactions on Systems, Man and Cybernatics*-Part B: Cybernetics, 34(2), 997-1006. [7]

Dashora, Y. ,Kumar, S., Shankar, R. and Tiwari, M. K., Ant Colony Optimization based approach to select the optimum Process Plan in Automated Manufacturing Environment, communicated to *IIE Transactions*, UIIE-0061. [8]

Clerc, M. and Kennedy, J., 2002, The Particle Swarm—Explosion, Stability, and Convergence in a Multidimensional Complex Space, *IEEE Transactions on Evolutionary Computation*, 6(1), 58-73. [9]

Wachowiak, M. P., Smolíková, R., Zheng, Y., Zurada, J. M., Elmaghraby, A. S., 2004,An Approach to Multimodal Biomedical Image Registration Utilizing Particle Swarm Optimization, *IEEE Transactions on Evolutionary Computation*, 8(3), 289-301. [10]

Mendes, R., Kennedy, J. and Neves, J., 2004, The Fully Informed Particle Swarm: Simpler, Maybe Better, *IEEE Transactions on Evolutionary Computation*, 8(3), 204-210. [11]

Parsopoulos, K. E. and Vrahatis, M. N., 2004, On the Computation of All Global Minimizers Through Particle Swarm Optimization, *IEEE Transactions on Evolutionary Computation*, 8(3), 211-224. [12]

Ming, X.G., and Mak, K.L., 2000, A hybrid Hopfield network-genetic algorithm approach to optimal process plan selection, *International Journal of Production Research*, 38(8), 1823-1839. [13]

20

Job-shop scheduling and visibility studies with a hybrid ACO algorithm

Heinonen, J. and Pettersson, F.
Åbo Akademi University
Finland

1. Introduction

Manufacturing today is primarily cooked down to all-out efforts into profitability. Factories are moved to low-salary countries in order to ensure that profits are maintained and stockholders kept happy. Decisions like these are met with debates about morale, ethics and responsibilities that companies have to society, since losing an entire manufacturing plant can be devastating to a community. An alternative to industrial relocalization is trying to maintain profitability through development of effective production schedules, better utilization of resources and overall better planning in existing manufacturing plants. The significance of effective planning methods has, in other words, increased and will likely continue to do so.

The focus of this chapter is to solve the MT10 job-shop scheduling problem using 4 different variants of the Ant Colony Optimization (ACO) algorithm and to try to rank them. A hybrid model, that uses a postprocessing algorithm to improve the resulting schedule, is also tried for all four ACO versions. The term *visibility* is explained in the context of job-shop scheduling, and incorporated into the test runs.

When we are talking about job-shop scheduling problems (JSP), we mean a set of machines $\boldsymbol{M}$, a set of jobs $\boldsymbol{J}$ and a set of operations $\boldsymbol{O}$. For each operation there is a job to which it belongs, a machine on which it it has to be processed, a predetermined processing time on that machine as well as a predetermined processing order on the machines. The problem is to minimize the makespan while ensuring that no more than one job can be processed at the same time on the same machine, and seeing to that when a job starts, it must be completed (and can't be interrupted).

There have been numerous publications of successful algorithms applied to job-shop problems. Among exact mathematical methods are Mixed integer linear programming and Branch & Bound, among approximation methods there are List Scheduler Algorithms (see Panwalker & Iskander, 1977 for a survey), that assign one operation at a time from a list that is sorted by some priority rule, Shifting Bottleneck by Adams et al. (1988), Simulated Annealing by van Laarhoven et al. (1988), Tabu search was first used in job shop scheduling by Taillard (1989) and a Genetic algorithm approach by Nakano and Yamada (1991).

A newcomer in these approaches to the JSP, ant colony optimization has become an increasingly popular candidate when it comes to algorithms that mimic behaviour of processes that exist in nature. The first ACO algorithm was introduced by Marco Dorigo in his doctoral thesis (1992) and was called an Ant System (AS). Since then AS has matured into an algorithm that does very well when it comes to problem types that are formulated as a traveling salesman problem (TSP) as well as the quadratic assignment problem (QAP). As a result of research into ACO algorithms, some very successful variants have emerged.

We have the Elitist AS (EAS) proposed by Dorigo et al. (1996), in which the pheromone updating rules are biased towards the best solution found so far, the idea being to exploit the solution components within that solution.

Ant Colony System (ACS) by Dorigo and Gambardella (1997) has several modifications to the original AS. It uses a modified rule when an ant chooses the next travel node, it uses a best-so-far pheromone update rule but applies pheromone evaporation only to the trail that belong to solution components that are in the best-so-far solution. It also uses a local pheromone update rule to decrease the pheromone values on visited solution components, in order to encourage exploration.

Rank-based AS (RAS) by Bullnheimer et al. (1999), is a variant where the elite ant as well as a selection of ants with good solutions during that iteration get to update the pheromone trails.

MAX-MIN AS (*MM*AS) by Stützle and Hoos (2000), is an approach that updates the pheromone trails, according to some convergence measure, with either the iteration-best ant or the best-so-far ant. The algorithm uses a lower bound for the pheromones (>0) as well as restricting the maximum amount of pheromone a trail can have. The lower bound encourage ant exploratory behaviour and the upper bound is prohibiting premature convergence due to the elite solution dominating the other solutions.

Hypercube Framework (HCF) by Blum and Dorigo (2004) is more of a framework for implementing ACO algorithms. Among the benefits are automatic scaling of pheromone values to the interval [0,1].

In a paper by Colorni et al. (1993) AS was applied into job-shop scheduling and proved to be a noteworthy candidate when faced with the task of chosing a suitable algorithm for scheduling problems. The conclusions in the aforementioned paper were that AS is one of the most easily adaptable population-based heuristics so far proposed and that its computational paradigm is indeed effective under very different conditions.

As an example of ACO robustness, Jayaraman et al. (2000) used an ACO algorithm in solving a combinatorial optimization problem of multiproduct batch scheduling as well as the continuous function optimization problem for the design of multiproduct plant with single product campaigns and horizon constraints. Further real-world applications with regard to ACO algorithms would be using ACO to solve an established set of vehicle routing problems as done by Bell and McMullen (2004) and a dynamic regional nurse-scheduling problem in Austria by Gutjahr and Rauner (2005). The former paper concluded the results were competetive and in the latter paper ACO was compared to a greedy assignment algorithm and achieved highly significant improvements.

Kuo-Ching Ying et al. (2004) applied the ant colony system to permutation flow-shop sequencing and effectively solved the $n/m/P/C_{max}$ problem, and commented that this suggests that the ant colony system metaheuristic is well worth exploring in the context of solving different scheduling problems.

An example of ACO and flowshops in recent use would be a paper by Gajpal and Rajendran (2006), where they used a new ACO algorithm (NACO) to minimize the completion-

variance of jobs, showing that work with ACO algorithms is an ongoing process to modify and improve the original AS and apply it to a variety of scheduling problems.
For two of the top performing ACO algorithms, ACS and *MMAS*, convergence to the optimal solution has been proved (Dorigo and Stützle, 2004 as well as Stützle and Dorigo, 2002). It is worth to remember that convergence results do not allow prediction of how quickly an optimal solution can be found.

2. Problem description

The Job-Shop Scheduling Problem (JSP) can be characterized as n jobs to be processed on m machines. In general it is a set of concurrent and conflicting goals to be satisfied using a finite set of resources where resources are called machines and basic tasks are called jobs. Each job is a request for scheduling a set of operations according to a process plan which specifies precedence restrictions. We have

$$M = \{M_1, ..., M_m\} \qquad \text{a given set of machines}$$

$$J = \{J_1, ..., J_n\} \qquad \text{a given set of jobs}$$

$$O = \{O_1, ..., O_n\} \qquad \text{a set of operations}$$

For each operation $u_{ij} \in O$ there is a job J_i to which it belongs, a machine M_j on which it has to be run and a processing time p_{ij} of the operation u_{ij}, where p_{ij} is a nonnegative integer. Every job is a chain of operations and every operation has to be processed on a given machine for a given time. The task is to find the starting times of all operations such that the completion time of the very last operation is minimal. The chain order of each job has to be maintained and each machine can only process one job at the same time. No job can be preempted; once an operation starts it must be completed. The solution s to an instance of the n x m JSP specifies a processing order for all of the jobs on each machine and implicitly defines an earliest starttime and earliest completion time for each operation. The maximum of the completion times is called *makespan* and most research address the problem of makespan minimization.
Given an instance of JSP we can associate with it a disjunctive graph $G = (V, A, E)$, where V is the node set, A is the conjunctive arc set and E is the disjunctive arc set. The nodes V correspond to all of the operations and two dummy nodes, a source and a sink. The conjunctive arcs A represent the precedence relationships between the operations of a single job and the disjunctive arcs E represent all pairs of operations to be performed on the same machine. All arcs emanating from a node have the processing time of the operation performed at that node as their length. The source has conjunctive arcs with length zero emanating to all the first operations of the job and the sink has conjunctive arcs coming from all the last operations. A feasible schedule corresponds to a selection of one arc from each disjunctive arc pair such that the resulting directed graph is acyclic, i.e. no loops can be found. The problem of minimizing the makespan reduces to finding a set of disjunctive arcs which minimize the length of the critical path in the directed graph. An in-depth description of disjunctive graphs with regard to job-shop problems can be found in for instance the article about AS and JSP by Colorni et al. (1993).

The MT10 problem is a 10 x 10 instance formulated by Muth and Thompson in 1963. It consists of 10 jobs processed on 10 machines, and every job has 10 tasks to perform. The processing times vary greatly with shortest duration being only 2 time units and longest 99 time units. It has the reputation of being one of the most difficult combinatorial problems ever considered, and was not solved exactly until as late as 1989 by Carlier and Pinson using a branch and bound algorithm. It is a typical job-shop problem.

3. ACO

ACO belongs to the class metaheuristics. The term *metaheuristic* is derived from two greek words, *heuristic* which means "to find" and the prefix *meta*, which means "beyond, in the sense of an upper level". It has come to mean a high-level strategy for guiding heuristics in a search for feasible solutions as well as a framework that can be specialized to solve optimization problems. ACO is also a succesful example of swarm intelligence, whose purpose is to design intelligent multi-agent systems by taking inspirations from the collective behaviour of social insects.

ACO is modeled after the foraging behaviour of certain ant species. In the 1940s the French entomologist Pierre-Paul Grassé observed that some species of termites react to what he called "significant stimuli" (Grassé, 1946). He used the term "stigmergy" to describe the communication of ants, and he described this communication as workers being stimulated by the performance they have achieved. Ants alter their environment by means of pheromone trails. A pheromone is any chemical or set of chemicals produced by a living organism that transmits a message to other members of the same species. It is volatile and evaporates quickly, and ants secrete this chemical by walking and follow, in turn, other pheromone trails left by other ants. There are alarm pheromones, food trail pheromones and others that affect behavior or physiology. Strong food trail pheromone concentrations are perceived and stimulate ants to move into that direction. Ants are able to transport food through this mechanism by finding and maintaining the shortest path between the food source and the nest. Occasionally there will be the stray ant taking another route, and this event can be seen as exploration, the ants are constantly trying to find a more effective path. This mechanism was demonstrated by Denebourg et al. (1990), who in an experiment called "the double bridge" connected a nest of Argentine ants with a food source. Figure 1 (a) shows the experimental setup and figure 1 (b) another experimental setup by Goss et al. (1989). If the setup is that of figure 1 (a), initially, each ant randomly chooses one of the two bridges. Due to random fluctuations, after some time one of the two bridges presents a higher concentration of pheromone and attracts more ants. After a while almost the whole colony converges toward the use of the same bridge. With the setup illustrated in figure 1 (b) another mechanism besides random fluctuations was demonstrated: the ants randomly choosing the shorter path travel between the nest and the food source faster and, given time, this means that pheromone will accumulate faster on this path, converging the population towards using this shorter path.

The mechanism can be utilized in order to find the shortest path in, for instance, minimizing makespan for scheduling problems. The underlying problems are formulated as a TSP, that is, a connected, undirected graph $G = (V, E)$ with weights on the edges between the nodes. The nodes V denote the cities, and the edge weight is the distance between two cities. The goal is to find a tour in G that connects all cities once so that the overall length is minimal.

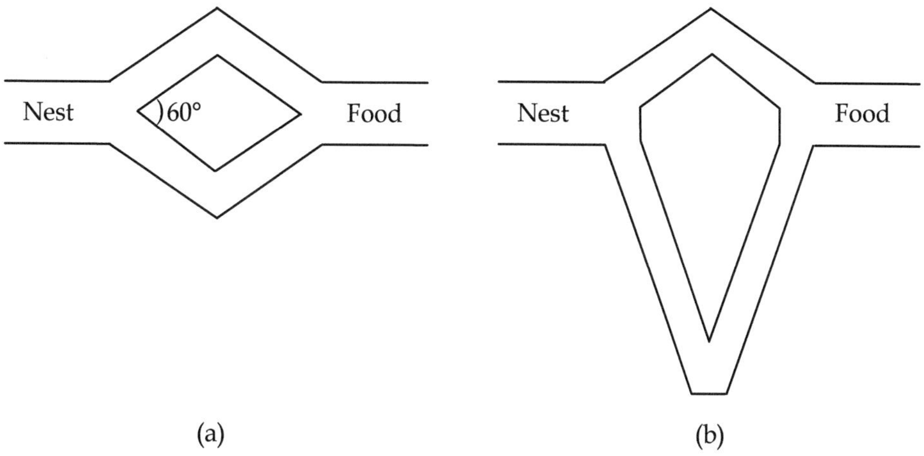

Figure 1. Experimental setup for the double bridge experiments: (a) branches have equal length; (b) branches have different lengths

Having artifical ants search the solution space simulate real ants searching their environment. The artifical ants can be equipped with some oddities that real life ants don't have, for instance a local heuristic function to guide their search through a set of feasible solutions only, or an adaptive memory corresponding to the pheromone trail so that they can remember visited nodes. Also we require the ants to be symmetrical in the sense that they move from the nest to the food and back using the same path. The ACO algorithm also keeps tracks of visited nodes, meaning the ants have a memory which helps them select the next node from a list of possible choices.

3.1 Ant System (AS)

Each edge e_{ij} has a pheromone value τ_{ij} associated with it, and this pheromone value can be read and modified by the ants. The algorithm starts with the user sprinkling some pheromone on random edges. All ants are initially in their home nest, and move to a node in their feasible list. When located at a node i an ant k uses the pheromone trails τ_{ij} to compute the probability of choosing node j as the next node:

$$p_{ij}^{k} = \begin{cases} \dfrac{\tau_{ij}^{\alpha}\eta_{ij}^{\beta}}{\sum_{l\in N_i^k} \tau_{il}^{\alpha}\eta_{il}^{\beta}}, j \in N_i^k \\ 0, j \notin N_i^k \end{cases} \quad (1)$$

N_i^k is the feasible neighbourhood of ant k when in node i, that is, the list of cities that ant k has not yet visited. The parameter $\eta_{ij} = C / d_{ij}$, where d_{ij} is the distance between nodes i and j, and C is a positive constant, is a measure of heuristic information, in other words η_{ij} is our *visibility*. Parameters a and β determine the relative influence of the pheromone trail and the heuristic information. If $a = 0$ then the closest cities are more likely to be selected. If $\beta = 0$ then only pheromone amplification is at work, which generally leads to the rapid emergence

of a stagnation situation, all ants eventually follow the same path and construct the same tour. Dorigo found in his studies (Dorigo et al. 1996) that typically $\beta > \alpha$.
Once all ants have completed their tour the pheromone trails get updated. The pheromone values are modified in order to bias ants in the future iterations to construct solutions similar to the best ones previously constructed. First the pheromone on all arcs is lowered by a constant, and then pheromone is added on the arcs that the ants have passed in their tour. Evaporation is implemented by:

$$\tau_{ij} \leftarrow (1-p)\tau_{ij} \tag{2}$$

where $0 < p \leq 1$ is the evaporation rate. This enables the algorithm to "forget" previous bad decisions and avoids unlimited accumulation on the edges. The deposition of pheromone on the edges is done by means of global trail update

$$\tau_{ij} \leftarrow (1-p)\tau_{ij} + \sum_{k=1}^{m} \Delta\tau_{ij}^{k}, \forall(i,j) \in L \tag{3}$$

where $\Delta\tau_{ij}^{k}$ is the amount of pheromone ant k deposits on the arcs it has visited, which usually amounts to the value Q / C^k, where C^k is the length of the tour and Q is a positive constant. This means that arcs used by many ants, and therefore part of short tours, receive more pheromone and are therefore more likely to be chosen by ants in future iterations of the algorithm. When using an elitist ant system, the solution presented by the best-solution-so-far adds extra pheromone on its arcs. Equation (3) becomes

$$\tau_{ij} \leftarrow (1-p)\tau_{ij} + \sum_{k=1}^{m} \Delta\tau_{ij}^{k} + e\Delta\tau_{ij}^{bs}, \forall(i,j) \in L \tag{4}$$

where e is a parameter that defines the weight given to the best-so-far tour and

$$\Delta\tau_{ij}^{bs} = 1/C^{bs} \text{ if } e_{ij} \text{ belongs to the ants tour, 0 otherwise} \tag{5}$$

where C^{bs} is the length of the best-so-far tour.
When initializing the system, all ants can be placed in the starting node or sprinkled randomly over all nodes. Dorigo studied the differences and came to the conclusion that it had little effect, though placing them randomly gave sometimes slightly better performance. Also, the differences between three AS algorithms, *ant-cycle*, *ant-density* and *ant-quantity* were studied in the same paper. In the latter two models each ant lay its trail at each step, without waiting for the end of the tour, whereas in the *ant-cycle* pheromone updates occur at the end of the tour. In the *ant-density* model a quantity Q of trail is left on edge (i,j) every time an ant goes from i to j, whereas in the *ant-quantity* model the amount of pheromone left was Q/d_{ij}. The *ant-cycle* model performed best and was chosen, and is the one depicted in the equations above.

3.2 Rank-based Ant System (RAS)

This version is an extension to the original AS. After all m ants have generated a tour, the ants are sorted by tour length and the contribution of an ant to the pheromone trail update is weighted according to the rank μ of the ant. An elitist strategy is used as well.
Only the ω best ants are considered and $\omega = \sigma - 1$, where σ is the number of elitist ants in the system. This means that equation (4) is modified accordingly

$$\tau_{ij} \leftarrow (1-p)\tau_{ij} + \sum_{\mu=1}^{\sigma-1} \Delta\tau_{ij}^{\mu} + \Delta\tau_{ij}^{*}, \forall (i,j) \in L \tag{6}$$

where $\Delta\tau_{ij}^{\mu} = \begin{cases} (\sigma-\mu)\dfrac{Q}{L_{\mu}} & \text{if the } \mu\text{-th best ant travels on edge } (i,j) \\ 0 & \text{otherwise} \end{cases}$

and $\Delta\tau_{ij}^{*} = \begin{cases} \sigma\dfrac{Q}{L^{*}} & \text{if edge } (i,j) \text{ is part of the best solution found} \\ 0 & \text{otherwise} \end{cases}$

where

μ ranking index

$\Delta\tau_{ij}^{\mu}$ increase of trail level on edge (i,j) caused by the μ-th best ant

L_{μ} tour length of the μ-th best ant

$\Delta\tau_{ij}^{*}$ increase of trail level on edge (i,j) caused by the elitist ants

σ number of elitist ants

L^{*} tour length of the best solution found

In the paper (Bullnheimer et al. 1999) RAS is put to the test against AS, EAS as well as simulated annealing and a genetic algorithm. The conclusion was that RAS could for all problem instances compete with the classical metaheuristics regarding speed and quality, and that the ranking improved the performance of the ant system algorithm in every respect.

3.3 Ant Colony System (ACS)

ACS proposed by Dorigo and Gambardella (1997) introduced a new state transition rule to provide a direct way to balance between exploration of new edges and exploitation of a priori and accumulated knowledge about the problem.

$$j = \begin{cases} \arg\max\limits_{j \in N_k^i} \left\{\tau_{ij} \cdot \eta_{ij}^{\beta}\right\} & \text{if } q < q_o \text{ (exploitation)} \\ J & \text{otherwise (biased exploration)} \end{cases} \tag{7}$$

where q is a random number uniformly distributed in $[0,1]$, q_o is a parameter ($0 \le q_o \le 1$) and J is a random node selected according to the probability distribution given in equation 1.
This means that every time an ant in city i has to choose a city j to move to, it samples a random number q. If $q \le q_o$ then the best edge according to equation 3 is chosen, otherwise and edge is chose according to equation 1.
While ants are constructing a solution a *local pheromone updating rule* is applied

$$\tau_{ij} \leftarrow (1-\sigma)\cdot\tau_{ij} + \sigma\cdot\Delta\tau_{ij}^{k}, \forall(i,j)\in L \tag{8}$$

and σ is a parameter $0 < \sigma < 1$ and $\Delta\tau_{ij}^{k}$ is $1/(nL_{nn})$, where n is the number of nodes in the problem and L_{nn} is the tour length produced by the nearest neighbour heuristic (see Rosenkrantz et al. 1977).
The *global pheromone updating rule* is applied only to edges that belong to the best ant tour

$$\tau_{ij} \leftarrow (1-p)\tau_{ij} + \sum_{k=1}^{m}\Delta\tau_{ij}^{k}, \forall(i,j)\in L \tag{9}$$

where $$\Delta\tau_{ij}^{k} = \begin{cases} \dfrac{1}{L_{gb}} & \text{if } (i,j) \text{ is part of the global best tour} \\ 0 & \text{otherwise} \end{cases}$$

and L_{gb} is the length of the globally best tour.
Noticeable in ACS is that the local updating rule is applied in parallel, every time an ant selects a new node to travel to, but the global updating rule after all ants have completed their tour.

3.4 Max-min Ant System (MMAS)

This version by Stützle and Hoos (2000) differs from the original AS in three ways. Only the iteration best ant is allowed to apply pheronome, the strength of the pheromone trails have lower and upper bounds, and at start, all trails are initialized to their upper bound value to encourage early exploration. Equation 4 is modified

$$\tau_{ij} \leftarrow (1-p)\tau_{ij} + \sum_{k=1}^{m}\Delta\tau_{ij}^{best}, \forall(i,j)\in L \tag{10}$$

where $\Delta\tau_{ij}^{best}$ is the amount of pheromone the iteration best ant deposits on the arcs it has visited.
The pheromone trail upper (τ_{max})and lower (τ_{min}) bounds for an edge can be calculated, a detailed description can be found in the paper by Stützle and Hoos.

$$[x]_{\tau_{\min}}^{\tau_{max}} = \begin{cases} \tau_{max} & \text{if } x > \tau_{max} \\ \tau_{min} & \text{if } x < \tau_{min} \\ x & \text{otherwise} \end{cases} \tag{11}$$

At all times should the algorithm see to that the pheromone strength is between the given bounds on any edge.
Studies were conducted in the paper to ascertain if the algorithm should use the iteration best ant or the global best (elite) ant as basis for the pheromone updates, and the results were that the iteration best ant performed better. Also the effects of using τ_{min} or τ_{max} as a starting value for the initial pheromone amount on the trails were studied, resulting in τ_{max} being the better approach.
An additional mechanism called *pheromone trail smoothing* was introduced in the paper for increased performance. Basically when the MMAS has converged, or is very close to convergence, the mechanism increases the pheromone trails proportionally to their difference to the maximum pheromone trail limit. As a conclusion it is stated that MMAS outperformed all other AS variants to date.

4. The hybrid-ACO algorithm

The algorithm consists of two parts. We have the ACO part, where ants crawl over the searchspace trying to construct a feasible tour. When all ants have constructed their tour, the timestamps have also been calculated for the individual operations in the schedule defined by a tour, which allows us to calculate the makespan. The postprocessing part springs to life when there is a complete schedule to operate on. The (global) pheromone update of the ACO occurs only after the postprocessing has finished, this is due to the postprocessing affecting the makespan of the schedule formed by the tour of the ant. After the pheromone update ACO continues with the next iteration.

4.1 The postprocessing algorithm

After all ants have constructed their tour, a postprocessing algorithm is applied. This algorithm is effectively a local search procedure, based upon the approach of Nowicki and Smutnicki (1996).
The local search begins by identifying the critical path in the constructed schedule. The critical path can be decomposed into a number of blocks where a block is a maximal sequence of adjacent operations that require the same machine. Block length can vary from just one operation to all operations that are scheduled on one machine. Given a block, swapping operations take place. We start from the last block in the critical path which has a size larger than 1 and its last operation in the block. The block size must be larger than 1 since otherwise no swap can be made. The identified operation is swapped with its predecessor in the same block, and the necessary changes are made into the tour of the ant as well as the timestamps of the scheduled operations. If the swap improves the makespan, it is accepted, otherwise the swap is undone and the next pair in the block is up for swapping. If a block contains no more swaps we move to the preceeding block. Note that an accepted swap means that the critical path may change and a new critical path must be identified. If no swap of operations in the critical path improve the makespan, the local search ends.
This means that the tour of an ant may change in the postprocessing part of the algorithm. The tour of the ants after the very first completed postprocessing run may differ radically from the one presented by the first iteration of the ACO, but succeeding postprocessing runs after the first round of calculations are much easier on the ants and are not interrupting the pheromone trails too much.

Figure 1 shows a critical path and possible swaps for an example schedule.

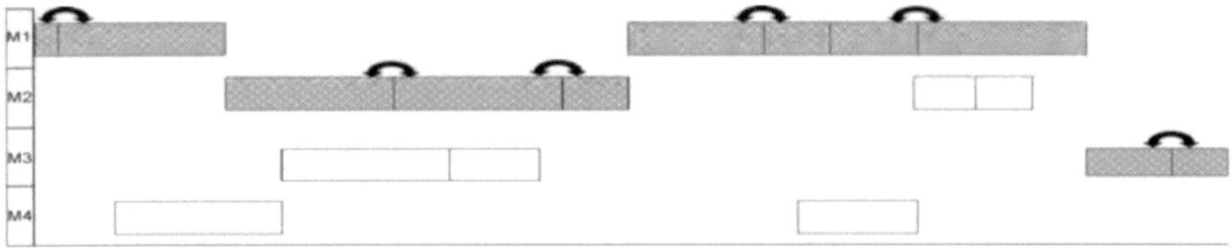

Figure 1. A sample 4-machine schedule with the critical path marked in grey and possible swap pairs with arrows. The path is made of 4 blocks with the largest block consisting of four scheduled operations.

5. What is visibility?

An additional problem when working with ant systems is that of visibility. There are similarities between priority rules used in heuristic approaches and the visibility of a single ant, both are trying to evaluate and make a choice of where to go next from a specific node. Usually visibility is referred to as the neighbourhood of the ant, i.e. the nodes that are close to the node the ant is currently staying on. It is a measure of what nodes the ant can see around it when standing on a specified node. In equation 1, the parameter η_{ij} is our measure of visibility and in TSP-problems the meaning is clear and all values of η_{ij} can be computed a priori, since the node distances are known. No matter which node the ant stands on, the distance to all other nodes can be fetched from a pre-calculated distance table. When it comes to schedules it is not entirely straightforward what visibility is and what effect it has on computations with regard to ACO. The distance in time units from a node in the tour to the next is not known until you have calculated the timestamps for the entire tour so far.

Another thing with ACO and the MT-10 problem is that the tabu list (already visited nodes) alone is not enough. Since the tasks in every job have to be done in correct order, that is, task A3 has to be done before A4 etc., a candidate list is needed. The candidate list has all the legal node choices an ant can make from the node it is currently standing on. This means that only the selection probabilities for the nodes in the candidate list need to be calculated, which speeds up the algorithm. In this case visibility for an ant is restricted to only the nodes in the candidate list. Figure 2 illustrates this phenomena.

In order to understand more about visibility and its effects, some various approaches to ACO-visibility in schedules are undertaken and studied. Table 1 shortly outlines some different types of visibility.

Type of visibility	Explanation
Distance	Distance-based, the starting time of an operation (counted from t_0)
SPT	Shortest processing time first
LPT	Longest processing time first
TLM	Length of unscheduled tasks left on machine
TLJ	Length of unscheduled tasks left in job
TLJ+TLM(30-70)	Length of unscheduled tasks left in job and on machine, weight 30%-70%
TLJ+TLM(50-50)	Length of unscheduled tasks left in job and on machine, weight 50%-50%
TLJ+TLM(70-30)	Length of unscheduled tasks left in job and on machine, weight 70%-30%

Table 1. Various types of visibility for ACO

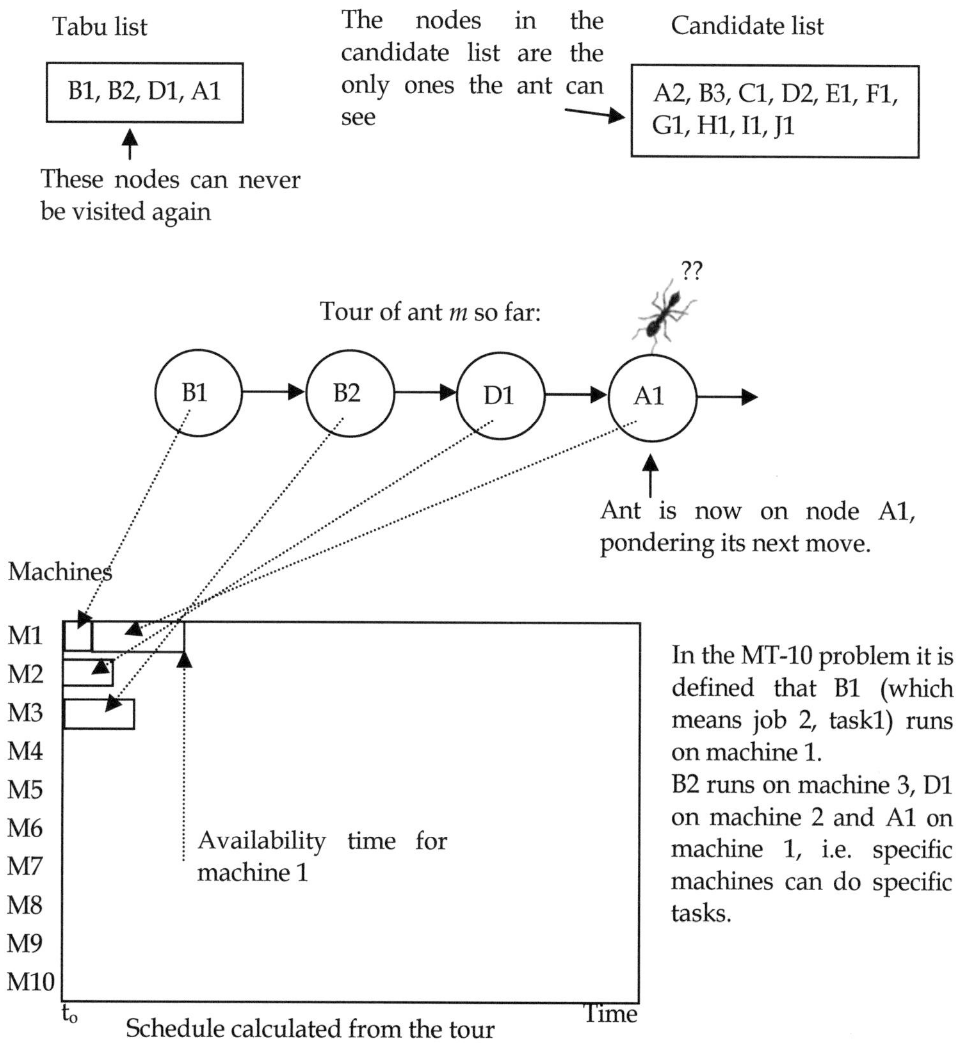

Figure 2. Visibility in scheduling. Since the ant has visited the nodes B1 and B2, the candidate list contains the next in the series, B3. Same for A2 and D2 since both A1 and D1 are in the tour. The rest of the candidates are jobs that have not started yet, the first in their series of tasks. Every time a node is added to the tour, it is placed into the schedule and the timestamps for starting and finishing that task on the specific machine are calculated. When choosing the next node to travel to, visibility can be calculated for all the nodes in the candidate list. The good choices get better visibility rating, according to selected visibility method, and thus a better chance of being selected

When the ant is selecting the next node to travel to, distance-based visibility is the earliest possible start time on the corresponding machine for the possible selections in its allowed list. The task that can start earlier than other candidates gets a higher probability of being chosen than a task that can start later and this can be achieved with a simple formula Q/t_{start}

that replaces the definition of η_{ij} in equation 1. SPT ranks the candidates according to length of their processing time, shorter processing time means a higher probability of being chosen, whereas LPT is the opposite; longer processing times means higher probability. TLM calculates the total processing time for all unscheduled tasks on the current machine. The longer the total processing time is, the higher the probability of being chosen. TLJ is similar, it calculates the total processing times for all the unscheduled tasks left in the current job. The longer the total processing time, the higher the probability. TLJ + TLM is a combination of TLJ and TLM, where each visibility is weighted differently. To get an outline of the impact of the weighting factors, 30-70, 50-50 and 70-30 proportional weights are used (percentage values).

6. Computational experience and results

The experiment setup was to take each ACO method and do 5 runs for each of the different types of visibility. Each run was 2,500 rounds of calculations, then the algorithm was halted. Two sets of runs were made, one without postprocessing, the other with. Average values and mean deviations were calculated. All units in table 3 and 4 are time units. Common parameter settings for ACO can be seen in table 2.

Parameter	value	meaning
m	40	number of ants
Q	80	pheromone deposited by an ant
a	1	bias towards pheromone amplification
β	2	bias towards closest nodes (visibility)
p	0.007	evaporation rate

Table 2. ACO parameter settings

These parameters were kept the same for all comparative runs, i.e. for all visibility types during the runs with and without postprocessing.

The column that dictates percentage deviation from optimum solution is calculated for the best found makespan of the runs.

AS and RAS perform about the same, with RAS having the slight edge, smaller standard deviation and better mean values. ACS outperforms both AS and RAS, and MMAS outperforms them all. This is in line with the findings in quoted papers.

The impact of the different visibilities vary for the different ACO methods, and it is quite an interesting read. As can be seen, best solution in table 3 was found by the TLJ visibility with ACS as the ACO method. The results for ACS with different visibilities are a bit jumpy, since ACS also holds the worst solution found. MMAS does good overall with all visibilities.

The best found solution after 2,500 rounds of calculations is really not a very good one, it is still 13.1% from optimum, however, the algorithm has not stagnated and it continues to explore the search space and comes up with new solutions. The meaning of these runs is not to solve to optimality, rather to study the visibility effects and get a feel for the performance of the different ACO methods.

Tweaking the parameter settings for each individual type of visibility may improve the results, but this way all the visibility types are on the same page for easy comparison. Same goes for the ACO methods.

ACO	Type of visibility	worst	best	mean	σ	% from optimum
AS	Distance	2174	1373	1954.0	294.4	32.3%
	SPT	2273	1582	2134.8	276.4	41.2%
	LPT	2314	1491	2121.8	316.8	37.6%
	TLM	2406	1482	2117.4	324.7	37.2%
	TLJ	2218	1502	2020.8	266.3	38.1%
	TLJ+TLM(30-70)	2322	1457	2072.2	311.6	36.2%
	TLJ+TLM(50-50)	2357	1464	2114.4	333.0	36.5%
	TLJ+TLM(70-30)	2127	1459	1975.8	259.1	36.3%
RAS	Distance	2102	1488	1946. 6	230.4	37.5%
	SPT	2121	1508	1981.6	237.6	38.3%
	LPT	2384	1519	2151.0	318.4	38.7%
	TLM	2119	1486	1852.6	205.6	37.4%
	TLJ	2230	1466	2032.8	284.8	36.6%
	TLJ+TLM(30-70)	2145	1364	1929.6	290.4	31.8%
	TLJ+TLM(50-50)	2265	1520	2090.8	286.8	38.8%
	TLJ+TLM(70-30)	2008	1494	1871.0	190.3	37.8%
ACS	Distance	1251	1137	1184.6	42.0	18.2%
	SPT	2072	1867	2001.0	71.2	50.2%
	LPT	2213	1638	2072.6	218.8	43.2%
	TLM	1473	1381	1431.4	32.1	32.6%
	TLJ	1108	1070	1093.8	13.1	13.1%
	TLJ+TLM(30-70)	1459	1234	1373.0	81.1	24.6%
	TLJ+TLM(50-50)	1404	1279	1335.0	50.6	27.3%
	TLJ+TLM(70-30)	1273	1168	1231.6	37.9	20.4%
MMAS	Distance	1272	1183	1243.6	31.8	21.4%
	SPT	1363	1241	1332.4	46.2	25.1%
	LPT	1303	1237	1276.8	25.83	24.8%
	TLM	1301	1209	1273.0	33.0	23.1%
	TLJ	1286	1267	1279.8	7.0	26.6%
	TLJ+TLM(30-70)	1286	1211	1260.4	30.6	23.2%
	TLJ+TLM(50-50)	1286	1235	1260.2	19.2	24.7%
	TLJ+TLM(70-30)	1295	1245	1269.0	18.1	25.3%

Table 3. Results from computational runs without postprocessing

ACO	Type of visibility	worst	best	mean	σ	% from optimum
AS	Distance	1341	1083	1231.6	84.4	14.1%
	SPT	1609	1055	1445.6	198.9	11.8%
	LPT	1608	1079	1464.4	195.2	13.8%
	TLM	1667	1048	1475.8	219.9	11.3%
	TLJ	1620	1061	1458.8	207.9	12.3%
	TLJ+TLM(30-70)	1599	1057	1437.8	195.1	12.0%
	TLJ+TLM(50-50)	1578	1059	1422.6	185.4	12.2%
	TLJ+TLM(70-30)	1580	1071	1420.6	183.3	13.2%
RAS	Distance	1292	1087	1207.6	71.8	14.4%
	SPT	1463	1069	1346.8	142.8	13.0%
	LPT	1538	1101	1351.2	148.3	15.5%
	TLM	1465	1088	1330.21	129.4	14.5%
	TLJ	1358	1068	1245.6	97.4	12.9%
	TLJ+TLM(30-70)	1457	1093	1339.0	127.3	14.9%
	TLJ+TLM(50-50)	1456	1067	1281.4	125.9	12.8%
	TLJ+TLM(70-30)	1502	1101	1378.6	145.9	15.5%
ACS	Distance	1053	1032	1045.0	7.4	9.9%
	SPT	1340	1123	1254.0	72.5	17.2%
	LPT	1178	1103	1157.2	27.5	15.7%
	TLM	1137	1038	1073.0	35.5	10.4%
	TLJ	988	981	982.8	2.7	5.2%
	TLJ+TLM(30-70)	1105	1008	1052.8	31.5	7.7%
	TLJ+TLM(50-50)	1060	999	1033.4	20.1	6.9%
	TLJ+TLM(70-30)	995	977	983.0	6.6	4.8%
MMAS	Distance	1013	1001	1003.8	4.6	7.1%
	SPT	1006	977	989.6	9.8	4.8%
	LPT	1019	991	1004.2	10.2	6.2%
	TLM	1014	988	1002.2	10.6	5.9%
	TLJ	1013	993	1001.2	6.7	6.3%
	TLJ+TLM(30-70)	994	982	987.4	5.1	5.3%
	TLJ+TLM(50-50)	1006	989	998.6	6.8	6.0%
	TLJ+TLM(70-30)	1003	979	990.4	8.8	5.0%

Table 4. Results from computational runs with postprocessing

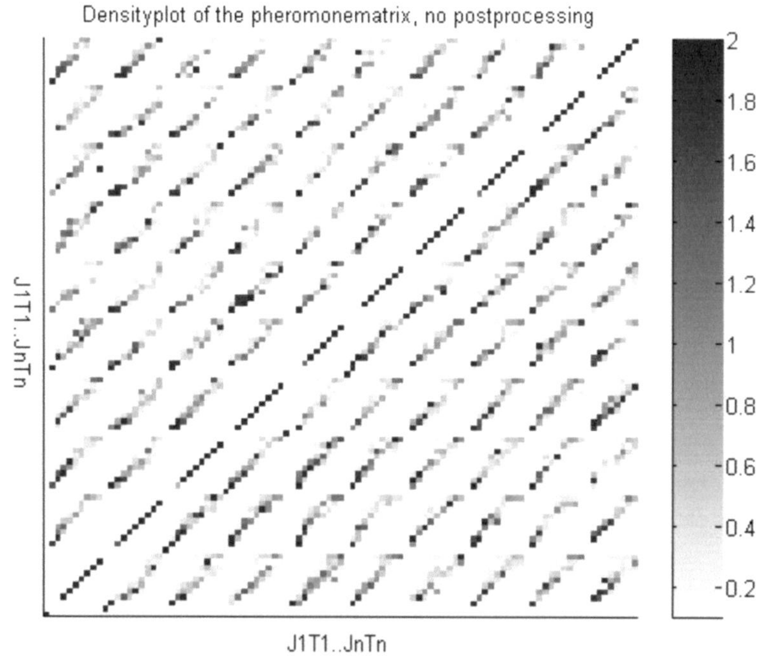

Figure 3. A plot of the pheromonematrix when no postprocessing present. Very clear pheromonetrails are visible

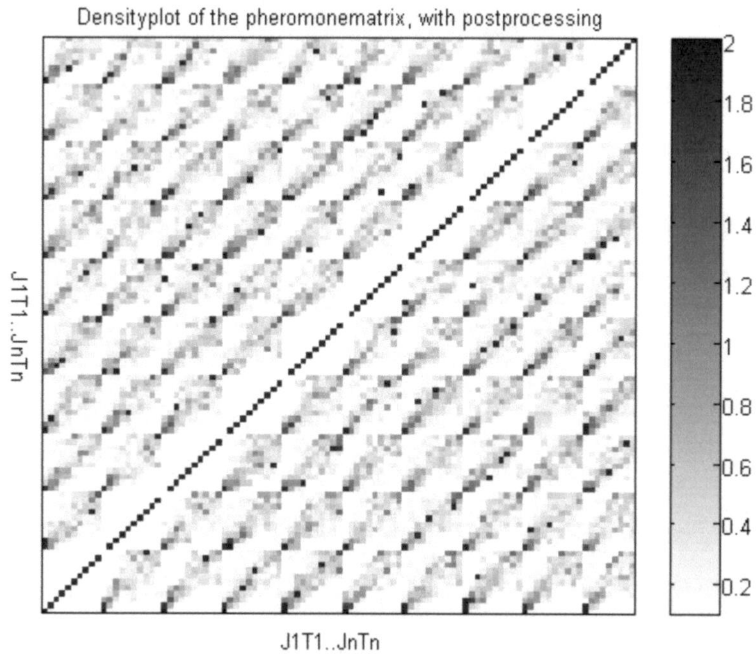

Figure 4. A plot of the pheromonematrix when using postprocessing. Clear pheromonetrails visible but distributed over more edges than in figure 4

As for the postprocessing version of the ACO methods, RAS beats AS in the sense that RAS has less deviation, which means it consistently gives good solutions, though AS did manage to find some better solutions. ACS is still a bit jumpy, it finds very good solutions for some visibility runs, but also performs poorly with for instance SPT and LPT. The various weighted combinations of TLJ + TLM seem to do better, overall, than other visibilities.

TLJ+TLM(70-30) visibility in MMAS seems to work best, after 2,500 rounds of calculations the best found solution is 5.0% from optimum, though TLJ visibility and ACS are very close with a 5.2% solution. MMAS has less deviation, and thus is more likely to continue to produce good solutions every time it runs.

It is clear that the postprocessing closes the performance gap between the different ACO methods, but the same internal ranking still holds true with postprocessing as without. The postprocessing also improves the performance dramatically for all versions of ACO algorithms tested.

The algorithms were stopped after 2,500 rounds of calculations, so the question arises, how good a solution can be found if allowed to run without interruptions for a longer time? An additional run with the best visibility and ACO method from table 3 landed after 30,000 rounds of calculations at a best found makespan of 1012 time units. which is 8.1% from optimum. An additional run with the best visibility and ACO method from table 4 landed after 30,000 rounds of calculations at a best found makespan of 948 time units, which is 1.9 % from optimum.

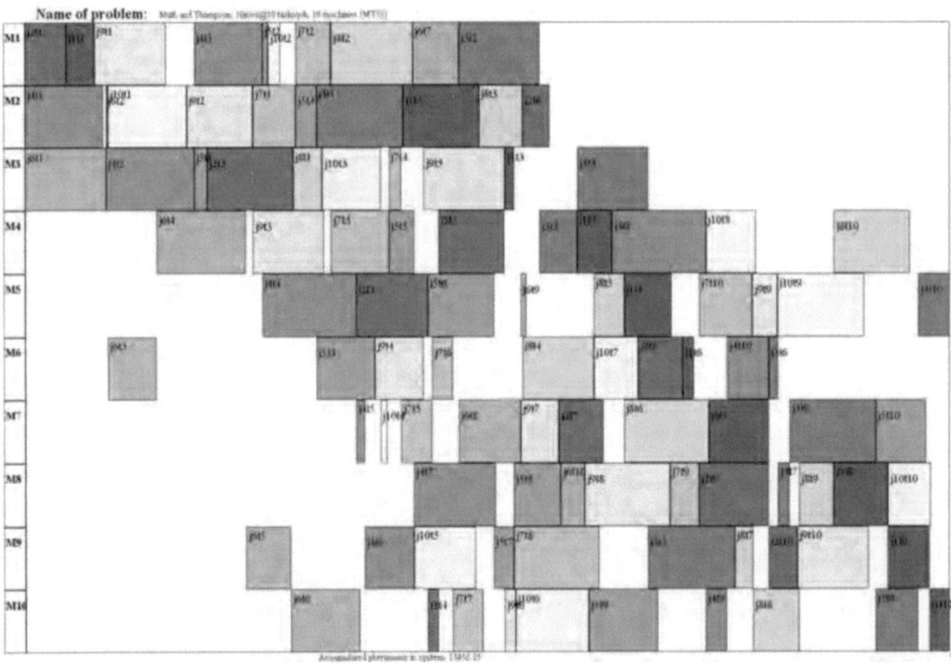

Figure 5. A finished schedule for the MT10 problem, made with the hybrid ACO (MMAS), with a makespan of 968 time units (3.9% from optimum)

Another question that can be asked is does the postprocessing disturb the forming of pheromone trails in the system in any way? Figure 3 is the pheromonematrix of the MMAS with no postprocessing, taken after 2,500 rounds, and figure 4 is a similar one with

postprocessing. The dark dots depict a high concentration of pheromone whereas the presence of a lighter dot means no or very little pheromone is present. As one can imagine, the presence of a postprocessing routine that modifies ant tours messes with the ant pheromone trails, and you can clearly see if you compare figure 3 and figure 4 with each other that figure 4 shows more pheromone distribution in the system. There are still dark dots in figure 4 signifying established pheromone trails so we are not dealing with random search. In light of these figures you could eventually tweak the evaporation setting higher when using postprocessing, or bias the parameters more towards an emphasis on visibility. You could argue that the larger distribution of pheromone over the trails as seen in figure 4 encourages ant exploration more and actually helps in finding better solutions.
A finished schedule produced by a hybrid ACO can be seen in figure 5.

7. Conclusion

When paired with the local search the ACO produces noteworthy results very fast (typically 5% from optimum within 200 rounds of calculations). The Max-Min Ant System outperformed all other ACO versions, and it did so for all types of visibility tested, showing that it is indeed a leading candidate for choosing your ant system.
There are various version of ACO available and this chapter served its purpose to both do an attempt at ranking them, showing the impact of various visibility methods as well as proving that pure ACO methods produce good results, but even better when combined with the postprocessing algorithm shown. Naturally, not every combination of ACO and a local search is guaranteed to work better than a pure ACO, but a hybrid version can improve the performance dramatically.
If you are looking for a good, quick solution rather than an all-out effort to find the best solution, ACO perfomance is a noteworthy competitor to existing job-shop scheduling approaches. ACO is an easy algorithm to implement, with roughly the same amount of code and difficulty as that of a genetic algorithm.
ACO is a good example of how harnessing, mimicking and utilizing processes occurring in nature for tough scientific problems can be a successful enterprise.

8. References

Adams J., Balas E., Zawack D. (1988). The shifting bottleneck procedure for job shop scheduling, *Management Science*, 34, pp. 391-401.

Bell J.E., McMullen P.R. (2004) Ant colony optimization techniques for the vehicle routing problem, *Advanced Engineering Informatics*, 18, pp. 41-48.

Blum C., Dorigo M. (2004). The hyper-cube framework for ant colony optimization, *IEEE Trans Syst Man Cybernet Part B*, 34(2), pp. 1161-1172.

Bullnheimer B., Hartl R., Strauss C. (1999). A new rank-based version of the Ant System: A computational study, *Central European J Operations Res Econom*, 7(1), pp. 25-38.

Colorni A., Dorigo M., Maniezzo V. and Trubian M. (1993). Ant System for Job-shop scheduling, *Belgian Journal of Operations Research, Statistics and Computer Science*, 34: pp. 39--54.

Denebourg, J.-L., Aron, S., Goss, S., Pasteels, J.-M. (1990) The self-organizing exploratory pattern of the Argentine ant, *Journal of insect behaviour*, vol. 3, p. 150.

Dorigo M. (1992). Optimization, Learning and Natural Algorithms. *PhD thesis*, Dipartemento di Elettronica, Politecnico di Milano.

Dorigo M., Gambardella L.M. (1997). Ant Colony System: A cooperative learning approach to the traveling salesman problem, *IEEE Trans Evolutionary Comput*,1(1), pp. 53-66.

Dorigo M., Maniezzo V., Colorni A. (1996). Ant system: Optimization by a colony of cooperating agents, *IEEE Trans Syst Man Cybernet Part B*, 26(1), pp. 29-41.

Dorigo, M. and Stützle, T. (2004). Ant colony optimization, MIT press, Cambridge, MA.

Gajpal Y., Rajendran C. (2006). An ant-colony optimization algorithm for minimizing the completion-time variance of jobs in flowshops, *International Journal of Production Economics*, 101, pp. 259-272.

Grassé, P.-P. (1946). Les Insects Dans Leur Univers, Paris, France, Ed. Du Palais de la découverte.

Gutjahr W.J., Rauner M.S. (2005). An ACO algorithm for a dynamic regional nurse-scheduling problem in Austria, *Computers & Operations Research* (in print).

Jayaraman V.K., Kulkarni B.D., Karale S., Shelokar P. (2000). Ant colony framework for optimal design and scheduling of batch plants, *Computers and Chemical Engineering*, 24, pp. 190-192.

Kuo-Ching Ying, Ching-Jong Liao (2004). An ant colony system for permutation flow-shop sequencing, *Computers & Operations Research*, 31, pp. 791-801.

Panwalker S.S., Iskander W. (1977). A survey of Scheduling Rules, *Oper.Res.*, 25, 1, pp. 45-61.

Rosenkrantz, D. J., Stearns, R. E., Lewis, P. M. (1977). An analysis of several heuristics for the traveling salesman problem, *SIAM Journal on Computing*, vol. 6, pp. 563-581.

Nakano R., Yamada T. (1991). Conventional Genetic Algorithm for Job Shop Problems, *Proc. of the 4th Int. Conference on Genetic Algorithms*, San Diego, Californa, pp. 474-479.

Nowicki E., Smutnicki C. (1996). A fast taboo search algorithm for the job-shop problem. *Management Science*, 42 (6), pp. 797-813.

Stützle T., Hoos H.H. (1996). Improving the Ant System: a detailed report on the *MAX-MIN* Ant system, *Technical Report AIDA-96-12*, FG Intellektik, TH Darmstadt.

Stützle T., Hoos H.H. (2000). *MAX-MIN* Ant system, *Future Generat Comput Syst*, 16(8), pp. 889-914.

Stützle, T. and Dorigo, M. (2002). A short convergence proof for a class of ACO algorithms, *IEEE Transactions on evolutionary computation*, vol.6, no. 4, pp. 358-365.

Taillard E. (1989). Parallel Tabu Search Technique for the Jobshop Scheduling Problem, *Internal Report ORWP 89/11*, Departemente de Mathematiques, Ecole Polytechnique Federale de Lausanne, Lausanne.

Van Laarhoven P. J. M., Aarts E.H.L., Lenstra J.K. (1992). Job shop scheduling by simulated annealing, *Operations Research*, 40, pp. 113-125.

21

Particle Swarm Optimization in Structural Design

Ruben E. Perez[1] and Kamran Behdinan[2]
[1]*University of Toronto, Institute for Aerospace Studies,*
[2]*Ryerson University, Department of Aerospace Engineering*
Canada

1. Introduction

Optimization techniques play an important role as a useful decision making tool in the design of structures. By deriving the maximum benefits from the available resources, it enables the construction of lighter, more efficient structures while maintaining adequate levels of safety and reliability. A large number of optimization techniques have been suggested over the past decades to solve the inherently complex problem posed in structural design. Their scope varies widely depending on the type of structural problem to be tackled. Gradient-based methods, for example, are highly effectively in finding local optima when the design space is convex and continuous and when the design problem involves large number of design variables and constraints. If the problem constraints and objective function are convex in nature, then it is possible to conclude that the local optimum will be a global optimum. In most structural problems, however, it is practically impossible to check the convexity of the design space, therefore assuring an obtained optimum is the best possible among multiple feasible solutions. Global non-gradient-based methods are able to traverse along highly non-linear, non-convex design spaces and find the best global solutions. In this category many unconstrained optimization algorithms have been developed by mimicking natural phenomena such as Simulated Annealing (Kirkpatrick et al., 1983), Genetic Algorithms (Goldberg, 1989), and Bacterial Foraging (Passino, 2002) among others. Recently, a new family of more efficient global optimization algorithms have been developed which are better posed to handle constraints. They are based on the simulation of social interactions among members of a specific species looking for food sources. From this family of optimizers, the two most promising algorithms, which are the subject of this book, are Ant Colony Optimization (Dorigo, 1986), and Particle Swarm Optimization or PSO. In this chapter, we present the analysis, implementation, and improvement strategies of a particle swarm optimization suitable for constraint optimization tasks. We illustrate the functionality and effectiveness of this algorithm, and explore the effect of the different PSO setting parameters in the scope of classical structural optimization problems.

1.1 The Structural Design Problem

Before we describe the implementation of the particle swarm approach, it is necessary to define the general structural design problem to understand the different modification and improvements made later to the basic algorithm. Mathematically, a structural design problem can be defined as:

$$\begin{aligned} &min \quad f(x,p) \quad s.t. \quad x \in D \\ &where \quad D = \{x \mid x \in [x_l, x_u] \subset \Re^n, g_j(x,p) \le 0 \forall j \in [1,m]\} \end{aligned} \tag{1}$$

where a specific structural attribute (e.g. weight) is defined as an objective or merit function f which is maximized or minimized using proper choice of the design parameters. The design parameters specify the geometry and topology of the structure and physical properties of its members. Some of these are independent design variables (x) which are varied to optimize the problem; while others can be fixed value parameters (p). From the design parameters, a set of derived attributes are obtained some of which can be defined as behaviour constraints (g) e.g., stresses, deflections, natural frequencies and buckling loads etc., These behaviour parameters are functionally related through laws of structural mechanics to the design variables. The role of an optimization algorithm in structural design will be then to find the best combination of design variables that lead to the best objective function performance, while assuring all constraints are met.

2. The Particle Swarm Algorithm

The PSO algorithm was first proposed in 1995 by Kennedy and Eberhart. It is based on the premise that social sharing of information among members of a species offers an evolutionary advantage (Kennedy & Eberhart, 1995). Recently, the PSO has been proven useful on diverse engineering design applications such as logic circuit design (e.g. Coello & Luna, 2003), control design (e.g. Zheng et al., 2003) and power systems design (e.g. Abido, 2002) among others. A number of advantages with respect to other global algorithms make PSO an ideal candidate for engineering optimization tasks. The algorithm is robust and well suited to handle non-linear, non-convex design spaces with discontinuities. It is also more efficient, requiring a smaller number of function evaluations, while leading to better or the same quality of results (Hu et al., 2003; and Hassan et al., 2005). Furthermore, as we will see below, its easiness of implementation makes it more attractive as it does not require specific domain knowledge information, internal transformation of variables or other manipulations to handle constraints.

2.1 Mathematical Formulation

The particle swarm process is stochastic in nature; it makes use of a velocity vector to update the current position of each particle in the swarm. The velocity vector is updated based on the "memory" gained by each particle, conceptually resembling an autobiographical memory, as well as the knowledge gained by the swarm as a whole (Eberhart & Kennedy, 1995). Thus, the position of each particle in the swarm is updated based on the social behaviour of the swarm which adapts to its environment by returning to promising regions of the space previously discovered and searching for better positions over time. Numerically, the position x of a particle i at iteration $k+1$ is updated as:

$$x_{k+1}^i = x_k^i + v_{k+1}^i \Delta t \tag{2}$$

where v_{k+1}^{i} is the corresponding updated velocity vector, and Δt is the time step value typically considered as unity (Shi & Eberhart, 1998a). The velocity vector of each particle is calculated as:

$$v_{k+1}^{i} = wv_{k}^{i} + c_1 r_1 \frac{\left(p_{k}^{i} - x_{k}^{i}\right)}{\Delta t} + c_2 r_2 \frac{\left(p_{k}^{g} - x_{k}^{i}\right)}{\Delta t} \tag{3}$$

where v_{k}^{i} is the velocity vector at iteration k, p_{k}^{i} & p_{k}^{g} are respectively the best ever position of particle i and the global best position of the entire swarm up to current iteration k, and r represents a random number in the interval [0,1]. The remaining terms are configuration parameters that play an important role in the PSO convergence behaviour. The terms c_1 and c_2 represent "trust" settings which respectively indicate the degree of confidence in the best solution found by each individual particle (c_1 - cognitive parameter) and by the swarm as a whole (c_2 - social parameter). The final term w, is the inertia weight which is employed to control the exploration abilities of the swarm as it scales the current velocity value affecting the updated velocity vector. Large inertia weights will force larger velocity updates allowing the algorithm to explore the design space globally. Similarly, small inertia values will force the velocity updates to concentrate in the nearby regions of the design space.
Figure 1 illustrates the particle position and velocity update as described above in a two-dimensional vector space. Note how the updated particle position will be affected not only by its relationship with respect to the best swarm position but also by the magnitude of the configuration parameters.

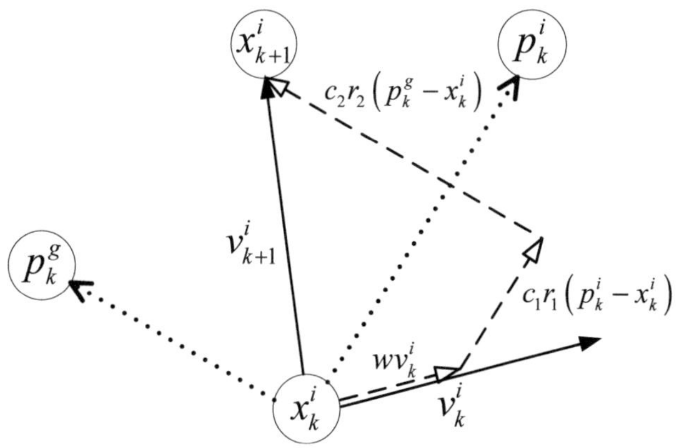

Figure 1. PSO Position and Velocity Update

2.2 Computational Algorithm

As with all numerical based optimization approaches the PSO process is iterative in nature, its basic algorithm is constructed as follows:

1. Initialize a set of particles positions x_{0}^{i} and velocities v_{0}^{i} randomly distributed throughout the design space bounded by specified limits.
2. Evaluate the objective function values $f\left(x_{k}^{i}\right)$ using the design space positions x_{k}^{i}. A total of n objective function evaluations will be performed at each iteration, where n is the total number of particles in the swarm.

3. Update the optimum particle position p_k^i at current iteration k and global optimum particle position p_k^g.
4. Update the position of each particle using its previous position and updated velocity vector as specified in Eq. (1) and Eq. (2).
5. Repeat steps 2-4 until a stopping criterion is met. For the basic implementation the typical stopping criteria is defined based on a number of iterations reached.

The iterative scheme behaviour for a two-dimensional variable space can be seen in Figure 2, where each particle position and velocity vector is plotted at two consecutive iterations. Each particle movement in the design space is affected based on its previous iteration velocity (which maintains the particle "momentum" biased towards a specific direction) and on a combined stochastic measure of the previous best and global positions with the cognitive and social parameters. The cognitive parameter will bias each particle position towards its best found solution space, while the social parameter will bias the particle positions towards the best global solution found by the entire swarm. For example, at the kth iteration the movement of the tenth particle in the figure is biased towards the left of the design space. However, a change in direction can be observed in the next iteration which is forced by the influence of the best design space location found by the whole swarm and represented in the figure as a black square. Similar behaviour can be observed in the other particles of the swarm.

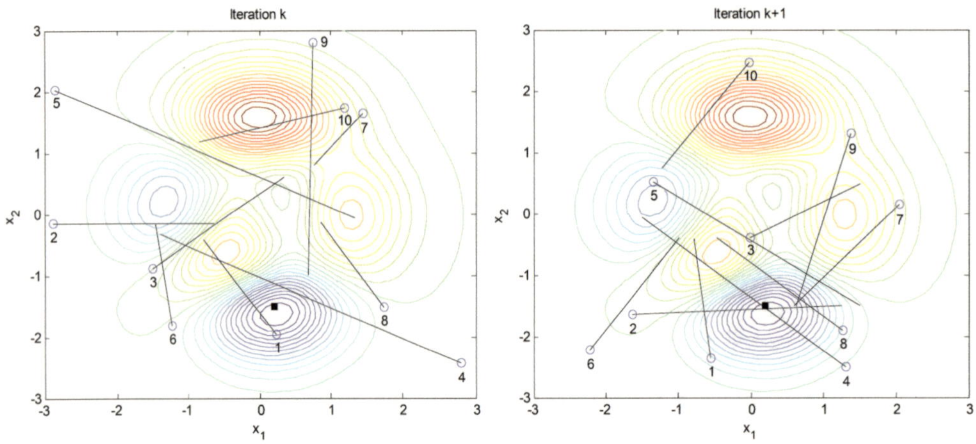

Figure 2. PSO Position and Velocity Update

An important observation is that the efficiency of the PSO is influenced to some extent by the swarm initial distribution over the design space. Areas not initially covered will only be explored if the momentum of a particle carries the particle into such areas. Such a case only occurs when a particle finds a new individual best position or if a new global best is discovered by the swarm. Proper setting of the PSO configuration parameters will ensure a good balance between computational effort and global exploration, so unexplored areas of the design space are covered. However, a good particle position initialization is desired. Different approaches have been used to initialize the particle positions with varying degrees of success. From an engineering design point of view, the best alternative will be to distribute particles uniformly covering the entire search space. A simpler alternative, which has been proven successfully in practice, is to randomly distribute the initial position and velocity vectors of each particle throughout the design space. This can be accomplished using the following equations:

$$x_0^i = x_{min} + r\left(x_{max} - x_{min}\right) \tag{4}$$

$$v_0^i = \frac{x_{min} + r\left(x_{max} - x_{min}\right)}{\Delta t} \tag{5}$$

where x_{min} and x_{max} represent the lower and upper design variables bounds respectively, and r represents a random number in the interval [0,1]. Note that both magnitudes of the position and velocity values will be bounded, as large initial values will lead to large initial momentum and positional updates. This large momentum causes the swarm to diverge from a common global solution increasing the total computational time.

2.2 Algorithm Analysis

A useful insight of the PSO algorithm behaviour can be obtained if we replace the velocity update equation (Eq. (3)) into the position update equation (Eq. (2)) to get the following expression:

$$x_{k+1}^i = x_k^i + \left(wV_k^i + c_1 r_1 \frac{\left(p_k^i - x_k^i\right)}{\Delta t} + c_2 r_2 \frac{\left(p_k^g - x_k^i\right)}{\Delta t} \right) \Delta t \tag{6}$$

Factorizing the cognitive and social terms from the above equation we obtain the following general equation:

$$x_{k+1}^i = x_k^i + wV_k^i \Delta t + \left(c_1 r_1 + c_2 r_2\right)\left(\frac{c_1 r_1 p_k^i + c_2 r_2 p_k^g}{c_1 r_1 + c_2 r_2} - x_k^i \right) \tag{7}$$

Note how the above equation has the same structure as the gradient line-search used in convex unconstrained optimization ($x_{k+1}^i = \hat{x}_k^i + a\overline{p}_k$) where:

$$\begin{aligned} \hat{x}_k^i &= x_k^i + wV_k^i \Delta t \\ a &= c_1 r_1 + c_2 r_2 \\ \overline{p}_k &= \frac{c_1 r_1 p_k^i + c_2 r_2 p_k^g}{c_1 r_1 + c_2 r_2} - x_k^i \end{aligned} \tag{8}$$

So the behaviour of each particle in the swarm can be viewed as a traditional line-search procedure dependent on a stochastic step size (α) and a stochastic search direction ($\overline{p}_k$). Both the stochastic step size and search direction depend on the selection of social and cognitive parameters. In addition, the stochastic search direction behaviour is also driven by the best design space locations found by each particle and by the swarm as a whole. Behaviour confirmed from the Fig. 2 observations. Knowing that $r_1, r_2 \in [0,1]$, then the step size will belong to the interval $[0, c_1 + c_2]$ with a mean value of $(c_1 + c_2)/2$. Similarly, the search direction will be bracketed in the interval $\left[-x_k^i, \left(c_1 p_k^i + c_2 p_k^g / c_1 + c_2\right) - x_k^i t\right]$.

Two questions immediately arise from the above analysis. The first question is what type of convergence behaviour the algorithm will have. The second one is which values of the social and cognitive parameters will guarantee such convergence. To answer both questions let us start by re-arranging the position terms in equation (6) to get the general form for the ith particle position at iteration $k+1$ as:

$$x_{k+1}^{i} = x_{k}^{i}\left(1 - c_1 r_1 - c_2 r_2\right) + wV_{k}^{i}\Delta t + c_1 r_1 p_{k}^{i} + c_2 r_2 p_{k}^{g} \tag{9}$$

A similar re-arrangment of the position term in equation (2) leads to:

$$V_{k+1}^{i} = -x_{k}^{i}\frac{\left(c_1 r_1 + c_2 r_2\right)}{\Delta t} + wV_{k}^{i} + c_1 r_1 \frac{p_{k}^{i}}{\Delta t} + c_2 r_2 \frac{p_{k}^{g}}{\Delta t} \tag{10}$$

Equations (8) and (9) can be combined and written in matrix form as:

$$\begin{bmatrix} x_{k+1}^{i} \\ V_{k+1}^{i} \end{bmatrix} = \begin{bmatrix} 1 - c_1 r_1 - c_2 r_2 & w\Delta t \\ -\dfrac{\left(c_1 r_1 + c_2 r_2\right)}{\Delta t} & w \end{bmatrix} \begin{bmatrix} x_{k}^{i} \\ V_{k}^{i} \end{bmatrix} + \begin{bmatrix} c_1 r_1 & c_2 r_2 \\ \dfrac{c_1 r_1}{\Delta t} & \dfrac{c_2 r_2}{\Delta t} \end{bmatrix} \begin{bmatrix} p_{k}^{i} \\ p_{k}^{g} \end{bmatrix} \tag{11}$$

which can be considered as a discrete-dynamic system representation for the PSO algorithm where $\left[x^{i}, V^{i}\right]^{T}$ is the state subject to an external input $\left[p^{i}, p^{g}\right]^{T}$, and the first and second matrices correspond to the dynamic and input matrices respectively.

If we assume for a given particle that the external input is constant (as is the case when no individual or communal better positions are found) then a convergent behaviour can be maintained, as there is no external excitation in the dynamic system. In such a case, as the iterations go to infinity the updated positions and velocities will become the same from the kth to the $k^{th}+1$ iteration reducing the system to:

$$\begin{bmatrix} 0 \\ 0 \end{bmatrix} = \begin{bmatrix} -\left(c_1 r_1 + c_2 r_2\right) & w\Delta t \\ -\dfrac{\left(c_1 r_1 + c_2 r_2\right)}{\Delta t} & w - 1 \end{bmatrix} \begin{bmatrix} x_{k}^{i} \\ V_{k}^{i} \end{bmatrix} + \begin{bmatrix} c_1 r_1 & c_2 r_2 \\ \dfrac{c_1 r_1}{\Delta t} & \dfrac{c_2 r_2}{\Delta t} \end{bmatrix} \begin{bmatrix} p_{k}^{i} \\ p_{k}^{g} \end{bmatrix} \tag{12}$$

which is true only when $V_{k}^{i} = 0$ and both x_{k}^{i} and p_{k}^{i} coincide with p_{k}^{g}. Therefore, we will have an equilibrium point for which all particles tend to converge as iteration progresses. Note that such a position is not necessarily a local or global minimizer. Such point, however, will improve towards the optimum if there is external excitation in the dynamic system driven by the discovery of better individual and global positions during the optimization process.

The system stability and dynamic behaviour can be obtained using the eigenvalues derived from the dynamic matrix formulation presented in equation (11). The dynamic matrix characteristic equation is derived as:

$$\lambda^{2} - \left(w - c_1 r_1 - c_2 r_2 + 1\right)\lambda + w = 0 \tag{13}$$

where the eigenvalues are given as:

$$\lambda_{1,2} = \frac{1 + w - c_1 r_1 - c_2 r_2 \pm \sqrt{\left(1 + w - c_1 r_1 - c_2 r_2\right)^{2} - 4w}}{2} \tag{14}$$

The necessary and sufficient condition for stability of a discrete-dynamic system is that all eigenvalues (λ) derived from the dynamic matrix lie inside a unit circle around the origin on the complex plane, so $|\lambda_{i=1,\dots,n}| < 1$. Thus, convergence for the PSO will be guaranteed if the following set of stability conditions is met:

$$\begin{gathered} c_1 r_1 + c_2 r_2 > 0 \\ \frac{(c_1 r_1 + c_2 r_2)}{2} - w < 1 \\ w < 1 \end{gathered} \tag{15}$$

Knowing that $r_1, r_2 \in [0,1]$ the above set of conditions can be rearranged giving the following set of parameter selection heuristics which guarantee convergence for the PSO:

$$\begin{gathered} 0 < (c_1 + c_2) < 4 \\ \frac{(c_1 + c_2)}{2} - 1 < w < 1 \end{gathered} \tag{16}$$

While these heuristics provide useful selection bounds, an analysis of the effect of the different parameter settings is essential to determine the sensitivity of such parameters in the overall optimization procedure. Figure 3 shows the convergence histories for the well-known 10-bar truss structural optimization problem (described in more detail on Section 4) under different social and cognitive parameter combinations which meet the above convergence limits. The results are representative of more than 20 trials for each tested case, where the algorithm was allowed to run for 1000 iterations, with a fixed inertia weight value of 0.875, and the same initial particles, velocity values, and random seed.

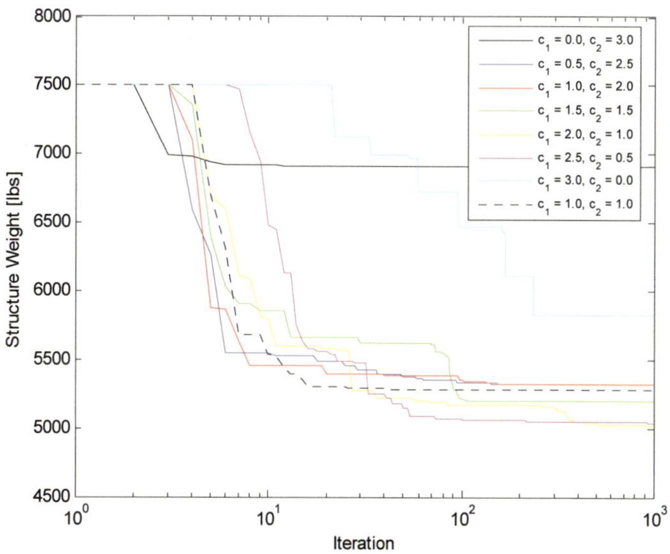

Figure 3. Cognitive (c_1) and Social (c_2) Parameters Variation Effect

From the figure we can clearly see that when only social values are used to update the particle velocities, as is the case when c_1=0 & c_2=3, the algorithm converges to a local optimum within the first ten iterations. As no individual (local) exploration is allowed to improve local solutions, all the particles in the swarm converge rapidly to the best initial optimum found from the swarm. We can also see that by increasing the emphasis on the cognitive parameter while reducing the social parameters, better solutions are found requiring less number of iterations for convergence. When we place slightly higher emphasis in the local exploration by each particle, as is the case with c_1=2.0 & c_2=1.0 and c_1=2.5 & c_2=0.5, the algorithm provides the best convergence speed to accuracy ratio. This result is due to the fact that individuals concentrate more in their own search regions thus avoiding overshooting the best design space regions. At the same time, some global information exchange is promoted, thus making the swarm point towards the best global solution. However, increasing local exploration at the expense of global agreement has its limits as shown in the case where only cognitive values are used to update the particle velocities (c_1=3 and c_2=0). In this case, each particle in the swarm will explore around its best-found solution requiring a very large number of iterations to agree into a common solution, which for this example is not the global optimum.
In a similar way to the above analysis, Figure 4 shows the effect of varying the inertia weight between its heuristic boundaries for a fixed set of "trust" settings parameters with c_1=2.0 and c_2=1.0 values. As before, the results are representative of more than 20 trials for each tested case where the algorithm was allowed to run for 1000 iterations with the same initial position, velocity and random seed. From the figure it is clear that reducing the inertia weight promotes faster convergence rates, as it controls the particle "momentum" bias towards a specific direction of the search space. Reducing the inertia weight beyond its allowable convergence limits comes at a cost as particles are forced to reduced their momentum stagnating at local optima as shown in the figure for the w=0.5 case.

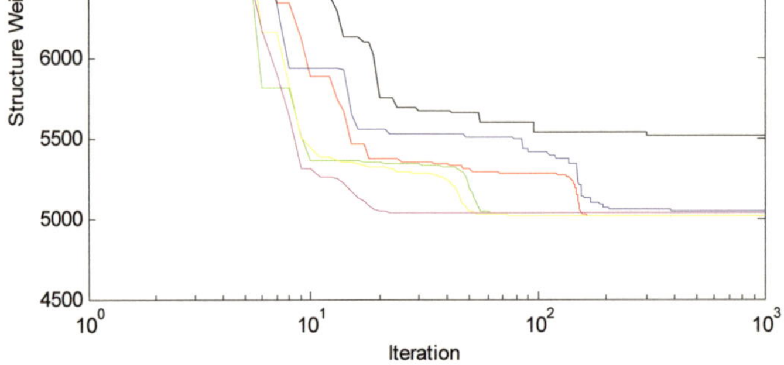

Figure 4. Inertia Weight Variation Effect

It is important to note at this stage that the optimal selection of the PSO parameters is in general problem-dependent. However, the obtained results for our example confirms the expectations as derived from the theoretical analysis (see i.e. van den Bergh & Engelbrecht, 2006; Trelea, 2003; and Clerc & Kennedy, 2002) and experiments (see i.e. Shi & Eberhart, 1998b; Shi & Eberhart, 1999; and Eberhart & Shi, 2000) regarding the sensitivity and behaviour of such tuning parameters. As long as the stability conditions presented in Eq. (16) are met, it is observed that maintaining an approximately equal or slightly higher weighting of the cognitive vs. the social parameter (in the interval of 1.5 to 2.5) will lead to the optimal convergent behaviour for the PSO.

3. Algorithm Improvements

Thus far, we have only dealt with the most basic PSO algorithm. Two important concerns when dealing with practical engineering problems have been left out up to now: how to improve the convergence rate behaviour as particles converge to a solution, and how to handle constraints. As we will see below, different modifications can be made to the original algorithm to address these concerns making it much stronger to deal with constrained optimization problems such as those traditionally present in structural design.

3.1 Updating the Inertia Weight

As shown before, the PSO global convergence is affected by the degree of local/global exploration provided by the "trust" settings parameters while the relative rate of convergence is provided by the inertia weight parameter. An interesting observation can be made from the inertia weight analysis presented in Figure 4. For a fixed inertia value there is a significant reduction in the algorithm convergence rate as iterations progresses. This is the consequence of excessive momentum in the particles, which results in detrimentally large steps sizes that overshoot the best design areas. By observing the figure, an intuitive strategy comes to mind: during the initial optimization stages, allow large weight updates so the design space is searched thoroughly. Once the most promising areas of the design space have been found (and the convergence rate starts to slow down) reduce the inertia weight, so the particles momentum decreases allowing them to concentrate in the best design areas. Formally, different methods have been proposed to accomplish the above strategy. Notably, two approaches have been used extensively (see Shi & Eberhart, 1998a; and Fourie & Groenwold, 2002). In the first one, a variation of inertia weight is proposed by linearly decreasing w at each iteration as:

$$w_{k+1} = w_{max} - \frac{w_{max} - w_{min}}{k_{max}} k \tag{17}$$

where an initial inertia value w_{max} is linearly decreased during k_{max} iterations.

The second approach provides a dynamic decrease of the inertia weight value if the swarm makes no solution improvement after certain number of iterations. The updated is made from an initial weight value based on a fraction multiplier $k_w \in [0,1]$ as:

$$w_{k+1} = k_w w_k \tag{18}$$

The effect of the described inertia update methods against a fixed inertia weight of 0.875 is shown in Figure 5 for the 10-bar truss example used before. For the linear decrease method, the inertia weight is varied in the interval [0.95, 0.55]. This interval meets the specified convergence conditions (Eq. (16)) with c_1=2.0 and c_2=1.0 values. For the dynamic decrease case a fraction multiplier of k_w = 0.975 is used if the improved solution does not change after five iterations, with an initial inertia weight specified as 0.95. As expected, an initial rapid convergence rate can be observed for the fixed inertia test, followed by a slow convergence towards the global optimum. The effect of dynamically updating the inertia weight is clear as both the linear and dynamic decrease methods present faster overall convergence rates. The dynamic update method provide the fastest convergence towards the solution, taking approximately 100 iterations as compared to 300 iterations taken by the linear decrease method, and the 600 iterations taken by the fixed inertia weight test. An intrinsic advantage is also provided by the dynamic decrease method as it depends solely on the value of past solutions adapting well to algorithmic termination and convergence check strategies.

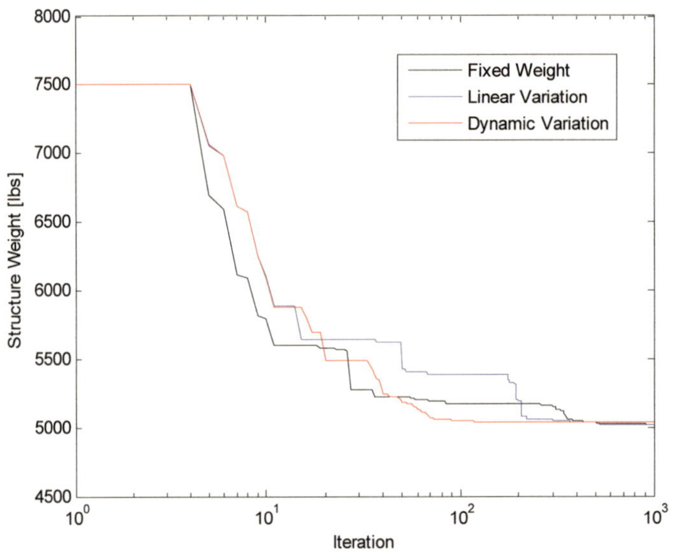

Figure 5. Inertia Weight Update Strategies Effect

3.2 Dealing with Constraints

Similar to other stochastic optimization methods, the PSO algorithm is formulated as an unconstrained optimizer. Different strategies have been proposed to deal with constraints, making the PSO a strong global engineering optimizer. One useful approach is to restrict the velocity vector of a constrained violated particle to a usable feasible direction as shown in Fig. 6. By doing so, the objective function is reduced while the particle is pointed back towards the feasible region of the design space (Venter & Sobieszczanski-Sobieski, 2004). A new position for the violated constraint particles can be defined using Eq. (2) with the velocity vector modified as:

$$v_{k+1}^{i} = c_1 r_1 \frac{\left(p_k^i - x_k^i\right)}{\Delta t} + c_2 r_2 \frac{\left(p_k^g - x_k^i\right)}{\Delta t} \tag{19}$$

where the modified velocity vector includes only the particle self information of the best point and the information of the current best point in the swarm. The new velocity vector is only influenced then by the particle best point found so far and by the current best point in the swarm. If both of these best points are feasible, the new velocity vector will point back to a feasible region of the design space. Otherwise, the new velocity vector will point to a region of the design space that resulted in smaller constraint violations. The result is to have the violated particle move back towards the feasible region of the design space, or at least closer to its boundary, in the next design iteration.

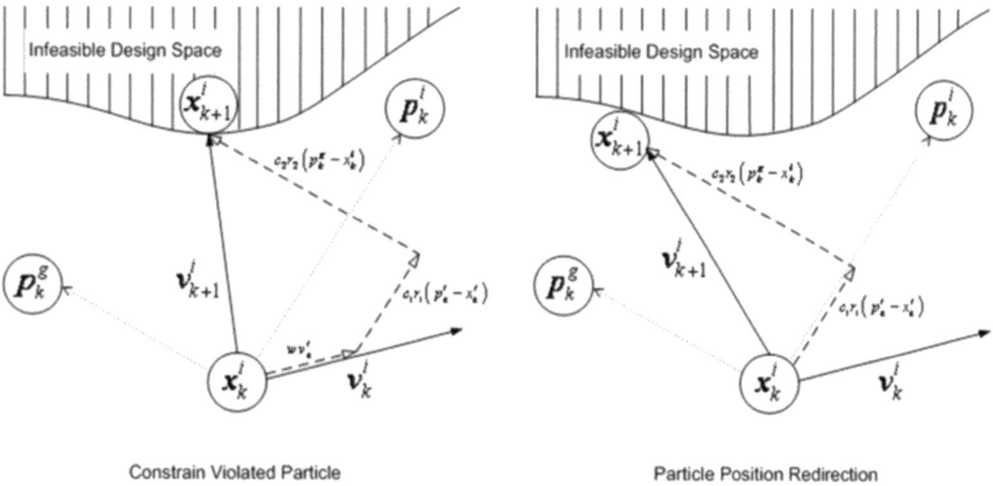

Figure 5. Violated Design Points Redirection

The velocity redirection approach however, does not guarantee that for the optimum solution all constraints will be met as it does not deal with the constraint directly. One classic way to accommodate constraints directly is by augmenting the objective function with penalties proportional to the degree of constraint infeasibility as:

$$f'(x_k) = \begin{cases} f(x_k) & if \quad x_k \quad is \quad feasible \\ f(x_k) + \sum_{j=1}^{m} k_j \hat{g}_j(x_k) & otherwise \end{cases} \tag{20}$$

where for m constraints k_j is a prescribed scaling penalty parameter and $\overline{g}_j(x_k)$ is a constraint value multiplier whose values are larger than zero if the constraint is violated:

$$\hat{g}_j(x_k) = \max\left(0, \left[g_j(x_k)\right]^2\right) \tag{21}$$

In a typical optimization procedure, the scaling parameter will be linearly increased at each iteration step so constraints are gradually enforced. The main concern with this method is that the quality of the solution will directly depend on the value of the specified scaling parameters. A better alternative will be to accommodate constraints using a parameter-less scheme. Taking advantage of the available swarm information Eq. (22) and Eq. (23) show a useful adaptive penalty approach, where penalties are defined based on the average of the objective function and the level of violation of each constraint during each iteration step:

$$k_j = \left|\bar{f}(x_k)\right| \frac{\bar{g}_j(x_k)}{\sum_{l=1}^{m}\left[\bar{g}_l(x_k)\right]^2} \tag{22}$$

with

$$\bar{g}_j(x_k) = \frac{1}{n}\sum_{k=1}^{n}\max\left(0, \hat{g}_j(x_k)\right) \tag{23}$$

where $\bar{f}(x_k)$ is the average of the objective function values in the current swarm, and $\bar{g}_j(x_k)$ is the violation of the lth constraint averaged over the current population. The above formulation distributes the penalty coefficients in a way that those constraints which are more difficult to be satisfied will have a relatively higher penalty coefficient. Such distribution is achieved by making the jth coefficient proportional to the average of the violation of the jth constraint by the elements of the current population. An individual in the swarm whose j^{th} violation equals the average of the jth violation in the current population for all j, will have a penalty equal to the absolute value of the average objective function of the population. Similarly, the average of the objective function equals $\bar{f}(x_k)+\left|\bar{f}(x_k)\right|$.

While the penalty based method works well in many practical cases, the numerically exact constrained optimum feasible solution can only be obtained at the infinite limit of the penalty factor. Recently, a new approach which circumvents the need for infinite penalty factors has been proposed by Sedlaczek & Eberhard (2005). It directly uses the general Lagrange function defined for an ith particle as:

$$\Im_i\left(x_k^i, \lambda^i\right) = f\left(x_k^i\right) + \sum_{j=1}^{m}\lambda_j^i g_j\left(x_k^i\right) \tag{24}$$

where λ are Lagrange multipliers. This function can be used as an unconstrained pseudo objective function by realizing that the solution of a constrained optimization problem (Eq. (1)) with the correct set of multipliers is a stationary point for the function. The stationary is not necessarily a minimum of the Lagrange function. To preserve the stationary properties of the solution while assuring that it is a minimum, the Lagrange function is augmented using a quadratic function extension θ as (Gill et al. 1981):

$$\Im_i\left(x_k^i, \lambda^i, r_p^i\right) = f\left(x_k^i\right) + \sum_{j=1}^{m}\lambda_j^i\theta_j\left(x_k^i\right) + \sum_{j=1}^{m} r_{p,j}\theta_j^2\left(x_k^i\right) \tag{25}$$

with

$$\theta_j\left(x_k^i\right) = max\left[g_j\left(x_k^i\right), \frac{-\lambda_j}{2r_{p,i}}\right] \tag{26}$$

where the $-\lambda_j/2r_{p,i}$ term is arbitrarily chosen from gradient-based optimization problems. Note from Eq. (25) how each constraint violation is penalized separately using an r_p penalty factor. It can be shown that each constrain penalty factor will be of finite value in the solution of the augmented Lagrange function (Eq. (25)) hence in the solution of the original constrained problem (Eq. (1)). The multipliers and penalty factors values that lead to the optimum are unknown and problem dependent. Therefore, instead of the traditional single unconstrained optimization process, a sequence of unconstrained minimizations of Eq. (25) is required to obtain a solution. In such a sequence, the Lagrange multiplier is updated as:

$$\lambda_j^i\big|_{v+1} = \lambda_j^i\big|_v + 2r_{p,j}\big|_v\,\theta_j\left(x_k^i\right) \tag{27}$$

In a similar way, the penalty factor is updated in a way such that it penalizes infeasible movements as:

$$r_{p,j}\big|_{v+1} = \begin{cases} 2r_{p,j}\big|_v & \textit{if} \quad g_j\left(x_v^i\right) > g_j\left(x_{v-1}^i\right) \wedge g_j\left(x_v^i\right) > \varepsilon_g \\ \frac{1}{2}r_{p,j}\big|_v & \textit{if} \quad g_j\left(x_v^i\right) \le \varepsilon_g \\ r_{p,j}\big|_v & \textit{otherwise} \end{cases} \tag{28}$$

where ε_g is a specified constrained violation tolerance. A lower bound limit of $r_{p,j} \ge (1/2)\sqrt{\left|\lambda_j^i\right|/\varepsilon_g}$ is also placed in the penalty factor so its magnitude is effective in creating a measurable change in Lagrange multipliers. Based on the above formulation the augmented Lagrange PSO algorithm can be then constructed as follows:

1. Initialize a set of particles positions x_0^i and velocities v_0^i randomly distributed throughout the design space bounded by specified limits. Also initialize the Lagrange multipliers and penalty factors, e.g. $\lambda_j^i\big|_0 = 0$, $r_{p,j}\big|_0 = r_0$, and evaluate the initial particles corresponding function values using Eq. (25).
2. Solve the unconstrained optimization problem described in Eq. (25) using the PSO algorithm shown in section 2.2 for k_{max} iterations.
3. Update the Lagrange multipliers and penalty factors according to Eq. (27) and Eq. (28).
4. Repeat steps 2-4 until a stopping criterion is met.

4. PSO Application to Structural Design

Particle swarms have not been used in the field of structural optimization until very recently, where they have show promising results in the areas of structural shape optimization (Fourie & Groenwold, 2002; Venter & Sobieszczanski-Sobieski, 2004) as well as topology optimization (Fourie & Groenwold, 2001). In this section, we show the application of the PSO algorithm to three classic non-convex truss structural optimization examples to demonstrate its effectiveness and to illustrate the effect of the different constraint handling methods.

4.1 Example 1 – The 10-Bar Truss

Our first example considers a well-known problem corresponding to a 10-bar truss non-convex optimization shown on Fig. 6 with nodal coordinates and loading as shown in Table 1 and 2 (Sunar & Belegundu, 1991). In this problem the cross-sectional area for each of the 10 members in the structure are being optimized towards the minimization of total weight. The cross-sectional area varies between 0.1 to 35.0 in^2. Constraints are specified in terms of stress and displacement of the truss members. The allowable stress for each member is 25,000 psi for both tension and compression, and the allowable displacement on the nodes is ±2 in, in the x and y directions. The density of the material is 0.1 lb/in^3, Young's modulus is E = 10^4 ksi and vertical downward loads of 100 kips are applied at nodes 2 and 4. In total, the problem has a variable dimensionality of 10 and constraint dimensionality of 32 (10 tension constraints, 10 compression constraints, and 12 displacement constraints).

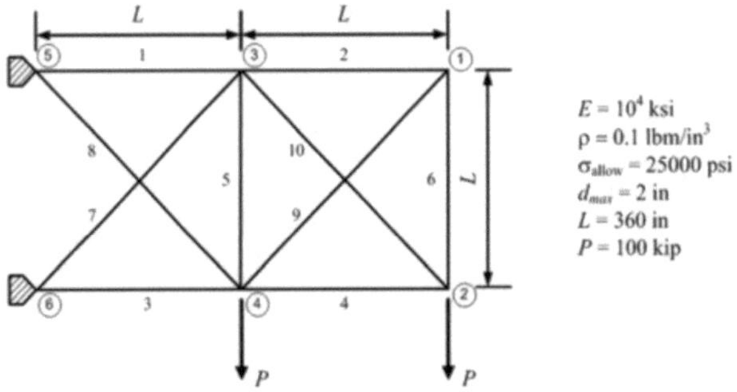

Figure 6. 10-Bar Space Truss Example

Node	x (in)	y (in)
1	720	360
2	720	0
3	360	360
4	360	0
5	0	360
6	0	0

Table 1. 10-Bar Truss Members Node Coordinates

Node	Fx	Fy
4	0	-100
6	0	-100

Table 2. 10-Bar Truss Nodal Loads

Three different PSO approaches where tested corresponding to different constraint handling methodologies. The first approach (PSO1) uses the traditional fixed penalty constraint while the second one (PSO2) uses an adaptive penalty constraint. The third approach (PSO3) makes use of the augmented Lagrange multiplier formulation to handle the constraints. Based on the derived selection heuristics and parameter settings analysis, a dynamic inertia weight variation method is used for all approaches with an initial weight of 0.95, and a fraction multiplier of k_w = 0.975 which updates the inertia value if the improved solution does not change after five iterations. Similarly, the "trust" setting parameters where specified as c_1=2.0 and c_2=1.0 for the PSO1 and PSO2 approaches to promote the best global/local exploratory behaviour. For the PSO3 approach the setting parameters where reduced in value to c_1=1.0 and c_2=0.5 to avoid premature convergence when tracking the changing extrema of the augment multiplier objective function.

Table 3 shows the best and worst results of 20 independent runs for the different PSO approaches. Other published results found for the same problem using different optimization approaches including gradient based algorithms both unconstrained (Schimit & Miura, 1976), and constrained (Gellatly & Berke, 1971; Dobbs & Nelson, 1976; Rizzi, 1976; Haug & Arora, 1979; Haftka & Gurdal, 1992; Memari & Fuladgar, 1994), structural approximation algorithms (Schimit & Farshi, 1974), convex programming (Adeli & Kamal, 1991, Schmit & Fleury, 1980), non-linear goal programming (El-Sayed & Jang, 1994), and genetic algorithms (Ghasemi et al, 1997; Galante, 1992) are also shown in Tables 3 and 4.

Truss Area	PSO1 Best	PSO1 Worst	PSO2 Best	PSO2 Worst	PSO3 Best	PSO3 Worst	Gellatly & Berke, 1971	Schimit & Miura, 1976	Ghasemi, 1997	Schimit & Farshi, 1974	Dobbs & Nelson, 1976
01	33.50	33.50	33.50	33.50	33.50	30.41	31.35	30.57	25.73	33.43	30.50
02	0.100	0.100	0.100	0.100	0.100	0.380	0.100	0.369	0.109	0.100	0.100
03	22.76	28.56	22.77	33.50	22.77	25.02	20.03	23.97	24.85	24.26	23.29
04	14.42	21.93	14.42	13.30	14.42	14.56	15.60	14.73	16.35	14.26	15.43
05	0.100	0.100	0.100	0.100	0.100	0.110	0.140	0.100	0.106	0.100	0.100
06	0.100	0.100	0.100	0.100	0.100	0.100	0.240	0.364	0.109	0.100	0.210
07	7.534	7.443	7.534	6.826	7.534	7.676	8.350	8.547	8.700	8.388	7.649
08	20.46	19.58	20.47	18.94	20.47	20.83	22.21	21.11	21.41	20.74	20.98
09	20.40	19.44	20.39	18.81	20.39	21.21	22.06	20.77	22.30	19.69	21.82
10	0.100	0.100	0.100	0.100	0.100	0.100	0.100	0.320	0.122	0.100	0.100
Weight	5024.1	5405.3	5024.2	5176.2	5024.2	5076.7	5112.0	5107.3	5095.7	5089.0	5080.0

Table 3. 10-Bar Truss Optimization Results

Truss Area	Rizzi, 1976	Haug & Arora, 1979	Haftka & Gurdal, 1992	Adeli & Kamal, 1991	El-Sayed & Jang, 1994	Galante, 1992	Memari & Fuladgar, 1994
01	30.73	30.03	30.52	31.28	32.97	30.44	30.56
02	0.100	0.100	0.100	0.10	0.100	0.100	0.100
03	23.934	23.274	23.200	24.65	22.799	21.790	27.946
04	14.733	15.286	15.220	15.39	14.146	14.260	13.619
05	0.100	0.100	0.100	0.10	0.100	0.100	0.100
06	0.100	0.557	0.551	0.10	0.739	0.451	0.100
07	8.542	7.468	7.457	7.90	6.381	7.628	7.907
08	20.954	21.198	21.040	21.53	20.912	21.630	19.345
09	21.836	21.618	21.530	19.07	20.978	21.360	19.273
10	0.100	0.100	0.100	0.10	0.100	0.100	0.100
Weight	5061.6	5060.9	5060.8	5052.0	5013.2	4987.0	4981.1

Table 4. 10-Bar Truss Optimization Results (Continuation)

We can see that all three PSO implementations provide good results as compared with other methods for this problem. However, the optimal solution found by the fixed penalty approach has a slight violation of the node 3 and node 6 constraints. This behaviour is expected from a fixed penalty as the same infeasibility constraint pressure is applied at each iteration; it also indicates that either we should increase the scaling penalty parameter or dynamically increase it, so infeasibility is penalized further as the algorithm gets closer to the solution. The benefit of a dynamic varying penalty is demonstrated by the adaptive penalty PSO which meets all constraints and has only two active constraints for the displacements at nodes 3 and 6. The augmented Lagrange multiplier approach also converges to the same feasible point as the dynamic penalty result. Furthermore, it does it in fewer number of iterations as compared to the other two approaches since convergence is checked directly using the Lagrange multiplier and penalty factor values. Note as well how the fixed penalty approach has a larger optimal solution deviation as compared to the dynamic penalty and Lagrange multiplier approaches.

4.2 Example 2 – The 25-Bar Truss

The second example considers the weight minimization of a 25-bar transmission tower as shown on Fig 7 with nodal coordinates shown on Table 5 (Schmit & Fleury, 1980). The design variables are the cross-sectional area for the truss members, which are linked in eight member groups as shown in Table 6. Loading of the structure is presented on Table 7. Constraints are imposed on the minimum cross-sectional area of each truss (0.01 in^2), allowable displacement at each node (±0.35 in), and allowable stresses for the members in the interval [-40, 40] ksi. In total, this problem has a variable dimensionality of eight and a constraint dimensionality of 84.

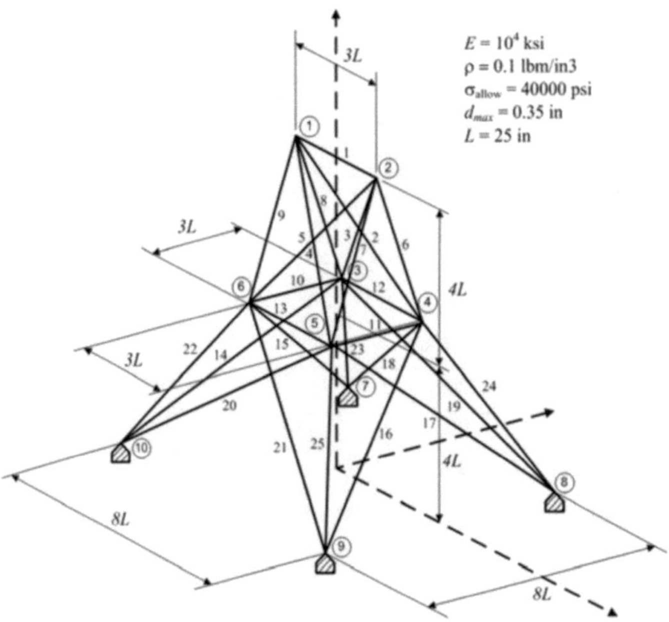

Figure 7. 25-Bar Space Truss Example

Node	x (in)	y (in)	z (in)
1	-37.5	0	200.0
2	37.5	0	200.0
3	-37.5	37.5	100.0
4	37.5	37.5	100.0
5	37.5	-37.5	100.0
6	-37.5	-37.5	100.0
7	-100.0	100.0	0.0
8	100.0	100.0	0.0
9	100.0	-100.0	0.0
10	-100.0	-100.0	0.0

Table 5. 25-Bar Truss Members Node Coordinates

Group	Truss Members
A1	1
A2	2-5
A3	6-9
A4	10,11
A5	12,13
A6	14-17
A7	18-21
A8	22-25

Table 6. 25-Bar Truss Members Area Grouping

Node	Fx	Fy	Fz
1	1000	-10000	-10000
2	0	-10000	-10000
3	500	0	0
6	600	0	0

Table 7. 25-Bar Truss Nodal Loads

As before, three different PSO approaches that correspond to different constraint handling methods were tested. The best and worst results of 20 independent runs for each tested method are presented on Table 8 as well as results from other research efforts obtained from local (gradient-based) and global optimizers. Clearly, all PSO approaches yield excellent solutions for both its best and worst results where all the constraints are met for all the PSO methods. The optimal solutions obtained have the same active constraints as reported in other references as follows: the displacements at nodes 3 and 6 in the Y direction for both load cases and the compressive stresses in members 19 and 20 for the second load case. As before, a larger solution deviation in the fixed penalty results is observed as compared to the other two PSO approaches. In addition, results from the augmented Lagrange method are obtained in less number of iterations as compared to the penalty-based approaches.

Area Group	PSO1 Best	PSO1 Worst	PSO2 Best	PSO2 Worst	PSO3 Best	PSO3 Worst	Zhou & Rosvany, 1993	Haftka & Gurdal, 1992	Erbatur, et al., 2000	Zhu, 1986	Wu, 1995
A1	0.1000	0.1000	0.1000	0.1000	0.1000	0.1000	0.010	0.010	0.1	0.1	0.1
A2	0.8977	0.1000	1.0227	0.9895	0.4565	1.0289	1.987	1.987	1.2	1.9	0.5
A3	3.4000	3.3533	3.4000	3.4000	3.4000	3.4000	2.994	2.991	3.2	2.6	3.4
A4	0.1000	0.1000	0.1000	0.1000	0.1000	0.1000	0.010	0.010	0.1	0.1	0.1
A5	0.1000	0.1000	0.1000	3.4000	1.9369	0.1000	0.010	0.012	1.1	0.1	1.5
A6	0.9930	0.7033	0.6399	0.6999	0.9647	0.8659	0.684	0.683	0.9	0.8	0.9
A7	2.2984	2.3233	2.0424	1.9136	0.4423	2.2278	1.677	1.679	0.4	2.1	0.6
A8	3.4000	3.4000	3.4000	3.4000	3.4000	3.4000	2.662	2.664	3.4	2.6	3.4
Weight	489.54	573.57	485.33	534.84	483.84	489.424	545.16	545.22	493.80	562.93	486.29

Table 8. 25-Bar Truss Optimization Results

4.3 Example 3 – The 72-Bar Truss

The final example deals with the optimization of a four-story 72-bar space truss as shown on Fig. 8. The structure is subject to two loading cases as presented on Table 9. The optimization objective is the minimization of structural weight where the design variables are specified as the cross-sectional area for the truss members. Truss members are linked in 16 member groups as shown in Table 10. Constraints are imposed on the maximum allowable displacement of 0.25 in at the nodes 1 to 16 along the x and y directions, and a maximum allowable stress in each bar restricted to the range [-25,25] ksi. In total, this problem has a variable dimensionality of 16 and a constraint dimensionality of 264.

Load Case	Node	Fx	Fy	Fz
1	1	5	5	-5
2	1	0	0	-5
2	0	0	-5	0
3	0	0	-5	0
4	0	0	-5	0

Table 9. 72-Bar Truss Nodal Loads

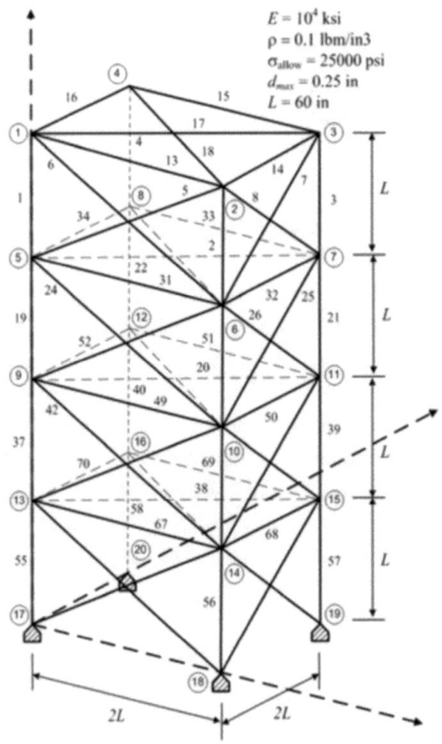

Figure 8. 72-Bar Space Truss Example

Results from the three PSO approaches as well as other references are shown in Table 11. As before, comparisons results include results from traditional optimization (Venkayya, 1971; Gellatly & Berke, 1971; Zhou & Rosvany, 1993), approximation concepts (Schimit & Farshi, 1974), and soft-computing approaches (Erbatur, et al., 2000). Similar to the previous examples, all the tested PSO approaches provide better solutions as those reported in the literature, with the augmented Lagrange method providing the best solution with the lowest number of iterations. The obtained optimal PSO solutions meet all constraints requirements and have the following active constraints: the displacements at node 1 in both the X and Y directions for load case one, and the compressive stresses in members 1-4 for load case two. The above active constraints agree with those reported by the different references.

Area Members Group	Truss Members
A1	1, 2, 3, 4
A2	5, 6, 7, 8, 9, 10, 11, 12
A3	13, 14, 15, 16
A4	17, 18
A5	19, 20, 21, 22
A6	23, 24, 25, 26, 27, 28, 29, 30
A7	31, 32, 33, 34
A8	35, 36
A9	37, 38, 39, 40
A10	41, 42, 43, 44, 45, 46, 47, 48
A11	49, 50, 51, 52
A12	53, 54
A13	55, 56, 57, 58
A14	59, 60, 61, 62, 63, 64, 65, 66
A15	67, 68, 69, 70
A16	71, 72

Table 10. 72-Bar Truss Members Area Grouping

Area Group	PSO1 Best	PSO1 Worst	PSO2 Best	PSO2 Worst	PSO3 Best	PSO3 Worst	Zhou & Rosvany, 1993	Venkayya, 1971	Erbatur, et al., 2000	Schimit & Farshi, 1974	Gellatly & Berke, 1971
A01	0.1561	0.1512	0.1615	0.1606	0.1564	0.1568	0.1571	0.161	0.155	0.1585	0.1492
A02	0.5708	0.5368	0.5092	0.5177	0.5553	0.5500	0.5356	0.557	0.535	0.5936	0.7733
A03	0.4572	0.4323	0.4967	0.3333	0.4172	0.3756	0.4096	0.377	0.480	0.3414	0.4534
A04	0.4903	0.5509	0.5619	0.5592	0.5164	0.5449	0.5693	0.506	0.520	0.6076	0.3417
A05	0.5133	2.5000	0.5142	0.4868	0.5194	0.5140	0.5067	0.611	0.460	0.2643	0.5521
A06	0.5323	0.5144	0.5464	0.5223	0.5217	0.4948	0.5200	0.532	0.530	0.5480	0.6084
A07	0.1000	0.1000	0.1000	0.1000	0.1000	0.1000	0.100	0.100	0.120	0.1000	0.1000
A08	0.1000	0.1000	0.1095	0.1000	0.1000	0.1001	0.100	0.100	0.165	0.1509	0.1000
A09	1.2942	1.2205	1.3079	1.3216	1.3278	1.2760	1.2801	1.246	1.155	1.1067	1.0235
A10	0.5426	0.5041	0.5193	0.5065	0.4998	0.4930	0.5148	0.524	0.585	0.5793	0.5421
A11	0.1000	0.1000	0.1000	0.1000	0.1000	0.1005	0.1000	0.100	0.100	0.1000	0.1000
A12	0.1000	0.1000	0.1000	0.1000	0.1000	0.1005	0.1000	0.100	0.100	0.1000	0.1000
A13	1.8293	1.7580	1.7427	2.4977	1.8992	2.2091	1.8973	1.818	1.755	2.0784	1.4636
A14	0.4675	0.4787	0.5185	0.4833	0.5108	0.5145	0.5158	0.524	0.505	0.5034	0.5207
A15	0.1003	0.1000	0.1000	0.1000	0.1000	0.1000	0.1000	0.100	0.105	0.1000	0.1000
A16	0.1000	0.1000	0.1000	0.1000	0.1000	0.1000	0.1000	0.100	0.155	0.1000	0.1000
Weight	381.03	417.45	381.91	384.62	379.88	381.17	379.66	381.20	385.76	388.63	395.97

Table 11. 72-Bar Truss Optimization Results

7. Summary and Conclusions

Particle Swarm Optimization is a population-based algorithm, which mimics the social behaviour of animals in a flock. It makes use of individual and group memory to update each particle position allowing global as well as local search optimization. Analytically the PSO behaves similarly to a traditional line-search where the step length and search direction are stochastic. Furthermore, it was shown that the PSO search strategy can be represented as a discrete-dynamic system which converges to an equilibrium point. From a stability analysis of such system, a parameter selection heuristic was developed which provides an initial guideline to the selection of the different PSO setting parameters. Experimentally, it was found that using the derived heuristics with a slightly larger cognitive pressure value leads to faster and more accurate convergence. Improvements of the basic PSO algorithm were discussed. Different inertia update strategies were presented to improve the rate of convergence near optimum points. It was found that a dynamic update provide the best rate of convergence overall. In addition, different constraint handling methods were shown. Three non-convex structural optimization problems were tested using the PSO with a dynamic inertia update and different constraint handling approaches. Results from the tested examples illustrate the ability of the PSO algorithm (with all the different constraint handling strategies) to find optimal results, which are better, or at the same level of other structural optimization methods. From the different constraint handling methods, the augmented Lagrange multiplier approach provides the fastest and more accurate alternative. Nevertheless implementing such method requires additional algorithmic changes, and the best combination of setting parameters for such approach still need to be determined. The PSO simplicity of implementation, elegant mathematical features, along with the lower number of setting parameters makes it an ideal method when dealing with global non-convex optimization tasks for both structures and other areas of design.

8. References

Abido M. (2002). Optimal design of power system stabilizers using particle swarm optimization, *IEEE Trans Energy* Conversion, Vol. 17, No. 3, pp. 406–413.

Adeli H, and Kamal O. (1991). Efficient optimization of plane trusses, *Adv Eng Software*, Vol. 13, No. 3, pp. 116–122.

Clerc M, and Kennedy J. (2002). The particle swarm-explosion, stability, and convergence in a multidimensional complex space, *IEEE Trans Evolut. Comput.*, Vol. 6, No. 1, pp 58–73.

Coello C, and Luna E. (2003). Use of particle swarm optimization to design combinational logic Circuits, Tyrell A, Haddow P, Torresen J, editors. *5th International conference on evolvable systems: from biology to hardware, ICES 2003. Lecture notes in computer science*, vol. 2606. Springer, Trondheim, Norway, pp. 398–409.

Dobbs M, and Nelson R. (1976). Application of optimality criteria to automated structural design, *AIAA Journal*, Vol. 14, pp. 1436–1443.

Dorigo M, Maniezzo V, and Colorni A. (1996). The ant system: optimization by a colony of cooperating agents, *IEEE Trans Syst Man Cybernet B*, Vol. 26, No. 1, pp. 29–41.

Eberhart R, and Kennedy J. (1995). New optimizer using particle swarm theory, *Sixth Int. symposium on micro machine and human science*, Nagoya, Japan, pp. 39–43.

Eberhart R, and Shi Y. (2000). Comparing inertia weights and constriction factors in particle swarm optimization, *IEEE congress on evolutionary computation (CEC 2000)*, San Diego, CA, pp. 84–88.

El-Sayed M, and Jang T. (1994). Structural optimization using unconstrained non-linear goal programming algorithm, *Comput Struct*, Vol. 52, No. 4, pp. 723–727.

Erbatur F, Hasantebi O, Tntnncn I, Kilt H. (2000). Optimal design of planar and space structures with genetic algorithms, *Comput Struct*, Vol. 75, pp. 209–24.

Fourie P, and Groenwold A. (2001). The particle swarm optimization in topology optimization, *Fourth world congress of structural and multidisciplinary optimization*, Paper no. 154, Dalian, China.

Fourie P, and Groenwold A. (2002). The particle swarm optimization algorithm in size and shape optimization, *Struct Multidiscip Optimiz*, Vol. 23, No. 4, pp. 259–267.

Galante M. (1992). Structures Optimization by a simple genetic algorithm, *Numerical methods in engineering and applied sciences*, Barcelona, Spain, pp. 862–70.

Gellatly R, and Berke L. (1971). Optimal structural design, *Tech Rep AFFDLTR-70-165*, Air Force Flight Dynamics Laboratory (AFFDL).

Ghasemi M, Hinton E, and Wood R. (1997). Optimization of trusses using genetic algorithms for discrete and continuous variables, *Eng Comput*, Vol. 16, pp. 272–301.

Gill P.E., Murray W., and Wright M.H. (1981). *Practical Optimization*. Academic Press, London.

Goldberg D. (1989). Genetic algorithms in search, optimization, and machine learning. Addison- Wesley, New York, NY.

Haftka R, and Gurdal Z. (1992). *Elements of structural optimization*, 3rd ed. Kluwer Academic Publishers.

Hassan R, Cohanim B, de Weck O, and Venter G. (2005). A comparison of particle swarm optimization and the genetic algorithm, *1st AIAA multidisciplinary design optimization specialist conference*, Paper No. AIAA-2005-1897, Austin, TX.

Haug E, and Arora J. (1979). *Applied optimal design*, Wiley, New York, NY. Hu X, Eberhart R, and Shi Y. (2003). Engineering optimization with particle swarm, *IEEE Swarm intelligence symposium (SIS 2003)*, Indianapolis, IN, pp. 53–57.

Kennedy J, and Eberhart R. (1995). Particle swarm optimization, *IEEE international conference on neural networks*, Vol. IV, Piscataway, NJ, pp. 1942–1948.

Kirkpatrick S, Gelatt C, and Vecchi M. (1983). Optimization by simulated annealing. *Science*, Vol. 220, No. 4598, pp. 671–680.

Memari A, and Fuladgar A. (1994). Minimum weight design of trusses by behsaz program, *2nd International conference on computational structures technology*, Athens, Greece.

Passino K. (2002). Biomimicry of bacterial foraging for distributed optimization and control, *IEEE Control Syst Mag*, Vol. 22, No. 3, pp. 52–67.

Rizzi P. (1976). Optimization of multiconstrained structures based on optimality criteria, 17th *Structures, structural dynamics, and materials conference*, King of Prussia, PA.

Schimit L, and Farshi B. (1974). Some approximation concepts in structural synthesis, *AIAA Journal*, Vol. 12, pp. 692–699.

Schimit L, and Miura H. (1976). A new structural analysis/synthesis capability: access 1. *AIAA Journal*, Vol. 14, pp. 661–671.

Schmit L, and Fleury C. (1980). Discrete-continuous variable structural synthesis using dual methods, *AIAA Journal*, Vol. 18, pp. 1515–1524.

Sedlaczek K. and Peter Eberhard (2005). Constrained Particle Swarm Optimization of Mechanical Systems, *6th World Congresses of Structural and Multidisciplinary Optimization*, Rio de Janeiro, 30 May - 03 June 2005, Brazil

Shi Y, and Eberhart R. (1998a). A modified particle swarm optimizer, *IEEE international conference on evolutionary computation*, IEEE Press, Piscataway, NJ, pp. 69–73.

Shi Y, and Eberhart R. (1998b). Parameter selection in particle swarm optimization, *7th annual conference on evolutionary programming*, New York, NY, pp. 591–600.

Shi Y, and Eberhart R. (1999). Empirical study of particle swarm optimization, *IEEE congress on evolutionary computation (CEC 1999)*, Piscataway, NJ, pp. 1945–50.

Sunar M, and Belegundu A. (1991). Trust region methods for structural optimization using exact second order sensitivity, *Int J. Numer Meth Eng*, Vol. 32, pp. 275–293.

Trelea I. (2003). The particle swarm optimization algorithm: convergence analysis and parameter selection, *Information Processing Letters*, Vol. 85, No. 6, pp. 317–325.

Van den Bergh F, and Engelbrecht A. (2006). A study of particle swarm optimization particle trajectories, *Information Science*, Vol. 176, pp. 937-971.

Venkayya V. (1971). Design of optimum structures, *Comput Struct*, Vol. 1, No. 12, pp. 265–309.

Venter G, and Sobieszczanski-Sobieski J. (2003). Particle swarm optimization, *AIAA Journal*, Vol. 41, No. 8, pp 1583–1589.

Venter G, and Sobieszczanski-Sobieski J. (2004). Multidisciplinary optimization of a transport aircraft wing using particle swarm optimization, *Struct Multidiscip Optimiz*, Vol. 26, No. 1-2, pp. 121–131.

Wu S, Chow P. (1995). Steady-state genetic algorithms for discrete optimization of trusses, *Comput Struct*, Vol. 56, No. 6, pp. 979–991.

Zheng Y, Ma L, Zhang L, Qian J. (2003). Robust pid controller design using particle swarm optimizer, *IEEE international symposium on intelligence control*, pp. 974–979.

Zhou M, Rozvany G. (1993). Dcoc: an optimality criteria method for large systems. Part ii: algorithm, *Struct Multidiscip Optimiz*, Vol. 6, pp. 250–62.

Zhu D. (1986). An improved templemans algorithm for optimum design of trusses with discrete member sizes, *Eng Optimiz*, Vol. 9, pp. 303–312.

22

Reserve-Constrained Multiarea Environmental/Economic Dispatch Using Enhanced Particle Swarm Optimization

Lingfeng Wang and Chanan Singh
Department of Electrical and Computer Engineering,
Texas A&M University College Station
USA

1. Introduction

Development of the power dispatch problem can be divided into several stages. The traditional economic dispatch (ED) has only one objective for minimizing fuel costs (Lee, et al., 1998). With the increasing awareness of environmental protection in recent years, environmental/economic dispatch (EED) is proposed as an alternative to achieve simultaneously the minimization of fuel costs and pollutant emissions (Abido, 2003; Talaq, et al., 1994). At the same time, only limited work has been carried out to deal with the multiarea economic dispatch (MAED), where power is dispatched within multiple areas (Chen & Chen, 2001; Jayabarathi, et al., 2000; Streiffert, 1995; Wang & Shahidepour, 1992; Yalcinoz & Short, 1998; Zhu, 2003). In this chapter, we further extend the concept of EED into the MAED scenario and a new concept termed multiarea environmental/economic dispatch (MAEED) is proposed by also minimizing the pollutant emissions in the MAED context. The MAEED problem is first presented and then an enhanced multiobjective particle swarm optimization (MOPSO) algorithm is developed to handle the MAEED problem. PSO has turned out to be capable of dealing with a variety of complex engineering optimization problems like MAEED considered in this study. In the problem formulation, the tie-line transfer capacities are treated as a set of design constraints to increase the system security. Furthermore, area spinning reserve requirements are also incorporated in order to ensure the system reliability. Reserve-sharing scheme is used to enable the area without enough capacity to meet its reserve demand. A four-area test power system is then used as an application example to verify the effectiveness of the proposed method through numerical simulations. A comparative study is also carried out to illustrate the different solutions obtained based on different problem formulations.

The remainder of the chapter is organized as follows: In Section 2, the MAEED problem is formulated. The inner working of the particle swarm optimization (PSO) algorithm is discussed in Section 3. In Section 4, the proposed method for optimal MAEED is presented. Simulation results and analysis are given in Section 5. Finally, conclusions are drawn and future research directions are suggested.

2. Problem Formulation

The optimal MAEED problem can be modeled as a bi-criteria optimization problem. The two conflicting objectives, i.e., operational costs and pollutant emissions, should be minimized simultaneously while fulfilling certain system constraints.

2.1 Design objectives

- Objective 1: Minimization of operational costs

The generator cost curves are represented by quadratic functions. The total $/h fuel cost $FC(P_G)$ can be represented as follows:

$$FC(P_G) = \sum_{j=1}^{N} \sum_{i=1}^{M_j} a_{ij} + b_{ij} P_{G_{ij}} + c_{ij} P_{G_{ij}}^2 \tag{1}$$

where N is the number of areas, M_j is the number of generators committed to the operating system in area j, a_{ij}, b_{ij}, c_{ij} are the cost coefficients of the i-th generator in area j, and $P_{G_{ij}}$ is the real power output of the i-th generator in area j. P_{A_j} is the vector of real power outputs of generators in area j and defined as

$$P_{A_j} = [P_{G_{1j}}, P_{G_{2j}}, \ldots, P_{G_{M_j j}}] \tag{2}$$

Thus,

$$P_G = [P_{A_1}, P_{A_2}, \ldots, P_{A_N}] \tag{3}$$

Another operational cost in MAEED is the transmission cost $TC(P_T)$ for power transfer between areas. It can be expressed as follows:

$$TC(P_T) = \sum_{j=1}^{N-1} \sum_{k=j+1}^{N} f_{jk} P_{T_{jk}} \tag{4}$$

where $P_{T_{jk}}$ is the tie line flow from area j to area k, f_{jk} is the transmission cost coefficient relevant to $P_{T_{jk}}$. P_T is the vector of real power transmission between areas and defined as

$$P_T = [P_{T_{1,2}}, \ldots, P_{T_{1,N}}, P_{T_{2,3}}, \ldots, P_{T_{2,N}}, \ldots, P_{T_{N-1,N}}] \tag{5}$$

As a result, the total operational costs can be calculated as

$$F_1 = FC(P_G) + TC(P_T) \tag{6}$$

- Objective 2: Minimization of pollutant emissions

The SO_2 and NO_x emissions can be approximated by a quadratic function of the generator output:

$$F_2 = \sum_{j=1}^{N} \sum_{i=1}^{M_j} \alpha_{ij} + \beta_{ij} P_{G_{ij}} + \gamma_{ij} P_{G_{ij}}^2 \tag{7}$$

where α_{ij}, β_{ij}, and γ_{ij} are coefficients of the *i-th* generator emission characteristics in area j.

2.2 Design constraints

There are three kinds of constraints considered in the problem, i.e, the generation capacity of each generator, area power balance, and tie line transfer limits.

- Constraint 1: Generation capacity constraint

For normal system operations, real power output of each generator is restricted by lower and upper bounds as follows:

$$P_{G_{ij}}^{min} \leq P_{G_{ij}} \leq P_{G_{ij}}^{max} \tag{8}$$

where $P_{G_{ij}}^{min}$ and $P_{G_{ij}}^{max}$ are the minimum and maximum power produced by generator *i* in area *j*.

- Constraint 2: Area power balance constraint

In area *j*, the total power generation must cover the total demand P_{D_j} with the consideration of imported and exported power. The power transmission loss is not considered in this study. This relation can be expressed as

$$\sum_{i=1}^{M_j} P_{G_{ij}} = P_{D_j} + \sum_{k,k \neq j} P_{T_{jk}}, j = 1, 2, \ldots, N. \tag{9}$$

- Constraint 3: Area spinning reserve constraint

In area *j*, the spinning reserve requirement should be satisfied through multiarea reserve sharing:

$$\sum_{i=1}^{M_j} P_{S_{ij}} \geq P_{S_{Req_j}} + \sum_{k,k \neq j} P_{RC_{jk}}, j = 1, 2, \ldots, N \tag{10}$$

where the spinning reserve of unit *i* in area *j* $P_{S_{ij}}$ equals to $P_{G_{ij}}^{max} - P_{G_{ij}}$, $P_{S_{Req_j}}$ is the required spinning reserve in area *j*, and $P_{RC_{kj}}$ is the reserve contribution from area *k* to area *j*.

A new vector P_{RC} is defined here to represent the reserve sharing between areas:

$$P_{RC} = [P_{RC_{1,2}}, \ldots, P_{RC_{1,N}}, P_{RC_{2,3}}, \ldots, P_{RC_{2,N}}, \ldots, P_{RC_{N-1,N}}]. \tag{11}$$

- Constraint 4: Tie line constraint

The transfer including both generation and reserve from area *j* to area *k* should not exceed the tie line transfer capacities for security consideration:

$$P_{T_{jk,min}} \leq P_{T_{jk}} + P_{RC_{jk}} \leq P_{T_{jk,max}} \tag{12}$$

where $P_{T_{jk,min}}$ and $P_{T_{jk,max}}$ specify the tie-line transmission capability.

In summary, the objective of MAEED optimization is to minimize F_1 and F_2 simultaneously subject to the constraints (8), (9), (10), and (12).

3. Particle Swarm Optimization

Particle swarm optimization (PSO) is inspired from the collective behavior exhibited in swarms of social insects (Kennedy & Eberhart, 1995). It has turned out to be an effective optimizer in dealing with a broad variety of engineering design problems. In PSO, a swarm is made up of many particles, and each particle represents a potential solution (i.e., individual). PSO algorithms are global optimization algorithms and do not need the operations for obtaining gradients of the cost function. Initially the particles are randomly generated to spread in the feasible search space. A particle has its own position and flight velocity, which keep being adjusted during the optimization process. The update equations determine the position of each particle in the next iteration. Let $k \in \mathbb{N}$ denote the generation number, let $N \in \mathbb{N}$ denote the swarm population in each generation, let $x_i(k) \in \mathbb{R}^M$, $i \in \{1,..., N\}$, denote the i-th particle of the k-th iteration, let $v_i(k) \in \mathbb{R}^M$ denote its velocity, let $c_1, c_2 \in \mathbb{R}_+$ and let $r_1(k), r_2(k) \sim U(0,1)$ be uniformly distributed random numbers between 0 and 1, let w be the inertia weight factor, and let $\chi \in [0,1]$ be the constriction factor for controlling the particle velocity magnitude. Then, the update equation is, for all $i \in \{1,..., N\}$ and all $k \in \mathbb{N}$,

$$\begin{aligned} v_i(k+1) &= \chi * (wv_i(k) + c_1r_1(k)(pbest_i(k) - x_i(k)) \\ &+ c_2r_2(k)(gbest(k) - x_i(k))), \end{aligned} \tag{13}$$

$$x_i(k+1) = x_i(k) + v_i(k+1), \tag{14}$$

where $Vi(0) \triangleq 0$ and

$$pbest_i(k) \triangleq \text{argmin}_{x \in \{x_i(j)\}_{j=0}^{k}} f(x), \tag{15}$$

$$gbest(k) \triangleq \text{argmin}_{x \in \{\{x_i(j)\}_{j=0}^{k}\}_{i=1}^{N}} f(x). \tag{16}$$

Hence, $pbest_i(k)$ is the position that for the i-th particle yields the lowest cost over all generations, and $gbest(k)$ is the location of the best particle in the entire population of all generations. The inertia weight w is considered to be crucial in determining the PSO convergence behavior. It regulates the effect of the past velocities on the current velocity. By doing so, it controls the wide-ranging and nearby search of the swarm. A large inertia weight facilitates searching unexplored areas, while a small one enables fine-tuning the current search region. The inertia is usually set to be a large value initially in order to achieve better global exploration, and gradually it is reduced for obtaining more refined solutions. The term $c_1r_1(k)(pbest_i(k) - x_i(k))$ is relevant to cognition since it takes into account the particle's own flight experience, and the term $c_2r_2(k)(gbest(k) - x_i(k))$ is associated with social interaction between the particles. Therefore, the learning factors c_1 and c_2 are also known as *cognitive acceleration constant* and *social acceleration constant,* respectively. The constriction factor χ should be chosen to enable appropriate particle movement steps. Under the guidance of these two updating rules, the particles will be attracted to move toward the best position found thus far. That is, the optimal or near-optimal solutions can be sought out due to this driving force.

4. The Proposed Solution Method

PSO-based approaches have shown advantages in resolving a wide variety of engineering optimization problems in terms of simplicity, convergence speed, and robustness (Kennedy & Eberhart, 2001). In this study, an enhanced particle swarm optimization algorithm (i.e., MOPSO) is proposed and it is then applied to deal with the MAEED problem.

4.1 Encoding scheme

The first step in defining a PSO algorithm is to connect the "real world" to the "PSO world", that is, to build a bridge between the practical problem and the problem solver by which the optimization is performed. Encoding is to define a mapping from the phenotypes onto a set of genotypes. In PSO, each particle flying in the search space is a potential solution. The power output of each generating unit and the tie line flow is selected as the position of the particle in each dimension to constitute the individual, which is a potential solution for the MAEED problem. The position values in all dimensions are all real-coded and the *i*-th individual P_i can be represented as follows:

$$P_i = [P_G, P_{RC}, P_T], \qquad i = 1, 2, \ldots, PS \tag{17}$$

where *PS* is the population size.

4.2 Constraints handling

Constraints lie at the heart of all constrained engineering optimization applications. Practical constraints, which are oftentimes nonlinear and non-trivial, confine the feasible solutions to a small subset of the entire design space. There are several prime approaches which can be applied to treat the constrained optimization problems, i.e., feasibility preservation, penalty functions, repair functions, restricting search to the feasible region, decoder functions, and other hybrid approaches (Eiben & Smith, 2003). Since PSO is essentially an unconstrained optimization algorithm, the constraints handling scheme needs to be incorporated into it in order to deal with the constrained power dispatch problem. Here a straightforward constraint-checking procedure is added. A feasible solution needs to satisfy all the constraints. Thus, for each potential solution, once a constraint is violated, it is not necessary to test its validity against other constraints anymore, which may be very many or highly complicated. In doing so, the overall time consumption is not proportional to the number of computational iterations and the computation time is significantly reduced. Furthermore, this approach is easy to implement as no pre-processing measures and complex numerical manipulations are needed. Since the individual fitness evaluation and its constraints are dealt with in a separate fashion, the approach can be commonly used in other optimization applications. In the selection of Pareto-optimal solutions, when any two individuals are compared, their constraints are examined first. If both satisfy the constraints, the concept of Pareto-dominance is then applied to determine which potential solution should be chosen. If both are infeasible solutions, then they are not qualified to be stored in the archive. If one is feasible and the other is not, the feasible dominates. Though this scheme is simple, it turns out to be quite effective in guaranteeing the feasibility of the non-dominated solutions throughout the optimization run.

4.3 Guides selection

A challenging task in applying PSO to handle multi-objective problems is to design a scheme for choosing both local and global guides for each particle in the swarm. Unlike single objective (SO) problems, there are no explicit concepts on how personal and global best positions can be identified in multi-objective (MO) problems. In the single-objective PSO, the global best particle can be readily found by choosing the particle with the best position. In MO optimization problems, the optimum solutions are Pareto-optimal. Thus, each particle should select the globally best particle based on the Pareto-optimal concept.

Oftentimes, the key task in MOPSO is to determine the best global search guide for each particle in the population. A fuzzification mechanism is introduced to the proposed multi-objective particle swarm optimization algorithm for the selection of global best position *gbest*. Here we interpret *gbest* not just as a point but as an area, and each point in the area has different possibilities of being chosen as the *gbest*. The fuzzification formula used in the study is $N(gbest, std^2)$, which represents a set of normally distributed particles with *gbest* as their mean value and *std* as standard deviation. First, in each iteration, the original *gbest* is selected from the archive, which is however not used directly to update the particle speed and position. Instead, an area around it is randomly generated based on the normal distribution. Then, tournament selection is applied to choose the *gbest* from this area, which will be used to update the particle speed and position. It is obvious that large *std* values will result in large generated selection regions. Furthermore, in tournament selection, local competition is used to determine survivors. In this study, binary tournament selection is used where the individual with the higher fitness in the group of two individuals is selected, and the other is removed. This selection scheme can be deemed as an effective measure to increase the population diversity during the optimization process.

4.4 Archiving

The major function of the archive is to store a historical record of the non-dominated solutions found along the heuristic search process. The archive interacts with the generational population in each iteration so as to absorb superior current non-dominated solutions and eliminate inferior solutions currently stored in the archive. The non-dominated solutions obtained at every iteration in the generational population (swarm) are compared with the contents of archive in a one-per-one basis. A candidate solution can be added to the archive if it meets any of the following conditions:

- There is no solution currently stored in the archive;
- The archive is not full and the candidate solution is not dominated by or equal to any solution currently stored in the archive;
- The candidate solution dominates any existing solution in the archive;
- The archive is full but the candidate solution is non-dominated and is in a sparser region than at least one solution currently stored in the archive.

4.5 Optimization procedure

The computational flow of the proposed optimization procedure is laid out as follows:

- Step 1: Specify the lower and upper bound generation power of each unit as well as the tie-line transfer limits; specify the area loads and reserves.
- Step 2: Randomly initialize the individuals of the population.
- Step 3: Evaluate each individual P_i in the population based on the concept of Pareto-dominance.
- Step 4: Store the non-dominated members found thus far in the archive.
- Step 5: Initialize the memory of each particle where a single local best *pbest* is stored. The memory is contained in another archive.
- Step 6: Increase the iteration counter.
- Step 7: Choose the personal best position *pbest* for each particle based on the memory record; Choose the global best *gbest* from the fuzzi-fied region using binary

tournament selection. The niching and fitness sharing mechanism is also applied throughout this process for enhancing solution diversity (Wang & Singh, 2007).

- Step 8: Update the member velocity v of each individual P_i, based on (13) as follows:

$$\begin{aligned} v_{id}^{(t+1)} &= w * v_i^{(t)} + c_1 * \mathrm{rand}() * (pbest_{id} - P_{id}^{(t)}) \\ &+ c_2 * \mathrm{Rand}() * (gbest_d - P_{id}^{(t)}), \\ & i = 1, \ldots, PS; d = 1, \ldots, (GN + 2 * TLN) \end{aligned} \tag{18}$$

where *GN* is the total number of generators, and *TLN* is the number of tie lines.

- Step 9: Modify the member position of each individual P_i, based on (14) as follows:

$$P_{id}^{(t+1)} = P_{id}^{(t)} + v_{id}^{(t+1)} \tag{19}$$

- Step 10: Update the archive which stores non-dominated solutions according to the four selection criteria as discussed earlier.
- Step 11: If the current individual is dominated by the $pbest$ in the memory, then keep the $pbest$ in the memory; Otherwise, replace the $pbest$ in the memory with the current individual.
- Step 12: If the maximum iterations are reached, then go to Step 13. Otherwise, go to Step 6.
- Step 13: Output a set of Pareto-optimal solutions from the archive as the final solutions for further decision-making selection.

5. An Application Example

In this study, a four-area test system is used to investigate the effectiveness of the proposed MOPSO algorithm. There are four generators in each area with different fuel and emission characteristics, which are shown in Table 1 and Table 2, respectively. The tie-line transfer limits are shown in Table 3. The system base is 100 MVA. The area loads are 0.3, 0.5, 0.4, and 0.6 p.u., respectively. The area spinning reserve is 30% of the load demand in each area. The transmission cost is not considered in simulations since it is normally small as compared with the total fuel costs.

In the simulations, after some trials, both the population size and archive size are set to 100, and the number of generations is set to 500. The constants c_1 and c_2 are both chosen as 1. The inertia weight factor w decreases linearly during the optimization run according to

$$w = w_{max} - \frac{w_{max} - w_{min}}{iter_{max}} \times iter \tag{20}$$

where $iter_{max}$ is the number of generations and $iter$ is the current number of iterations. In the first 200 generations, the $gbest$ is fuzzified using a large standard deviation to generate a region around the $gbest$ according to Gaussian distribution. In the remaining 300 generations, its value is decreased. This makes sense since, similar to the choice of w values, initial large standard deviation enables global search while the following small standard deviation facilitates local exploration using small movement in each iteration. The minimum fuel costs and minimum emissions obtained with and without inter-area aid are shown in Table 4 and Table 5, respectively. It should be noted that the negative values of tie-line flow $P_{T_{jk}}$, where $k > j$, indicate that the flow is sent from area k to area j.

Generator ij	a_{ij}	b_{ij}	c_{ij}	$P_{G_{ij}}^{min}$	$P_{G_{ij}}^{max}$
$G_{1,1}$	150	189	0.50	0.0005	0.14
$G_{1,2}$	115	200	0.55	0.0005	0.10
$G_{1,3}$	40	350	0.60	0.0005	0.13
$G_{1,4}$	122	315	0.50	0.0005	0.12
$G_{2,1}$	125	305	0.50	0.0005	0.25
$G_{2,2}$	70	275	0.70	0.0005	0.12
$G_{2,3}$	70	345	0.70	0.0005	0.20
$G_{2,4}$	70	345	0.70	0.0005	0.18
$G_{3,1}$	130	245	0.50	0.0005	0.30
$G_{3,2}$	130	245	0.50	0.0005	0.30
$G_{3,3}$	135	235	0.55	0.0005	0.30
$G_{3,4}$	200	130	0.45	0.0005	0.30
$G_{4,1}$	70	345	0.70	0.0005	0.11
$G_{4,2}$	45	389	0.60	0.0005	0.20
$G_{4,3}$	75	355	0.60	0.0005	0.30
$G_{4,4}$	100	370	0.80	0.0005	0.30

Table 1. Fuel cost coefficients and generator capacities (p.u.)

Generator ij	a_{ij}	b_{ij}	c_{ij}
$G_{1,1}$	0.016	-1.500	23.333
$G_{1,2}$	0.031	-1.820	21.022
$G_{1,3}$	0.013	-1.249	22.050
$G_{1,4}$	0.012	-1.355	22.983
$G_{2,1}$	0.020	-1.900	21.313
$G_{2,2}$	0.007	0.805	21.900
$G_{2,3}$	0.015	-1.401	23.001
$G_{2,4}$	0.018	-1.800	24.003
$G_{3,1}$	0.019	-2.000	25.121
$G_{3,2}$	0.012	-1.360	22.990
$G_{3,3}$	0.033	-2.100	27.010
$G_{3,4}$	0.018	-1.800	25.101
$G_{4,1}$	0.018	-1.810	24.313
$G_{4,2}$	0.030	-1.921	27.119
$G_{4,3}$	0.020	-1.200	30.110
$G_{4,4}$	0.040	-1.400	22.500

Table 2. Pollutant emissions coefficients (p.u.)

Tie line *jk*	$P_{T_{jk}}^{min}$	$P_{T_{jk}}^{max}$
$P_{T_{1,2}}$	0.001	0.060
$P_{T_{1,3}}$	0.001	0.040
$P_{T_{1,4}}$	0.001	0.200
$P_{T_{2,3}}$	0.001	0.035
$P_{T_{2,4}}$	0.001	0.055
$P_{T_{3,4}}$	0.001	0.009

Table 3. Tie-line transfer limits (p.u.)

Generation/objectives	w/ inter-area aid (p.u.)	w/o inter-area aid (p.u.)
$P_{G_{1,1}}$	0.1320	0.1074
$P_{G_{1,2}}$	0.0649	0.0943
$P_{G_{1,3}}$	0.1201	0.0503
$P_{G_{1,4}}$	0.1128	0.0533
$P_{G_{2,1}}$	0.2047	0.2507
$P_{G_{2,2}}$	0.0657	0.0671
$P_{G_{2,3}}$	0.1316	0.0980
$P_{G_{2,4}}$	0.1503	0.0846
$P_{G_{3,1}}$	0.0572	0.1083
$P_{G_{3,2}}$	0.0971	0.1646
$P_{G_{3,3}}$	0.0663	0.0662
$P_{G_{3,4}}$	0.2278	0.0622
$P_{G_{4,1}}$	0.0759	0.0754
$P_{G_{4,2}}$	0.1123	0.1587
$P_{G_{4,3}}$	0.0520	0.1071
$P_{G_{4,4}}$	0.1402	0.2604
$P_{T_{1,2}}$	-0.0316	-
$P_{T_{1,3}}$	-0.0088	-
$P_{T_{1,4}}$	0.1699	-
$P_{T_{2,3}}$	-0.0320	-
$P_{T_{2,4}}$	0.0516	-
$P_{T_{3,4}}$	0.0048	-
Mininium cost ($/hour)	2166.82	2191.14
Emission (ton/hour)	3.3152	3.7493

Table 4. Minimum fuel costs with and without inter-area aid

Generation/objectives	w/ inter-area aid (p.u.)	w/o inter-area aid (p.u.)
$P_{G_{1,1}}$	0.1277	0.1089
$P_{G_{1,2}}$	0.0625	0.0940
$P_{G_{1,3}}$	0.1188	0.0500
$P_{G_{1,4}}$	0.0945	0.0500
$P_{G_{2,1}}$	0.1684	0.2464
$P_{G_{2,2}}$	0.0677	0.0676
$P_{G_{2,3}}$	0.1891	0.1022
$P_{G_{2,4}}$	0.1604	0.0852
$P_{G_{3,1}}$	0.0619	0.1089
$P_{G_{3,2}}$	0.0722	0.1659
$P_{G_{3,3}}$	0.0901	0.0658
$P_{G_{3,4}}$	0.1948	0.0619
$P_{G_{4,1}}$	0.0900	0.0794
$P_{G_{4,2}}$	0.1172	0.1639
$P_{G_{4,3}}$	0.0595	0.1075
$P_{G_{4,4}}$	0.1498	0.2512
$P_{T_{1,2}}$	-0.0469	-
$P_{T_{1,3}}$	-0.0020	-
$P_{T_{1,4}}$	0.1427	-
$P_{T_{2,3}}$	-0.020	-
$P_{T_{2,4}}$	0.0499	-
$P_{T_{3,4}}$	-0.0089	-
Minimum emission (ton/hr)	3.2301	3.6923
Fuel cost ($/hour)	2178.20	2191.27

Table 5. Minimum emissions with and without inter-area aid

From the simulation results, it is evident that both fuel costs and emissions of the MAEED with inter-area aid dominate those of the separate areas case. Thus, it is desirable to connect the multiple areas for achieving lower fuel costs and emissions while satisfying the load demands of different areas. Based on the above simulation results, we can find that except for area 1, other three areas are all capable of satisfying the reserve requirements by themselves. Only area 1 needs reserve sharing from other area in order to cover the additional power for reserve satisfaction. Here, it is assumed that the reserve sharing scheme is applied unless the capacity in the area cannot fulfill the area reserve demand itself. Table 6 illustrates the reserve sharing for the minimum cost and minimum emission cases. $P_{RCG_{i,j}}$ represents the reserve contribution from generator G_{ij}. Again, the negative

values of reserve sharing $P_{RC_{jk}}$ where $k > j$, indicate that the reserve is sent from area k to area j when needed.
From the simulation results, we can appreciate that when the area spinning reserve requirements are considered, higher operational costs and higher emissions are inevitably caused for achieving higher power system reliability.

Reserve combination	Minimum cost solution (p.u.)	Minimum emission solution (p.u)
$P_{S_{1,1}}$	0.0080	0.0123
$P_{S_{1,2}}$	0.0351	0.0375
$P_{S_{1,3}}$	0.0099	0.0112
$P_{S_{1,4}}$	0.0072	0.0255
$P_{RCG_{2,1}}$	0.0005	0.0005
$P_{RCG_{2,2}}$	0.0005	0
$P_{RCG_{2,3}}$	0.0005	0
$P_{RCG_{2,4}}$	0.0005	0
$P_{RCG_{3,1}}$	0.0070	0.0012
$P_{RCG_{3,2}}$	0.0007	0
$P_{RCG_{3,3}}$	0.0080	0.0008
$P_{RCG_{3,4}}$	0.0100	0.0010
$P_{RCG_{4,1}}$	0.0005	0
$P_{RCG_{4,2}}$	0.0005	0
$P_{RCG_{4,3}}$	0.0006	0
$P_{RCG_{4,4}}$	0.0005	0
$P_{RC_{1,2}}$	-0.0020	-0.0005
$P_{RC_{1,3}}$	-0.0257	-0.0030
$P_{RC_{1,4}}$	-0.0021	0

Table 6. Reserve sharing for enabling area 1 to satisfy the reserve demand

6. Concluding Remarks

In this chapter, a new concept termed multiarea environmental/economic dispatch (MAEED) is proposed, and an enhanced multiobjective particle swarm optimization (MOPSO) algorithm is used to derive a set of Pareto-optimal solutions. The tie-line transfer limits between areas are considered to ensure the power system security. Also, the area spinning reserve requirements are incorporated in order to increase the system reliability. A comparison is made between the solutions obtained from different problem formulations. In this work, reserve sharing is only applied when there exists an area without sufficient generation capacity for reserve requirement fulfillment. In the future work, the reserve can be simultaneously scheduled with the generation. Moreover, the power flow in each area can be considered to further increase the system security. Other issues such as transmission losses, transmission costs, and buying and selling policies between areas can also be considered in MAEED problems.

7. References

Abido, M. A. (2003). Environmental/economic power dispatch using multiobjective evolutionary algorithms, *IEEE Transactions on Power Systems,* Vol. 18, No. 4, pp. 1529-1537.

Chen, C.-L. & Chen, N. (2001). Direct search method for solving economic dispatch problem considering transmission capacity constraints, *IEEE Trans. on Power Systems,* Vol. 16, No. 4, pp. 764-769.

Eiben, A. E. & Smith, J. E. (2003). *Introduction to Evolutionary Computing,* Springer-Verlag.

Jayabarathi, T.; Sadasivam, G. & Ramachandran, V. (2000). Evolutionary programming-based multi-area economic dispatch with tie line constraints, *Electric Machines and Power Systems,* Vol. 28, pp. 1165-1176.

Kennedy, J. & Eberhart, R. (1995). Particle swarm optimization, *IEEE Proceedings of the International Conference on Neural Networks,* Perth, Australia, pp. 1942-1948.

Kennedy, J. & Eberhart, R. (2001). *Swarm Intelligence,* Morgan Kauf-mann Publishers, San Francisco.

Lee, K.Y.; Yome, A.S. & Park, J.H. (1998). Adaptive Hopfield neural networks for economic load dispatch, *IEEE Transactions on Power Systems,* Vol. 13, No. 2, pp. 519-526.

Streiffert, D. (1995). Multi-area economic dispatch with tie line constraints, *IEEE Trans. on Power Systems,* Vol. 10, No. 4, pp. 1946-1951.

Talaq, J. H.; El-Hawary, F. & El-Hawary, M. E. (1994). A summary of environmental/economic dispatch algorithms, *IEEE Transactions on Power Systems,* Vol. 9, No. 3, pp. 1508-1516.

Wang, C. & Shahidepour, S. M. (1992). A decomposition approach to non-linear multi-area generation scheduling with tie line constraints using expert systems, *IEEE Trans, on Power Systems,* Vol. 7, No. 4, pp. 1409-1418.

Wang, L. F. & Singh, C. (2007). Environmental/economic power dispatch using a fuzzified multi-objective particle swarm optimization algorithm, *Electric Power Systems Research,* in press.

Yalcinoz, T. & Short, M. J. (1998). Neural neworks approach for solving economic dispatch problems with transmission capacity constraints, *IEEE Trans. Power Systems,* Vol. 13, No. 2, pp. 307-313.

Zhu, J. Z. (2003). Multiarea power systems economic power dispatch using a nonlinear optimization neural network approach, *Electric Power Components and Systems,* Vol. 31, No. 6, pp. 553-563.

23

Hybrid Ant Colony Optimization for the Channel Assignment Problem in Wireless Communication

Peng-Yeng Yin and Shan-Cheng Li
Department of Information Management, National Chi Nan University
Taiwan

1. Introduction

Wireless communication is a central technology to many applications such as wireless TV, radio broadcasting, global positioning, satellite-based cellular systems, mobile telephony, wireless LAN, to name a few. The research and development of wireless products have also bloomed the wireless communication applications to a new era. However, the available bandwidth does not grow as fast as the exploding demands from the consumer markets, so we need an algorithm to effectively and repetitively assign the available channels to multiple demanding cells such that no electromagnetic interference is induced. The aim of the *channel assignment problem* (CAP) is to minimize the span, the spectrum between the maximum and minimum used frequency, of allocated channels with an associated assignment that satisfies the bandwidth demands without incurring electromagnetic interference among them. The CAP can be polynomially reduced to the graph-coloring problem which has been known to be NP-hard. This means the derivation of the exact solution to the CAP in the general case is computationally prohibitive.

Most existing methods for tackling CAP are based on three approaches, namely, *mathematical programming*, *heuristics*, and *metaheuristics*. The mathematical programming techniques such as *integer linear programming* (Janssen & Kilakos, 1999; Mathar & Schmeink, 2002) and *branch-and-bound* (Tcha et al., 1997) are efficient in finding the exact solutions, however, they are limited to the application of small-sized problems only. Heuristics such as *ordering* technique (Sivarajan et al., 2000) and *sequential packing* technique (Sung & Wong, 1997) use a heuristic function for determining the order or packing of radio cells to allocate channels. These methods can quickly obtain a feasible solution even for a large problem but the solution quality varies a lot with the instances of the problem. Alternatively, more and more CAP researchers are attracted by the promising results on some applications using metaheuristics including genetic algorithms (Ngo & Li, 1998; Ghosh et al., 2003), simulated annealing (Aardal et al., 2003), tabu search (Hao & Perrier, 1999), and ant colony optimization (Montemanni, 2002). Their results have demonstrated some advantanges in problem scalability, easy implementation, economic computation, and high quality solutions over other approaches.

Inspired by the success of metaheuristics, in this chapter we present a hybrid ant colony optimization (HACO) algorithm embodied with several problem-dependent heuristics to take advantages of various approaches. The HACO algorithm provides an elegant framework for maintaining a good balance between *exploration* and *exploitation* trajectories in the solution space during the search, while the embedded heuristics are customized to the properties of CAP and is helpful in intensifying the promising area previously found in the search history. The performance of our algorithm is evaluated using a set of benchmark problems named *Philadelphia* that has been broadly used in early literature. Compared to existing approaches, our algorithm manifests the robustness and efficicency in solving the tested problems.

The remainder of this chapter is organized as follows. Section 2 presents the formulation of CAP considered in the chapter. Section 3 renders the details of the proposed HACO algorithm. In Section 4, the experimental results and discussions are presented. Finally, a conclusion is given in Section 5.

2. Problem Formulation

The objective of the CAP is to find an economic channel assignment with the minimum span of frequency spectrum to a number of demanding cells such that no electromagnetic interference is induced. There are three broadly considered electromagnetic compatibility (EMC) constraints as described as follows.

- Co-channel constraint The same channel cannot be assigned simultaneously to certain pairs of cells that are within a stipulated distance.
- Adjacent channel constraint The adjacent channels are not allowed to be assigned to adjacent cells simultaneously.
- Co-cell constraint The separation in channel units between any pair of channels assigned to a cell should be larger than a minimum separation threshold.

This chapter considers the CAP scenario involving the three EMC constraints. Assume that we are given n radio cells and m available channels, the three EMC constraints can be described together by a compatibility matrix $C = \{c_{ij}\}_{1 \le i,j \le n}$ which stipulates the minimum separation in channel units between any pair of channels assigned to cell i and cell j simultaneously. The demands of the n radio cells can be described by a demanding vector $D = \{d_i\}_{1 \le i \le n}$ where d_i indicates the amount of channels requested by cell i. The decision variables can be defined as $F = \{f_{ij}\}_{1 \le i \le n, 1 \le j \le d_i}$ where f_{ij} denotes the index of the jth allocated channel to cell i. The addressed CAP can be formulated as follows.

$$\text{Min} \max_{\forall i,j,k,l} \left| f_{ij} - f_{kl} + 1 \right| \tag{1}$$

subject to

$$\left| f_{ij} - f_{kl} \right| \ge c_{ik} \;\; \forall\, i, j, k, l \text{ and } (i, j) \ne (k, l). \tag{2}$$

The objective function (1) describes the goal of the optimization problem that is to minimize the span in the channels assigned to the demanding cells. The constraint (2) stipulates that the channel assignment must satisfy all of the three EMC constraints described in terms of the compatibility matrix C.

3. Hybrid Ant Colony Optimization for the CAP

In addition to the good generalization of metaheuristics, many successful applications using metaheurisitcs rely on an elaborately designed procedure for handling the problem-specific constraints. There are two different approaches for constraint handling. The *relaxation* method releases the constraints by adding a penalty to the objective value where the penalty is a monotonically increasing function of the degree of the solution infeasibility with respect to the constraints. The *hybrid* method employs a problem-specific heuristic to guide the generation of new solutions that satisfy the constraints. As the convergence rate of the relaxation method could be slow if the constraints are too complicate, we adopt the hybrid method to design our algorithm. In particular, the ordering technique (Sivarajan et al., 2000) and the sequential packing technique (Sung & Wong, 1997) that have been developed for solving the CAP are embedded into an ant colony optimization framework to create an efficient hybrid algorithm. Moreover, a local optimizer is proposed to improve the candidate solutions generated in each iteration such that the quality of the candidate solutions is guaranteed.

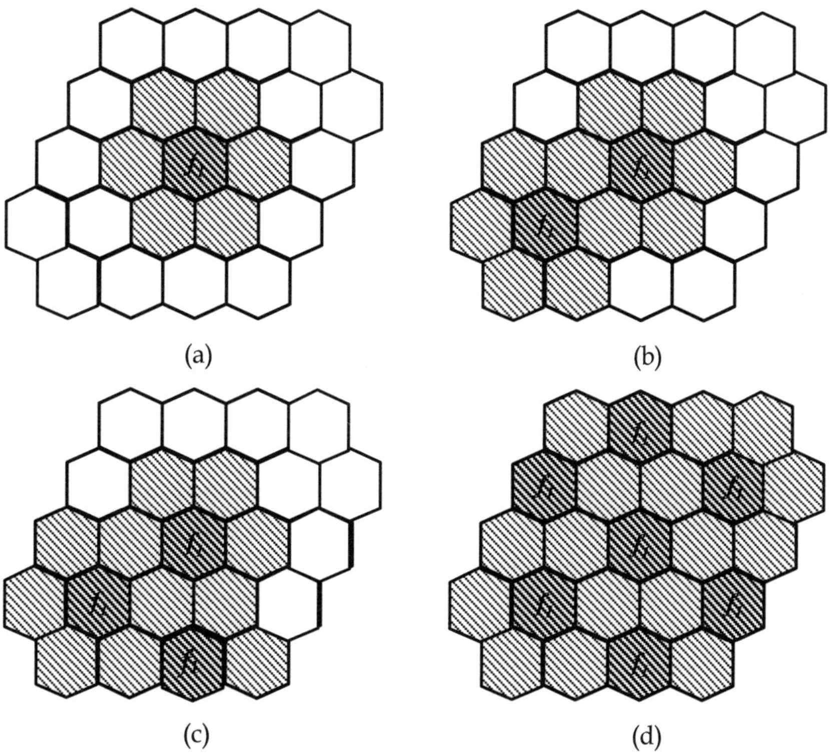

Figure 1. Illustration of the sequential packing method

3.1 Ordering and sequential packing

The ordering heuristic (Sivarajan et al., 2000) determines the order of the cells with which the channels are assigned in turn. In particular, the order of the cell is given according to the cell sequence in decreasing value of the cell degree, which is defined as $\delta_i = \sum_{j=1}^{n} d_j c_{ij} - c_{ii}$ taking into account the demands and the EMC constraints. The cell with a greater demand

and inducing more EMC interference with its surrounding cells is associated with a greater degree and will be considered for assigning channels earlier.
The sequential packing heuristic (Sung & Wong, 1997) sequentially packs the cells that are the "best" for the assignment of a particular channel considering the partial channel assignment already done. The "best" criterion is according to the heuristic that maximizes the overlap between the interfering area induced by the next cell which the channel is assigned to and that by the cells already been assigned channels. Fig. 1 gives an illustration of the sequential packing procedure. Assume that we start with packing with frequency f_1 and it is first assigned to the central cell as shown in Fig. 1(a). The interfering area induced by the electromagnetic effect is marked by light stripes. It should be noted here, although there is only one assigned channel shown in this illustration, the interfering area induced by all of the already assigned channels should be marked. Thus, the unmarked cells are interference free and are candidates for the next cell to assign the channel. The sequential packing heuristic arbitrarily selects one from those that have the maximal interfering overlap with the marked area such that the usage of the assigned channel is maximized. All the unmarked cells surrounding the marked area in Fig. 1(a) are candidates for selecting the next cell to assign the same channel except the bottom-left and upper-right cells. Thus, we can select an arbitrary one as shown in Fig. 1(b). Again, the interfering area due to the new assignment of the channel is marked with light stripes. The process is iterated until all the cells are marked and no interference free cells can be selected, as shown in Figs. 1(c) and 1(d). The sequential packing heuristic starts with the assignment of the first channel and continues with the assignment of the rest channels in turn until the demands of all cells are fulfilled.

3.2 The HACO algorithm

Dorigo developed the first framework of ant colony optimization (ACO) in his Ph.D. dissertation (Dorigo, 1992). He related his ant algorithm to the natural metaphor that ants are able to construct the shortest feasible path from their colony to the feeding source by the use of pheromone trails. An ant leaves some quantities of pheromone on the path it walks along, the next ant senses the pheromone laid on different paths and chooses one to follow with a probability that is proportional to the intensity of pheromone on the path, then leaves its own pheromone. This is an autocatalytic (positive feedback) process that is prone to select the preferable path along which more ants have previously traversed. The ACO has manifested successful applications such as the travelling salesman problem (Dorigo & Gambardella, 1997), quadratic assignment problem (Maniezzo et al., 1994), combined heat and power economic dispatch problem (Song et al., 1999), and the digital curve segmentation problem (Yin, 2003).
To circumvent the CAP problem by using the ACO, we propose a hybrid framework that embodies the ordering and sequential packing heuristics and a local optimiser into the ACO iterations. The details will be articulated in the following subsections.

3.2.1 Graph representation

ACO is a solution-construction algorithm that enables each of the artificial ants (which will be called ants hereafter for simplicity) to sequentially construct a solution by traversing a path on a problem-dependent graph. By iterating the solution construction process, the graph forms a pheromone field contributed by all the ants. Therefore, near-optimal solution can be constructed according to the pheromone attractiveness.

The conversion of a CAP problem to a corresponding graph is straightforward. Assume there are n radio cells, we can construct a graph $G = <S, E>$, where $S = (s_1, s_2, \ldots, s_n)$ is the set of all radio cells and $E = \{e_{ij} | 1 \le i, j \le n,\ i \ne j\}$ is the set of edges connecting any pairs of cells. Note that there is no loop, i.e., the edge connecting a cell to itself, in E because the co-cell constraint prohibits the same channel to be assigned twice within a cell.

3.2.2 Node transition rule

To allow the ant to traverse a path (in fact, it is to construct a solution), a node transition rule needs to be devised. The node transition rule is a probabilistic function which is defined on a biased probability distribution that is proportional to the product values of the pheromone intensity τ_{ij} and the visibility value η_{ij} associated with the edges. The value of τ_{ij} is initially set equal to a small constant and is iteratively updated using the pheromone updating rule as will be noted. While the value of η_{ij} is determined by a greedy heuristic $\eta_{ij} = A_{ij}\delta_j$ where A_{ij} is the overlap area of the electromagnetic interference if cell j is selected as the next cell to assign the channel as explained in the sequential packing heuristic, and δ_j is the degree of cell j defined in the ordering heuristic. Hence, the visibility greedily prefers to transit to the next cell which causes a greater overlap interference area and has a larger demand and is located in a more complex topology with its surrounding cells.
We now define the probability p_{ij} with which the ant transits from node i to node j as

$$p_{ij} = \frac{(\tau_{ij})^{\alpha}(\eta_{ij})^{\beta}}{\sum_{h \notin tabu}(\tau_{ih})^{\alpha}(\eta_{ih})^{\beta}}, \tag{3}$$

where *tabu* is the set of cells containing those violating the EMC constraints and those whose demands have been fulfilled (so there is no need to be considered for channel assignemnt further), parameters α and β are the weights for the relative importance of pheromone and visibility. The ties with respect to p_{ij} are broken randomly.
The solution construction process starts with the assignment of the first channel. When all cells are marked as interfering area due to this channel, the algorithm clears all the marks and continues with the assignment of the next channel. The assignment process is iterated until the demands of all the cells are fulfilled. As such, a feasible channel assignment is obtained.

3.2.3 Pheromone Updating Rule

After each ant has finished constructing a solution by traversing a path, the pheromone field (the pheromone intensity at the edges of the graph) should be updated according to the quality of the constructed solutions. As such, the experience can be accumulated in order to guide the future traverse conducted by the ants. In particular, the pheromone intensity at edge e_{ij} is updated by

$$\tau_{ij} \leftarrow (1-\rho)\tau_{ij} + \sum_{k=1}^{P} \Delta\tau_{ij}^{k}, \tag{4}$$

where $\rho \in (0,1)$ is the evaporation rate of previous pheromone trails, and P is the number of ants used in the algorithm. We define $\Delta\tau_{ij}^{k}$ as the quantity of new pheromone trails left at edge e_{ij} by the kth ant and it is computed by

$$e_{ij} = Q/Span_k, \text{ if } e_{ij} \text{ was traversed by ant } k \text{ at the current iteration;} \quad (5)$$
$$= 0, \quad \text{otherwise,}$$

where Q is a constant and $Span_k$ is the span of the channel assignment constructed by the kth ant. Therefore, the edges that constitute shorter spans will receive greater amount of pheromone and serve as building blocks for constructing elite solutions in future iterations. This is an autocatalytic process and the near-optimal solution is more likely to be constructed as the pheromone field converges.

3.2.4 Local optimizer

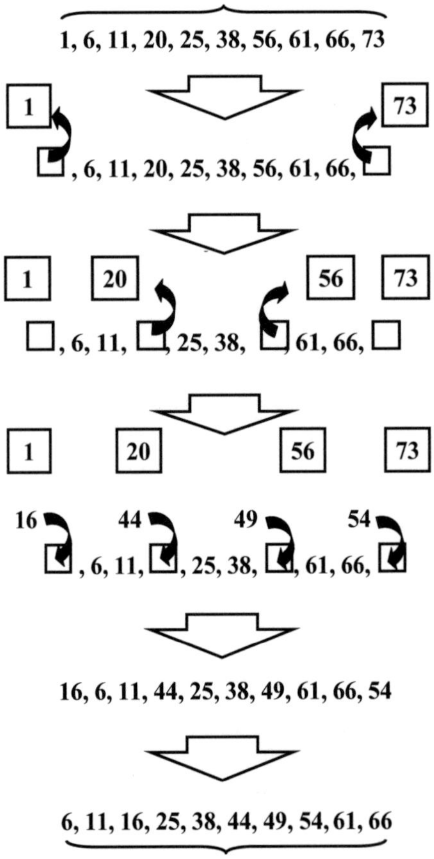

Figure 2. Illustration of the local optimizer process

In order to ensure the quality of the solution that is used for pheromone updating, a local optimizer is devised to modify the solution found by each ant to a local optimum in a definite local neighborhood. The local optimizer randomly selects certain allocated channels and replaces them with the best available channels under the EMC constraints. As the span can be shorten only when the least indexed and the greatest indexed allocated channels are replaced, we always include the two channels for replacement. An illustration of the local optimizer process is given in Fig. 2. Assume that the span of the currently allocated channels is equal to 73. The local optimizer will move the first (1) and the last indices (73) of the allocated channels to a tempary memory. However, the indices of the rest of the allocated channels are moved subject to a replacement probability. In this illustration, say, channels 20 and 56 are selected for replacement. Then, for each of the holes left by the moves, the local optimizer tries to fill it with the best among available channels under the EMC constraints. In this illustration, say, the holes are filled with channels 16, 44, 49, and 54, respectively. After re-sorting the allocated channels, we observe that the span is equal to 61 which is shorter than that of the previous channel assignment.

3.2.5 The algorithm

The pseudo code of the HACO algorithm for the CAP problem is summarized in Fig. 3.

```
1.  Initialize
    Convert the CAP problem into the corresponding graph G = <S, E>
    Set the initial pheromone to a constant value
2.  Repeat
        For each ant do
            Randomly select a starting node
            Repeat
                Move to the next node according to the node transition rule
            Until the demands of all radio cells are fulfilled
            Improve the channel assignment using the local optimizer
        End For
        For each edge do
            Update the pheromone intensity using the pheromone updating rule
        End For
    Until a maximal number of iterations are experienced
3.  Output the minimal span channel assignment found
```

Figure 3. Pseudo code of the HACO algorithm

4. Experimental Results and Discussions

In this section, we present the computational results and evaluate the performance of the HACO algorithm. The platform of the experiments is a PC with a 2.4 GHz CPU and 256 MB RAM. The algorithm is coded in C++.

4.1 Benchmark instances

The Philadelphia benchmark is one of the most widely used testing set of instances in the literature. It contains 21 hexagonal cells of a cellular phone network in Philadelphia. The hexagonal network structure is shown in Fig. 4. Following the literature, we use two nonhomogeneous demand vectors D_1 and D_2 detailed in Table 1 and four different settings of EMC constraints C_1, C_2, C_3 and C_4 in terms of specific values of the minimum separation threshold, as shown in Table 2. With the combinations of these settings, we get a set of eight problem instances shown in Table 3.

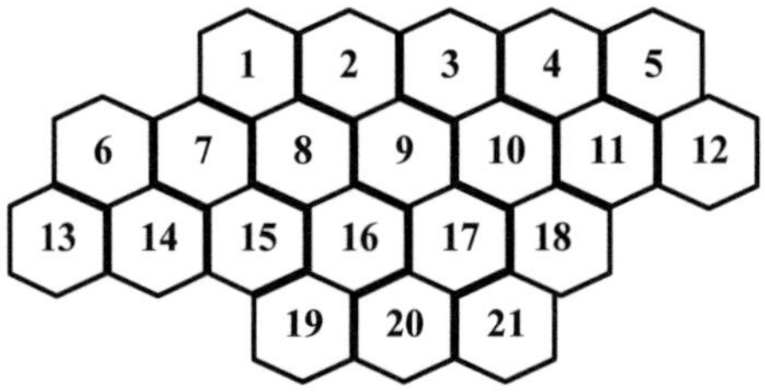

Figure 4. Hexagonal network structure of Philadelphia

Cell	1	2	3	4	5	6	7	8	9	10	11	12	13
D_1	8	25	8	8	8	15	18	52	77	28	13	15	31
D_2	5	5	5	8	12	25	30	25	30	40	40	45	20
Cell	14	15	16	17	18	19	20	21					
D_1	15	36	57	28	8	10	13	8					
D_2	30	25	15	15	30	20	20	25					

Table 1. Two nonhomogeneous demand vectors

	C_1	C_2	C_3	C_4
S_0	5	5	7	7
S_1	1	2	1	2
S_2	1	1	1	1

Table 2. Four different settings of EMC constraints

Problem	1	2	3	4	5	6	7	8
EMC constraints	C_1	C_2	C_3	C_4	C_1	C_2	C_3	C_4
Demand vectors	D_1	D_1	D_1	D_1	D_2	D_2	D_2	D_2

Table 3. Eight testing problem instances

4.2 Comparative results

As we use the benchmark instances, the comparative performances of the proposed HACO algorithm and some representitives in the literature can be evaluated. The parameters involved in the HACO algorithm are optimally tuned based on intensive experiments. They are set as the values tabulated in Table 4. For the application of the HACO algorithm in real-world cases, we set the stopping criterion of the algorithm to a fixed execution time intead of setting to different execution times according to the hardness of the problems because it is hard to know in advance the hardness of the problem in hand by observing on the compatibility matrix and the demand vectors. For example, it is hard to know which of the eight problems listed in Table 3 is the most difficult at this stage, although it turns out that problems 2 and 6 are the most difficult in this set after conducting the experiments as will be noted. In the following, the maximal execution time of the HACO algorithm for each of the benchmark problems is set to 10 min.

Parameter	Value
Number of ants (P)	20
Pheromone weight (α)	2
Visibility weight (β)	9
Evaporation rate (ρ)	0.2

Table 4. Parameter values used in the HACO algorithm

Ghosh et al. (2003) summarized the numerical results of a number of representitives in the literature tested on the same eight instances listed in Table 3. We only quoted the most recent results no earlier than 1999 from their report. Table 5 shows the comparative performances of the competing algorithms. The lower bound for each of the problems is also listed. It is seen that the methods proposed by Ghosh et al. (2003) and Beckmann & Killat (1999) are able to solve each of the benchmark problems optimally. Both of the two approaches are based on genetic algorithms, manifesting the promising direction of solving CAP using metaheuristics. The HACO can optimally solve problems 1, 3, 4, 5, 7, and 8, but obtains near-optimal solutions for problems 2 and 6, which have been known to be the most difficult problems in Philadelphia dataset. Nonetheless, the HACO spent 10 min for solving either problem 2 or problem 6, the GA-based method in Ghosh et al. (2003) spent 12-80 h for solving the two problems. The method in Beckmann & Killat (1999) starts with a lower bound and increases one channel at a time if a feasible channel assignment cannot be found by their algorithm, however, a reachable lower bound is not available in the general cases. The rest of the competing algorithms are based on heuristics, their performances are not comparable to those based on metaheuristics such as GA or ACO. While the heuristic proposed in Battiti et al. (2001) can obtain competitive results, the method they adopted involves randomisation process, which is a central feature of metaheuristics.

Problem	1	2	3	4	5	6	7	8
Lower bound	381	427	533	533	221	253	309	309
HACO	381	433	533	533	221	258	309	309
Ghosh et al., 2003	381	427	533	533	221	253	309	309
Chakraborty, 2001	381	463	533	533	221	273	309	309
Battiti et al., 2001	381	427	533	533	221	254	309	309
Tcha et al., 2000	381	433	533	533	-	260	-	309
Beckmann & Killat, 1999	381	427	533	533	221	253	309	309

Table 5. Comparative performances of the HACO algorithm and a number of representative algorithms in the literature

4.3 Convergence analysis

It is important to analyze the convergence behavior of the practiced algorithm because even a pure random search can report a solution improving with elapsed execution time, but the explored solutions never converge. The information entropy was used here to measure the amount of information observed in the pheromone field. The expected information entropy E over all radio cells is defined as

$$E = -\sum_{i=1}^{n}\sum_{\forall j} p_{ij} \log_2 p_{ij} \Big/ n \tag{6}$$

where p_{ij} is the node transition probability defined in Eq. (3). Hence, the less the value of E, the purer the information exhibited by p_{ij} related for each cell, which means the node transition rule becomes more deterministic due to a dominating probability and less information can be explored further.

Fig. 5 shows the variations of the expected information entropy as the number of HACO iterations increases. It is observed that the value of the expected information entropy decreases rapidly during the first 20 iterations (note that, to clearly demonstrate this phenomenon, the scale on the x-axis is varied in different intervals). This is because the node transition probabilities are uniformly distributed at the initialization phase of the algorithm and the transition probabilities related to the preferable paths (with shoter frequency span) are reinforced by the pheromone updating rule during the iterations, thus the expected information entropy is quickly decreased. After the 20th iteration, the decreasing rate of the expected information entropy becomes moderate, and gradually reaches stagnation as the number of iterations approaches 2000. This is due to the fact that the node transition rule becomes more deterministic and guides the ants to the paths corresponding to elite solutions. Although the information (building blocks) exchange among the elite solutions is still ungoing in order to finely improve the best solution found, the information gain is less than that obtained at the earlier iterations, because there is a large overlap at the building blocks of the elite solutions. So the solution improving ratio per unit time becomes less economic as the elapsed execution time increases. The practitioners must determine the best stopping criterion according to the allocated computational resource for their applications.

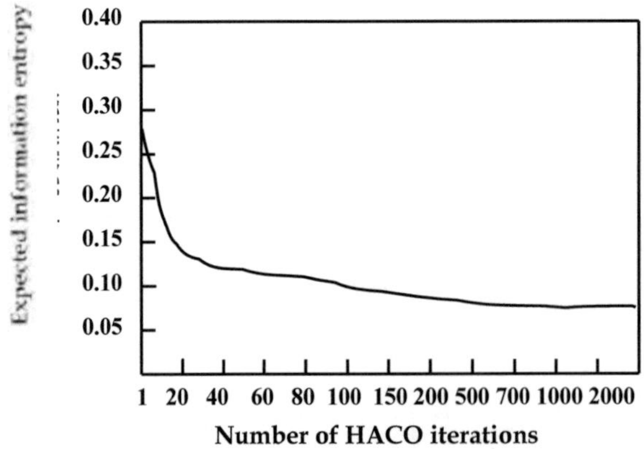

Figure 5. Variations of the expected information entropy as the number of HACO iterations increases

5. Conclusion

In this chapter, we investigate the channel assignment problem (CAP) that is critical in wireless communication applications. Researchers strive to develop algorithms that are able to effectively assign limited channels to a number of cells with nonhomogeneous demands. Inspired by the recent success of metaheuristics, a hybrid ant colony optimisation (HACO) is proposed in this chapter. The HACO embodies several problem-dependent heuristics including ordering, sequential packing, and a local optimiser into an ACO framework. The advantages of this hybrid are two-fold. First, the EMC constraints can be effectively handled by the problem-dependent heuristics instead of using a penalty function as observed in other works which may lengthen the elapsed time in order to reach convergence. Second, the embedded heuristics serve as intensification strategies conducted by the metaheuristic framework and help improve the generated solutions from different view points.
The performance of the HACO algorithm is evaluated on the Philadelphia benchmark set, such that it can be compared to that of existing approaches. It is observed from the experimental results that the HACO algorithm can solve optimally six of the eight benchmark problems and obtain near-optimal solutions for the other two problems which have been known to be the most difficult in the literature. For practical reasons, we only allow the HACO algorithm to run for a relatively short time compared to that used by other approaches. It is plausible to get a better result if more computational time is allocated.

6. References

Aardal, K. I.; Hoesel, P. M.; Koster, M. C. A.; Mannino, C. & Sassano, A. (2003). Models and Solution Techniques for Frequency Assignment Problems. A slightly revised version appeared in: *4OR: A Quarterly Journal of Operations Research*, Vol. 1, 261-317.

Battiti, R.; Bertossi, A. & Cavallaro, D. (2001). A randomized saturation degree heuristic for channel assignment in cellular radio networks. *IEEE Transactions on Vehicular Technology*, Vol. 50, pp. 364-374

Beckmann, D. & Killat, U. (1999). A new strategy for the application of genetic algorithms to the channel-assignment problem. *IEEE Transactions on Vehicular Technology*, Vol. 48, pp. 1261-1269

Chakraborty, G. (2001). An efficient heuristic algorithm for channel assignment problem in cellular radio networks. *IEEE Transactions on Vehicular Technology*, Vol. 50, pp.1528-1539

Dorigo, M. (1992). *Optimization, learning, and natural algorithms*. Ph.D. Thesis, Dip. Elettronica e Informazione, Politecnico di Milano, Italy

Dorigo, M. & Gambardella, L. (1997). Ant colony system: a cooperative learning approach to the traveling salesman problem. *IEEE Transaction on Evolutionary Computation*, Vol. 1, pp. 53-66

Ghosh, S. C.; Sinha, B. P. & Das, N. (2003). Channel Assignment Using Genetic Algorithm Based on Geometric Symmetry. *IEEE Transactions on Vehicular Technology*, Vol. 52, No. 4, pp. 860-875

Hao, J. K. & Perrier, L. (1999). Tabu search for the frequency assignment problem in cellular radio networks. Technical report LGI2P, EMA-EERIE, Parc Scientifique Georges Besse, Nimes, France.

Janssen, J. & Kilakos, K. (1999). An optimal solution to the "Philadelphia" channel assignment problem. *IEEE Transactions on Vehicular Technology*, Vol. 48, No. 3, pp. 1012-1014

Maniezzo, V.; Colorni, A. & Dorigo, M. (1994). The ant system applied to the quadratic assignment problem. Universite Libre de Bruxelles, Belgium, Technical Report IRIDIA/94-28

Mathar, R. & Schmeink, M. (2002). Optimal base station positioning and channel assignment for 3G mobile networks by integer programming. *Annals of Operations Research*, Vol. 107:1-4 , pp. 225-236

Montemanni, R.; Smith, D. H. & Allen, S. M. (2002). An ANTS Algorithm for the Minimum-Span Frequency Assignment Problem With Multiple Interference. *IEEE Transactions on Vehicular Technology*, Vol. 51, No. 5

Ngo, C. Y. & Li, V. O. K. (1998). Fixed channel assignment in cellular radio networks using a modified genetic algorithm. *IEEE Transactions on Vehicular Technology*, Vol. 47, pp. 163-172

Sivarajan, K. N.; McEliece, R. J. & Ketchum, J. W. (2000) Channel assignment in cellular radio. *Proceedings of the 39th IEEE Transactions on Vehicular Technology* to appear

Song, Y. H.; Chou, C. S. & Stonham, T. J. (1999). Combined heat and power economic dispatch by improved ant colony search algorithm. *Electric Power Systems Research*, Vol. 52, pp. 115-121

Sung, C. W. & Wong, W. S. (1997). Sequential Packing Algorithm for Channel Assignment under Cochannel and Adjacent Channel Interference Constraint. *IEEE Transactions on Vehicular Technology*, Vol. 46, pp. 676-685.

Tcha, D. W.; Chung, Y. & Choi, T. J. (1997). A new lower bound for the frequency assignment problem. *IEEE/ACM Transactions on Networking*, Vol. 5, pp. 34-39

Tcha, D. W.; Kwon, J. H.; Choi, T. J. & Oh, S. H. (2000). Perturbation-minimizing frequency assignment in a changing TDMA/FDMA cellular environment, *IEEE Transactions on Vehicular Technology*, Vol. 49, pp. 390-396

Yin, P.Y. (2003). Ant colony search algorithm for optimal polygonal approximation of plane curves. *Pattern Recognition*, Vol. 36, pp. 1783-1797

24

Case Study Based Convergence Behaviour Analysis of ACO Applied to Optimal Design of Water Distribution Systems

Aaron C. Zecchin, Holger R. Maier and Angus R. Simpson
School of Civil and Environmental Engineering,The University of Adelaide Australia

1. Introduction

Based on its analogical link with nature, ant colony optimisation (ACO) aims to determine the least cost solution to an optimisation problem via the process of stigmergy (Dorigo *et al.* 2000). That is, the colony of artificial ants repeatedly stochastically constructs solutions and utilises the information gained from these solutions to guide the construction of future solutions. This process occurs in an attempt to increase the likelihood of the colony constructing the optimal solution. Each individual ant operates essentially randomly, but through alteration of its environment, a colony learns and assimilates information as a collective.

A conceptualised characteristic of this process is that the colony's searching behaviour changes with time. That is, it undergoes a highly variable, and broad reaching, initial search as the colony learns about the solution space, followed by a subsequent intensified searching in smaller regions of the solution space that the colony has learned as being promising. As such, ACO can be visualised as an initially widely spread colony converging to a point, or region, within the solution space.

Typically algorithms, such as ACO, are assessed only based on their performance in terms of the quality of the solutions found, and the computational effort required to find them. In addition to these performance based indicators, much can be learned about the different algorithms by considering the behaviour of their searching and converging process. Algorithm developers qualitatively discuss mechanisms as being exploration encouraging or exploitation encouraging (Colorni *et al.* 1996). The question arises as to the actual manifestation of these mechanisms in an algorithm's searching behaviour in terms of measurable quantities.

Within this chapter, two simple statistics for achieving this are implemented. A statistic is formulated that describes the topological nature of the *spread* of solutions through the solution space, termed the *mean colony distance*. Combining this statistic with a measure of the quality of the solutions being found, it is shown to give significant insight into the behaviour of selected ACO algorithms as the colonies converge. This chapter presents a purely computational analysis. For a theoretical treatment of ACO, the reader is referred to other work (e.g. Gutjahr, 2002).

In this chapter, a case study based analysis of the convergence behaviour of four ACO algorithms applied to the water distribution system problem (WDSP) is presented. Water distribution systems are one of the largest and most costly infrastructure in all developed societies. As such, the problem of the optimal design of such systems has been a large area of active research within the Civil Engineering field since the late 1960s. The WDSP represents a difficult, highly constrained combinatorial optimisation problem.

The four ACO algorithms studied are: ant system (AS), the first and most basic form of ACO (Dorigo *et al.* 1996); the elitist AS (AS_{elite}), a version of AS utilising an elitism strategy (Dorigo *et al.* 1996); the elitist-rank AS (AS_{rank}), similar to AS_{elite} but with a rank based prioritisation of information about the solution space obtained by the ants (Bullnheimer *et al.* 1999); the max-min AS (MMAS), an ACO algorithm that bounds the evolution of the artificial pheromone trails (Stützle & Hoos 2000). On a macro level, these algorithms differ in their assimilation of new information with previously learned information. By considering the comparative convergence behaviour of these algorithms, insight into the practical outworking of their different formulations is gained.

The chapter is structured as follows. Firstly, in section 2 ACO is briefly presented and the pheromone updating mechanisms of the four algorithms are outlined. In section 3, the WDSP is explained and defined. Section 4 presents the application of ACO to the WDSP, where the issues of unconstrained problem transformation and problem graph structure are discussed. In section 5, a topology of the solution space is defined and the topological measure used to quantify the *spread* of the colony's solutions through the solution space is presented. In section 6, a detailed case study based analysis of the convergence behaviour of the algorithms is undertaken. Finally, the conclusions are given in section 7.

2. Ant Colony Optimisation Algorithms

This section is intended to provide a brief overview of ACO for the purpose of representing it in a multi-graph framework, so that its application to the WDSP in section 4 is easier to understand. For a detailed discussion of the traditional formulation, the reader is referred to Dorigo *et al.* (1999).

ACO is an evolutionary algorithmic optimisation process based on the analogy of a colony of foraging ants determining the shortest path between a food source and its nest (see Dorigo *et al.* (1996) for examples). The colony is able to *optimise* the excursions of its ants through the process of stigmergy (Dorigo *et al.* 2000), where stigmergy refers to the indirect form of communication between the ants that arises from their deposition of pheromone trails. These trails act as sign posts encouraging ants to follow them. Gradually, over time increasingly shorter pheromone trails will be reinforced with greater amounts of pheromone. This in turn will encourage more ants to follow them, potentially finding small improvements, leaving the pheromone on the less frequently used, and longer, paths to evaporate into non-existence.

ACO deals with a combinatorial optimisation problem organised as a graph $G(N, L)$, where N is the set of nodes and L is the set of edges linking the nodes (the structure of the graph is unique for each problem type). A candidate solution S to the problem is constructed by an ant selecting a feasible path through $G(N, L)$. The feasibility of the path is ensured by a special constraint function Θ, which lists the edges that are available for selection based on the previously constructed path of the ant. That is, given an ant has constructed a path S',

then $\Theta(S')$ describes the set of edges available for selection. An ant's tour is complete when $\Theta(S') = \emptyset$, at which point, $S' \in \mathcal{S}$, the set of all feasible tours through the graph.
A probabilistic decision policy is implemented at each sequential node in an ant's path for the selection of a new edge from the set Θ to add to their partially constructed path S'. This policy is dependent on the pheromone intensity on a particular edge (representative of the colony's learned information) and the desirability of the edge (a measure of the local effect that the selection of a particular edge will have on the value of the objective function (Dorigo *et al.* 1996)). More precisely, the probability $p_{j|S'}(t)$ that edge $j \in \Theta(S')$ will be selected in iteration t given an ant's partially constructed tour S' is

$$p_{j|S'}(t) = \frac{[\tau_j(t)]^\alpha [\eta_j]^\beta}{\sum_{l \in \Theta(S')} [\tau_l(t)]^\alpha [\eta_l]^\beta}, \tag{1}$$

where $\tau_j(t)$ is the pheromone concentration associated with edge j at iteration t, η_j is the desirability factor and, α and β are the parameters controlling the relative importance of pheromone and desirability, respectively, in the decision process. If $\alpha >> \beta$ the algorithm will make decisions based mainly on the learned information, as represented by the pheromone, and if $\beta >> \alpha$ the algorithm will act as a greedy heuristic selecting mainly the lowest cost options, disregarding the impact of these decisions on the final solution quality.
At the end of an iteration, all ants from the colony have constructed feasible paths through $\mathcal{G}(\mathcal{N}, \mathcal{L})$. The edge pheromone values τ_j, $j \in \mathcal{L}$ are updated to include the new information gained by the colony from the set of the new paths created by the colony $\Sigma(t) = \{S_1(t), \ldots, S_m(t)\}$, where $S_k(t) \in \mathcal{S}$ is the path chosen by ant k, and m is the number of ants in the colony. The pheromone is updated from one iteration to the next by the transitional relationship

$$\tau_j(t+1) = \rho\tau_j(t) + \Delta\tau_j(\Sigma(t), t) \tag{2}$$

where $\rho \in (0, 1)$ is the pheromone persistence factor that mimics the natural operation of pheromone decay, and governs the influence of previously learned information on future decisions, and $\Delta\tau_j(\Sigma(t),t)$ is the pheromone addition for edge j, which governs the influence of the newly acquired information from iteration t, on future decisions. The function $\Delta\tau_j(\Sigma(t),t)$ can be viewed as the value placed on edge j based on the information contained in $\Sigma(t)$, where value can be interpreted to mean the likelihood that edge j is contained in S^*, the optimal solution to the problem. Practically, this means that edge $j \in S$ is considered to have more value than $j' \in S'$ if $f(S) < f(S')$. The information in this set is essentially the resulting sample of relationships between the edges of the solutions in $\Sigma(t)$ and the corresponding function values of these solutions. The premise of ACO is that by repeated iteration of this process the colony of ants will collectively guide itself to find the optimal path through $\mathcal{G}(\mathcal{N}, \mathcal{L})$.
The main differentiating factor between ACO variants is the formulation of $\Delta\tau_j(\Sigma(t),t)$, as this describes the manner in which new information is assimilated with existing learned information. In the following subsections, the pheromone updating procedures of the four ACO variants studied in this chapter are described. All of these algorithms use the decision policy from (1).

2.1 Ant System (AS)

Ant System (AS) (Dorigo *et al.* 1996) is the original and simplest ACO algorithm. For AS, all of the ants within the colony add pheromone to their paths, and as such $\Delta\tau_j(t)$ is a function of all the solutions found at iteration t and is given by

$$\Delta\tau_j(t) = \sum_{k=1}^{m} \frac{Q}{f(S_k(t))} I_{S_k(t)}\{j\}, \tag{3}$$

where m is the number of ants in the colony (*i.e.* the number of solutions generated at each iteration), Q is the pheromone addition factor, $f(\cdot)$ is the objective function to be minimised and $I_A\{a\}$ is the indicator function (equal to one if $a \in A$ and zero otherwise). From (3), it is clear that better solutions (*i.e.* solutions with lower objective f values) are rewarded with greater pheromone addition.

2.2 Elitist Ant System (AS$_{elite}$)

To exploit information about the current global-best solution, Dorigo *et al.* (1996) proposed the use of an algorithm known as Elitist Ant System (AS$_{elite}$). This algorithm uses *elitist ants,* which only reinforce the path of the current global-best solution after every iteration (analogous to elitism strategies used in genetic algorithms). Thus, the pheromone addition is given by

$$\Delta\tau_j(t) = \sum_{k=1}^{m} \frac{Q}{f(S_k(t))} I_{S_k(t)}\{j\} + \sigma \frac{Q}{f(S_{gb}(t))} I_{S_{gb}(t)}\{j\} \tag{4}$$

where the first part of (4) corresponds to the pheromone addition from the colony, as defined for AS in (3), and the second part corresponds to the pheromone addition from the elitist ants, where σ is the number of elitist ants and $S_{gb,}(t)$ is the set of edges comprising the global best solution found up until iteration t (*i.e.* this is equivalent to the addition of pheromone from σ ants). The updating rule for AS$_{elite}$ allows for exploration, as each of the m solutions found by the colony receives a pheromone addition, but also encourages exploitation, as the global-best path is reinforced with the greatest amount of pheromone. As σ increases, so does the emphasis on exploitation.

2.3 Elitist-Rank Ant System (AS$_{rank}$)

Proposed by Bullnheimer *et al.* (1999), the Elitist-Rank Ant System (AS$_{rank}$) further develops the idea of elitism used in AS$_{elite}$ to involve a rank-based updating scheme. In AS$_{rank}$, σ elitist ants reinforce the current global-best path, as in AS$_{elite}$, and the ants that found the top $\sigma - 1$ solutions within the iteration add pheromone to their paths with a scaling factor related to the rank of their solution. The pheromone update formula for AS$_{rank}$ is given by

$$\Delta\tau_j(t) = \sigma \frac{Q}{f(S_{gb}(t))} I_{S_{gb}(t)}\{j\} + \sum_{k=1}^{\sigma-1} (\sigma - k) \frac{Q}{f(S_{(k)}(t))} I_{S_{(k)}(t)}\{j\}, \tag{5}$$

where the first part of (5) corresponds to the addition from the elitist ants, and the second part from the ranked ants, where $S_{(k)}(t)$ is the set of edges selected by the kth ranking ant in iteration t. The edges that are selected by the kth ranking ant receive pheromone equivalent to the addition from ($\sigma - k$) ants. The potential advantages of this formulation, compared with AS and AS$_{elite}$, are (i) only the top $\sigma - 1$ ranked ants are used to lay pheromone (and not all m ants), which allows for the retention of only good information, and (ii) greater importance is given to the higher ranking ants (*i.e.* the top ranked solution receives $\sigma - 1$ times the normal amount of pheromone and the $(\sigma - 1)^{th}$ ranked solution receives only the normal pheromone amount), so that better edges receive more pheromone.

2.4 Max-Min Ant System (MMAS)

To overcome the problem of premature convergence whilst still allowing for exploitation, Stützle and Hoos (2000) developed the Max-Min Ant System (MMAS). The basis of MMAS is the provision of dynamically evolving bounds on the pheromone trail intensities such that the pheromone intensity on all paths is always within a specified lower bound $\tau_{min}(t)$ of a theoretically asymptotic upper limit $\tau_{max}(t)$, that is $\tau_{min}(t) \le \tau_j(t) \le \tau_{max}(t)$ for all edges j. As a result of stopping the pheromone trails from decaying to zero, all paths always have a non-trivial probability of being selected, and thus wider exploration of the search space is encouraged. The pheromone bounds at iteration t are given by (Stützle & Hoos 2000)

$$\tau_{\min}(t) = \frac{\tau_{\max}(t)\left(1 - \sqrt[n]{P_{best}}\right)}{\left(NO_{avg} - 1\right)\sqrt[n]{P_{best}}}, \quad \tau_{\max}(t) = \frac{1}{1-\rho}\frac{Q}{f\left(S^{gb}(t)\right)} \tag{6}$$

where P_{best} is the (user selected) probability that the current global-best path, $S_{gb}(t)$, will be selected, given that all non-global best edges have a pheromone level of $\tau_{min}(t)$ and all global-best edges have a pheromone level of $\tau_{max}(t)$, and NO_{avg} is the average number of edges at each decision point. It should be noted that lower values of P_{best} indicate tighter bounds.
As the bounds serve to encourage exploration, MMAS adds pheromone only to the iteration-best ant's path $S_{(1)}(t)$ at the end of an iteration in order to ensure the exploitation of good solutions. To further exploit good information, the global-best solution $S_{gb}(t)$ is updated every T_{gb} iterations. The MMAS pheromone update is given by

$$\Delta\tau_j(t) = \frac{Q}{f\left(S_{(1)}(t)\right)} I_{S_{(1)}(t)}\{j\} + \frac{Q}{f\left(S_{gb}(t)\right)} I_{S_{gb}(t)}\{j\} \cdot I_{\mathrm{N}}\left\{t/T_{gb}\right\}, \tag{7}$$

where the first part of (7) corresponds to the addition from the iteration best ant, and the second part from the global best ant, where N is the set of natural numbers.
MMAS also utilises another mechanism known as pheromone trail smoothing (PTS). This reduces the relative difference between the pheromone intensities, and further encourages exploration. The PTS operation is given by

$$\tau_j(t) \leftarrow \tau_j(t) + \delta\left(\tau_{\max}(t) - \tau_j(t)\right), \tag{8}$$

where $0 \le \delta \le 1$ is the PTS coefficient. If $\delta = 0$, PTS has no effect, whereas if $\delta = 1$, all pheromone paths are scaled up to $\tau_{max}(t)$. The pheromone updating process of MMAS can be summarised as the three step process of: (i) decay and addition by (2) and (7), (ii) bounding by (6), and (iii) smoothing by (8).

3. The Water Distribution System Optimisation Problem

Water distribution systems (WDSs) consist of the system of pipes, pumps, valves *etc.* that delivers water from sources to consumers. From an optimisation perspective, the water distribution system problem (WDSP) is defined as the selection of the lowest cost combination of appropriate component sizes (*e.g.* pipes) and settings (*e.g.* valve settings) such that the criteria of water demands and other design constraints (*e.g.* minimum pressures) are satisfied. A simple example of this is as follows. Consider two networks, the first comprising pipes with small diameters and the second comprising pipes with large diameters. The first network has a low cost, but as the pipe diameters are small, the frictional pressure loss through the network will be greater, which is likely to result in insufficient pressure at the demand points (nodes). The second system is likely to provide more than adequate pressure, as the pipe diameters are large, but is also more expensive. The optimal design is the least cost combination of pipe sizes that are able to provide adequate pressure at each of the nodes. Within the WDSP, the decision variables are associated with the pipes within the system where, more specifically, the design options are the following, (i) a diameter for a new pipe, (ii) the cleaning of an existing pipe to reduce the hydraulic resistance, and (iii) no action.

As outlined in Zecchin *et al.* (2005), for the WDSP, a design involves the selection of a series of design options for all or some of the pipes within the network. A WDS design $\Omega = \{\Omega_1, ..., \Omega_n\}$ is defined as a set of n decisions where n is the number of pipes to be sized and/or rehabilitated, and Ω_i is the selected option for pipe i, and is defined as $\Omega_i \in \Lambda_i = \{\omega_{i,1}, \ldots, \omega_{i,NO_i}\}$, where Λ_i is the set of all NO_i options available for pipe i. For each option there is an associated cost, $c(\Omega_i)$, of implementing that option, and one of three actions as listed above.

The constraints on a solution are categorized as design constraints and hydraulic constraints. A design constraint is an inequality constraint that defines the minimum acceptable performance of a design, whereas hydraulic constraints are equality constraints that describe the distribution of the flow of water through the WDS (based on the fundamental equations for fluid flow within a closed conduit and the governing equations for fluid flow within a looped network). The design constraint for the WDSP specifies the minimum allowable pressure at each node, and is given as

$$H_{i,j} \geq \underline{H}_{i,j} \quad \forall i = 1,.., N_{node} \quad \forall j = 1,.., N_{pattern}\,, \tag{9}$$

where $H_{i,j}$ is the actual head at node i for demand pattern j, $\underline{H}_{i,j}$ is the minimum allowable head at node i for demand pattern j, N_{node} is the total number of nodes and $N_{pattern}$ is the number of demand patterns.

The hydraulic equations for fluid flow within a WDS are the conservation of mass and the pipe headloss equations. As the fluid is assumed to be incompressible, the conservation of mass equations dictate that the flow rate into a node is equal to the flow rate out of a node. This can be expressed as

$$\underline{Q}_{i,j} + \sum_{k \in \Theta_{u,i}} Q_{k,j} - \sum_{k \in \Theta_{d,i}} Q_{k,j} = 0 \qquad \forall i = 1,.., N_{node} \quad \forall j = 1,.., N_{pattern}\,, \tag{10}$$

where $Q_{i,j}$ is the demand for node i and demand pattern j (by definition, a positive demand is one that draws water from the node), $Q_{k,j}$ is the flow in pipe k for demand pattern j, $\Theta_{u,j}$ is the set of all pipes for which node i is the upstream node, and $\Theta_{d,j}$ is the set of pipes for which node i is the downstream node (note that the sign convention is that positive pipe flow occurs from upstream to downstream).
The headloss equation is written as (Streeter & Wylie 1997)

$$H_{i_u,j} - H_{i_d,j} = r_{\Omega_i} \left|Q_{i,j}\right| Q_{i,j}^{\,a-1} \qquad i = 1, ..., N_{pipe}, \; j = 1,.., N_{pattern}, \tag{11}$$

where r_{Ω_i} is a hydraulic resistance term associated with decision Ω_i, a is the flow exponent, and N_{pipe} is the number of pipes, including new pipes. The headloss equation used within most WDSPs is the Hazen-Williams equation, for which r_{Ω_i} is expressed as

$$r_{\Omega_i} = A C_{\Omega_i}^{-a} D_{\Omega_i}^{-b} L_i \qquad \forall i = 1,.., N_{pipe} \quad \forall j = 1,.., N_{pattern}, \tag{12}$$

where L_i is the length of pipe i, D_{Ω_i} is the diameter of pipe i for design Ω, C_{Ω_i} is the Hazen-Williams coefficient for pipe i for design Ω, A is a constant that is dependent on the units used, and a and b are regression coefficients. The adopted values of A, a, and b are those used in the hydraulic solver software EPANET2 (Rossman 2000).
The objective is the minimization of the material and installation costs, and so the WDSP can be expressed as

$$\min \; C(\Omega) = \sum_{i=1}^{n} c(\Omega_i), \text{ Subject to (9) - (11)} \tag{13}$$

where $C(\Omega)$ is the cost of design Ω and $c(\Omega_i)$ is the cost of decision Ω_i. As is seen from (13), despite the simplicity of the objective function, the complexity of the optimisation problem arises from the nonlinear nature of the constraints dependency on the design options Ω_i.

4. Application of Ant Colony Optimisation to Water Distribution System Optimisation

4.1 Transformation of constrained problem

The WDSP is a constrained optimisation problem. ACO is unable to deal directly with constrained optimisation problems as, within its solution generation, it cannot adhere to constraints that separate feasible regions of a search space from infeasible regions (here feasibility refers to constraints (9)-(11) and not the Θ function). The standard technique to convert constrained problems to unconstrained problems is to use a penalty function (Coello Coello 2002). ACO algorithms direct their search solely based on information provided by the objective function. To guide the search away from the infeasible region and towards the feasible region, a penalty function increases the cost of infeasible solutions such that they are considered to be poor quality solutions. The unconstrained optimisation problem for the WDSP takes the form of minimising the sum of the real cost plus the penalty cost, that is

$$\min \quad NC(\Omega) = C(\Omega) + PC(\Omega) \tag{14}$$

where $NC(\Omega)$ is the network cost for design Ω, $C(\Omega)$ is the material and installation cost given by (13) and $PC(\Omega)$ is the penalty cost incurred by Ω. When evaluating a potential design, the set of heads $\{H_{i,j} : i = 1, \ldots, N_{node}, j = 1, \ldots, N_{pattern}\}$ is calculated by a hydraulic solver. Therefore (10)-(11) are automatically satisfied, and hence, only (9) is required to be considered in the penalty cost. Within this study, $PC(\Omega)$ was taken to be proportional to the maximum nodal pressure deficit induced by Ω as in Maier *et al.* (2003). That is

$$PC(\Omega) = \begin{cases} 0 & \text{if } H_{i,j} \geq \underline{H}_{i,j}, i = 1, \ldots, N_{node}, j = 1, \ldots, N_{pattern} \\ \left(\max_{(i,j)\in[1,N_{node}]\times[1,N_{pattern}]} \left\{ \underline{H}_{i,j} - H_{i,j} \right\} \right) \cdot PEN & \text{otherwise} \end{cases} \quad (15)$$

where PEN is the penalty factor (user defined) with units of dollars per meter of pressure violation.

4.2 Modification of ACO elements

As in used in previous studies (Maier *et al.* 2003; Zecchin *et. al.* 2005; Zecchin *et. al.* 2006; Zecchin *et. al.* 2007), but formalised here, the graph $\mathcal{G}(\mathcal{N}, \mathcal{L})$ of the WDSP can be represented as a multi-graph, with the set of nodes $\mathcal{N} = \{1, 2, \ldots, n + 1\}$. Each node $i \leq n$ is connected to the next via a set of directed edges $\theta_i = \{(i, i{+}1)_j : j = 1, 2, \ldots, NO_i\}$, where $(i, i{+}1)_j$ is the jth edge connecting node i to node $i + 1$, NO_i is the number of edges connecting node i to node $i + 1$ and the set of all edges is $\mathcal{L} = \{s : s \in \theta_1 \cup \ldots \cup \theta_n\}$. The edge set θ_i is associated with the set of design options Λ_i, and the edge $(i, i{+}1)_j$ is associated with option $\omega_{i,j}$. A solution S, associated with design Ω, is a feasible tour through the graph and is an element of the solution space $\mathcal{S} = \{S : S = \{s_1, \ldots, s_n\}, s_i \in \theta_i, i = 1, \ldots, n\}$, where the constraint function Θ is given by $\Theta(\{s_1, \ldots, s_i\}) = \theta_i$ for $i \leq n$.

As the objective is to minimise cost, lower cost options are more desirable. Therefore the desirability of an option is taken as the inverse of the cost of implementing that option (Maier *et al.* 2003). In other words

$$\eta_{(i,i+1)_j} = 1/c(\omega_{i,j}) \cdot \quad (16)$$

As lower cost diameter options are more desirable, a bias in the probability towards the selection of lower cost diameters results. For options with zero cost (*i.e.* the null option), a virtual-zero-cost was selected.

4.3 Parameter Settings

One of the limitations of ACO is that an extensive calibration phase is required to determine appropriate parameter settings. From an extensive analysis of ACO applied to the WDSP, Zecchin *et al.* (2005) determined a series of parameter guidelines relating the five fundamental ACO parameters (α, β, ρ, Q, τ_0, and m) to WDSP characteristics (such as the number of decision points n, the average number of options per decision NO_{avg}, and the cost of key design configurations such as $\Omega^{\max}$, the maximum cost design, and Ω^*, the optimum, or near optimum, design). These are summarised in Table 1.

Contrary to other problem types (Dorigo & Gambardella 1997), Zecchin *et al.* (2005) found that, for the WDSP, better performance was achieved when the ants gave greater emphasis to the learned pheromone values τ as opposed to the visibility values η, as manifested through $\alpha > \beta$. Better performance was achieved when the pheromone persistence factor was relatively high, facilitating slow convergence and long memory times for learned information. Zecchin *et al.* (2005) showed that the ratio of Q to τ_0 is important (not the actual values of each) and empirical guidelines were determined accordingly. The best number of ants m was also found to be dependent on the number of options per decision, not just the number of decisions, as for other problem types (Dorigo *et al.* 1996).

Parameter	Heuristic
α	1.0
β	0.5
ρ	0.98
Q	$C(\Omega^{max})$
τ_0	$Q\sqrt{nNO_{avg}}/NC(\Omega^*)$
M	$n\sqrt{NO_{avg}}$

Table 1. Parameter guidelines for ACO parameters from Zecchin *et al.* (2005)

In addition to the guidelines derived for the ACO parameters, the following semi-deterministic expression for *PEN* was derived in Zecchin *et al.* (2005)

$$PEN = \left|C(\Omega^{\max}) - C(\Omega^{\min})\right| / \Delta H \tag{17}$$

where Ω^{min} is the minimum cost network design, and ΔH is a user selected pressure deficit, based on the maximum acceptable pressure deficit for a feasible solution as defined by (9). The value of *PEN* ensures that all networks with a pressure violation greater than or equal to ΔH (an extremely small value) are made more expensive than the maximum feasible network cost $C(\Omega^{min})$.

5. Analysis of Algorithm Convergence Behaviour

The standard approach to the analysis of optimisation algorithms is to assess their performance on a particular problem from statistics based on the lowest cost achieved by the algorithm (termed *best-cost*) and the computational time required for the algorithm to find the associated solution (termed *search-time*). A richer understanding of the performance of an algorithm can be achieved by considering statistics from the solutions generated by the algorithms during their run-time. A typical approach used by many authors (Simpson *et al.*, 1994; Cunha & Ribeiro, 2004; Afshar & Marino, 2007) is to track the minimum cost generated in each iteration as a means of assessing the algorithm's convergence behaviour. This statistic is important, as it indicates the effectiveness of the search, but acts only as a surrogate measure of the actual convergence behaviour of the algorithm.

This work aims to extend this qualitative performance assessment to include a topologically based statistic to describe an algorithm's convergence behaviour. From the perspective of ACO, convergence is defined as the point in time at which all ants select the same path through the problem graph (*i.e.* the colony's population of solutions is fixed at a certain point in the solution space $\mathfrak{S}$) from that point onward. Thus, convergence behaviour is the nature of the colony's solution generation up until the point of convergence. Topologically, convergence means that the distance between all solutions generated by the colony is zero. Conversely, a non-converged search will have some *spread* of the solutions throughout the solution space. It is the quantification and tracking of this *spread* that is of interest in describing an algorithm's convergence behaviour.

The motive behind convergence analysis is to gain a greater understanding of how the different explorative and exploitative mechanisms in the ACO algorithms considered actually impact the algorithm's search. Below, the topology of the solution space is first defined, and then the adopted convergence metric, the *mean colony distance*, is presented.

It is important to note that the use of metrics is widely used in evolutionary algorithm based multi-objective optimisation (Deb 2001). However, this is fundamentally different to what is considered here. In multi-objective optimisation, the distribution of solutions throughout the multi-dimensional objective space is of primary interest, and thus the metrics operate in this space. Conversely, this chapter is concerned with the distribution of solutions within the solution space, and, as such, the mean colony distance is defined on this space.

5.1 Topology of the Solution Space

Fundamental to any topologically based statistic is the notion of distance between points (solutions) in the solution space. A measure of distance for all elements within the set $\mathfrak{S}$ is equivalent to defining a metric $d : \mathfrak{S} \times \mathfrak{S} \rightarrow \mathbb{R}_+$ associated with $\mathfrak{S}$ that defines the distance between two elements S, $S' \in \mathfrak{S}$ (Cohen 2003). For sets whose elements have no specific numerical relation, the Hamming distance is a natural metric. This has been used by Bose *et al.* (1994) and Stützle & Hoos (2000) for the travelling salesperson problem. A generalisation that applies to sets whose elements are equal length lists of objects is

$$d(S,S') = \sum_{i=1}^{n} d_i(s_i, s_i'), \tag{18}$$

where $S=\{s_1, \ldots, s_n\}$, $S'=\{s_1', \ldots, s_n'\}$, $s_i, s_i' \in \theta_i$ and $d_i : \theta_i \times \theta_i \rightarrow \mathbb{R}_+$ is itself a metric for the set of all possible i^{th} elements in the list. For the Hamming distance, $d_i(\cdot,\cdot)$ is either zero or one, depending whether s_i and s_i' are equal or not. However, if the elements in the set have some other attribute that can be exploited, such as a meaningful ordering based on some property, then the metric can be defined so as to include this information.

Considering (12), it is seen that the selection of an option Ω_i is essentially equivalent to selecting a resistance parameter r_{Ω_i}. Therefore, it is meaningful to say that an option is closer to one option than another based purely on the relative differences between their associated resistance parameter values. The list of options Λ_i for pipe i can therefore be meaningfully ordered by the magnitude of their associated resistance parameter. That is, consider the following ordering of Λ_i, based on the resistance parameter $\underline{\Lambda}_i = \{\underline{\omega}_{i,1}, \ldots, \underline{\omega}_{i,NO_i}\}$, where $r_{\underline{\omega}_{i,1}} \leq \ldots \leq r_{\underline{\omega}_{i,NO_i}}$, and the distance d_i between any two of these options $\underline{\omega}_{i,j}$ and $\underline{\omega}_{i,k}$, is given by

$$d_i(\underline{\omega}_{i,j}, \underline{\omega}_{i,k}) = |j-k| \quad \text{where } \underline{\omega}_{i,j}, \underline{\omega}_{i,k} \in \Lambda_i \,. \tag{19}$$

In this context, the distance between two options is the number of positions in the ordered list $\underline{\Lambda}_i$ that separates the two options.

5.2 Mean colony distance

By ascribing a topology to the search space, the colony of solutions generated within an iteration can be considered to be spread, in some manner, over the topology. This spread of solutions gives an indication of how widely, or tightly, an algorithm is searching. To use the terminology of Colorni *et al.* (1996), whether the algorithm is *exploring* broadly through the search space or *exploiting* smaller regions of the search space. In order to quantify this spread, the mean of the distances between each of the ants' solutions has been used in this chapter, which is henceforth referred to as the mean colony distance d_Σ. Mathematically this is given as the summation of the distances of each unique pair of solutions divided by the total number of pairs, and is expressed as the map $d_\Sigma : \mathcal{S}^m \rightarrow \mathrm{R}_+$ where

$$d_\Sigma(t) = \frac{2}{m(m-1)} \sum_{k=1}^{m-1} \sum_{l=k+1}^{m} d(S_k(t), S_l(t)) \text{ ,} \tag{20}$$

where $m(m-1)/2$ is the number of unique pairs that exist in a colony of m ants. The usefulness of d_Σ as a behavioural analysis measure is fully realised when considering its variation with time. For example: periods of high exploration when solutions are spread broadly throughout the search space correspond to large values of d_Σ; periods during which the algorithm converges correspond to a series of decreasing d_Σ values; the point at which the algorithm converges is given by $d_\Sigma = 0$, as this indicates that all solutions in $\Sigma(t)$ are equal. As such, d_Σ provides a direct measure of an algorithm's convergence behaviour.

6. Case Studies

Experiments were performed on four different case studies, the Two Reservoir Problem (TRP), the New York Tunnels Problem (NYTP), the Hanoi Problem (HP) and the Doubled New York Tunnels Problem (2-NYTP). The ACO algorithms were coded in FORTRAN 90 with EPANET2 (Rossman 2000) as the hydraulic solver. Parameter settings from Zecchin *et al.* (2005), summarised in Table 1, were used for parameters α, β, ρ, τ_0, m, and Q for all algorithms with the adjustment that τ_0 was scaled by σ for AS_{elite} and AS_{rank} (in accordance with the logic of the derivation of Q in Zecchin *et al.* (2005)) and for MMAS, τ_0 was set to an arbitrarily high number, as proposed by Stützle & Hoos (2000). For AS_{elite} and AS_{rank}, σ required calibration for each case study. For MMAS, f_{global} was set to 10, as in Stützle & Hoos (2000) and P_{best} and δ were calibrated for each case study. The best-cost and search-time statistics for AS, AS_{elite}, and AS_{rank} and MMAS are as presented in Zecchin *et al.* (2007).

6.1 Case Study 1: Two-Reservoirs Problem

6.1.1 Preliminaries

The TRP was initially studied by Gessler (1985), and Simpson *et al.* (1994) introduced the metric version. The TRP is a 14-pipe network with two reservoirs (Figure 1). The TRP involves three demand cases: a peak hour demand case and two fire loading demand cases. There are nine existing pipes, of which three are considered for rehabilitation, duplication with one of eight pipe sizes, or to be left alone. There are five new pipes that must be sized with one of eight diameters. The reader is referred to Simpson *et al.* (1994) for case study details. The problem, consists of 32,768,000 possible combinations.

6.1.2 Results

Based on the heuristics given in Table 1, $\{\tau_0, m\}$ = {27, 25} and preliminary testing showed that a maximum number of iterations of I_{max} = 400 was sufficient for the algorithms to not significantly improve on their solution quality after this point. For each algorithm, a single run for the TRP consisted of 10,000 function evaluations. The range of parameters tested was: $\sigma \in [2, 20]$ for AS_{elite}; $\sigma \in [2, 20]$ for AS_{rank}; $\{P_{best}, \delta\} \in [1 \times 10^{-5}, 0.99] \times [0, 0.99]$ for MMAS. AS_{elite} achieved a mean performance within 1% of the known optimum for most of the tested values of σ, with better performances observed using $3 \leq \sigma \leq 5$. Similarly, AS_{rank} achieved a mean performance within 1% of the known optimum for all tested values of $\sigma > 2$ with lower mean best-cost values occurring for $10 \leq \sigma \leq 14$. AS_{rank} tended to be less sensitive to variations in σ than AS_{elite}, as it was able to find the optimum in each run for a broader range of values for this parameter. MMAS achieved a mean performance within 1% of the optimum for values of $P_{best} \geq 0.001$ and $\delta \leq 0.001$, with the solution quality deteriorating for parameter values outside these ranges. The optimal parameter values were as follows: for AS_{elite}, $\sigma = 4$; for AS_{rank}, $\sigma = 10$; for MMAS, $\{P_{best}, \delta\} = \{0.5, 10^{-6}\}$.

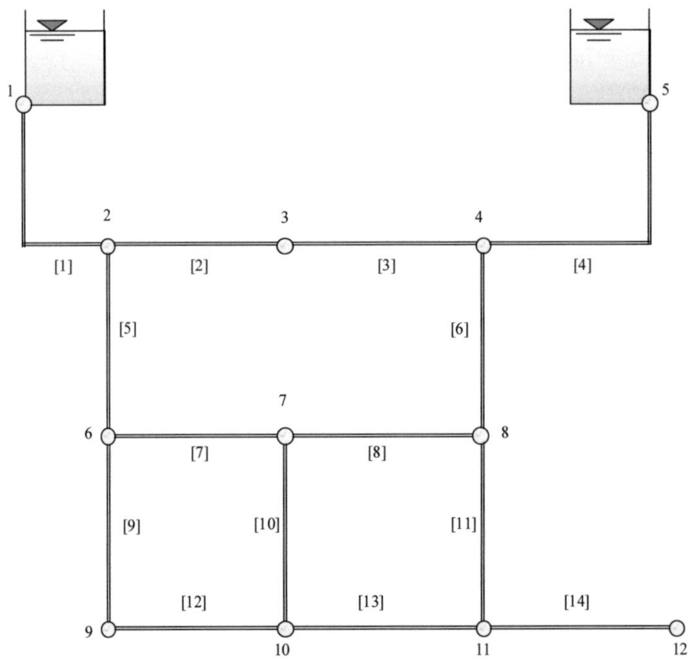

Figure 1. Network layout for the Two-Reservoir Problem

Table 2 gives a comparison of the results obtained using the ACO algorithms considered and those obtained from a selection of other best performing algorithms that have been applied to the discrete version of the TRP previously. A detailed statistical analysis of these algorithms was given in Zecchin *et al.* (2007), but it is clear that all algorithms performed extremely well (finding the optimum for all 20 runs) and were, comparatively, computationally efficient.

Plots of the iteration best-costs $f_{min}(t)$ and the mean colony distance $d_{\Sigma}(t)$, averaged over 20 runs, are given in Figure 2 (a) and (b). In addition to this, other run-time properties (to be discussed) are given in Figure 2 (c). With regard to $f_{min}(t)$, three distinct phases are observed. The first part of the search, phase-I, is a relatively short phase in which all algorithms find relatively poor quality solutions, which is followed by the second phase, phase-II, in which a dramatic increase in solution quality (reduction in the minimum cost) takes place, which leads into the third phase, phase-III, in which the rate of increase of the solution quality plateaus and the algorithms seem to not find any better solutions (or in some cases, the optimum is found repeatedly).

Algorithm	Best-cost ($M) *(% deviation from optimum)*						Mean search-time (evaluation no.)
	Minimum		Mean		Maximum		
AS	1.750	*(0.00)*	1.750	*(0.00)*	1.750	*(0.00)*	2,084
AS_{elite}	1.750	*(0.00)*	1.750	*(0.00)*	1.750	*(0.00)*	1,842
AS_{rank}	1.750	*(0.00)*	1.750	*(0.00)*	1.750	*(0.00)*	1,523
MMAS	1.750	*(0.00)*	1.750	*(0.00)*	1.750	*(0.00)*	2,993
PE[a]	1.834	*(4.80)*	-		-		900
GA_{prop}[b]	1.750	*(0.00)*	1.759	*(0.51)*	1.812	*(3.54)*	23,625
GA_{tout}[c]	1.750	*(0.00)*	1.750	*(0.00)*	1.750	*(0.00)*	8,700
SA[d]	1.750	*(0.00)*	NA		NA		NA
ACOA[e]	1.750	*(0.00)*	1.769	*(1.09)*	1.813	*(3.60)*	12,455
TS[f]	1.728[i]	-	NA		NA		~10,000
$ACOA_{i\text{-}best}$[g]	1.750	*(0.00)*	1.750	*(0.00)*	1.750	*(0.00)*	8,509
ACS[h]	1.750	*(0.00)*	1.770	*(1.13)*	1.904	*(8.81)*	5,014

[a] Partial enumeration (Gessler 1985). [b] GA based on a proportionate selection rule (Simpson *et al.* 1994). [c] Tournament selection GA (Simpson & Goldberg 1994). [d] Simulated Annealing (Sousa & Cunha 1999). [e] An AS variant that subtracts pheromone (Maier *et al.* 2003). [f] Tabu Search (Cunha & Ribeiro 2004). [g] Iteration-best updating version of ACOA (Maier *et al.* 2003). [h] Ant Colony System (Zecchin *et. al* 2007). [i] Not feasible by complete enumeration results (Simpson *et al.* 1994).

Table 2. Comparison of performance of AS, AS_{elite}, AS_{rank}, MMAS, and other algorithms from the literature applied to the Two-Reservoir Problem. Results for AS, AS_{elite}, AS_{rank}, and MMAS are based on 20 runs. NA means that the information is not available

These three phases can also be seen clearly when considering the behaviour of d_{Σ} in Figure 2 (b). To make the distinction between the phases clearer, the bar chart in Figure 2 (c) indicates when the algorithms are in each of the phases (dark grey for phase-I, light grey for phase-II and the remaining white space for phase-III). For d_{Σ}, phase-I corresponds to a brief period of extremely broad searching where almost no convergence behaviour is displayed, followed by phase-II, in which relatively rapid convergence is observed, and phase-III, in which the rate of convergence either plateaus or decreases gradually to $d_{\Sigma}(t) = 0$, the point of convergence.

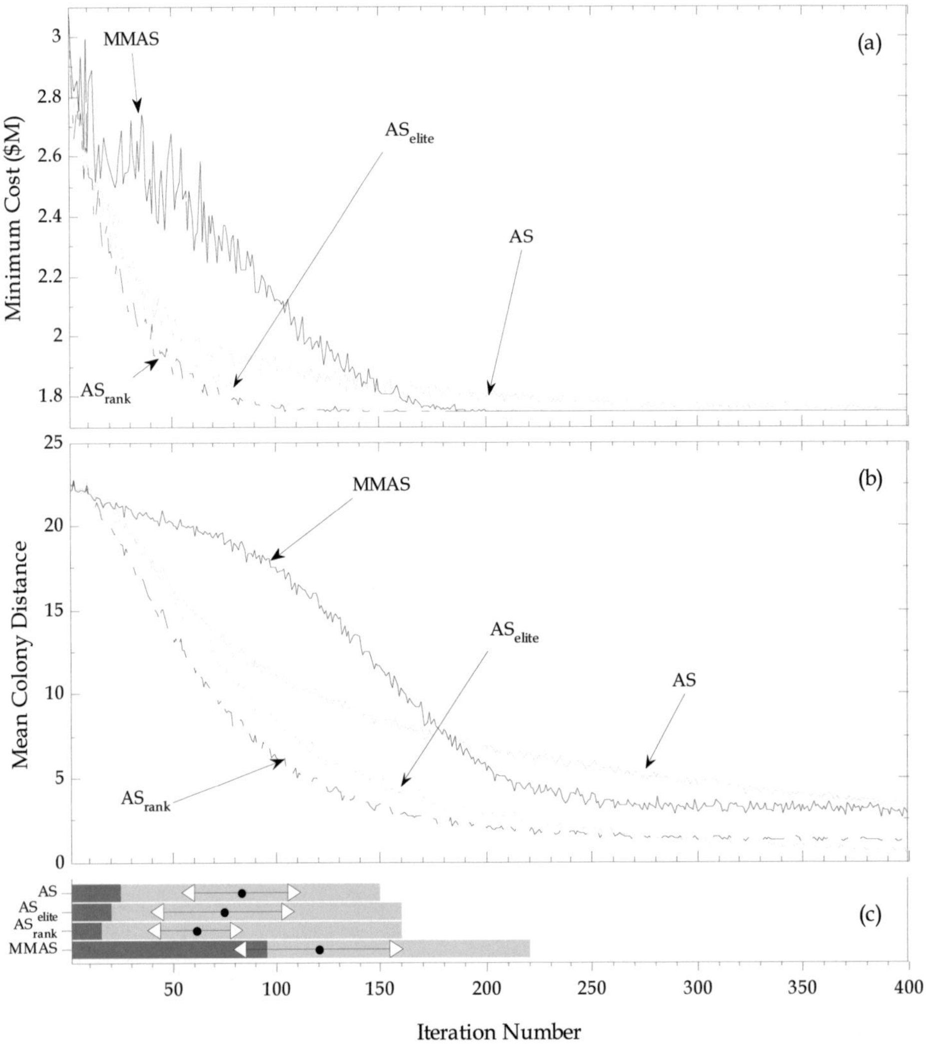

Figure 2. Plots of (a) the minimum cost ($M) found in each iteration $f_{min}(t)$, (b) the mean colony distance $d_{\Sigma}(t)$, and (c) run-time statistics for AS, AS_{elite}, AS_{rank}, and MMAS applied to the Two Reservoir Problem. Plots (a) and (b) are averaged from 20 runs. Plot (c) depicts the three convergence phases: phase-I (dark grey); phase-II (light grey); phase-III (remaining white space). The line graphs overlaying the bar charts in (c) indicate the search-time statistics (based on 20 runs) with the dot indicating the mean search-time, and the left and right arrows indicating the mean minus and plus a standard deviation, respectively

The nature and time spent in each of these three phases is different for each algorithm. As seen in Figure 2, AS, AS_{elite}, and AS_{rank} have a relatively short broad searching phase-I, followed by a rapid convergence in phase-II. In contrast, MMAS has a relatively long broad searching phase-I, followed eventually by rapid phase-II convergence. The relatively long phase-I for MMAS may be attributed to the exploration encouraging mechanisms of pheromone bounding and pheromone smoothing. AS_{elite} and AS_{rank} have faster phase-II convergence than AS, which can possibly be attributed to the elitist exploitation mechanisms in these algorithms driving the search to converge faster. In phase-III, AS and AS_{elite} experience a gradually reducing, but steady, convergence, albeit AS_{elite} in a much tighter region after phase-II. In contrast to this, AS_{rank} and MMAS plateau in their convergence, as seen by $d_\Sigma(t)$ tending to a constant value in phase-III.

This difference in phase-III behaviour can be explained by a consideration of the pheromone adjustment operations of each algorithm. For ACO, convergence cannot only be defined in the context of the distribution of solutions throughout the solution space (*i.e.* the point at which $d_\Sigma(t) = 0$), but also in a pheromone value context. That is, an ACO algorithm has converged when the pheromone value on all paths, except for a single path $S \in \mathcal{S}$, is effectively zero (*i.e.* zero for all computational purposes). At such a point, ants will only select edges from path S. For both AS and AS_{elite}, as pheromone values of paths become more dominant, the natural positive feedback process of the colony's path selection will dictate that the pheromone value on all edges, other than that of the increasingly dominant path, will decay to zero. Thus, these algorithms will converge to the point where $d_\Sigma(t) = 0$. However, both AS_{rank} and MMAS contain mechanisms that moderate this positive feedback process. Firstly, in the update process for AS_{rank}, in addition to the elitist ants, there are σ-1 unique paths that receive a weighted pheromone addition within each iteration. What this means for AS_{rank} is that there are always multiple paths for which the pheromone value does not decay to zero. Within MMAS, the pheromone bounding ensures that the pheromone values on all paths do not go below $\tau_{min}(t)$.

The search-time statistics in Figure 2(c) (the triangle and dot lines plots superimposed over the bar charts) indicate the range of iteration numbers in which each algorithm found S_{gb}, the global best solution for the run. Interestingly, all four algorithms tended to find their global best solutions towards the end of phase-I and the beginning of phase-II, albeit MMAS at a later stage than the other three algorithms. AS_{elite} and AS had a greater variation in their search-times than AS_{rank}, with MMAS having the greatest variation in its search-times.

6.2 Case Study 2: New York Tunnels Problem

6.2.1 Preliminaries

The New York Tunnels Problem (NYTP) was first considered by Schaake and Lai (1969) while Dandy *et al.* (1996) was the first to apply an evolutionary algorithm to this problem. The network is a gravity system fed from a single reservoir, and consists of 20 nodes connected via 21 tunnels (Figure 3). There is a single demand case for the problem. Each tunnel has a null option, or the option to provide a duplicate tunnel with one of 15 different diameter sizes. The reader is referred to Dandy *et al.* (1996) for the case study details. This case study is the second smallest considered in this chapter, and has a search space of approximately 1.934×10^{25} possible combinations.

6.2.2 Results

Based on the heuristics given in Table 1 $\{\tau_0, m\} = \{140, 90\}$ and based on preliminary analyses $I_{max} = 500$ was found to be sufficient. A single run of the NYTP consisted of 45,000 function evaluations. The range of parameters tested was: $\sigma \in [2, 80]$ for AS_{elite}; $\sigma \in [2, 80]$ for AS_{rank}; $\{P_{best}, \delta\} \in [1\times10^{-5}, 0.99]\times[0, 0.99]$ for MMAS. For $2 \leq \sigma \leq 20$ the performance of AS_{elite} varied less than 1%, but for $\sigma > 20$ the solution quality was increasingly worse. For AS_{rank}, the performance varied less than 1% for the entire parameter range, with the better values being $8 \leq \sigma \leq 12$. For MMAS, the performance varied less than 1% for $0.005 \leq P_{best} \leq 0.99$ and $\delta \leq 0.0005$, with the solution quality degrading for lower values of P_{best} and higher values of δ. The optimal parameter settings were as follows: $\sigma = 8$ for AS_{elite}; $\sigma = 8$ for AS_{rank}; $\{P_{best}, \delta\} = \{0.05, 5\text{x}10^{-5}\}$ for MMAS.

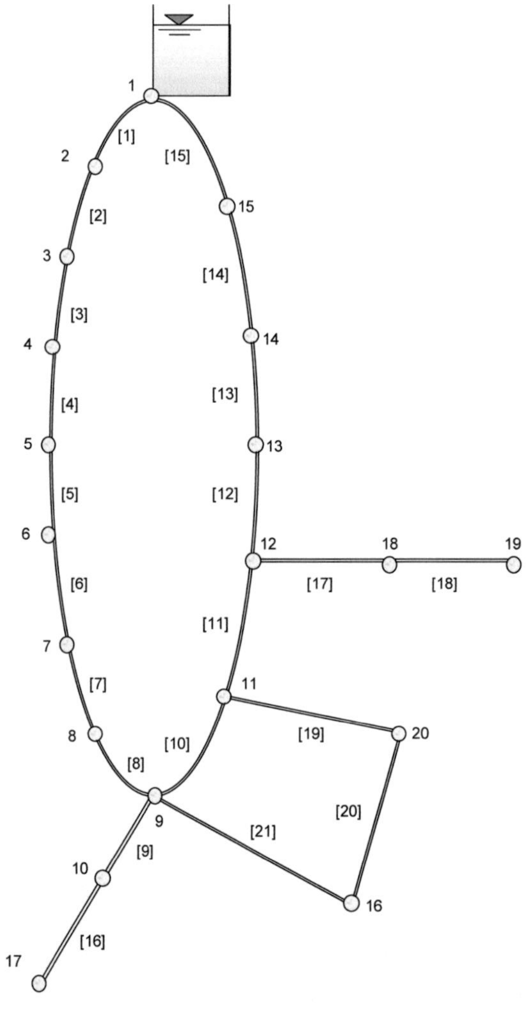

Figure 3. Network layout for New York Tunnels Problem

Table 3 gives a comparison of the performance of the ACO algorithms considered in this paper with that of the current best performing algorithms from the literature for the NYTP. A detailed statistical analysis of these algorithms was given in Zecchin *et al.* (2007), but all algorithms performed well, with AS_{elite}, AS_{rank} and MMAS, on average, finding solutions within a 1% cost of the known-optimum.

Algorithm	Best-cost ($M) *(% deviation from optimum)*						Mean search-time (evaluation no.)
	Minimum		Mean		Maximum		
AS	39.204	*(1.47)*	39.910	*(3.29)*	40.922	*(5.91)*	34,877
AS_{elite}	38.638	*(0.00)*	38.988	*(0.91)*	39.511	*(2.26)*	21,945
AS_{rank}	38.638	*(0.00)*	38.777	*(0.36)*	39.221	*(1.51)*	19,319
MMAS	38.638	*(0.00)*	38.836	*(0.51)*	39.415	*(2.01)*	30,711
PE[a]	41.800	*(8.18)*	-		-		NA
GA_{imp}[b]	38.796	*(0.41)*	NA		NA		96,750
GA[c]	37.13[i]	-	NA		NA		~1,000,000
$ACOA_{i\text{-}best}$[d]	38.638	*(0.00)*	NA		NA		13,928
TS[e]	37.13[i]	-	NA		NA		~10,000
$AS_{i\text{-}best}$[f]	38.638	*(0.00)*	38.849	*(0.55)*	39.492	*(2.21)*	22,052
ACS[g]	38.638	*(0.00)*	39.629	*(2.57)*	41.992	*(8.68)*	23,972
GA_{adapt}[h]	38.638	*(0.00)*	38.770	*(0.34)*	39.07	*(1.12)*	15,680

[a] Partial enumeration (Gessler, 1982). [b] Improved GA that used a variable exponent in fitness scaling, an adjacency mutation operator, and Gray code representation (Dandy *et al.* 1996). [c] Genetic algorithm (Savic & Walters, 1997). [d] Iteration-best updating version of ACO (Maier, *et al.* 2002). [e] Tabu search (Cunha & Ribeiro, 2004). [f] An improved iteration-best version of AS (Zecchin *et al.* 2005). [g] Ant colony system (Zecchin *et al.* 2007). [h] Parameter free, self-adapting, boundary searching genetic algorithm (Afshar & Marino, 2007). [i] Not assessed as feasible by EPANET2 (Maier *et al.*, 2002).

Table 3. Comparison of performance of AS, ACS, AS_{elite}, AS_{rank}, MMAS, and other algorithms from the literature applied to the New York Tunnels Problem. Results for AS, AS_{elite}, AS_{rank}, and MMAS are based on 20 runs. NA means that the information was not available

Plots of the iteration best-costs $f_{min}(t)$, the mean-colony-distance $d_\Sigma(t)$, and the searching phases and search-time statistics for the algorithms applied to the NYTP are given in Figure 4(a)-(c). Again, the three distinct searching phases observed for the TRP are observed in the behaviour of f_{min} and d_Σ. The relative behaviours of the algorithms applied to the NYTP are similar to that for the TRP, except for the faster convergence of AS in phase-I than that of both AS_{elite} and AS_{rank}. The effectiveness of the additional pheromone adjustment mechanisms in AS_{elite}, AS_{rank} and MMAS is made clear in Figure 4(a). This is seen by the fact that, for the majority of the phase-III searching, these algorithms have confined the search to the high quality region of the solution space, as indicated by the near optimal f_{min}. In contrast, by the end of the run-time, AS has converged to a smaller region than MMAS, but the higher value of f_{min} indicates that the search is not in a near optimal region. This behaviour is also exhibited in the performance statistics of Table 3.

Figure 4(c) gives a plot of the search-time statistics (the distribution of iteration times taken by the algorithms to find their global best run-time cost S_{gb}) for the NYTP. In contrast to the TRP, the algorithms tended to find their S_{gb} relatively later in the searching phases. AS_{elite} and AS_{rank} tended to find their best cost just after the descent in phase-II, whereas AS and MMAS found their best cost well into phase-III. This observation is interesting, as even though AS_{elite} and AS_{rank} had clearly not converged (as $d_{\Sigma} > 0$), and their search was intensified within a near optimal region of the solution space, they were both unable to find higher quality solutions in phase-III of their search. The implications of this are that the phase-III search for AS_{elite} and AS_{rank} is not an effective phase in their searching behaviour.

6.3 Case Study 3: Hanoi Problem

6.3.1 Preliminaries

The Hanoi Problem (HP), first published by Fujiwara and Khang (1990), has been considered by numerous authors in its discrete problem formulation (Savic & Walters 1997; Cunha & Sousa 1999; Wu *et al.* 2001). This case study is for a new design that consists of 34 pipes and 32 nodes organised in three loops (Figure 5). The system is gravity fed by a single reservoir and has only a single demand case. For each link, there are six different new pipe options where a minimum diameter constraint is enforced. For case study details, the reader is referred to Cunha & Sousa (1999). This case study is the second largest considered in this chapter, having a problem size of approximately 2.87×10^{26} combinations.

Based on the heuristics given in Table 1 $\{\tau_0, m\} = \{26, 80\}$ and $I_{max} = 1{,}500$ were found to be sufficient, implying that a single run for the HP consisted of 120,000 function evaluations. The range of parameters tested was: $\sigma \in [2, 70]$ for AS_{elite}; $\sigma \in [2, 70]$ for AS_{rank},; for MMAS, $\{P_{best}, \delta\} \in [1 \times 10^{-5}, 0.99] \times [0, 0.005]$. In general, the performances of AS_{elite}, AS_{rank}, and MMAS were much more sensitive to their respective parameter settings for this case study, such that only moderate variations from the parameters selected resulted in the inability to find feasible solutions for some runs. For AS_{elite}, no feasible solutions were found for $\sigma \leq 10$, with the best performance occurring with $\sigma = 40$. For values of $\sigma > 20$, no feasible solutions were found within a greater number of runs for AS_{rank}. For MMAS, no feasible solutions were found for $P_{best} \leq 0.1$ and $\delta \geq 0.001$, however, there was a less than 1% variation in solution quality for $0.5 \leq P_{best} \leq 0.65$. The selected parameter values were as follows: for AS_{elite}, $\sigma = 40$; for AS_{rank}, $\sigma = 20$; for MMAS, $\{P_{best}, \delta\} = \{0.5, 0\}$. An important point to note is that the best parameter settings for this case study vary greatly from those of all the other case studies. A common thread is that the optimal parameter settings for this case study increased each of the algorithms' emphasis on exploitation. For example: for AS_{elite}, and to a lesser degree AS_{rank}, the number of elitist ants for this case study was far greater than for the other case studies; for MMAS, P_{best} was higher (indicating looser pheromone bounds) and δ was set to a low value, both of these indicating a reduction in exploration potential. Despite this notable sensitivity, the parameter heuristics proposed by Zecchin *et al.* (2005) resulted in extremely good performance for MMAS and AS_{rank}.

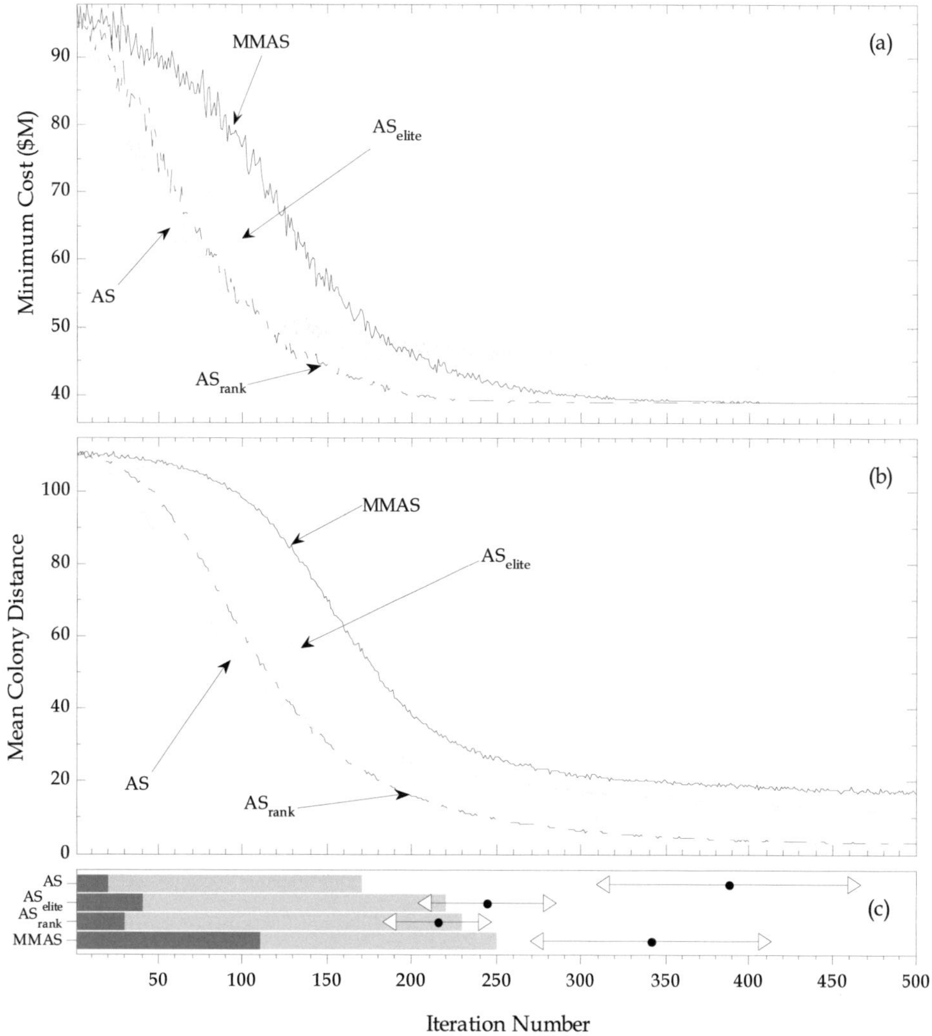

Figure 4. Plots of (a) the minimum cost ($M) found in each iteration $f_{min}(t)$, (b) the mean colony distance $d_{\Sigma}(t)$, and (c) run-time statistics for AS, AS_{elite}, AS_{rank}, and MMAS applied to the New York Tunnels Problem. Plots (a) and (b) are averaged from 20 runs. Plot (c) depicts the three convergence phases: phase-I (dark grey); phase-II (light grey); phase-III (remaining white space). The line graphs overlaying the bar charts in (c) indicate the search-time statistics (based on 20 runs) with the dot indicating the mean search-time, and the left and right arrows indicating the mean minus and plus a standard deviation, respectively

6.3.2 Results

Table 4 shows a comparison of the performance of the ACO algorithms with the other best performing algorithms in the literature. A detailed statistical analysis of the algorithms was given in Zecchin *et al.* (2007), but as a summary, MMAS, and to a lesser extent AS_{rank}, were the only algorithms that performed well on the HP. AS_{elite} was unable to find high quality solutions, and AS was not able to find any feasible solutions. Other authors have also noted that the HP has a small feasible region (Eusuff & Lansey 2003).

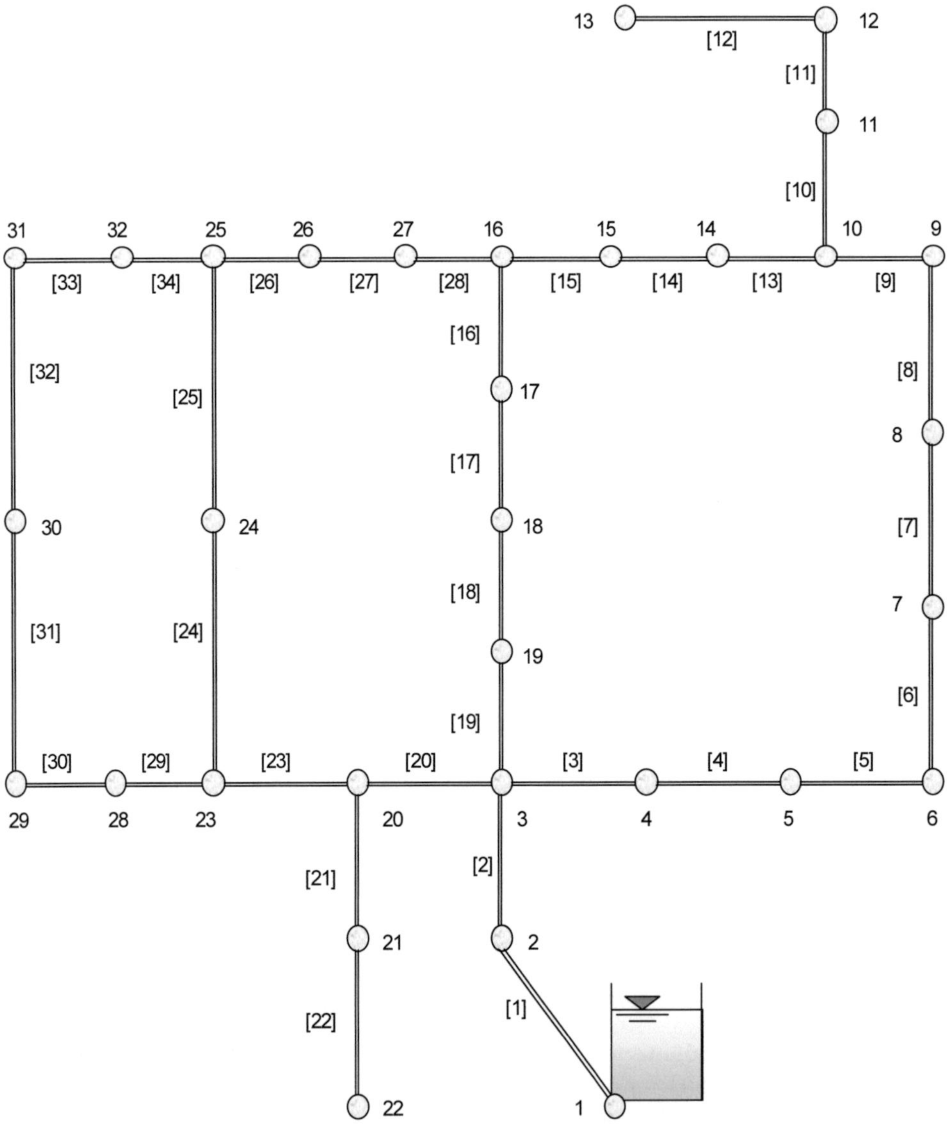

Figure 5. Network layout for the Hanoi Problem

Algorithm	Best-cost ($M) *(% deviation from optimum)*						Mean search-time (evaluation no.)
	Minimum		Mean		Maximum		
AS	NFS		NFS		NFS		-
AS_{elite}	6.827	*(11.30)*	7.295	*(18.93)*	8.187	*(33.48)*	59,917
AS_{rank}	6.206	*(1.17)*	6.506	*(6.07)*	6.788	*(10.66)*	75,328
MMAS	6.134	*(0.00)*	6.394	*(4.24)*	6.635	*(8.17)*	85,571
GA[a]	6.195	*(1.00)*	NA		NA		~1,000,000
SA[b]	6.053[g]	-	NA		NA		~53,000
GA_{fm}[c]	6.182	*(0.78)*	NA		NA		113,626
TS[d]	6.053[g]	-	NA		NA		~10,000
$AS_{i\text{-}best}$[e]	6.367	*(3.80)*	6.842	*(11.54)*	7.474	*(21.95)*	67,136
ACS[f]	7.754	*(26.41)*	8.109	*(32.20)*	8.462	*(37.96)*	61,324

[a] Genetic algorithm (Savic & Walters, 1997). [b] Simulated annealing (Cunha & Sousa, 1999). [c] The fast messy genetic algorithm (Wu *et al.*, 2001). [d] Tabu search (Cunha & Ribeiro, 2004). [e] An iteration-best pheromone updating version of AS (Zecchin *et al.* 2005); [f] Ant colony system (Zecchin *et al.* 2007).
[g] Infeasible by EPANET2 (Zecchin *et al.*, 2005).

Table 4. Comparison of performance of AS, ACS, AS_{elite}, AS_{rank}, MMAS, and other algorithms from the literature applied to the Hanoi Problem. Results for AS, AS_{elite}, AS_{rank}, and MMAS are based on 20 runs. NFS means no feasible solution was found, NA means that the information was not available

Plots of the iteration best-costs $f_{min}(t)$, the mean-colony-distance $d_{\Sigma}(t)$, and the searching phases and search-time statistics for the algorithms applied to the HP are given in Figure 6(a)-(c). Vastly different behaviours were observed for the HP in comparison to the other case studies, but the three phases of searching are still distinct. A marked difference though is the relative lengths of the phase-I searching, (AS, AS_{elite}, and AS_{rank} all have a far longer phase-I search than MMAS) and the distinct hump in the phase-II convergence of MMAS. The differences in the trends of f_{min} and d_{Σ} for this case study can be explained by the small feasible region. The maximum cost of a feasible solution for the HP, which is also the maximum network cost (for which the penalty cost *PC* from (15) is zero), is $C(\Omega^{max})$ = $M 10.96. Therefore, any solutions with costs higher than this are infeasible. With this in mind, the appearance of the data points of f_{min} in Figure 6(a) can be interpreted as the iteration times at which each algorithm first found feasible solutions. This is why no plot of f_{min} for AS is seen in Figure 6(a), as AS found no feasible solutions for the HP.

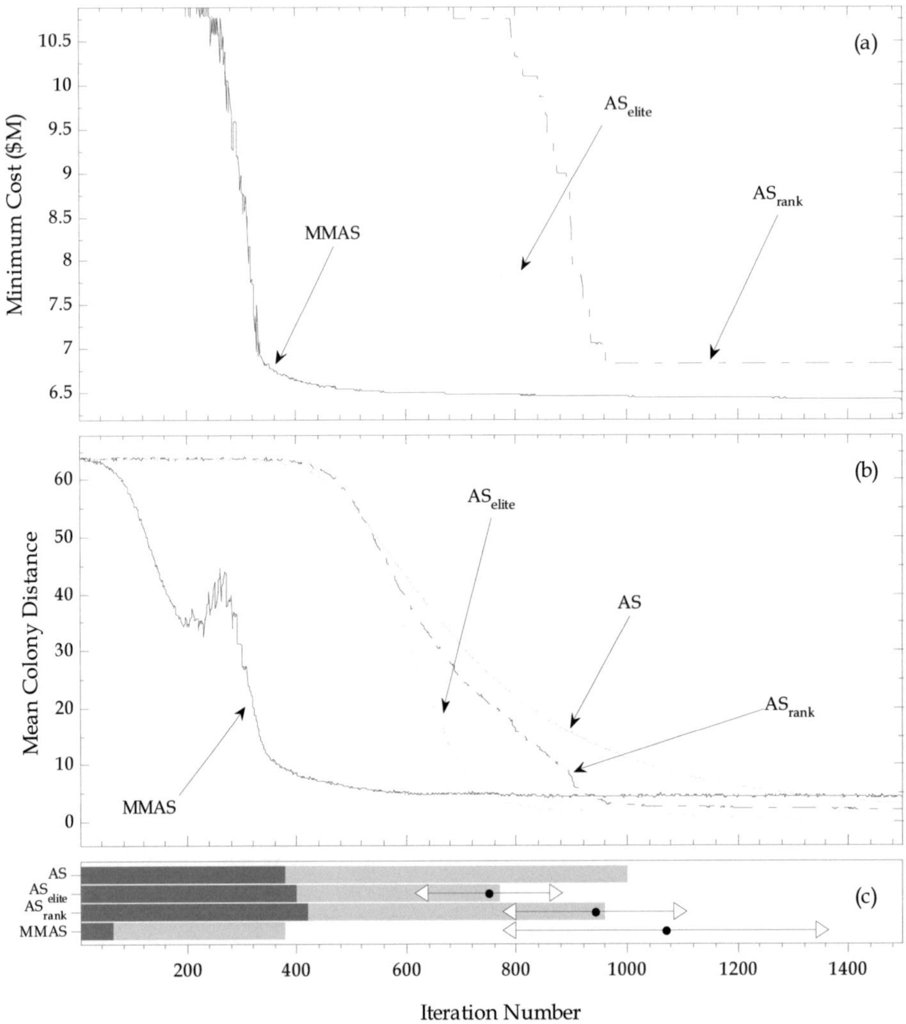

Figure 6. Plots of (a) the minimum cost ($M) found in each iteration $f_{min}(t)$, (b) the mean colony distance $d_{\Sigma}(t)$, and (c) run-time statistics for AS, AS_{elite}, AS_{rank}, and MMAS applied to the Hanoi Problem. Plots (a) and (b) are averaged from 20 runs. Plot (c) depicts the three convergence phases: phase-I (dark grey); phase-II (light grey); phase-III (remaining white space). The line graphs overlaying the bar charts in (c) indicate the search-time statistics (based on 20 runs) with the dot indicating the mean search-time, and the left and right arrows indicating the mean minus and plus a standard deviation, respectively

This entry into the feasible region for AS_{elite}, AS_{rank} and MMAS occurred well into the phase-II search (for MMAS, it is seen to coincide with the hump in the phase-II convergence). This means that the phase-I search was entirely within the infeasible region, and furthermore, it took the algorithms some time to effectively use the information in the infeasible region before they could begin the phase-II convergence to guide the search into the feasible region. Interestingly, only the algorithms that contain exploitive mechanisms were able to find the feasible region.

Considering the search-time statistics in Figure 6(c), it is seen that AS_{elite} and AS_{rank} found their best-costs towards the end of the phase-II search, with AS_{rank} consistently finding higher quality solutions than AS_{elite}. For MMAS however, the best-cost was found well into the phase-III search, again illustrating the effectiveness of MMAS's confined phase-III searching.

Algorithm	Best-cost ($M) (*% deviation from optimum*)						Mean search-time (evaluation no.)
	Minimum		Mean		Maximum		
AS	80.855	*(4.63)*	83.572	*(8.15)*	85.267	*(10.34)*	131,769
AS_{elite}	77.922	*(0.84)*	79.806	*(3.28)*	81.986	*(6.10)*	90,404
AS_{rank}	77.434	*(0.21)*	78.492	*(1.58)*	79.863	*(3.35)*	72,276
MMAS	77.275	*(0.00)*	78.213	*(1.21)*	79.353	*(2.69)*	238,264
$AS_{i\text{-}best}$[a]	77.275	*(0.00)*	78.302	*(1.33)*	79.922	*(3.43)*	75,760
ACS[b]	77.275	*(0.00)*	80.586	*(4.28)*	86.682	*(12.17)*	471,977

[a] An iteration-best pheromone updating version of AS (Zecchin *et al.* 2005); [b] The ACO algorithm ant colony system (Zecchin *et al.* 2007).

Table 5. Comparison of performance of AS, AS_{elite}, AS_{rank}, MMAS, and other algorithms from the literature applied to the Doubled New York Tunnels Problem. Results for AS, AS_{elite}, AS_{rank}, and MMAS are based on 20 runs

6.4 Case Study 4: Doubled New York Tunnels Problem

6.4.1 Preliminaries

The Doubled New York Tunnels Problem (2-NYTP), first studied in Zecchin *et al.* (2005), consists of two NYTP networks connected via the single reservoir at node 1 in Figure 3. The link and node details are as for the NYTP. This problem has a search space size of 3.741 x 10^{50} and is the largest case study considered in this chapter.

6.4.2 Results

Based on the heuristics given in Table 1, $\{\tau_0, m\} = \{200, 170\}$, and from a preliminary analysis, I_{max} = 3,000, therefore, a single run for the 2-NYTP consisted of 510,000 function evaluations. The range of parameters tested was: $\sigma \in [1, 160]$ for AS_{elite}; $\sigma \in [2, 160]$ for AS_{rank}; for MMAS, $\{P_{best}, \delta\} \in [1 \times 10^{-6}, 0.99] \times [0, 0.99]$.

AS_{elite} achieved a less than 1% variation in the performance for $1 \leq \sigma \leq 5$, with the solution quality deteriorating for higher values of σ. AS_{rank}'s performance varied less than 5% for the entire parameter range of σ, with the best values occurring for $6 \leq \sigma \leq 10$. For MMAS, the performance varied less than 1% for $0.0005 \leq P_{best} \leq 0.5$ and $\delta \leq 0.0001$, with the solution quality degrading for parameter values outside these ranges. The selected parameter values were: $\sigma = 3$ for AS_{elite}; $\sigma = 8$ for AS_{rank}; $\{P_{best}, \delta\} = \{0.001, 0\}$ for MMAS.

Table 5 shows a comparison of the performance of the ACO algorithms considered for the 2-NYTP with that obtained using other algorithms from the literature. A detailed statistical analysis of these algorithms was given in Zecchin *et al.* (2007), but as a summary, AS_{rank} and MMAS performed consistently well (the former with extremely computationally efficient search times), with AS_{elite} performing only moderately inferior to that the above two, algorithms but significantly better than AS.

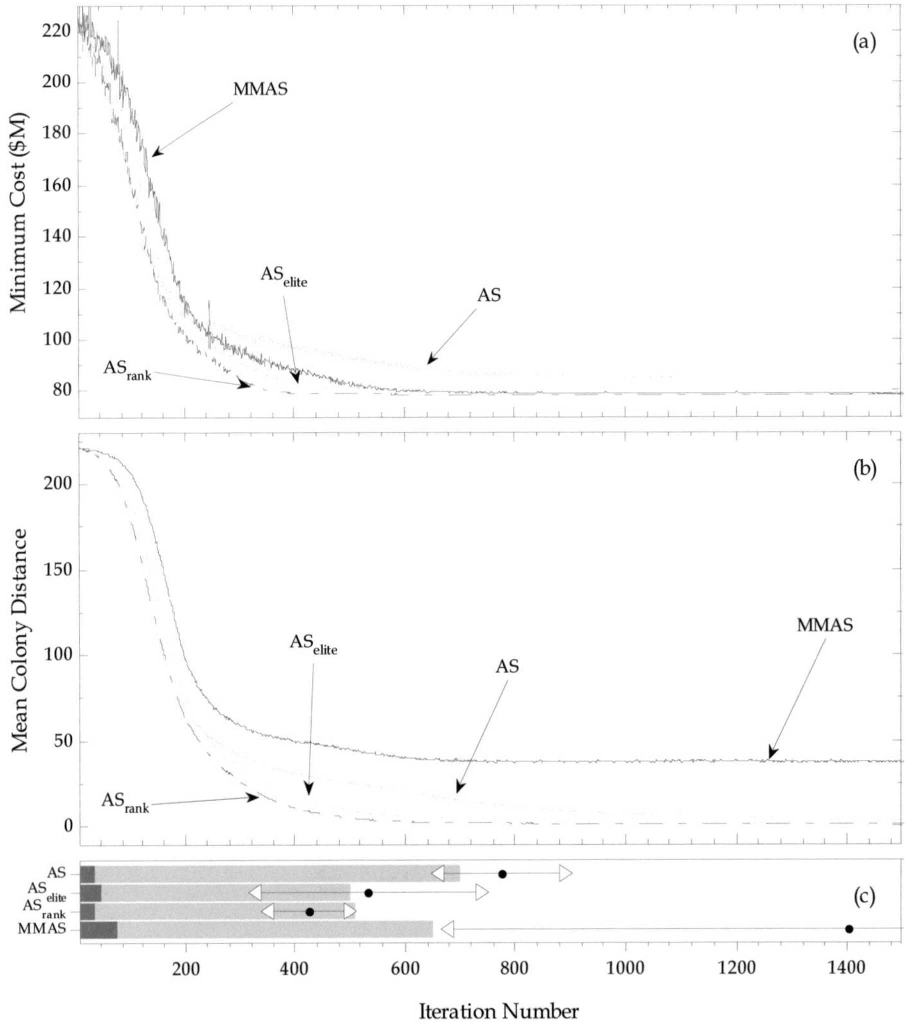

Figure 7. Plots of (a) the minimum cost ($M) found in each iteration $f_{min}(t)$, (b) the mean colony distance $d_{\Sigma}(t)$, and (c) run-time statistics for AS, AS_{elite}, AS_{rank}, and MMAS applied to the Doubled New York Tunnels Problem. Plots (a) and (b) are averaged from 20 runs. Plot (c) depicts the three convergence phases: phase-I (dark grey); phase-II (light grey); phase-III (remaining white space). The line graphs overlaying the bar charts in (c) indicate the search-time statistics (based on 20 runs) with the dot indicating the mean search-time, and the left and right arrows indicating the mean minus and plus a standard deviation, respectively

Plots of the iteration best-costs $f_{min}(t)$, the mean-colony-distance $d_{\Sigma}(t)$, and the searching phases and search-time statistics for the algorithms applied to the 2-NYTP are given in Figure 7(a)-(c). These figures show behaviour quite similar to that for the NYTP, just on a larger time scale. The main difference between the two is the relative size of d_{Σ} in MMAS's phase-III search with respect to the other algorithms. In other words, MMAS still seems to be searching a relatively broad area of the solution space in phase-III. This explorative behaviour is seen as being effective, as the distribution of search-times in Figure 7(c) shows that, as with the other case studies, MMAS finds many of its best-cost solutions in this phase of the search.

6.5 Discussion

As in a previous study (Zecchin *et al.* 2007), the additional pheromone adjustment mechanisms in AS_{elite}, AS_{rank} and MMAS were shown to improve the performance of ACO, in comparison to AS, when applied to the WDSP. AS_{elite} and AS_{rank} were seen to be relatively fast algorithms, finding high quality solutions for all case studies except the difficult HP. MMAS was observed as a slower algorithm, but able to consistently find high quality solutions for all the case studies considered. Below is a discussion of the convergence behaviour of each algorithm as observed in the case studies considered.

AS was observed to converge quickly initially (*i.e.* typically a short phase-I search), with an accompanied increase in solution quality. However, by the end of its (also relatively short) phase-II, AS's search was still typically broad, and it did not seem to be able to focus the colony to find solutions that were as good as those found by the other algorithms. AS was also not able to find the feasible region at all for the HP.

Despite AS_{elite}'s emphasis on exploitation, its phase-II convergence was not consistently faster than that of AS, implying an initially more explorative phase-I. The exploitative nature of AS_{elite} was seen at the end of phase-II, at which point AS_{elite} converged to a comparatively small region of high quality solutions. AS_{elite} tended to find its best-cost solutions towards the end of phase-II and at the beginning of phase-III. AS_{elite}'s ability to find the feasible region for the HP can be directly attributed to the exploitive nature of its elitist ants, which effectively used the information in the infeasible region to guide the search into the feasible region. However, once in the feasible region, AS_{elite} was not able to find high quality solutions.

AS_{rank} consistently converged faster than AS_{elite}, and to a tighter searching region (lower d_Σ), by the end of phase-II. AS_{rank} had a typically lower, and less variable, search-time than the other algorithms, with best-cost solutions generally found towards the end of phase-II. Given its speed of convergence, and the high quality of the solutions found, AS_{rank}'s pheromone updating scheme, although highly exploitative, is considered to be very effective. However, in situations, such as the small feasible region of the HP or the relatively large solution space of the 2-NYTP, AS_{rank}'s inability to conduct an explorative phase-III search, means that it does not perform as well as MMAS for these case studies.

MMAS typically had the longest phase-I search, which can be attributed to its exploration encouraging pheromone bounding and pheromone smoothing mechanisms. MMAS maintained a relatively broad search after its phase-II convergence, but unlike AS, it was still able to find high quality solutions. This aspect of relatively broad phase-III searching, coupled with high solution quality, can be attributed to MMAS's effective management of exploitation, by updating only the iteration best path, and exploration, by lower bounding all paths' pheromone values. As such, MMAS tended to find its best cost solutions well into phase-III.

This lower bounding of the pheromone values also explains MMAS's ability to effectively explore the feasible region of the HP. As the discovery of the higher quality solutions in the feasible region raised the lower pheromone bound once MMAS entered the feasible region, the pheromone values were all partially replenished, with the information concerning the feasible region being retained. From this perspective, the hump observed in Figure 6(b) can be considered as another phase-I period for the MMAS search as it entered the feasible region. That is, due to the replenishing nature of the lower pheromone bound, the searching phases seemed to start again once the feasible region was found.

7. Conclusions

To gain a more complete understanding of ACO algorithms, it is important to not only consider their performance with respect to their solution quality and computational efficiency, but also the algorithms' searching behaviour. In this chapter, two statistics of searching behaviour have been considered, (i) the minimum cost found within an iteration, which is an indication of search quality, and (ii) the mean colony distance, a topological measure that describes the spread of solutions through the solution space and thus provides an indication of the degree of convergence of an algorithm.

Four ACO algorithms were considered in this chapter, namely, Ant System (AS), Elitist Ant System (AS_{elite}), Elitist-Rank Ant System (AS_{rank}), and Max-Min Ant System (MMAS). The focus of this chapter was a case study based computational analysis of the convergence behaviour of these four algorithms. The problem type considered was the water distribution system problem, a classical combinatorial optimisation problem in the field of civil engineering. The case studies considered were the Two-Reservoir Problem (TRP), the New York Tunnels Problem (NYTP), the Hanoi Problem (HP), and the Doubled New York Tunnels Problem (2-NYTP).

From studying the convergence behaviour as exhibited by the mean colony distance, three distinct searching phases were observed for all algorithms. Phase-I was observed to be a broad searching phase in which only low quality solutions were found. In phase-II, a rapid convergence was observed, where increasingly good solutions were found and the colonies search was guided into smaller and higher quality regions of the solution space. Phase-III consisted of compact and dense searching in the high quality regions discovered in phase-II, where the convergence rate was much reduced.

Each algorithm exhibited different behaviour in each phase. These differences were interpreted from the perspective of the algorithms' formulations. For example, the exploitative algorithms, AS_{elite} and AS_{rank} experienced an extremely short phase-I, followed by a rapid convergence in phase-II. In contrast, the exploration encouraging MMAS had a significantly longer phase-I search and tended to converge to a much broader region than the other algorithms at the end of phase-II. AS tended to converge quickly initially, but its lack of exploitative mechanisms meant that, even by the end of phase-II, it was not able to focus its search in the high quality regions of the search space.

Combining this qualitative three phase description with the search-time statistics (the time in the search at which the algorithms found their best-cost) leads to a deeper understanding of the productive stages in the algorithms' search. In almost all instances, AS_{rank}'s search-time occurred near the end of phase-II. What this means is that the phase-III searching for AS_{rank} was seen to be unproductive. AS_{elite} performed similarly to AS_{rank}, but with slightly longer search-times. The search-times for the explorative MMAS were typically much longer than those of the others algorithms, and the best-cost solutions tended to occur in the phase-III searching stage. The implications of this are that, even though MMAS maintained a relatively broad phase-III search, this longer term exploration was fruitful as solutions of higher quality were found.

This chapter illustrates how relatively simple run-time statistics can yield significant insight into the convergence behaviour of ACO algorithms. The type of analysis presented in this chapter shows potential to be useful for the purpose of both research and application. In terms of research (and algorithmic development), considering run-time behavioural statistics could aid in understanding the behavioural impacts of algorithmic mechanisms, and also provide a more informative comparison of different algorithms. In terms of application, run-time statistics could aid in understanding the influence of parameter variations, and facilitate the determination of appropriate parameter values, both online and offline.

8. References

Afshar, M.H., & Marino, M.A. (2007). A parameter-free self-adapting boundary genetic search for pipe network optimization. *Comput. Optim. App.*, 37, 83-102

Boese, K. D.; A. B. Kahng, & S.Muddu (1994). A new adaptive multi-start technique for combinatorial global optimization. *Operations Research Letters, 16*, 2, 101–113

Bullnheimer, B.; Hartl, R. F. & Strauss, C. (1999). A new rank based version of the Ant System: A computational study. *Central European Journal for Operations Research and Economics*, 7, 1, 25–38

Coello Coello, C.A. (2002). Theoretical and numerical constraint-handling techniques used with evolutionary algorithms: A survey of the state of the art, *Computer methods in applied mechanics and engineering*, 191, 1245-1287

Cohen, G. (2003), A course in modern analysis and its applications, *Australian Mathematical Society lecture series*, vol. 17, Cambridge University Press, Port Melbourne, Australia

Colorni, A.; Dorigo, M.; Maffoli, F.; Maniezzo, V.; Righini, G. & Trubian, M. (1996). Heuristics from nature for hard combinatorial optimisation problems. *International Transactions in Operational Research*, 3, 1, 1–21

Cunha, M.C., & Ribeiro, L. (2004). Tabu search algorithms for water network optimization. *European Journal of Operational Research*, 157, 746-758

Cuhna, M.C. & Sousa, J. (1999). Water distribution network design optimization: Simulated annealing approach. *Journal of Water Resources Planning and Management*, ASCE, 125, 4, 215–221

Dandy, G.C.; Simpson, A.R. & Murphy, L.J. (1996). An improved genetic algorithm for pipe network optimisation. *Water Resources Research*, 32, 2, 449–458

Deb, K. (2001). Multi-objective optimization using evolutionary algorithms, Wiley, Chichester, U.K.

Dorigo, M.; Bonabeau E., & Theraulaz, G. (2000). Ant algorithms and stigmergy. *Future Generation Computer Systems*, 16, 851–871

Dorigo, M.; Di Caro, G. & Gambardella, L.M. (1999). Ant algorithms for discrete optimisation. *Artificial Life*, 5, 2, 137–172

Dorigo, M. & Gambardella, L.M. (1997). Ant colony system: A cooperative learning approach to TSP. *IEEE Transactions on Evolutionary Computation*, 1, 1 , 53–66

Dorigo, M.; Maniezzo, V. & Colorni, A. (1996). The ant system: Optimisation by a colony of cooperating agents. *IEEE Transactions on Systems, Man, and Cybernetics – Part B*, 26 1, 29–41

Eusuff, M.M. & Lansey, K.E. (2003). Optimisation of water distribution network design using the shuffled frog leaping algorithm. *Journal of Water Resources Planning and Management*, ASCE, 129, 3, 210–225

Fujiwara, O. & Khang, D.B. (1990). A two phase decomposition method for optimal design of looped water distribution networks. *Water Resources Research*, 26, 4, 539–549

Gessler, J. (1982). Optimisation of pipe networks. *Proceedings of International Symposium on Urban Hydrology, Hydraulics and Sediment Control*. University of Kentucky, Lexington, 165-171

Gessler, J. (1985). Pipe network optimisation by enumeration. *Computer Applications for Water Resources*, ASCE, Buffalo, NY, 76, 579–581

Gutjahr, W.J. (2002). ACO algorithms with guaranteed convergence to the optimal solution. *Information Processing Letters*, 82, 145-153

Maier, H.R.; Simpson, A.R., Zecchin, A.C.; Foong, W.K.; Phang, K.Y.; Seah, H.Y. & Tan, C.L. (2003). Ant colony optimisation for the design of water distribution systems. *Journal of Water Resources Planning and Management*, ASCE, 129, 3, 200–209

Rossman (2000). *EPANET 2 Users Manual*. National Risk Management Research Laboratory Office of Research and Development U.S. Environmental Protection Agency. Cincinnati, Ohio, USA.

Savic, D.A. & Walters, G.A. (1997). Genetic algorithms for least-cost design of water distribution networks. *Journal of Water Resources Planning and Management*, ASCE, 123, 2, 67–77

Schaake, J. & Lai, D. (1969). Linear programming and dynamic programming applications to water distribution network design. *Research Report No. 116*, Department of Civil Engineering, Massachusetts Institute of Technology

Simpson, A.R.; Murphy, L.J. & Dandy, G.C. (1994). Genetic algorithms compared to other techniques for pipe optimization. *Journal of Water Resources Planning and Management*, ASCE, 120, 4, 423–443

Simpson, A.R., & Goldberg, D.E. (1994). Pipeline optimization via genetic algorithms: From theory to practice. *Proc. 2nd Int. Conf. On Pipeline Systems*, Edinburgh, Scotland, May, 309–320

Sousa, J. & Cunha, M.C. (1999), On the quality of simulated annealing for water network optimization problems, In: *Water Industry Systems: Modelling and Optimisation Applications*, Vol. 2, Savic, D., Walters, G. (Eds.), 333-345, Research Studies Press Ltd.

Streeter, V. L.; Wylie, E. B. & Bedford, K. W. (1997), *Fluid mechanics*, 9th ed.,WCB/McGraw Hill, Boston, Mass.

Stützle, T. & Hoos, H.H. (2000). MAX-MIN Ant System. *Future Generation Computer Systems*, 16, 889–914

Wu, Z.Y.; Boulos, P.F.; Orr, C.H. & Ro, J.J. (2001). Using genetic algorithms to rehabilitate distribution systems. *Journal for American Water Works Association*, November 2001, 74–85

Zecchin, A.C.; Simpson, A.R.; Maier H.R., & Nixon, J.B. (2005). Parametric study for an ant algorithm applied to water distribution system optimization. *IEEE Transactions on Evolutionary Computation*, 9, 2, 175-191

Zecchin, A.C.; Maier, H.R.; Simpson, A.R.; Leonard, M.; Roberts, A.J., & Berrisford, M.J. (2006). Application of two ant colony optimisation algorithms to water distribution system optimisation. *Mathematical and Computer Modelling*, 44, 451-468

Zecchin, A.C.; Maier, H.R.; Simpson, A.R.; Leonard, M., & Nixon, J.B. (2007). Ant Colony Optimization Applied to Water Distribution System Design: Comparative Study of Five Algorithms. *ASCE Journal of Water Resources, Planning & Management*, 133, 1, 84-92

25

A CMPSO algorithm based approach to solve the multi-plant supply chain problem

Felix T. S. Chan[1], Vikas Kumar[2] and Nishikant Mishra[3]
[1] *The University of Hong Kong,* [2]*University of Exeter,* [3]*University of Warwick*
[1]*Hong Kong S.A.R.,* [2,3] *United Kingdom*

1. Introduction

In the era globalisation the emerging technologies are governing the manufacturing industries to a multifaceted state. The escalating complexity has demanded researchers to find the possible ways of easing the solution of the problems. This has motivated the researchers to grasp ideas from the nature and implant it in the engineering sciences. This way of thinking led to emergence of many biologically inspired algorithms that have proven to be efficient in handling the computationally complex problems with great ease and competence such as Genetic Algorithm (GA), Ant Colony Optimization (ACO), Particle Swarm Optimization (PSO), etc. Motivated by the capability of the biologically inspired algorithms the present research proposes a new Cooperative Multiple Particle Swarm Optimization (CMPSO) algorithm. The idea behind this proposed CMPSO algorithm came from the limitations associated with the existing PSO algorithm under the discussed problem scenario. The proposed CMPSO algorithm has been applied in multi-plant supply chain environment which has proven to be NP hard problem. To prove the efficacy and robustness of the proposed CMPSO algorithm it has been compared with the existing evolutionary algorithms (EAs). Furthermore the authors have also shown the statistical validation of CMPSO algorithm.

The changing scenario of the global business urges efficient ways of performing various tasks to sustain the impact of market uncertainty. Especially manufacturing industries are looking for the competent ways of managing their processes. Supply chain being the backbone of any industrial organization demands its efficient management for the shake of profitability, and customer satisfaction point of view. Meeting delivery dates is an increasingly important objective in today's competitive market, because delivery delays often result in a considerable loss of goodwill and eventually market share. Realizing this important contribution of the effective supply chain management, this research aims to optimize the efficiency of the supply chain by handling the complex task of planning and scheduling. In the context of supply chain management the integrated process planning and scheduling has a key role to play. In order to satisfy timeliness and cost criteria imposed by market competition, generally manufacturing industries are opting for *Multi-Plant Supply Chain* (MPSC). MPSC can be seen as a part of supply chain in which coordination, cooperation, and synchronization actions are deliberately strong and binding, so as to guarantee the accomplishment of the predefined objectives. More specifically, the MPSC represents an extended integration ahead of a single manufacturing site by means of strong distribution management capability; electronic data interchange, and adequately coordinated multiple plant management to ensure the real motives of Computer Integrated Manufacturing (CIM). The intricacy of the problem under such conditions increases exponentially with the increase in number of operations, plants, and customers. The increasing applicability and popularity of the biologically inspired tools, in particular, the growing interest among the researchers in PSO techniques motivated us to use it in our present problem scenario. However, PSO in the original form could not be applied under multiple dimensions problem scenario. This limitation prompted us to propose a new artificial intelligence tool known as Cooperative Multiple Particle Swarm Optimization (CMPSO) algorithm which can solve such computationally intricate problem efficiently. CMPSO algorithm takes its governing traits from the PSO. The proposed algorithm is marked by the cooperation among 'sister swarms' that makes it compatible to the problems pertaining to multiple dimensions. The limitation of restricted applicability to the multi-dimensional problems has been the prime reason of thinking behind the cooperative PSO. The objective of the proposed research aims to generate an efficient operating sequence which would explore maximum utilization of the manufacturing resources simultaneously meeting the customer's due date. To ease the solution strategy the underlying problem has been modelled as a travelling salesman problem (TSP). The traditional PSO uses a random number to determine the position and velocity of the particle during fitness evaluation. In the proposed research the random number has been replaced by the chaotic function because of the ergodic and stochastic properties of the chaotic systems. The idea behind this approach was to overcome the demerits associated with the random number generators such as requirement of more number of generations to converge towards an optimal/near optimal solution, tendency to generate the higher-order part more randomly than their lower-order counterpart etc. The chaotic sequences have been successfully applied in the area of natural phenomena modelling, neural network, DNA computing procedures etc. Different researchers use four chaotic sequences (Logistic Map, Tent Map, Sinusoidal Iterator, and Gauss Map) to generate optimal/near optimal solution preventing the premature convergence. Each of these functions are also associated with some merits and demerits, hence in this present research a hybrid chaotic sequence has also been proposed to overcome these demerits. The proposed research aims towards exploring the applicability of PSO technique under diverse situations by inheriting some new concepts. These hybrid PSO techniques (such as CMPSO) could be applied to efficiently solve number of computationally complex problems prevailing in manufacturing environment.

The chapter is organized as follows. Section 2 of the chapter discusses the literature review and attempts to find the gap in the research work in the proposed filed. Section 3 along with some sub-sections gives a brief idea of the problem scenario, and its mathematical formulation. Section 4 gives a background of the PSO algorithm further discussing the proposed CMPSO in detailed i.e. explaining the steps of the algorithm as well as about the chaotic functions. Section 5 explains a case study. Section 6 discusses the outcomes of the proposed CMPSO algorithm and shows a comparative performance measurement with other existing evolutionary algorithms. And finally, section 7 concludes the chapter with some future research directions.

2. Literature Review

In recent years, the changing business scenarios and escalating complexity especially in manufacturing plants have shifted the inclination of the researchers towards issues that have great impact on overall performance of the plants. The supply chain being one of the important aspects of profitability and performance of any plant have gained considerable attention these days. In the past the attention on the operational issues and the supply chain issues were dealt separately. Even process planning and the scheduling part were independent entities to be handled. However, increased competence & complexity prompted to integrate them together which led to the rigorous researches carried out to integrate the process planning and scheduling problems. Scheduling issues have been discussed by many researchers. Hankins *et al.* (1984) emphasized the advantages of alternative machines to increase the productivity of a machine shop, it also shows how mathematical programming techniques tends to become unaffordable when jobs have to be assigned and scheduled on a large set of alternative machines. To deal with such complexity, Khoshnevis and Chen (1991) suggested the use of various dispatching rules, which however suffers from context-dependence and performance unpredictability issues. Similar strategies are also suggested by Brandimarte and Calderini (1995) and Lin (2001).
The challenges associated to the computational complexity of integrated optimization problems in various types of manufacturing systems have stimulated many researchers to apply advanced approaches based on evolutionary computation (Dimopoulos and Zalzala, 2000) and related forms of meta-heuristics. Palmer (1996) applied Simulated Annealing based random search optimization technique to produce an integrated process plan and schedule for a manufacturing unit. Tiwari and Vidyarthi (2000) recognized the machine loading problem as one of the important planning problem in FMS. They utilized Genetic Algorithm based random search heuristic to determine the part type sequence and operation machine allocations to maximize the throughput and minimize the system unbalance. Swarnkar and Tiwari (2004) applied a hybrid Tabu Simulated Annealing based approach to model the machine loading in flexible manufacturing system (FMS). Similarly Tabu and constructive heuristic-based approaches have been proposed by Kolisch, and Hess (2000), Tan and Khoshnevis (2004), and Kolisch (2000). Hybrid approaches combining evolutionary computation with other tools have also gained increasing attention. Rai *et al.* (2002) solved a machine-tool selection and operation allocation problem in FMS based on a fuzzy goal programming model using a GA-based approach. Chiu and Lin (2004) introduced an approach based on Artificial Neural Networks (ANN) to achieve complete order fulfillment and increased resource utilization in a collaborative supply chain planning problem. Naso *et al.* (2007) have proposed a hybrid meta-heuristic in which Genetic Algorithm has been used as master search algorithm that guides and modifies the operations of subordinate algorithm (a set of very fast constructive heuristics) to achieve efficient solutions in acceptable search time for an integrated production and distribution problem with strict time delivery constraints. Chang and Lee (2004) provided a detailed discussion of a two-stage (production and distribution) case in which the case of one production center and one vehicle with makespan minimization is shown to be a NP-hard problem. Additionally, the authors have proposed number of heuristics with guaranteed worst case performances. Garcia *et al.* (2002) proposes GA based approach for the coordination between production and transportation operations in multi- plant supply chain environment.

The literature review gives a clear indication of the ever growing interest in problems related to distributed production planning and scheduling. It may be worth mentioning that while the broad umbrella of distributed scheduling also covers research studies on distributed optimization e.g. Nishi & Konishi (2005), this paper is focused on multi-plant (hence distributed) environments governed by a centralized decision system. This problem is also referred to as distributed scheduling (Chan *et al.,* 2005) with reference to the fact that the assignment of jobs to alternative suitable factories must be solved before (or jointly with) the overall production scheduling. Integrated process planning and scheduling problem is a NP hard problem. In order to solve such problems in past various types of evolutionary algorithms (EAs), heuristics and Meta heuristics have been proposed. However, all those heuristics were not able to completely solve the problem efficiently in real time. In the present research integrated process planning and scheduling problem under MPSC environment has been considered which is more complex than previous scenarios. Recently Particle Swarm Optimization (PSO) algorithm has appeared to be one of the powerful tools to solve such complex problems, which could be envisaged by its implementation in health sectors, manufacturing sectors, etc.

PSO being one of the emerging computational techniques for optimality has received a lot of attention in recent years. This could be visualized both in terms of number of research output produced, as well as conferences organized on this topic in past few years, such as Congress on Evolutionary Computation (CEC) and Genetic and Evolutionary Computation Conference (GECCO), (Hu *et al.* 2004). The successful applicability of PSO ranges in a broad domain of research areas such as in artificial neural network training (Eberhart and Shi 1998b, Messerschmidt and Engelbrecht 2004), the optimal power flow (OPF) problem (Abido 2002), the task assignment problem (Salman *et al.* 2002), the unit commitment (UC) problem (Ting *et al.* 2003), quantitative structure–activity relationship (QSAR) model construction (Cedeno and Agrafiotis 2003), multiple sequence alignment (MSA) (Rasmussen and Krink 2004), multi-modal biomedical image registration (Wachowiak *et al.* 2004), multi-objective optimization (Coello *et al* 2004), electromagnetic optimizations (Robinson and Rahmat-Samii 2003, Boeringer and Werner 2004), blind source separation (BBS) (Gao and Xie 2004), protein motif discovery (Chang *et al.* 2004), etc.

The accomplishment of the PSO technique lies in its ability to produce competitive or even better results in a faster way, compared to other heuristic methods such as GA. The general applicable areas where the other evolutionary computation techniques are practiced are the good application areas for PSO (Eberhart and Shi 2004). PSO and GA have many similarities, such as both the algorithm starts with the random population generation and both of them have fitness values to evaluate the population. Also in both cases the updation process and optimality search procedure is based on the random techniques. The difference lies in the fact that PSO does not have genetic operators such as crossover and mutation. In PSO particles update themselves with the internal velocity and have memory of the previous best solution which is an important aspect of the algorithm. Several key issues related to PSO and GA has been pointed out by Rahmat-Samii (2003). The prime advantage of the PSO over the GA is its algorithmic simplicity. Both GA and PSO have several numerical parameters that need to be carefully selected. However, the robustness to control parameters makes their selection even easier for PSO (Trelea 2003). Another advantage of PSO over GA is the ability to control convergence. It has been shown that the decrease of inertial weight dramatically increases the swarm's convergence. Stagnation may occur in

GA however, in case of PSO this effect can be controlled or prevented easily, for example, by decreasing the inertial weight during the evolution process (Eberhart and Shi 1998a, Clerc and Kennedy 2002). The capability of PSO to converge towards optimality or near optimality faster makes it a preferable option as compared to GA.
However, certain limitations are as applicable to PSO, as in case of other evolutionary algorithms. To overcome these limitations many researchers have proposed numerous variants of PSO. Angeline (1998) in his study showed that though PSO converges to reasonable quality solutions much faster than other evolutionary algorithms, the quality of the solutions does not improves with the increased number of generations. Xie *et al.* (2002) proposed an opening Dissipative System (DPSO) to prevent the stagnation in PSO by introducing negative entropy through additional chaos for particles. Overshooting in PSO is an important situation that is often used to occur, which causes premature convergence and is essential for the performance of PSO. The overshooting problem affects the velocity update mechanism leading the particles to the wrong or opposite directions against the direction of the global optimum. As a consequence, the pace of convergence of the whole swarm to the global optimum slows down. In order to overcome the this Liu *et al.* (2005) proposed a novel Memetic-Particle Swarm Optimization that integrates the standard PSO with the Solis and Wets local search strategy to avoid the overshooting problem, and that is based on the recent probability of success to efficiently generate a new candidate solution around the current particle.
The present work considers the MPSC environment where it is very difficult to apply normal PSO because of its inability to handle multi-dimensional problems. The shifting trend of the industries towards the new supply chain environment prompts to develop an evolutionary algorithm that could be efficiently employed to solve the complex problems. Realizing the applicability and efficacy of PSO in solving the complex operational sequencing problems prompted us to use as a powerful tool in the present research. Hence, to overcome the difficulty/limitation of applicability of normal PSO in multi-supply chain scenario the present research attempts to propose a new type of PSO termed as Cooperative Multi plant particle Swarm Optimization (CMPSO) algorithm that could be successfully applied in case of Multi-plant supply chain problem. In order to solve Multi-dimensional problem scenario in the proposed CMPSO algorithm the sister swarms explores the search space to reach towards optimality/sub-optimal by cooperating each other.

3. Problem Formulation

Globalization, increased competence, and continuously changing business environment have driven the manufacturing industries to a new era of enhanced complexity and uncertainty. These changes have great impact on the performance of the manufacturing industries. The manufacturing entities are suffering from operational difficulties, such as due to economies of scale of production and long operational time preparation; it has been quite difficult for them to prepare the production schedule in accordance with their due dates. A schematic representation of integrated process planning and scheduling model describing its various components in a multi plant supply chain environment has been shown in Figure 1. The process planning module is responsible for the generation of an effective process plan, incorporating the features of part design specification, available machine characteristics and their mutual relationship. The scheduling module is responsible for allocating the available resources in the shop floor as well as overall management of the flow of production order and their attendant information flows (Huang *et al.*, 1995).

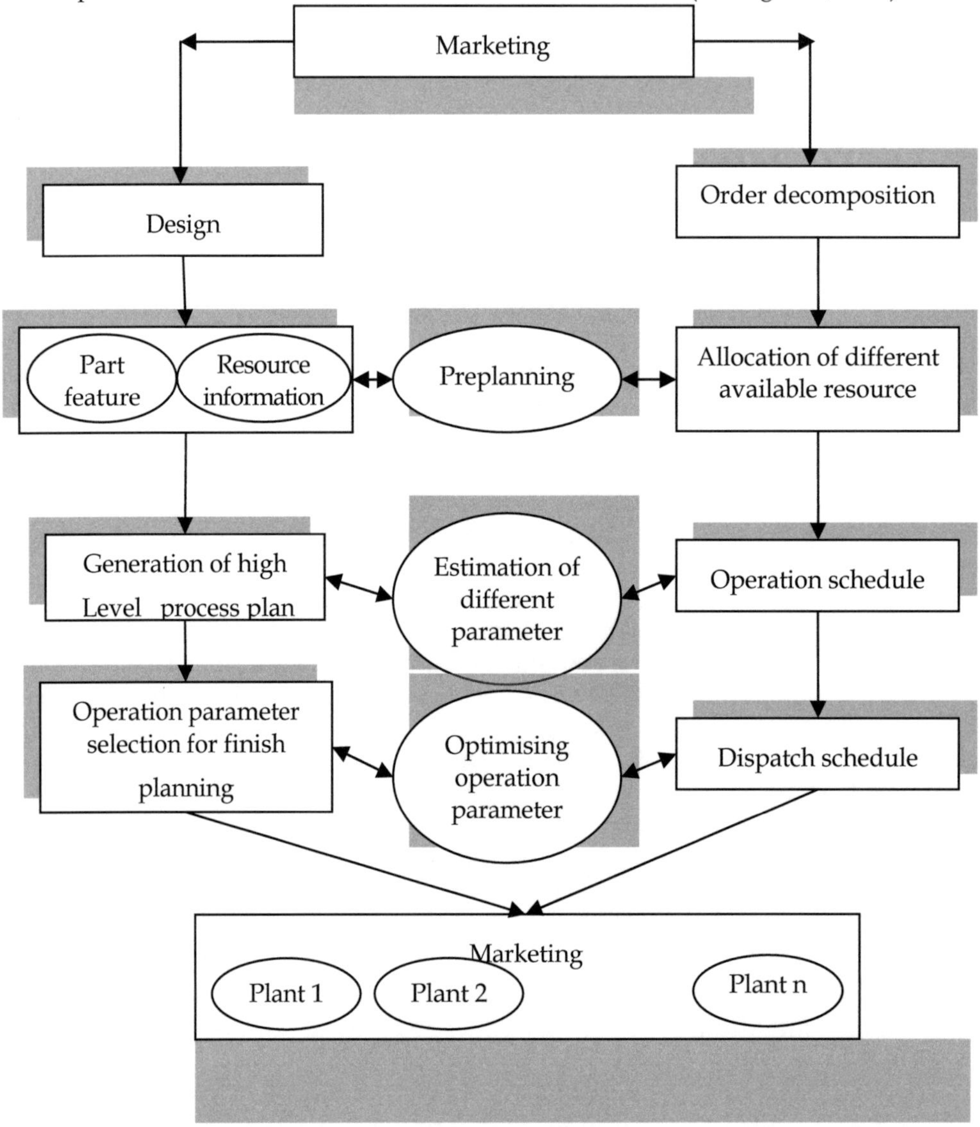

Figure 1. General architecture of integrated process planning and scheduling model

This model consists of four layers: (a) Supply (b) Fabrication (c) Assembly and (d) Customers, respectively. Out of these four layers, fabrication layer and assembly layers can be treated as directly linked to the production process which needs to be optimized. Hence, these two layers play a crucial role in the MPSC optimization. In general, MPSC industries posses the property of having multiple orders with different due dates. Under such scenario each order may have several parts with dissimilar array of operations. Some of these operations may have precedence constraints relation, whilst some others might be iterative in nature. These variations typically make the nature of Integrated Process Planning and

Scheduling a NP hard problem. The proper representation of such types of problems were proposed by, Finke *et al.*(1984) who modeled such problem state as a *Traveling Salesman Problem* (TSP) model with precedence relationships [Weiqi *et al.* (2002), Pepper *et al.* (2002)]. The travel distance between the two nodes corresponds to the transition costs between the operations. The selection of machine for each operation is not uncomplicated, because there may be numerous alternative machines for each operation. A classic selection criterion considers operational time, set up time and transportation time as decision attributes. Moreover, each TSP determines the process planning and scheduling for each part type. Accordingly, for multiple part type problems, multiple TSP has been considered. The fundamental characteristic for these types of systems are constituted by lot sizes (Nasr and Elsayed, 1990). The TSP model is based on some rules which involve transferring of the parts. In TSP environment if the transfer batch is equal to the process batch, then the part is transferred to subsequent stage after the completion of the entire batch processing, whereas if transferred batch differs from the process batch, then the part is immediately moved to the subsequent operation after the completion of current operation.

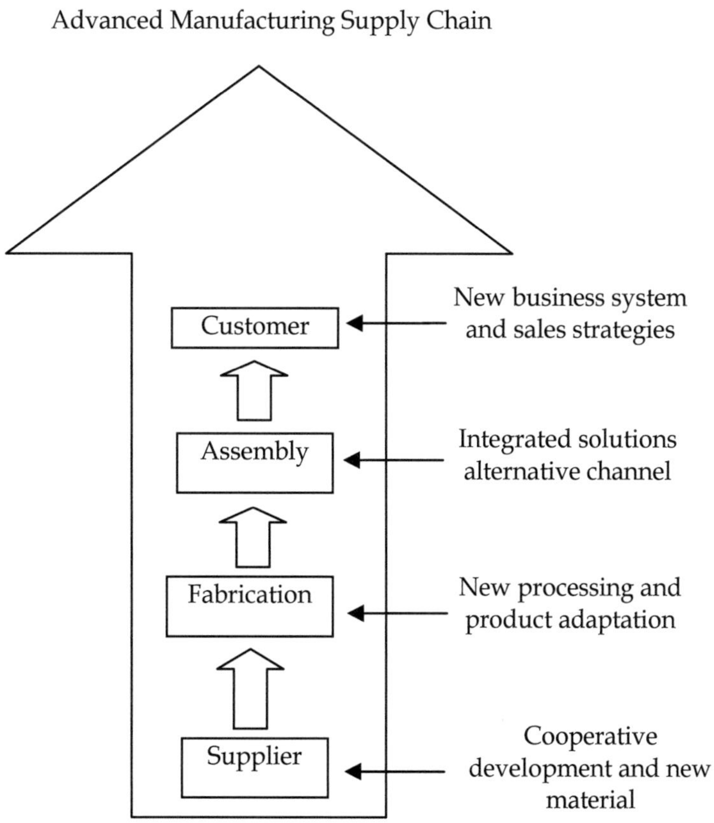

Figure 2. Schematic structure of flexible manufacturing processes

Two-commodity network flow model can be used to generate a feasible operation sequence with precedence constraints criteria in TSP problems (Kusiak and Finke, 1987). The edges of the flow network symbolize the precedence constraints. Let q and r be two distinct commodities in the network with k nodes. The selected starting node q provides k-1 units to the commodity q whereas, on the rest of the nodes, q is used by one unit each. On the other hand, r represents the commodity that utilizes $k-1$ units at the starting node and is supplied by one unit at the other nodes. Such network flows of the commodities are characterized by two properties, first the sum of the commodities q and r in any feasible tour should be equal to $k-1$ (Moon *et al.*, 2002). Also, as the tour proceeds, the quantity of commodity q or r out bonded from a node decreases. Precedence relationships of constrained TSP are modeled using these characteristics.

3.1 Operation Sequence

In this research, we develop a CMPSO algorithm with amalgamated features of directed graph and *Topological Sort* (TS) techniques to generate an optimal/nearly-optimal feasible solution. In a directed graph, vertices represent operations and edges represent precedence relations between different operations. The directed edge of the directed graph can be represented by *emi* , *emj*; where vertex *emi* must be completed before the vertex *emj*. The search algorithm is executed first to assign a fixed priority number corresponding to each vertex of the directed graph. Thereafter, TS technique is applied to generate a unique feasible operation sequence according to the assigned priority numbers. Directed graph of a manufacturing process carried out in the two plants is illustrated in the Figure 3.

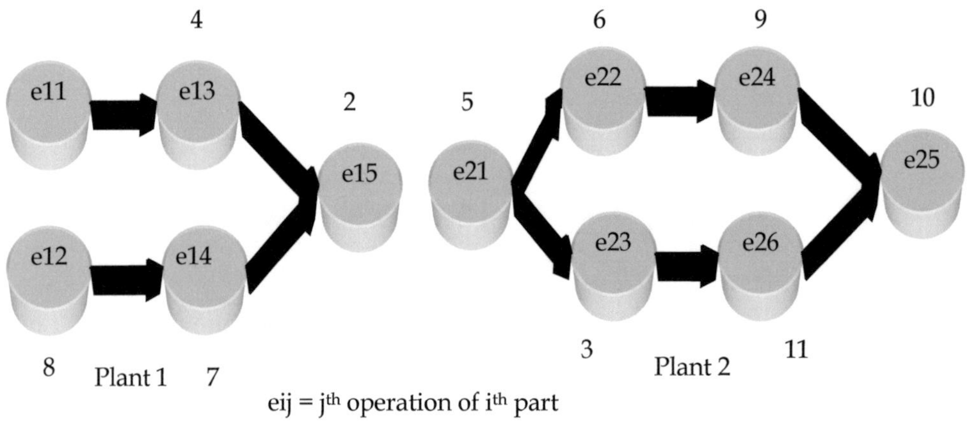

Figure 3. Directed graph of a manufacturing process with precedence relationship

The vertex *e11* is selected as first operation because it has no precedence edge and has higher priority number as compared to vertex *e12* and *e13*. Select vertex *e11* as the first operation and remove the edges connecting to the vertex *e11-e13*. This procedure is repeated until all the vertices are selected. Finally, a feasible path {*e11, e13, e21, e23, e22, e12,,e14, e15, e24, ,e26, e25* } is uniquely obtained. Therefore, operation sequence for each part types may be written as follows.

Part1 = { *e11,e13,e12,e14,e15*}, Part2 = { *e21,e23,e22,e24,e26* , *e25*}.

3.2 Objective Function

The main objective considered in the proposed research involves the generation of a feasible optimal/near optimal operational sequence with minimum tardiness. The solution generated by the proposed CMPSO algorithm is also subjected to satisfy all the constraints and decision variables imposed by the considered manufacturing scenario. The mathematical formulations of the objective function including the various constraints, and decision variables have been explained below. The notations used in the equations have been explained in the Appendix A attached at the end of the chapter.

Decision Variables:

$$\phi_{pij} = \begin{cases} 1; \textit{if operation of part type is performed immediately after the completion of opertation j} \\ 0; \textit{otherwise} \end{cases}$$

$$\phi_{pij} = \begin{cases} 1; \textit{if machine m is selected for operation i of the part type} \\ 0; \textit{otherwise} \end{cases}$$

$$\phi_{pij} = \begin{cases} 1; \textit{if operation i precedes opertation j on the machine m} \\ 0; \textit{otherwise} \end{cases} \qquad \forall [i, j] \in \beta_m, m = 1,2,3,...M$$

Constraints:

C_1: Commodity feasibility constraints:

Between the operations w_{pi} to w_{pj} commodity q of the part type p is feasible if it satisfied the following constraints.

$$\sum_{j=1}^{J_p} \phi_{pij}^q - \sum_{j=1}^{J_p} \phi_{pji}^q = \begin{cases} J_p - 1, & \text{for } i = \eta_p \\ -1, & \text{otherwise} \end{cases} \qquad \forall \text{ P} \tag{1}$$

$$\phi_{pij}^q , \phi_{pji}^q \geq 0 \ \forall \text{ p, i, j} \tag{2}$$

Similarly between the operations w_{pi} to w_{pj} commodity r is feasible if it satisfied the following constraints.

$$\sum_{j=1}^{J_p} \phi_{pij}^r - \sum_{j=1}^{J_p} \phi_{pji}^r = \begin{cases} -(J_p - 1), & \text{for } i = \eta_p \\ -1, & \text{otherwise} \end{cases} \qquad \forall \text{ P} \tag{3}$$

$$\phi_{pij}^r , \phi_{pji}^r \geq 0 \ \forall \text{ p, i, j} \tag{4}$$

C_2 Precedence constraints:

Precedence relations between operations are feasible if the difference between sum of the commodity q from operation $w_{p\alpha}$ to w_{pj} and from operation $w_{p\beta}$ to w_{pj} for all the part type p is greater then or equal to 1.

$$\sum_{j=1}^{J_p} \phi_{p\alpha j}^q - \sum_{j=1}^{J_p} \phi_{p\beta j}^q = \sum_{j=1}^{J} \phi_{\beta j}^q \geq 1, \qquad \forall \text{ P and } (w_{p\alpha} \to w_{p\beta})(w_{p\beta} \neq \eta_p) \tag{5}$$

C_3: Sum of commodity constraints:

For a feasible operation sequence sum of commodities q and r between the operation w_{pi} and w_{pj} is equal to J_p-1..

$$\phi_{pij}^q + \phi_{pij}^r = (J_p - 1)\phi_{pij} \qquad \forall \text{ p, i and j.} \tag{6}$$

C_4: Machine Constraints:
This constraint implies that machine will start a new operation only after completing the previous operation. This constraint can be express as:

$$\xi_{hjm} - \xi_{pim} + \theta(1 - \gamma_{ijm}) \geq \mu_{pjm} \tag{7}$$

Where θ is a very large positive number
C_5: Operational time constraints:
The completion time of each operation should always be positive or zero.

$$\xi_{pim} \geq 0 \tag{8}$$

C_6: Feasibility of tour constraints:
Operation sequence of the part type p is feasible if sum of commodities q and r is equal to J_p-1.

$$\sum_{j=1}^{J_P}\left(\phi^q_{pij} + \phi^r_{pij}\right) = J_p - 1 \qquad \forall \text{p and i,} \tag{9}$$

Objective Function:

The number of transportation from the operation w_{pi} to w_{pj} for the part type p having lot size of production r_p is

$$\hbar_{pij} = \left[\frac{1_p}{\alpha_{pij}}\right] \tag{10}$$

Symbol $[\ ]$ represents the greatest integer function.
The transition time from operation i performed on the machine m to operation j performed on the machine n of the part type p can be expressed as follows

$$t_{pij} = \{r_p\ \mu_{pim}\ \varphi_{pim} + \hbar_{pij}\ \upsilon_{mn}\ \varphi_{pim}\ \varphi_{pjn} + \delta_{pij}\ \phi_{pij}\} \tag{11}$$

Total transition time for all the part types in 0-1 integer programming model is given by

$$T = \sum_{p=1}^{P}\sum_{j=1}^{J_p}\sum_{i=1}^{I_p}\sum_{m=1}^{M}\sum_{n=1}^{N}\frac{1}{J_p - 1} t_{pij}\left(\varphi^q_{pij} + \varphi^r_{pij}\right) \tag{12}$$

Subjected to

$$\sum_{m=1}^{M}\varphi_{pim} = 1 \qquad \forall\ p\ and\ i \tag{13}$$

And

$$\varphi_{pim} \in \{0,1\} \qquad \forall_p, i\ and\ m \tag{14}$$

For part type p tardiness of an order Ω_p is the amount of time by which the completion time of it exceeds from its due date. It can be express as

$$\Omega_p = \max\begin{cases} C_p - du_p \\ 0 \end{cases} \tag{15}$$

Total tardiness of all the part type of an order Ω is

$$\Omega = \sum_{p=1}^{P} \Omega_p \tag{16}$$

The overall objective of integrated process planning and scheduling is to minimize the total tardiness of all the part type of an order.

$$\min imize \sum_{p=1}^{P} \Omega_p \tag{17}$$

It is possible only if total transition time T for all the part type is minimum that is

$$Minimize \sum_{p=1}^{P} \sum_{j=1}^{J_p} \sum_{i=1}^{I_p} \sum_{m=1}^{M} \sum_{n=1}^{N} \frac{1}{J_p - 1} t_{pij} \left(\varphi_{pij}^{q} + \varphi_{pij}^{r}\right) \quad i \neq j \tag{18}$$

Where,

$$t_{pij} = \{r_p \, \mu_{pim} \, \varphi_{pim} + \hbar_{pij} \, \upsilon_{mn} \, \varphi_{pim} \, \varphi_{pjn} + \delta_{pij} \, \phi_{pij}\} \tag{19}$$

The next section gives an insight on the PSO algorithm further expalining the necessity to propose the CMPSO algorithm to find the optimal/sub-optimal solution of the abovementioned objective funtion. The section also breifly explains the steps of the proposed algorithm, a hybrid chaotic sequencing, and a case study.

4. Particle Swarm Optimization (PSO)

The inclination of the researchers towards the implementation of the biologically inspired algorithms in solving the engineering problems have led to the invention of many algorithms such as Genetic Algorithm, Ant colony optimization, Artificial Immune System based algorithms etc. Particle swarm optimization (PSO) is one of the biologically inspired evolutionary algorithms which drive the idea from the flocking of birds. Abundant examples could be extracted from the nature that demonstrates that social sharing of information among the individuals of a population may provide an evolutionary advantage. PSO was first proposed by Kennedy and Eberhart (1995) and it has been deserved considerable attention in recent years in the global optimization areas. PSO originally intends to graphically mimic the elegant way in which swarms find their food sources and save themselves from predators (Eberhart and Kennedy 1995). It is a population-based stochastic optimization paradigm, in which each individual termed as *particle* from the population of *swarm* changes their position with time and represent a potential solution. PSO in some ways resembles with the other existing Evolutionary Algorithms, such as Genetic Algorithm, but the difference lies in its definition in a social context rather than biological context. According to Eberhart and Shi (2001) PSO is based on simple concepts with the ease of implementation and computational efficacy.

Particle Swarm Optimization (PSO) algorithm motivated by the flocking of the birds works on the social behavioral interaction among the particles in the swarm. It begins with the random initialization of a population of particles in the search space. These particles are considered to be in multidimensional space (*D*-dimensional) where each particle has a position and velocity. These two factors i.e. the position and velocity demonstrates the particles status in the search space. Hence in a PSO system, particles fly/move around in multi directions in the search space, and the position of each particle is guided accordingly by the memory of their own best position, as well as of a neighbouring particle. These particles communicate the best positions to each other and adjust their own position and velocity accordingly. Parsopoulos and Vrahatis (2002) proposed basically two main variants of the PSO algorithm:

- Global neighhborhood, where best global position is communicated to all partilces and updated immeditely in the swarm
- Local neighborhood, where each particle moves towards its best previous position and towards the best particle in its restricted neighborhood.

In the proposed work the global variant has been adapted. The reason behind opting for the global neighborhood is due to the fact that local neighborhood even though allows better exploration of the search space and reduces the susceptibility of PSO to falling into local minima; it slows down the convergence speed. The position and velocity vectors of the *i*th particle can be represented as

$$xi = (xi1, xi2, \ldots, xiD) \tag{20}$$

$$pi = (pi1, pi2, \ldots, piD) \tag{21}$$

The fittest particle among all the particles in the population is represented by

$$F = (f1, f2, fD) \tag{22}$$

The velocity vector for the *i*th particle can be represented as

$$Vi = (vi1, vi2, \ldots viD) \tag{23}$$

The updated velocity and position for the next fitness evaluation of each particle could be determined according to the following equations:

$$\upsilon_{id}^{k+1} = \omega \bullet \upsilon_{id}^{k} + c_1 \bullet R_1() \bullet \left(p_{id}^{k} - x_{id}^{k}\right) + c_2 \bullet R_2() \bullet \left(f_d^{k} - x_{id}^{k}\right) \tag{24}$$

$$x_{id}^{k+1} = x_{id}^{k} + \upsilon_{id}^{k+1} \tag{25}$$

Here k is the iteration number, $d = 1, 2. \ldots D$; $i = 1, 2. \ldots N$, and N is the size of the population (swarm). $c1$ and $c2$ are two positive values called acceleration constants, $R_1(\,)$ and $R_2(\,)$ are two independent random numbers that uniformly distribute between 0 and 1 and are used to stochastically vary the relative pull of *pi* and *f* (Clerc andKennedy 2002). The introduction of such random elements into the optimization is intended to simulate the slightly unpredictable component of natural swarm behavior. 'ω' is the inertial weight introduced by Shi and Eberhart (1998b) in order to improve the performance of the particle swarm optimizer.

The equation (24) contains the three terms on the right hand side in which the inertial effects of the movement is represented by the first term. The memory of the individual and whole is referred by second and third terms respectively. Basically, equation (24) is used to calculate the particle's new velocity which depends on its preceding velocity and the distances of its present position from both its own best past position and the group's best past position. All the other particles follow the best position found and moves closer to it, exploring the region more thoroughly in the process. According to Robinson and Rahmat-Samii (2004) equation (24) is the central constituent of the entire optimization. The stochastic tendency to return towards particle's preceding best position is represented by the second term of the equation (24). The third term in equation (24) is referred as *social influence* term. The variable *F* keeps moving towards the best solution i.e. optimal solution found by the neighbor particles in the search space. Particle farther from the global best is more strongly pulled from its location, and moves rapidly than a closer particle. The particles velocity comes to halt after it reaches the locations of best fitness. This is the point from where the particles are pulled back in the opposite direction. The performances of the individual particles are evaluated by a predefined fitness function dependent on the problem during the evolution of the swarm. In case of maximization of the fitness function Fitness *(xi)*, the individual best position of each particle *pi* and the global best position *f* are updated after each iteration using the following two equations, respectively:

$$p_i^{k+1} = \begin{cases} x_i^{k+1} & : Fit(x_i^{k+1}) > Fit(p_i^{k+1}) \\ p_i^k & : Fit(x_i^{k+1}) \leq Fit(p_i^{k+1}) \end{cases} \quad (26)$$

$$F^{k+1} = \arg\max Fit(p_i^{k+1}) \quad (27)$$

Where 'Fit' refers to the fitness value for the respective iteration.

4.1 CMPSO Algorithm & its implementation

This section describes the formulations of the CMPSO algorithm for the process planning and scheduling in multi plant supply chain scenario. The prime objective of the problem considered is to generate an operation sequence and simultaneously select an appropriate machine corresponding to each operation from existing alternatives. It is a multiple dimensional problem as shown in the Figure 4. In the figure, first row represents an operation sequence while the second row represents the machine corresponding to each operation. In order to resolve the complexity of the problem in this piece of research CMPSO algorithm has been proposed. One of the key issues in successful implementation of PSO to a specified engineering problem is the representation scheme, i.e. finding a suitable mapping between the problem solution and the PSO particle. In the proposed methodology during the exploration of the search space the sister swarms cooperate with each other.

4	7	9	2	1	5	3	6	8	1
2	3	1	2	2	4	3	2	1	2

Figure 4. Systematic representation of solution

In this paper each bit of solution are positive integers and comprises a non-continuous integer search space. Since the original PSO works on a real-valued search space, especially on the particle positions (i.e., the operation sequence and corresponding machine in this paper) is calculated using equation (25) which are real numbers. Hence, a conversion is needed between the real-valued positions and the positive-integer-valued indices. In order to meet the criteria the sign is ignored and value is changed to the closest integer. After calcualting the x_{id}^{k+1} term in equation (25) the changes mentioned earlier are applied leaving the rest part of the equations (24) and (25) same as in the original PSO. These changes does not have any affect on the performance of the algorithm and has been proven to be feasible (Salman *et al.* 2002, Laskari *et al.* 2002, Parsopoulos and Vrahatis 2002).

The individuals in the swarm are initialized by randomly setting their positions and velocities using operation sequence or machine depending on the nature of the swarm. During the iteration, reset is performed only when the value of a new position component calculated from equation (25) is greater than the upper limitation of the search space. It should be noted that, in the first row at any time of the operation process two bits cannot have the same values. Hence, if a new component value is calculated using equation (25) (for first row) that already exists, a random small integer will be added to this value till no collision exists. This combination pfacilitates fast convergence and ensures near-optimal solutions by establishing a proper balance between exploration and exploitation. In case of simple PSO in equation (24) random numbers were genrated using the Randon function. Howver, during experimentation it has been found that random function are associated with some demerits. Hence, in order to overcome the demerits of the random number in this research not only it is being replaced by chaotic sequences, but also a new hybrid chaotic sequence has been proposed.

This paragraph explains the significance of applying a chaotic sequence generator to update the velocity instead of the random number generator. The random function used in equation (24) has been replaced with a chaotic function because of the ergodic and stochastic properties of the chaotic systems. One of the limitations coupled with the random number generators is that the solution becomes conserved by sequential correlation of successive cells; hence requiring more number of generations to converge towards an optimal or near-optimal solution. Also the commonly used random number generators have a tendency to generate the higher-order part more randomly than their lower-order counterpart (Caponetto *et al.*, 2003). Therefore, it requires a consistent random number generator which can explore search space without being biased. Recently, various chaotic sequences have been applied in areas related to secure transmission, neural networks, natural phenomena modelling, deoxyribonucleic acid computing procedures, and non-linear circuits (Arena *et al.*, (2000), Determan and Foster (1999), Manganaro and Pineda (1997), Sugantahn (1999), Nozawa (1992), and Wang and Smith (1998)) and encouraging results have been obtained with random number generators. The unpredictability characteristics, i.e. spread spectrum characteristics, justify theoretically the use of a chaotic sequence. Thus, the recent research drift towards the implementation of chaotic sequence generators in various AI tools motivated us to use in the present problem scenario. The commonly used chaotic equations by researchers are Logistic map-based chaos equation (LM), Tent map-based chaos equation (TM), Sinusoidal integrator-based chaos equation (SI), and Gauss map-based chaos equation (GM). As usual each equation has some advantage and some disadvantage and in order to overcome the demerit of each chaotic equation in this present research a hybrid chaotic equation termed as Chaotic Sequence-based Hybrid chaos equation (HC) has been proposed. The proposed chaotic equation incorporates the advantages of each chaotic equations mentioned below;

(A) Logistic map-based chaos equation (LM): In this method logistic map-based chaotic sequence is used to generate random numbers. It is one of the simplest dynamic systems evidencing chaotic behavior. The logistic map chaotic equation is delineated as follows.

$$Y_{k+1} = \omega Y_k (1 - Y_k) \tag{28}$$

Where ω is tuning parameter

(B) Tent map-based chaos equation (TM): In this method, random numbers are generated using Tent map-based chaotic sequence. It resemble as the logistic map which follows the following equations.

$$Y_{k+1} = \mu_k (Y_k) \tag{29}$$

$$\mu(Y_k) = \begin{cases} \dfrac{Y_k}{0.7}, & \text{if } Y_k < 0.7 \\ \dfrac{1}{0.3} Y_k (1 - Y_k), & \text{Otherwise} \end{cases} \tag{30}$$

(C) Sinusoidal integrator-based chaos equation (SI): In this chaotic equation, random numbers are generated using the following Sinusoidal Integrator relation:

$$Y_{k+1} = \sin(\pi Y_k) \tag{31}$$

(D) Gauss map-based chaotic equation(GM): In this chaotic equation, Gauss Map function is used to generate the random numbers and it transfers from one stage to another stage in a quadratic manner. Gauss Map function can be expressed as follows:

$$Y_{k+1} = \mu_k (Y_k) \tag{32}$$

$$\mu(Y_k) = \begin{cases} 0, & \text{if } Y_k = 0 \\ \dfrac{1}{Y_k} \bmod 1, & Y_k \in (0,1) \end{cases} \tag{33}$$

(F) Chaotic sequence-based hybrid chaotic equation (HC): Randomly select a chaotic sequence strategy among aforementioned four strategies and generate random number using selected chaotic equation.

As mentioned earlier first row of each solution represents the operation sequence and second row represents the corresponding machine. For each individual row the proposed CMPSO algorithm runs separately. After updating the position and velocity for each row the sister swarm will cooperate with each other to evaluate the fitness function. On the basis of the computed fitness value the global and local best positions are decided. And after certain number of iterations the solution will tend to converge towards the optimality or sub-optimality. The stpes of the proposed CMPSO algorithm are shown below:

Step 1: Generate discrete search space for first and second row of solution i.e. maximum numbers of operation and number of possible machine corresponding to each option.

Step 2: Generate random initial solution, and assign random position X and velocity V vectors corresponding to each particle swarm (For both sister swarms) and assign number of generation (num_gen=1)

Step 3: Calculate the fitness value by the help of sister swarm and update the personal best position and global best position of each of sister swarm using equation (26) and (27) respectively.

Step 4: Update the velocity and position of the each swarm using the chaotic sequence mentioned above.

Step 5: num_gen=num_gen+1;

Step 6: If num_gen=max num_gen; go to step 7 otherwise go to step 3

Step7: Terminate the algorithm and global position is the optimal solution obtained by the algorithm.

Corresponding to the global best solution the optimal sequence and the corresponding machines are decided. A case study has been discussed in the next section.

5. Case Study

A case study has been taken from Moon *et al.* (2002) in this present work to reveal the efficacy and robustness of the proposed model, and to disclose the quality of the solutions found with the CMPSO. The case study involves an illustrative example which has been derived considering a constrained integrated process planning and scheduling problem. The case study involves three coupled decision problems i.e. selection of parts, priority of operation sequences and selection of appropriate machine for each operation to minimize the total tardiness in context of Advanced Integrated Process Planning and Scheduling (AIPPS) model. To make the case study more realistic additionally, various system constraints (precedence, commodity feasibility, sum of commodity, machine, operational time, and feasibility of tour constraints) have been considered. In the present case study the process planning and scheduling has been carried out simultaneously. The study also involves consideration of set up times between the operations, and transportation times between machines, thus closely resembling to the typical characteristics of industrial contexts. The case study consists of 5 different parts with different due dates {d1=1000, d2=1300, d3=2000, d4=1600, d5=1400}. These parts are manufactured in two plants (plant 1 and plant 2) having six different machine. Plant 1 consists of machines {M1, M2, M3} and plant 2 consists of machines {M4, M5, M6}. The production lot size for the each part type is considered {40, 70, 60, 30, 60} respectively. Also, the transportation time between plants is assumed to be 50, and unit size is considered equal to the lot size of each part. The remaining data needed in the problem such as initial load, transportation time, and set up time between alternative machines etc., are shown in Table 1-3, whereas the operation and there precedence constraints relation are shown in Figure 5.

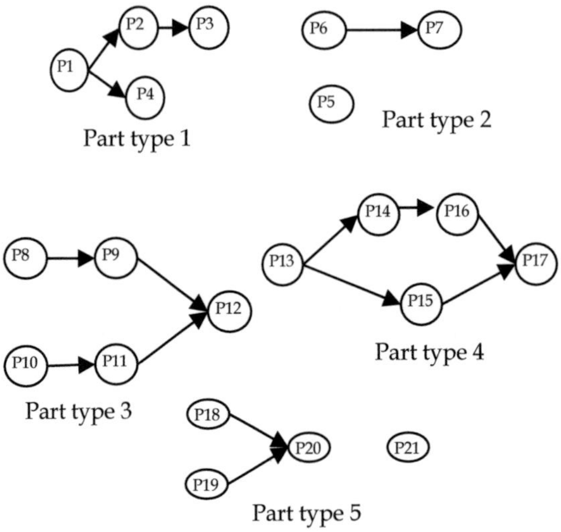

Figure 5. Precedence Relationship between different Operations

Operations performed in different plants	Operation performed in different plants																				
	1	2	3	4	5	6	7	8	9	10	11	12	13	14	15	16	17	18	19	20	21
01	00	35	46	39	28	32	20	16	12	39	40	23	49	08	26	20	47	14	03	36	40
02	39	00	36	23	47	33	46	36	06	08	34	02	48	15	12	04	12	24	30	44	34
03	15	08	00	27	21	34	33	25	33	13	49	08	35	40	26	32	46	28	14	41	26
04	13	38	19	00	01	44	14	27	48	36	38	35	37	39	14	32	22	10	26	25	29
05	34	48	24	10	00	36	12	48	09	24	28	19	08	36	17	06	28	06	22	22	45
06	05	18	30	12	01	00	12	32	00	39	12	18	19	19	05	27	42	37	16	24	31
07	28	37	48	15	17	13	00	44	38	15	09	01	05	36	02	20	17	15	06	10	34
08	17	15	00	42	41	13	17	00	30	22	33	25	02	33	26	35	41	35	04	09	22
09	37	10	41	27	35	46	30	16	00	35	33	15	28	06	08	30	22	25	39	10	36
10	06	05	49	47	00	01	18	37	06	00	44	30	23	07	04	02	04	30	03	16	19
11	44	30	21	11	46	15	30	17	46	14	00	44	06	04	06	14	48	29	27	29	15
12	34	25	34	04	10	14	27	07	26	49	13	00	40	20	15	15	49	07	28	43	47
13	09	09	04	42	01	36	21	15	36	27	20	11	00	33	41	46	02	33	44	02	07
14	29	29	29	24	47	28	28	30	46	23	26	20	49	00	39	24	33	26	06	29	36
15	07	19	10	14	17	44	27	13	10	14	09	17	48	15	00	28	17	46	45	21	36
16	31	01	37	03	21	09	23	46	13	41	21	47	15	16	43	00	18	03	24	27	11
17	29	39	03	30	48	39	02	45	03	39	36	26	28	23	40	29	00	32	17	38	23
18	02	13	10	09	32	14	45	11	24	43	15	02	16	06	32	15	30	00	15	37	38
19	09	20	35	08	18	48	27	12	41	30	47	16	02	41	13	29	23	07	00	08	08
20	27	49	40	29	09	36	29	12	24	45	30	10	16	34	05	06	08	33	38	00	31
21	27	04	34	31	29	03	32	47	12	09	44	30	42	21	25	02	40	26	26	25	00

Table 1. Set up time between different operations

To further prove the efficacy of the proposed CMPSO algorithm, it has been tested on several randomly generated data set problems with increasing complexity as shown in the Table 4.

6. Result & Discussion

It has been concluded after comprehensive survey of research contributions in the broad domain of PSO application that number of iterations required to achieve optimal/near optimal solution is relatively high. Therefore, it is not only desirable but also inevitable to develop a meta-heuristic, which can overcome the drawbacks associated with simple PSO, and can solve large size combinatorial problems in lesser number of iterations and CPU time. The incapability associated with simple PSO algorithm in solving multidimensional problem prompted to develop an evolutionary meta-heuristic termed as CMPSO algorithm. The CMPSO algorithm has been proposed to solve Multi plant supply chain problem in the distributed manufacturing environments.

CMPSO algorithm achieves the optimal/near optimal solutions for the objective considered (Tardiness minimization) and emphasizes it as a powerful meta-heuristic algorithm. Use of hybrid chaotic sequence function empowers the algorithm to obtain optimal/near optimal results in significantly less number of generations. These features of the algorithm make it more effective as compared to simple PSO algorithm. Performance of the proposed CMPSO algorithm is found superior, when compared with GA and Tabu Search, on a set of problems adopted from the literature. For the case study mentioned in section 5, total tardiness obtained in 35 iterations is 32. The optimal operation sequence obtained by CMPSO algorithm is shown in Table 5. Table 6 presents a comparative analysis of proposed approach with others. Figure 6, shows a convergence trend of CMPSO algorithm along with number of generations. It is evident from the Table 6 that proposed approach outperformed the results obtained using existing methodologies. The operation sequence generated by Genetic Algorithm (Li *et al.*, 2005) shows total tardiness to be 39 in 42 generations.

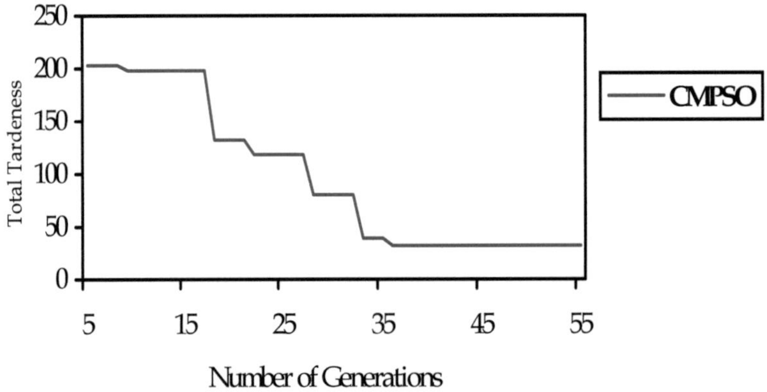

Figure 6. Convergence trend of CMPSO with number of generations

Various chaotic sequence operators that are used in literature were tested on sample problem and found that hybrid chaotic sequence based particle swarm optimization outperforms other PSOs. Their comparative results are shown in Figure 7. To have a better appraisal of the algorithm performance, a new parameter 'percentage Heuristic Gap (PHG)' (Huang et al. (2002)) has been utilized. Percentage heuristic gap can be mathematically defined as:

$$PHG = \frac{Best\ uppper\ bound - Best\ lower\ bound}{Best\ lower\ bound} \times 100 \qquad (34)$$

Here, lower bound is defined as the objective value obtained by relaxing some of the bounds or constraints pertaining to the problem environment, whereas upper bound is the objective function value of the feasible solution that fulfils all the constraints. In our case, one of the precedence constraints has been relaxed to obtain the lower bound. From the definition of PHG, it can be envisaged that the near optimal solution of the problem is guaranteed if its value is very small (Huang *et al.* (2002)) as shown in Figure 8. PHG for the test problems defined in the table 4 are shown in table 7-10. While average value of PHG for different size of data sets are shown in Table 11 which are less than 3%. Thus, from the definition of heuristic gap, it is inferred that solution obtained by CMPSO algorithm is near optimal one. A two way ANOVA without replication was also performed to assess the significance of the problem parameters. The results of the ANOVA test are in listed the Table 12-13. The results obtained by ANOVA test, performed at 99.5 % confidence level, validates the robustness of the CMPSO algorithm pertaining to MPSC problems.

The CMPSO algorithm has been coded in C++ programming language and experiments have been carried out on an Intel Pentium IV 2.4 GHz processor. In the nutshell, aforementioned computational results not only authenticate the efficacy and supremacy of the proposed algorithm, but also provide new dimensions to the solution of complex combinatorial problems like integrated process planning and scheduling problem in MPSC environment.

Plant	-	1	1	1	2	2	2
part	Operation	M1	M2	M3	M4	M5	M6
1	1	7	-	-	5	-	-
1	2	7	-	-	6	-	-
1	3	-	6	5	-	8	-
1	4	6	-	-	-	-	5
2	5	-	9	-	8	-	-
2	6	3	5	-	-	6	-
2	7	8	-	12	9	-	8
3	8	-	-	5	-	8	-
3	9	10	-	-	10	-	7
3	10	6	5	-	-	6	-
3	11	15	-	-	6	-	5
3	12	-	6	-	-	5	-
4	13	-	-	6	6	-	8
4	14	-	5	-	-	9	-
4	15	-	-	6	4	-	-
5	18	-	8	-	6	-	8
5	19	-	7	10	-	8	-
5	20	13	-	-	-	8	9
5	21	-	-	7	6	-	-

Where M1, M2, M3, M4, M5, M6 are different machines in plant 1 and 2.

Table 2. Machining time for different operation and alternative available

7. Conclusions

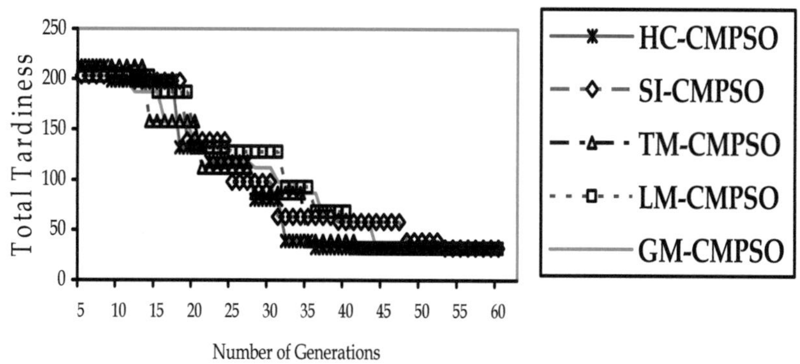

Figure 7. Comparative plot of CMPSO based on different chaotic equations

The efficient process planning and scheduling in multi-plant supply chain environment is gaining prime importance these days. Especially the manufacturing units are keen on finding efficient ways of handling such problems. This popularity and interest motivated our present research to build a realistic MPSC model and emphasize on its proper scheduling aiming to reduce the overall tardiness. Recognizing the fact that MPSC problem is a NP hard problem and quite complex to be solved by most of the existing evolutionary algorithms (EAs), this paper also proposes a new Cooperative Multiple Particle Swarm Optimization (CMPSO) algorithm to overcome the drawbacks of existing EAs. The prime objective considered in this paper was to reduce the overall tardiness considering several constraints, selection criteria's, decision variables and operational sequences. To build the model more close to realistic situation the setup time and transportation time has also been considered during problem formulation. The limitations associated with normal PSO while its application in multi plant situation was overcome by the newly proposed CMPSO algorithm. The comparative analysis of the CMPSO algorithm with other existing EAs shows its superiority over others. The CMPSO algorithm has also been statistically validated by performing ANOVA and Percentage heuristic gap analysis. The comparative analysis reveals that CMPSO algorithm not only does performs well to converge towards optimality/sub-optimality, the computational time required is also relatively less as compared to others. The paper also attempts to overcome the demerit of the normal PSO regarding the random number generators by using the newly proposed chaotic function instead.

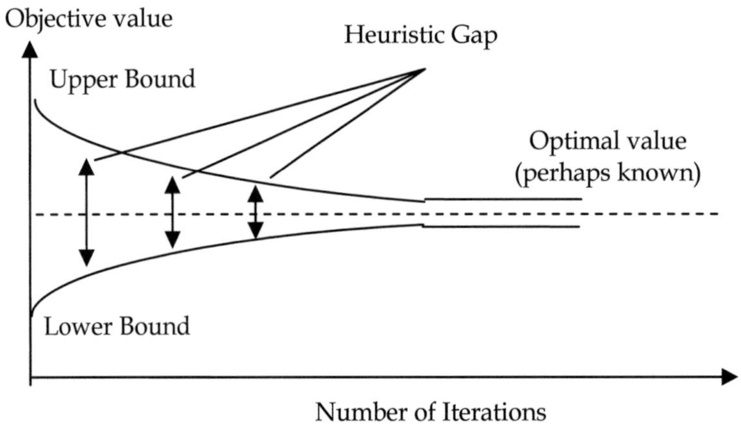

Figure 8. Heuristic gaps as a function of number of iterations

		Plant 1			Plant2		
	Machine	M1	M2	M3	M4	M5	M6
Plant 1	M1	0	5	6	-	-	-
	M2	5	0	7	-	-	-
	M3	6	7	0	-	-	-
Plant 2	M4	-	-	-	0	5	6
	M5	-	-	-	5	0	7
	M6	-	-	-	6	7	0

Table 3. Transportation times between machines

Though, CMPSO algorithm possesses many advantages over the traditional PSO and other existing evolutionary algorithms it has plenty of scope for its future extension. Future research can be directed towards its implementation in diverse areas of manufacturing fields. CMPSO algorithm also needs to be tested on multi-objective problems under various constraints, decision variables etc. to disclose its capability of handling diverse complex problems. The proposed algorithm has promising aspects that deserve further investigations; therefore work also needs to be focussed on further improving its efficacy and robustness.

Classification	Number of jobs	Number of operations
Very Small problem (VSP)	3	10-20
	12	20-30
Small Problem (SP)	15	30-40
	20	40-50
Large Problem (LP)	22	50-60
	25	60-70
Very Large Problem (VLP)	28	70-80
	35	80-90

Table 4. Detailed randomly generated data sets

		Operation		Operation		Operation		Operation	
Plant	Machine	start time	end time	start time	end time	start time	end time	start time	end time
	M1	10		7		17			
1			709	727	1287	1413	1563		
	M2	6		3		14		16	
		100	450	775	1015	1062	1212	1243	1393
	M3	8		13		21			15
		250	550	552	732	782	1202	1227	1407
	M4		1	2		5			
2		250	450	485	725	772	1332		
	M5		19	20			12		
		187	667	675	1155	1357	1657		
	M6	18		4		9		11	
		100	580	589	789	839	1257	1290	1590

Table 5. Final operations schedules of the Case Study using CMPSO

Total Tardiness	Using GA (Moon *et al.* 2002)	Using Tabu Search (Moon *et al.* 2002)	CMPSO Algorithm
Total Tardiness	39	39	32
Number of generations	42	>>GA	35
CPU Time	7 sec	48 sec	4 sec

Table 6. Comparative Result of the proposed CMPSO algorithm

Number of Jobs	Number of operations	% Heuristic gap (HG)
3	10	1.382
3	15	2.052
12	20	1.678
12	25	2.236

Table 7. Computational results for very small sized problem

Number of Jobs	Number of operations	% Heuristic gap (HG)
15	30	1.302
15	35	1.524
20	40	2.134
20	45	1.182

Table 8. Computational results for small sized problem

Number of Jobs	Number of operations	% Heuristic gap (HG)
22	50	2.167
22	55	2.005
25	60	2.761
25	65	1.755

Table 9. Computational results for largel sized problem

Number of Jobs	Number of operations	% Heuristic gap (HG)
28	70	1.854
28	75	2.530
35	80	2.345
35	85	2.449

Table 10. Computational results for very large sized problem

	L	H	Average
VSP	1.717	1.957	1.837
SP	1.413	1.658	1.6005
LP	2.087	2.258	2.1675
VLP	2.192	2.397	2.2943

L : Average *PHP* values for the smaller number of customers in the respective categories.
H : Average *PHP* values for the larger number of customers in the respective categories.
Table 11. Average heuristic gap for different problem sizes

SUMMARY	Row 1	Row 2	Row 3	Row 4	Column 1	Column 2
Count	2	2	2	2	4	4
Sum	3.674	3.071	4.345	4.589	7.409	8.27
Average	1.837	1.5355	2.1725	2.2945	1.85225	2.0675
Variance	0.0288	0.030013	0.01462	0.021012	0.127257	0.108254

Table 12. Intermediate values of the two way ANOVA test without replication

Source of Variation	Rows	Columns	Error	Total
SS	0.704751	0.092665	0.00178	0.799197
Df	3	1	3	7
MS	0.234917	0.092665	0.000593	
F	395.8443	156.1443		
P-value	0.000215	0.001105		
F crit*	47.46835	55.55194		
* α =0.005				

Table 13. Results of ANOVA test

Appendix A: List of notations used in the Mathematical Formulation

C_P	:	Completion time of the part type *p*.
du_p	:	Due date of the part type *p*.
$\hbar_{pij}$	:	Number of transportation from the operation w_{pi} to w_{pj} of the part type *p*.
IML_m	:	Initial mean load on the machines *m*
J_P	:	Total number of operations of part type p.
M	:	Set of different machines, $M=\{1,2,\ldots,\ldots,m,\ldots M\}$
$MT_{K,J}$	:	Machining time for k th operation corresponding to the machine assign in the i th male chromosome.
$MT_{k,j}$	:	Machining time for k th operation corresponding to the machine assign in the j th female chromosome.
n	:	Number of male or female population.
P	:	Set of different part types, $P=\{1, 2, 3, 4, \ldots, P\}$
R	:	Lot size of production of different part type, $R=\{r_1, r_2, r_3, \ldots, r_p\}$ where r_p is lot size of the part type p.
t_{pij}	:	Transition time from operation i to j for the part type p.
w_{pi}	:	i th operation of the part type *p*.
w_p	:	Set of operations for part type p, $W_p=\{w_{pi} \mid \forall\ i=1,2,3,4, \ldots, j_p\}$, where w_{pi} is i th operation of the part type *p*.
$Z_{i,k}$	:	k^{th} bit of i th chromosome.
α_{pij}	:	Lot size of transportation between the operation w_{pi} to w_{pj}.
β_m	:	Set of operations on the machine *m*.
δ_{pij}	:	Setup time of machine between the operation w_{pi} to w_{pj} of the part type *p*.
ε_i	:	Number of alternative machine available for the operation i.
η_p	:	First selected operation for the part type *p*.
θ	:	An arbitrarily large positive number.
μ_{pim}	:	Processing time of *i* th operation of the part type *p* on the machine m.
ξ_{pim}	:	Completion time of operation i for part type *p* on the machine *m*.

ξ_{hjm}	:	Completion time of operation j for part type *h* on the machine *m*.
υ_{mn}	:	Transportation time from machines *m* to *n*.
ϕ^{q}_{pji}	:	Quantity of commodity q transferred from operation w_{pj} to w_{pi} for the part type P
ϕ^{r}_{pij}	:	Quantity of commodity r transferred from operation w_{pi} to w_{pj} for the part type P.
ϕ^{r}_{pji}	:	Quantity of commodity r transferred from operation w_{pj} to w_{pi} for the part type P
$\phi^{q}_{p\alpha j}$	:	Quantity of commodity q transferred from operation $w_{p\alpha}$ to w_{pj} for the part type P.
$\phi^{q}_{p\beta j}$	:	Quantity of commodity q transfer from operation $w_{p\beta}$ to w_{pj} for the part type P.
Ω_p	:	Total tardiness of part type p.
Ω	:	Total tardiness of all jobs.

8. References

Abido, M A., (2002). Optimal power flow using particle swarm optimization, *Electric Power Energy Systems*, Vol.26, Pages 563–571

Angeline, P.J. (1998). Using selection to improve particle swarm optimization, *The 1998 IEEE International Conference and IEEE World Congress on Computational Intelligence*, Evolutionary Computation Proceedings, Anchorage, AK, USA, Pages 84-89, ISBN: 0-7803-4869-9

Boeringer, D., and WandWerner, D. H (2004). Particle swarm optimization versus genetic algorithms for phased array synthesis, *IEEE Trans. Antennas Propag.*, Vol. 52, Pages 771–779

Brandimarte, P., and Calderini, M., (1995). A heuristic bi-criterion approach to integrated process plan selection and job shop scheduling. *International Journal of Production Research*, Vol.33, Pages 161-181

Carlisle, A., and Dozier, G. (2001). An off-the-shelf PSO, *Proceedings of the Particle Swarm Optimization Workshop*, Pages 1–6

Caponetto, R., Fortuna, L., Fazzino, S., and Xibilia, M. G. (2003).Chaotic sequences to improve the performance of evolutionary algorithm. *IEEE Trans.*, Vol.7, No.3, Pages 289–304.

Cedeño Walter , and Agrafiotis, Dimitris K. (2003). Using particle swarms for the development of QSAR models based on K-nearest neighbor and kernel regression, *Journal of Computer-Aided Molecular Design*, Vol.17, No.2-4, Pages 255-263, ISSN0920-654X (Print) 1573-4951 (Online)

CedenoWand, Agrafiotis, D K., (2003) Using particle swarms for the development of QSAR models based on K-nearest neighbor and kernel regression, *Journal of Computer Aided Mol. Des.*, Vol.17, Pages 255–263

Chan, F.T.S., Chung, S.H., and Chan, P.L.Y. (2005). An adaptive genetic algorithm with dominated genes for distributed scheduling problems, *Expert Systems with Applications*, Vol. 29, Pages 364–371.

Chang, H., Ratnaweera. A., Halgamuge, S. K., and Watson, H. C. (2004). Particle swarm optimization for protein motif discovery Genet. Program., *Evol. Mach.*, Vol. 5, Pages 203–214

Chang, Y. C., Lee, C. Y. (2004). Machine scheduling with job delivery coordination, *European Journal of Operational Research*, Vol. 158, Pages 470487

Chiu, M. and Lin, G. (2004). Collaborative supply chain planning using the artificial neural network approach, *Journal of Manufacturing Technology Management*, Vol.15, No.8, Pages 787-796

Dimopoulos, C. and Zalzala, A.M.S. (2000). Recent developments in Evolutionary computation for manufacturing optimisation: problems, solutions, and comparisons, *IEEE Trans. Evolutionary Computation*, Vol.4, No.2, Pages 93-113, ISSN: 1089-778X

Eberhart, R. C., and Shi, Y. (1998a) Comparison between genetic algorithms and particle swarm optimization, *Proc. 7th Ann. Conf. on Evolutionary Programming*, Berlin, Springer, Pages 611–15

Eberhart, R C., and Shi,Y., (1998b). Evolving artificial neural networks *Proc. Int. Congress on Neural Networks and Brain*, Beijing, China, Pages 5–13

Eberhart, R. C., and Kennedy, J. (1995) A new optimizer using particle swarm theory, *Proc. 6th Int. Symp. on Micro Machine and Human Science*, Nagoya, Japan, (Piscataway, NJ: IEEE) Pages 39–43

Eberhart, R. C., and Shi, Y. (2001). Particle swarm optimization: developments, applications and resources, *Proc. Congress on Evolutionary Computation, Hawaii*, Pages 81–6

Eberhart, R. C., and Shi, Y (2004). Guest Editorial special issue on particle swarm optimization. *IEEE Trans. Evolutionary Computation*, Pages 201–203

Finke, G., Claus, A., and Gunn, E. (1984). A two- commodity network flow approach to traveling salesman problem. *Congressus Numerantium*, Vol.41, Pages167-178

Gao, Y., and Xie, S. (2004). A blind source separation algorithm using particle swarm optimization, *Proceedings of the IEEE 6th Circuits and Systems Symposium*, Shanghai, China, Pages 297–300

Garcia, J. M., Lozano, S., Smith, K., Kwok, T., Villa, G. (2002). Coordinated scheduling of production and delivery from multiple plants and with time windows using genetic algorithms. *Proceedings of the 9th International Conference on Neural Information Processing, ICONIP '02*, Vol. 3, Pages 1153 1158.

Hankins, S.L., Wysk, R.A., and Fox, K.R. (1984). Using a CATS database for alternative machine loading, *Journal of Manufacturing Systems*, Vol. 3, Pages 115-120,

Hu X, Shi Y and Eberhart, R C., (2004). Recent advances in particle swarm *Proc. IEEE Int. Conf. on Evolutionary Computation*, Pages 90–97

Huang, F., Zhang H., Li, Xiaodong, and Li Heng. (2006). Particle swarm optimization-based schemes for resource-constrained project scheduling, *Automation in Construction*, Vol. 15, No. 2, Page 252

Huang, S.H., Zhang, H.C., and Smith, M.L. (1995). A Progressive Approach for the Integration of Process Planning and Scheduling. *IIE Transaction*, Vol.27, No.4, Pages 456-464, ISSN: 0740-817X

Kennedy. J., and Eberhart, R. C 1995 Particle swarm optimization Proc. IEE 1110 se kab takE *Int. Conf. on Neural Networks (Piscataway,NJ: IEEE)*, Pages 1942–48

Khoshnevis, B., and Chen, Q. (1991). Integration of Process Planning and Scheduling Functions. *Journal of Intelligent Manufacturing*, Vol.2, No.3, Pages 165-176, 1990, ISSN0956-5515 (Print) 1572-8145 (Online)

Kolisch, R. (2000). Integrated assemble and fabrication for make-to-order production, *International Journal of Production Economy*, Vol.65, Pages 189-306

Kolisch, R., and Hess, K. (2000). Efficient methods for scheduling make-to-order assemblies under resource assembly area and part availability constraints, *International Journal of Production Research*, Vol.38, No.1, Pages 207-228

Kusiak, A., and Finke, G., (1987). Modeling and solving the flexible forging module scheduling problem. *Engineering Optimization*, Vol. 12, No. 1, Pages 1-12

Laskari, E. C, Parsopoulos, K. E., and Vrahatis, M. N. (2002). Particle swarm optimization for integer programming, *Proc. IEEE Congress on Evolutionary Computation*, Pages 1582–7

Li ,Y., Yao, J., and Yao, D., (2004) Automatic beam angle selection in IMRT planning using genetic algorithm, *Phys. Med. Biol.*, Vol. 49, Pages 1915–32

Lin, B.M.T. (2001). Scheduling in the two- machine flow shop with due date constraints, *International Journal of Production Economy*, Vol.70, No.2, Pages 117-123

Liu, Bo-Fu, Chen, Hung-Ming, Chen, Jian-Hung, Hwang, Shiow-Fen, and Ho, Shinn-Ying, (2005). MeSwarm: Memetic Particle Swarm Optimization, *Proceedings of the 2005 conference on Genetic and evolutionary computation Washington DC*, USA, Poster Session: Ant colony optimization and swarm intelligence, Pages: 267 - 268

Messerschmidt, L., and Engelbrecht, A P., (2004). Learning to play games using a PSO-based competitive learning approach, *IEEE Trans. Evolutionary Computing*, Vol. 8, Pages 280–288

Moon, C., Kim, J., and Hur, S., (2002). Integrated Process Planning and Scheduling with minimizing total tardiness in multi-plants supply chain. *Computers and Industrial Engineering*, Vol. 43, No. 1-2, Pages 331-349, ISSN:0360-8352

Naso D., Surico, M., Turchiano, B., Kaymak, U. (2007), Genetic algorithms for supply chain scheduling:a case study on ready mixed concrete, *Erasmus Research Institute of Management – Report ERS-2004-096-LIS, European Journal of Operation Research.* Vol.177, No. 3, Pages 2069-2099

Nasr, N. and Elsayed, A. (1990). Job shop scheduling with alternative machines, *International Journal of Production Research.* Vol. 28, No. 9, Pages 1595-1609. 1990

Nishi, Tatsushi, Konishi, Masami. (2005). An autonomous decentralized supply chain planning system for multi-stage production processes, *Journal of Intelligent Manufacturing*, Vol.16, Pages 259-275

Palmer, G.J. (1996), A simulated annealing approach to integrated production scheduling, *Journal of Intelligent Manufacturing*, Vol.7 No.3, Pages 163-176, ISSN0956-5515 (Print) 1572-8145 (Online)

Parsopoulos, K. E., and Vrahatis, M. N. (2002). Recent approaches to global optimization problems through particle swarm optimization, *Nat. Comput.* Vol.1, Pages 235–306

Pepper, J.W. Golden, B.L. Wasil, E.A. (2002). Solving the traveling salesman problem with annealing-basedheuristics: a computational study, *IEEE Transactions on man, machine, and cybernetics- part A: Systems, Man and Cybernetics*, Vol.32, No.1, Pages 72-77, ISSN: 1083-4427

Pugachev, A., and Xing, L., (2002) Incorporating prior knowledge into beam orientation optimization in IMRT, *Int. J. Radiat. Oncol. Biol. Phys.*, Vol. 54, Pages 1565–74

Rahmat-Samii, Y., (2003) Genetic Algorithm (GA) and particle swarm optimization (PSO) in engineering electromagnetics *17th Int. Conf. on Applied Electromagnetics and Communications*, Pages 1–5

Rai, R., Kameshwaran, S. and Tiwari, M.K. (2002). Machine-tool selection and operation allocation in FMS: solving a fuzzy goal programming model using a genetic algorithm. *International Journal of Production Research*, Vol.40, No.3, Pages 641-665

Robinson, J., and Rahmat-Samii,Y (2004). Particle swarm optimization in electromagnetics, *IEEE Trans. Antennas Propag.* Vol. 52, Pages 397–407

Robinson, J., and Rahmat-SamiiY. (2004) Particle swarm optimization in electromagnetics *IEEE Trans. Antennas Propag.* Vol. 52, Pages 397–407

Salman A, Ahmad I and Al-Madani, S., (2002) Particle swarm optimization for task assignment problem, *Microprocess. Microsyst.* 26 363–71

Salman, A., Ahmad, I., and Al-Madani, S. (2002). Particle swarm optimization for task assignment problem, *Microprocess. Microsyst.* Vol. 26, Pages 363–71

Shi, Y., and Eberhart, R. C., (1998b) A modified particle swarm optimizer, *Proc. the IEEE Int. Conf. on Evolutionary Computation (Piscataway, NJ: IEEE)*, Pages 69–73

Swarnkar R. and Tiwari M.K. (2004). Modeling machine loading problem of FMSs and its solution methodology using hybrid Tabu search and simulated annealing based heuristic approach, *Robotics and Computer Integrated Manufacturing*, Vol. 20, No.3, Pages 199-209

Tan, W. and Khoshnevis, B. (2004). A linearized polynomial mixed integer programming model for the integration of process planning and scheduling. *Journal of Intelligent Manufacturing*, Vol. 15, Pages 539-605

Ting, Tiew-On, Rao, M.V.C., Loo, C. K. and Ngu, S.S. (2003). Solving Unit Commitment Problem Using Hybrid Particle Swarm Optimization, *Journal of Heuristics*,Vol.9, No.6, Pages 507-520, ISSN1381-1231 (Print) 1572-9397 (Online)

Tiwari, M.K., and Vidyarthi, N.K. (2000). Solving machine loading problem in a flexible manufacturing system using a genetic algorithm based heuristic approach. *International Journal of Production Research*, Vol.38, No.14, Pages 3357-3384

Trelea, I. C. (2003). The particle swarm optimization algorithm: convergence analysis and parameter selection, *Inf. Process. Lett.* Vol. 85, Pages 317–25

Weiqi, L.I., and Alidaee, B. (2002). Dynamics of Local Search Heuristics for the Traveling Salesman Problem, *IEEE Transactions on man, machine, and cybernetics- part A: Systems, Man and Cybernetics*, Vol. 32, No. 2, Pages 173- 184, ISSN: 1083-4427

Xie, Xiao-Feng, Zhang, Wen-Jun, Yang, Zhi-Lian.(2002). A Dissipative Particle Swarm Optimization, *Congress on evolutionary computing (CEC)*,Hawaii, USA, Pages 1456-1461

Xing, L. (1999) A medical knowledge based system for the selection of beam orientations in intensity modulated radiation therapy (IMRT), *Int. J. Radiat. Oncol. Biol. Phys.* Vol. 45, Pages 246–247

Arena, P., Caponetto, R., Fortuna, L., Rizzo, A., and La Rosa, M. (2000), Self organization in non recurrent complex system. *Int. J. Bifurcation Chaos*, Vol.10, No.5, Pages1115–1125.

Determan, J. and Foster, A. (1999). Using chaos in genetic algorithm. *In Proceedings of the IEEE Conference on Evolutionary computation*, IEEE, Piscataway, New Jersey, Vol.3, Pages 2094-2101

Manganaro, G. and Pineda, D. G. J. (1997). DNA computing based on chaos. *In Proceedings of the IEEE International Conference on Evolutionary Computation*, Piscataway, New Jersey, IEEE, Pages. 255–260

Suganthan, N. (1999). Particle swarm optimizer with neighbourhood operator. *In Proceedings of the IEEE International Conference on Evolutionary computation*, IEEE, Piscataway, New Jersey, Vol. 3, Pages 1958–1962

Nozawa, H. A (1992). A neural network model as globally coupled map and application based on chaos, *Chaos*, Pages 377–386.

Wang, L. and Smith, K. (1998). On chaotic simulated annealing. *IEEE Trans. Neural Networks*, Vol.9, Pages 716–718.

26

Ant colonies for performance optimization of multi-components systems subject to random failures

Nabil Nahas, Mustapha Nourelfath and Daoud Ait-Kadi
Universite Laval, Mechanical Engineering Department CIRRELT
Canada

1. Introduction

Reliability has been considered as an important design measure in industry. The design of a system involves in general numerous discrete choices among available component types based on reliability, cost, performance, weight, etc. If the design objective is to maximize reliability for a certain cost requirement, then a strategy is required to identify the optimal combination of components and/or design configuration. This leads to combinatorial optimization problems which are NP-hard. For large industrial problems, exact methods are lacking since they require a very large amount of computation time to obtain the solution of the problem. This chapter will focus on the use of ant colonies to solve three optimal design problems which are among the most important in practice:

1. The reliability optimization of series systems with multiple-choice constraints incorporated at each subsystem, to maximize the system reliability subject to the system budget. This is a nonlinear binary integer programming problem and characterized as an NP-hard problem.
2. The redundancy allocation problem (RAP) of binary series-parallel systems. This is a well known NP-hard problem which involves the selection of elements and redundancy levels to maximize system reliability given various system-level constraints. As telecommunications and internet protocol networks, manufacturing and power systems are becoming more and more complex, while requiring short developments schedules and very high reliability, it is becoming increasingly important to develop efficient solutions to the RAP.
3. Buffers and machines selections in unreliable series-parallel production lines: we consider a series-parallel manufacturing production line, where redundant machines and in-process buffers are included to achieve a greater production rate. The objective is to maximize production rate subject to a total cost constraint. Machines and buffers are chosen from a list of products available in the market. The buffers are characterized by their cost and size. The machines are characterized by their cost, failure rate, repair rate and processing time. To estimate series-parallel production line performance, an analytical decomposition-type approximation is proposed. Simulation results show that this approximate technique is very accurate. The optimal design problem is formulated

as a combinatorial optimization one where the decision variables are buffers and types of machines, as well as the number of redundant machines.

For each problem, a literature review will be presented. This review will focus on meta-heuristics in general, and on ant colonies in particular. Recent advances on efficient solution approaches based on Hybrid Ant Colony Optimization (HACO) will be detailed.

2. Reliability optimization of a series system

2.1. Literature review

As it is often desired to consider the practical design issue of handling a variety of different component types, this paper considers a reliability optimization problem with multiple-choice constraints incorporated. To deal with such reliability optimization problems with multiple-choice constraints incorporated, Sung and Cho [9] have used an efficient branch-and-bound method. Nourelfath and Nahas [6] have solved the reliability optimization problem by using quantized neural networks. [11] deals with a reliability optimization problem for a series system with multiple choice constraints incorporated to maximize the system reliability subject to the system budget. The problem is formulated as a binary integer programming problem with a non linear objective function [1], which is equivalent to a knapsack problem with multiple-choice constraints, so that it is NP-hard [3]. Some branch-and-bound methods for such knapsack problems with multiple-choice constraints have been suggested in the literature [5,7,8]. However, for large industrial problems, these methods are lacking since they require a very large amount of computation time to obtain the solution of the problem. This section describes the use of an *ant system* to obtain optimal or nearly optimal solutions very quickly.

2.2. Optimal design problem

Let us consider a series system of n components. For each component, there are different technologies available with varying costs, reliabilities, weights and other characteristics. The design problem we propose to study is to select the best combination of technologies to maximize reliability given cost. Only one technology will be adopted for each component. In order to formulate the problem in mathematical expression, the following notations are introduced first:

n the number of components

Mi the number of technologies available for the component i

C_i^j the cost of a component i using the technology j (C_i^j is assumed to be known)

R_i^j the reliability of the component i when the technology j is used

B the available budget

TC the total cost.

We specify the decision variable x_i^j (with $j = 1, 2, \ldots, M$; and $i = 1, 2, \ldots, n$) as:

$$x_i^j = \begin{cases} 1 \text{ if the component } i \text{ uses the technology } j \\ 0 \text{ otherwise} \end{cases}$$

Considering these notations, the proposed series-system reliability optimization problem is expressed in the following binary nonlinear integer programming problem:

Maximize
$$Z = \prod_{i=1}^{n}\left(\sum_{j=1}^{M_i} x_i^j R_i^j\right)$$

Subject to
$$\sum_{i=1}^{n}\sum_{j=1}^{M_i} x_i^j C_i^j \leq B \qquad (1)$$

$$\sum_{j=1}^{M_i} x_i^j = 1 \ \forall \ i = 1, 2, \ldots, n \qquad (2)$$

$$x_i^j = \{0,\ 1\} \ \forall \ j = 1, 2, \ldots, M_j \text{ and } i = 1, 2, \ldots, n \qquad (3)$$

Constraint (1) represents the budget constraint; without loss of generality, we consider that B is an integer. Constraint (2) represents the multiple-choice constraint, and constraint (3) defines the decision variables.

When a solution satisfies all the constraints, it is called a feasible solution; otherwise, the solution is said to be infeasible. Our goal is to find an optimal solution or sometimes a nearly optimal solution. This is motivated by the fact that in real size industrial systems, the search space of the reliability optimization problem formulated in this paper is very large, taking the use on non heuristic approaches infeasible. Ant system is a recent kind of meta-heuristic which has been shown to be suitable (especially when combined with local search) for combinatorial optimization problems with a good neighborhood structure (see e.g. [6,10]), as in the case of the reliability optimization problem formulated in this paper.

2.3. Solution approach of the reliability optimization problem

To apply the ant system (AS) algorithm to a combinatorial optimization problem, it is convenient to represent the problem by a graph $G = (\varsigma, \Lambda)$, where ς are the nodes and Λ is the set of edges. To represent our problem as such a graph, the set of nodes g is given by components and technologies, and edges connect each component to its available technologies. Ants cooperate by using indirect form of communication mediated by pheromone they deposit on the edges of the graph G while building solutions.

Informally, our algorithm works as follows: m ants are initially positioned on the node representing the first component. Each ant will construct one possible structure of the entire system. In fact, each ant builds a feasible solution (called a tour) by repeatedly applying a stochastic greedy rule, called, the *state transition rule*. Once all ants have terminated their tour, the following steps are performed:

- An improvement procedure is applied. This procedure, which will be detailed later, is composed of a specific *improvement algorithm* (called algorithm 1) and a local search.
- The amount of pheromone is modified by applying the *global updating rule*.

Ants are guided, in building their tours, by both heuristic information and by pheromone information. Naturally, an edge with a high amount of pheromone is a very desirable choice. The pheromone updating rules are designed so that they tend to give more pheromone to edges which should be visited by ants.

The state transition rule used by the ant system is given in equation (4). This represents the probability with which ant k selects a technology j for component i:

$$p_{ij}^k(t) = \frac{[\tau_{ij}(t)]^{\alpha}.[\eta_{ij}]^{\beta}}{\sum_{m=1}^{M_i}[\tau_{im}(t)]^{\alpha}.[\eta_{im}]^{\beta}} \qquad (4)$$

where τ_{ij} and η_{ij} are respectively the pheromone intensity and the heuristic information between component i and technology j . α is the relative importance of the trail and β is the relative importance of the heuristic information η_{ij}. The problem specific heuristic j information used is $\eta_{ij} = \frac{R_i^j}{C_i^j}$ where R_i^j and C_i^j represent the associated reliability and cost. That is, technologies with higher reliability and smaller cost have greater probability to be chosen.

During the construction process, no guarantee is given that an ant will construct a feasible solution which obeys the budget constraint (i.e. $\sum_{i=1}^{n}\sum_{j=1}^{M_i} x_i^j C_i^j \leq B$). The unfeasibility of solutions is treated in the pheromone update: the amount of pheromone deposited by an ant is set to a high value if the generated solution is feasible and to a low value if it is infeasible. These values are dependent of the solution quality. Infeasibilities can then be handled by assigning penalties proportional to the amount of budget violations. In the case of feasible solutions, an additional penalty proportional to the obtained solution is introduced to improve its quality.

Following the above remarks, the trail intensity is updated as follows:

$$\Delta\tau_{ij} = \sum_{k=1}^{m} \Delta\tau_{ij}^k \tag{5}$$

ρ is a coefficient such that (1 - ρ) represents the evaporation of trail and $\Delta\tau_{ij}$ is :

$$\tau_{ij}(new) = \rho\tau_{ij}(old) + \Delta\tau_{ij} \tag{6}$$

where m is the number of ants and $\Delta\tau_{ij}^k$ is given by:

$$\Delta\tau_{ij}^k = \begin{cases} Q.penalty_k & \text{if the k}^{\text{th}}\text{ ant chooses technology } j \text{ for component } i \\ 0 & \text{otherwise} \end{cases} \tag{7}$$

where Q is a positive number, and $penalty_k$ is defined as follows:

$$penalty_k = \begin{cases} \left(\frac{B}{TC_k}\right)^a & \text{if } B < TC_k \\ \left(\frac{R_k}{R^*}\right)^b & \text{if } B \geq TC_k \end{cases} \tag{8}$$

B is the available budget, TCk is the total cost obtained by ant k, R_k is the reliability obtained by ant k and R^* is the best obtained solution. Parameters a and b represent the relative importance of penalties. It can be easily seen from the above equations that by introducing a penalty function, we aim at encouraging the AS algorithm to explore the feasible region and infeasible region that is near the border of feasible area and discouraging, but allowing, search further into infeasible region.

It is well known that the performance of AS algorithms can be greatly enhanced when coupled to local improvement procedures [2]. Following this, two local improvement algorithms are included in our AS approach (called local search algorithm and algorithm 1). Algorithm 1 uses the remaining budget (the amount not used by the ant) to improve the solution. In fact, some generated feasible solutions do not use the entire available budget.

This algorithm improves the initial solution by using this remaining budget to exchange some actual technologies by more reliable other technologies. A similar idea can be found in [10] where a neural network is presented to solve the job-shop scheduling problem, and where a similar procedure is used to improve the obtained solutions by eliminating the time segments during which all machines are idle.
The local search algorithm proceeds to change in turn each pair of chosen technologies by another pair. For each component, technologies are indexed in ascending order in accordance with their reliability. A solution $S = \{u, v, ...\}$ indicates that component 1 uses technology with index u, component 2 uses technology with index v, etc. Let consider for example a series system with 3 components and 6 available technologies for each component. Suppose that the obtained solution at a given cycle is $S = \{3, 2, 5\}$. The local search will evaluate the following solutions:

$$S=\{4, 1,5\},\ S = \{4, 2, 4\},\ S = \{2, 3, 5\},\ S = \{2, 2, 6\},\ S = \{3, 3, 4\},\ S = \{3, 1,6\}.$$

Among all these evaluated solutions, whenever an improvement feasible solution is detected, the new solution replaces the old one. It has been shown in [11] that the experimental results showed that the optimal or nearly optimal solutions could be obtained quickly. In the next section, Hybrid Ant Colony Optimization (HACO) will be used to solve the redundancy allocation problem. This HACO uses rather the extended great deluge algorithm as a local search within the proposed ant colony algorithm.

3. Redundancy allocation problem

3.1. Problem description

The redundancy allocation problem (RAP) is a well known combinatorial optimization problem where the design goal is achieved by discrete choices made from elements available on the market. The system consists of n components in series. For each component i ($i = 1, 2, ..., n$) there are various versions of elements, which are proposed by the suppliers on the market. Elements are characterized by their cost and weight according to their version. Each component i contains a number of elements connected in parallel. Different elements can be placed in parallel. A component i is functioning properly if at least k_i of its p_i elements are operational (k-out-of-n: G).
The series-parallel system is a logic-diagram representation for many design problems encountered in industrial systems. As it is pointed out in [18] and [31], electronics industry is an example where the RAP is very important. In fact, in this industry most systems require very high reliability and the products are usually assembled and designed using off-the-shelf elements (capacitors, transistors, microcontrollers, etc.) with known characteristics. Other examples where the above type of structure is becoming increasingly important include telecommunications systems and power systems. In all these systems, redundancy is indeed a necessity to reach the required levels of reliability and the RAP studied in this paper is therefore one of the major problems inherent to optimal design of reliable systems.
Assumptions

1. Elements and the system may experience only two possible states: good and failed.
2. The system weight and cost are linear combinations of element weight and cost.
3. The element attributes (reliability, cost and weight) are known and deterministic.
4. Failed elements do not damage the system, and are not repaired.

5. All redundancy is active: failure rates of elements when not in use are the same as when in use.
6. The supply of elements is unlimited.
7. Failures of individual elements are *s*-independent.

Notation

R_{sys}	overall reliability of the series-parallel system
R^*	optimal solution
C	cost constraint
W	weight constraint
n	number of components
i	index for components
a_i	number of available elements choices (i.e., versions) for component i
r_{ij}	reliability of element j available for component i
w_{ij}	weight of element j available for component i
c_{ij}	cost of element j available for component i
x_{ij}	number of element j used in component i
$\mathbf{x}_i$	$\left(x_{i1}, x_{i2}, \ldots, x_{ia_i}\right)$
p_i	total number of elements used in component i
p_{max}	maximum number of elements in parallel
k_i	minimum number of elements in parallel required for component i
$\mathbf{k}$	$(k_1, k_2, \ldots, k_n)$
$R_i(\mathbf{x}_i \mid k_i)$	reliability of component i, given k_i
$C_i(\mathbf{x}_i)$	total cost of component i
$W_i(\mathbf{x}_i)$	total cost of component i

The RAP is formulated to maximize system reliability given restrictions on system cost and weight. That is,

Maximize
$$R_{sys} = \prod_{i=1}^{n} R_i\left(\mathbf{x}_i \mid k_i\right) \tag{9}$$

Subject to
$$\sum_{i=1}^{n} C_i(\mathbf{x}_i) \le C, \tag{10}$$

$$\sum_{i=1}^{n} W_i(\mathbf{x}_i) \le W. \tag{11}$$

Constraints (10) and (11) represent respectively the budget and the weight constraints. If there is a pre-selected maximum number of elements which are allowed in parallel, the following constraint (12) is added:

$$k_i \le p_i \le p_{\max} \quad \forall\, i = 1, 2, \ldots, n \tag{12}$$

3.2. Literature review

The RAP is NP-hard [17] and has previously been solved using many different optimization approaches and for different formulations as summarized in [39], and more recently in [32]. Optimization approaches to determine optimal or very good solutions for the RAP include dynamic programming, e.g. [12,25,35,41], mixed-integer and nonlinear programming, e.g.

[32], and integer programming, e.g. [14,27,28,34]. Nevertheless, these methods are limited to series-parallel structures where the elements used in parallel are identical. This constitutes a drawback since in practice many systems designs use different elements performing the same function, to reach high reliability level [31]. For example, as explained in [18], (airplanes use a primary electronic gyroscope and a secondary mechanical gyroscope working in *parallel*, and most new automobiles have a redundant (spare) tire with different size and weight characteristics forming a 4-out-of-5: G standby redundant system). Because of the above-mentioned drawback and of the exponential increase in search space with problem size, heuristics have become a popular alternative to exact methods. Meta-heuristics, in particular, offer flexibility and a practical way to solve large instances of the relaxed RAP where different elements can be placed in parallel.

Genetic algorithm (GA) is a well-known meta-heuristic used to solve combinatorial reliability optimization problems [18,33,37,42,43]. In addition to genetic algorithms, other heuristic or meta-heuristic approaches have also been efficiently used to deal with system reliability problems. A tabu search (TS) meta-heuristic [30] has been developed in [31] to efficiently solving the RAP, while the ant colony optimization meta-heuristic [20] is used in [4] to solve the problem.

In light of the aforementioned approaches, the method presented here gives a heuristic approach to solve the RAP. This method combines an *ant colony* optimization approach and a degraded *ceiling local* search technique. This approach is said to be *hybrid* and will be called *ACO/DC* (for Ant Colony Optimization and Degraded Ceiling).

The idea of employing a colony of cooperating agents to solve combinatorial optimization problems was recently proposed in [21]. The ant colony approach has been successfully applied to the classical traveling salesman problem [22,23], to the quadratic assignment problem [26], and to scheduling [13]. Ant colony shows very good results in each applied area. The ant colony has also been adapted with success to other combinatorial optimization problems such as the vehicle routing problem [15], telecommunication networks management [24], graph coloring [19], constraint satisfaction [38] and Hamiltonian graphs [44]. In [11], the authors used ant system to solve the optimal design problem of series system under budget constraints. The ant colony approach has also been applied for the RAP of multi-state systems in [36]. For the RAP in the binary state case, which is the focus of the present paper, the only existing work is that of [4].

3. 3. Hybrid solution approach: ACO/DC

As for the problem studied in section 2, to apply the AGO meta-heuristic to this problem, it is convenient to represent the problem by a graph $G = (\varsigma, \Lambda)$, where ς are the nodes and Λ is the set of edges. To represent our problem as such a graph, we introduce the following sets of nodes and edges [55]:

- *Three sets of nodes*:
  1. The first set of nodes (N_1) represents the components.
  2. The second set of nodes (N_2) represents, for each component, the numbers of elements which can be used in parallel. For example, if the maximum number of elements in parallel is three (p_{max} = 3), the set N_2 will be given by three nodes corresponding to one element, two parallel elements and three parallel elements.
  3. The third set (N_3) represents the versions of elements available for each component.

- *Two sets of edges*:
  1. The first set of edges is used to connect each component node in the set N_1 to the corresponding nodes in N_2.
  2. The second set of edges is used to connect the nodes in N_2 to the nodes in N_3 of their available versions.

Informally, our algorithm works as follows: m ants are initially positioned on a node representing a component. Each ant represents one possible structure of the entire system. This entire structure is defined by the vectors $\mathbf{x}_i$ (i = 1, ..., n). Each ant builds a feasible solution (called a tour) to our problem by repeatedly applying stochastic greedy rules (i.e., the *state transition rules*). Once all ants have terminated their tour, the amount of pheromone on edges is modified by applying the *global updating rule*. Ants are guided, in building their tours, by both heuristic information (they prefer to choose "less expansive" edges), and by pheromone information. Once an ant has built a structure, the obtained solution is improved by using a local search algorithm. This step is performed only in the following cases:

- the obtained solution by the ant is feasible and,
- the quality of the solution is "good". The term "good" means here that the reliability R_{sys} of the structure should be either better than the best solution R^*, i.e., $R_{sys} \geq R^*$,or close to this best solution R^*, i.e., $0 \leq \frac{R^* - R_{sys}}{R^*} \leq +l$ where l represents the solution quality level.

Ants can be guided, in building their tours, by pheromone information and heuristic information. Naturally, an edge with a high amount of pheromone is a very desirable choice. The pheromone updating rules are designed so that they tend to give more pheromone to edges which should be visited by ants.

In the following we discuss the state transition rules and the global updating rules.

State transition rules

In the AGO algorithm, each ant builds a solution (called a tour) to our problem by repeatedly applying two different *state transition rules*. At each step of the construction process, ants use: (1) pheromone trails (denoted by τ_{ij}) to select the number of elements connected in parallel and the versions of elements; (2) and a problem- specific heuristic information (denoted by η_{ij}) related to the versions of elements.

An ant positioned on node i (i.e. component i) chooses the total number p_i of elements to be connected in parallel. This choice is done by applying the rule given by:

$$P_{ip_i} = \begin{cases} \dfrac{(\tau_{ip_i})^{\alpha_1}}{\sum_{k=1}^{p_{max}} (\tau_{ik})^{\alpha_1}} & if \quad p_i \in \{1, \ 2, \ ..., p_{max}\} \\ 0 & otherwise \end{cases} \tag{13}$$

where α_1 is a parameter that controls the relative weight of the pheromone (τ_{ip_i}). We favour the choice of edges which are weighted with greater amount of pheromone.

When an ant is positioned on node p_i representing the selected number of elements connected in parallel in component i, it has to choose these p_i versions of elements. This choice is done by applying the rule given by:

$$P_{p_i j} = \begin{cases} \dfrac{\left(\tau_{p_i j}\right)^{\alpha_2} \left(\eta_{p_i j}\right)^{\beta}}{\sum_{k=1}^{a_i} \left(\tau_{p_i k}\right)^{\alpha_2} \left(\eta_{p_i k}\right)^{\beta}} & if \quad j \in \{1, 2, \ldots, a_i\} \\ 0 \quad otherwise & \end{cases} \tag{14}$$

where α_2 and β are respectively parameters that control the relative weight of the pheromone ($\tau_{p_i j}$) and the local heuristic ($\eta_{p_i j}$).

We tested different heuristic information and the most efficient was $\eta_{p_i j} = (r_{ij})/(w_{ij}^3)$, where r_{ij} and w_{ij} represent respectively the associated reliability and weight of version j for component i. In equation (14) we multiply the pheromone on edges by the corresponding heuristic information. In this way we favour the choice of edges which are weighted with smaller weight and greater reliability and which have a greater amount of pheromone.

Global updating rule

During the construction process, no guarantee is given that an ant will construct a feasible solution which obeys the constraints (11) and (12). The unfeasibility of solutions is treated in the pheromone update: the amount of pheromone deposited by an ant is set to a high value if the generated solution is feasible and to a low value if it is infeasible. These values are dependent of the solution quality. Infeasibilities can then be handled by assigning penalties proportional to the amount of cost and weight violations. Thus, the trail intensity is updated as follows:

$$\tau_{ij}(new) = \rho \tau_{ij}(old) + \Delta \tau_{ij} \tag{15}$$

ρ is a coefficient such that (1 - ρ) represents the evaporation of trail and $\Delta \tau_{ij}$ is :

$$\Delta \tau_{ij} = \sum_{k=1}^{m} \Delta \tau_{ij}^k \tag{16}$$

where m is the number of ants. Furthermore, $\Delta \tau_{ij}^k$ is given by:

$$\Delta \tau_{ij}^k = \begin{cases} Q \ penalty_k \ R_{sys}^k & \text{if the edge } (i, j) \text{ is visited by the } k^{\text{th}} \text{ ant} \\ 0 & \text{otherwise} \end{cases} \tag{17}$$

where Q is a positive number, R_{sys}^k is the system reliability for ant k, and $penalty_k$ is defined as follows:

$$penalty_k = \begin{cases} \left(\dfrac{C}{TC_k}\right)^a & if \ (C < TC_k) \\ \left(\dfrac{W}{TW_k}\right)^b & if \ (W < TW_k) \\ \left(\dfrac{C}{TC_k}\right)^a \left(\dfrac{W}{TW_k}\right)^b & if \ (C < TC_k \ and \ W < TW_k) \end{cases} \tag{18}$$

and TW_k are respectively the total cost and the total weight obtained by ant k. Parameters α and β represent the relative importance of penalties.

The degraded ceiling local search meta-heuristic

The principle of the degraded ceiling meta-heuristic

The performance of algorithms based on the AGO meta-heuristic can be greatly enhanced when coupled to local improvement procedures. A degraded ceiling (DC) based algorithm is included in our AGO approach to improve the solutions obtained by the ants.

The degraded ceiling is a local search meta-heuristic recently introduced in [6a] and [6b]. Like other local search methods, the degraded ceiling iteratively repeats the replacement of a current solution s by a new one s^*, until some stopping condition has been satisfied. The new solution is selected from a neighbourhood $N(s)$. The mechanism of accepting or rejecting the candidate solution from the neighbourhood is different of other methods. In degraded ceiling approach, the algorithm accepts every solution whose objective function is more or equal (for the maximization problems) to the upper limit L, which is monotonically increased during the search by ΔL.

The initial value of ceiling (L) is equal to the initial cost function $f(s)$ and only one input parameter ΔL has to be specified. In [16], the authors applied successfully the degraded ceiling on exam timetabling problem and demonstrated that it outperformed well-known best results found by others meta-heuristics, such as simulated annealing and tabu search. They showed two main properties of the degraded ceiling algorithm:

- The search follows the degrading of the ceiling. Fluctuations are visible only at the beginning, but later, all intermediate solutions lie close to a linear line.
- When a current solution reaches the value where any further improvement is impossible, the search rapidly converges. The search procedure can then be terminated at this moment.

The degraded ceiling algorithm is an extension of the "great deluge" method which was introduced as an alternative to simulated annealing. Degraded ceiling, simulated annealing and "great deluge" algorithms share the characteristic that they may both accept worse candidate solutions than the current one. The difference is in the acceptance criterion of worse solutions. The simulated annealing method accepts configurations which deteriorate the objective function only with a certain probability. The degraded ceiling algorithm incorporates both the worse solution acceptance (of the "great deluge" algorithm) if the solution fitness is less than or equal to some given upper limit L, i.e. ($f(s^*) \geq L$), and the well-known hill climbing rule ($f(s^*) \geq f(s)$).

Like simulated annealing, the degraded ceiling algorithm may accept worse candidate solutions during its run. The introduction of the dynamic parameter has an important effect on the search. As explained in [16], the decreasing of L may be seen as a control process, which drives the search towards a desirable solution. Note finally that degraded ceiling algorithm has the advantage to require only one parameter (ΔL) to be tuned.

3.4. Test problems and results

The test problems, used to evaluate the performance of the ACO/DC methodology for the RAP, were originally proposed by Fyffe *et al.* in [25] and modified by Nakagawa and Miyazaki in [35]. Fyffe *et al.* [25] specified constraint limits of 130 units of system cost, 170 units of system weight and $k_i = 1$ (i.e., l-out-of-n:G). Nakagawa and Miyazaki [35] developed 33 variations of the original problem, where the cost constraint C is set to 130 units and the

weight constraint W varies from 159 units to 191 units. The system is designed with 14 components. For each component, there are three or four element choices [55].
Earlier optimization approaches to the problem (e.g., [25] and [35]), required that only identical elements be placed in redundancy. Such approaches determined optimal solutions through dynamic programming and IP models, but only a restricted set of solutions was considered due to computational or formulation limitations of exact solution methods. Nevertheless, for the ACO/DC approach, as in [81], [31] and [4], different types are allowed to reside in parallel. In [18], Coit and Smith first solved the RAP with a genetic algorithm without restricting the search space. More recently, Kulturel-Konak *et al.* solved this problem in [31] with a tabu search algorithm, while Liang and Smith [31] used an ant colony optimization approach improved by a local search. Because the heuristic benchmarks for the RAP where elements mixing is allowed are the methods in [18], [31] and [4], there are chosen for comparison. Our approach will be compared also with [35] and [29]. By comparing the proposed ACO/DC methodology to all the above-mentioned papers (e.g., [18], [31], [4], [35] and [29]), we compare it to the best-known solutions found in literature at the best of our knowledge.
In meta-heuristics such as AGO, simulated annealing and degraded ceiling, it is necessary to tune a number of parameters to have good performance. The user-specified parameters of the ACO/DC algorithm were varied to establish the values most beneficial to the optimization process. Following the tuning procedure used in [21-23], we tested various values for each parameter, while keeping the others constant. Based on these initial experiments the values found to be most appropriate are:

$$\alpha_1 = 0.1, \alpha_2 = 0.5, \beta=1, Q = 0.01, \rho = 0.9, a = 1, b = 10, \tau_0 = 1, \Delta L = 0.0001 \text{ and } l = 0.01.$$

These parameters values are used for all test problems. 50 ants are used in each iteration. When combined to the degraded ceiling algorithm, AGO converges quickly to optimal or near optimal solutions. Note that the degraded ceiling is called only if the obtained solutions are very good. For the considered problem instances, the maximum number of iterations needed does not exceed 300 iterations.
Comparing the results obtained by our approach with those of previous works [18,29,31,4,35], it has been shown in [55] that:

1. The solutions found by our algorithm are all better than those of Hsieh [19].
2. In 31 of the 33 test cases, the solutions found by our algorithm are better than those of Nakagawa and Miyazaki [27] while the rest (i.e., 2 cases) are as good as those they found.
3. Cases 22 to 29 and 31 to 32 are as good as those found by the genetic algorithm of Coit and Smith [8] while the rest (i.e., 24 instances) are all better than those they found.
4. In 6 of the 33 test cases, the ACO/DC outperformed the tabu search algorithm of Kulturel-Konak *et al.* [21] while it was very close but at a lower reliability in only 2 instances.
5. In 9 of the 33 test cases, the solutions found by our algorithm are better than those of Liang and Smith [24] while the rest are as good as those they found.

Both the degraded ceiling and the ant colony algorithms are meta-heuristics. Our contribution is based on the ACO/DC hybridization and very good results are obtained. The RAP is one of the most difficult combinatorial optimization problems inherent to optimal design of reliable systems. We believe and we show that two efficient metaheuristics have to cooperate in order to solve efficiently this problem, namely the AGO and the DC meta-heuristics.

The study conducted in this section shows again that hybridization of meta-heuristics is a very promising methodology for NP-hard reliability design problems.

4. Selecting machines and buffers in series-parallel production lines

4.1. Optimal design problem

Consider the series-parallel production line. Buffers are inserted to limit the propagation of disruptions, and this increases the average production rate of the line. This line consists of n components and n-1 buffers. Each component of type i (i = 1,2,..., n) can contain several identical machines connected in parallel. For each component i, there are a number of machine versions available in the market.

In order to formulate the problem in mathematical expression, the following notations are introduced first:

h_i version number of machine i

H_i maximum h_i available

$\mathbf{h}$ $\{ h_i \}$, $h_i \in \{1,2,.., H_i \}$

r_i number of elements connected in parallel in i

R_i maximum r_i allowed

$C(h_i)$ cost of each machine of version h_i

$P(h_i)$ isolated production rate of machine with version h_i

$T(h_i)$ processing time of machine with version h_i

$\lambda(h_i)$ failure rate of each machine with version h_i

$\mu(h_i)$ repair rate of each machine with version h_i

$u(h_i)$ speed of the machine's version h_i

We assume that a buffer is also chosen from a list of available buffers. The buffers of different versions f differ by their size $N^b{}_f$ and cost $C^b{}_f$. The total number of different buffer versions available for m^{th} component is denoted by F_m. The vector $\mathbf{f} = \{f_m\}$, where $0 \le f_m \le F_m$, defines versions of buffers chosen for each component. The entire production line structure is defined by the vectors **h**, **r** and $\mathbf{f} = \{f_m\}$.

For the given **h**, **r** and **f**, the total cost of the production line can be calculated as:

$$C_T = \sum_{m=1}^{n-1} C^B_{f(m)} + \sum_{i=1}^{n} r_i . C(h_i) \tag{19}$$

The optimal design problem of production system can be formulated as follows: find the system configuration **f**, **h** and **r** that maximizes the total production rate P_T such that the total cost C_T is less or equal to a specified value C*. That is,

Maximize P_T (**f**, **h**, **r**) (20)

Subject C_T (**f**, **h**, **r**) $\le$ C* (21)

The input of this problem is C* and the outputs are the optimal production rate P_{TMax} and the corresponding configuration determined by the vectors **f**, **h**, **r**. The resulting maximum value of P_T is written P_{TMax} (C*).

4.2. Literature review

There is a substantial literature on the analysis of production lines with buffers [45]. This literature is mainly concerned with the prediction of performance. Much of it is aimed at evaluating the average production rate (throughput) of a system with specified machines and buffers. In [46], the authors present a set of algorithms that select the minimal buffer space in a flow line to achieve a specified production rate. The algorithms are based on analytical approximations of the Buzacott model of a production line [47,48]. For a recent review of the literature on production line optimization, the reader is referred to [46]. The goal of the existing works is to choose buffers sizes for a production line. They all assume that the number of machines is specified, and the only parameters to find are buffers sizes. The proposed approach to optimal design aims at *selecting both buffers and machines*; it gives also the number of redundant machines used in parallel.

To deal with the optimal design problem considered in this work, it is mandatory to develop a method for throughput evaluation of series-parallel manufacturing production lines. This method has to take into account two characteristics:

(i) Components may consist of banks of parallel machines. Concerning this first characteristic, we attempt to represent each stage by an equivalent single component.

(ii) The processing rate may differ from component to component. To deal with this second characteristic, we use a continuous (or fluid) material model type which produces very good results. This consists of two main steps. First, the non homogeneous line is transformed into an approximately equivalent homogeneous one. In a second step, the resulting homogeneous line is analysed by using the well-known decomposition method for homogeneous lines [49].

The effect of the used simplifications for estimating throughput is examined by comparing the results provided by our approximate technique to simulation results on many examples. This comparison shows that the proposed approximate technique is very accurate.

As the formulated problem is a complicated combinatorial optimization one, an exhaustive examination of all possible solutions is not realistic, considering reasonable time limitations. Because of this, we develop two heuristics to solve the problem. The first heuristic is inspired from the *ant colony system* meta-heuristic: a recent kind of biologically inspired algorithms [48,49]. The second proposed heuristic is based on the *simulated annealing* meta-heuristic [50].

4.3. Throughput evaluation of series-parallel production lines

4.3.1. Summary of the method

The proposed method approximates each component (i.e. each set of parallel machines) of the original production line as a single unreliable machine. The system is then reduced to a single machine per component production line of the type represented in figure 2. The equivalent machines may have different processing rates. To determine the steady state behaviour of this *non-homogeneous* production line, it is first transformed into an approximately equivalent homogeneous line. Then, the well-known Dallery-David-Xie algorithm (DDX) is used to solve the decomposition equations of the resulting (homogenous) line [51].

4.3.2. Replacing each component by an equivalent machine

The decomposition techniques developed in the literature are efficient in estimating performance characteristics of series production lines. In these techniques it is necessary for

each component to be described by three parameters: *failure rate, repair rate* and *processing rate*. By limiting the description of the equivalent machine to these three parameters, our analysis of the new system is reduced in complexity to that of the existing decomposition techniques. Furthermore, the state space of a series-parallel line grows large with the number of parallel machines in the components. Replacing each set of parallel machines by one equivalent machine leads advantageously to a reduction of the state space.
Let denote by λ_{ij}, μ_{ij} and P_{ij}, respectively, the failure rate, the repair rate and the processing rate of a machine M_{ij}, and by λ_i, μ_i and P_i, respectively, the failure rate, the repair rate and the processing rate of a machine M_i. To calculate the three unknown quantities λ_i, μ_i and P_i, we have to formulate three equations. Assuming that machines within the set of parallel machines are fairly similar, the following approximation is proposed in [52] :

$$\lambda_i = \sum_{j=l}^{J_i} \lambda_{ij} \qquad i = 1, 2, \ldots, n \tag{22}$$

$$\mu_i = \sum_{j=1}^{J_i} \mu_{ij} \qquad i = 1, 2, \ldots, n \tag{23}$$

$$P_i = \sum_{j=l}^{J_i} P_{ij} \qquad i = 1, 2, \ldots, n \tag{24}$$

It is shown in [52] that it is a good approximation. However, when buffers are small, this heuristic is inaccurate. In the present work, we assume that the available buffers are large enough. Thus, each set of parallel machines is approximated as an equivalent single machine by using equations (22), (23) and (24). This leads to a non-homogenous line. Therefore, a homogenisation technique is required, as explained in the next subsection.

4.3.3. Homogenisation technique

It is known that in the case of non-homogenous lines (*i.e.* production lines in which the machines do not have the same processing time), two approaches can be used. The first approach is based on an extension to the case of homogenous lines of the decomposition technique developed in [49]. The second approach relies on the modification of the non-homogeneous line into an approximately equivalent homogeneous line by means of *homogenisation techniques* [53]. The analysis of the obtained homogeneous line is therefore based on the use of the decomposition method for homogeneous line. In this way, it is possible to rely on the DDX algorithm which has been proven to be very fast and reliable. In [53], the authors showed that the homogenization method of [54], referred to as the completion time approximation, provides fairly accurate results. In this method, each machine M_i of the original non-homogeneous line is replaced by an approximately equivalent machine M_i^e, such that its completion time distribution is close to that of the original machine. The processing time of machine M_i^e is set to the processing time of the fastest machine in the original line: $T^e = \min(T_1, T_2, \ldots, T_k)$. Since the processing time of M_i^e is given (equal to T^e) there are two parameters per machine that must be determined, namely the failure and repair rates. Let λ_i^e and μ_i^e be the failure and repair rates of machine M_i^e. The principle of the method developed in [53] is to determine λ_i^e and μ_i^e in such a way that the distribution of completion times of machine M_i^e has the same first and second moments as those of the distribution of completion times of machine M_i. The values of λ_i^e and μ_i^e are given in [53] by:

$$\lambda_i^e = \left[\frac{T_i}{T^e}\left(1+\frac{\lambda_i}{\mu_i}\right)-1\right]^2 \frac{T^e}{T_i}\frac{\mu_i^2}{\lambda_i} \text{ and } \mu_i^e = \left[\frac{T_i}{T^e}\left(1+\frac{\lambda_i}{\mu_i}\right)-1\right]\frac{T^e}{T_i}\frac{\mu_i^2}{\lambda_i}.$$

4.3.4. Decomposition equations and DDX algorithm

As said before, we denote by λ_i^e, μ_i^e and T_i^e respectively, the failure rate, the repair rate and the processing time of the machine M_i^e in the equivalent homogenous line. In [51], the authors developed decomposition equations for homogenous lines and propose an efficient algorithm (DDX) to solve these equations.

Production line decomposition methods typically work as follows. An original line is divided into *k-1* lines with only two machines. The method requires the derivation of a set of equations that link the decomposed systems together. Such methods are efficient because systems with two machines can be rapidly analyzed. In general, systems may be represented by discrete or continuous flow models. In both, the processing time is deterministic. The discrete material model has the advantage of better representing the discrete nature of typical factories, but it is limited to systems with equal processing times. The continuous (or fluid) model is better suited in our case because it can be used for systems where the machines have different processing rates. The fluid modelling approach is an approximation which consists in using continuous variables to characterize the flow of parts. Therefore, the quantity of material in each buffer B_i at any time t is a real number taking its value in the interval $[0, N_i]$.

The DDX algorithm [51] is the quickest and most reliably convergent algorithm for solving decomposition-type equations. In our optimal design problem, the DDX algorithm can be used to solve the decomposition equations for each configuration. Let recall that in our analytical method the DDX algorithm is applied after approximating each set of parallel machines as a single machine and transforming the resulting non-homogenous production line into an approximate equivalent homogenous line. For more details about DDX algorithm, the reader is referred to [51].

4.4. The hybrid ant colony optimization (HACO) and the simulated annealing

4.4.1. Applying ACS to select machines and buffers: the general algorithm

Following [21], with respect to the problem of selecting machines and buffers in a series-parallel line, each ant is an agent that leaves a pheromone trail, called a trace, on the edges of a graph representing the problem. To represent our problem as such a graph, we introduce the following sets of nodes and edges [56] :

- *Three sets of nodes*:

1. The first set of nodes (N_1) represents the components and the buffers.
2. The second set (N_2) represents the versions of elements available for each component and buffer.
3. The third set of nodes (N_3) represents, for each component, the numbers of elements which can be used in parallel. For example, if the maximum number of elements in parallel is two, the set N_3 will be given by two nodes corresponding to one element and two parallel elements.

- *Two sets of edges*:

1. The first set of edges is used to connect each node in the set N_1 to the corresponding nodes in N_2.
2. The second set of edges is used to connect some nodes in N_2 to the nodes in N_3.

Informally, our algorithm works as follows: *m* ants are initially positioned on a node representing a component. Each ant represents one possible structure of the entire system. This entire production line structure is defined by the vectors **f**, **h** and **r**. Each ant builds a feasible solution (called a tour) to our problem by repeatedly applying *three* different stochastic greedy rules (i.e., the *state transition rules*). While constructing its solution, an ant also modifies the amount of pheromone on the visited edges by applying the *local updating rule*. Once all ants have terminated their tour, the amount of pheromone on edges is modified again (by applying the *global updating rule*). Ants are guided, in building their tours, by both heuristic information (they prefer to choose "less expensive and more efficient edges"), and by pheromone information.

Note that when an ant builds a solution, it can be feasible or unfeasible. When the obtained solution is unfeasible, it is automatically rejected and it is not taken into account in the comparison with the other feasible solutions obtained by the other ants. It should be noted also that the global update of the pheromone is done only for the best obtained feasible solution.

In the following we discuss the state transition rules, the global updating rule, and the local updating rule.

State transition rules

In the above algorithm, at each step of the construction process, ants use: (1) pheromone trails (denoted by τ_{ij}) to select the versions of machines and buffers and the number of machines connected in parallel; (2) a problem-specific heuristic information (denoted by η_{ij}). The value of η_{ij} depends of the nature of the node (i.e. machine's version or buffer's version). Note that the choice of the number of machines to be connected in parallel is not function of the heuristic information η_{ij}.

An ant positioned on node *i* (representing a machine or a buffer) chooses the version *j* ($j = h_i$ if *i* is a machine and $j = f_i$ if *i* is a buffer) according to following:

$$j = \begin{cases} \arg\max_{k \in \Gamma_i} \left\{ (\tau_{ik})^{\alpha} (\eta_{ik})^{\beta} \right\} & \text{if} \quad q \le q_o \\ J & \text{otherwise} \end{cases} \tag{25}$$

where Γ_i is the set of nodes representing the available versions for node *i* ($\Gamma_i = \{1, \ldots, H_i\}$ if *i* is a machine or $\Gamma_i = \{1, \ldots, F_i\}$ if *i* is a buffer).

And *J* is a random variable selected according to the probability distribution given by:

$$p_{ij} = \begin{cases} \dfrac{(\tau_{ij})^{\alpha} (\eta_{ij})^{\beta}}{\sum_{k \in \Gamma_i} (\tau_{ik})^{\alpha} (\eta_{ik})^{\beta}} & \text{if} \quad j \in \Gamma_i \\ 0 & \text{otherwise} \end{cases} \tag{26}$$

In the above equations (25) and (26), α and β are parameters that control the relative weight of the pheromone (τ_{ij}) and the local heuristic (η_{ij}), respectively. The value of β depends on the type of a given node. The variable q is a random number uniformly distributed in [0, 1]; and q_0 is a parameter ($0 \le q_0 \le 1$) which determines the relative importance of exploitation versus exploration $\eta_{ij} = \frac{P(h_i)}{C(h_i)}$ if i represents a machine and $\eta_{ij} = \frac{N(f_i)}{C(f_i)}$ represents a buffer.

Similarly, when an ant is positioned on node i representing a version of a machine, it has to select a number j of machines to be connected in parallel. In this case, the used rule is similar to (7) and (8) except for the heuristic information which is set to 1 and $\Gamma_i = \{1,..., R_i\}$.

Global updating rule

Once all ants have built a complete solution, pheromone trails are updated. Only the globally best ant (i.e., the ant which constructed the best design solution from the beginning of the trial) is allowed to deposit pheromone. A quantity of pheromone $\Delta\tau_{ij}$ is deposited on each edge that the best ant has used, where the indices i and j refer to the edges visited by the best ant. The quantity $\Delta\tau_{ij}$ is given by the total production rate P_{Tbest} of the design feasible solution constructed by the best ant. Therefore, the global updating rule is:

$$\tau_{ij} \leftarrow (1-\rho)\tau_{ij} + \rho\Delta\tau_{ij} \tag{27}$$

where $0 < \rho < 1$ is the pheromone decay parameter representing the evaporation of trail.

Global updating is intended to allocate a greater amount of pheromone to greater design solution. Equation (27) dictates that only those edges belonging to the globally best solution will receive reinforcement.

Local updating rule

While building a solution of the problem, ants visit edges on the graph G, and change their pheromone level by applying the following local updating rule:

$$\tau_{ij} \leftarrow (1-\rho)\tau_{ij} + \rho\tau_o \tag{28}$$

where τ_o is the initial value of trail intensities.

The application of the local updating rule, while edges are visited by ants, has the effect of lowering the pheromone on visited edges. This favours the exploration of edges not yet visited, since the visited edges will be chosen with a lower probability by the other ants in the remaining steps of an iteration of the algorithm.

Improving constructed solutions

As said before, it is well known that the performance of ACS algorithms can be greatly improved when coupled to local search algorithms [2]. Following this idea again, an improvement procedure is included in our ACS algorithm, once all ants have terminated their tour and before applying the global updating rule.

This procedure consists of two steps:

1. The remaining budget (the amount not used by the ant) of the obtained structure is first used to improve the solution. In fact, some generated feasible solutions do not use the entire available budget. The procedure improves the initial solution by using this remaining budget to increase the number of machines connected in parallel.
2. In this step, two types of evaluation are performed depending of the nature of the component (*i.e.* machine or buffer). For each pair of components representing the machines, the number of machines is changed by adding one for the first component and subtracting one for the second component. In the case of buffers, the algorithm proceeds to change in turn each pair of chosen versions by another pair.

The above steps are illustrated in the following example. Let us consider a series-parallel line with 3 machines (5 available versions for each machine) and 2 buffers (6 available versions for each buffer). Suppose that the solution at a given cycle is **f** = {3, 2}, **h** = {2, 1, 1} and **r** = {2, 3, 3}. The improvement procedure will evaluate the structures with the following numbers of parallel machines:

r ={1,4,3}, **r** ={1,3,4}, **r** ={2,2,4}, **r** ={3,2,3}, **r** ={3,3,2} and **r** ={2,4,2},

and the following versions of buffers:

f = {2,3} and **f** = {4,1}.

Note finally that when this improvement procedure is used, only the neighbouring feasible solutions are evaluated and compared with the current solution.

4.4.2. Simulated annealing for the optimal design of series-parallel lines

The simulated annealing (SA) exploits the analogy between the way in which a metal cools and freezes into a minimum crystalline energy and the search for a minimum in a more general energy. The connection between this algorithm and mathematical minimization was first noted by [57], but it was Kirckpatrick *et al.* in 1983 [50] who proposed that it forms the basis of optimization technique for combinatorial problems.

The simulated annealing technique is an optimization method suitable for combinatorial minimization problems. A new solution is generated and compared against the current solution. The new solution is accepted as the current solution if the difference in quality does not exceed a dynamically selected threshold. The solutions corresponding to larger increases in cost have a small probability of being accepted. A parameter that regulates the threshold is called the temperature and the function that determines the values for the temperature over time is called the cooling scheduling. The temperature decreases over time to decrease the probability of non improving moves.

Initial feasible solution

The initial feasible solution can be generated in many ways. We tried two generation methods. The first one generates a feasible initial solution by taking the least expensive solution (i.e. only one machine in each component and version 1 for all buffers and machines). The second way starts with the least expensive solution and tries to improve it by an iterative improvement procedure. The experimental tests show that the first method is better.

Neighbouring solution

There are many ways to define neighbourhood for this problem. On the one hand, two types of neighbourhood structures have been tested. Regarding the number of machines in parallel for example, the first type was adding or subtracting one machine. The second one consisted in choosing a random number of machines in parallel. This kind of neighbourhood move has been proposed also in [58] when solving the buffer allocation problem. The carried out experiments showed that the second way is slightly more effective. On the other hand, the versions of the machines are indexed in ascending order of the production rate $P(h_i)$.

Our adopted neighbouring structure can be summarized by the following steps:

Step 1.

Randomly select a component COMP representing either a machine or a buffer.

Step 2.

If COMP = Machine, randomly select one of these two actions:

Action 1: Change the number of machines in parallel by choosing a random number less than k_{max} (k_{max} is the maximum number of machines allowed to be connected in parallel).

Action 2: Change the version of machine VERSION(Machine) by VERSION(Machine)+1 or VERSION(Machine)-1.

If COMP = Buffer, change its version VERSION(Buffer) by VERSION(Buffer)+1 or VERSION(Buffer)-1.

When a neighbour solution is randomly selected, it can be either feasible or unfeasible. If the solution is unfeasible, it is automatically rejected without using the criterion of acceptance and the algorithm passes to the next iteration.

Before introducing the numerical results, it should be noted that it would be straightforward to iterate the improvement procedure until no further improvements are found, i.e. to turn it into a local hill-climber. The coupling of a local search procedure such as the hill-climbing with the ACES may give a good idea on the quality of the obtained solutions. However, this will increase considerably the total computation time. Because the calculation of the objective function depends greatly on the convergence of the DDX algorithm whose time is not negligible, we proposed a local search procedure which does not require much evaluations of the objective function as the hill-climbing.

Numerical results

To prove the efficiency of our algorithm when combined with the local search, we proposed four examples of production line with respectively 4, 10, 15 and 20 components. Tables A.1-A.7 (in Appendix) show the corresponding data. The versions are indexed in ascending order of the production rate $P(h_i)$. The available budgets are respectively 160$, 300$, 450$ and 750$ and the maximum number of machines allowed to be connected in parallel is 3 for the first example and 4 for the other examples. The search space size is respectively larger than 5.5×10^5, 2.684×10^{18}, 8.796×10^{27} and 2.88×10^{37}. All the algorithms were implemented using MATLAB on a PC with 1.8 GHz processor.

	Example 1 ($n = 4$)	Example 2 ($n = 10$)	Example 3 ($n = 15$)	Example 4 ($n = 20$)
ACO(*)	α=0.1, β_1=0.5, β_2=1, ρ=0.01, τ_o=1/25, q_0=0.75.	α=0.1, β_1=0.1, β_2=0.3, ρ=0.01, τ_o=1/25, q_0=0.75.	α=1, β_1=1.5, β_2=1, ρ=0.05, τ_o=1/15, q_0=0.80.	α=1, β_1=1.5, β_2=1, ρ=0.05, τ_o=1/15, q_0=0.80.
ACO(*) with improving procedure	α=0.1, β_1=0.1, β_2=1, ρ=0.05, τ_o=1/25, q_0=0.80.	α=0.5, β_1=1, β_2=1, ρ=0.05, τ_o=1/50, q_0=0.80.	α=0.5, β_1=1, β_2=1, ρ=0.05, τ_o=1/50, q_0=0.75.	α=1, β_1=0.3, β_2=0.5, ρ=0.05, τ_o=1/35, q_0=0.75.
Simulated annealing	c=0.98, T=5, length inner loop=40, $T_{min}=5.10^{-5}$, V_{max}=40	c=0.99, T=5, inner loop=100n, $T_{min}=5.10^{-5}$, V_{max}=35n	c=0.95, T=5, inner loop=100n, $T_{min}=5.10^{-5}$, V_{max}=35n	c=0.975, T=5, inner loop=100n, $T_{min}=5.10^{-5}$, V_{max}=35n

Table 1. Parameters data for three typical examples taken from [52]
(*) $\beta=\beta_1$ when the node i of equations (25) and (26) is a machine and (*) $\beta=\beta_2$ otherwise

We implemented the simulated annealing and ACS algorithm, and we ran simulations to set the parameters. For the ACS algorithm, the parameters considered are those that effect directly or indirectly the computation of the probability in formulas (25) and (26) (*i.e.* α, β, ρ, τ_o and q_0). We tested several values for each parameter, while all the others were held constant (over ten simulations for each setting in order to achieve some statistical information about the average evolution). Based on these initial experiments the values found to be most appropriate are determined. Furthermore, in all our experiments, the number of ants is set to 5. Note that the ACS is not very sensitive to changes in these values, and tested well for quite a range of them. The parameters considered for the simulated annealing are the initial temperature T, length of the inner loop, the final temperature T_{min}, the maximum of success solution V_{max} and the cooling rate c. Initially, the temperature T is set to a sufficiently high value to accept all solutions during the initial phase of the simulated annealing. The cooling rate c should be generally greater than 0.7. Table 1 shows the values of all the parameters considered in the three algorithms.

Each algorithm was tested by performing ten trials. Figures 2 to 5 show the highest throughput versus the number of evaluations. By 6000, 200.000, 250.000 and 400.000 evaluations of throughput, respectively, for example 1, 2, 3 and 4, the highest throughput has been leveled out. These numbers of evaluations are used to assess the performance of the algorithms.

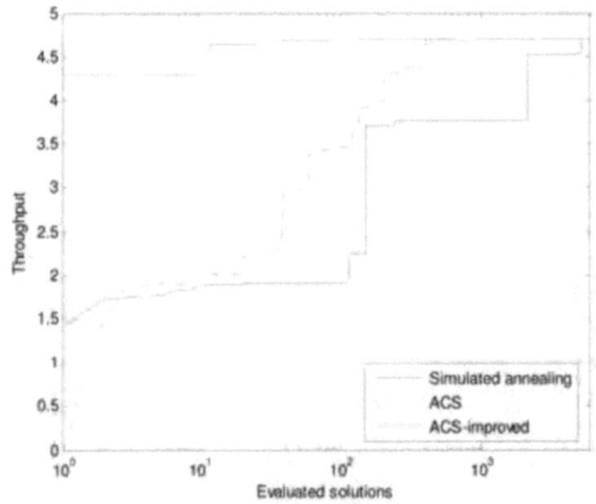

Figure 2. Convergence results for example 1

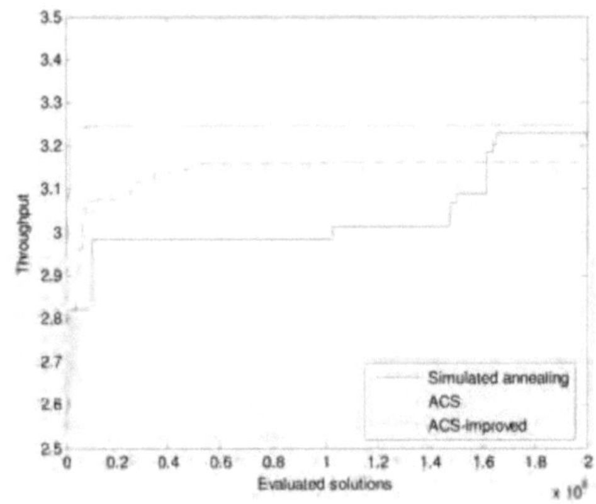

Figure 3. Convergence results for example 2

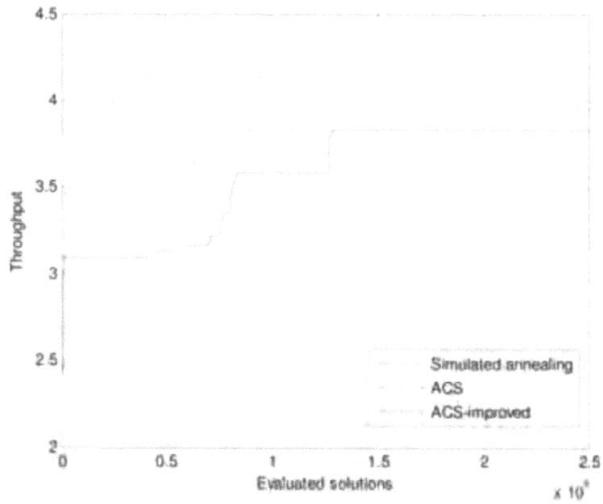

Figure 4. Convergence results for example 3

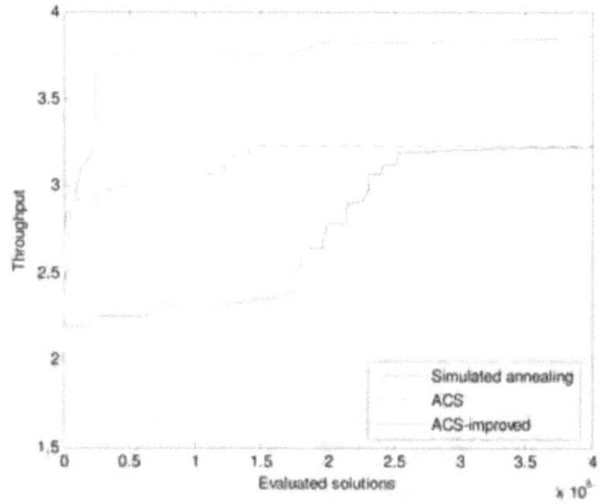

Figure 5. Convergence results for example 4

The convergence curves in figures 2 to 5 show that the ACS algorithm performs better when coupled with the improvement procedure. Generally, the convergence is faster and the quality is better than the other algorithms. The ACS algorithm when coupled with the local improvement procedure starts with a good solution, because the initial solutions built by the ants are improved by the procedure at the *first iteration* and before being reported in the graph. It is important to note that *all* the evaluated solutions are taken into account including those generated by the local improvement procedure. The results obtained by simulated annealing and ACS without the improvement procedure are fairly similar in the 4 examples.

The results obtained after 10 trials are given in tables 2 and 3. The solutions obtained by the ACS when coupled with the improvement procedure are the best obtained solutions. The application of the improvement procedure with the ACS improves the quality of solutions and the time required to produce near optimal solutions. Table 6 shows that the best results obtained by the simulated annealing and ACS (without the improvement procedure) are almost similar. However, we remark that:

(i) The mean values of the results obtained by the simulated annealing are clearly better than those obtained by the ACS algorithm.

(ii) The execution times of simulated annealing and ACS when coupled with the improvement procedure are lower than the execution time of ACS alone. For instance, in example 4 the mean execution time is 3960 seconds for ACS alone and it is about 1172 and 2030 seconds for SA and ACS coupled with the improvement procedure, respectively.

	P_{Tmax}	C_T($)	**H**	**r**	**f**
Example 1	4.7074	160	(1,3,1,1)	(3,3,3,3)	(2,1,2)
Example 2	3.2467	250	(1,1,1,1,5,5,1,2,1,2)	(2,2,2,3,1,1,2,1,1,1)	(1,1,1,1,3,1,1,1,1)
Example 3	4.4406	450	(1,1,1,1,1,1,1,1,1,1,1,1,2,1,1)	(3,2,2,4,2,2,2,2,2,2,2,2,4,2,2)	(1,1,2,1,1,1,1,1,1,1,1,2,1,1)
Example 4	3.8991	750	(2,4,3,1,5,4,2,4,1,2,1,2,1,2,1,1,2,3,4,2)	(3,2,2,4,2,2,2,2,4,2,3,2,3,2,4,3,2,2,2,2)	(1,2,2,1,1,3,1,2,2,1,1,1,1,1,1,2,1,1,1)

Table 2. Results for examples 1, 2, 3 and 4

	Simulated annealing					**ACS**					**ACS with improving procedure**				
	Min	**Mean**	**STD**	**Max**	t_{mea}	**Min**	**Mean**	**STD**	**Max**	t_{mea}	**Min**	**Mean**	**STD**	**Max**	t_{mea}
Example 1	**4.7074**	**4.7074**	**0**	**4.7074**	**<1**	**4.7074**	**4.7074**	**0**	**4.7074**	**<1**	**4.7074**	**4.7074**	**0**	**4.7074**	**<1**
Example 2	3.1162	3.1694	0.0478	3.2467	352s	3.1162	3.1291	0.0522	3.2282	1130s	**3.2452**	**3.2463**	**0.0005**	**3.2467**	**186s**
Example 3	3.5855	3.7107	0.1243	3.8282	933s	3.5855	3.6649	0.1411	3.9738	1644s	**3.8282**	**4.0746**	0.1274	**4.4406**	**788 s**
Example 4	2.9096	3.0663	0.1252	3.2206	1172s	2.4375	2.9607	0.3082	3.2325	3960s	**3.2169**	**3.4577**	0.2154	**3.8991**	**2030s**

Table 3. Results for examples 1, 2, 3 and 4

In order to compare the performance of the three algorithms, the stopping criterion is the number of evaluated solutions. The computation time of the ACS algorithm, for the same number of evaluated solutions, is higher than that of the other algorithms. This is because the ACS algorithm constructs an *entire solution* (*i.e.*, selects versions and number of machines for each sub-system), at each iteration and for each ant. It implies that a complete loop is used. Thus, each solution construction requires considerable computation time. On the other hand, when the ACS is coupled with the improvement procedure, each generated solution by an ant can be improved by evaluating the neighbour solutions while carrying out *minor changes in the current solution*. Consequently, since it does *not require a complete construction of the solution,* the computation time is decreased. On the other hand, the simulated annealing algorithm constructs the solutions by making minor changes in the current solutions, requiring less computation time than the ACS algorithm when coupled or not with the improvement procedure.

Additional tests

A set of 10 test instances are also randomly generated for n = 20 and used to evaluate the performance of the proposed algorithms. Note that the parameters used for these 10 test instances are those set by using example 4 as a typical problem (see Table 3, for n = 20). By running the algorithms without further tuning on the 10 test instances, we avoid any parameters over-fitting.

The proposed algorithms are evaluated in terms of solutions quality. For each instance, five trials are performed. It has been observed again for these randomly generated instances that the ACS coupled with the Improvement procedure (ACS-I) out-performs ACS and SA algorithms.

5. Conclusion

Three optimal design problems were studied in this chapter. The first problem is related to the reliability optimization of series systems with multiple-choice and budget constraints. The second problem concerns the redundancy allocation problem of series-parallel systems, while the third deals with the selection of machines and buffers in unreliable series-parallel production lines. As the formulated problems are complicated combinatorial optimization ones, an exhaustive examination of all possible solutions is not realistic, considering reasonable time limitations. Because of this, we developed efficient heuristics to solve the formulated problems. This heuristic was inspired by the ant system meta-heuristic. The experimental results showed that the optimal or nearly optimal solutions are obtained very quickly. Through several numerical examples, the effectiveness of HACO with respect to the quality of solutions and the computing time will be discussed by performing comparisons with others approaches based on mate-heuristics.

6. References

Ait-Kadi D, Nourelfath M. Availability optimization of fault-tolerant systems. *Int Conf Ind Engng Prod Manage* (IEPM'2001) Quebec 2001; August. [1]

Dorigo M, Stutzle T. The ant colony optimization metaheuristic: Algorithms, applications and advances. *Handbook of Metaheuristics* 2001: F. Glover and G. Kochenberger. [2]

Garey MR, Johnson DS. Computers and Intractability. San Francisco:Freeman, 1979. [3]

Liang YC, Smith AE. An ant system approach to redundancy allocation. *Proceedings of the 1999 Congress on Evolutionary Computation,* 1999 (CEC 99);2: 1999 -1484. [4]

Nauss RM. The 0-1 knapsack problem with multiple choice constraints. *European Journal of Operational Research* 1978. p 121-131. [5]

Nourelfath M, Nahas N. Quantized Hopfield networks for reliability optimization. Reliab *Engng Sys Safety,* Volume 81, Issue 2, pages 191-196. [6]

Sinha P, Zoltners AA. The multiple choice knapsack problem. *Operations Research* 1979. p 503-515. [7]

Sung CS, Lee HK. A branch-and-bound approach for spare unit allocation in a series system. *European Journal of Operational Research* 1994. p 217-232. [8]

Sung CS, Cho YK. Reliability optimization of a series system with multiple-choice and budget constraints. *European Journal of Operational Research* 2000. p 159-171. [9]

Yang S, Dingwei W. Constraint satisfaction adaptive neural network and heuristics combined approaches for generalized job-shop scheduling. *IEEE Transactions on Neural Networks* 2000; ll(2):474-486. [10]

Nahas N, Nourelfath M. Ant system for reliability optimization of a series system with multiple-choice and budget constraints. *Reliab Eng Syst Saf* 2005;87(1):1-12. [11]

Bellman RE, Dreyfus E. Dynamic programming and reliability of multi-component devices. *Operations Research* 1958;6: 200-206. [12]

Besteo MD, Stutzle T, Dorigo M. Ant colony optimization for the total weighted tardiness problem. *Proc. 6th Int. Conf. Parallel Problem Solving From Nature* (PPSN VI), Berlin, 2000; pp. 611-620. [13]

Bulfin RL, Liu CY. Optimal allocation of redundant components for large systems. *IEEE Transactions on Reliability* 1985;34: 241-247. [14]

Bullnheimer B, Hartl RF, Strauss C. Applying the Ant System to the vehicle Routing problem. *2nd Metaheuristics International Conference* (MIC-97), Sophia-Antipolis, France, 1997; pp. 21-24. [15]

Burke EK, Bykov Y, Newall JP, Petrovic S. A New Local Search Approach with Execution Time as an Input Parameter. *Computer Science Technical Report No.* NOTTCS-TR-2002-3. School of Computer Science and Information Technology. University of Nottingham. [16]

Chern MS. On the computational complexity of reliability redundancy allocation in a series system. *Operations Research Letter* 1992; 11:309-15. [17]

Coit DW, Smith AE. Reliability Optimization of Series-Parallel Systems Using a Genetic Algorithm. *IEEE Transactions on Reliability* 1996;45(2): 254-260. [18]

Costa D, Hertz A. Ants can color graphs. *J. Oper. Res. Soc.* 1997; 48: 295-305. [19]

Dorigo M. Optimization, Learning and Natural Algorithms. *Ph.D Thesis*, Politecnico di Milano, Italy, 1992. [20]

Dorigo M, Maniezzo V, Colorni A. The Ant System: Optimization by a colony of cooperating agents. *IEEE Transactions on Systems*, Man and Cybernetics- Part B 1996; [21]

Dorigo M, Gambardella LM. Ant colonies for the traveling salesman problem. *BioSystems* 1997;43: 73-81. [22]

Dorigo M, Gambardella LM. Ant colony system: a cooperative learning approach to the traveling salesman problem. *IEEE Transactions on Evolutionary Computation* 1997; 1(1): 53-66. [23]

Di Caro G, Dorigo M. Mobile Agents for Adaptive Routing. *Proceedings for the 31st Hawaii International Conference on System Sciences*, Big Island of Hawaii, January 6-9, 1998, pp. 74-83. [24]

Fyffe DE, Hines WW, Lee NK. System Reliability Allocation And a Computational Algorithm. *IEEE Transactions on Reliability* 1968; vol. R-17(2):64-69. [25]

Gambardella LM, Taillard E, Dorigo M. Ant Colonies for the Quadratic Assignment Problem. *Journal of the Operational Research Society* 1999; 50:167-176. [26]

Gen M, Ida K, Tsujimura Y, Kim CE. Large scale 0-1 fuzzy goal programming and its application to reliability optimization problem. *Computers & Industrial Engineering* 1993; 24: 539-549. [27]

Ghare M, Taylor RE. Optimal redundancy for reliability in series system. *Operations research* 1969;17:838-847. [28]

Hsieh YC. A linear approximation for redundant reliability problems with multiple components choices. *Computers and Industrial Engineering* 2002; 44:91-103. [29]

Glover F. Future paths for integer programming and links to artificial intelligence. *Computers & Operations Research* 1986;13:533-549. [30]

Kulturel-Konak S, Smith AE, Coit D.W. Efficiently solving the redundancy allocation problem using tabu search. *HE transactions* 2003;35: 515-526. [31]

Kuo W, Prasad VR. An annotatedoverview of system-reliability optimization. *IEEE Transactions on Reliability* 2000;49(2): 176-87. [32]

Levitin G, Lisnianski A, Ben-Haim H, Elmakis D. Redundancy optimization for series-parallel multi-state systems. *IEEE Transactions on Reliability* 1998;47(2): 165-172. [33]

Misra KB, Sharma U. An Efficient Algorithm to Solve Integer-Programming Problems Arising in System-Reliability Design. *IEEE Transactions on Reliability* 1991;40(1): 81-91. [34]

Nakagawa Y, Miyazaki S. Surrogate Constraints Algorithm for Reliability Optimization Problems with Two Constraints. *IEEE Transactions on Reliability* 1981;R-30(2): 175-180. [35]

Nourelfath M, Nahas N, Ait-Kadi D. Optimal design of series production lines with unreliable machines and finite buffers. *Journal of Quality in Maintenance Engineering* 2005;11(2): 121-138. [36]

Painton L, Campbell J. Genetic Algorithms in Optimization of System Reliability. *IEEE Transactions on Reliability* 1995;44(2): 172-178. [37]

Schoofs L, Naudts B. Ant colonies are good at solving constraint satisfaction problems. *Proc. 2000 Congress on Evolutionary Computation*, San Diego, CA, July 2000, pp. 1190-1195. [38]

Tillman FA, Hwang CL, Kuo W. Optimization techniques for system reliability with redundancy- a review. *IEEE Transaction on Reliability* 1977;R-26(3): 147-155. [39]

Tillman FA, Hwang C-L, Kuo W. Determining Component Reliability and Redundancy for Optimum System Reliability. *IEEE Transactions on Reliability* 1977;R-26(3): 162-165. [40]

Yalaoui A, Chatelet E, Chu C. A New Dynamic Programming Method for Reliability and Redundancy Allocation in a Parallel-Series System. *IEEE transactions on Reliability* 2005; 54 (2):254-261. [41]

Yokota T, Gen M, Ida K. System reliability of optimization problems with several failure modes by genetic algorithm. *Japanese Journal of Fuzzy Theory and Systems* 1995; 7(l):117-35. [42]

Yokota T, Gen M, Li YX. Genetic algorithm for nonlinear mixed-integer programming and its applications. *Computers and Industrial Engineering* 1996;30(4):905-17. [43]

Wagner IA, Bruckstein AM. Hamiltonian(t)—an ant inspired heuristic for recognizing Hamiltonian graphs. *Proc. 1999 Congress on Evolutionary Computation*, Washington, D.C., July 1999, pp. 1465-1469. [44]

Dallery, Y. and Gershwin, S.B., 1992, Manufacturing Flow Line Systems: A Review of Models and Analytical Results, Queueing Systems theory and Applications, *Special Issue on Queueing Models of Manufacturing Systems*, 12(1-2), 3-94. [45]

Gershwin, S.B. and Schor, J.E., 2000, Efficient Algorithms for Buffer Space Allocation, *Annals of Operations Research*, 93, 117-144. [46]

Buzacott, J.A. 1967, Automatic Transfer Lines with Buffer Stocks, *International Journal of Production Research*, 5(3), 182-200. [47]

Buzacott, J.A., 1968, Prediction of Efficiency of Production Systems without Internal Storage, *International Journal of production Research*, 6(3), 173-188. [48]

Gershwin, S.B., 1987, An Efficient Decomposition Algorithm for The Approximate Evaluation of Tandem Queues with Finite Storage Space and Blocking, *Operations Research*, 35, 291-305. [49]

Kirckpatrick, S., GERLATT C.D. Jr and VECCHI M.P., 1983, Optimization by Simulated Annealing, *Science*, 220, 671-680. [50]

DALLERY, Y., DAVID, R. and Xffi, X.L., 1988, An Efficient Algorithm for Analysis of Transfer Lines with Unreliable machines and Finite Buffers, *HE transactions*, 20(3), 280-283. [51]

Burman, M.H., 1995, New Results in Flow Line Analysis, *Ph. D. Thesis*, MIT, Cambridge MA. [52]

Le Bihan, H. and Dallery, Y., 1997, Homogenisation Techniques for the Analysis of Production Lines with Unreliable Machines Having Different Speeds, *European Journal of Control*, 3, 200-215. [53]

Liu X-G and Buzacott, J.A., 1990, Approximate models of assembly systems with finite banks, *European Journal of Operational Research*, 45, 145-154. [54]

N. Nahas, D., M. Nourelfath et Ait-Kadi (2007). Coupling ant colony and the degraded ceiling algorithm for the redundancy allocation problem of series-parallel systems. *Reliability Engineering and System Safety*. Volume 92, Issue 2, Pages 211-222. [55]

N. Nahas, M. Nourelfath et D. Ait-Kadi (2006). Selecting machines and buffers in unreliable series-parallel production lines. *International Journal of Production Research*. (Submitted). [56]

PENCUS, M., 1970, A monte carlo method for the approximate solution of certain types of constrained optimization problems, *Oper. Rese.*, 18, 1225-1228. [57]

SPINELLIS, D. and PAPADOPOULOS, C.T., 2000, A simulated annealing approach for buffer allocation in reliable production lines. *Annals of Operations Research*, 93, 373-384. [58]

7. Appendix

		Version 1	Version 2	Version 3	Version 4
Machine 1	μ, λ, P	0.0735, 0.0121, 2.2238	0.1470, 0.0289, 2.3338	0.0438, 0.0075, 2.3764	0.0392, 0.0068, 2.4643
	Cost($)	5	10	13	15
Machine 2	μ, λ, P	0.1557, 0.0530, 2.027	0.1588, 0.0446, 2.0396	0.1495, 0.0375, 2.1153	0.0358, 0.0082, 2.1273
	Cost($)	10	15	20	25
Machine 3	μ, λ, P	0.0521, 0.0053, 2.1849	0.0447, 0.0051, 2.2222	0.1383, 0.0205, 2.2924	0.0523, 0.0062, 2.3265
	Cost($)	10	12	15	20
Machine 4	μ, λ, P	0.0336, 0.0023, 2.1568	0.0916, 0.0037, 2.3087	0.1007, 0.0044, 2.3541	0.1074, 0.0055, 2.4084
	Cost($)	9	15	23	30

Table A. 1. Data for example 1

		Version 1	Version 2	Version 3
Buffer 1	Capacity, Cost($)	30, 5	40, 8	55, 15
Buffer 2	Capacity, Cost($)	45,10	60, 20	65, 25
Buffer 3	Capacity, Cost($)	35, 5	50, 10	60, 18

Table A.2. Data for example 1

		Version 1	Version 2	Version 3	Version 4	Version 5
Machine 1	μ, λ, P	0.2645, 0.0438, 3.1145	0.1544, 0.0268, 3.3136	0.2468, 0.0433, 3.3426	0.1593, 0.0269, 3.3977	0.3688, 0.0622, 3.5288
	Cost($)	5	7	10	12	13
Machine 2	μ, λ, P	0.2085, 0.0303, 2.9765	0.2171, 0.0283, 3.1229	0.3707, 0.0522, 3.4287	0.195, 0.0315, 3.5041	0.2525, 0.0339, 3.5389
	Cost($)	7	10	12	13	14
Machine 3	μ, λ, P	0.2351, 0.1242, 2.5327	0.2691, 0.0861, 2.783	0.1953, 0.0574, 2.9909	0.2192, 0.0484, 3.07	0.199, 0.0547, 3.2178
	Cost($)	10	11	12	15	17
Machine 4	μ, λ, P	0.1528, 0.0289, 2.9659	0.2796, 0.0535, 3.0089	0.2921, 0.0617, 3.2554	0.3878, 0.0798, 3.3826	0.1809, 0.0318, 3.398
	Cost($)	5	8	9	10	14
Machine 5	μ, λ, P	0.2314, 0.0242, 3.1254	0.2567, 0.0254, 3.1522	0.2103, 0.0175, 3.4252	0.1982, 0.021, 3.4279	0.1957, 0.0155, 3.5828
	Cost($)	20	22	23	25	26
Machine 6	μ, λ, P	0.1599, 0.0108, 3.2422	0.3256, 0.0221, 3.292	0.234, 0.018, 3.481	0.218, 0.0148, 3.5796	0.2695, 0.0196, 3.629
	Cost($)	20	22	23	25	26
Machine 7	μ, λ, P	0.2612, 0.0323, 3.0859	0.1718, 0.0217, 3.3243	0.1827, 0.0221, 3.3351	0.1552, 0.0172, 3.6137	0.3862, 0.047, 3.6151
	Cost($)	10	13	15	16	17
Machine 8	μ, λ, P	0.2287, 0.0108, 3.6734	0.3794, 0.015, 3.7013	0.1845, 0.0072, 3.818	0.2565, 0.0088, 3.8469	0.2403, 0.0096, 3.9015
	Cost($)	10	11	12	14	15
Machine 9	μ, λ, P	0.2494, 0.0153, 3.4925	0.2221, 0.0115, 3.5739	0.3126, 0.0198, 3.6441	0.1941, 0.0113, 3.7465	0.2547, 0.0126, 3.8411
	Cost($)	5	6	8	10	11
Machine 10	μ, λ, P	0.2285, 0.0051, 3.4271	0.3272, 0.0074, 3.6841	0.3721, 0.0124, 3.7248	0.1863, 0.0051, 3.828	0.3115, 0.0097, 3.9345
	Cost($)	15	16	18	20	21

Table A.3. Data for example 2

		Version 1	Version 2	Version 3	Version 4
Buffer 1	Capacity, Cost($)	40, 5	55, 8	70, 14	80, 20
Buffer 2	Capacity, Cost($)	30, 5	40, 8	50, 14	65, 20
Buffer 3	Capacity, Cost($)	30, 7	40, 10	45, 15	60, 18
Buffer 4	Capacity, Cost($)	45, 10	55, 15	60, 19	70, 23
Buffer 5	Capacity, Cost($)	35, 12	50, 15	67, 20	70, 30
Buffer 6	Capacity, Cost($)	40, 10	50, 15	65, 19	70, 23
Buffer 7	Capacity, Cost($)	50, 5	65, 8	75, 14	85, 20
Buffer 8	Capacity, Cost($)	30, 15	55, 20	65, 24	80, 28
Buffer 9	Capacity, Cost($)	30, 10	35, 15	40, 20	45, 25

Table A.4. Data for example 2

		Version 1	Version 2	Version 3	Version 4	Version 5
Machine 1	μ, λ, P	0.2304, 0.1166, 2.6313	0.1973, 0.0972, 2.676	0.2139, 0.1336, 2.7256	0.0714, 0.0447, 2.8628	0.106, 0.0448, 2.9109
	Cost($)	5	7	10	12	13
Machine 2	μ, λ, P	0.1898, 0.0507, 3.1064	0.0923, 0.0205, 3.5717	0.1508, 0.0344, 3.7054	0.0792, 0.0204, 3.7109	0.0912, 0.019, 3.7525
	Cost($)	7	10	12	13	14
Machine 3	μ, λ, P	0.17, 0.025, 3.4031	0.0788, 0.0118, 3.4336	0.2261, 0.0327, 3.5206	0.0609, 0.0087, 3.8141	0.0615, 0.0092, 4.0129
	Cost($)	10	11	12	15	17
Machine 4	μ, λ, P	0.1093, 0.0404, 2.81	0.0682, 0.0222, 2.9181	0.1566, 0.0444, 3.0724	0.1804, 0.0562, 3.4688	0.1919, 0.0516, 3.667
	Cost($)	5	8	9	10	14
Machine 5	μ, λ, P	0.105, 0.0202, 3.4092	0.2216, 0.0352, 3.4678	0.1866, 0.0309, 3.6719	0.0751, 0.0113, 3.9665	0.0801, 0.0126, 3.9949
	Cost($)	20	22	23	25	26
Machine 6	μ, λ, P	0.1022, 0.0103, 3.5011	0.0719, 0.0073, 3.6115	0.1238, 0.0127, 3.652	0.0806, 0.0085, 3.6843	0.1755, 0.019, 4.243
	Cost($)	20	22	23	25	26
Machine 7	μ, λ, P	0.2373, 0.0236, 3.6365	0.1379, 0.0134, 4.1087	0.1587, 0.0156, 4.2079	0.1497, 0.0143, 4.212	0.1063, 0.0103, 4.2268
	Cost($)	10	13	15	16	17
Machine 8	μ, λ, P	0.0804, 0.0091, 3.4941	0.1803, 0.0206, 3.5102	0.1389, 0.0188, 3.6295	0.0767, 0.0089, 3.7977	0.1837, 0.0253, 4.0229
	Cost($)	10	11	12	14	15
Machine 9	μ, λ, P	0.1958, 0.0157, 3.6803	0.158, 0.0112, 3.8792	0.1185, 0.0094, 4.006	0.0979, 0.0077, 4.1912	0.0717, 0.0054, 4.2743
	Cost($)	5	6	8	10	11
Machine 10	μ, λ, P	0.166, 0.0147, 4.0969	0.0918, 0.0083, 4.1199	0.0975, 0.0082, 4.1955	0.0949, 0.0086, 4.2948	0.1807, 0.0148, 4.313
	Cost($)	15	16	18	20	21
Machine 11	μ, λ, P	0.1157, 0.008, 3.7438	0.1402, 0.0095, 3.8245	0.087, 0.0059, 3.9554	0.0641, 0.0045, 3.9678	0.0964, 0.0065, 4.0083
	Cost($)	8	13	15	16	17
Machine 12	μ, λ, P	0.079, 0.0013, 3.7965	0.0952, 0.0023, 4.019	0.2368, 0.0047, 4.2889	0.1972, 0.0044, 4.5438	0.0787, 0.0015, 4.5666
	Cost($)	9	11	12	15	17
Machine 13	μ, λ, P	0.1524, 0.1524, 1.9293	0.1309, 0.1309, 2.0227	0.1779, 0.1779, 2.1252	0.0762, 0.0762, 2.149	0.0983, 0.0983, 2.1636
	Cost($)	5	7	10	12	13
Machine 14	μ, λ, P	0.1997, 0.0077, 3.8336	0.0854, 0.0035, 4.1152	0.0791, 0.0034, 4.1519	0.0972, 0.0032, 4.1718	0.0688, 0.0019, 4.2924
	Cost($)	10	12	13	15	16
Machine 15	μ, λ, P	0.1573, 0.0099, 3.6318	0.0904, 0.0053, 3.7954	0.1232, 0.008, 4.0276	0.0637, 0.0039, 4.2929	0.1181, 0.0066, 4.3657
	Cost($)	5	8	10	12	15

Table A.5. Data for example 3

		Version 1	Version 2	Version 3	Version 4
Buffer 1	Capacity, Cost($)	40, 5	55, 8	70, 14	80, 20
Buffer 2	Capacity, Cost($)	30, 5	40, 8	50, 14	65, 20
Buffer 3	Capacity, Cost($)	30, 7	40, 10	45, 15	60, 18
Buffer 4	Capacity, Cost($)	45, 10	55, 15	60, 19	70, 23
Buffer 5	Capacity, Cost($)	35, 12	50, 15	67, 20	70, 30
Buffer 6	Capacity, Cost($)	40, 10	50, 15	65, 19	70, 23
Buffer 7	Capacity, Cost($)	50, 5	65, 8	75, 14	85, 20
Buffer 8	Capacity, Cost($)	30, 15	55, 20	65, 24	80, 28
Buffer 9	Capacity, Cost($)	30, 10	35, 15	40, 20	45, 25
Buffer 10	Capacity, Cost($)	30, 7	40, 10	45, 15	60, 18
Buffer 11	Capacity, Cost($)	35, 10	55, 15	60, 19	70, 23
Buffer 12	Capacity, Cost($)	30, 12	40, 15	67, 20	70, 30
Buffer 13	Capacity, Cost($)	40, 10	50, 15	65, 19	70, 23
Buffer 14	Capacity, Cost($)	40, 5	55, 8	65, 14	85, 20

Table A.6. Data for example 3

		Version 1	Version 2	Version 3	Version 4	Version 5
Machine 1	μ, λ, P	0.0185, 0.0113, 1.7486	0.0813, 0.0115, 2.152	0.0931, 0.018, 2.2771	0.0353, 0.0072, 2.3781	0.0245, 0.0024, 2.6762
	Cost($)	5	7	10	12	13
Machine 2	μ, λ, P	0.0371, 0.0178, 1.9237	0.0202, 0.0042, 2.0775	0.0295, 0.0040, 2.3179	0.0303, 0.0019, 2.3961	0.0189, 0.0006, 2.7135
	Cost($)	7	10	12	13	14
Machine 3	μ, λ, P	0.0382, 0.0114, 1.8927	0.1223, 0.0204, 2.2257	0.128, 0.0098, 2.2937	0.0297, 0.0042, 2.2937	0.0186, 0.001, 2.8012
	Cost($)	10	11	12	15	17
Machine 4	μ, λ, P	0.0823, 0.0254, 1.9109	0.0585, 0.0226, 2.1123	0.0231, 0.001, 2.4097	0.0219, 0.0032, 2.4536	0.1037, 0.0205, 2.4773
	Cost($)	5	8	9	10	14
Machine 5	μ, λ, P	0.068, 0.0257, 1.8233	0.076, 0.0117, 2.1325	0.0611, 0.0022, 2.3506	0.08, 0.0134, 2.4409	0.1092, 0.0026, 2.7139
	Cost($)	20	22	23	25	26
Machine 6	μ, λ, P	0.0295, 0.0044, 2.2169	0.035, 0.0046, 2.5357	0.04804, 0.0068, 2.5703	0.033, 0.001, 2.7065	0.0354, 0.0012, 2.8585
	Cost($)	20	22	23	25	26
Machine 7	μ, λ, P	0.0353, 0.0139, 1.8043	0.03, 0.0029, 2.2432	0.1072, 0.0044, 2.3552	0.0294, 0.0006, 2.3913	0.0285, 0.0026, 2.5494
	Cost($)	10	13	15	16	17
Machine 8	μ, λ, P	0.0994, 0.0312, 1.8479	0.0359, 0.0072, 2.2335	0.0518, 0.0052, 2.2525	0.0285, 0.0007, 2.5563	0.0226, 0.0012, 2.7477
	Cost($)	10	11	12	14	15
Machine 9	μ, λ, P	0.0207, 0.0045, 2.1397	0.0988, 0.0286, 2.2173	0.0179, 0.0029, 2.3142	0.0891, 0.0126, 2.5253	0.0212, 0.0008, 2.5373
	Cost($)	5	6	8	10	11
Machine 10	μ, λ, P	0.094, 0.0142, 2.1576	0.1087, 0.013, 2.2653	0.0588, 0.0098, 2.4437	0.0931, 0.0058, 2.5515	0.0225, 0.0014, 2.6952
	Cost($)	15	16	18	20	21
Machine 11	μ, λ, P	0.0377, 0.0053, 2.152	0.1138, 0.0111, 2.3944	0.1134, 0.0107, 2.437	0.0216, 0.0012, 2.6218	0.1068, 0.0135, 2.6254
	Cost($)	8	13	15	16	17
Machine 12	μ, λ, P	0.0181, 0.0078, 1.8908	0.1131, 0.0068, 2.3775	0.0182, 0.0025, 2.4526	0.0572, 0.0042, 2.4693	0.1201, 0.0086, 2.4944
	Cost($)	9	11	12	15	17
Machine 13	μ, λ, P	0.0612, 0.006, 2.3013	0.0612, 0.0027, 2.5733	0.0594, 0.0055, 2.6149	0.0321, 0.0021, 2.6493	0.1287, 0.0065, 2.6888
	Cost($)	5	7	10	12	13
Machine 14	μ, λ, P	0.0281, 0.0123, 1.8713	0.0317, 0.0029, 2.3124	0.0192, 0.0036, 2.3596	0.0613, 0.0073, 2.6254	0.0764, 0.0072, 2.688
	Cost($)	10	12	13	15	16
Machine 15	μ, λ, P	0.0279, 0.0071, 2.06	0.0296, 0.0054, 2.1132	0.1134, 0.0182, 2.3418	0.1072, 0.0046, 2.5759	0.0311, 0.0012, 2.7956
	Cost($)	5	8	10	12	15
Machine 16	μ, λ, P	0.0307, 0.0034, 2.3659	0.0339, 0.0035, 2.5748	0.1291, 0.011, 2.6265	0.017, 0.0012, 2.6318	0.1279, 0.0044, 2.7025
	Cost($)	5	8	9	10	14
Machine 17	μ, λ, P	0.0888, 0.0449, 1.7617	0.0831, 0.0135, 2.3343	0.0346, 0.0029, 2.3881	0.0248, 0.0017, 2.3942	0.0175, 0.0005, 2.8557
	Cost($)	20	22	23	25	26
Machine 18	μ, λ, P	0.0316, 0.0097, 1.9782	0.03, 0.0022, 2.3827	0.0659, 0.0053, 2.5769	0.0704, 0.0078, 2.6572	0.0215, 0.0013, 2.775
	Cost($)	20	22	23	25	26
Machine 19	μ, λ, P	0.0615, 0.0183, 2.2777	0.0334, 0.0076, 2.3789	0.0172, 0.0026, 2.3951	0.123, 0.0084, 2.6452	0.032, 0.0009, 2.6673
	Cost($)	10	13	15	16	17
Machine 20	μ, λ, P	0.0244, 0.0073, 1.9532	0.0715, 0.0075, 2.4901	0.1182, 0.0061, 2.6246	0.0291, 0.0019, 2.644	0.0719, 0.0057, 2.6495
	Cost($)	10	11	12	14	15

Table A.7. Data for example 4

		Version 1	Version 2	Version 3	Version 4
Buffer 1	Capacity, Cost($)	40, 5	55, 8	70, 14	80, 20
Buffer 2	Capacity, Cost($)	30, 5	40, 8	50, 10	65, 13
Buffer 3	Capacity, Cost($)	30, 7	40, 10	45, 11	60, 15
Buffer 4	Capacity, Cost($)	45, 10	55, 12	60, 15	70, 20
Buffer 5	Capacity, Cost($)	35, 12	50, 15	67, 20	70,30
Buffer 6	Capacity, Cost($)	40, 10	50, 11	65, 13	70, 14
Buffer 7	Capacity, Cost($)	50, 5	65, 8	75, 10	85, 13
Buffer 8	Capacity, Cost($)	30, 17	55, 20	65, 24	80, 28
Buffer 9	Capacity, Cost($)	30, 10	35, 12	40, 15	45, 16
Buffer 10	Capacity, Cost($)	30, 7	40, 10	45, 15	60, 18
Buffer 11	Capacity, Cost($)	35, 10	55, 12	60, 15	70, 18
Buffer 12	Capacity, Cost($)	30, 12	40, 15	67, 20	70, 23
Buffer 13	Capacity, Cost($)	40, 10	50, 15	65, 19	70, 23
Buffer 14	Capacity, Cost($)	40, 5	55, 8	65, 13	85, 17
Buffer 15	Capacity, Cost($)	50, 5	65, 8	75, 12	85, 15
Buffer 16	Capacity, Cost($)	30, 15	55, 16	65, 18	80, 21
Buffer 17	Capacity, Cost($)	30, 10	35, 15	40, 20	45, 25
Buffer 18	Capacity, Cost($)	30, 7	40, 10	45, 12	60, 15
Buffer 19	Capacity, Cost($)	35, 10	55, 15	60, 19	70, 23

Table A. 8. Data for example 4

27

Distributed Particle Swarm Optimization for Structural Bayesian Network Learning

Ferat Sahin and Archana Devasia
Rochester Institute of Technology
USA

1. Introduction

Particle Swarm Optimization (PSO) was first introduced as a concept for a non-linear optimizer by Kennedy and Eberhart in 1995. Their seminal work articulates a technique of evolutionary computation, which has its origin in artificial intelligence and simplified social models such as bird flocking and fish schooling (Kennedy & Eberhart, Nov. 1995; Kennedy & Eberhart, Oct. 1995). Its early appeal lay in its use of only primitive mathematical operators and computational economy with regard to both memory and speed. The authors were influenced by the work of Reynolds, Heppner and Grenander in modeling bird flocking and recognized that the fundamental hypothesis to the development of PSO is that an evolutionary advantage is obtained by the social sharing of information among members of the same species. They stated that the simulation of the graceful but unpredictable choreography of a bird flock by collision-proof agents could be used as an effective optimizer for a wide range of functions.

1.1 PSO concept

The PSO technique involves casting a population of co-operative agents, randomly in the multidimensional search space. Each agent has an associated fitness value, which is evaluated by the fitness function to be optimized, and a velocity that directs its motion. Each agent can keep track of its solution that resulted in the best fitness as well as the solutions of the best performing agents in its neighborhood. The trajectory of each agent is dynamically governed by its own and its companions' historical behavior. Kennedy and Eberhart view this adjustment as conceptually similar to the crossover operation utilized by genetic algorithms (Kennedy & Eberhart, Nov. 1995). Such an adjustment maximizes the probability that the agents are moving toward a region of space that will result in a better fitness. At each step of the optimization, the agent is allowed to update its position by evaluating its own fitness and the fitness of the neighboring agents. The PSO algorithm is terminated when the specified maximum number of generations is reached or when the best particle position of the entire population cannot be improved further after a sufficiently large number of generations.

A simple pseudo code describing the functioning of the optimizer taken from (Taşgetiren & Liang, 2003) is shown below.

Initialize parameters
Initialize population
Evaluate
Do{
Find particlebest
Find globalbest
Update velocity
Update position
Evaluate
}While (Termination)

Kennedy and Eberhart realized that the behavior of the population of agents was more comparable to a swarm rather than a flock. This swarm behavior or swarm intelligence rests on five basic principles put forth by Millonas. These have been obtained from (Kennedy & Eberhart, Nov. 1995) and (Kennedy & Eberhart, Oct. 1995) and are listed as follows:

1. *Proximity principle*: The population should be able to carry out simple space and time computations.
2. *Quality principle*: The population should be able to respond to quality factors in the environment.
3. *Principle of diverse response*: The population should not commit its activities along excessively narrow channels.
4. *Principle of stability*: The population should not change its mode of behavior every time the environment changes
5. *Principle of adaptability*: The population must be able to change its behavior when its worth the computational price.

They found that the PSO concept seemed to be consistent with the checklist above. It could inherently carry out multidimensional space calculations over a series of time steps thus following the proximity principle. The agents could respond to quality factors such as their own best fitness values as well as the neighborhood best, in accordance with the quality principle. The algorithm could allocate responses between the individual best fitness value and the neighborhood best thus ensuring the fulfillment of the principle of diverse response. The population could change its mode of behavior only with a change in global best thereby suggesting stability. And finally, the change of state with a change in neighborhood best was in itself an indication of adaptability. The population was hence branded as a swarm. The authors called each agent of the swarm, a particle and hence the label particle swarm.

1.2 Mathematical formulation

The dynamic behavior of the swarm can be quantified as given in equation (1).

$$v(t+1) = v(t) + \phi_1\left(x - x_p\right) + \phi_2\left(x - x_n\right) \tag{1a}$$

$$x(t+1) = x(t) + v(t+1) \tag{1b}$$

Here, v is the particle velocity and x is the particle position which represents a test solution. In addition, ϕ_1 and ϕ_2 are uniform random variables which introduce an element of uncertainty. The inclusion of such a stochastic factor facilitates an exhaustive search of the hyperspace under consideration thereby preventing the swarm from converging on to a local solution. Historically ϕ_1 and ϕ_2 are a combination of a positive constant and a random function. Thus (1a) becomes,

$$v(t+1) = v(t) + c_1 \times rand_1() \times (x - x_p) + c_2 \times rand_2() \times (x - x_n) \quad (2)$$

Here c_1 and c_2 are acceleration constants called cognition and social constants respectively, the functions $rand_1()$ and $rand_2()$ are random functions usually uniformly distributed between [0, 1]. The values of the constants determine the tension in the system (Shi & Eberhart, 2001). Low values allow the particles to roam far from the target regions before being pulled back, while high values result in abrupt movement toward or past target regions. Kennedy and Eberhart chose the both the acceleration constants to have a value of "2" in order to give the random factor a mean of "1" thereby causing the particles to overfly local optima and enable search in the region between local solutions. Variables ϕ_1 and ϕ_2 are clamped by an upper limit which is a parameter of the system.

The introduction of stochastic factors may cause the system to enter a state of explosion because of increased global exploration resulting in the particle velocities and positional co-ordinates tending to infinity. In order to prevent such a scenario, a maximum value of velocity $v_{\max}$ is usually defined. The second term in equation (1a) is the cognition part of the particle with the variable x_p representing the (previous) position of the particle that resulted in the best fitness so far. Kennedy and Eberhart referred to this as *simple nostalgia* (Kennedy & Eberhart, Nov. 1995). The last term of (1a) is the communal part which involves exchange of public knowledge. Here the variable x_n is the neighborhood position that resulted in the best fitness so far. Equation (1b) directs the new position of the particle based upon its current position and its new velocity.

1.3 Neighborhood size

In PSO, a neighborhood is defined for an individual particle as the subset of particles it is able to communicate with (Kennedy & Eberhart, April 2007). According to Bratton and Kennedy, since the earliest PSO model was a simulation of the social milieu, the neighborhood of choice was largely Euclidian. However it proved to be unwieldy and cumbersome in mathematical computations and hence was dispensed with to be replaced by topological neighborhoods. A number of neighborhood configurations have been discussed in literature. Some significant ones listed below are taken from (Kennedy, 1999; Guo et. al., July 2006) as shown in Fig. 1:

1. *Stars*: Every individual is connected to every other individual making the best performing individual the social source of influence.
2. *Circles*: Every individual is connected to only *K* of its immediate neighbors. This results in slower information propagation as compared to the stars topology. In this type of neighborhood, clusters are created that may converge onto different local optima. But due to neighbor to neighbor interaction, once the global solution is found, all the

clusters are pulled in towards it. For a $K = 2$ neighborhood (called a ring), it would take swarmsize/K number of steps for information about a new global best to be transmitted to the other side of the ring.

3. *Wheels*: One individual called the focal individual is connected to all the others and they are connected to only that one. The performance of the population is supervised by this central individual so as to determine the best and adjust its course according to it. If the adjustment results in improvement in the focal individual's performance then that improvement is communicated out to the rest of the population. This topology is faster than the ring topology.
4. *Random edges*: For N individuals, there are N random symmetrical connections between pairs of individuals.
5. *Von Neumann*: This topology is in the form of a 2-D lattice that wraps around itself as can be seen in Fig. 1(d).

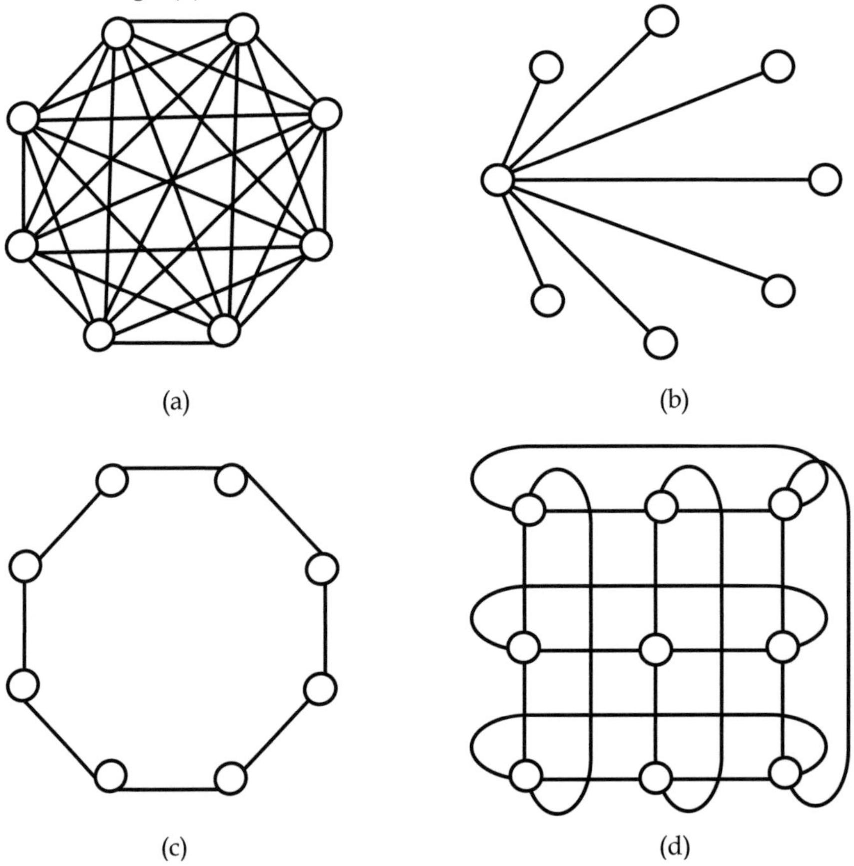

Figure 1. Neighborhood Topologies found in (Guo et. al, July 2006, Venayagamoorthy et. al, 2007): (a) Star, (b) Wheel, (c) Ring, (d) Von Neumann

1.3.1 Global neighborhood

A global neighborhood (also referred to as the GBEST model) has a star topology. The GBEST PSO algorithm as proposed in (Kennedy & Eberhart, Oct. 1995) is shown in Fig. 2.

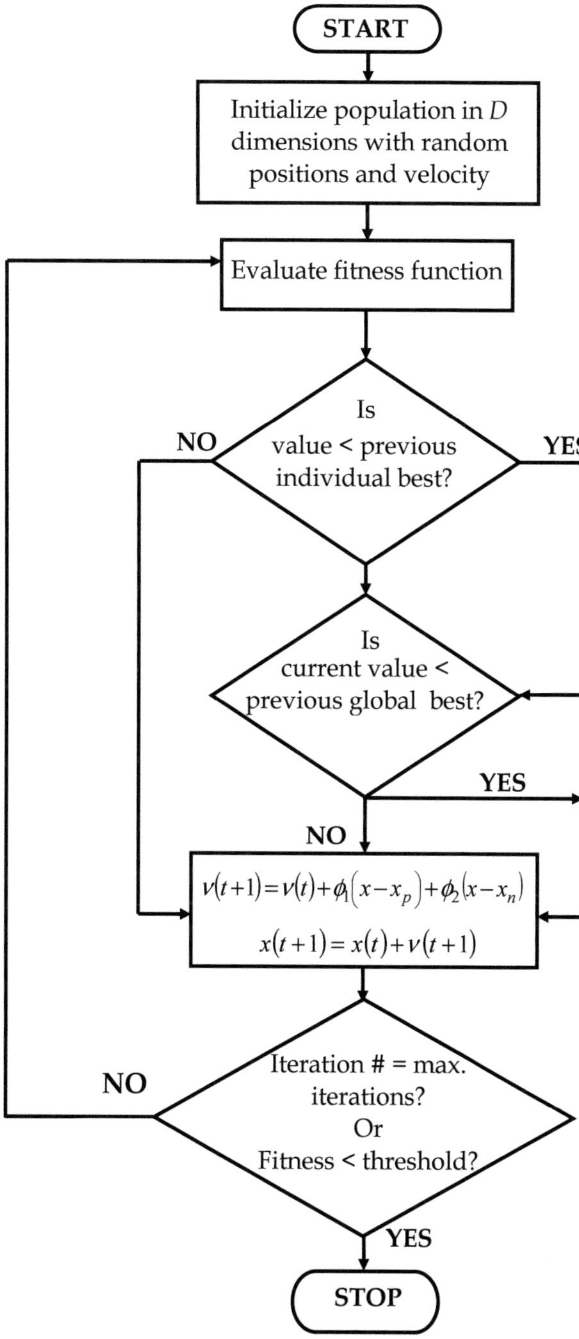

Figure 2. Flowchart of the GBEST PSO Algorithm

All the particles in the GBEST model try to reach the global solution. Hence even when a local solution is reached, all particles feel a tug in that direction. This may reduce the chances of the particles exploring the entire search space and may even cause the swarm to converge at the local solution. However since every particle keeps track of every other particle in the swarm convergence rate is fast, which makes the GBEST approach an ideal candidate for uni-modal problems.

1.3.2 Neighborhood of *K*

This refers to the Circle topology. It is called the LBEST or local version of the PSO. The number of nearest neighbors is decided by the size of the neighborhood. As discussed previously, for a neighborhood of size *K*, each particle can communicate directly with only *K* other particles. Hence instead of moving toward the stochastic average of particle best and global best, the particles move toward the points defined by particle best and local best, which is the position of the particle with the best evaluation in the neighborhood (Kennedy & Eberhart, Oct. 1995). Kennedy and Eberhart found this local approach to be more flexible than the GBEST approach while trying to solve a three layer feed forward neural network designed to solve the XOR problem (Kennedy & Eberhart, Oct. 1995). They have attributed the insensitivity of this version to local solution to the fact that a number of groups of particles spontaneously separate and explore different regions. The LBEST ring model has been found to be suited for multi-model problems on account of its immunity to local optima convergence. The flipside to this limited interaction between swarm particles is the slower convergence rate in comparison to the GBEST model.

1.4 Other particle swarm parameters

In 2002, El Gallad *et al* have studied the various inputs required for working the particle swarm optimizer. Some of their findings are described below.

1) *Population of the swarm*: This factor depends upon the problem being optimized. Smaller swarms may be more successful for some problems while larger ones may be useful for others. However if the swarm size is too small it may result in convergence upon a local optimum while on the other hand very large swarms may increase computational time. Hence as suggested in (El Gallad *et al*, 2002) a balance has to be struck between the complexity of the algorithm and the risk of getting trapped in local optima by selecting a proper swarm size specific to the application at hand.
2) *Number of iterations*: The uncertainty in the velocity update equation introduced by the stochastic factors results in a global exploration of the search space that makes arriving at the global optimum extremely likely if the algorithm is run for a sufficiently long period of time. The use of the word *sufficient* is in itself indicative of the problem specific nature of this parameter. Indeed the permissible error margin, which strongly dictates the computational time, varies with the problem at hand. In cases where the time required to converge onto the global solution appears to be very long, it is more advantageous to run the algorithm for multiple short replications rather than running one very long replication. This is indeed a sound suggestion since it is possible that the time required for getting the particles out of local optima could be greater than the time required to reinitialize a new replication in (El Gallad *et al*, 2002). The stopping criterion for such multiple replications can be evaluated by observing if successive generations show any significant improvement or not.
3) *Velocity of particles*: This factor determines the fineness with which the hyperspace under consideration is searched. If the value of this parameter is too high, then the

particles may fly past the optimal solution and may even oscillate about a certain position. On the other hand if this value is too low, then the particles could get stuck at a local optimum. In order to circumvent this issue, an adaptive velocity technique can be applied. According to this approach, in the event that the solution found is oscillatory, the value of velocity is allowed to gradually decrease in a random fashion thereby helping the particles to get out of the oscillation and at the same time allowing the swarm to explore new areas.

1.5 Evolution of PSO through the ages

This section elucidates the development of PSO and details the various adjustments and modifications made to the original algorithm in order to maximize it performance.

1.5.1 Addition of inertia weight

Shi and Eberhart modified the PSO algorithm by introducing the concept of inertia weight. They argued that such a factor was necessary in order to bring a balance between global search and local search (Shi and Eberhart, 1998). Consider equation (1a). In the absence of the term representing the current velocity of the particle, the velocity would be memory less. If initially a particle, *i*, is at the best global position then it would be stationary at that position. The other particles would move toward the weighted centroid of their own best position and the global best causing the swarm to statistically contract toward the global best. This continues till another particle reaches a better global solution causing the particles to now statistically contract toward the new global best. The described scenario represents a search space that statistically shrinks over generations thus resembling a local search. Shi and Eberhart pointed out that in this case the global solution could be found only if it existed within the initial search space. Thus the search ability (i.e. global or local) could be varied by the presence or absence of the current velocity term in equation (1a). In order to fine tune the search ability, the inertia weight, w, was introduced which modified (1a) as follows.

$$v(t+1) = wv(t) + \phi_1\left(x - x_p\right) + \phi_2\left(x - x_n\right) \tag{3}$$

Shi and Eberhart used the problem of *Schaffer's f6* function to test this algorithm using w values ranging from 0 to 1.4. They found that the inertia weight in the range of [0.9, 1.2] resulted in a higher success rate of finding the global solution within a reasonable number of iterations as compared w values outside this range. They also experimented with time decreasing inertia weights and found that as w was linearly decreased from 1.4 to 0 from the first to the last iteration, the PSO showed significantly improved performance as regards success rate of finding the global optimum and number of iterations required to reach this optimum when compared to the case of using a fixed value of w. Further investigations were carried out in (Shi & Eberhart, 2000) using a linearly decreasing inertia weight starting at 0.9 and terminating at 0.4 on four benchmark functions viz. *spherical, Rosenbrock, Rastrigrin,* and *Griewank*. The mathematical expression for these functions can be found in Table 1. It was observed that the PSO algorithm converged quickly for all the four cases but reduced its convergence speed when reaching the optimum. Shi and Eberhart attributed this to the inability of the linearly decreasing inertia weighted PSO to perform a global search at the end of a run. If w_{int} and w_{fin} represent the initial and final values of w respectively,

MAX is the maximum number of optimization steps and *iter* represents the current iteration number, then a linearly decreasing w is defined in equation (4) (Iwamatsu, 2006),

$$w = (w_{\text{int}} - w_{fin}) \times (\text{MAX} - iter) / \text{MAX} + w_{fin} \tag{4}$$

Name	Mathematical Representation
Spherical	$f = \sum_{i=1}^{D} x_i^2$
Rosenbrock	$f = \sum_{i=1}^{D-1} \left\{ 100\left(x_{i+1} - x_i^2\right)^2 + \left(x_i - 1\right)^2 \right\}$
Rastrigrin	$f = \sum_{i=1}^{D} \left\{ x_i^2 - 10\cos(2\pi x_i) + 10 \right\}$
Griewank	$f = \frac{1}{4000} \sum_{i=1}^{D} x_i^2 - \prod_{i=1}^{D} \cos\left(\frac{x_i}{\sqrt{i}}\right) + 1$
Schaffer's f6	$f = 0.5 - \frac{\left(\sin\sqrt{x^2 + y^2}\right)^2 - 0.5}{\left(1 + 0.001\left(x^2 + y^2\right)\right)^2}$

Table 1. Benchmark functions used to test PSO in literature (Taşgetiren & Liang, 2003; Shi & Eberhart, 1998; Clerc & Kennedy, 2002)

1.5.2 Introduction of constriction coefficient

Clerc and Kennedy demonstrated that constriction coefficients could be used to prevent system explosion, which hitherto had been contained using $v_{\max}$ (Clerc & Kennedy, 2002). A constriction factor is defined as follows:

$$\chi = \frac{2}{\left|2 - \phi - \sqrt{\phi^2 4\phi}\right|} \tag{5}$$

Here $\phi = \phi_1 + \phi_2$. The mathematical development leading to (5) is beyond the scope of this work but can be obtained from [13]. The constriction factor when inserted into the velocity update equation modifies equation (2) as follows,

$$v(t+1) = \chi\left[v(t) + c_1 \times rand_1() \times \left(x - x_p\right) + c_2 \times rand_2() \times \left(x - x_n\right)\right] \tag{6}$$

They also showed that for values of $\phi > 4$, the particles would quickly converge onto the global solution while for $\phi < 4$ the swarm would most likely get stuck at a local optimum. Such a behavior is similar to that exhibited by the inclusion of inertia weight, w, into the system response. This similarity spawned a study comparing the performance of a PSO using a constriction factor with that using an inertia weight by (Eberhart & Shi, 2006). Five benchmark functions viz. *spherical, Rosenbrock, Rastrigrin, Griewank* and *Schaffer's f6* function were investigated during this performance analysis. It was found that even though it is not essential to specify the value of $v_{\max}$ in the constriction factor approach, limiting it to the dynamic range of each variable in each dimension (i.e. $x_{\max}$) of the system under consideration resulted in the fastest and most consistent way to obtain good results. The authors have shown that by setting $w = \chi$ and $\phi = c_1 + c_2$, the PSO algorithm using constriction factor can be considered as a special case of the PSO using inertia weight.

1.5.3 Use of adaptive scaling term

Sometimes situations are encountered wherein the evaluation of the objective function may not be feasible within a restricted time frame. In such cases the algorithm is limited to operate within an acceptable time resulting in a solution that is sub-optimal. The ideal choice here would be to accelerate the PSO in order to reduce convergence time and also increase the probability of finding the global optimum. This is the motivation for considering speed-up strategies for PSO. One such strategy proposed in (Fan, 2002) involved the use of an adaptive scaling term into the algorithm. As discussed previously the behavior of the swarm is modeled as shown in equation (1) and the necessary velocity limitations are applied as shown below,

$$\begin{aligned} v(t) &= V_{\max}, \text{ if } v(t) > V_{\max} \\ v(t) &= -V_{\max}, \text{ if } v(t) < -V_{\max} \end{aligned} \tag{7}$$

Fan explains that at the beginning of a search it is desirable that the particles be spread all over the search space in order to explore all possible regions to maximize the chances of finding the global solution. However as the search progresses, the searching scale should be reduced in order to allow the found solution to be refined. For this purpose he introduced a scaling term $\left(1-(t/T)^h\right)$ that revises (7) as,

$$\begin{aligned} v(t) &= \left(1-(t/T)^h\right)V_{\max}, \text{ if } v(t) > \left(1-(t/T)^h\right)V_{\max} \\ v(t) &= -\left(1-(t/T)^h\right)V_{\max}, \text{ if } v(t) < -\left(1-(t/T)^h\right)V_{\max} \end{aligned} \tag{8}$$

Here, t is the number of the current generation (i.e. optimization step), T is the maximum number of iterations and h is a positive constant chosen by trial and error. The velocity update and position update equations remain the same as shown in equation (1). Changes are effected only in setting the limits of velocity. Benchmark experiments revealed that this modified PSO performed better as compared to the original PSO on test functions such as spherical, Rosenbrock and Griewank's function. The modified PSO had a higher convergence rate than the original when used to solve these three function minimization problems. Fan found that the original PSO rapidly stagnated when no improvement was exhibited by its searched solution. However the modified PSO could still search progressively till the global solution was found indicating a higher reliability rate. Even with a fixed number of generations, the modified PSO exhibited better convergence reliability. It was also found that in case of the original PSO the parameter $v_{\max}$ strongly influences the best function value, making the selection of v_{max} crucial. However in the case of the modified PSO, this parameter can be selected quite arbitrarily within a relatively large range. A preliminary study was also performed to examine the effect of the exponent h that controls the reducing speed of the searching scale on the algorithm. It was found that similar to v_{max}; this parameter can also be arbitrarily selected over a wide range.

1.5.4 Inclusion of Boundary Conditions

In order to prevent the swarm searching outside the solution space, boundary conditions can be specified. These conditions are highly dependent upon factors such as problem dimensionality and the location of global optimum. The following list of boundary conditions has been taken from (Xu & Rahmat-Samii, 2007) who have also proposed two hybrids.

1. *Absorbing:* This is a type of restricted boundary condition in the sense that if a particle of the swarm flies outside the solution space in a particular dimension then it is tugged back to the boundary of the space of that dimension and its velocity is assigned a zero value. In 2007, Xu and Rahmat-Samii liken this situation to the energy of the errant particle being absorbed by a soft wall so that the particle is stuck on it, and eventually gets pulled back by its memory of best locations only.
2. *Reflecting:* This is another type of restricted boundary condition in which the deviant particle is pulled back to the boundary of the solution space of the dimension it overshot and the direction of its velocity in that dimension is altered. This is equivalent to the particle being reflected by a hard wall, and the energy driving it outside the boundary being totally reversed in order to accelerate it back toward the solution space.
3. *Damping:* This is the third type of restricted boundary condition and bears a resemblance to the reflecting boundary condition. In this case also the errant particle is drawn back into the solution space and is relocated at the boundary of the dimension under consideration where its velocity component is reversed and assigned a random number between 0 and 1. The only difference between a damping and a reflecting boundary condition is the introduction of this uncertainty factor, which makes the reflection imperfect.
4. *Invisible:* This is an unrestricted boundary condition in which the particle that leaves the solution space is not brought back but allowed to stay there. The fitness of that particle's position is not assessed and instead it is assigned a bad fitness value. In due course, the particle comes back into the solution space because of its inherent characteristic of setting its trajectory towards the weighted sum of global and individual best.
5. *Invisible/Reflecting:* This is the first of the two new unrestricted boundary conditions proposed in (Xu & Rahmat-Samii, 2007) and is a hybrid of the invisible and reflecting boundary conditions. In this case the errant particle is not pulled back to the solution space boundary and instead gets assigned a bad fitness score. Also, the direction of the velocity of the particle in the dimension under consideration is reversed because of which it accelerates back toward the solution space.
6. *Invisible/Damping:* This is the other new boundary condition proposed in (Xu & Rahmat-Samii, 2007) and is a combination of the invisible and reflecting boundary conditions. Again, the deviant particle is allowed to stay outside the solution space and gets assigned a bad fitness value while the direction of the velocity of the particle in that dimension is

reversed with a random factor between 0 and 1. As a result the particle comes back into the solution space.

1.6 Recent applications of PSO

Since its inception in 1995, the PSO algorithm has been used extensively; in some cases being tailored to suit the problem at hand and in other cases to solve issues that have not been attempted so far. In this section a brief description of some of the recent applications of the PSO algorithm have been described.

1. *Micro-PSO (μPSO)*: Recently a microparticle swarm optimizer (μPSO) is proposed for reconstructing the dielectric properties of normal and malignant breast tissues (Huang & Mohan, 2007). This is a type of high-dimensional microwave imaging which requires a large population of co-operative agents in order to find the global optimum for accurate image reconstruction. The population size adversely affects the computational effort required. Huang and Mohan have proposed an algorithm that utilizes a smaller population and implements a set of restart operations after the population has converged. If the population converges to a solution that is inferior or equal to the available best solution, the solution is blacklisted for future searches and all particles are prevented from converging onto the same solution again. They utilized the concept of the guaranteed convergence PSO and introduced a force of repulsion modeled on the lines of Coulomb's law of electrostatics between particles and blacklisted solutions. This repulsive force is inversely proportional to some power of the distance between the particle under consideration and a given blacklisted solution. The authors suggested the value of this power should be chosen in such a way that it cause enough force to repel the particles away from blacklisted solutions while at the same time allowing them to search spaces surrounding the blacklisted solutions. While selecting the value of the inertia parameter, the authors have employed an adaptive technique that sets the value of w depending on the quality of solutions found. As regards the type of neighborhood, since a μPSO typically consists of only 3-5 agents, the authors have suggested the use the GBEST topology.
2. Application to Electromagnetic Devices: The PSO is successfully applied for the purpose of optimizing the design of electromagnetic devices, particularly the problem of a super conducting magnetic energy storage (SMES) configuration with eight free parameters (Ho et al, 2006). In their attempt they have suggested certain enhancements in order to balance the exploration and exploitation capabilities of PSO. Stagnation may be introduced into the PSO algorithm due to sharing of information between the particles of the swarm. In order to boost up the diversity of the algorithm, the authors have proposed the introduction of an age variable, which is representative of the age of a global best, or an individual particle's best. If this age exceeds a certain threshold value then that particular solution is disposed and replaced by a new randomly generated solution thus improving global search ability. The authors also recommend that in order to further ensure the solution diversity of the particles, a Roulette wheel scheme should be adopted for selecting the individual and global bests from their respective sets. For the purpose of balancing personal and social experience as well as exploration and exploitation two new random factors are introduced by the authors. The former in this case is actually a combination of rand1() and rand2() (defined in equation (2)) set in such a way that the sum of rand1() and rand2() equals 1. Ho et al

also proposed the inclusion of an intensified search into the algorithm for accurately identifying the global optimum. They have explained this method as follows. When a global best is found, an intensification search is activated in the neighborhood around this point using only its speed vector with the cognitive and social influences being deliberately excluded in the velocity updating formula. In this iterative process, if a search is successful, the algorithm will keep the velocity vector unchanged while continuing its exploitation using this speed vector; otherwise, the algorithm will generate randomly a new speed vector to begin the next refinement search. The intensification search process will be repeated until the number of consecutive unsuccessful explorations around a new reaches a previously decided number.

3. Application to Circuit Partitioning: The PSO is applied to a circuit partitioning problem (Venayagamoorthy et al. 2007). Such a partitioning is essential in order to reduce the number of test vectors required to detect faults in VLSI circuits. The authors have compared the performance of a standard I-PIFAN (improved primary input and fanout based partitioning approach) algorithm in partitioning combinational CMOS circuits into a number of sub-circuits with that of a modified version employing PSO (called PSO-PIFAN). In the I-PIFAN, the circuit can be partitioned depending upon the combinations of the maximum node fan in size N and the minimum partitioning fanout value F. Venayagamoorthy et al showed that I-PIFAN's search is exhaustive and hence slow and is constrained within a pre-specified range of N and F combinations. The best result has to be selected from this range. Thus, if the optimal solution is outside the specified range of N and F values then it will not be found. In the case of the PSO-PIFAN, all combinations of N and F are searched simultaneously without necessitating a specified range. The authors have concluded that the PSO-PIFAN performs a directed search of the solution space and uses its memory to accelerate the PSO particles towards the global solution in a shorter time and will always converge to the optimal solution.
4. Application in Power Systems: Recently, there has been an attempt to demonstrate the feasibility and robustness of PSO in solving a transient stability constrained optimal power flow problem (TSCOPF) (Mo et al, 2007). They tested the algorithm on two test systems viz. the IEEE 30-bus system and the New England 39-bus systems with promising results. Comparison with GA revealed PSO to be better equipped for solving multi-contingency TSCOPF. In order to accelerate the process of computation, the authors have proposed the use of a parallel computing environment.

1.7 Binary PSO

In order to easily solve combinatorial problems such as scheduling and routing issues that involve ordering or arranging of discrete elements, Kennedy and Eberhart proposed a binary version of the PSO optimizer, which could operate on two valued functions (Kennedy & Eberhart, 1997). In this adaptation of the original PSO, the position of each particle is described either by a 0 or a 1 in each dimension. In this case, the velocity of the particle in a particular dimension represents the probability of the position of the particle in that dimension being 0 or 1. A sigmoid limiting transformation $\sigma(v(t+1))$ is used to update the position of the particle under consideration by comparing it to a random number ρ. This is expressed in the equation (9).

$$\text{If } \sigma(v(t+1)) > \rho \text{ then } x(t+1) = 1 \text{ otherwise } x(t+1) = 0 \tag{9}$$

The random number, ρ , is considered to be uniformly distributed in the range [0, 1].

The pseudo code for the discrete PSO developed by Kennedy, Eberhart and Shi and taken from (Guo et al, 2006) is described as follows:

Loop
    For $i = 1$ to N_p // N_p is the number of particles
        If $G(X^t_i) > G(P^t_i)$ then   // $G(\ )$ evaluates the objective function, X^t_i is a potential solution i.e. $X^t_i = (x^t_{i1}, x^t_{i2},\ldots x^t_{iD})$, x^t_{id} □{1,0}, D is the number of dimensions, t is the iteration number and $P^t_i = (p^t_{i1}, p^t_{i2},\ldots p^t_{iD})$ is the best solution that particle i has obtained until iteration t
            For $d = 1$ to D bits
                $p^t_{id} = x^t_{id}$ // p^t_{id} is best so far
            Next d
        End if
        $g = i$ // arbitrary
        For j = indices of neighbors (or population)
            If $G(P^t_j) > G(P^t_g)$ then $g = j$ // $P^t_g = (p^t_{g1}, p^t_{g2},\ldots p^t_{gD})$ is the best solution in the population or neighborhood at iteration t and g is index of best performer in neighborhood (or population)
            Next j
            For $d = 1$ to D
                $v^t_{id} = v^{t-1}_{id} + c_1 r_1(p^t_{id} - x^t_{id}) + c_2 r_2(p^t_{gd} - x^t_{id})$
                v^t_{id} □ $[-V_{\max}, +V_{\max}]$
                If random number $< \rho(v^t_{id})$ then
                    $x^{t+1}_{id} = 1$
                else
                    $x^{t+1}_{id} = 0$
            Next d
        Next i
    Until criterion

1.7.1 Recent Applications of Binary PSO

Recently, the binary PSO approach is applied to the problem of polygonal approximation of digital curves (Yin, 2004). This problem is of significance since it is used in a number of image analysis tasks such as object recognition, image matching and target tracking. A polygon can be used to represent a shape in an image since the information of a shape is mainly preserved at the corners that have the maximal measure of significance. The problem at hand is to approximate the curve along the corners as closely as possible while at the same time keeping the number of vertices at the corners of the polygon (called degree of the polygon) as small as possible. Yin employed the binary PSO technique developed in (Kennedy & Eberhart, 1007) with a slight modification. He introduced a local search heuristic in between successive generations of the discrete PSO so that once the algorithm found a good region within a given iteration, it could exploit that region thoroughly before moving onto another region. This hybrid PSO showed significantly improved performance in terms of the number of polygon vertices necessary for the same error and variations in results between different runs as compared to the original binary PSO.

Another work has showed the use of binary PSO in optimizing flowshop scheduling problems (Liao *et al,* 2007). They used a variant of the GBEST model to search for the best global solution. Instead of determining the global best for a given iteration from the individual bests of the individual particles up to that iteration, the global best was determined from the positions of the particles at the current iteration. Liao *et al* showed this technique to perform better than the conventional GBEST model. Even though it spent more time on converging, it increased the probability of not getting stuck at a local solution. In an attempt to further improve the PSO performance, Liao *et al* introduced a local search scheme to be carried out once, every fixed number of iterations within the PSO loop. The main idea was that given a current solution, the PSO mechanism would lead the solution to an intermediate solution. The local search would be applied to this intermediate solution in order to reach the global solution. The binary PSO method has been applied to define a preliminary short/medium range aircraft configuration, fully compliant with given requirements, that allows a minimum direct operating cost (Blasi & Del Core, 2007). In this work they tested two different boundary conditions viz. absorbing wall technique and reflecting wall. The authors found the latter technique to provide a slightly improved performance over the former. They also compared the PSO method with that of a previously studied genetic optimizer and found the PSO method to be quite promising.

2. Application of PSO to fault diagnosis of airplane engines

The work discussed in this work involves using PSO in conjunction with Bayesian Networks (BN) for diagnosing and predicting faults in airplane engines. A distributed Particle Swarm Optimization approach is explored in order to construct the best BN from a large dataset comprising of raw data taken from the sensors of airplane engines during actual flights. The inherent parallelism of the PSO technique has been exploited with the algorithm being implemented on a cluster of 48 processors using Message Passing Interface (MPI) in Linux. The seamless blend of graph theory and probability theory that makes uncertainty representation both instinctive and spontaneous is an inherent characteristic of Bayesian Networks and this makes it a highly appealing option for fault diagnosis. This work attempts to employ Bayesian Networks for the purpose of creating a fault diagnosis system. Initially no expert information is available as regards the relationship between the variables forming the network and it is discovered solely from the available engine data. After the network is conceptualized, expert information is incorporated for a more accurate modeling of the dependencies associated between fault and other system variables. The task of determining the Bayesian Network that best fits the data is accomplished by means of PSO.

As mentioned previously, the parallel behavior exhibited by the PSO technique is employed in fitness evaluation of the processed data on a cluster of 48 CPUs running parallel, using MPI in Linux. Such an arrangement serves to substantially reduce computational time.

2.1 Overview of Bayesian Networks

A Bayesian Network (BN) is a probabilistic network that provides a cogent and coherent depiction of the dependencies and independencies between the variables of interest. Such a network is a graphical model in the form of a directed acyclic graph (DAG), which has a causal semantics thereby enabling an effortless incorporation of causal prior knowledge. The strength of these causal relationships is encoded in the form of conditional independence assertions between the variables (Heckerman, 1995). Consider a domain of random variables given by $U = (X_1, X_2, \ldots, X_n)$. These signify the nodes of a network. Conditional dependencies are represented in the form of directed links between variables. An arrow from node X_1 to node X_2 indicates X_1 to be the parent of X_2. In order to quantify the effect of the parents on the node, a conditional probability distribution is associated with it defining its local semantics, e.g. each node X_i, has a conditional probability distribution $P(X_i \mid Parents(X_i))$. The product of these local conditional distributions evolves into global semantics of the problem at hand with the Chain rule being its mathematical manifestation. The Chain rule expresses the relationship between the unconditional probabilities $P(X_i)$, the conditional probabilities $P(X_i \mid e)$, where e is the evidence and the joint probability $P(U)$ as shown in equation (10). Here $P(U) = P(X_1, X_2, \ldots, X_n)$. An exponential enhancement in $P(U)$ is observed as the number of variables escalates.

$$P(U) = \prod_{i=1}^{n} P(X_i \mid Parents(X_i)) \tag{10}$$

2.2 Bayesian Learning

Incomplete knowledge spawns learning. It is a means of obtaining information through experience. Bayesian Learning uses hypotheses as intermediaries between data and predictions (Russell & Norvig, 1995). The main steps are:

- Estimating the probability of each hypothesis given the data
- Making predictions from the hypotheses, using the posterior probabilities of the hypotheses to weight the predictions

Four classes of *Bayesian Network Learning* arise based on whether the structure of the network is known or unknown and the variables are observable or hidden. These include the following:

1. *Known structure complete data:* This is the case where the network is specified and the data does not contain any missing values. It involves evaluation of the conditional probability tables for each node of the network from the complete data.
2. *Known structure incomplete data:* For this case the network is specified but the data is by no means complete and consists of missing values or hidden variables. The missing data can be estimated on the basis of the available data and the information about the missing data - an approach that is adopted by the *Expectation-Maximization* (EM)

algorithm (Friedman, 1995) and by *Gibbs' Sampling*. *Bound and Collapse* (BC) (Sebastiani & Ramoni, 2000) is another technique which can be explored given such a scenario.

3. *Unknown structure incomplete data:* Such a problem involves an unspecified network structure coupled with data having missing vales. Exact solutions are not viable and hence such problems call for sub optimal networks which can be determined using gradient based algorithms using *structural* EM and BC (Sebastiani & Ramoni, 2000).
4. *Unknown structure complete data:* The problem dealt with in this chapter belongs to this category. It attempts to learn the structure of the BN using the complete sensor data and on the basis of the developed structure endeavors to diagnose presence/absence of faults in airplane engines. Here the network topology has to be generated such that it fits the data the best. The number of structures grows super-exponentially as the number of variables multiplies, making such a problem computationally expensive. Thus applying distributed PSO could help greatly.

2.3 Structural Learning

In order to demonstrate the suitability of Bayesian Networks as an inference tool for predictive maintenance of airplane engines, the network has to be built first and this requires learning its topology using the available sensor data. This is structural BN learning. Given a training set D, the problem of learning a BN involves finding a network B that best matches D (Friedman, 1995). Structural BN learning can be addressed using either constraint based or score based learning. The former deals with conducting statistical tests on the given data and then determining a unique DAG that is consistent with the observed (in)dependencies. The latter approach focuses on optimization. It involves finding a network structure that maximizes a defined scoring function that represents how well each network structure fits the data. Less vulnerability to errors in individual tests gives score based methods an edge over constraint-based techniques. The approach in this work is score based. Literature provides an assortment of scoring functions which include *log-likelihood* (Heckerman, 1995) , the *minimal description length* (MDL) score (Lam & Bacchus, 2000), *Bayesian score* (Heckerman, 1995) etc. Of these, the *K2* scoring metric (based on a Bayesian approach) provided in (Cooper & Herskovits, 1992) has been found to be the most successful. The technique applied in the presented work is Bayesian score, which can be described as having the following form:

$$Score(B:D) = P(B \mid D) = \frac{P(D \mid B)P(B)}{P(D)} \tag{11}$$

$$P(D \mid B) = \int P(D \mid \theta_B, B) P(\theta_B \mid B) \mathrm{d}\theta_B \tag{12}$$

Here, D represents the data and B represents a network candidate. The network structure that maximizes $P(D \mid B)P(B)$, maximizes the score as well. The probability $P(D \mid B)$ is evaluated in the equation (12), where θ_B is a parameter of the network B.

As discussed previously, the goal of score based methods is to find the highest scoring network structure. This is accomplished by means of a search algorithm. This score + search approach is NP-hard (Chickering et al, 2004) justifying a heuristic approach (Djan-Sampson & Sahin, 2004). The most commonly used algorithm is a simple greedy hill-climbing algorithm. However it suffers from the ills of local maxima and plateaus that have adverse effects on the score. Heuristic searches generally assume that ordering of variables is known and many do not scale well with networks having a large number (more than five) of variables. Additional scaling difficulties arise while dealing with large datasets such as gene and census data (Sahin et al, 2007; Yavuz et al, 2006). In order to avoid the pitfalls of heuristic searches we use a PSO based approach, as it is highly compatible with large datasets and large networks.

2.4 Applying Binary PSO

In this problem each particle of the swarm represents a BN. The position of each particle is made up of a string of 0s and 1s where each bit represents whether an edge exists between the nodes indexed by the bit. Assuming no node can be its own parent, the binary string will contain $n(n-1)$ bits. The fitness is calculated using the scoring function given below (Herskovits, 1992):

$$Fitness = 1/\log_{10}\left(\prod_{i=1}^{n}\prod_{j=1}^{q_i}\frac{(r_i-1)!}{(N_{ij}+r_j-1)!}\prod_{k=1}^{r_i}N_{ijk}\right) \tag{13}$$

Here r_i is the number of states for node i, the first product is over the nodes in the network, the second product is over the set of permutations of the parents of node i, and the third product is over the states of node. Also N_{ij} is defined as

$$N_{ij} = \sum_{k=1}^{r_i} N_{ijk} \tag{14}$$

Here, N_{ijk} is an entry in the conditional probability table for node i. The conditional probability table elements contain occurrences of joint instantiations of the parents, (each permutation is indexed with *j*) of node *i* for which node *i* is in state *k*. Hence, the sum N_{ij} is a total of a column of the conditional probability table, where each column enumerates occurrences of node i in each state for a specific instantiation set of parents. At each step of the optimization, equations (1a) and (9) are used to update the particle velocities and positions respectively.

3. Fault Diagnosis

Fault diagnosis using PSO based Bayesian Network learning is accomplished in two steps: preprocessing and network discovery. Preprocessing generates the input dataset. Network discovery is accomplished by the PSO algorithm that is run in a computer cluster. The output is a network that correctly models the system dependencies and serves as a tool for system diagnosis and monitoring as well as fault prediction.

3.1 Preprocessing

Extensive information pertaining to an assortment of airplane engine parameters viz. temperature, altitude, pressure, flight phase etc. is furnished by sensors connected to the airplane engines. MATLAB is used for the purpose of storing this raw data as structure files. Each structure file comprises of sensor information pertaining to a single flight. The raw data has to be suitably condensed in order to optimize computational efforts. The fact that oil related variables account for most number of airplane engine faults forms the basis of such a condensation. Hence, from each raw data file the features corresponding to only oil related variables are extracted. Another aspect necessitating preprocessing of raw data is data sampling. In order to allow all the oil related variables in a given file to have equal lengths, a sampling interval adjustment is vital. The necessity of sampling uniformity stems from the fact the sampling rate of different sensors is different.

In an effort to further reduce computational expense, focus is restricted to information obtained during the approach phase of the flight. The rationale behind the choice of flight phase is the fact that the sensors relevant for lube diagnosis record a broad range of values during the approach phase thereby allowing us to delineate distinct states for the BN nodes (Sahin et al, 2007). Such a choice also helps extend the coverage of flight data analysis since unlike take-off and cruise, the approach phase has not been studied as well (Sahin et al, 2007) . The adjusted data pertaining to a particular flight now constitutes equal sized arrays of sensor readings corresponding to only engine oil failure related variables, further narrowed down to include only approach phase readings. In a Bayesian Network, the maximum number of states corresponding to each node directly influences the total run time of the network structure learning algorithm. Hence it is crucial to reduce the variation of the values in the adjusted dataset. This is accomplished by means of an *equal frequency data binning algorithm*. Similar data are grouped together into bins while at the same time ensuring that that each bin contains a fairly equal number of elements. The data is tagged based on the bin numbers, which represent the probable states a given variable would be at a particular point in time. Thus a reduction in the maximum number of states associated with each node is brought about. In the presented work, each node is chosen to have four states (four bins). The equal frequency binning algorithm works as follows:

1. Initially a minimum number of elements (say *n*) are considered to be clustered together in one bin.
2. The first bin is filled up with the first n number of elements, the second bin by the next n number of elements and so on. This may cause the last bin to contain more or less than n number of elements.
3. To ensure that similar elements are in the same bin some elements are transferred to or from adjacent bins
4. Any resulting empty bins are discarded.
5. The bins are checked to see if similar elements are grouped together in the same bin. If not the control goes back to step (3)
6. The original data is represented by the bin number.

3.1.1 Addition of Fault

The binned data is classified as faulty or non faulty by introducing an additional column named Fault in the data. Information regarding the presence or absence of Fault is determined from the maintenance records of the airplane engines. For example, a flight before an oil related repair on an engine is categorized as faulty while the very first flight after that maintenance is considered to have non faulty flight data. The entries of the Fault column are set to 1 or 0 respectively depending on whether the raw data file is faulty or not.

3.1.2 Packing data and compression

In order to reduce the size of the data, we have packed the data by combining data elements in bytes and applied compression techniques. The size reduction in the data file improved the performance of the distributed PSO algorithm since smaller data can be sent to the slaves faster in the cluster. Thus, less time was required to complete the algorithm. After packing and compression, it was possible to condense the original file by about 40-75 times. Details of this approach can be found in (Sahin et al, 2007).

3.2 Using Particle Swarm Optimization for Searching the best Bayesian Network

Parallelism is the hallmark of the PSO algorithm and this feature can be efficiently exploited for fitness calculation, as it is the most computationally demanding aspect of a BN search, especially when the problem at hand involves a large number of variables or large datasets. The following sections explore the characteristics of the implemented PSO. Fig. 3 shows the distributed PSO in master-slave framework.

3.2.1 Parallel Computing for Particle Swarm Optimization

The PSO algorithm was run on a cluster of 48 CPUs operating in parallel. An MPI (Message Passing Interface) having a master slave framework was implemented. The particle swarm was managed and initialized by the master. Each slave process received a particle from the master and was required to calculate its fitness and send it back. After all the fitness results for the swarm were received by the master, the algorithm was advanced by one step i.e. one iteration. The master again sent out the newly evolved particles to the slaves and the procedure was repeated.

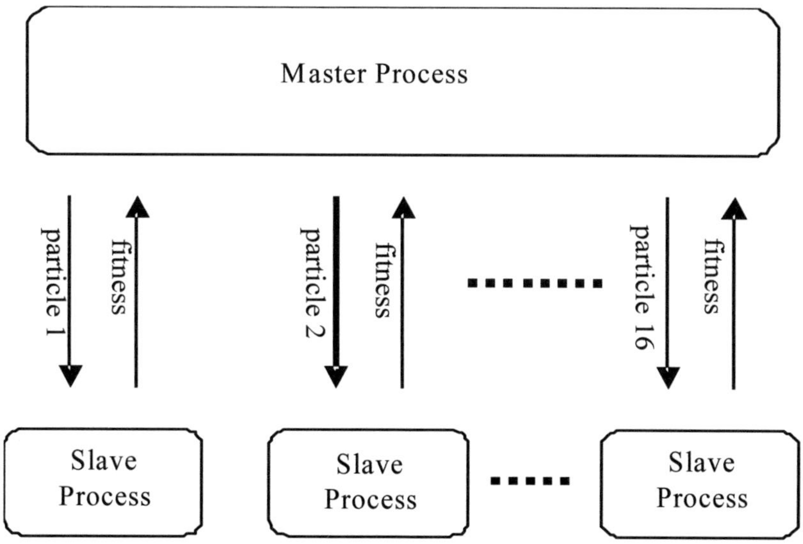

Figure 3. Parallel implementation of PSO algorithm

For dynamic evolution of the swarm, all the processes must wait for each other to complete their current fitness calculation. Such implementation architecture is termed as *synchronous PSO*. Efficient parallel implementation of the PSO algorithm was accomplished by keeping the number of slave processes equal to or greater than the number of particles. This is because with an adequate number of processes there is a high probability that all the processes up to the number of particles will compute fitness and return the values at approximately the same time resulting in a small idle process time.

3.2.2 Particle and Velocity Initialization

The particles in the swarm were heuristically initialized. If there were *N* nodes in the network, each particle was initialized to contain a randomly selected set of *N/2* edges. If this resulted in a cyclic particle then it had to be axed and recreated. This was critical since the chosen fitness function was designed to handle only acyclic graphs. The maximum number of arcs was restricted to *2N*. Such a restriction did not impact the particle initialization. There was a possibility of encountering the problem of cyclic particles yet again when the particles were allowed to 'fly'. At such instances the cyclic particles were identified and rendered acyclic by repeated removal of edges. For velocity initialization, each component of each particle's velocity was randomly initialized on the interval

$$-v_{\max} \le v_o \le v_{\max} \tag{15}$$

This initialization lead to particles having approximately $N(N-1)/2$ arcs after they were moved for the first time. This ensured adequate initial exploration of the BN bit string particle swarm. Effectual exploration of the search space demanded intelligent selection of maximum velocity in order to prevent greediness from creeping in.

3.3 Training and testing

For the purpose of network generation and fault prediction, the PSO based structural BN learning code is developed in two modes: simulation and inference. The simulation mode is also referred to as training. This mode involved using a set of preprocessed data files (called training files) for exploring the optimal representation of the system dependencies by execution of the PSO algorithm. Other input parameters of significance included the number of PSO particles, type of neighborhood, and the number of optimization steps. This resulted in a BN that was representative of the input preprocessed (training) data. Inference mode is also called the testing mode. In this mode the accuracy of the generated BN in diagnosing faults in known and unknown datasets was investigated. A collection of preprocessed files different from those used for training was tested by using the BN. For this purpose a preprocessed training sample set, its corresponding BN realization and the set of files to be tested were fed into the inference engine. Correct diagnosis of known files served to validate the use of the BN for fault prediction in unknown datasets. Table 2 shows the list of engine oil failure variables under investigation that directly or indirectly influences Fault. The problem of coming up with the best BN that models the dependencies between the listed variables has been attempted in our previous work (Sahin et al, 2007; Yavuz et al, 2006). Here we incorporate expert information in order to make our model more accurate. This expert input is of two types. Firstly we tag certain variables to be independent of others as a result of which they show absence of parents in the resulting DAG. Secondly, we determine and discard those variables that have no influence on the system.

4. Experimental Tests and Results

Oil related variable	Symbol	Remarks
Pressure Altitude	ALT	-
Engine Cycle	ECYC	Independent variable
Engine Hours	EHRS	Independent variable
Exhaust Gas Temperature	EGT	-
Fuel Flow	FF	-
Mach	MACH	-
Fan Speed	N1	-
Core Speed	N2	-
Oil Pressure	OIP	-
Oil Temperature	OIT	-
Power Lever Angle	PLA	-
Total Pressure	PT	-
Total Air Temperature	TAT	Independent variable
Thrust Mode	TMODE	-
Engine Vibration	VIB	-

Table 2. List of oil related variables

4.1 Incorporation of independent variables

Based on experts at Honeywell Inc., three oil related variables viz. *Engine Cycle* (*ECYC*), *Engine Hours* (*EHRS*) and *Total Air Temperature* (*TAT*) are considered to be unaffected by others and hence are marked as independent variables. Initially a set of 10 files comprising of an equal number of faulty and non-faulty files are selected. After preprocessing, this data is fed into the simulation mode of the software that utilizes PSO to generate the required best BN. An accurate BN entails an appropriate PSO, the efficacy of which depends upon judicious selection of its parameters. To come up with the most efficient optimizer, four parameters viz. number of optimization steps, swarm size, maximum velocity of particles and type of neighborhood were investigated. These are enumerated in Table 3. The training data was subjected to an exhaustive series of simulations in order to study the inter-dependencies between the various PSO parameters and construct the best BN. As perceived from the Table 3, a total of 450 simulations were carried out.

PSO parameters	Values	Remarks
Number of optimization steps	1000, 2000, 3000, 4000, 5000	In a single run the PSO parameters take up specified values from column 2. Each run is repeated five times and the quality of the network generated by using those values for the parameters is assessed by considering the average fitness score of the five runs
Type of neighborhood	Global, neighborhood of 2	
Number of particles	8, 16, 24	
Maximum velocity of particles	6, 8, 10	

Table 3. List of PSO Parameters

Based on these 450 runs with different PSO parameter, we see that the behavior of a network generated using PSO is highly dependent upon the inter-relationship between the PSO parameters. Hence the choice of parameter values is always problem specific.

The quality of the generated BNs was evaluated on the basis of the fitness score and the number of parents to the Fault node. Networks with higher number (three or more) of parents to Fault were desirable since these provided better inference results (Sahin et al, 2007). Also networks with smaller fitness scores tended to differentiate faulty and non faulty files better (Sahin et al, 2007). As a result of the 450 different simulations carried, 23 networks having four or more parents to Fault were obtained. They are as listed in Table 4.

Network	Steps	No. of particles	Neigh-borhood	Velocity	No. of parents	Fitness Score	Percentage Fault	
							Faulty Test File	Non-Faulty Test file
Network1	3000	24	0	10	5	-3.6058E-06	92.61%	50.03%
Network2	5000	24	2	6	5	-3.4560E-06	96.65%	45.57%
Network3	5000	16	2	6	4	-3.4486E-06	49.99%	80.00%
Network4	3000	24	2	10	4	-3.4283E-06	99.90%	38.17%
Network5	5000	24	2	10	4	-3.4095E-06	58.50%	79.01%
Network6	5000	24	2	8	4	-3.3882E-06	88.26%	69.40%
Network7	5000	24	0	6	4	-3.3345E-06	60.28%	80.92%
Network8	5000	24	2	10	4	-3.3232E-06	58.54%	60.62%
Network9	4000	16	0	6	4	-3.2829E-06	98.00%	55.01%
Network10	2000	24	2	10	5	-3.2558E-06	67.59%	47.20%
Network11	4000	16	0	6	5	-3.2409E-06	52.43%	59.44%
Network12	2000	8	2	8	5	-3.2369E-06	49.99%	81.41%
Network13	2000	24	2	8	4	-3.2255E-06	78.73%	80.66%
Network14	3000	24	0	10	4	-3.2123E-06	33.60%	71.63%
Network15	3000	8	0	6	4	-3.1994E-06	87.59%	79.55%
Network16	4000	16	0	8	5	-3.1810E-06	63.27%	79.90%
Network17	5000	24	2	10	5	-3.1687E-06	81.30%	77.34%
Network18	2000	16	0	8	4	-3.1684E-06	96.13%	45.82%
Network19	2000	16	2	6	4	-3.1497E-06	50.08%	69.40%
Network20	4000	24	2	10	4	-3.1247E-06	99.50%	53.97%
Network21	3000	16	0	6	5	-3.1185E-06	77.55%	47.44%
Network22	3000	8	2	6	4	-3.0115E-06	98.53%	46.34%
Network23	1000	16	0	6	4	-3.0060E-06	67.87%	50.03%

Table 4. Simulation and inference results

Each network was tested on a set of seven known files in order to determine its diagnostic capability. The results are indicated in the final two columns of Table 4. Let us examine Network 2. It has five parents to Fault and a very good fitness score. It indicated a fault probability of about 97% and above for faulty files and a fault probability of about 46% and below for non-faulty files, thus exhibiting acceptable proficiency in fault diagnosis. Now consider Network 1. It also has five parents to Fault and in fact the best (i.e. lowest) fitness score as compared to the other networks. It was able to successfully diagnose faulty files as seen by the high value of fault probability for faulty files. However it demonstrated some ambiguity while diagnosing non-faulty files. This irregularity can be attributed to data over fitting. Increase in the number of parents to the Fault node does not always ensure successful diagnosis. In fact overfitting may introduce excessive variance thereby reducing the prediction quality of the model. More than the number, it is *which* variables are parents to the Fault node is what is significant. Network 10 may also be the victim of such an overfitting as is indicated by the diminished capability of the network in diagnosing faulty files. The inferior diagnostic capability of Networks 11, 12, 16 and 17 can be attributed to poor fitness score in addition to overfitting. On the other hand, Network 4 with 4 parents to Fault exhibited excellent diagnostic capability even surpassing Network 2. Networks 5 through Network 8 have low (i.e. good) fitness scores but are weak representations of the system as observed by the excessively high fault probabilities predicted by these networks for non-faulty data. On the other hand, Networks 21 and 22 with relatively high (i.e. poor) fitness scores function as effective diagnostic tools. This may be considered as an indication towards the significance of the variables that affect Fault directly (i.e. are parents to Fault) as opposed to their number. Table 5 lists the parent variables to Fault for the networks discussed in Table 4.

Network	Fault Percentage		Parents to Fault
	Faulty Test File	Non-faulty Test File	
Network1	92.614632%	50.034897%	EHRS, MACH, PT, TMODE, VIB
Network2	96.649025%	45.570953%	ECYC, EGT, MACH, N2, TMODE
Network3	49.987072%	80.001564%	ALT, EGT, EHRS, OIP
Network4	99.900787%	38.174068%	ALT, EGT, EHRS, OIT
Network5	58.498676%	79.011688%	ECYC, EHRS, OIP, PLA
Network6	88.262665%	69.401489%	EGT, EHRS, OIP, PLA
Network7	60.278790%	80.917755%	OIP, PLA, PT, TAT
Network8	58.544533%	60.622322%	ALT, MACH, N1, TAT
Network9	98.004845%	55.009872%	EHRS, N2, PT, TMODE
Network10	67.592590%	47.199936%	ECYC, EGT, N1, OIT, TMODE
Network11	52.425045%	59.435143%	ALT, ECYC, EHRS, N1, VIB
Network12	49.987072%	81.405655%	ALT, ECYC, OIP, PLA, TAT
Network13	78.727547%	80.657501%	PT, TAT, TMODE, VIB
Network14	33.595486%	71.633659%	OIP, PLA, PT, TMODE
Network15	87.590485%	79.550301%	ECYC, OIP, PT, VIB
Network16	63.271446%	79.898872%	EGT, MACH, OIP, PT, TAT
Network17	81.295242%	77.337982%	ECYC, MACH, N1, OIP, TMODE
Network18	96.130951%	45.815529%	ALT, EGT, EHRS, PLA
Network19	50.079407%	69.395515%	FF, PLA, PT, TMODE
Network20	99.503967%	53.965019%	ECYC, PLA, TMODE, VIB
Network21	77.546539%	47.442135%	EHRS, N1, N2, OIT, TMODE
Network22	98.533943%	46.341629%	ECYC, N2, TAT, TMODE
Network23	67.869797%	50.034897%	EGT, N2, FF, PT

Table 5. Parents to Fault node

From Table 5 it is observed that all the networks with acceptable diagnostic capability viz. Networks 2, 4, 18, 21 and 22, include the variables ALT and/or N2 and/or TMODE as parents to Fault. Since the amount of data is limited for such a study no generalizations will be made. However it must be pointed out that the presence of these variables as well as that of others not identified here but which may very well appear repeatedly as parents to Fault in further studies can be considered of certain consequence while deciding the suitability of a network for diagnosing or testing new data. In summary, while evaluating the quality of the BN for inference purposes, it is essential to consider the fitness score and, not only the number of parents but also the variables that act as parents to Fault.

4.2 Removal of irrelavent variables

Another effective way to enhance the accuracy of modeling and accelerate the algorithm is to determine and discard those variables that have no influence on the network. Such variables appear in the form of leaf nodes or islands. In order to obtain a visual representation of the networks generated from the simulations, a program called GraphViz was employed (GraphViz software). These graphical depictions were examined in order to ascertain the unnecessary variables. Three variables viz. EGT, MACH and VIB consistently appeared as leaf nodes in a number of networks. Fig. 4 (a) and (b) illustrate networks having these variables as leaf nodes.

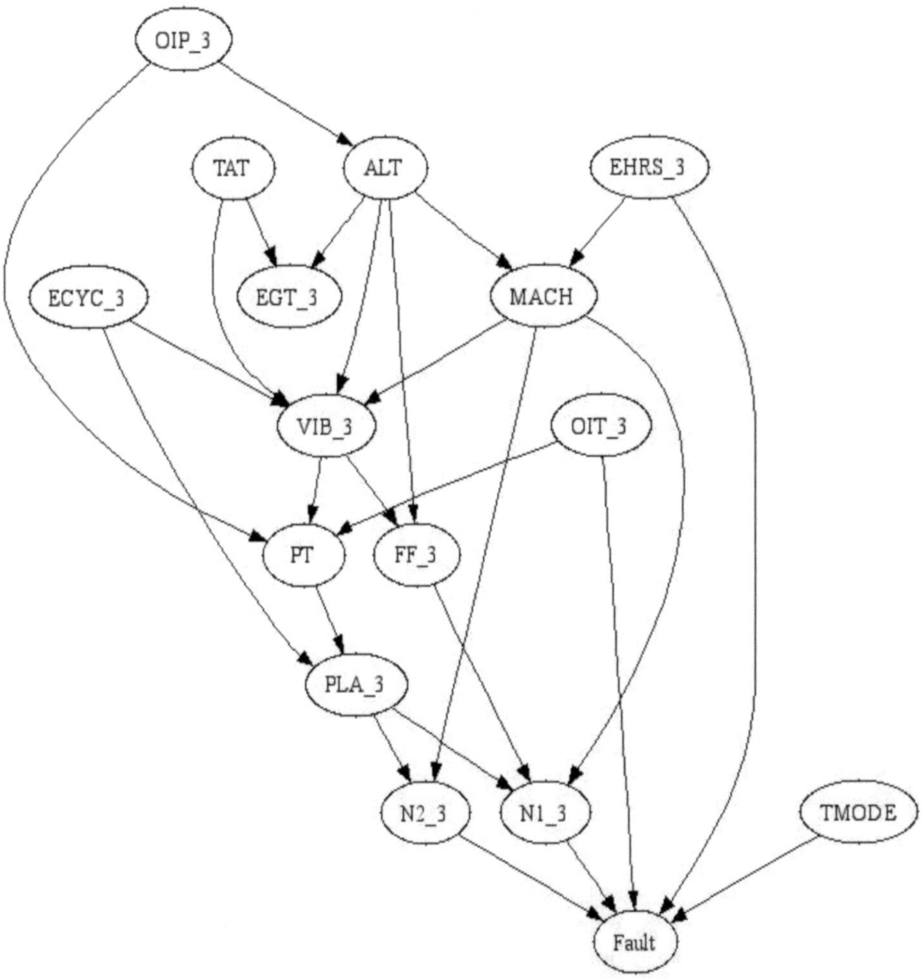

Figure 4(a). BN generated exhibiting variable EGT as a leaf node

Once the variables were identified, they were not included while pre-processing the raw data. An appropriate training set consisting of five faulty and five non-faulty files was selected and fed into the simulation mode of the software. The PSO parameters were chosen corresponding to those that resulted in the best diagnostic capability. The diagnostic proficiency of the resulting BNs was tested on a group of seven known files. The results are as presented in Table 6.

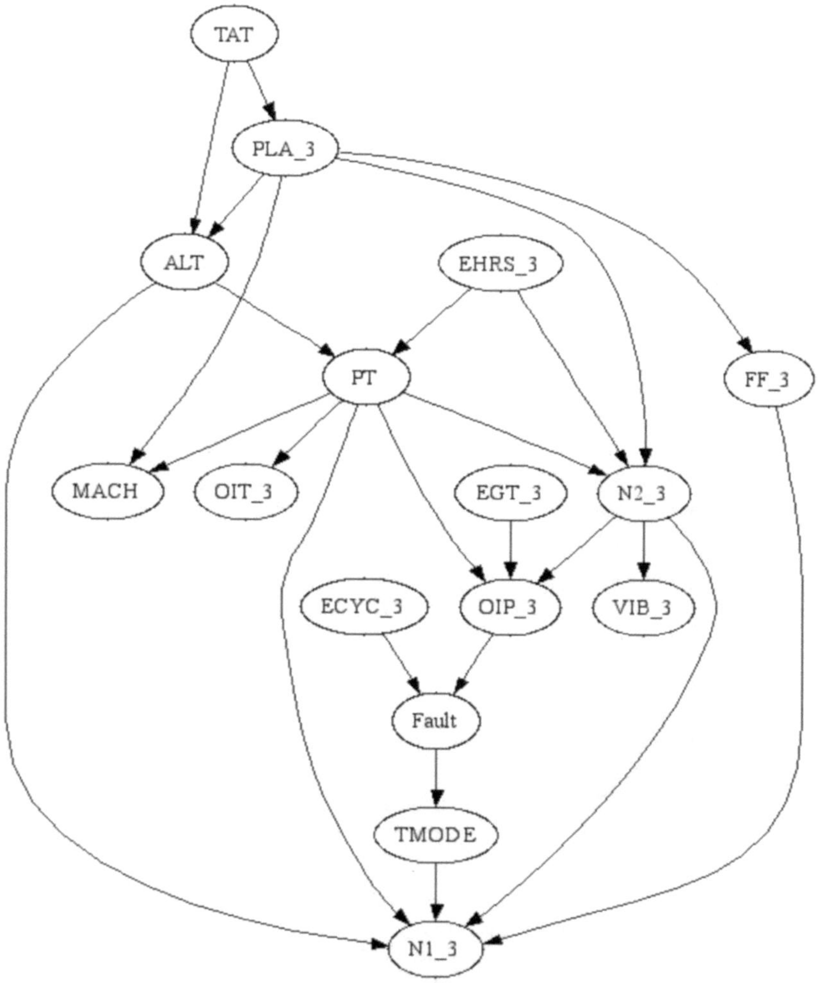

Figure 4 (b). BN generated using the proposed software exhibiting variable VIB as a leaf node

Five good networks were obtained by following the procedure indicated in Section 4.1. The values of the PSO parameters of these networks were selected while training the data with variables EGT, MACH and VIB removed. For each set of PSO parameters, four different runs were executed with an aim to obtain at least one network having three or more parents to Fault. As seen in Table 6, only one run out of 20 runs resulted in Fault having four parents. Three parents to Fault were found in nine runs. These 10 networks were then used to diagnose fault in a set of files consisting of two faulty and five non-faulty files. The results are indicated in the last two columns of Table 6. Networks 2, 10 and 17 are able to successfully diagnose faulty files. Though there seems to be some uncertainty in diagnosing non-faulty files this approach looks promising. Further study is on to better the predictive capability for non-faulty files by performing extensive number of simulations and assessing the influence of the remaining variables on the network.

Network	Optimization steps	No. of particles	Neighborhood	Velocity	Parents to Fault	Fitness Score	Fault Percentage	
							Faulty Test Files	Non Faulty Test Files
Network 1	5000	24	2	6	3	-	58.50%	53.10%
Network 2	5000	24	2	6	3	-4.0015E-06	99.97%	55.24%
Network 3	5000	24	2	6	1	-	-	-
Network 4	5000	24	2	6	2	-	-	-
Network 5	3000	24	2	10	1	-	-	
Network 6	3000	24	2	10	2	-	-	-
Network 7	3000	24	2	10	2	-	-	-
Network 8	3000	24	2	10	0	-	-	-
Network 9	2000	16	0	8	3	-4.2130E+06	58.50%	49.70%
Network 10	2000	16	0	8	3	-4.1461E-06	99.97%	51.96%
Network 11	2000	16	0	8	1	-	-	-
Network 12	2000	16	0	8	1	-	-	-
Network 13	3000	16	0	6	4	-4.4827E-06	62.37%	56.54%
Network 14	3000	16	0	6	3	-4.0790E-02	45.63%	60.02%
Network 15	3000	16	0	6	1	-	-	-
Network 16	3000	16	0	6	3	-4.0195E-06	0.00%	48.76%
Network 17	3000	8	2	6	3	-3.7565E-06	98.57%	52.61%
Network 18	3000	8	2	6	3	-3.8662E+06	47.86%	72.62%
Network 19	3000	8	2	6	3	-3.6141E-06	89.88%	76.83%
Network 20	3000	8	2	6	2	-	-	-

Table 6. Simulation and inference results with variable removal

5. Conclusion

This work involved the implementation of a highly successful technique for fault diagnosis and predictive maintenance of airplane engines. Some of the highlights of the discussed Bayesian Network approach include creation of the network without prior information and later incorporating expert information for better modeling, monitoring, and diagnosing faults in known systems, predicting faults in unknown systems, ability to handle large systems and the possibility of modifying the technique for diagnosing and distinguishing different types of faults. The presented Particle Swarm Optimization technique was effectual in reducing the computational complexity of the problem at hand by capitalizing on its innately parallel behavior thereby enabling the application of a cluster of 48 CPUs for faster network creation. Thus the developed software had several advantages of being generic, robust, scalable and modifiable.

6. References

Kennedy J. & Eberhart R. (Nov. 1995), Particle Swarm Optimization, *Proceedings of the IEEE International Conference on Neural Networks*, vol. 4, Nov 1995, pp. 1942-1948.

Kennedy J. & Eberhart R. (Oct. 1995), A New Optimizer using Particle Swarm Theory, *Proceedings of the 6th International Symposium on Micro Machine and Human Science*, Oct. 1995, pp. 39-43.

Taşgetiren M. F. & Liang Y.-C. (2003), A Binary Particle Swarm Optimization Algorithm for Lot Sizing Problem, *Journal of Economic and Social Research*, vol. 5, No. 2, 2003, pp. 1-20.

Shi Y. & Eberhart R. (2001), Particle Swarm Optimization: Developments, Applications and Resources, *Proceedings of the Congress on Evolutionary Computation*, vol. 1, 2001, pp. 81-86.

Kennedy J. & Eberhart R. (2007), Defining a Standard for Particle Swarm Optimization, *Proceedings of the IEEE Swarm Intelligence Symposium*, April 2007, pp. 120-127.

Kennedy J. (1999), Small Worlds and Mega-Minds: Effects of Neighborhood Topology on Particle Swarm Performance, *Proceedings of the Congress on Evolutionary Computation*, vol. 3, July 1999, pp. 6-9.

Guo Q.-J., Yu H.-B., & Xu A.-D. (2006), A Hybrid PSO-GD based Intelligent Method for Machine diagnosis, *Digital Signal* Processing, vol. 16, No. 4, July 2006, pp. 402-18.

El-Gallad A., El-Hawary M., Sallam A. & Kalas A. (2002), Enhancing the Particle Swarm Optimizer via Proper Parameters Selection, *IEEE Canadian conference on Electrical and Computer Engineering*, vol. 2, May 2002, pp. 792-797.

Shi Y. & Eberhart R. (1998), A Modified Particle Swarm Optimizer, *Proceedings of the IEEE International Conference on Evolutionary Computation*, May 1998, pp. 69-73.

Kennedy J. & Eberhart R. (1997), A Discrete Binary Version of the Particle Swarm Algorithm, *IEEE International Conference on Systems, Man and Cybernetics*, vol. 5, Oct. 1997, pp. 4104-4108.

Shi Y. & Eberhart R. (2000), Empirical Study of Particle Swarm Optimization, *Proceedings of the Congress on Evolutionary Computation*, vol. 1, July 2000, pp. 6-9.

Iwamatsu M. (2006), Locating All the Global Minima Using Multi-Species Particle Swarm Optimizer: The Inertia Weight and The Constriction Factor Variants, *Proceedings of the Congress on Evolutionary Computation*, vol. 3, July 2006, pp. 816-822.

Clerc M. & Kennedy J. (2002), The Particle Swarm - Explosion, Stability and Convergence in a Multidimensional Space, IEEE Transactions on Evolutionary Computation, vol. 6, No. 1, Feb 2002, pp. 58-73.

Eberhart R. & Shi Y. (2006), Comparing Inertia Weights and Constriction Factors in Particle Swarm Optimization, *Proceedings of the Congress on Evolutionary Computation*, vol. 3, July 2006, pp. 816-822.

Fan H. (2002), A Modification to Particle Swarm Optimization Algorithm, *Engineering Computations*, vol. 19, No. 8, 2002, pp. 970-989.

Xu S. & Rahmat-Samii Y. (2007), Boundary Conditions in Particle Swarm Optimization Revisited, *IEEE Transactions on Antennas and Propagation*, vol. 55, No. 3, March 2007, pp. 760-765.

Huang T. & Mohan A. S. (2007), A Microparticle Swarm Optimizer for the Reconstruction of Microwave Images, *IEEE Transactions on Antennas and Propagation*, vol. 55, No. 3, March 2007, pp. 568-576.

Ho S. L, Shiyou Y., Guangzheng N. & Wong H. C. (2006), A Particle Swarm Optimization Method with Enhanced Global Search Ability for Design Optimizations of Electromagnetic Devices, *IEEE Transactions on Magnetics,* vol. 42, No. 4, April 2006, pp. 1107-1110.

Venayagamoorthy G. K., Smith S. C. & Singhal G. (2007), Particle swarm-based optimal partitioning algorithm for combinational CMOS circuits, *Engineering Applications of Artificial Intelligence*, vol. 20, 2007, pp.177-184.

Yin P.-Y. (2004), A Discrete Particle Swarm Algorithm for Optimal Polygonal Approximation of Digital Curves *J. Vis. Comm. Image R.*, vol. 15, 2004, pp. 241-260.

Liao C.-J., Tseng C.-T. & Luarn P. (2007), A Discrete Version of Particle Swarm Optimization for Flowshop Scheduling Problems, *Computer & Operations Research*, vol. 34, 2007, pp. 3099-3111.

Blasi L. & Del Core G. (2007), Particle Swarm Approach in Finding Optimum Aircraft Configuration, *Journal of Aircraft*, vol. 44, No. 2, March-April 2007, pp 679-683.

Heckerman D. (1995), A Tutorial on Learning Bayesian Networks, Microsoft Research, 1995.

Russell S. & Norvig P. (1995), *Artificial Intelligence: A Modern Approach,* 1995, Prentice Hall.

Friedman N. (1995), Learning Belief Networks in the Presence of Missing Values and Hidden Variables, *Proceedings of the 14th International Conference on Machine Learning*, 1995, pp. 125-133.

Sebastiani P. & Ramoni M. (2000), Bayesian Inference with Missing Data using Bound and Collapse, *Journal of Computational and Graphical Statistics*, vol. 9, No. 4, Dec. 2000, pp.779-800.

Lam W. & Bacchus F. (1994), Learning Bayesian Belief Networks: An Approach Based on the MDL Principle, *Computational Intelligence*, vol. 10, 1994, pp. 269-293.

Cooper G. & Herskovits E. (1992), A Bayesian method for the Induction of Probabilistic Networks from Data, *Machine Learning*, vol. 9, No. 4, Oct. 1992, pp. 309-347.

Chickering D. M., Heckerman D. & Meek C. (2004), Large-Sample Learning of Bayesian Networks is NP-Hard, *Journal of Machine Learning Research*, vol. 5, 2004, pp. 1287-1330.

Djan-Sampson P. and Sahin F. (2004), Structural Learning of Bayesian Networks from Complete Data using Scatter Search Documents, *Proceedings of the IEEE Conference on Systems, Man and Cybernetics*, vol. 4, Oct 2004, pp. 3169-3624.

Sahin F., Yavuz M. C., Arnavut Z. & Uluyol O. (2007), Fault Diagnosis for Airplane Engines using Bayesian Networks and Distributed Particle Swarm Optimization, *Journal of Parallel Computing*, vol. 33, No. 2, March 2007, pp. 124-143.

Yavuz M. C., Sahin F., Arnavut Z. & Uluyol O. (2006), Generating and Exploiting Bayesian Networks for Fault Diagnosis in Airplane Engines, *Proceedings of the IEEE International Conference on Granular Computing,* April 2006, pp. 250-255.

Herskovits E. (1992), Computer-based probabilistic network construction, Stanford University, CA.

Mo N., Zou Z. Y., Chan K. W., & Pong T. Y. G. (2007), Transient stability constrained optimal power flow using particle swarm optimisation, *IET Generation, Transmission, and Distribution*, vol. 1, issue 3, May 2007, pp. 476-483.

GraphViz Software website. http://www.graphviz.org.